CCNP Data Center Application Centric Infrastructure

DCACI 300-620

Official Cert Guide

AMMAR AHMADI CCIE No. 50928

Cisco Press

CCNP Data Center Application Centric Infrastructure DCACI 300-620 Official Cert Guide

Ammar Ahmadi

Copyright© 2021 Pearson Education, Inc.

Published by:
Cisco Press
Hoboken, NJ

ScoutAutomatedPrintCode

Library of Congress Control Number: 2020948500

ISBN-13: 978-0-13-660266-8

ISBN-10: 0-13-660266-5

Warning and Disclaimer

This book is designed to provide information about the CCNP Implementing Cisco Application Centric Infrastructure DCACI 300-620 certification exam. Every effort has been made to make this book as complete and as accurate as possible, but no warranty or fitness is implied.

The information is provided on an "as is" basis. The authors, Cisco Press, and Cisco Systems, Inc. shall have neither liability nor responsibility to any person or entity with respect to any loss or damages arising from the information contained in this book or from the use of the discs or programs that may accompany it.

The opinions expressed in this book belong to the author and are not necessarily those of Cisco Systems, Inc.

Trademark Acknowledgments

All terms mentioned in this book that are known to be trademarks or service marks have been appropriately capitalized. Cisco Press or Cisco Systems, Inc., cannot attest to the accuracy of this information. Use of a term in this book should not be regarded as affecting the validity of any trademark or service mark.

Special Sales

For information about buying this title in bulk quantities, or for special sales opportunities (which may include electronic versions; custom cover designs; and content particular to your business, training goals, marketing focus, or branding interests), please contact our corporate sales department at corpsales@pearsoned.com or (800) 382-3419.

For government sales inquiries, please contact governmentsales@pearsoned.com.

For questions about sales outside the U.S., please contact intlcs@pearson.com.

Feedback Information

At Cisco Press, our goal is to create in-depth technical books of the highest quality and value. Each book is crafted with care and precision, undergoing rigorous development that involves the unique expertise of members from the professional technical community.

Readers' feedback is a natural continuation of this process. If you have any comments regarding how we could improve the quality of this book, or otherwise alter it to better suit your needs, you can contact us through email at feedback@ciscopress.com. Please make sure to include the book title and ISBN in your message.

We greatly appreciate your assistance.

Editor-in-Chief: Mark Taub

Alliances Manager, Cisco Press: Arezou Gol

Director, ITP Product Management: Brett Bartow

Executive Editor: James Manly

Managing Editor: Sandra Schroeder

Development Editor: Ellie Bru

Senior Project Editor: Tonya Simpson

Copy Editor: Kitty Wilson

Technical Editors: Akhil Behl, Nikhil Behl

Editorial Assistant: Cindy Teeters

Cover Designer: Chuti Prasertsith

Composition: codeMantra

Indexer: Erika Millen

Proofreader: Donna Mulder

Americas Headquarters	Asia Pacific Headquarters	Europe Headquarters
Cisco Systems, Inc.	Cisco Systems (USA) Pte. Ltd.	Cisco Systems International BV Amsterdam,
San Jose, CA	Singapore	The Netherlands

Cisco has more than 200 offices worldwide. Addresses, phone numbers, and fax numbers are listed on the Cisco Website at www.cisco.com/go/offices.

Cisco and the Cisco logo are trademarks or registered trademarks of Cisco and/or its affiliates in the U.S. and other countries. To view a list of Cisco trademarks, go to this URL: www.cisco.com/go/trademarks. Third party trademarks mentioned are the property of their respective owners. The use of the word partner does not imply a partnership relationship between Cisco and any other company. (1110R)

About the Author

Ammar Ahmadi, CCIE No. 50928, has nearly a decade of experience in data center design, implementation, optimization, and troubleshooting. He currently consults for Cisco Gold partner AHEAD INC, where he has been designing and supporting large-scale ACI fabrics since the early days of ACI. Occasionally, he breaks from design work to produce network modernization roadmaps or demonstrate the possibilities of software-defined networking (SDN) to customers.

Ammar also owns and operates Networks Reimagined LLC, which focuses on SDN enablement and training. He can be reached at ammar.ahmadi@networksreimagined.com.

About the Technical Reviewers

Akhil Behl, CCIE No. 19564, is a passionate IT executive with a key focus on cloud and security. He has more than 16 years of experience in the IT industry, working across several leadership, advisory, consultancy, and business development profiles with various organizations. His technology and business specialization includes cloud, security, infrastructure, data center, and business communication technologies. Currently he leads business development for cloud for a global systems integrator.

Akhil is a published author. Over the past few years, he has authored multiple titles on security and business communication technologies. He has contributed as technical editor to more than a dozen books on security, networking, and information technology. He has published several research papers in national and international journals, including *IEEE Xplore*, and presented at various IEEE conferences, as well as other prominent ICT, security, and telecom events. He is passionate about writing and mentoring.

He holds CCIE Emeritus (Collaboration and Security), Azure Solutions Architect Expert, Google Professional Cloud Architect, CCSK, CHFI, ITIL, VCP, TOGAF, CEH, ISM, CCDP, and many other industry certifications. He has a bachelor's degree in technology and an MBA.

Nikhil Behl, CCIE No. 23335, is a seasoned IT professional with exposure to a broad range of technologies. He has more than 15 years of experience working in the IT industry. He has worked in several ICT roles, including solutions architect, pre-sales lead, network architect, business consultant, and CISCO TAC engineer, and he has worked with system integration and managed network services.

Nikhil has expertise in various technologies, including cloud, core networking, data center networking, software-defined networking, Wi-Fi, SD-WAN, and Software-Defined Access. He actively participates in several industry conferences and IT forums as a speaker.

Nikhil holds CCIE (Enterprise Infrastructure), Azure Solutions Architect Expert, Cisco SD-WAN Blackbelt, CCNP (Enterprise), CCDP, CCNA, CCDA, JNCIA (Junos), JNCIS, and many other industry leading certifications. He has a bachelor's degree in computer applications.

Dedication

I dedicate this book to my loving wife, Sophia, and my two children, Kiyana and Daniel. Sophia, your unrelenting support and patience made this book possible. I am forever grateful! Kiyana, you are full of life! You remind me every day that life is wonderful and that every moment should be cherished. Daniel, your nice big hugs have energized me at times when I really needed them. I look forward to spending more time with you and getting to know you more.

Acknowledgments

First, I would like to thank all the people who helped get this book to print. My special thanks go to Pearson product manager James Manly for his patience and understanding during this long process. I am also grateful to development editor Eleanor Bru, whose keen eye for detail has contributed tremendously to the quality of this book. Thank you, Brett Bartow, for the opportunity. And thanks to all the other people who contributed behind the scenes.

Second, I would like to thank all the people who have helped me grow in my career. I thank Peter Thompson, whom I saw as a mentor early in my career at Cisco. You helped me make several tough decisions that each greatly influenced my career. Also, thank you to Ryan Alt from AHEAD and John Rider from Cisco for allowing me the freedom to pick my projects. And thanks to all the unnamed folks at AHEAD who have made the past few years enjoyable. Thank you, Anthony Wilde, for showing me that you actually can have your cake and eat it, too. I would also like to acknowledge my wife, Sophia, for never letting me fall into the trap of complacency.

Finally, I would like to thank my mom, whose greatest desire has always been for me and my siblings to succeed, be happy, and achieve our dreams.

Contents at a Glance

Reader Services

Other Features

In addition to the features in each of the core chapters, this book has additional study resources on the companion website, including the following:

Practice exams: The companion website contains an exam engine that enables you to review practice exam questions. Use these to prepare with a sample exam and to pinpoint topics where you need more study.

Interactive exercises and quizzes: The companion website contains interactive hands-on exercises and interactive quizzes so that you can test your knowledge on the spot.

Glossary quizzes: The companion website contains interactive quizzes that enable you to test yourself on every glossary term in the book.

Video training: The companion website contains unique video samples from the author's complete video course.

To access this additional content, simply register your product. To start the registration process, go to www.ciscopress.com/register and log in or create an account.* Enter the product ISBN 9780136602668 and click Submit. After the process is complete, you will find any available bonus content under Registered Products.

*Be sure to check the box that you would like to hear from us to receive exclusive discounts on future editions of this product.

Contents

Icons Used in This Book

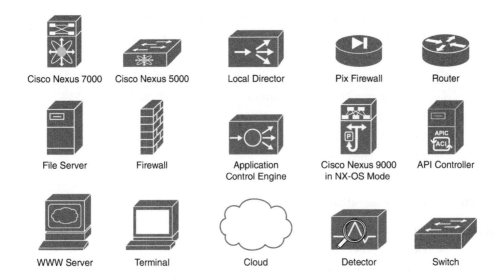

| Cisco Nexus 7000 | Cisco Nexus 5000 | Local Director | Pix Firewall | Router |

| File Server | Firewall | Application Control Engine | Cisco Nexus 9000 in NX-OS Mode | API Controller |

| WWW Server | Terminal | Cloud | Detector | Switch |

Command Syntax Conventions

The conventions used to present command syntax in this book are the same conventions used in the IOS Command Reference. The Command Reference describes these conventions as follows:

- **Boldface** indicates commands and keywords that are entered literally as shown. In actual configuration examples and output (not general command syntax), boldface indicates commands that are manually input by the user (such as a **show** command).

- *Italic* indicates arguments for which you supply actual values.

- Vertical bars (|) separate alternative, mutually exclusive elements.

- Square brackets ([ ]) indicate an optional element.

- Braces ({ }) indicate a required choice.

- Braces within brackets ([{ }]) indicate a required choice within an optional element.

Introduction

Welcome to the brave new world of Cisco ACI! This book strives to help you to:

- Understand the benefits of Cisco ACI and unlock its often-untapped potential

- Gain the expertise necessary to design, deploy, and support single-pod ACI fabrics

- Pass the Implementing Cisco Application Centric Infrastructure DCACI 300-620 exam.

The order of these three objectives is very important. An exam candidate who has an in-depth understanding of the fundamentals of a solution not only has an easier time on exam day but is also, arguably, a more capable engineer. That is why this book places an extraordinary amount of emphasis on the fundamentals of ACI rather than tips and tricks, corner-case scenarios, and platform-specific caveats.

This does not mean that this book is lacking in coverage of the DCACI blueprint. On the contrary, this book covers all the exam topics and then some. It does so with plain language and example after example of how particular features can be deployed and how they fit into the bigger picture of enabling ACI to be the data center SDN platform of the future.

Perspectives on the DCACI 300-620 Exam

In June 2019, Cisco announced that it was making substantial changes to certification products at all levels.

Cisco Application Centric Infrastructure (ACI) is a case in point for why these changes were necessary. Previous Cisco Certified Network Professional (CCNP) certifications followed a monolithic approach that necessitated major changes at both the CCNP and Cisco Certified Network Associate (CCNA) levels before a newer solution like ACI could be retrofitted into an overall curriculum. It commonly took several years for even immensely popular products (like ACI) to make it into the CCNP—and some never made it.

Newer Cisco certifications, on the other hand, take a more modular approach and encourage specialization in solutions most relevant to candidate job roles. If, for example, you are only interested in ACI, you can just take the DCACI 300-620 exam and obtain a specialist designation instead of a CCNA or CCNP. In the case of ACI, the Cisco certification evolution translates into greater depth of coverage without having content dispersed into a daunting number of exams alongside unrelated content.

One challenge that remains is that designing a certification covering all facets of a network product can require candidates to learn several thousand pages of content. This would unnecessarily discourage exam takers. Cisco has therefore divided coverage of ACI into two main exams:

- The DCACI 300-620 exam covers the fundamentals of ACI single-pod fabrics, such as endpoint learning, forwarding, management, monitoring, and basic integrations.

In addition to being a specialization exam, the DCACI 300-620 exam also counts as a concentration toward the CCNP Data Center certification.

■ The Implementing Cisco Application Centric Infrastructure—Advanced (300-630 DCACIA) exam addresses the implementation of more advanced ACI architectures, such as ACI Multi-Pod and ACI Multi-Site. It also covers route leaking, advanced contract implementation, and service insertion via policy-based redirect (PBR).

The DCACI 300-620 exam addresses at least 70% of the concepts a typical ACI engineer deals with on a day-to-day basis and provides an excellent on ramp for engineers seeking to build the foundational knowledge necessary to implement the most complex of ACI designs.

As you might have noticed, one essential topic still missing from the blueprints of these two exams is network automation. Cisco has released a dedicated exam for data center automation that includes ACI, called the Automating and Programming Cisco Data Center Solutions (300-635 DCAUTO) exam. Therefore, this book does not cover network automation, opting instead to serve as a tool to help engineers build a solid foundation in ACI.

Who Should Read This Book?

This book has been written with you in mind!

For engineers new to ACI, this book attempts to demystify the complex language of ACI by using unambiguous wording and a wide range of examples. It includes detailed configuration steps and can even be used as a lab guide. This book recognizes ACI newcomers as a significant part of its target audience and has been written to be the most comprehensive and up-to-date book on ACI while also being the easiest to read.

For more advanced engineers who have experience with ACI but need a guide to prepare for the DCACI 300-620 exam or to address knowledge gaps, this book is comprehensive enough to address the topics on the exam while also taking a look under the hood of ACI to enable these engineers to better appreciate how ACI works.

This book can also help network automation engineers build a solid foundation of ACI design and implementation concepts. Even though this book does not cover automation in ACI, it does address, in detail, how some of the most significant and often-used objects interact with one another.

This book is not an introduction to general networking and does expect readers to understand the basics of switching and routing. But this book does not assume that readers have any prior knowledge of ACI or even basic knowledge of data center overlay technologies. For this reason, this book can be used as a network engineer's first introduction to ACI.

The Companion Website for Online Content Review

All the electronic review elements, as well as other electronic components of the book, exist on this book's companion website.

To access the companion website, start by establishing a login at www.ciscopress.com and registering your book. To do so, simply go to www.ciscopress.com/register and enter the ISBN of the print book: 9780136602668. After you have registered your book, go to your account page and click the Registered Products tab. From there, click the Access Bonus Content link to get access to the book's companion website.

Note that if you buy the Premium Edition eBook and Practice Test version of this book from Cisco Press, your book will automatically be registered on your account page. Simply go to your account page, click the Registered Products tab, and select Access Bonus Content to access the book's companion website.

How to Access the Pearson Test Prep (PTP) App

You have two options for installing and using the Pearson Test Prep application: a web app and a desktop app. To use the Pearson Test Prep application, start by finding the access code that comes with the book. You can find the code in these ways:

- **Print book:** Look in the cardboard sleeve in the back of the book for a piece of paper with your book's unique access code.

- **Premium edition:** If you purchase the Premium edition eBook and Practice Test directly from the Cisco Press website, the code will be populated on your account page after purchase. Just log in at www.ciscopress.com, click Account to see details of your account, and click the Digital Purchases tab.

- **Amazon Kindle:** For those who purchase a Kindle edition from Amazon, the access code will be supplied directly by Amazon.

- **Other bookseller eBooks:** Note that if you purchase an eBook version from any other source, the practice test is not included because other vendors to date have not chosen to vend the required unique access code.

NOTE   Do not lose the access code because it is the only means with which you can access the QA content with the book.

Once you have the access code, to find instructions about both the Pearson Test Prep web app and the desktop app, follow these steps:

Step 1.   Open this book's companion website.

Step 2.   Click the **Practice Exams** button.

Step 3.   Follow the instructions listed there for installing the desktop app and for using the web app.

If you want to use the web app only at this point, just navigate to www.pearsontestprep. com, establish a free login if you do not already have one, and register this book's practice tests using the access code you just found. The process should take only a couple of minutes.

NOTE   Amazon eBook (Kindle) customers: It is easy to miss Amazon's email that lists your Pearson Test Prep access code. Soon after you purchase the Kindle eBook, Amazon should send an email; however, the email uses very generic text and makes no specific mention of PTP or practice exams. To find your code, read every email from Amazon after you purchase the book. Also do the usual checks for ensuring your email arrives, like checking your spam folder.

NOTE   Other eBook customers: As of the time of publication, only the publisher and Amazon supply Pearson Test Prep access codes when you purchase their eBook editions of this book.

How This Book Is Organized

Although this book could be read cover-to-cover, it is designed to be flexible and allow you to easily move between chapters and sections of chapters to cover just the material that you are interested in learning. Chapters 1 through 16 cover topics that are relevant to the DCACI 300-620 exam:

- **Chapter 1, "The Big Picture: Why ACI?":** This chapter describes some of the challenges inherent in traditional network switches and routers and how ACI is able to solve these challenges.

- **Chapter 2, "Understanding ACI Hardware and Topologies":** This chapter addresses the prominent ACI topologies in use today as well as ACI hardware platforms.

- **Chapter 3, "Initializing an ACI Fabric":** This chapter covers planning parameters that are important for fabric initialization, the fabric initialization process itself, and some common post-initialization tasks, such as assignment of static out-of-band IP addresses to ACI nodes as well as making fabric backups and restoring configurations.

- **Chapter 4, "Exploring ACI":** This chapter explores ACI access methods, the ACI object model, and some basic fabric health monitoring and fault management concepts.

- **Chapter 5, "Tenant Building Blocks":** This chapter examines from a conceptual viewpoint the various objects present under the tenant hierarchy and how they relate to one another.

- **Chapter 6, "Access Policies":** This chapter examines the concepts behind configuration of switch downlinks to servers, external switches, and routers. It also addresses how switch port configurations tie in with the tenant hierarchy.

- **Chapter 7, "Implementing Access Policies":** This chapter focuses on configuration of individual switch ports, port channels, vPCs, and fabric extenders (FEX) down to servers, external switches, and routers.

- **Chapter 8, "Implementing Tenant Policies":** This chapter covers endpoint learning and forwarding in ACI as well as deployment of multitier applications and the enforcement of contracts to whitelist data center communications.

- **Chapter 9, "L3Outs":** This chapter examines implementation of ACI route peering with outside Layer 3 devices as well as inbound and outbound route filtering.

- **Chapter 10, "Extending Layer 2 Outside ACI":** This chapter addresses ACI Layer 2 connectivity with non-ACI switches and interaction with Spanning Tree Protocol. It also provides basic coverage of network migrations into and out of ACI.

- **Chapter 11, "Integrating ACI into vSphere Using VDS":** This chapter addresses implementation of the most popular ACI integration and why it is important.

- **Chapter 12, "Implementing Service Graphs":** This chapter tackles the introduction of firewalls and load balancers into ACI fabrics using service graphs.

- **Chapter 13, "Implementing Management":** This chapter revisits the topic of in-band and out-of-band management in ACI and dives into the implementation of in-band management.

- **Chapter 14, "Monitoring ACI Using Syslog and SNMP":** This chapter covers how ACI can forward faults and other monitoring information to syslog or SNMP servers.

- **Chapter 15, "Implementing AAA and RBAC":** This chapter dives into role-based access control and how multitenancy can be enforced from a management perspective.

- **Chapter 16, "ACI Anywhere":** This chapter provides a primer on additional ACI solutions within the ACI portfolio, including ACI Multi-Pod and ACI Multi-Site, which allow extension of ACI policies between data centers, between remote locations, and between public clouds.

How to Use This Book

The questions for each certification exam are a closely guarded secret. However, Cisco has published exam blueprints that list the topics you must know to *successfully* complete the exams. Table I-1 lists the exam topics listed in the DCACI 300-620 exam blueprint along with a reference to the book chapter that covers each topic. These are the same topics you should be proficient in when designing and implementing ACI fabrics in the real world.

Table I-1   CCNP DCACI 300-620 Exam Topics and Chapter References

Exam Topic	Chapter(s) in Which Topic Is Covered
1.0 ACI Fabric Infrastructure	
1.1 Describe ACI topology and hardware	2
1.2 Describe ACI Object Model	4
1.3 Utilize faults, event record, and audit log	4
1.4 Describe ACI fabric discovery	3

Exam Topic	Chapter(s) in Which Topic Is Covered
1.5 Implement ACI policies 1.5.a access 1.5.b fabric	5, 6, 7
1.6 Implement ACI logical constructs 1.6.a tenant 1.6.b application profile 1.6.c VRF 1.6.d bridge domain (unicast routing, Layer 2 unknown hardware proxy, ARP flooding) 1.6.e endpoint groups (EPG) 1.6.f contracts (filter, provider, consumer, reverse port filter, VRF enforced)	5, 8, 9, 10
2.0 ACI Packet Forwarding	
2.1 Describe endpoint learning	8
2.2 Implement bridge domain configuration knob (unicast routing, Layer 2 unknown hardware proxy, ARP flooding)	8
3.0 External Network Connectivity	
3.1 Implement Layer 2 out (STP/MCP basics)	10
3.2 Implement Layer 3 out (excludes transit routing and VRF route leaking)	9
4.0 Integrations	
4.1 Implement VMware vCenter DVS integration	11
4.2 Describe resolution immediacy in VMM	11
4.3 Implement service graph (managed and unmanaged)	12
5.0 ACI Management	
5.1 Implement out-of-band and in-band	3, 13
5.2 Utilize syslog and snmp services	14
5.3 Implement configuration backup (snapshot/config import export)	3
5.4 Implement AAA and RBAC	15
5.5 Configure an upgrade	3
6.0 ACI Anywhere	
6.1 Describe multipod	16
6.2 Describe multisite	16

Each version of the exam may emphasize different topics, and some topics are rather broad and generalized. The goal of this book is to provide comprehensive coverage to ensure that you are well prepared for the exam. Although some chapters might not address specific exam topics, they provide a foundation that is necessary for a clear understanding of important topics. Your short-term goal might be to pass this exam, but your long-term goal should be to become a qualified CCNP data center engineer.

It is important to understand that this book is a static reference, whereas the exam topics are dynamic. Cisco can and does change the topics covered on certification exams often.

This book should not be your only reference when preparing for the certification exam. You can find a wealth of information at Cisco.com that covers each topic in great detail. If you think you need more detailed information on a specific topic, read the Cisco documentation that focuses on that topic.

Note that as ACI features and solutions continue to evolve, Cisco reserves the right to change the exam topics without notice. Although you can refer to the list of exam topics in Table I-1, you should check Cisco.com to verify the current list of topics to ensure that you are prepared to take the exam. You can view the current exam topics on any current Cisco certification exam by visiting the Cisco.com website and choosing Menu > Training & Events and selecting from the Certifications list. Note also that, if needed, Cisco Press might post additional preparatory content on the web page associated with this book at http://www.ciscopress.com/title/9780136602668. It's a good idea to check the website a couple weeks before taking the exam to be sure you have up-to-date content.

Figure Credits

Figure 11-03: Screenshot of a VMkernel adapter with management services enabled © 2020 VMware, Inc

Figure 11-4: Screenshot of selecting Ephemeral - No Binding as the port binding type © 2020 VMware, Inc

Figure 11-5: Screenshot of teaming and failover settings for port groups © 2020 VMware, Inc

Figure 11-6: Screenshot of data center, cluster, and ESXi host hierarchy in vCenter © 2020 VMware, Inc

Figure 11-11: Screenshot of validating VDS creation in vCenter © 2020 VMware, Inc

Figure 11-12: Screenshot of navigating to the Add and Manage Hosts Wizard in vCenter © 2020 VMware, Inc

Figure 11-13: Screenshot of selecting add hosts © 2020 VMware, Inc

Figure 11-14: Screenshot of clicking new hosts © 2020 VMware, Inc

Figure 11-15: Screenshot of choosing the hosts to add on the Select New Hosts page © 2020 VMware, Inc

Figure 11-16: Screenshot of assigning uplinks to a VDS © 2020 VMware, Inc

Figure 11-17: Screenshot of the Manage VMkernel Adapters page © 2020 VMware, Inc

Figure 11-18: Screenshot of the Manage VM Networking page © 2020 VMware, Inc

Figure 11-19: Screenshot of confirming the addition of ESXi hosts to the VDS © 2020 VMware, Inc

Figure 11-22: Screenshot of verifying distributed port group generation in vCenter © 2020 VMware, Inc

Figure 11-23: Screenshot of reassigning a VM vNIC to a distributed port group © 2020 VMware, Inc

Figure 11-25: Screenshot of verifying the result of custom EPG naming and delimiter modification © 2020 VMware, Inc

Figure 11-26: Screenshot of verifying the result of active uplinks and standby uplinks settings © 2020 VMware, Inc

Figure 11-28: Screenshot of assigning ESXi host uplinks to a link aggregation group © 2020 VMware, Inc

Figure 11-30: Screenshot of verifying distributed port group mapping to uplinks © 2020 VMware, Inc

## CHAPTER 1

The Big Picture: Why ACI?

This chapter covers the following topics:

Understanding the Shortcomings of Traditional Networks: This section discusses some of the challenges related to traditional data center networks.

Recognizing the Benefits of Cisco ACI: This section outlines how ACI addresses the major limitations of traditional networks.

The only way for businesses to be able to deploy and operationalize a technical solution in a way that takes full advantage of the benefits offered by the product is for engineers to develop a solid understanding of the product so that as they deploy it, they can keep its capabilities, corporate challenges, and industry challenges in mind.

This chapter provides a 10,000-foot view of Cisco Application Centric Infrastructure (ACI) and explores the reasons companies commonly deploy ACI. To this end, this chapter revisits the challenges that plagued more traditional networks and discusses how ACI addresses such challenges. The concepts outlined also set the stage for the more technical deep dives that follow in later chapters.

"Do I Know This Already?" Quiz

The "Do I Know This Already?" quiz allows you to assess whether you should read this entire chapter thoroughly or jump to the "Exam Preparation Tasks" section. If you are in doubt about your answers to these questions or your own assessment of your knowledge of the topics, read the entire chapter. Table 1-1 lists the major headings in this chapter and their corresponding "Do I Know This Already?" quiz questions. You can find the answers in Appendix A, "Answers to the 'Do I Know This Already?' Questions."

Table 1-1 "Do I Know This Already?" Section-to-Question Mapping

Foundation Topics Section	Questions
Understanding the Shortcomings of Traditional Networks	1–3
Recognizing the Benefits of Cisco ACI	4–10

CAUTION The goal of self-assessment is to gauge your mastery of the topics in this chapter. If you do not know the answer to a question or are only partially sure of the answer, you should mark that question as wrong for purposes of the self-assessment. Giving yourself credit for an answer you correctly guess skews your self-assessment results and might provide you with a false sense of security.

1. Which of the following items contribute to network management complexity? (Choose all that apply.)
   a. Level of engineering expertise needed
   b. Open standards
   c. Number of managed endpoints
   d. Correlation of information across devices

2. How many bits does the IEEE 802.1Q frame format use to define VLAN IDs, and what is the maximum number of VLAN IDs that can be used to segment Layer 2 traffic?
   a. 12 bits and 4094 VLAN IDs
   b. 10 bits and 1024 VLAN IDs
   c. 11 bits and 2048 VLAN IDs
   d. 24 bits and 8096 VLAN IDs

3. True or false: Firewalls in traditional data centers focus primarily on securing east–west traffic.
   a. True
   b. False

4. True or false: ACI uses VLANs internally to segment traffic.
   a. True
   b. False

5. Which of the following solutions can be used as a single point of orchestration for multiple ACI fabrics?
   a. vPod
   b. ACI Multi-Pod
   c. The APIC GUI
   d. Multi-Site Orchestrator

6. True or false: In ACI, you can decommission a switch and then replace it in a few mouse clicks by reallocating a node ID.
   a. True
   b. False

7. Which of the following is the term for allowing all traffic except that which is denied by access lists and similar security mechanisms?
   a. Blacklisting
   b. Whitelisting
   c. Multitenancy
   d. Firewalling

8. True or false: Customers that avoid automation and orchestration cannot use ACI to achieve more agility.
   a. True
   b. False

9. Which ACI solution enables engineers to run additional control plane instances within a single ACI fabric?

   a. Multisite

   b. Configuration zones

   c. Multipod

   d. Security zones

10. Which one of the following items is not a reason to implement multitenancy?

   a. Limiting the impact of configuration mishaps

   b. Handing off network containers to business units

   c. Administrative separation of network resources

   d. Microsegmentation

Foundation Topics

Understanding the Shortcomings of Traditional Networks

In response to questions about the nature and purpose of Application Centric Infrastructure (ACI), engineers sometimes tend to answer simply that ACI is Cisco's response to the popularity of software-defined networking (SDN). Although it *is* controller based, agile, and highly programmable, ACI has actually been designed to address the broader range of industrywide headaches that have plagued traditional data center networks.

To better appreciate ACI, therefore, it's important to understand the context in which ACI was introduced to the market.

Network Management

Networks are complex to manage for a variety of reasons. The following are several of the common reasons for the complexity of network management:

- **Number of managed endpoints:** It is common for large enterprises to have hundreds of switches and routers in each data center. In addition to endpoints managed by network teams, storage nodes, compute nodes, firewalls, and load balancers further contribute to the number of endpoints that need to be individually managed. As the number of devices in a network increases, the probability of configuration drift also increases, and so does the possibility of incorrect configurations going unnoticed for long periods of time. The number of devices also has a direct impact on the feasibility and effort needed for periodic end-to-end audits.

- **Correlating information between devices:** When complex issues occur and reactive mitigation is required, it can be cumbersome to correlate information across large numbers of switches, routers, compute nodes, virtualized environments, firewalls, and load balancers to reach resolutions.

- **Level of expertise:** Network maintenance is not always straightforward. A typical enterprise network leverages multiple networking vendors or at least multiple network operating systems. Each network is also configured differently. While it is common for network engineers to specialize in several platforms, it is not always common for all engineers to become subject matter experts in all areas of a corporate network. For this reason, interaction between multiple engineers is typically required, and a high level of expertise is therefore needed to keep networks performant.

- **Human error:** Even the most knowledgeable engineers may overlook some aspect of a network design or fat-finger a line of configuration. Any type of human error can be devastating and could lead to major downtime.

- **Differences in protocol implementations:** While open standards are often detailed, they are also very flexible, and a lot is left open to interpretation. Vendors therefore end up deploying solutions that have slight differences across platforms, which can sometimes lead to network management headaches.

Scalability and Growth

Traditionally, networks have been built based on hierarchical designs that call for three layers. Within the data center, the three-tier design recommended by Cisco has consisted of an access layer, an aggregation layer, and a core layer. Figure 1-1 shows a conceptual view of the three-tier data center architecture.

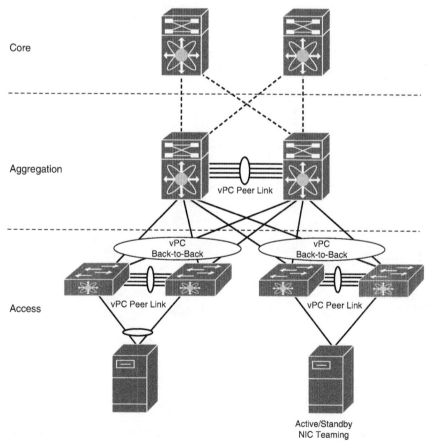

Figure 1-1 *Conceptual View of the Traditional Three-Tier Data Center Architecture*

Within the three-tier data center model, servers are typically housed in the access layer, where relatively low-cost switches are used to perform line-rate intra-VLAN forwarding. A set of access switches connecting to a dedicated pair of aggregation layer switches forms a switch block.

The aggregation layer serves as the root of spanning tree for VLANs within data center switch blocks and also as a point for service aggregation. Inter-VLAN routing is performed at the aggregation layer, where default gateways are typically implemented using a first-hop redundancy protocol (FHRP), enabling an aggregation block to potentially sustain the loss of a single aggregation switch.

For aggregation layer downlinks to the access layer, Cisco recommends using Layer 2 virtual port channels (vPCs) or some other form of Multichassis EtherChannel (MEC) technology. Access layer switches are also often configured as vPC pairs to allow downstream servers to be dual-homed to the access layer using vPCs.

By definition, the data center core layer is intended to be formed of routed links and to support low-latency rapid forwarding of packets. The goal of the core layer is to interconnect the aggregation and access layers with other network zones within or outside the enterprise.

Historically, the three-tier data center hierarchical design enabled a substantial amount of predictability because use of aggregation switch blocks simplified the spanning-tree topology. The need for scalability and sometimes requirements for traffic separation pushed the three-tier model toward modularization, which in turn further increased predictability within the data center. Figure 1-2 depicts a sample modular data center network design.

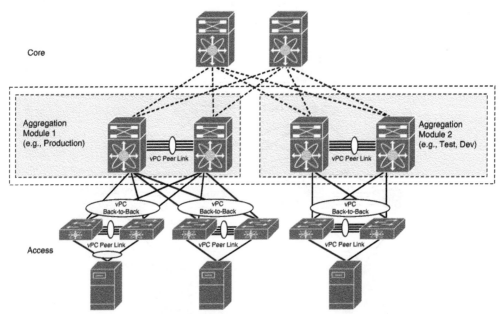

Figure 1-2 *Example of Network Modularization Within the Data Center*

The main challenge inherent in the three-tier model is that it is difficult to scale. To eliminate spanning-tree blocked links and maximize bandwidth between tiers, access and aggregation switches are typically paired into vPC domains, but each vPC domain can be formed using a maximum of two switches. Spanning-tree implications within the three-tier design prevented scaling out the aggregation layer through addition of a third aggregation switch to a given switch block. In these traditional networks, to prevent bandwidth oversubscription within switch blocks from becoming a costly bottleneck, companies taking on data center redesign projects had to predict and often inflate their target-state network scalability requirements and purchase equipment accordingly. Knowing that applications tend to become more and more bandwidth hungry over time, companies that had deployed the 1 Gbps and 10 Gbps architectures of the time began to expect that vendors introduce newer and more flexible 40 Gbps and 100 Gbps architectures. The clear expectation in the industry was that application owners should be able to scale their applications knowing that the network could also be rapidly scaled to accommodate them.

An additional challenge that also guided the development of network solutions within data centers at the time was the growth in east–west traffic. The term *east–west traffic* refers to traffic between servers and is used to differentiate between traffic remaining in the data center and traffic to servers from the rest of the network (*north–south*). Server virtualization, distributed applications, and changes in the amount of data stored and replicated within data centers meant that traffic flows shifted in the east–west direction, and the network had to be able to support this growth. This shift coincided with demands for more agility and stability inside the data center, giving rise to a desire for subsecond failovers and a move away from spanning tree in favor of routed overlay networks.

This evolution continued with the emergence of technologies such as Cisco FabricPath, with which large enterprises were able to build extremely scalable topologies that did not suffer from spanning-tree blocked links and eliminated the need for modularization of data center switch blocks. Using these new routed fabrics, companies also managed to optimize their data centers for east–west traffic flows. The popularity of routed fabrics and the industrywide embrace of a data center design approach that collapsed VLANs from all switch blocks within a data center into a single fabric and enabled any given VLAN to be available on any top-of-rack switch was enough for the industry to concede to routed fabrics being the way forward.

The fabric-based approach simplified the deployment of new switches and servers in data centers from a facilities standpoint and therefore decreased the time to deploy new services.

While these early fabrics were a step forward, each network switch within these fabrics still had to be configured independently. The early fabrics also did not address the issue of the number of managed network endpoints. Furthermore, the move of all VLANs into a single fabric also made apparent that some data center fabrics could be adversely impacted by IEEE 802.1Q limitations on the maximum number of VLANs.

NOTE   The IEEE 802.1Q standard that defines frame formats for supporting VLANs over Ethernet calls for the use of 12 bits to identify VLAN IDs; therefore, a maximum of 4096 VLANs are possible. With two VLANs (0 and 4095) reserved for system use, a total maximum of 4094 VLANs can be used to segment Layer 2 data plane traffic.

Although modularization is still desired in networks today, the general trend in large enterprise environments has been to move away from traditional architectures that revolve around spanning tree toward more flexible and scalable solutions that are enabled by VXLAN and other similar Layer 3 overlay architectures.

Network Agility

The network underpins all IT services that modern businesses have come to rely on. For this reason, the network is almost always considered mission critical, and requests for changes to the network are understandably met with resistance.

The word *agility* in the context of IT refers to making configuration changes, deploying services, and generally supporting the business at the speed it desires; therefore, one company's definition of its expectations for agility will be different from that of another. In some environments, a network team may be considered agile if it can deploy new services in a matter of weeks. In others, agility may mean that business units in a company should be able to get applications to production or scale core services on demand through automation and orchestration with zero intervention from network engineers or even corporate IT.

Regardless of how a company decides to define agility, there is very little disagreement with the idea that network agility is vital to business success. The problem is that network agility has traditionally been hard to achieve.

Security

Switches and routers use access lists to enforce data plane security. However, companies have seldom been able to effectively leverage access lists on switches and routers for granular lockdown of server-to-server traffic.

Outside of server firewalls, the most common form of data plane security enforcement within data centers has been the use of physical firewalls, which are very effective in locking down north–south traffic flowing between security zones. Because firewalls are expensive and there is a latency impact associated with traffic inspection, redirecting east–west traffic that remains inside a single security zone is not always desirable.

Figure 1-3 shows the typical firewall security zones deployed in most data centers today. Almost every data center has an Internet zone, a demilitarized zone (DMZ), and an inside security zone, but the exact number of security zones, the names associated with the zones, and the implementation details are very environment specific.

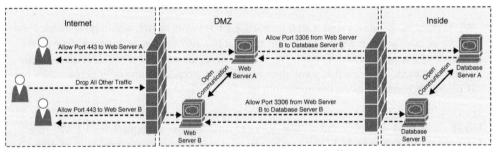

Figure 1-3   *A Data Center Network Built Using Three Firewall Security Zones*

The challenge with the traditional model of solely locking down north–south traffic via perimeter and inside firewalls is that once a server within a firewall security zone is compromised, other servers can then be impacted through lateral movement. For example, in Figure 1-3, if Database Server A in the inside security zone were to become infected, the malware could potentially move laterally to infect other servers, such as Database Server B, in the inside security zone without intervention from the north–south firewalls. Likewise, if a hacker were to compromise Web Server A, the hacker could then launch exploits laterally against Web Server B without firewall intervention. Even though Web Server A and Database Server A form an entirely different application instance than Web Server B and Database Server B, this type of lateral movement is common in traditional networks due to the complexities of enforcing and managing access lists on traditional switches and routers.

Network Visibility

Virtualization has muddied the boundaries between servers and the network. As more and more servers were deployed as virtual machines, troubleshooting of network connectivity issues became more complex because network teams only had visibility down to the hypervisor level and no visibility down to the VM level.

Even though solutions like Cisco's Nexus 1000v distributed virtual switch alleviate some visibility concerns, a lot of enterprises prefer to use hypervisor switches produced by the hypervisor vendors to simplify support and prevent interoperability issues.

Lack of end-to-end network visibility continues to be a concern for many network teams, especially now that container networking is becoming more popular.

Recognizing the Benefits of Cisco ACI

Fully embracing ACI requires a dramatic paradigm shift for most engineers. One motivation for outlining the ideal target-state objectives for ACI-based networks is to give those transitioning into ACI a taste of the brave new world of data center networking. In addition, we want to provide very basic guideposts that may help inform engineers of blind spots as well as alternative approaches to ACI that may require different thinking in terms of design or configuration.

Some of the benefits listed in this section are inherent to ACI and some are products of good design and configuration practices. Not all of the benefits described in the following sections are exclusive to ACI. This section is not intended to provide a competitive comparison of data center network solutions available in the market today. It is also *not* intended to call out benefits in order of priority.

Network Management Touchpoints

Cisco ACI is deployed in a two-tier spine-and-leaf architecture in which every *leaf* connects to every *spine* in the topology. The leaf switches are the attachment points for all servers in the network. The spines serve to interconnect leaf switches at high speeds. The brain and central management point for the entire fabric is the *Cisco Application Policy Infrastructure Controller (APIC) cluster,* which is a set of (typically three) specialized servers that connect to leaf switches within the ACI fabric.

Figure 1-4 shows the components of an ACI fabric and their placement in a two-tier spine-and-leaf architecture.

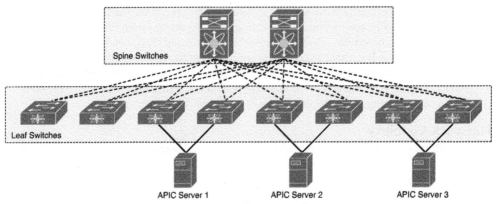

Figure 1-4   *Architecture and Components of an ACI Fabric*

In ACI, engineers do not directly configure switches. They send configurations to the APICs, which are the only configuration management points in the fabric, thereby reducing the number of touchpoints for configuration changes compared to traditional data center networks. Using APICs as a centralized component for fabric configuration also reduces the potential for human error because the APICs often identify when a new configuration conflicts with previously deployed configurations and may prevent the deployment of problematic configurations.

With ACI, engineers still have access to the individual switches for verification and troubleshooting purposes.

Traffic Flow Optimizations

Spine-and-leaf architectures optimize east–west traffic forwarding by ensuring that server-to-server traffic within a data center needs to traverse no more than a single spine and two leaf switches to reach the intended destination, making latency between servers more deterministic.

In addition to east–west traffic flow optimizations through the use of a spine-and-leaf physical topology, ACI has a number of data plane and control plane enhancements that lead to better traffic handling; these enhancements are covered in detail in Chapter 8, "Implementing Tenant Policies."

Scalability Optimizations

Spine-and-leaf architectures that rely on routing protocols and not spanning tree enable a scale-out approach to growing the network. When more servers need to be deployed in a data center, you can expand ACI without outage and during regular work hours simply by adding new leaf switches. If oversubscription becomes a concern, you can introduce more leaf uplinks and/or spines into the fabric.

Another reason ACI fabrics are more scalable than traditional networks is that they are built around VXLAN, which uses 24 bits and provides over 16 million unique IDs. Note that ACI is VLAN aware, but VLANs in ACI are mostly used to encapsulate traffic egressing to external devices such as servers and routers as well as map inbound traffic entering the fabric to corresponding VXLAN network identifiers (VNIDs).

Programmability

ACI uses an advanced object-based model that allows for network constructs to be fully configured using an open representational state transfer (REST) API. In addition to providing this interface, ACI also provides a number of access methods that enable reading and manipulating of data.

In legacy network devices, APIs are an afterthought; in contrast, programmability is at the foundation of ACI. In fact, the ACI GUI programs the fabric using API calls.

The programmatic nature of ACI enables network agility; it allows for network and security engineers to script out changes and repeatable tasks to save time and enforce configuration standardization. For companies that seek to eliminate the need for manual changes through automation and orchestration, ACI programmability has even wider implications.

Stateless Network

An engineer who wants to configure an ACI fabric sends configurations to an APIC, which in turn configures the leaf and spine switches accordingly. Configurations are not associated with physical switches but with node IDs. A *node ID* is a logical representation of an ACI switch or APIC that can be associated with or disassociated from physical hardware. Because configurations are not bound to the physical devices, ACI hardware can be considered stateless.

In practice, statelessness enables engineers to look at switches as infrastructure that can be easily decommissioned and replaced with newer-model switches faster and with minimal impact. Once a switch is replaced, an engineer assigns the node ID of the decommissioned switch to the new switch and the APIC and then configures the switch with all the same port assignments and configurations that were assigned to the old switch. Because platform-specific configuration parameters, such as interface names, are abstracted from node configurations as much as possible, and because it is the APICs and not the engineers that are tasked with interpreting how to deploy node configurations to physical switches, subsequent data center migrations can be dramatically expedited. Stateless networking, therefore, attempts to address the need for network agility.

By lowering data center migration times as well as the time to migrate off of faulty switches, stateless networking introduces additional cost savings that cannot be easily calculated. By saving costs in the long term and enabling an architecture that can be leveraged for decades to come, ACI frees up engineering time that can be refocused on more business-critical tasks, such as enforcement of enhanced security.

Multitenancy

Multitenancy is the ability to logically separate management as well as data plane forwarding of different logical environments that reside on top of common physical infrastructure.

Because multitenancy means different things to different people, it might be best to first examine characteristics of multitenant environments in general and then clarify how multitenancy should be understood within the context of ACI.

A natural analogy for multitenancy in IT can be found in the operation of apartment buildings, and an analysis of how apartments enable multitenancy is therefore a great place to start.

An apartment building usually consists of several apartments, each of which is rented out to a different tenant. The apartment building is cost-effective for the owner because it uses shared infrastructure such as land, walls, parking lots, water pipes, natural gas infrastructure, and the electrical system.

A tenant who rents an apartment is given a key and has relative freedom to do as he or she pleases within the confines of the apartment. Renters can invite guests and can come and go as they please, regardless of the time of day or night.

Even though the electrical system is a shared infrastructure, a tenant does not need to worry too much about blowing the fuse on occasion due to use of high-amperage appliances. As a core design consideration, the building owner is expected to provide each tenant with core services and a reasonable amount of fault isolation. In other words, it is reasonable to expect that the loss of electricity within a single apartment should not impact the entire building or complex.

Tenants also have certain rights and responsibilities that govern their relationships with neighbors and the apartment owner as well as his or her representatives. A tenant has the right to privacy and understands that the apartment owner cannot enter his or her dwelling unless either there is an emergency or the tenant has been notified well in advance. Tenants also have a right to good living conditions. On the other hand, the apartment owner expects that tenants pay rent in a timely fashion and avoid disruptive behavior or cause damage to the building.

An apartment owner typically signs a binding contract with a tenant. The law complements these contracts by enabling lawsuits against negligent owners and making evictions possible, where tenants may abandon their responsibilities.

All in all, the tenant/owner relationship benefits both parties. The owner performs maintenance where reasonable within apartments and is responsible for keeping the property grounds clean. The owner is also responsible for maintaining all shared infrastructure within the property. Since the tenants are not responsible for maintenance, they have more time to focus on the things that matter most to them.

Moving on to ACI, one can easily see that shared infrastructure is primarily a reference to the ACI fabric itself. But the idea of shared infrastructure also applies to servers and appliances residing within the fabric.

ACI inherits support for multitenancy through its use of the Multiprotocol Border Gateway Protocol Ethernet Virtual Private Network (MP-BGP EVPN) control plane for VXLAN. The MP-BGP EVPN control plane and other control plane instruments play a role similar to that of the law and the binding contract between the apartment owner and tenant in the previous example.

In addition to control plane dependencies, data plane and management plane aspects are at work to enable multitenancy capabilities similar to those outlined for apartments:

- **Data plane multitenancy:** As in the world of apartment rentals, in a network, there is a need to ensure that tenants remain exclusive and in controlled environments and that issues within one tenant space do not impact other tenants. In ACI, a tenant is simply an object under which an administrator may configure one or more virtual routing and forwarding (VRF) instances. VRF instances segment traffic at Layer 3 by virtualizing the routing tables of routers. Because any given network subnet is always associated with a VRF instance and traffic originating within a subnet cannot traverse VRF boundaries unless intentionally leaked or advertised into the destination VRF, full data plane traffic segmentation is possible. ACI also enables multitenancy at Layer 2.

- **Management multitenancy:** Just as an apartment renter expects to have almost exclusive access to apartment keys and have the freedom to do as he or she pleases within the rented apartment, ACI multitenancy employs mechanisms to enable and enforce relevant users the freedoms they need within their tenant space. ACI introduces the concept of security domains to define the part of the object-based hierarchy within ACI that a user can access. ACI also controls the amount of access the user has by using role-based access control (RBAC).

Some common drivers for the implementation of multiple tenants in ACI are as follows:

- **Administrative separation:** When network administration for different applications or devices is handled by different teams within a company, a simple solution is to use multitenancy to carry over the same administrative separation into ACI. A good example of this is hospitals that have a for-profit division as well as a nonprofit division. Each division may employ different engineers who manage different applications and servers, but they may be able to cut costs through the use of shared infrastructure.

- **Alignment with software development lifecycles:** There are a lot of use cases for leveraging tenants in software development. For example, in some environments, applications may be deployed in a tenant that mirrors production and serves as a staging ground for testing. Once the application is fully tested, it can then be moved into a production tenant without IP address changes.

- **Overall IT strategy:** IT is generally seen as a cost center. Some companies cross-charge departments for services as part of an effort to transform from a cost center to a provider of services to the business. In such cases, IT may intend to provide one or more tenants to each business unit to allow them to configure their own networking constructs, applications, and security so they can deploy IT services at the pace they expect. Decisions around tenant design often come down to overall IT strategy, and a wide range of reasons exist for tenant deployment that may be specific to an individual environment.

- **Partnerships, mergers, and acquisitions:** Let's say two companies enter into a partnership and need a common space to set up applications that will be owned jointly by both companies. In these types of scenarios, a tenant can be deployed with a security domain that employees from both companies are assigned to. Mergers and acquisitions create similar situations, where granular control over networking environments may allow additional flexibility and agility.

- **Limiting fault domain sizes:** Similar to the case in which an apartment tenant blows a fuse and the expectation is that there will be no cascading effect leading to power outages across the entire apartment building, some customers use ACI multitenancy to limit and isolate fault domains from one another. Imagine that an IT organization creates a tenant for a series of applications that are business critical and makes a firm decision that management of that individual tenant will always remain under the control of the central IT organization. It then creates a separate tenant and hands off management of the tenant to a specific business unit that has specific requirements for more agile changes to the network in support of an important software development project. Let's say the IT team is more network savvy than the business unit in question. It understands that route overlaps between the new tenant and the business-critical tenant will have minimal considerations, but it is worried about the possibility of the new tenant owner incorrectly configuring subnets that propagate throughout the enterprise network and causing outages to other systems. Because the egress point for all VRF instances within the tenant is the default VRF instance on the data center core, IT has decided to implement very basic route filtering in the inbound direction on the core layer, allowing only subnets that are within a single supernet to be advertised out of ACI from the tenant in question. This basic solution, when combined with well-defined security domains and RBAC, can prevent any configuration mishap in the new development tenant from causing wider issues within the corporate network.

It is worth noting that multitenancy did exist in traditional networks using VRF instances and RBAC. However, multitenancy in ACI provides more granular control and is easier to configure.

Zero-Trust Security

In traditional data centers, north–south firewalls are the primary enforcers of security within the data centers. By default, switches and routers do not block any traffic and do little in terms of data plane security enforcement. If switches and routers use tools such as access lists to lock down data plane traffic, they are basically *blacklisting* certain traffic.

ACI is different from traditional switches and routers in that all traffic flows crossing VXLAN boundaries within the fabric are denied by default. Contracts define which subset of endpoints within ACI can communicate with one another. This default behavior in which traffic is dropped unless it is explicitly allowed via contracts is called whitelisting.

Whitelisting is more feasible in ACI than in traditional networks because the configuration of contracts is fundamentally different from that of CLI-based access lists, even though they are enforced nearly the same way.

The benefits of whitelisting can be better understood through analysis of a multitier application. Figure 1-3, shown earlier in the chapter, actually depicts two multitier applications, each consisting of a web tier and a database tier. When ACI and whitelisting come into the picture, the same traffic flows exist. However, only the minimally required ports between the application tiers are opened due to whitelisting rules, as depicted in Figure 1-5. With this change, Web Server A can no longer talk to Web Server B. Likewise, Database Server A is also unable to communicate with Database Server B.

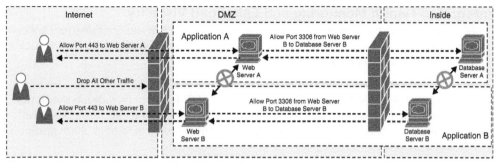

Figure 1-5 *Whitelisted Two-Tier Application*

ACI supports a ***zero-trust security*** architecture through whitelisting, allowing administrators to block non-essential communications other than those explicitly specified through contracts. Where more granular application-level inspection is also desired, ACI can redirect desired traffic to a firewall for inspection prior to forwarding to the destination server.

Cross-Platform Integrations

One of the challenges in traditional networks is cross-platform and cross-vendor visibility and integration. ACI has a large partner ecosystem and has integrations with an extensive number of vendors.

Although there is a wide variety of use cases for integrations with ACI, some of the more common include integrations with hypervisor environments and L4–L7 service insertion. ACI integration with VMware vCenter, for example, enables ACI to automatically push port groups into vSphere. One use case for L4–L7 service insertion is to selectively redirect traffic to a firewall or a pool of firewalls for more granular inspection of traffic.

Compared to legacy architectures, ACI cross-platform integrations provide a lot of benefits and primarily address the need for visibility and agility within data centers.

New Architectural Possibilities

In addition to attempting to address the challenges inherent in traditional data centers, ACI also creates new architectural possibilities.

ACI Multi-Pod, for instance, offers a way of segmenting a fabric into pods that each run separate control plane instances and is very effective in creating active/active data centers or staging equipment across data centers within a single campus environment.

ACI Multi-Site, on the other hand, is a solution that is enabled by Multi-Site Orchestrator (MSO), which can serve as a single point of policy orchestration across multiple ACI fabrics to enable flexible and even dual active/active architectures that allow for seamless policy movement between data centers, among other things. It can also integrate with the Cisco Cloud APIC to allow homogenous security policy across on-premises data centers and public clouds, ensuring operational consistency and visibility across clouds.

Other ACI solutions include remote leaf and vPod.

Integrated Health Monitoring and Enhanced Visibility

ACI is a controller-based system, and by virtue of being a system and not a disparate collection of switches, ACI allows visibility into traffic flow and issues that may be causing packet loss and performance degradation.

ACI uses faults and health scores to determine the state of an overall system. Because of the deep visibility of the APIC controllers into the fabric, ACI is able to provide more analytics than regular monitoring tools such as syslog and SNMP typically provide. Integrated health monitoring and enhanced visibility within ACI typically translate to faster problem resolution and more proactive problem resolution.

Policy Reuse

While automation through scripting greatly helps agility, not all companies will embrace scripting and orchestration in the near future. Some companies simply expect to save as much time as possible without having to learn scripting. In such cases, policy reuse can help. For instance, by creating profiles for server interface configurations that can be instantiated anywhere in the data center, IT teams can reduce the amount of time needed to deploy new servers while also decreasing the possibility of configuration drift.

Exam Preparation Tasks

As mentioned in the section "How to Use This Book" in the Introduction, you have a couple of choices for exam preparation: Chapter 17, "Final Preparation," and the exam simulation questions in the Pearson Test Prep Software Online.

Review All Key Topics

Review the most important topics in this chapter, noted with the Key Topic icon in the outer margin of the page. Table 1-2 lists these key topics and the page number on which each is found.

Table 1-2 Key Topics for Chapter 1

Key Topic Element	Description	Page Number
Paragraph	Lists the components of an ACI fabric	9
Paragraph	Explains how a node ID enables stateless networking	11
Paragraph	Defines multitenancy	11
List	Explains how data plane and management multitenancy work together to make multitenancy possible	12
Paragraph	Describes blacklisting	14
Paragraph	Describes whitelisting	14
Paragraph	Explains the high-level mechanisms ACI uses to establish zero-trust security	15

Complete Tables and Lists from Memory

There are no memory tables or lists in this chapter.

Define Key Terms

Define the following key terms from this chapter and check your answers in the glossary:

blacklisting, whitelisting, node ID, APIC cluster, leaf, spine, zero-trust security, multitenancy

## CHAPTER 2

Understanding ACI Hardware and Topologies

This chapter covers the following topics:

ACI Topologies and Components: This section describes the key hardware components and acceptable topologies for ACI fabrics.

APIC Clusters: This section covers available APIC hardware models and provides an understanding of APIC cluster sizes and failover implications.

Spine Hardware: This section addresses available spine hardware options.

Leaf Hardware: This section outlines the leaf platforms available for deployment in ACI fabrics.

This chapter covers the following exam topics:

- 1.1 Describe ACI topology and hardware
- 6.1 Describe Multi-Pod
- 6.2 Describe Multi-Site

ACI is designed to allow small and large enterprises and service providers to build massively scalable data centers using a relatively small number of very flexible topologies.

This chapter details the topologies with which an ACI fabric can be built or extended. Understanding supported ACI topologies helps guide decisions on target-state network architecture and hardware selection.

Each hardware component in an ACI fabric performs a specific set of functions. For example, leaf switches enforce security rules, and spine switches track all endpoints within a fabric in a local database.

But not all ACI switches are created equally. Nor are APICs created equally. This chapter therefore aims to provide a high-level understanding of some of the things to consider when selecting hardware.

"Do I Know This Already?" Quiz

The "Do I Know This Already?" quiz allows you to assess whether you should read this entire chapter thoroughly or jump to the "Exam Preparation Tasks" section. If you are in doubt about your answers to these questions or your own assessment of your knowledge of the topics, read the entire chapter. Table 2-1 lists the major headings in this chapter and their corresponding "Do I Know This Already?" quiz questions. You can find the answers in Appendix A, "Answers to the 'Do I Know This Already?' Questions."

Table 2-1 "Do I Know This Already?" Section-to-Question Mapping

Foundation Topics Section	Questions
ACI Topologies and Components	1–5
APIC Clusters	6
Spine Hardware	7, 8
Leaf Hardware	9, 10

CAUTION The goal of self-assessment is to gauge your mastery of the topics in this chapter. If you do not know the answer to a question or are only partially sure of the answer, you should mark that question as wrong for purposes of the self-assessment. Giving yourself credit for an answer you correctly guess skews your self-assessment results and might provide you with a false sense of security.

1. An ACI fabric is being extended to a secondary location to replace two top-of-rack switches and integrate a handful of servers into a corporate ACI environment. Which solution should ideally be deployed at the remote location if the deployment of new spines is considered cost-prohibitive and direct fiber links from the main data center cannot be dedicated to this function?

   a. ACI Multi-Site

   b. ACI Remote Leaf

   c. ACI Multi-Tier

   d. ACI Multi-Pod

2. Which of the following is a requirement for a Multi-Pod IPN that is not needed in an ACI Multi-Site ISN?

   a. Increased MTU support

   b. OSPF support on last-hop routers connecting to ACI spines

   c. End-to-end IP connectivity

   d. Multicast PIM-Bidir

3. Which of the following connections would ACI definitely block?

   a. APIC-to-leaf cabling

   b. Leaf-to-leaf cabling

   c. Spine-to-leaf cabling

   d. Spine-to-spine cabling

4. Which of the following are valid reasons for ACI Multi-Site requiring more specialized spine hardware? (Choose all that apply.)

   a. Ingress replication of BUM traffic

   b. IP fragmentation

   c. Namespace normalization

   d. Support for PIM-Bidir for multicast forwarding

5. Which of the following options best describes border leaf switches?

   a. Border leaf switches provide Layer 2 and 3 connectivity to outside networks.

   b. Border leaf switches connect to Layer 4–7 service appliances, such as firewalls and load balancers.

   c. Border leaf switches are ACI leaf switches that connect to servers.

   d. Border leaf switches serve as the border between server network traffic and FCoE storage traffic.

6. Which of the following statements is accurate?

   a. A three-node M3 cluster of APICs can scale up to 200 leaf switches.

   b. Sharding is a result of the evolution of what is called horizontal partitioning of databases.

   c. The number of shards distributed among APICs for a given attribute is directly correlated to the number of APICs deployed.

   d. A standby APIC actively synchronizes with active APICs and has a copy of all attributes within the APIC database at all times.

7. Out of the following switches, which are spine platforms that support ACI Multi-Site? (Choose all that apply.)

   a. Nexus 93180YC-EX

   b. Nexus 9364C

   c. Nexus 9736C-FX line card

   d. Nexus 9396PX

8. Which of the following is a valid reason for upgrading a pair of Nexus 9336PQ ACI switches to second-generation Nexus 9332C spine hardware? (Choose all that apply.)

   a. Namespace normalization for ACI Multi-Site support

   b. Support for 40 Gbps leaf-to-spine connectivity

   c. Support for CloudSec

   d. Support for ACI Multi-Pod

9. True or false: The Nexus 93180YC-FX leaf switch supports MACsec.

   a. True

   b. False

10. Which of the following platforms is a low-cost option for server CIMC and other low-bandwidth functions that rely on RJ-45 connectivity?

   a. Nexus 9336C-FX2

   b. Nexus 93180YC-FX

   c. Nexus 9332C

   d. Nexus 9348GC-FXP

Foundation Topics

ACI Topologies and Components

Like many other current data center fabrics, ACI fabrics conform to a Clos-based leaf-and-spine topology.

In ACI, leaf and spine switches are each responsible for different functions. Together, they create an architecture that is highly standardized across deployments. Cisco has introduced several new connectivity models and extensions for ACI fabrics over the years, but none of these changes break the core ACI topology that has been the standard from day one. Any topology modifications introduced in this section should therefore be seen as slight enhancements that help address specific use cases and not as deviations from the standard ACI topology.

Clos Topology

In his 1952 paper titled "A Study of Non-blocking Switching Networks," Bell Laboratories researcher Charles Clos formalized how multistage telephone switching systems could be built to forward traffic, regardless of the number of calls served by the overall system.

The mathematical principles proposed by Clos also help address the challenge of needing to build highly scalable data centers using relatively low-cost switches.

Figure 2-1 illustrates a three-stage Clos fabric consisting of one layer for ingress traffic, one layer for egress traffic, and a central layer for forwarding traffic between the layers. Multistage designs such as this can result in networks that are not oversubscribed or that are very close to not being oversubscribed.

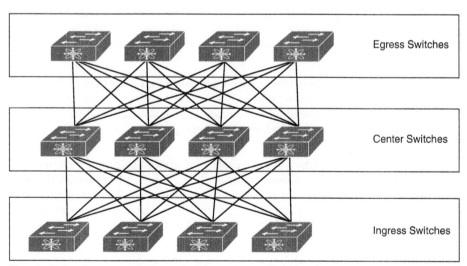

Figure 2-1   *Conceptual View of a Three-Stage Clos Topology*

Modern data center switches forward traffic at full duplex. Therefore, there is little reason to depict separate layers for ingress and egress traffic. It is possible to fold the top layer from the three-tier Clos topology in Figure 2-1 into the bottom layer to achieve what the industry refers to as a "folded" Clos topology, illustrated in Figure 2-2.

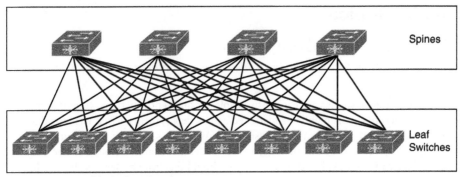

Figure 2-2 *Folded Clos Topology*

As indicated in Figure 2-2, a leaf switch is an ingress/egress switch. A spine switch is an intermediary switch whose most critical function is to perform rapid forwarding of traffic between leaf switches. Leaf switches connect to spine switches in a full-mesh topology.

NOTE At first glance, a three-tier Clos topology may appear to be similar to the traditional three-tier data center architecture. However, there are some subtle differences. First, there are no physical links between leaf switches in the Clos topology. Second, there are no physical links between spine switches. The elimination of cross-links within each layer simplifies network design and reduces control plane complexity.

Standard ACI Topology

An ACI fabric forms a Clos-based spine-and-leaf topology and is usually depicted using two rows of switches. Depending on the oversubscription and overall network throughput requirements, the number of spines and leaf switches will be different in each ACI fabric.

NOTE In the context of the Implementing Cisco Application Centric Infrastructure DCACI 300-620 exam, it does not matter whether you look at a given ACI fabric as a two-tiered Clos topology or as a three-tiered folded Clos topology. It is common for the standard ACI topology to be referred to as a two-tier spine-and-leaf topology.

Figure 2-3 shows the required components and cabling for an ACI fabric. Inheriting from its Clos roots, no cables should be connected between ACI leaf switches. Likewise, ACI spines being cross-cabled results in ACI disabling the cross-connected ports. While the topology shows a full mesh of cabling between the spine-and-leaf layers, a fabric can operate without a full mesh. However, a full mesh of cables between layers is still recommended.

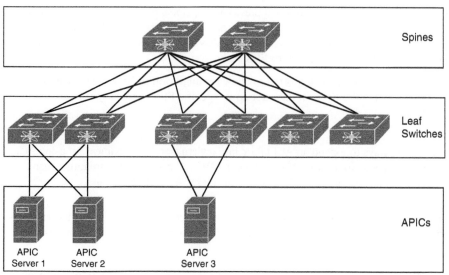

Figure 2-3 *Standard ACI Fabric Topology*

In addition to optics and cabling, the primary hardware components required to build an ACI fabric are as follows:

- **Application Policy Infrastructure Controllers (APICs):** The APICs are the brains of an ACI fabric and serve as the single source of truth for configuration within the fabric. A clustered set of (typically three) controllers attaches directly to leaf switches and provides management, policy programming, application deployment, and health monitoring for an ACI fabric. Note in Figure 2-3 that APICs are not in the data path or the forwarding topology. Therefore, the failure of one or more APICs does not halt packet forwarding. An ACI fabric requires a minimum of one APIC, but an ACI fabric with one APIC should be used only for lab purposes.

- **Spine switches:** ACI spine switches are Clos intermediary switches that have a number of key functions. They exchange routing updates with leaf switches via Intermediate System-to-Intermediate System (IS-IS) and perform rapid forwarding of packets between leaf switches. They provide endpoint lookup services to leaf switches through the Council of Oracle Protocol (COOP). They also handle route reflection to leaf switches using Multiprotocol BGP (MP-BGP), allowing external routes to be distributed across the fabric regardless of the number of tenants. (All three of these are control plane protocols and are covered in more detail in future chapters.) Spine switches also serve as roots for multicast trees within a fabric. By default, all spine switch interfaces besides the mgmt0 port are configured as fabric ports. *Fabric ports* are the interfaces that are used to interconnect spine and leaf switches within a fabric.

- **Leaf switches:** Leaf switches are the ingress/egress points for traffic into and out of an ACI fabric. As such, they are the connectivity points for endpoints, including servers and appliances, into the fabric. Layer 2 and 3 connectivity from the outside world into an ACI fabric is also typically established via leaf switches. ACI security policy enforcement occurs on leaf switches. Each leaf switch has a number of high-bandwidth uplink ports preconfigured as fabric ports.

In addition to the components mentioned previously, optional hardware components that can be deployed alongside an ACI fabric include fabric extenders (FEX). Use of FEX solutions in ACI is not ideal because leaf hardware models currently on the market are generally low cost and feature heavy compared to FEX technology.

FEX attachment to ACI is still supported to allow for migration of brownfield gear into ACI fabrics. The DCACI 300-620 exam does not cover specific FEX model support, so neither does this book.

> **NOTE**   There are ways to extend an ACI fabric into a virtualized environment by using ACI Virtual Edge (AVE) and Application Virtual Switch (AVS). These are software rather than hardware components and are beyond the scope of the DCACI 300-620 exam.

Engineers may sometimes dedicate two or more leaf switches to a particular function. Engineers typically evaluate the following categories of leaf switches as potential options for dedicating hardware:

- **Border Leaf:** *Border leaf* switches provide Layer 2 and 3 connectivity between an ACI fabric and the outside world. Border leaf switches are sometimes points of policy enforcement between internal and external endpoints.

- **Service Leaf:** *Service leaf* switches are leaf switches that connect to Layer 4–7 service appliances, such as firewalls and load balancers.

- **Compute Leaf:** *Compute leaf* switches are ACI leaf switches that connect to servers. Compute leaf switches are points of policy enforcement when traffic is being sent between local endpoints.

- **IP Storage Leaf:** *IP storage leaf* switches are ACI leaf switches that connect to IP storage systems. IP storage leaf switches can also be points of policy enforcement for traffic to and from local endpoints.

There are scalability benefits associated with dedicating leaf switches to particular functions, but if the size of the network does not justify dedicating leaf switches to a function, consider at least dedicating a pair of leaf switches as border leaf switches. Service leaf functionality can optionally be combined with border leaf functionality, resulting in the deployment of a pair (or more) of collapsed border/service leaf switches in smaller environments.

Cisco publishes a Verified Scalability Guide for each ACI code release. At the time of this writing, 500 is considered the maximum number of leaf switches that can be safely deployed in a single fabric that runs on the latest code.

ACI Stretched Fabric Topology

A *stretched ACI fabric* is a partially meshed design that connects ACI leaf and spine switches distributed in multiple locations. The stretched ACI fabric design helps lower deployment costs when full-mesh cable runs between all leaf and spine switches in a fabric tend to be cost-prohibitive.

Figure 2-4 shows a stretched ACI fabric across two sites.

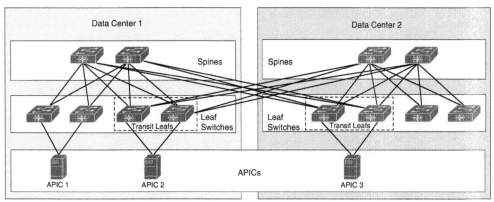

Figure 2-4 *ACI Stretched Fabric Topology*

A stretched fabric amounts to a single administrative domain and a single availability zone. Because APICs in a stretched fabric design tend to be spread across sites, cross-site latency is an important consideration. APIC clustering has been validated across distances of 800 kilometers between two sites.

A new term introduced in Figure 2-4 is *transit leaf*. A *transit leaf* is a leaf switch that provides connectivity between two sites in a stretched fabric design. Transit leaf switches connect to spine switches in both sites. No special configuration is required for transit leaf switches. At least one transit leaf switch must be provisioned in each site for redundancy reasons.

While stretched fabrics simplify extension of an ACI fabric, this design does not provide the benefits of newer topologies such as ACI Multi-Pod and ACI Multi-Site and stretched fabrics are therefore no longer commonly deployed or recommended.

ACI Multi-Pod Topology

The *ACI Multi-Pod* topology is a natural evolution of the ACI stretched fabric design in which spine and leaf switches are divided into pods, and different instances of IS-IS, COOP, and MP-BGP protocols run inside each pod to enable a level of control plane fault isolation.

Spine switches in each pod connect to an interpod network (IPN). Pods communicate with one another through the IPN. Figure 2-5 depicts an ACI Multi-Pod topology.

An ACI Multi-Pod IPN has certain requirements that include support for OSPF, end-to-end IP reachability, DHCP relay capabilities on the last-hop routers that connect to spines in each pod, and an increased maximum transmission unit (MTU). In addition, a Multi-Pod IPN needs to support forwarding of multicast traffic (PIM-Bidir) to allow the replication of broadcast, unknown unicast, and multicast (BUM) traffic across pods.

One of the most significant use cases for ACI Multi-Pod is active/active data center design. Although ACI Multi-Pod supports a maximum round-trip time latency of 50 milliseconds between pods, most Multi-Pod deployments are often built to achieve active/active functionality and therefore tend to have latencies of less than 5 milliseconds.

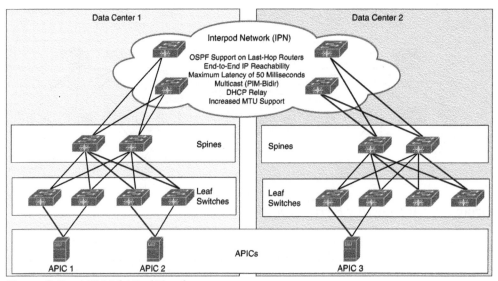

Figure 2-5   *ACI Multi-Pod Topology*

NOTE   Another solution that falls under the umbrella of ACI Multi-Pod is Virtual Pod (vPod). ACI vPod is not a new topology per se. It is an extension of a Multi-Pod fabric in the form of a new pod at a remote location where at least two ESXi servers are available, and deployment of ACI hardware is not desirable. ACI vPod components needed at the remote site for this solution include virtual spine (vSpine) appliances, virtual leaf (vLeaf) appliances, and the Cisco ACI Virtual Edge. ACI vPod still requires a physical ACI footprint since vPod is managed by the overall Multi-Pod APIC cluster.

On the issue of scalability, it should be noted that as of the time of writing, 500 is the maximum number of leaf switches that can be safely deployed within a single ACI fabric. However, the Verified Scalability Guide for the latest code revisions specifies 400 as the absolute maximum number of leaf switches that can be safely deployed in each pod. Therefore, for a fabric to reach its maximum supported scale, leaf switches should be deployed across at least 2 pods within a Multi-Pod fabric. Each pod supports deployment of 6 spines, and each Multi-Pod fabric currently supports the deployment of up to 12 pods.

Chapter 16, "ACI Anywhere," covers ACI Multi-Pod in more detail. For now, understand that Multi-Pod is functionally a single fabric and a single availability zone, even though it does not represent a single network failure domain.

ACI Multi-Site Topology

ACI Multi-Site is a solution that interconnects multiple ACI fabrics for the purpose of homogenous policy deployment across ACI fabrics, homogenous security policy deployment across on-premises ACI fabrics and public clouds, and cross-site stretched subnet capabilities, among others.

In an ACI Multi-Site design, each ACI fabric has its own dedicated APIC cluster. A clustered set of three nodes called Multi-Site Orchestrator (MSO) establishes API calls to each fabric independently and can configure tenants within each fabric with desired policies.

NOTE   Nodes forming an MSO cluster have traditionally been deployed as VMware ESXi virtual machines (VMs). Cisco has recently introduced the ability to deploy an MSO cluster as a distributed application (.aci format) on Cisco Application Services Engine (ASE). Cisco ASE is a container-based solution that provides a common platform for deploying and managing Cisco data center applications. ASE can be deployed in three form factors: a physical form factor consisting of bare-metal servers, a virtual machine form factor for on-premises deployments via ESXi or Linux KVM hypervisors, and a virtual machine form factor deployable within a specific Amazon Web Services (AWS) region.

Figure 2-6 shows an ACI Multi-Site topology that leverages a traditional VM-based MSO cluster.

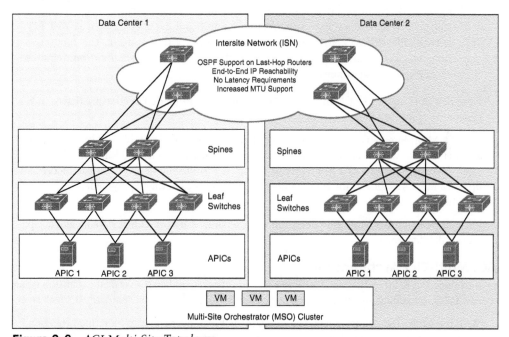

Figure 2-6   *ACI Multi-Site Topology*

As indicated in Figure 2-6, end-to-end communication between sites in an ACI Multi-Site design requires the use of an intersite network (ISN). An ACI Multi-Site ISN faces less stringent requirements compared to ACI Multi-Pod IPNs. In an ISN, end-to-end IP connectivity between spines across sites, OSPF on the last-hop routers connecting to the spines, and increased MTU support allowing VXLAN-in-IP encapsulation are all still required. However, ACI Multi-Site does not dictate any cross-site latency requirements, nor does it require support for multicast or DHCP relay within the ISN.

ACI Multi-Site does not impose multicast requirements on the ISN because ACI Multi-Site has been designed to accommodate larger-scale ACI deployments that may span the globe. It is not always feasible or expected for a company that has a global data center footprint to also have a multicast backbone spanning the globe and between all data centers.

Due to the introduction of new functionalities that were not required in earlier ACI fabrics, Cisco introduced a second generation of spine hardware. Each ACI fabric within an ACI Multi-Site design requires at least one second-generation or newer piece of spine hardware for the following reasons:

- **Ingress replication of BUM traffic:** To accommodate BUM traffic forwarding between ACI fabrics without the need to support multicast in the ISN, Multi-Site-enabled spines perform ingress replication of BUM traffic. This function is supported only on second-generation spine hardware.

- **Cross-fabric namespace normalization:** Each ACI fabric has an independent APIC cluster and therefore an independent brain. When policies and parameters are communicated between fabrics in VXLAN header information, spines receiving cross-site traffic need to have a way to swap remotely significant parameters, such as VXLAN network identifiers (VNIDs), with equivalent values for the local site. This function, which is handled in hardware and is called *namespace normalization*, requires second-generation or newer spines.

Note that in contrast to ACI Multi-Site, ACI Multi-Pod *can* be deployed using first-generation spine switches.

For ACI Multi-Site deployments, current verified scalability limits published by Cisco suggest that fabrics with stretched policy requirements that have up to 200 leaf switches can be safely incorporated into ACI Multi-Site. A single ACI Multi-Site deployment can incorporate up to 12 fabrics as long as the total number of leaf switches in the deployment does not surpass 1600.

Each fabric in an ACI Multi-Site design forms a separate network failure domain and a separate availability zone.

ACI Multi-Tier Architecture

Introduced in Release 4.1, ACI Multi-Tier provides the capability for vertical expansion of an ACI fabric by adding an extra layer or tier of leaf switches below the standard ACI leaf layer.

With the Multi-Tier enhancement, the standard ACI leaf layer can also be termed the Tier 1 leaf layer. The new layer of leaf switches that are added to vertically expand the fabric is called the Tier 2 leaf layer. Figure 2-7 shows these tiers. APICs, as indicated, can attach to either Tier 1 or Tier 2 leaf switches.

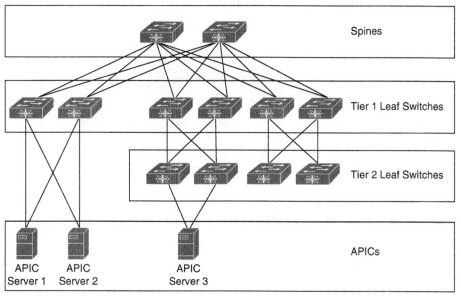

Figure 2-7 *ACI Multi-Tier Topology*

NOTE The topology shown in Figure 2-7 goes against the requirement outlined earlier in this chapter, in the section "Standard ACI Topology," *not* to cross-connect leaf switches. The ACI Multi-Tier architecture is an exception to this rule. Leaf switches within each tier, however, still should never be cross-connected.

An example of a use case for ACI Multi-Tier is the extension of an ACI fabric across data center halls or across buildings that are in relatively close proximity while minimizing long-distance cabling and optics requirements. Examine the diagram in Figure 2-8. Suppose that an enterprise data center has workloads in an alternate building. In this case, the company can deploy a pair of Tier 1 leaf switches in the new building and expand the ACI fabric to the extent needed within the building by using a Tier 2 leaf layer. Assuming that 6 leaf switches would have been required to accommodate the port requirements in the building, as Figure 2-8 suggests, directly cabling these 6 leaf switches to the spines as Tier 1 leaf switches would have necessitated 12 cross-building cables. However, the use of an ACI Multi-Tier design enables the deployment of the same number of switches using 4 long-distance cable runs.

ACI Multi-Tier can also be an effective solution for use within data centers in which the cable management strategy is to minimize inter-row cabling and relatively low-bandwidth requirements exist for top-of-rack switches. In such a scenario, Tier 1 leaf switches can be deployed end-of-row, and Tier 2 leaf switches can be deployed top-of-rack.

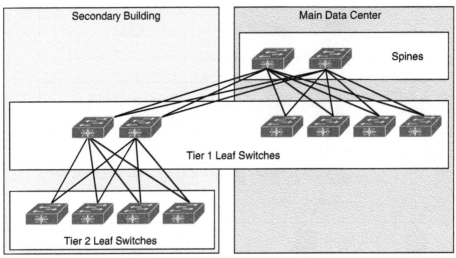

Figure 2-8   *Extending an ACI Fabric by Using ACI Multi-Tier in an Alternative Location*

> **NOTE**   ACI Multi-Tier *might not* be a suitable solution if the amount of bandwidth flowing upstream from Tier 2 leaf switches justifies the use of dedicated uplinks to spines.

Not all ACI switch platforms support Multi-Tier functionality.

Remote Leaf Topology

For remote sites in which data center endpoints may be deployed but their number and significance do not justify the deployment of an entirely new fabric or pod, the ACI *Remote Leaf* solution can be used to extend connectivity and ensure consistent policies between the main data center and the remote site. With such a solution, leaf switches housed at the remote site communicate with spines and APICs at the main data center over a generic IPN. Each Remote Leaf switch can be bound to a single pod.

There are three main use cases for Remote Leaf deployments:

- **Satellite/small colo data centers:** If a company has a small data center consisting of several top-of-rack switches and the data center may already have dependencies on a main data center, this satellite data center can be integrated into the main data center by using the Remote Leaf solution.

- **Data center extension and migrations:** Cross-data center migrations that have traditionally been done through Layer 2 extension can instead be performed by deploying a pair of Remote Leafs in the legacy data center. This approach often has cost benefits compared to alternative Layer 2 extension solutions if there is already an ACI fabric in the target state data center.

- **Telco 5G distributed data centers:** Telcom operators that are transitioning to more distributed mini data centers to bring services closer to customers but still desire centralized management and consistent policy deployment across sites can leverage Remote Leaf for these mini data centers.

In addition to these three main use cases, disaster recovery (DR) is sometimes considered a use case for Remote Leaf deployments, even though DR is a use case more closely aligned with ACI Multi-Site designs.

In a Remote Leaf solution, the APICs at the main data center deploy policy to the Remote Leaf switches as if they were locally connected.

Figure 2-9 illustrates a Remote Leaf solution.

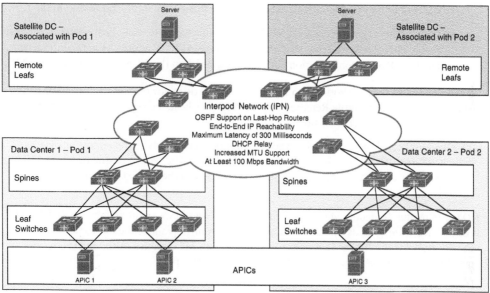

Figure 2-9 *Remote Leaf Topology and IPN Requirements*

IPN requirements for a Remote Leaf solution are as follows:

- **MTU:** The solution must support an end-to-end MTU that is at least 100 bytes higher than that of the endpoint source traffic. Assuming that 1500 bytes has been configured for data plane MTU, Remote Leaf can be deployed using a minimum MTU of 1600 bytes. An IPN MTU this low, however, necessitates that ACI administrators lower the ACI fabricwide control plane MTU, which is 9000 bytes by default.

- **Latency:** Up to 300 milliseconds latency between the main data center and remote location is acceptable.

- **Bandwidth:** Remote Leaf is supported with a minimum IPN bandwidth of 100 Mbps.

- **VTEP reachability:** A Remote Leaf switch logically associates with a single pod if integrated into a Multi-Pod solution. To make this association possible, the Remote Leaf should be able to route traffic over the IPN to the VTEP pool of the associated pod. Use of a dedicated VRF for IPN traffic is recommended where feasible.

- **APIC infra IP reachability:** A Remote Leaf switch needs IP connectivity with all APICs in a Multi-Pod cluster at the main data center. If an APIC has assigned itself IP addresses from a VTEP range different than the pod VTEP pool, the additional VTEP addresses need to also be advertised over the IPN.

- **OSPF support on upstream routers:** Routers northbound of both the Remote Leaf switches and the spine switches need to support OSPF and must be able to encapsulate traffic destined to directly attached ACI switches using VLAN 4. This requirement exists only for directly connected devices and does not extend end-to-end in the IPN.

- **DHCP relay:** The upstream router directly connected to Remote Leaf switches needs to enable DHCP relay to relay DHCP packets to the APIC IP addresses in the infra tenant. The DHCP relay configuration needs to be applied on the VLAN 4 subinterface or SVI.

Note that unlike a Multi-Pod IPN, a Remote Leaf IPN does not require Multicast PIM-Bidir support. This is because the Remote Leaf solution uses headend replication (HER) tunnels to forward BUM traffic between sites.

In a Remote Leaf design, traffic between known local endpoints at the remote site is switched directly, whether physically or virtually. Any traffic whose destination is in ACI but is unknown or not local to the remote site is forwarded to the main data center spines.

NOTE   Chapter 16 details MTU requirements for IPN and ISN environments for ACI Multi-Pod and ACI Multi-Site. It also covers how to lower control plane and data plane MTU values within ACI if the IPN or ISN does not support high MTU values. Although it does not cover Remote Leaf, the same general IPN MTU concepts apply.

Not all ACI switches support Remote Leaf functionality. The current maximum verified scalability number for Remote Leaf switches is 100 per fabric.

APIC Clusters

The ultimate size of an APIC cluster should be directly proportionate to the size of the Cisco ACI deployment. From a management perspective, any active APIC controller in a cluster can service any user for any operation. Controllers can be transparently added to or removed from a cluster.

APICs can be purchased either as physical or virtual appliances. Physical APICs are 1 rack unit (RU) Cisco C-Series servers with ACI code installed and come in two different sizes: M for medium and L for large. In the context of APICs, "size" refers to the scale of the fabric and the number of endpoints. Virtual APICs are used in ACI mini deployments, which consist of fabrics with up to two spine switches and four leaf switches.

As hardware improves, Cisco releases new generations of APICs with updated specifications. At the time of this writing, Cisco has released three generations of APICs. The first generation of APICs (M1/L1) shipped as Cisco UCS C220 M3 servers. Second-generation APICs (M2/L2) were Cisco UCS C220 M4 servers. Third-generation APICs (M3/L3) are shipping as UCS C220 M5 servers.

Table 2-2 details specifications for current M3 and L3 APICs.

Table 2-2   M3 and L3 APIC Specifications

Component	M3	L3
Processor	2x 1.7 GHz Xeon scalable 3106/85W 8C/11MB cache/DDR4 2133MHz	2x 2.1 GHz Xeon scalable 4110/85W 8C/11MB cache/DDR4 2400MHz
Memory	6x 16 GB DDR4-2666-MHz RDIMM/PC4-21300/single rank/ x4/1.2v	12x 16 GB DDR4-2666-MHz RDIMM/PC4-21300/single rank/ x4/1.2v
Hard drive	2x 1 TB 12G SAS 7.2K RPM SFF HDD	2x 2.4 TB 12G SAS 10K RPM SFF HDD (4K)
Network cards	1x Cisco UCS VIC 1455 Quad Port 10/25G SFP28 CNA PCIE	1x Cisco UCS VIC 1455 Quad Port 10/25G SFP28 CNA PCIE

Note in Table 2-2 that the only differences between M3 and L3 APICs are the sizes of their CPUs, memory, and hard drives. This is because fabric growth necessitates that increased transaction rates be supported, which drives up compute requirements.

Table 2-3 shows the hardware requirements for virtual APICs.

Table 2-3   Virtual APIC Specifications

Component	Virtual APIC
Processor	8 vCPUs
Memory	32 GB
Hard drive*	300 GB HDD
	100 GB SSD
Supported ESXi hypervisor version	6.5 or above

* A VM is deployed with two HDDs.

APIC Cluster Scalability and Sizing

APIC cluster hardware is typically purchased from Cisco in the form of a bundle. An APIC bundle is a collection of one or more physical or virtual APICs, and the bundle that needs to be purchased depends on the desired target state scalability of the ACI fabric.

Table 2-4 shows currently available APIC cluster hardware options and the general scalability each bundle can individually achieve.

Table 2-4   APIC Hardware Bundles

Part Number	Number of APICs	General Scalability
APIC-CLUSTER-XS (ACI mini bundle)	1 M3 APIC, 2 virtual APICs, and 2 Nexus 9332C spine switches	Up to 2 spines and 4 leaf switches
APIC-CLUSTER-M3	3 M3 APICs	Up to 1200 edge ports
APIC-CLUSTER-L3	3 L3 APICs	More than 1200 edge ports

APIC-CLUSTER-XS specifically addresses ACI mini fabrics. ACI mini is a fabric deployed using two Nexus 9332C spine switches and up to four leaf switches. ACI mini is suitable for lab deployments, small colocation deployments, and deployments that are not expected to span beyond four leaf switches.

APIC-CLUSTER-M3 is designed for medium-sized deployments where the number of server ports connecting to ACI is not expected to exceed 1200, which roughly translates to 24 leaf switches.

APIC-CLUSTER-L3 is a bundle designed for large-scale deployments where the number of server ports connecting to ACI exceeds or will eventually exceed 1200.

Beyond bundles, Cisco allows customers to purchase individual APICs for the purpose of expanding an APIC cluster to enable further scaling of a fabric. Once a fabric expands beyond 1200 edge ports, ACI Verified Scalability Guides should be referenced to determine the optimal number of APICs for the fabric.

According to Verified Scalability Guides for ACI Release 4.1(1), an APIC cluster of three L3 APICs should suffice in deployments with up to 80 leaf switches. However, the cluster size would need to be expanded to four or more APICs to allow a fabric to scale up to 200 leaf switches.

NOTE   Cisco recommends against deployment of APIC cluster sizes of 4 and 6. Current recommended cluster sizes are 3, 5, or 7 APICs per fabric.

Each APIC cluster houses a distributed multi-active database in which processes are active on all nodes. Data, however, is distributed or sliced across APICs via a process called *database sharding*. *Sharding* is a result of the evolution of what is called horizontal partitioning of databases and involves distributing a database across multiple instances of the schema. Sharding increases both redundancy and performance because a large partitioned table can be split across multiple database servers. It also enables a scale-out model involving adding to the number of servers as opposed to having to constantly scale up servers through hardware upgrades.

ACI shards each attribute within the APIC database to three nodes. A single APIC out of the three is considered active (the leader) for a given attribute at all times. If the APIC that houses the active copy of a particular slice or partition of data fails, the APIC cluster is able to recover via the two backup copies of the data residing on the other APICs. This is why the deployment of a minimum of three APICs is advised. Any APIC cluster deployed with fewer than three APICs is deemed unsuitable for production uses. Note that only the APIC that has been elected leader for a given attribute can modify the attribute.

Figure 2-10 provides a conceptual view of data sharding across a three-APIC cluster. For each data set or attribute depicted, a single APIC is elected leader. Assume that the active copy indicates that the APIC holding the active copy is leader for the given attribute.

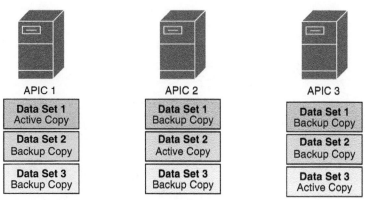

Figure 2-10 *Data Sharding Across Three APICs*

For a portion of a database to allow writes (configuration changes), a quorum of APICs housing the pertinent database attributes undergoing a write operation must be healthy and online. Because each attribute in an APIC database is sharded into three copies, a quorum is defined as two copies. If two nodes in a three-node APIC cluster were to fail simultaneously, the remaining APIC would move the entire database into a read-only state, and no configuration changes would be allowed until the quorum was restored.

When an APIC cluster scales to five or seven APICs, the sharding process remains unchanged. In other words, the number of shards of a particular subset of data does not increase past three, but the cluster further distributes the shards. This means that cluster expansion past three APICs does not increase the redundancy of the overall APIC database.

Figure 2-11 illustrates how an outage of Data Center 2, which results in the failure of two APICs, could result in portions of the APIC database moving into a read-only state. In this case, the operational APICs have at least two shards for Data Sets 1 and 3, so administrators can continue to make configuration changes involving these database attributes. However, Data Set 2 is now in read-only mode because two replicas of the attribute in question have been lost.

As Figure 2-11 demonstrates, increasing APIC cluster size to five or seven does not necessarily increase the redundancy of the overall cluster.

A general recommendation in determining APIC cluster sizes is to deploy three APICs in fabrics scaling up to 80 leaf switches. If recoverability is a concern, a standby APIC can be added to the deployment. A total of five or seven APICs should be deployed for scalability purposes in fabrics expanding beyond 80 leaf switches.

If, for any reason, a fabric with more than three APICs is bifurcated, the APIC cluster attempts to recover this split-brain event. Once connectivity across all APICs is restored, automatic reconciliation takes place within the cluster, based on timestamps.

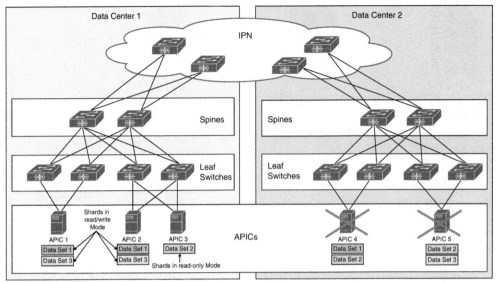

Figure 2-11 *Impact of APIC Failures in a Five-Node Cluster*

What would happen if Data Center 1 in Figure 2-11 failed instead of Data Center 2, and all shards for a specific subset of data resided in Data Center 1 at the time of the outage? In such a scenario, the failure of three APICs could lead to the hypothetical loss of all three shards of a specific subset of data. To ensure that a total loss of a given pod does not result in the loss of all shards for a given attribute, Cisco recommends that no more than two APICs be placed in a single pod.

NOTE Standby APICs allow an administrator to commission an APIC to allow recoverability of a fabric during failure scenarios in which the APIC quorum has been lost. When a standby APIC is deployed in a fabric, it acts as a passive player. It does not actively service users or configure ACI switches. It also does not synchronize data with active APICs. When first deploying a controller as a standby APIC, at least three APICs in the cluster need to be active.

Spine Hardware

Cisco ACI spine hardware options includes Nexus 9300 Series fixed form factor switches as well as Nexus 9500 modular switches. Not all switches in the noted switch families can be deployed in ACI mode.

The primary factors that guide spine purchasing decisions are desired port bandwidths, feature requirements, hardware generation, and the required number of target state ports.

Whereas a fixed spine switch has a limited number of ports, a port in a modular platform can scale with the addition of more line cards to a chassis. For this reason, modular chassis are more suitable for fabrics that require massive scale.

Fixed spine platforms satisfy the scalability requirements of small to medium fabrics without problem.

First-Generation Spine Switches

As noted earlier in this chapter, first-generation spine switches are not supported as spines interconnecting ACI fabrics in ACI Multi-Site deployments. Other new solutions, such as Remote Leaf and ACI Multi-Tier also require second-generation spine switches. Understanding first-generation spine platforms is, however, beneficial for historical purposes because a large number of ACI deployments still contain first-generation hardware.

First-generation ACI spine switch models on the market at the time of this writing have model numbers that end in PQ. Table 2-5 lists first-generation Nexus spine switches.

Table 2-5   First-Generation Spine Switches

Characteristic	Nexus 9336PQ	Nexus 9736PQ
Form factor	2 RU fixed switch	Line card for modular chassis
Supported modular platforms	N/A	Nexus 9504
		Nexus 9508
		Nexus 9516
40 Gigabit Ethernet ports	36 ports	36 ports
100 Gigabit Ethernet ports	N/A	N/A
ACI Multi-Pod support	Yes	Yes
CloudSec support	No	No
Remote Leaf support	No	No
ACI Multi-Tier support	No	No
ACI Multi-Site support	No	No

Even though first-generation spine switches do not support namespace normalization or ingress replication of BUM traffic, they can coexist with second-generation spine switches within a fabric. This coexistence enables companies to integrate fabrics into ACI Multi-Site without having to decommission older spines before the regular hardware refresh cycle.

NOTE   First-generation spine switches can no longer be ordered from Cisco.

Second-Generation Spine Switches

In addition to providing support for ACI Multi-Site, Remote Leaf, and ACI Multi-Tier, second-generation spine switch ports operate at both 40 Gigabit Ethernet and 100 Gigabit Ethernet speeds and therefore enable dramatic fabric bandwidth upgrades.

Second-generation spine switches also support MACsec and CloudSec. MACsec enables port-to-port encryption of traffic in transit at line rate. CloudSec enables cross-site encryption at line rate, eliminating the need for intermediary devices to support or perform encryption. Cross-site encryption is also referred to as *VTEP-to-VTEP encryption.*

Second-generation ACI spine switch models on the market at the time of this writing have model numbers that end in C, EX, and FX. Table 2-6 provides additional details about second-generation spine platforms.

Table 2-6 Second-Generation Spine Switches

Characteristic	Nexus 9364C	Nexus 9332C	Nexus 9732C-EX	Nexus 9736C-FX
Form factor	2 RU fixed	1 RU fixed	Line card for modular chassis	Line card for modular chassis
Supported modular platforms	N/A	N/A	Nexus 9504 Nexus 9508 Nexus 9516	Nexus 9504 Nexus 9508 Nexus 9516
40/100 Gigabit Ethernet ports	64	32	32	36
ACI Multi-Pod support	Yes	Yes	Yes	Yes
CloudSec support	Last 16 ports	Last 8 ports	N/A	All ports
Remote Leaf support	Yes	Yes	Yes	Yes
ACI Multi-Tier support	Yes	Yes	Yes	Yes
ACI Multi-Site support	Yes	Yes	Yes	Yes

In addition to the hardware listed in Table 2-6, Nexus 9732C-FX line cards will be supported as ACI spine line cards in the near future.

New spine switches with 100/400 Gigabit Ethernet ports are also on the horizon. The Nexus 9316D-GX is already available and is supported as an ACI spine. This platform is also in the roadmap for support as a leaf switch. The 100/400 Gigabit Ethernet Nexus 93600CD-GX switch, which is supported as an ACI leaf, is also in the roadmap for use as a spine.

Cisco uses the term *cloud scale* to refer to the newer Nexus switch models that contain the specialized ASICs needed for larger buffer sizes, larger endpoint tables, and visibility into packets and flows traversing the switch without impacting CPU utilization. Second-generation ACI spine switches fall into the category of cloud-scale switches.

Leaf Hardware

Cisco ACI leaf hardware options include Nexus 9300 Series fixed form factor switches. Not all switches in the noted switch families can be deployed in ACI mode.

The primary factors that guide leaf purchasing decisions are the desired port bandwidths, feature requirements, hardware generation, and the required number of target state ports.

First-Generation Leaf Switches

First-generation ACI leaf switches are Nexus 9300 Series platforms that are based on the Application Leaf Engine (ALE) ASICs.

The hardware resources that enable whitelisting of traffic are ternary content-addressable memory (TCAM) resources, referred to as the *policy CAM*.

Policy CAM sizes vary depending on the hardware. The policy CAM size and behavior limitations in first-generation switches tended to sometimes limit whitelisting projects.

There are also a number of other capability differences between first- and second-generation leaf hardware, such as handling of Layer 4 operations and multicast routing.

NOTE The majority of first-generation leaf switches can no longer be ordered from Cisco. All Nexus 9300 Series ACI leaf switches whose model numbers end in PX, TX, PQ, PX-E, and TX-E are considered first-generation leaf switches.

Second-Generation Leaf Switches

Second-generation ACI leaf switches are Nexus 9300 Series platforms that are based on cloud-scale ASICs. Second-generation leaf switches support Remote Leaf and ACI Multi-Tier, have significantly larger policy CAM sizes, and offer enhanced hardware capabilities and port speeds.

NOTE MACsec is supported on all ports with speeds greater than or equal to 10 Gbps on Nexus 9300 ACI switches whose model numbers end in FX. Check specific support levels for other platforms.

ACI leaf switches whose model numbers end in EX, FX, FX2, and FXP are considered second-generation leaf switches. Table 2-7 provides details about second-generation switches that have 1/10 Gigabit Ethernet copper port connectivity for servers.

Table 2-7   Second-Generation 1/10 Gigabit Ethernet Copper Leaf Switches

Characteristic	Nexus 93108TC-EX	Nexus 9348GC-FXP	Nexus 93108TC-FX	Nexus 93216TC-FX2
Form factor	1 RU fixed	1 RU fixed	1 RU fixed	2 RU fixed
100 Mbps and 1 Gigabit Ethernet copper ports	N/A	48	N/A	N/A
100 Mbps and 1/10 Gigabit Ethernet copper ports	48	N/A	48	96
10/25 Gigabit Ethernet ports	N/A	N/A	4	N/A
40/100 Gigabit Ethernet ports	6	2	6	12
ACI Multi-Pod support	Yes	Yes	Yes	Yes
Remote Leaf support	Yes	Yes	Yes	Yes
Can be used as a Tier 1 leaf	Yes	Yes	Yes	Yes
Can be used as a Tier 2 leaf	Yes	Yes	Yes	Yes

The Nexus 9348GC-FXP switch has 48 ports, offering 100 Mbps or 1 Gigabit Ethernet connectivity. These ports have RJ-45 connections, eliminating the need for transceivers. Due to its low cost and support for cloud-scale features, the Nexus 9348GC-FXP is an ideal replacement for Fabric Extenders.

NOTE Support for ACI Multi-Site is dependent on spine switches in the fabric and not leaf switches. Also, at the time of writing, CloudSec is most relevant to spine switches.

Table 2-8 details second-generation switches that provide 1/10/25 Gigabit Ethernet fiber port connectivity for servers.

Table 2-8 Second-Generation 1/10/25 Gigabit Ethernet Fiber Leaf Switches

Characteristic	Nexus 93180YC-EX	Nexus 93180YC-FX	Nexus 93240YC-FX2	Nexus 93360YC-FX2
Form factor	1 RU fixed	1 RU fixed	1.2 RU fixed	2 RU fixed
1/10/25 Gigabit Ethernet ports	48	48	48	96
40/100 Gigabit Ethernet ports	6	6	12	12
ACI Multi-Pod support	Yes	Yes	Yes	Yes
Remote Leaf support	Yes	Yes	Yes	Yes
Can be used as a Tier 1 leaf	Yes	Yes	Yes	Yes
Can be used as a Tier 2 leaf	Yes	Yes	Yes	Yes

Table 2-9 lists details on the only second-generation switch available at the time of writing that provides 40/100 Gigabit Ethernet connectivity for servers.

Table 2-9 Second-Generation 40/100 Gigabit Ethernet Leaf Switches

Characteristic	Nexus 9336C-FX2
Form factor	1 RU fixed
40/100 Gigabit Ethernet ports	36
ACI Multi-Pod support	Yes
Remote Leaf support	Yes
Can be used as a Tier 1 leaf	Yes
Can be used as a Tier 2 leaf	Yes

Exam Preparation Tasks

As mentioned in the section "How to Use This Book" in the Introduction, you have a couple of choices for exam preparation: Chapter 17, "Final Preparation," and the exam simulation questions in the Pearson Test Prep Software Online.

Review All Key Topics

Review the most important topics in this chapter, noted with the Key Topic icon in the outer margin of the page. Table 2-10 lists these key topics and the page number on which each is found.

Table 2-10   Key Topics for Chapter 2

Key Topic Element	Description	Page Number
List	Describes APICs, spine switches, and leaf switches	23
List	Describes some functions engineers commonly evaluate when deciding whether to dedicate leaf switches to functions	24
Paragraph	Describes ACI Multi-Pod	25
Paragraph	Calls out requirements for an ACI Multi-Pod IPN	25
Paragraph	Describes ACI Multi-Site	26
Paragraph	Explains APIC cluster separation in ACI Multi-Site fabrics and MSO communication with each cluster	27
Paragraph	Calls out requirements for an ACI Multi-Site ISN	27
Paragraph	Explains why ACI Multi-Site requires the use of at least one Gen 2 spine in each site	28
Paragraph	Describes Remote Leaf	30
Paragraph	Explains the significance of sizes in APIC purchases and the relevance of M versus L models	32
Paragraph	Explains APIC hardware generations and correlation with UCS C-Series server generations	32
Table 2-5	Lists first-generation spine switches	37
Table 2-6	Lists second-generation spine switches	38
Table 2-7	Lists second-generation 1/10 Gigabit Ethernet copper leaf switches	39
Table 2-8	Lists second-generation 1/10/25 Gigabit Ethernet fiber leaf switches	40
Table 2-9	Lists second-generation 40/100 Gigabit Ethernet leaf switches	40

Complete Tables and Lists from Memory

There are no memory tables or lists in this chapter.

Define Key Terms

Define the following key terms from this chapter and check your answers in the glossary:

fabric port, border leaf, service leaf, compute leaf, IP storage leaf, stretched ACI fabric, transit leaf, ACI Multi-Pod, ACI Multi-Site, sharding

## CHAPTER 3

Initializing an ACI Fabric

This chapter covers the following topics:

Understanding ACI Fabric Initialization: This section describes the planning needed prior to fabric initialization and the process of initializing a new ACI fabric.

Initializing an ACI Fabric: This section walks through the process of initializing an ACI fabric.

Basic Post-Initialization Tasks: This section touches on some of the basic tasks often performed right after fabric initialization.

This chapter covers the following exam topics:

- 1.4 Describe ACI fabric discovery

- 5.1 Implement out-of-band and in-band

- 5.3 Implement configuration backup (snapshot/config import export)

- 5.5 Configure an upgrade

Not all ACI engineers will be initializing new fabrics. Some will be more operations focused; others will be more implementation or design focused. But understanding the fabric discovery and initialization process is important for all ACI engineers.

For operations engineers, there is a possibility that new switch onboarding may necessitate troubleshooting of the switch discovery process. Implementation-focused individuals, on the other hand, may be more interested in understanding the planning necessary to deploy ACI fabrics.

This chapter first reviews the fabric discovery process. It then reviews the steps necessary for initializing an ACI fabric, discovering and onboarding switches, and completing basic post-initialization tasks, such as APIC and switch upgrades.

"Do I Know This Already?" Quiz

The "Do I Know This Already?" quiz allows you to assess whether you should read this entire chapter thoroughly or jump to the "Exam Preparation Tasks" section. If you are in doubt about your answers to these questions or your own assessment of your knowledge of the topics, read the entire chapter. Table 3-1 lists the major headings in this chapter and their corresponding "Do I Know This Already?" quiz questions. You can find the answers in Appendix A, "Answers to the 'Do I Know This Already?' Questions."

Table 3-1 "Do I Know This Already?" Section-to-Question Mapping

Foundation Topics Section	Questions
Understanding ACI Fabric Initialization	1–4
Initializing an ACI Fabric	5, 6
Basic Post-Initialization Tasks	7–10

CAUTION The goal of self-assessment is to gauge your mastery of the topics in this chapter. If you do not know the answer to a question or are only partially sure of the answer, you should mark that question as wrong for purposes of the self-assessment. Giving yourself credit for an answer you correctly guess skews your self-assessment results and might provide you with a false sense of security.

1. A company has purchased APICs for an ACI deployment. Which of the following switch platforms is the best candidate for connecting the APICs to the fabric?

   a. Nexus 9364C

   b. Nexus 9336PQ

   c. Nexus 9332C

   d. Nexus 93180YC-FX

2. Changing which of the following parameters necessitates a fabric rebuild? (Choose all that apply.)

   a. Infrastructure VLAN

   b. APIC OOB IP address

   c. Fabric ID

   d. Active or standby status of a controller

3. At the end of which stage in the switch discovery process are switches considered to be fully activated?

   a. Switch software upgrades

   b. IFM establishment

   c. LLDP neighbor discovery

   d. TEP IP assignment to nodes

4. An ACI engineer is initializing a fabric, but the first APIC is unable to add a seed switch to the Fabric Membership view. Which of the following could potentially be the causes? (Choose all that apply.)

   a. No spines have yet been discovered.

   b. The active APIC in-band interface connects to an NX-OS switch.

   c. The APIC has not received a DHCP Discover message from the seed leaf.

   d. The APICs need to form a cluster first.

5. An administrator has made several changes pertinent to the Cisco IMC while boot-strapping an APIC. Which of the following might be preventing fabric discovery?

   a. The IP address assigned to the Cisco IMC is incorrect.

   b. The NIC mode has been updated to Shared LOM.

   c. The Cisco IMC default gateway settings is incorrect.

   d. The Cisco IMC firmware has been updated.

6. Which of the following is associated exclusively with spine switches?

   a. VTEP

   b. PTEP

   c. DTEP

   d. Proxy-TEP

7. Which of the following import types and modes enables a user to overwrite all current configurations with settings from a backup file?

   a. Atomic Merge

   b. Best Effort Merge

   c. Atomic Replace

   d. Best Effort Replace

8. Which of the following are valid protocols for forwarding ACI backups to a remote server? (Choose all that apply.)

   a. TFTP

   b. FTP

   c. SFTP

   d. SCP

9. An administrator wants to conduct an upgrade of an ACI fabric. How can he best group the switches to ensure minimal outage, assuming that servers are dual-homed?

   a. Create two upgrade groups: one for spines and one for leafs.

   b. Create two upgrade groups: one for odd switch node IDs and one for even switch node IDs.

   c. Create four upgrade groups and randomly assign node IDs to each.

   d. Create four upgrade groups: one for odd leafs, one for even leafs, one for odd spines, one for even spines.

10. True or false: ACI can take automated scheduled backups.

    a. True

    b. False

Foundation Topics

Understanding ACI Fabric Initialization

Before administrators can create subnets within ACI and configure switch ports for server traffic, an ACI fabric needs to be initialized.

The process of fabric initialization involves attaching APICs to leaf switches, attaching leaf switches to spines, configuring APICs to communicate with leaf switches, and activating the switches one by one until the APICs are able to configure all switches in the fabric. Let's look first at the planning needed for fabric initialization.

Planning Fabric Initialization

The planning necessary for fabric initialization can be divided into two categories:

- **Cabling and physical deployment planning:** This category of tasks includes racking and stacking of hardware, cabling, powering on devices, and guaranteeing proper cooling. This book addresses only some of the basic cabling requirements because facilities issues are not the focus of the Implementing Cisco Application Centric Infrastructure DCACI 300-620 exam.

- **Planning of minimal configuration parameters:** This includes preparation of all the configurations needed to bootstrap the APICs, enable all ACI switches, and join APICs to a cluster.

One way to approach planning an ACI fabric initialization is to create a fabric initialization checklist or a basic table that includes all the information needed to set up the fabric.

Understanding Cabling Requirements

Before initializing a fabric, you need to run cabling between leaf and spine fabric ports. By default, fabric ports are the high-order ports on the right side of leaf switches. They are generally high-bandwidth ports compared to the server downlinks. Figure 3-1 shows a Nexus 93180YC-FX leaf switch. The six ports to the right are all fabric ports by default. The phrase "by default" is intentional here: On leaf switches, fabric ports can be converted to server downlinks and vice versa, but the switch must first be initialized into a fabric.

Figure 3-1   *Nexus 93180YC-FX Leaf with Six Fabric Ports*

Unlike the Nexus 93180YC-FX, a number of leaf platforms have default fabric ports that cannot be easily distinguished by their physical appearance.

Leaf fabric ports can generally be connected to any spine ports (except the spine out-of-band [OOB] management port and any 10 Gbps ports), as long as the transceivers and port speeds are compatible.

Not all leaf-to-spine connections need to be run for fabric discovery to be possible, but there needs to be enough physical connectivity to allow all switches and APICs to have at least a single path to one another.

For example, Figure 3-2 does not represent a full-mesh connectivity between the leaf and spine layers, but it is a perfectly valid topology for the purpose of enabling a full fabric initialization.

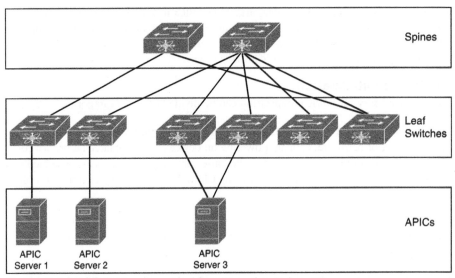

Figure 3-2   *Sample Topology Enabling Complete Fabric Discovery*

Connecting APICs to the Fabric

In addition to leaf-to-spine fabric port connectivity, the APICs need to be able to establish an in-band communication path through the fabric.

On the back of an APIC, you can see a number of different types of ports. Figure 3-3 shows a rear-panel view of a third-generation APIC populated with a VIC 1455 card.

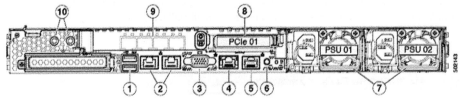

Figure 3-3   *Rear View of a Third-Generation APIC*

Table 3-2 provides a legend highlighting the components shown in Figure 3-3.

Table 3-2   Legend for Components Numbered in Figure 3-3

Number	Component	Number	Component
1	USB 3.0 ports (2)	6	Rear unit identification button/LED
2	Dual 1 /10 Gigabit Ethernet ports (LAN1 and LAN2)	7	Power supplies (two, redundant as 1+1)
3	VGA video port (DB-15 connector)	8	PCIe riser 1/slot 1 (x16 lane)
4	1 Gigabit Ethernet dedicated management port	9	VIC 1455 with external 10/25 Gigabit Ethernet ports (4)
5	Serial port (RJ-45 connector)	10	Threaded holes for dual-hole grounding lug

Out of the components depicted in Figure 3-3, the VIC 1455 ports are of most importance for the fabric discovery process because they form the in-band communication channel into the fabric. The VIC 1455 card has four 10/25 Gigabit Ethernet ports. VIC adapters in earlier generations of APICs had two 10 Gigabit Ethernet ports instead. At least one VIC port on each APIC needs to be cabled to a leaf to enable full APIC cluster formation. For redundancy purposes, it is best to diversify connectivity from each APIC across a pair of leaf switches by connecting at least two ports.

In first- and second-generation APICs sold with variants of dual-port VIC 1225 cards, ports 1 and 2 would need to be cabled up to leaf switches to diversify connectivity. In third-generation APICs, however, ports 1 and 2 together represent logical port eth2-1, and ports 3 and 4 together represent eth2-2. Ports eth2-1 and eth2-2 are then bundled together into an active/standby team at the operating system level. For this reason, diversifying in-band APIC connectivity across two leaf switches in third-generation APICs requires that one cable be connected to either port 1 or port 2 and another cable be attached to either port 3 or port 4. Connecting both ports that represent a logical port (for example, ports 1 and 2) to leaf switches in third-generation APICs can result in unpredictable failover issues.

Not all ACI leaf switches support 10/25 Gigabit Ethernet cabling. During the deployment planning stage, it is important to ensure that the leaf nodes to which the APICs connect actually support the available VIC port speeds and that proper transceivers and cabling are available.

Initial Configuration of APICs

Out of the box, APICs come with ACI code installed. Normally, switch configuration involves establishing console connectivity to the switch and implementing a basic configuration that allows remote SSH access to the switch. APICs, on the other hand, are servers and not network switches. As such, it is easiest to configure APICs using a crash cart with a standard DB-15 VGA connector and a USB keyboard.

APIC OOB Configuration Requirements

In addition to cabling the in-band communication channel, APICs have two embedded LAN on motherboard (LOM) ports for out-of-band management of the APIC. In third-generation APICs, these dual LAN ports support both 1 and 10 Gigabit Ethernet. (In Figure 3-3, these two LOM ports are shown with the number 2.) As part of the initialization process, users enter an out-of-band IP address for each APIC. The APIC then bonds these two LOM interfaces together and assigns the out-of-band IP address to the bond. From the out-of-band switch to which these ports connect, these connections appear as individual links and should not be misinterpreted as port channels. Basically, the APIC binds the OOB MAC and IP address to a single link and repins the traffic over to the second link if the active interface fails.

OOB management interfaces should not be confused with the Cisco Integrated Management Controller (Cisco IMC) port on the APICs. The *APIC Cisco IMC* allows lights-out management of the physical server, firmware upgrades, and monitoring of server hardware health. While the dual 1/10 Gigabit Ethernet LOM ports enable out-of-band access to the APIC operating system, the Cisco IMC provides out-of-band access to the server hardware itself. With Cisco IMC access, an engineer can gain virtual KVM access to the server and reinstall the APIC operating system remotely in the event that the APIC is no longer accessible. But the Cisco IMC cannot be used to gain HTTPS access to the ACI management interface. Because of the significance of Cisco IMC in APIC recovery, assigning an IP address to the Cisco IMC is often viewed as a critically important fabric initialization task.

APIC OOB IP addresses and Cisco IMC IP addresses are often selected from the same subnet even though it is not required for them to be in the same subnet.

Out-of-Band Versus In-Band Management

By default, administrators configure ACI fabrics through the dual OOB interfaces on the APICs. The APICs, in turn, configure switches and communicate with one another using the in-band channel over the VIC adapters.

If the default behavior of managing the fabric through the OOB interfaces is not desirable, administrators can implement in-band management.

There are many factors to consider when determining whether to use in-band management, but the only configuration option available during APIC initialization is to implement OOB management. Administrators can then log in to the ACI GUI and manually implement in-band management.

Out-of-band management of ACI fabrics is the most popular deployment option.

Chapter 13, "Implementing Management," discusses in-band management, its implications, and implementation in detail.

Configuration Information for Fabric Initialization

Table 3-3 describes the basic configuration parameters that need to be planned before an ACI fabric can be initialized and that you need to understand for the DCACI 300-620 exam.

Table 3-3   Basic Configuration Parameters for Fabric Initialization

Configuration Parameter	Description
Fabric Name	A user-friendly name for the fabric. If no name is entered, ACI uses the name ACI Fabric1.
Fabric ID	A numeric identifier between 1 and 128 for the ACI fabric. If no ID is entered, ACI uses 1 as the fabric ID.
Number of active controllers	A self-explanatory parameter whose valid values are 1 through 9. The default value is 3 for three APICs. If the intent is to add additional APICs to the fabric in the future, select 3 and modify this parameter when it is time to add new APICs.
Pod ID	A parameter that determines the unique pod ID to which the APIC being configured is attached. When ACI Multi-Pod is not being deployed, use the default value 1.
Standby Controller	An APIC added to a fabric solely to aid in fabric recovery and in reestablishing an APIC quorum during a prolonged outage. If the APIC being initialized is a standby APIC, select Yes for this parameter.

Configuration Parameter	Description
Controller ID	The unique ID number for the APIC being configured. Valid values are between 1 and 32. The first three active APICs should always be assigned IDs between 1 and 3. Valid node ID values for standby APICs range from 16 to 32.
Controller Name	The unique APIC hostname.
Pod 1 TEP Pool	The TEP pool assigned to the seed pod. A *TEP pool* is a subnet used for internal fabric communication. This subnet can potentially be advertised outside ACI over an IPN or ISN or when a fabric is extended to virtual environments using the AVS or AVE. TEP pool subnets should ideally be unique across an enterprise environment. Cisco recommends that TEP pool subnet sizes be between /16 and /22. TEP pool sizes *do* impact pod scalability, and use of /16 or /17 ranges is highly advised. Each pod needs a separate TEP pool. However, during APIC initialization, the TEP pool assigned to the seed pod (Pod 1) is what should be entered in the initialization wizard because all APICs in Multi-Pod environments pull their TEP addresses from the Pod 1 TEP pool.
Infrastructure (infra) VLAN	The VLAN ID used for control communication between ACI fabric nodes (leaf switches, spine switches, and APICs). The *infrastructure VLAN* is also used for extending an ACI fabric to AVS or AVE virtual switches. The infra VLAN should be unique and unused elsewhere in the environment. Acceptable IDs are 2 through 4094. Because the VLAN may need to be extended outside ACI, ensure that the selected infrastructure VLAN does not fall into the reserved VLAN range of non-ACI switches.
BD Multicast Addresses (GiPo)	The IP address range used for multicast within a fabric. In ACI Multi-Site environments, the same range can be used across sites. If the administrator does not change the default range, 225.0.0.0/15 will be selected for this parameter. Valid ranges are between 225.0.0.0/15 and 231.254.0.0/15. A prefix length of 15 must be used.
APIC OOB Addresses and Default Gateway	Addresses assigned to OOB LOM ports for access to the APIC GUI. These ports are separate from the Cisco IMC ports.
Password Strength	A parameter that determines whether to enforce the use of passwords of a particular strength for all users. The default behavior is to enforce strong passwords.

Some of the configuration parameters listed in Table 3-3 cannot be changed and require that a fabric be wiped clean and re-initialized in case of a misconfiguration. Specifically, the parameters to which attention is most critically important include Fabric Name, Fabric ID, Pod 1 TEP Pool, and Infrastructure VLAN.

Switch Discovery Process

Following a minimal configuration bootstrap of the first APIC, switch discovery can begin. So how do APICs use the parameters in Table 3-3 to discover switches and enable them to join the fabric? Figure 3-4 provides a high-level illustration of the process that takes place.

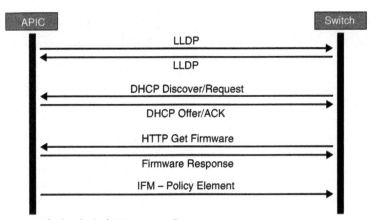

Figure 3-4 *Switch Discovery Process*

The process depicted in Figure 3-4 includes the following steps:

Step 1.   **LLDP neighbor discovery:** After a minimal configuration bootstrap, the first APIC begins sending out LLDP packets on its in-band interfaces. Unregistered leaf switches send LLDP packets on all operational ports. The APIC should eventually pick up LLDP packets from the neighboring leaf if the switch is fully operational and has ACI code installed. From the LLDP packets, the APIC can determine the serial number and hardware platform of the attached device.

Step 2.   **TEP IP assignment to nodes:** In addition to LLDP packets, unregistered ACI switches send DHCP Discover packets on operational interfaces. Once an APIC detects a switch via LLDP and is able to process DHCP Discover packets from the leaf, it adds the device to the Fabric Membership tab. An administrator then needs to register the switch to authorize it to join the fabric. The registration process maps a node ID to the switch and configures its hostname. The switch registration begins with the APIC responding to the switch DHCP requests with a DHCP Offer packet. The leaf confirms that it does want the offered IP address using a DHCP Request message, following which the APIC confirms the IP assignment with a DHCP ACK packet. APICs pull the IP addresses assigned during this process from the TEP pool range configured during APIC initialization. Each leaf switch is assigned a TEP address. These TEP addresses reside in a VRF instance called overlay-1 in a tenant called infra.

Step 3.   **Switch software upgrades, if necessary:** APICs are able to communicate to switches that they need to undergo upgrades to a particular code level before they can be moved into production status. If a switch upgrade is required, the switch downloads the necessary firmware from the APICs, performs an upgrade, and reboots. The Default Firmware Version setting determines whether a switch upgrade is necessary. This setting is detailed later in this chapter.

Step 4.   **Policy element intra-fabric messaging (IFM) setup:** After the switch boots up with the intended code revision, the APIC authenticates the switch by using the switch certificate signed at the factory and opens communication with the switch TEP address over the infrastructure VLAN using ***intra-fabric messaging (IFM)***. All IFM channel communication over the infrastructure VLAN is encrypted using TLS Version 1.2, and every message that comes to the switch over the IFM channel must be decrypted before it is processed by the switch. Once APICs establish IFM communication with a switch, the switch is fully activated. Any policy push from the APICs to switches rides this encrypted IFM communication channel.

Depending on the switch being discovered, some minor tasks may be added to the overall discovery process. For example, a Remote Leaf discovery would additionally require DHCP relay functionality to be enabled for DHCP packets from the Remote Leaf to reach the APICs. (The task of enabling DHCP relay does not conflict with the four primary steps outlined for switch discovery.) Another example of minor tasks added to the process is establishment of IS-IS adjacencies between leaf and spine switches using the switch loopback 0 interfaces.

Fabric Discovery Stages

After the bootstrapping of the first APIC, fabric initialization happens in the following three phases:

1. **Seed leaf initialization:** Even when an APIC VIC adapter attaches to two or more operational leaf switches, the APIC can detect only one of the leaf switches. This is because APIC VIC adapters operate in active/standby mode. Activation of the first leaf switch by an administrator allows the leaf to function as a seed switch for further discovery of the fabric.

2. **Spine initialization:** After the seed leaf initialization, any spines with fabric ports attached to the seed leaf are detected and added to the Fabric Membership view to allow spine activation.

3. **Initialization of leaf switches and additional APICs:** As spines are brought into the fabric, ACI can detect other leaf switches connected to them. Administrators can then activate the leaf switches. Once the leaf switches connected to additional APICs join the fabric, the APIC cluster forms, and APIC synchronization begins. Controllers join the cluster based on node ID. In other words, the third APIC (whose node ID is 3) joins the cluster only after the first and second APICs have joined. If any critical bootstrap configuration parameters have been entered incorrectly on the additional controllers, the APIC fails to join the cluster and needs to be wiped clean and re-initialized.

Note that the phases outlined here describe cluster formation as part of the final leaf initialization phase. However, if active in-band interfaces on all APICs connect to the seed leaf switch, the APIC cluster can form during the seed leaf initialization phase.

Switch Discovery States

During the discovery process, switches transition between various states. Table 3-4 describes the different discovery states.

Table 3-4   Fabric Node Discovery States

State	Description
Unknown	The node has been detected, but a node ID has not yet been assigned by an administrator in the Fabric Membership view.
Undiscovered	An administrator has prestaged a switch activation by manually mapping a switch serial number to a node ID, but a switch with the specified serial number has not yet been detected via LLDP and DHCP.
Discovering	The node has been detected, and the APICs are in the process of mapping the specified node ID as well as a TEP IP address to the switch.
Unsupported	The node is a Cisco switch, but it is not supported or the firmware version is not compatible with the ACI fabric.
Disabled/ Decommissioned	The node has been discovered and activated, but a user disabled or decommissioned it. The node can be reenabled.
Maintenance	An ACI administrator has put the switch into maintenance mode (graceful insertion and removal).
Inactive	The node has been discovered and activated, but it is not currently accessible. For example, it may be powered off, or its cables may be disconnected.
Active	The node is an active member of the fabric.

Initializing an ACI Fabric

Once all cabling has been completed and the APICs and ACI switches have been turned on, it is time to initialize the fabric. The tasks in this section lead to the configuration of the APIC Cisco IMC addresses, the initialization of the APICs, and the activation of ACI switches.

Changing the APIC BIOS Password

One of the things ACI implementation engineers usually do during APIC setup is to change the default BIOS password.

To change the BIOS password, you press the F2 key during the boot process to enter the BIOS setup. Then you can enter the default BIOS password **password** in the Enter Password dialog box and navigate to the Security tab, choose Set Administrator Password, and enter the current password in the Enter Current Password dialog box. When the Create New Password dialog box appears, enter the new password and then enter the new password again in the Confirm New Password dialog box. Finally, navigate to the Save & Exit tab and choose Yes in the Save & Exit Setup dialog box. The next time BIOS setup is accessed, the new BIOS password will be needed.

Configuring the APIC Cisco IMC

After changing the BIOS password, it is a good idea to configure a static IP address for the APIC Cisco IMC addresses.

To configure a static IP address for remote Cisco IMC access, press the F8 key during the boot process to enter Cisco IMC. Enter the desired IP addressing details in the section IP (Basic), as shown in Figure 3-5. Then press the F10 key to save the Cisco IMC configuration and wait up to 20 seconds for the configuration change to take effect before rebooting the server.

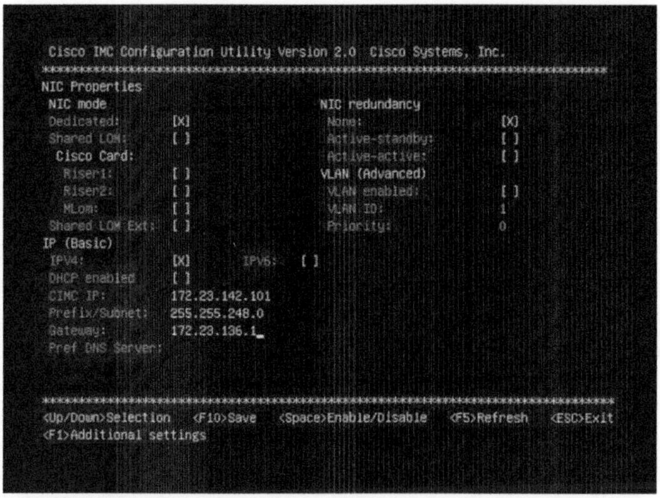

Figure 3-5 *Enter IP Addressing Details for Cisco IMC*

As a best practice, do not modify the NIC Mode or NIC Redundancy settings in Cisco IMC. If there are any discovery issues, ensure that Cisco IMC has been configured with the default NIC Mode setting Dedicated and not Shared. The NIC Redundancy setting should also be left at its default value None.

Initializing the First APIC

When the APIC boots up, basic configuration parameters need to be entered in line with the pre-installation data captured in earlier steps. Example 3-1 shows how the first APIC in a fabric with ID 1 and the name DC1-Fabric1 might be configured. Note that you can leave certain parameters at their default values by pressing the Enter key without modifying associated values. The BD multicast addresses range, for instance, is left at its default value of 225.0.0.0/15 in the following example.

Example 3-1 *Initialization of First APIC*

```
Cluster configuration ...
  Enter the fabric name [ACI Fabric1]: DC1-Fabric1
  Enter the fabric ID (1-128) [1]: 1
  Enter the number of active controllers in the fabric (1-9) [3]: 3
  Enter the POD ID (1-9) [1]: 1
  Is this a standby controller? [NO]: NO
  Enter the controller ID (1-3) [1]: 1
  Enter the controller name [apic1]: DC1-APIC1
  Enter address pool for TEP addresses [10.0.0.0/16]: 10.233.44.0/22
  Note: The infra VLAN ID should not be used elsewhere in your environment
        and should not overlap with any other reserved VLANs on other platforms.
  Enter the VLAN ID for infra network (2-4094): 3600
  Enter address pool for BD multicast addresses (GIPO) [225.0.0.0/15]:
```

```
Out-of-band management configuration ...
  Enable IPv6 for Out of Band Mgmt Interface? [N]:
  Enter the IPv4 address [192.168.10.1/24]: 172.23.142.29/21
  Enter the IPv4 address of the default gateway [None]: 172.23.136.1
  Enter the interface speed/duplex mode [auto]:

admin user configuration ...
  Enable strong passwords? [Y]:
  Enter the password for admin:


  Reenter the password for admin:

Cluster configuration ...
  Fabric name: DC1-Fabric1
  Fabric ID: 1
  Number of controllers: 3
  Controller name: DC1-APIC1
  POD ID: 1
  Controller ID: 1
  TEP address pool: 10.233.44.0/22
  Infra VLAN ID: 3600
  Multicast address pool: 225.0.0.0/15

Out-of-band management configuration ...
  Management IP address: 172.23.142.29/21
  Default gateway: 172.23.136.1
  Interface speed/duplex mode: auto

admin user configuration ...
  Strong Passwords: Y
  User name: admin
  Password: ********

The above configuration will be applied ...

Warning: TEP address pool, Infra VLAN ID and Multicast address pool
         cannot be changed later, these are permanent until the
         fabric is wiped.

Would you like to edit the configuration? (y/n) [n]:
```

After you complete the minimal configuration bootstrap for the first controller, the APIC starts various services, and the APIC web GUI eventually becomes accessible via the APIC out-of-band management IP address. Figure 3-6 shows the ACI login page. By default, APICs allow web access via HTTPS and not HTTP.

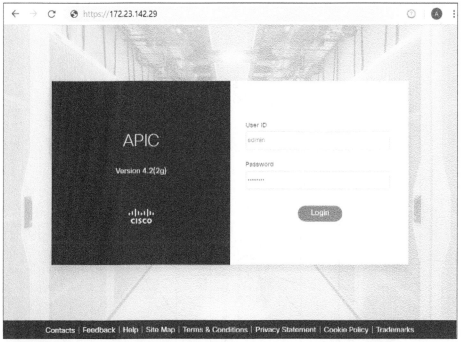

Figure 3-6   *The Default ACI Login Screen*

Enter **admin** as the username along with the password entered during setup to log in to the APIC.

Discovering and Activating Switches

The switch activation process involves selection of node IDs for all switches. The first three active APICs need to be assigned node IDs 1, 2, and 3. ACI design engineers have more flexibility in the selection of switch node IDs. As of ACI Release 4.2, valid switch node IDs are between 101 and 4000. Node IDs are cornerstones of ACI stateless networking. Once a switch is commissioned, node ID changes require that the node be decommissioned and cleanly rebooted.

Figure 3-7 shows a hypothetical node ID selection scheme in which spine switches have node ID numbers between 201 and 299 and leaf switches have node numbers between 101 and 199. It is a Cisco best practice to assign subsequent node IDs to leaf switches that are paired into a VPC domain.

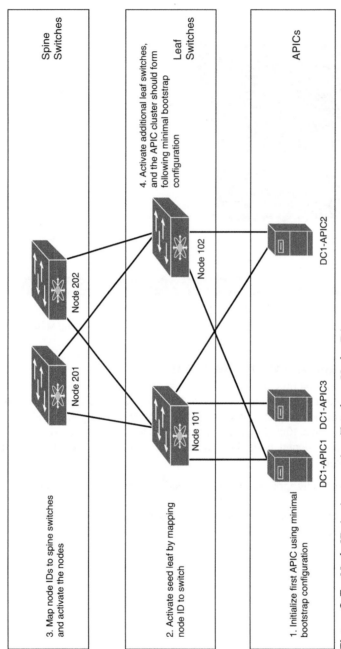

Figure 3-7   *Node ID Assignment in a Topology Under Discovery*

Following the initialization of DC1-APIC1 in Figure 3-7, the APIC should detect that a leaf switch is connected to its active VIC interface and add it to the Fabric Membership view. Navigate to Fabric, select Inventory, and then click on Fabric Membership. In the Fabric Membership view, select Nodes Pending Registration, right-click the detected switch entry, and select Register, as demonstrated in Figure 3-8. This first leaf switch added to the fabric will serve as the seed leaf for the discovery of the remaining switches in the fabric.

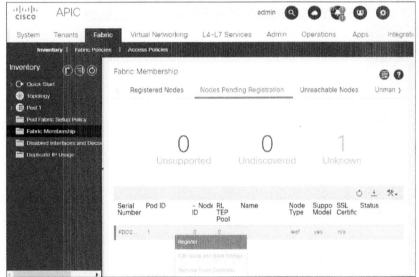

Figure 3-8 *Selecting the Entry for Unknown Switch and Launch Registration Wizard*

In the node registration wizard, enter values in the fields Pod ID, Node ID, and Node Name (hostname) and then click Register (see Figure 3-9). If the switch has been auto-detected by ACI, the role should be auto-populated. The Rack Name parameter is optional. The RL TEP Pool field should be populated only during configuration of a Remote Leaf switch.

Figure 3-9 *The Node Registration Wizard*

Aside from the leaf and spine roles, the node registration wizard allows assignment of *virtualleaf* and *virtualspine* roles for vPOD switches, the *controller* role for APICs, the *remoteleaf* role, and *tier-2-leaf* role for Tier 2 leaf switches.

Minutes after registering the seed switch, it should move into an active state. The state of commissioned fabric nodes can be verified under the Status column in the Registered Nodes subtab of the Fabric Membership menu.

Figure 3-10 shows that all node IDs depicted in Figure 3-7 earlier in this chapter have been initialized one by one and have moved to an active state, completing the fabric initialization process.

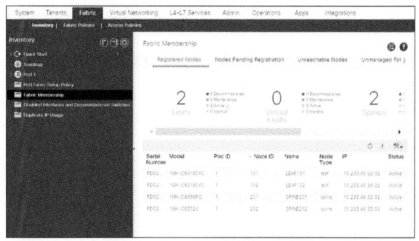

Figure 3-10 *Registered Nodes Submenu of the Fabric Membership View*

Understanding Graceful Insertion and Removal (GIR)

Figure 3-11 shows that one of the menu options that appears when you right-click a fabric node is Maintenance (GIR). Moving a switch into maintenance mode simulates an uplink failure from the perspective of downstream servers. This feature enables a more graceful way of moving a switch out of the data plane forwarding topology when minor maintenance or switch upgrades are necessary.

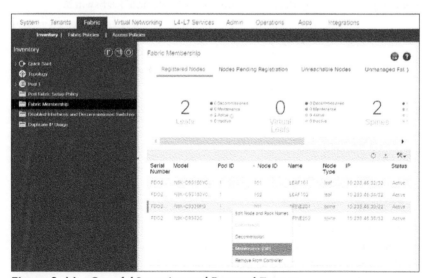

Figure 3-11 *Graceful Insertion and Removal Feature*

Initializing Subsequent APICs

The minimal configuration bootstrap for subsequent APICs can be performed simultaneously with the initialization of the first APIC. However, the APICs do not form a complete cluster until the end-to-end path between the APICs has been established over the infrastructure VLAN.

Remember that even when multiple APICs have connections to the seed leaf switch, it is still possible that they may not be able to form a cluster through the one seed leaf due to the active/standby status of the VIC adapter interfaces at the time of initialization.

But beyond the process and order of node activation, there is also the issue of bootstrapping requirements to form a cluster. If the fabric ID, fabric name, or Pod 1 TEP pool configured on the subsequent APICs are not the same as what has been configured for the initial controller, the APIC cluster will never form. In such cases, when the underlying problem is a misconfiguration on the second or third APIC, that APIC needs to be wiped clean and re-initialized. If the first APIC has been misconfigured, the entire fabric needs to be wiped clean and re-initialized.

Some APIC configuration parameters that should not be the same as those entered for the initial APIC include the out-of-band IP address and the APIC node ID.

After establishing end-to-end connectivity, you can verify the health of an APIC cluster by navigating to the System menu, selecting Controllers, opening the Controllers folder, double-clicking an APIC, and then selecting Cluster as Seen by Node. If the controllers are healthy and fully synchronized, all APICs should display Fully Fit in the Health State column, as shown in Figure 3-12.

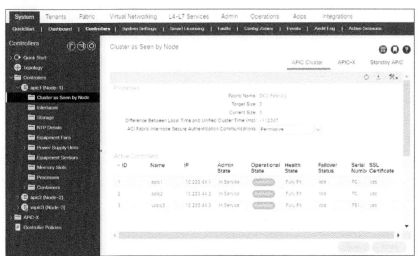

Figure 3-12 *Verifying Health and Synchronization Status of APICs*

Understanding Connectivity Following Switch Initialization

What actually happens during the switch node activation process from a routing perspective? One of the first things that happens is that IS-IS adjacencies are established between the leaf and spine switches, as shown in Example 3-2. Here, interfaces Ethernet 1/49 and 1/50 are the leaf fabric ports.

Example 3-2 *Verifying IS-IS Adjacencies Within the Fabric*

```
LEAF101# show isis adjacency detail vrf overlay-1
IS-IS process: isis_infra VRF:overlay-1
IS-IS adjacency database:
System ID        SNPA           Level  State  Hold Time  Interface
212E.E90A.0000   N/A            1      UP     00:01:01   Ethernet1/49.34
  Up/Down transitions: 1, Last transition: 21d17h ago
  Circuit Type: L1
  IPv4 Address: 10.233.46.33
232E.E90A.0000   N/A            1      UP     00:00:55   Ethernet1/50.35
  Up/Down transitions: 1, Last transition: 21d17h ago
  Circuit Type: L1
  IPv4 Address: 10.233.46.35
```

A look at the addresses with which LEAF101 has established adjacencies indicates that IS-IS adjacencies are sourced and destined from and to loopback 0 interfaces on leaf and spine switches. Furthermore, loopback 0 interfaces get associated with all operational fabric ports, as indicated in Example 3-3. The IP address ACI assigns to the loopback 0 interface of a given switch is a specific type of TEP address referred to as a *physical tunnel endpoint (PTEP)* address.

Example 3-3 *Verifying Switch TEP Addresses*

```
LEAF101# show ip int brief | grep -E "lo0|unnumbered"
eth1/49.34           unnumbered           protocol-up/link-up/admin-up
                     (lo0)
eth1/50.35           unnumbered           protocol-up/link-up/admin-up
                     (lo0)
lo0                  10.233.46.32/32      protocol-up/link-up/admin-up


SPINE201# show ip int brief | grep -E "lo0|unnumbered"
eth1/1.37            unnumbered           protocol-up/link-up/admin-up
                     (lo0)
eth1/2.38            unnumbered           protocol-up/link-up/admin-up
                     (lo0)
lo0                  10.233.46.33/32      protocol-up/link-up/admin-up
SPINE202# show ip int brief | grep -E "lo0|unnumbered"
eth1/1.35            unnumbered           protocol-up/link-up/admin-up
                     (lo0)
eth1/2.36            unnumbered           protocol-up/link-up/admin-up
                     (lo0)
lo0                  10.233.46.35/32      protocol-up/link-up/admin-up
```

In addition to loopback 0 interfaces, ACI creates loopback 1023 interfaces on all leaf switches. A loopback 1023 interface is used for assignment of a single fabricwide pervasive IP address called a *fabric tunnel endpoint (FTEP)* address. The FTEP address represents the entire fabric and is used to encapsulate traffic in VXLAN to an AVS or AVE virtual switch, if present.

ACI also assigns an SVI and IP address to leaf switches in the infrastructure VLAN. In Example 3-4, internal VLAN 8 on LEAF101 actually maps to VLAN 3600, which is the infrastructure VLAN configured during fabric initialization. Note that the infrastructure VLAN SVI should contain the same IP address for all leaf switches.

Example 3-4   *Additional Auto-Established Connectivity in the Overlay-1 VRF Instance*

```
LEAF101# show ip int brief vrf overlay-1
(...output truncated for brevity...)
IP Interface Status for VRF "overlay-1"(4)
Interface          Address            Interface Status
eth1/49            unassigned         protocol-up/link-up/admin-up
eth1/49.34         unnumbered         protocol-up/link-up/admin-up
                   (lo0)
eth1/50            unassigned         protocol-up/link-up/admin-up
eth1/50.35         unnumbered         protocol-up/link-up/admin-up
                   (lo0)
vlan8              10.233.44.30/27    protocol-up/link-up/admin-up
lo0                10.233.46.32/32    protocol-up/link-up/admin-up
lo1023             10.233.44.32/32    protocol-up/link-up/admin-up


LEAF101# show vlan extended

 VLAN Name                            Encap                Ports
 -------- ------------------------ -------------------- --------------------------
 ---
 8     infra:default                  vxlan-16777209,   Eth1/1, Eth1/2, Eth1/47
                                      vlan-3600
```

Once an ACI fabric has been fully initialized, each switch should have *dynamic tunnel endpoint (DTEP)* entries that include PTEP addresses for all other devices in the fabric as well as entries pointing to spine proxy (*proxy TEP*) addresses. Example 3-5 shows DTEP entries from the perspective of LEAF101 with the proxy TEP addresses highlighted.

Example 3-5   *Dynamic Tunnel Endpoint (DTEP) Database*

```
LEAF101# show isis dteps vrf overlay-1

IS-IS Dynamic Tunnel End Point (DTEP) database:
DTEP-Address       Role    Encapsulation   Type
10.233.46.33       SPINE   N/A             PHYSICAL
10.233.47.65       SPINE   N/A             PHYSICAL,PROXY-ACAST-MAC
10.233.47.66       SPINE   N/A             PHYSICAL,PROXY-ACAST-V4
10.233.47.64       SPINE   N/A             PHYSICAL,PROXY-ACAST-V6
10.233.46.34       LEAF    N/A             PHYSICAL
10.233.46.35       SPINE   N/A             PHYSICAL
```

If a leaf switch knows the destination leaf behind which an endpoint resides, it is able to tunnel the traffic directly to the destination leaf without using resources on the intermediary spine switches. If a leaf switch does not know where the destination endpoint resides, it can forward the traffic to the spine proxy addresses, and the recipient spine can then perform a lookup in its local Council of Oracle Protocol (COOP) database and forward the traffic to the intended recipient leaf. This spine proxy forwarding behavior is more efficient than forwarding via broadcasts and learning destination switches through ARP. Reliance on spine proxy forwarding instead of flooding of broadcast, unknown unicast, and multicast traffic is called *hardware proxy* forwarding. The benefit of using hardware proxy forwarding is that ACI is able to potentially eliminate flooding within the fabric, allowing the fabric to better scale while also limiting the amount of traffic servers need to process.

Because ACI leaf switches are able to use IS-IS to dynamically learn all PTEP and spine proxy addresses within the fabric, they are able to create tunnel interfaces to various destinations in the fabric. A tunnel in ACI can be simply interpreted as a reference to the next-hop addresses to reach a particular destination. Example 3-6 lists the tunnels on LEAF101. Tunnels 1, 3, and 4 are destined to leaf and spine PTEP addresses. Tunnels 5 through 7 reference proxy TEP addresses. Finally, tunnels 8, 9, and 10 refer to the TEP addresses assigned to APIC 1, APIC 2, and APIC 3, respectively.

Example 3-6   *Tunnel Interfaces Sourced from lo0 with Different Destinations*

```
LEAF101# show interface tunnel 1-20 | grep -E 'destination|up'
Tunnel1 is up
    Tunnel destination 10.233.46.33
Tunnel3 is up
    Tunnel destination 10.233.46.34
Tunnel4 is up
    Tunnel destination 10.233.46.35
Tunnel5 is up
    Tunnel destination 10.233.47.65
Tunnel6 is up
    Tunnel destination 10.233.47.66
Tunnel7 is up
    Tunnel destination 10.233.47.64
Tunnel8 is up
    Tunnel destination 10.233.44.1
Tunnel9 is up
    Tunnel destination 10.233.44.2
Tunnel10 is up
    Tunnel destination 10.233.44.3
```

Note that aside from IS-IS, ACI enables COOP functionality on all available spine switches as part of the fabric initialization process. This ensures that leaf switches can communicate endpoint mapping information (location and identity) to spine switches. However, fabric initialization does not result in the automatic establishment of control plane adjacencies for protocols such as MP-BGP. As of the time of this writing, a BGP autonomous system number needs to be selected, and at least one spine has to be designated as a route reflector before MP-BGP can be effectively used within an ACI fabric.

Basic Post-Initialization Tasks

After the initialization of APICs and switches, there are a number of tasks that are generally seen as basic prerequisites for putting a fabric into production. This section gives a rundown of such tasks.

Assigning Static Out-of-Band Addresses to Switches and APICs

Assigning out-of-band addresses to switches ensures that administrators can access switches via SSH. Out-of-band addresses can be assigned statically by an administrator or dynamically out of a pool of addresses.

Figure 3-13 shows how to assign static out-of-band addresses to fabric nodes through the Create Static Node Management Addresses page. To create static out-of-band addresses for a node, navigate to Tenants and select the tenant named mgmt. Within the tenant, double-click the Node Management Addresses folder. Then right-click the Static Node Management Addresses folder and select Create Static Node Management Addresses. Select default from the Out-of-Band Management EPG drop-down box. Chapter 5, "Tenants Building Blocks," describes EPGs thoroughly, but for now you just need to know that the default out-of-band management EPG is an object that represents one or more out-of-band subnets or specific out-of-band addresses used for ACI switches and APICs. Out-of-band management EPGs other than the default object can be created if desired to enable application of granular security policies to different nodes. After entering the node ID in both Node Range fields, the out-of-band IPv4 address, and the out-of-band IPv4 gateway details for a given switch or APIC, click Submit. The static node address mapping should then appear under the Static Node Management Addresses folder.

Figure 3-13 *Creating Static Out-of-Band Addresses for Switches and APICs*

Even though APIC addresses are manually assigned through the controller initialization process, they do not by default appear under the Static Node Management Addresses folder. This is a problem if monitoring solutions such as SNMP are used to query ACI. Assigning static out-of-band addresses to APICs following fabric initialization helps ensure that certain monitoring functions work as expected. Figure 3-14 illustrates how the original node IDs used during APIC initialization should be used to add static OOB IP addressing entries to APICs.

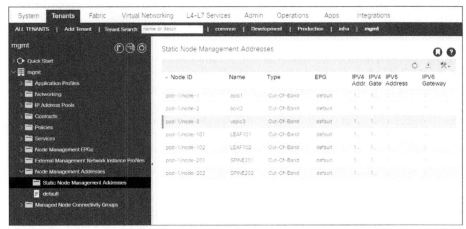

Figure 3-14 *Static Node Management Addresses View After OOB IP Configuration*

Chapter 13 covers dynamic out-of-band and in-band management in more detail.

Applying a Default Contract to Out-of-Band Subnet

From a high level, contracts enable the enforcement of security and other policies to the endpoints to which the contract associates. As a fabric initialization task, administrators can assign an out-of-the-box contract called default from a tenant called common to the OOB EPG to allow all communication to and from the OOB subnet.

While assignment of contracts permitting all communication is not an ideal long-term approach, it does enable the gradual enforcement of security policies as requirements are better understood. Moreover, the application of a contract is necessary when enabling certain management protocols, such as Telnet. Also, even though it is not required to implement an OOB contract for certain features like syslog forwarding to work, it is best practice to do so.

To apply the default OOB contract to the OOB management EPG, navigate to the mgmt tenant, open the Node Management EPG folder, and select Out-of-Band EPG - default. Then, in the Provided Out-of-Band Contracts section, select the contract common/default and click Update and click Submit (see Figure 3-15).

After application of a contract on an OOB EPG, a mechanism is needed to define the subnets outside the fabric that will have open access to the ACI out-of-band IP addresses assigned to the OOB management EPG. The mechanism used for management connectivity is an external management network instance profile. Navigate to the mgmt tenant, right-click the External Management Network Instance Profile folder, and select Create External Management Network Instance Profile. Provide a name for the object and select the default contract from the common tenant in the Consumed Out-of-Band Contracts section. Finally, enter the subnets that should be allowed to communicate with the ACI OOB EPG in the Subnets section, select Update, and then click Submit. To enable all subnets to communicate with ACI over the OOB interfaces, enter the subnet 0.0.0.0/0. Alternatively, you can enter all private IP address ranges or specific subnets assigned to administrators. Figure 3-16 shows the creation of an external management network instance profile.

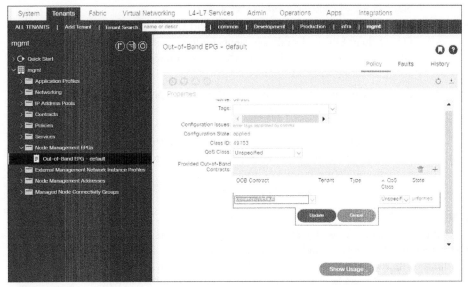

Figure 3-15   *Assigning a Contract to an OOB Management EPG*

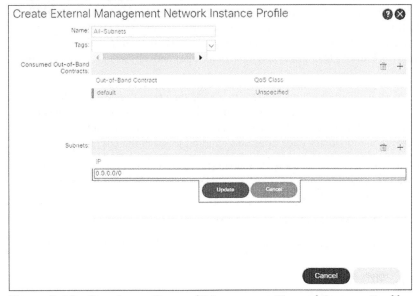

Figure 3-16   *Creating an External Management Network Instance Profile*

To recap, it is important to enforce contracts for access to the OOB management interface of an ACI fabric because certain configurations rely on contract enforcement. For open communication to the OOB subnets through use of contracts, take the following three steps:

Step 1. **Assign static node management addresses:** Assign out-of-band addresses to all switches and APICs in the fabric and ensure that all nodes are shown in the Static Node Management Addresses view.

Step 2. **Assign contract to the desired out-of-band EPG:** By default, the object called Out-of-Band EPGs - default represents OOB subnets. Assigning a contract that allows all traffic, such as the contract named common/default, can enable open communication to OOB subnets.

Step 3. **Define external management network instance profiles and associate contracts:** An external management network instance profile determines the subnets that can gain management access to ACI. Allocate the same contract applied in the previous step to the external management network instance profile you create to ensure that the contract is enforced between the external subnets you define and the ACI OOB subnets.

Upgrading an ACI Fabric

As a best practice, all nodes within an ACI fabric should operate at the same code revision. Upon purchasing ACI switches and APICs and setting up an ACI fabric, it is highly likely that components may have been shipped at different code levels. For this reason, it is common practice for engineers to upgrade ACI fabrics right after initialization.

If there are version disparities between APICs and ACI switch code, it is also possible for the APICs to flag certain switches as requiring electronic programmable logic device (EPLD) upgrades. EPLD upgrades enhance hardware functionality and resolve known issues with hardware firmware. EPLD upgrade code is sometimes slipstreamed into ACI firmware images, and therefore an EPLD upgrade may take place automatically as part of ACI fabric upgrades.

The first thing to do when upgrading a fabric is to decide on a target code. Consult the release notes for candidate target software revisions and review any associated open software defects. Also, use the APIC Upgrade/Downgrade Support Matrix from Cisco to determine if there are any intermediary code upgrades required to reach the targeted code.

After selecting a target software revision, download the desired APIC and switch code from the Cisco website. ACI switch and APIC firmware images that can be used for upgrades have the file extensions .bin and .iso, respectively.

The ACI fabric upgrade process involves three steps:

Step 1. Download APIC and switch software images and then upload them to the APICs.

Step 2. Upgrade APICs.

Step 3. Upgrade spine and leaf switches in groups.

To upload firmware images to ACI, navigate to the Admin tab, click on Firmware, select Images, click the Tools icon, and then select Add Firmware to APIC (see Figure 3-17).

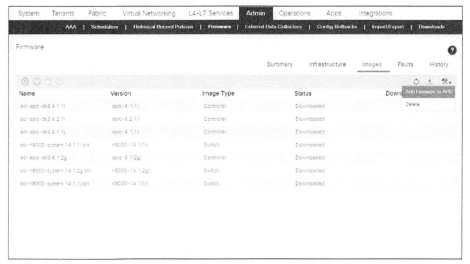

Figure 3-17 *Navigating to the Add Firmware to APIC Page*

In the Add Firmware to APIC page, keep Firmware Image Location set at its default value, Local, and then click Browse to select a file for upload from the local device from which the web session to the APIC has been established.

Alternatively, either HTTP or SCP (Secure Copy Protocol) can be used to download the target software code from a remote server. To download the image from a remote server, select the Remote option under Firmware Image Location and enter a name and URL for the download operation. SCP authenticates and encrypts file transfers and therefore additionally requires entry of a username and password with access to download rights on the SCP server. Instead of using a password, you can have ACI leverage SSH key data for the SCP download. Figure 3-18 shows sample data for downloading a file from an SCP server using a local username and password configured on the SCP server.

Once the firmware images have been uploaded to the APICs, they appear in the Images view (refer to Figure 3-17).

Unless release notes or the APIC Upgrade/Downgrade Support Matrix for a target release indicates otherwise, APICs should always be upgraded first. Navigate to the Admin menu, select Firmware, and click Infrastructure. Under the Controllers menu, click the Tools icon and select Schedule Controller Upgrade, as shown in Figure 3-19.

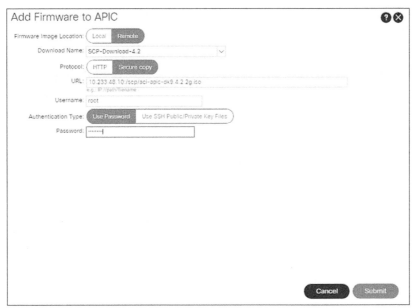

Figure 3-18 *Downloading Firmware from a Remote SCP Server*

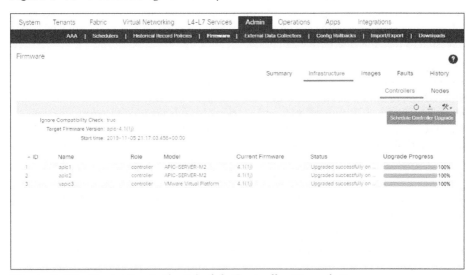

Figure 3-19 *Navigating to the Schedule Controller Upgrade Page*

The Schedule Controller Upgrade page opens. ACI advises against the upgrade if any critical or major faults exist in the fabric. These faults point to important problems in the fabric and can lead to traffic disruption during or after the upgrade. Engineers are responsible for fully understanding the caveats associated with active faults within a fabric. Do not upgrade a fabric when there are doubts about the implications of a given fault. After resolving any critical and major faults, select the target firmware version, define the upgrade mode via the Upgrade Start Time field (that is, whether the upgrade should begin right away or at a specified time in the future), and then click Submit to confirm the selected APIC upgrade schedule. During APIC upgrades, users lose management access to the APICs and need to reconnect.

Figure 3-20 shows how to kick off an immediate upgrade by selecting Upgrade Now and clicking Submit.

Figure 3-20 *Schedule Controller Upgrade Page*

By default, ACI verifies whether the upgrade path from the currently running version of the system to a specific newer version is supported. If, for any reason, ACI does not allow an upgrade due to the compatibility checks, and this is determined to be a false positive or if you wish to proceed with the upgrade anyway, you can enable the Ignore Compatibility Checks setting shown in Figure 3-20.

Following completion of any APIC upgrades, switch upgrades can begin. Cisco ACI uses the concept of upgrade groups to execute a group of switch upgrades consecutively. The idea behind upgrade groups is that if all servers have been dual connected to an odd and even switch, then an upgrade group consisting of all odd leaf switches should not lead to server traffic disruption as long as the even leaf upgrades do not happen until all odd leaf switches have fully recovered. Furthermore, if only half of all available spine switches are upgraded simultaneously and an even number of spines have been deployed, then there is little likelihood of unexpected traffic disruption.

In a hypothetical upgrade group setup, a fabric could be divided into the following four groups:

- Odd spine switches
- Even spine switches
- Odd leaf switches
- Even leaf switches

NOTE   Cisco only provides general guidance on configuration of upgrade groups. To maintain connectivity in a production environment, Cisco suggests that administrators define a *minimum of two* upgrade groups and upgrade one group at a time. Performing a minimally disruptive upgrade with two upgrade groups requires an administrator to group and upgrade a set of spine switches and leaf switches together. Most environments, however, tend to separate switches out into four or more upgrade groups to reduce the risk and extent of downtime if, for any reason, something goes wrong.

To configure an upgrade group, navigate to the Admin menu, select Firmware, click Infrastructure, and then select Nodes. Open the Tools menu and select Schedule Node Upgrade, as shown in Figure 3-21.

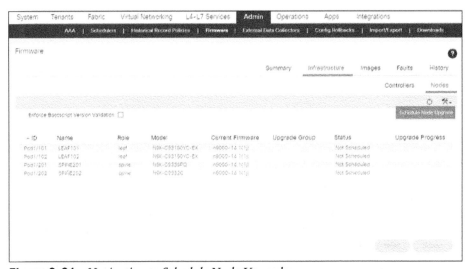

Figure 3-21   *Navigating to Schedule Node Upgrade*

In the Schedule Node Upgrade window, select New in the Upgrade Group field, choose a target firmware version, select an upgrade start time, and then select the switches that should be placed in the upgrade group by clicking the + sign in the All Nodes view. Nodes can be selected from a range based on node IDs or manually one by one. Finally, click Submit to execute the upgrade group creation and confirm scheduling of the upgrade of all switches that are members of this new upgrade group. Figure 3-22 shows the creation of an upgrade group called ODD-SPINES and scheduling of the upgrade of relevant nodes to take place right away. The completion of upgrades of all switches in an upgrade group can take anywhere from 12 to 30 minutes.

The Graceful Maintenance option ensures that the switches in the upgrade group are put into maintenance mode and removed from the server traffic forwarding path before the upgrade begins. The Run Mode option determines whether ACI will proceed with any subsequently triggered upgrades that may be in queue if a failure of the current upgrade group takes place. The default value for this parameter is Pause upon Upgrade Failure, and in most cases it is best not to modify this setting from its default.

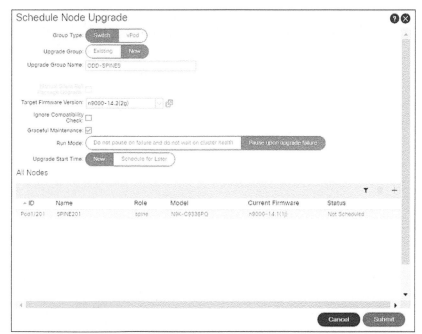

Figure 3-22 *Creating an Upgrade Group and Scheduling Node Upgrades*

One of the checkboxes shown but disabled in Figure 3-22 is Manual Silent Roll Package Upgrade. A silent roll package upgrade is an internal package upgrade for an ACI switch hardware SDK, drivers, or other internal components without an upgrade of the entire ACI switch software operating system. Typically, you do not need to perform a silent roll upgrade because upgrading the ACI switch operating system takes care of internal packages as well. Each upgrade group can be dedicated to either silent roll package upgrades or firmware upgrades but not both. Thus, the selection of a firmware code revision from the Target Firmware Version pull-down disables the Manual Silent Roll Package checkbox.

The triggering of an upgrade group places all switches in the specified upgrade group into queue for upgrades to the targeted firmware version. If upgrades for a group of nodes have been scheduled to start right away and no prior upgrade group is undergoing upgrades, the node upgrades can begin right away. Otherwise, the nodes are placed into queue for upgrades of previous upgrade groups to complete (see Figure 3-23). As indicated in Figure 3-23, the EVEN-SPINES group needs to wait its turn and allow upgrades of nodes in the ODD-LEAFS group to finish first.

Cisco recommends that ACI switches be divided into two or more upgrade groups. No more than 20 switches can be placed into a single upgrade group. Switches should be placed into upgrade groups to ensure maximum redundancy. If, for example, all spine switches are placed into a single upgrade group, major traffic disruption should be expected.

Once an upgrade group has been created, the grouping can be reused for subsequent fabric upgrades. Figure 3-24 shows how the selection of Existing in the Upgrade Group field allows administrators to reuse previously created upgrade group settings and trigger new upgrades simply by modifying the target firmware revision.

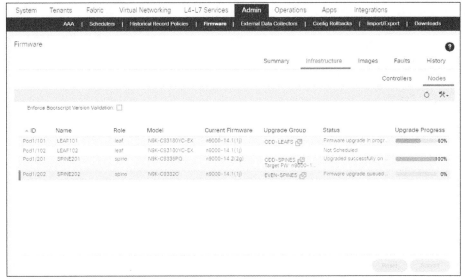

Figure 3-23 *An Upgrade Group Placed into Queue Due to Ongoing Upgrades*

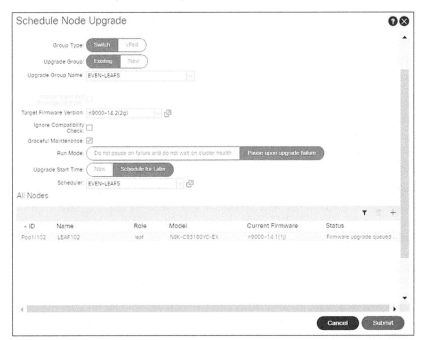

Figure 3-24 *Reusing a Previously Created Upgrade Group for Subsequent Upgrades*

Understanding Schedulers

An administrator can create a *scheduler* to specify a window of time for ACI to execute operations such as switch upgrades and configuration backups. Schedulers can be triggered on a one-time-only basis or can recur on a regular basis.

When an administrator creates an upgrade group, ACI automatically generates a scheduler object with the same name as the group.

In Figure 3-24 in the previous section, Schedule for Later has been selected for the Upgrade Start Time parameter, which in the installed APIC code version defaults to a scheduler with the equivalent name as the upgrade group name. The administrator can edit the selected scheduler by clicking on the blue link displayed in front of it. Figure 3-25 shows the Trigger Scheduler window, from which a one-time schedule can be implemented by hovering on the + sign and clicking Create.

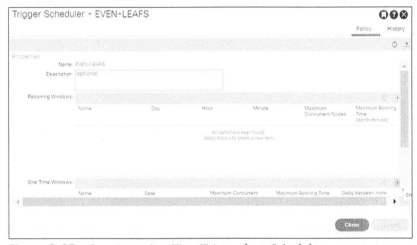

Figure 3-25   *Creating a One-Time Trigger for a Scheduler*

Figure 3-26 demonstrates the selection of a one-time window trigger, which involves the selection of a window name, the desired date and time, and the maximum number of nodes to upgrade simultaneously.

Figure 3-26   *Parameters Needed for Adding a One-Time Window Trigger to a Scheduler*

Enabling Automatic Upgrades of New Switches

Earlier in this chapter, we mentioned that APICs can force new switches to undergo upgrades to a certain firmware version prior to moving them into an active state.

The code version to which new switches should be upgraded needs to be selected using the Default Firmware Version setting. This setting, however, may be unavailable in certain APIC code versions by default. Figure 3-27 shows that after the Enforce Bootscript Version Validation setting is enabled, an administrator can then select a value for the Default Firmware Version setting.

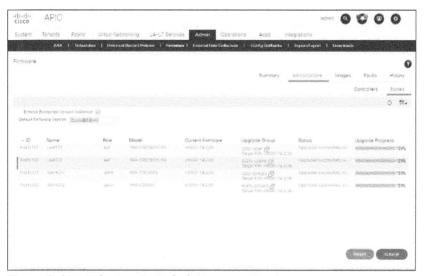

Figure 3-27   *Selecting the Default Firmware Version*

To execute the change, an administrator needs to click Submit. ACI then requests confirmation of the change by using an alert like the one shown in Figure 3-28.

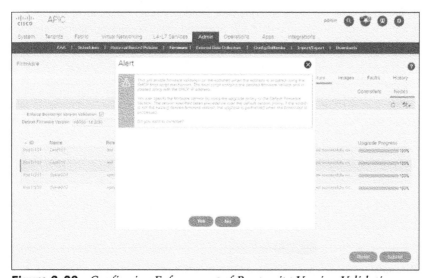

Figure 3-28   *Confirming Enforcement of Bootscript Version Validation*

From the alert message, it is clear that the code version selected for Default Firmware Version is indeed what is passed along to any new switches as part of the boot process. The alert message also clarifies that any switches whose node IDs have been added to an upgrade group will not be bound to the bootscript version requirements, as manual configuration supersedes the Default Firmware Version setting. Click Yes to confirm.

Understanding Backups and Restores in ACI

ACI allows both scheduled backups and on-demand backups of user configurations. The act of making a backup is referred to as a *configuration export*. Restoring ACI configurations from a backup is referred to as a *configuration import*.

ACI also enables recovery of the fabric configuration to a previous known good state. This process, called *configuration rollback*, is very useful when backing out of a change window is deemed necessary. For configuration rollback to a specific point in time (for example, prior to a change window), it is important for administrators to have taken a snapshot of the fabric configuration at the specified time. Snapshots are stored locally on the APICs.

In addition to snapshots, ACI can export configurations to remote FTP, SFTP, or SCP servers.

> **NOTE** For rapid rollback of configurations, it is best to take very regular configuration snapshots. To ease disaster recovery, administrators are also advised to retain two or more remote copies of recent backups at all times. These should be stored in easily accessible locations outside the local ACI fabric and potentially offsite. To automate backups, administrators can tie ACI backup operations to schedulers.

When performing a configuration import, ACI wants to know the desired import type and import mode. Import Type can be either set to Merge or Replace. As indicated in Table 3-5, the Import Type setting primarily determines what happens when the configuration being imported conflicts with the current configuration.

Table 3-5   Import Types

Import Type	Definition
Merge	The import operation combines the configuration in the backup file with the current configuration.
Replace	The import operation overwrites the current configuration with the configuration imported from the backup file.

The options for the Import Mode parameter are Best Effort and Atomic. The Import Mode parameter primarily determines what happens when configuration errors are identified in the imported settings. Table 3-6 describes the Import Mode options.

An import operation configured for atomic replacement, therefore, attempts to import all configurations from the backup and attempts to overwrite all settings to those specified in the backup file. Where a backup file may be used to import configurations to a different fabric, a best-effort merge operation may be a more suitable fit.

Table 3-6   Import Mode

Import Mode	Definition
Best Effort	Each shard is imported, but if there are objects within a shard that are invalid, these objects are ignored and not imported. If the version of the configuration being imported is incompatible with the current system, shards that can be imported are imported, and all other shards are ignored.
Atomic	The import operation is attempted for each shard, but if a shard has any invalid configuration, the shard is ignored and not imported. Also, if the version of the configuration being imported is incompatible with the current system, the import operation terminates.

Note that when an administrator selects Replace as the import type in the ACI GUI, the administrator no longer has the option to choose an import mode. This is because the import mode is automatically set at the default value Atomic to prevent a situation in which an import type Replace and an import mode Best Effort might break the fabric.

Another important aspect of backup and restore operations is whether secure properties are exported into backup files or processed from imported files. Secure properties are parameters such as SNMP or SFTP credentials or credentials used for integration with third-party appliances. For ACI to include these parameters in backup files and process secure properties included in a backup, the fabric needs to be configured with global AES encryption settings.

Making On-Demand Backups in ACI

To take an on-demand backup of an ACI fabric, navigate to the Admin tab, select Import/ Export, open the Export Policies folder, right-click Configuration, and select Create Configuration Export Policy, as shown in Figure 3-29.

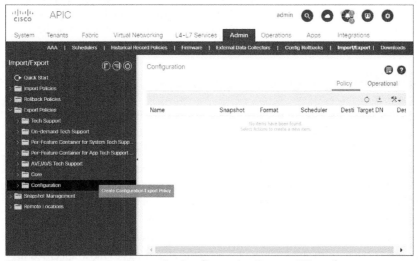

Figure 3-29   *Navigating to the Configuration Import Wizard*

In the Create Configuration Export Policy wizard, select a name, select whether the backup file should conform with JSON or XML format, indicate that a backup should be generated right after clicking Submit by toggling Start Now to Yes, and select to create a new remote server destination by right-clicking Export Destination and selecting Create Remote Location (see Figure 3-30).

Figure 3-30   *The Create Configuration Export Policy Wizard*

Figure 3-31 shows the Create Remote Location wizard. Enter the details pertinent to the remote server on which ACI should copy the file, and then click Submit.

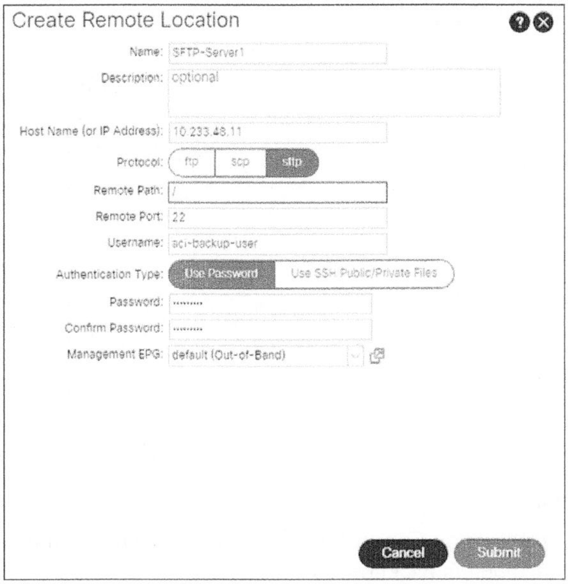

Figure 3-31   *The Create Remote Location Wizard*

Finally, back in the Create Configuration Export Policy wizard, update the global AES encryption settings, if desired. Click the Modify Global AES Encryption Settings checkbox to enable encryption of secure properties, as shown in Figure 3-32.

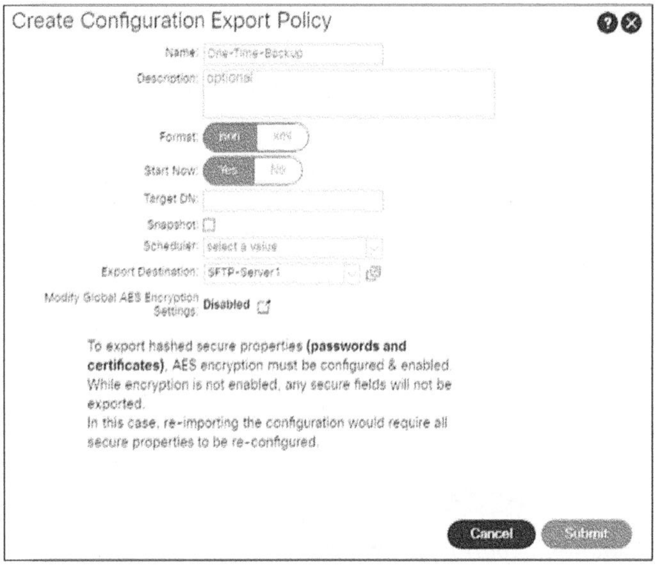

Figure 3-32   *Navigating to Global AES Encryption from the Export Window*

In the Global AES Encryption Settings for All Configuration Import and Export page, shown in Figure 3-33, select the Enable Encryption checkbox and then enter the passphrase for encryption. The passphrase needs to be between 16 to 32 characters.

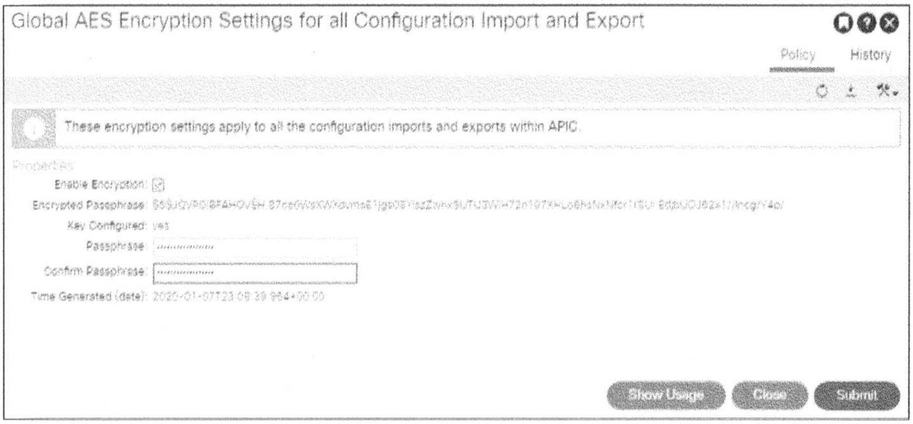

Figure 3-33   *Entering Encryption Settings in the Wizard*

Click Submit to return to the Create Configuration Export Policy wizard. With encryption enabled, secure properties will also be included in backup files.

Finally, click Submit to execute the configuration backup.

Note that one of the options available when making configuration backups is to specify the target DN field. This field limits the backup to a specific portion of the ACI object hierarchy.

When this field is not populated, the policy universe and all subtrees are captured in the backup file. Chapter 4, "Exploring ACI," introduces the ACI object hierarchy in detail.

Making Scheduled Backups in ACI

Scheduled backups are very similar to one-time backups. However, a scheduled backup also includes a reference to a scheduler object. For instance, an administrator who wants the entire fabric to be backed up every four hours could enter settings similar to the ones shown in Figure 3-34.

Figure 3-34 *Configuring Automated Backups Using a Recurring Schedule*

A scheduler that enables backups every four hours would need six entries, each configured for execution on a specific hour of day, four hours apart (see Figure 3-35).

Figure 3-35 *A Scheduler That Triggers an Action Every Four Hours*

Taking Configuration Snapshots in ACI

In addition to backing up configurations to remote locations, ACI allows users to take a snapshot of the configuration for local storage on the APICs. This can be done by enabling the Snapshot checkbox in the Create Configuration Export Policy wizard. Figure 3-36 shows that when the Snapshot checkbox is enabled, ACI removes the option to export backups to remote destinations.

Figure 3-36   *Creating Snapshots of ACI Configurations on a Recurring Basis*

Importing Configuration Backups from Remote Servers

To restore a configuration from a backup that resides on a remote server, navigate to the Admin tab, select Import/Export, drill into the Import Policies folder, right-click on Configuration, and then select Create Configuration Import Policy (see Figure 3-37).

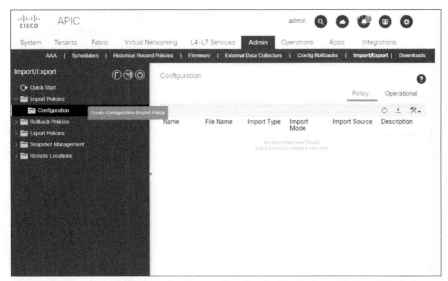

Figure 3-37   *Navigating to the Create Configuration Import Policy Wizard*

In the Create Configuration Import Policy wizard, enter a name for the import operation, enter details of the backup filename, select the import type and import mode, select the encryption settings, enter whether the process should start right away, and enter the remote destination from which the backup file should be downloaded. Figure 3-38 shows a sample import operation using Atomic Replace to restore all configuration to that specified in the backup file. Remember that when Import Type is set to Replace, Import Mode cannot be set to Best Effort.

Figure 3-38 *Restoring the Configuration from a Backup Residing on an External Server*

Once executed, the status of the import operation can be verified in the Operational tab of the newly created object, as shown in Figure 3-39.

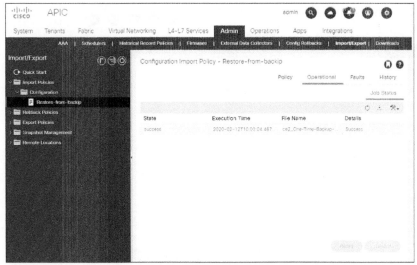

Figure 3-39 *Verifying the Status of an Import Operation*

In instances in which secure properties are not encrypted or a test of a backup and restore operation is desired, use of a configuration merge may be more desirable. Figure 3-40 shows that if Import Type is set to Merge, Import Mode can be set to Best Effort.

Figure 3-40   *Merging a Configuration Backup with Current Configurations*

Executing Configuration Rollbacks

When a misconfiguration occurs and there is a need to restore back to an earlier configuration, you can execute a configuration rollback. To do so, navigate to the Admin tab and select Config Rollback. Then select the configuration to which ACI should roll back from the list and select Rollback to This Configuration, as shown in Figure 3-41.

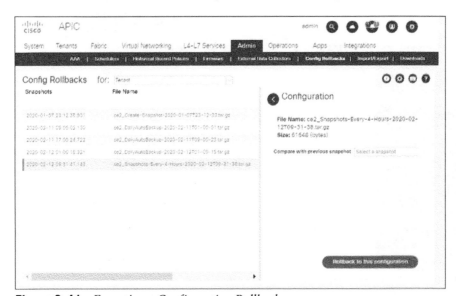

Figure 3-41   *Executing a Configuration Rollback*

Note that one of the beauties of configuration rollbacks and backups in ACI in general is that configurations can be backed up and restored fabricwide, for a single tenant, or for any specific portion of the ACI fabric object hierarchy.

ACI also simplifies pre-change snapshot creations by allowing users to take snapshots directly from within the Config Rollback page.

In instances in which a user does not know which snapshot is the most suitable to revert to, ACI can be directed to compare the contents of snapshots with one another and log differences between the selected snapshots.

Pod Policy Basics

All switches in ACI reside in a pod. This is true whether ACI Multi-Pod has been deployed or not. In single-pod deployments, ACI places all switches under a pod profile called default. Because each pod runs different control plane protocol instances, administrators need to have a way to modify configurations that apply to pods. Another reason for the need to tweak pod policies is that different pods may be in different locations and therefore may need to synchronize to different NTP servers or talk to different SNMP servers.

A *pod profile* specifies date and time, podwide SNMP, COOP settings, and IS-IS and Border Gateway Protocol (BGP) route reflector policies for one or more pods. Pod profiles map pod policy groups to pods by using pod selectors:

- A *pod policy group* is a group of individual protocol settings that are collectively applied to a pod.

- A *pod selector* is an object that references the pod IDs to which pod policies apply. Pod policy groups get bound to a pod through a pod selector.

Figure 3-42 illustrates how the default pod profile (shown as Pod Profile - default) in an ACI deployment binds a pod policy group called Pod-PolGrp to all pods within the fabric.

Figure 3-42   *Pod Profiles, Pod Policy Groups, and Pod Selectors*

Configuring Network Time Protocol (NTP) Synchronization

One of the day 0 tasks that may require changes to the default pod profile settings is NTP synchronization. Since multiple data centers may house pods from a single ACI Multi-Pod deployment, each pod may need to synchronize to different NTP servers. This is why NTP synchronization needs to be configured at the pod level.

To modify the list of NTP servers a pod points to, navigate to Fabric, select Fabric Policies, open the Pods folder, double-click Profiles, double-click the pod profile for the pod in question, select the relevant pod policy group, and click on the blue icon in front of the pod policy group to open the pod policy group applicable to the pod. Pod policy groups are also called fabric policy groups in several spots in the ACI GUI (see Figure 3-43).

Figure 3-43   *Opening the Pod Policy Group for the Relevant Pod*

In the Pod Policy Group view, validate the name of the date and time policy currently applicable to the pod in question. According to Figure 3-44, the date and time policy that ACI resolves for all pods in a particular deployment is a date and time policy called default.

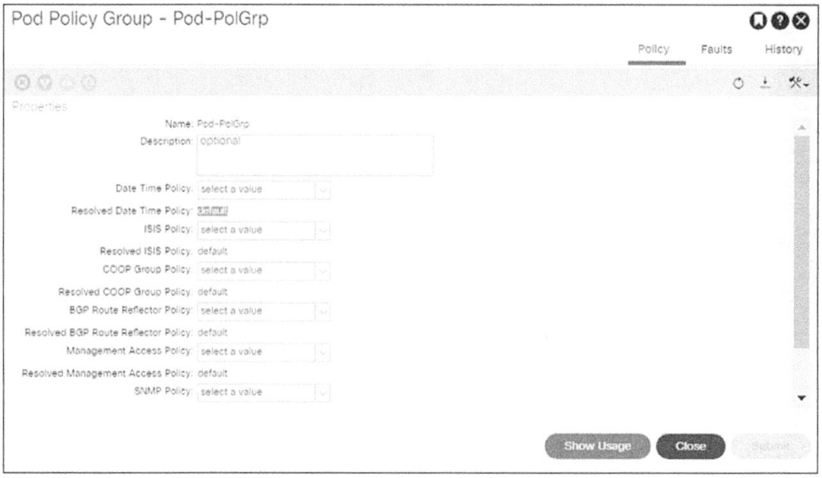

Figure 3-44   *Verifying the Date and Time Policy Applied to a Pod*

After identifying the date and time policy object that has been applied to the pod of interest, an administrator can either modify the applicable date and time policy or create and apply a new policy object. Figure 3-45 shows how the administrator can create a new date and time policy from the Pod Policy Group view.

Figure 3-45 *Creating a New Date and Time Policy in the Pod Policy Group View*

Enter a name for the new policy in the Create Date and Time Policy window and set the policy Administrative State to enabled, as shown in Figure 3-46, and click Next. Note that the Server State parameter allows administrators to configure ACI switches as NTP servers for downstream servers. The Authentication State option determines whether authentication will be required for any downstream clients in cases in which ACI functions as an NTP server.

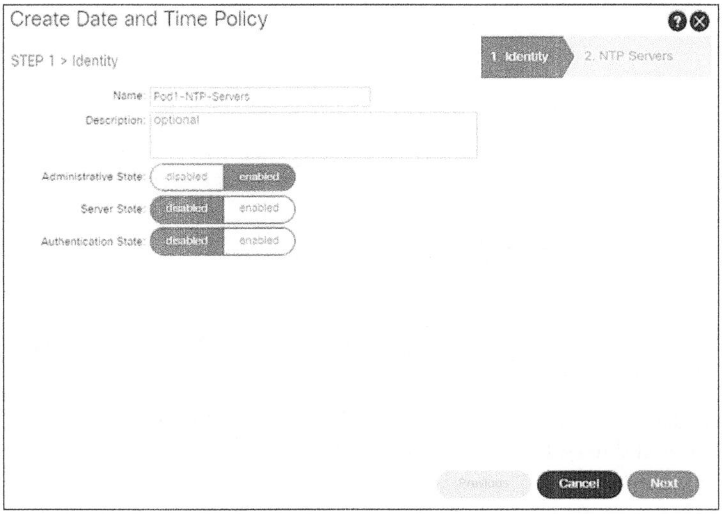

Figure 3-46 *Creating a Date and Time Policy*

Next, NTP servers need to be defined. Click the + sign on the top-right side of the NTP servers page to create an NTP provider, as shown in Figure 3-47. Enter the IP or DNS address of the NTP server in the Name field and set Minimum Polling Interval, Maximum Polling Interval, Management EPG (in-band or out-of-band) from which communication will be established. Finally, select whether the NTP server being configured should be preferred and then click OK.

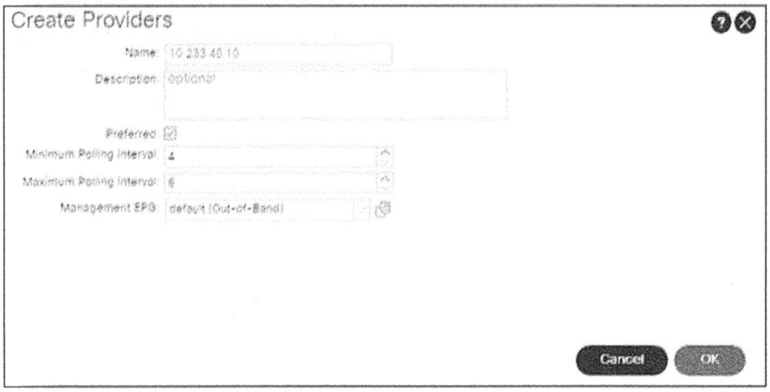

Figure 3-47　*Configuring NTP Providers*

Once all NTP providers have been configured, as shown in Figure 3-48, select Finish.

Figure 3-48　*Completing the NTP Provider Configuration*

As shown in Figure 3-49, the new date and time policy should appear to be selected in the Date Time Policy drop-down. Click Submit to apply the change.

To verify that the changes have taken effect, log in to the APIC CLI via SSH and run the commands **cat /etc/ntp.conf** and **netstat**, as shown in Example 3-7.

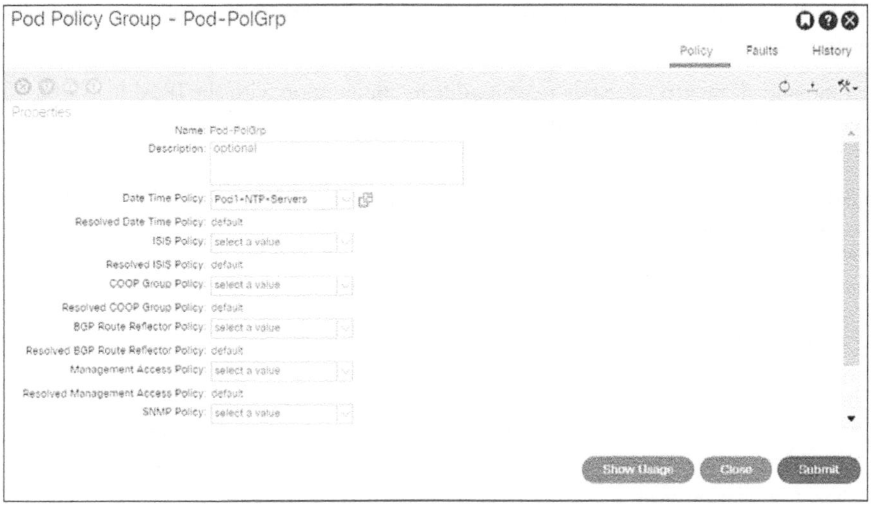

Figure 3-49 *Applying Changes to a Pod Policy Group*

Example 3-7 *Verifying NTP Configuration and Synchronization on an APIC*

```
apic1# cat /etc/ntp.conf
# Permit time synchronization with our time source, but do not
# permit the source to query or modify the service on this system.
tinker panic 501996547
restrict default kod nomodify notrap nopeer noquery
restrict -6 default kod nomodify notrap nopeer noquery

# Permit all access over the loopback interface.  This could
# be tightened as well, but to do so would effect some of
# the administrative functions.
#restrict default ignore
restrict 127.0.0.1
#restrict -6 ::1

keysdir /etc/ntp/
keys /etc/ntp/keys

server 10.233.48.10 prefer minpoll 4 maxpoll 6
server 10.133.48.10 minpoll 4 maxpoll 6

apic1# ntpstat
synchronised to NTP server (10.233.48.10) at stratum 4
   time correct to within 72 ms
   polling server every 16 s
```

Example 3-8 shows how to verify NTP settings on ACI switches. Execution of the commands **show ntp peers** and **show ntp peer-status** on a switch confirms that the APICs have deployed the NTP configuration to the switch and that an NTP server has been selected for synchronization.

Use the command **show ntp statistics peer ipaddr** in conjunction with the IP address of a configured NTP server to verify that the NTP server is consistently sending response packets to the switch.

Example 3-8   *Verifying NTP Configuration and Synchronization on an ACI Switch*

```
LEAF101# show ntp peers
------------------------------------------------------------------------------
---
  Peer IP Address                      Serv/Peer  Prefer  KeyId   Vrf
------------------------------------------------------------------------------
---
  10.233.48.10                         Server     yes     None    management
  10.133.48.10                         Server     no      None    management
LEAF101# show ntp peer-status
Total peers : 3
* - selected for sync, + - peer mode(active),
- - peer mode(passive), = - polled in client mode
    remote                       local           st poll reach delay
vrf
------------------------------------------------------------------------------
----
*10.233.48.10                   0.0.0.0          4  64   3    0.040  management
=10.133.48.10                   0.0.0.0          4  64   3    0.040  management
LEAF101# show ntp statistics peer ipaddr 10.233.48.10
remote host:          10.233.48.10
local interface:      Unresolved
time last received:   6s
time until next send: 59s
reachability change:  89s
packets sent:         3
packets received:     3
bad authentication:   0
bogus origin:         0
duplicate:            0
bad dispersion:       0
bad reference time:   0
candidate order:      0
```

Note that if you know the name of the date and time policy applicable to a pod of interest, you can populate the date and time policy directly by going to Fabric, selecting Fabric Policies, double-clicking Policies, opening Pod, and selecting the desired policy under the Date and Time folder (see Figure 3-50). If there is any question as to whether the right policy has been selected, you can click the Show Usage button to verify that the policy applies to the nodes of interest.

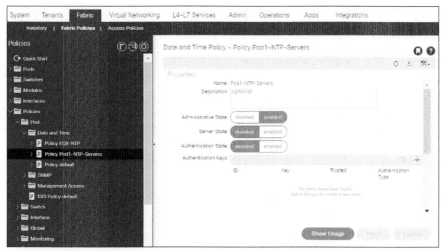

Figure 3-50 *Navigating Directly to a Specific Date and Time Policy*

If the time for a pod should reflect a specific time zone, the Datetime Format object needs to be modified. You can modify the Datetime Format object by navigating to System, selecting System Settings, and clicking on Date and Time.

The Display Format field allows you to toggle between Coordinated Universal Time (UTC) and local time. Selecting Local exposes the Time Zone field. Enabling the Offset parameter enables users to view the difference between the local time and the reference time. Figure 3-51 shows the Datetime Format object.

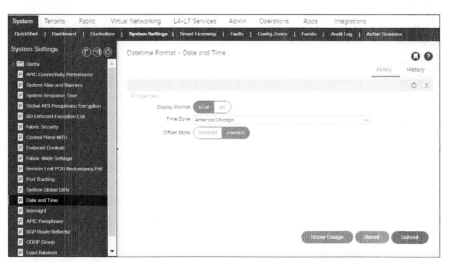

Figure 3-51 *Selecting a Time Zone via the Datetime Format Object*

NOTE NTP is considered a critical service for ACI fabrics. Atomic counters, a capability that measures traffic between leaf switches, requires active NTP synchronization across ACI fabrics. Without NTP synchronization, ACI is unable to accurately report on packet loss within the fabric.

Configuring DNS Servers for Lookups

Even though DNS is not explicitly within the scope of the DCACI 300-620 exam, DNS is considered a critical service. Various forms of integrations that are within the scope of the exam, such as VMM integration, sometimes rely on DNS. Therefore, this section provides basic coverage of ACI configurations for DNS lookups.

As a multitenancy platform, ACI needs a mechanism for each tenant to be able to conduct lookups against different DNS servers. ACI enables such a capability through DNS profiles. Each profile can point to a different set of DNS servers and leverage a different set of domains. Administrators can associate a different DNS profile or DNS label to each tenant to ensure that DNS lookups for endpoints within the specified tenant take place using DNS settings from the desired DNS profile.

Where multiple DNS profiles are not needed, a global DNS profile called default can be used to reference corporate DNS servers.

To create a DNS profile, navigate to the Fabric tab, select Fabric Policies, drill into the Policies folder, open the Global folder, right-click DNS Profiles, and select Create DNS Profile. Figure 3-52 shows that the DNS profile name, management EPG (in-band or out-of-band management connections of APICs), DNS domains, and DNS providers should be defined as part of the DNS profile creation process.

Figure 3-52 *Creating a DNS Profile*

Once a DNS profile has been created, the DNS label should then be associated with VRF instances within user tenants for ACI to be able to run queries against servers in the DNS profile. Figure 3-53 shows how to assign the DNS label Public to a VRF instance called DCACI within a tenant by navigating to the tenant and selecting Networking, opening VRF instances, selecting the desired VRF instance, clicking on the Policy menu, and entering the DNS profile name in the DNS Labels field.

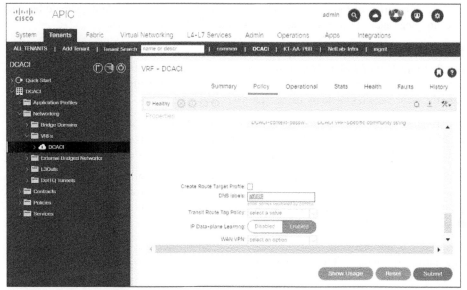

Figure 3-53   *Assigning a DNS Label Under a VRF Instance*

It is important to differentiate between manually selecting a DNS profile for a user tenant and associating a DNS profile that enables the APICs themselves to conduct global lookups. For the APICs to conduct lookups within the CLI and for use for critical functions, the DNS profile named default needs to be configured, and the label default needs to be associated with the in-band or out-of-band management VRF instances. Figure 3-54 shows the default label being associated with the VRF instance named oob. Association of any DNS label other than default with the inb and oob VRF instances triggers faults in ACI.

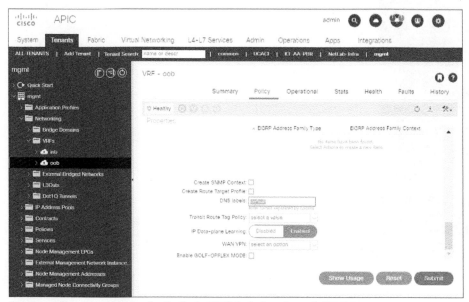

Figure 3-54   *Assigning the Default DNS Label to the oob VRF Instance*

Following association of the default label to the oob VRF instance, the APICs should be able to execute pings against servers using their fully qualified domain names.

Verifying COOP Group Configurations

Council of Oracle Protocol (COOP) is used to communicate endpoint mapping information (location and identity) to spine switches. A leaf switch forwards endpoint address information to the spine switch Oracle by using ZeroMQ.

COOP running on the spine nodes ensures that every spine switch maintains a consistent copy of endpoint address and location information and additionally maintains the distributed hash table (DHT) repository of endpoint identity-to-location mapping database.

COOP has been enhanced to support two modes: strict and compatible. In strict mode, COOP allows MD5 authenticated ZeroMQ connections only to protect against malicious traffic injection. In compatible mode, COOP accepts both MD5 authenticated and non-authenticated ZMQ connections for message transportation.

While COOP is automatically configured by ACI, it is helpful to be able to see the COOP configuration. To validate COOP settings, navigate to System, select System Settings, and click COOP Group.

Figure 3-55 shows COOP enabled on both spines with the authentication mode Compatible Type within a given fabric. When spines are selected to run COOP, ACI automatically populates the Address field with the loopback 0 address of the spines selected. If enforcement of COOP authentication is required within an environment, you need to update the authentication mode to strict type.

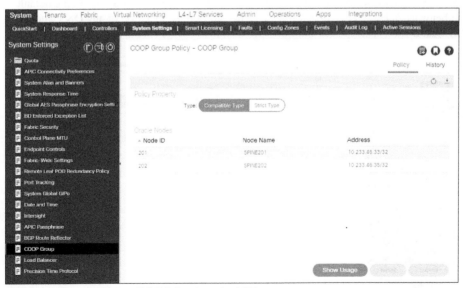

Figure 3-55 *Verifying COOP Settings in ACI*

Exam Preparation Tasks

As mentioned in the section "How to Use This Book" in the Introduction, you have a couple of choices for exam preparation: Chapter 17, "Final Preparation," and the exam simulation questions in the Pearson Test Prep Software Online.

Review All Key Topics

Review the most important topics in this chapter, noted with the Key Topic icon in the outer margin of the page. Table 3-7 lists these key topics and the page number on which each is found.

Table 3-7   Key Topics for Chapter 3

Key Topic Element	Description	Page Number
Paragraph	Describes APIC in-band ports and minimal versus recommended connectivity requirements	47
Paragraph	Describes APIC OOB ports and connectivity requirements	47
Paragraph	Contrasts APIC OOB ports with Cisco IMC ports	47
Table 3-3	Calls out basic configuration parameters that need to be planned for fabric initialization	48
List	Outlines the steps involved in ACI switch discovery	50
List	Describes fabric discovery stages	51
Table 3-4	Describes switch discovery states and what each one means	52
Paragraph	Describes the NIC mode and NIC redundancy settings required for proper fabric discovery	53
Paragraph	Describes the process of assigning OOB management addresses to ACI nodes	63
Paragraph	Explains why it is important to configure entries for APICs in the Static Node Management Addresses folder	64
Paragraph	Describes how to assign the default contract to the OOB management EPG	64
Paragraph	Outlines what external management network instance profiles are and how they can be used to define external subnets that should be allowed to communicate with ACI from a management perspective	64
List	Recaps the process of assigning an open contract to the out-of-band network	66
Paragraph	Describes how to upload firmware to APICs	67
Paragraph	Describes how to kick off APIC upgrades	67
Paragraph	Provides additional critical details on executing APIC upgrades	68
Paragraph	Explains how to configure an upgrade group	70
Paragraph	Provides additional critical details on configuring and triggering an upgrade group	70
Paragraph	Explains the use of schedulers in ACI	73

Key Topic Element	Description	Page Number
Paragraph	Describes the process of setting a default firmware version to enforce code upgrades for new switches that are introduced into the fabric	74
Table 3-5	Describes import types	75
Table 3-6	Describes import modes	76
Paragraph	Explains how all switches are by default placed into the default pod	83
Paragraph	Explains pod profiles, pod policy groups, and pod selectors	83

Complete Tables and Lists from Memory

Print a copy of Appendix C, "Memory Tables" (found on the companion website), or at least the section for this chapter, and complete the tables and lists from memory. Appendix D, "Memory Tables Answer Key" (also on the companion website), includes completed tables and lists you can use to check your work.

Define Key Terms

Define the following key terms from this chapter and check your answers in the glossary:

APIC in-band port, APIC OOB port, APIC Cisco IMC, TEP pool, infrastructure VLAN, intra-fabric messaging (IFM), physical tunnel endpoint (PTEP), fabric tunnel endpoint (FTEP), dynamic tunnel endpoint (DTEP), scheduler, pod profile, pod policy group, pod selector

## CHAPTER 4

Exploring ACI

This chapter covers the following topics:

> **ACI Access Methods:** This section reviews the methods available for managing and collecting data from ACI.

> **Understanding the ACI Object Model:** This section provides a high-level understanding of the policy hierarchy in ACI.

> **Integrated Health Monitoring and Enhanced Visibility:** This section explores mechanisms ACI uses to communicate problems and system health to users.

This chapter covers the following exam topics:

- 1.2 Describe ACI Object Model

- 1.3 Utilize faults, event record, and audit log

Before diving too deeply into configuration, it is important for an ACI administrator to understand some basics. For example, what are the methods with which one can interact with ACI?

Another important topic is the ACI object model. Everything in ACI is an object in a hierarchical policy model. Each object and its properties can be manipulated programmatically. Because of the importance of objects in ACI, this chapter touches on the ACI object hierarchy and how administrators can explore this hierarchy. It also provides a high-level understanding of why data pulled from the GUI may be organized slightly differently from the actual ACI object hierarchy.

Finally, this chapter covers how ACI provides feedback to administrators through faults, events, and audit logs.

"Do I Know This Already?" Quiz

The "Do I Know This Already?" quiz allows you to assess whether you should read this entire chapter thoroughly or jump to the "Exam Preparation Tasks" section. If you are in doubt about your answers to these questions or your own assessment of your knowledge of the topics, read the entire chapter. Table 4-1 lists the major headings in this chapter and their corresponding "Do I Know This Already?" quiz questions. You can find the answers in Appendix A, "Answers to the 'Do I Know This Already?' Questions."

Table 4-1 "Do I Know This Already?" Section-to-Question Mapping

Foundation Topics Section	Questions
ACI Access Methods	1–3
Understanding the ACI Object Model	4–6
Integrated Health Monitoring and Enhanced Visibility	7–10

CAUTION The goal of self-assessment is to gauge your mastery of the topics in this chapter. If you do not know the answer to a question or are only partially sure of the answer, you should mark that question as wrong for purposes of the self-assessment. Giving yourself credit for an answer you correctly guess skews your self-assessment results and might provide you with a false sense of security.

1. Which special login syntax should a user logging in to an ACI CLI use when trying to authenticate to the fabric by using a non-default login domain?
   a. No special syntax is needed.
   b. *username@apic-ip-address*
   c. apic#*domain\\username*
   d. apic#*username@apic-ip-address*

2. True or false: Using the ACI switch CLI is a suitable means for making configuration changes in an ACI fabric.
   a. True
   b. False

3. How can an administrator change the acceptable management access protocols and ports in an ACI fabric?
   a. Modify the active pod policy group.
   b. Modify the management access policy or policies associated with the active pod policy groups.
   c. Modify subobjects of the Policies folder under the tenant named mgmt.
   d. Modify subobjects of the Admin menu.

4. Which of the following changes can be made in the Access Policies view?
   a. Synchronizing switches to an NTP server
   b. Operationalizing a switch
   c. Configuring a port channel down to a server
   d. Integrating ACI into a hypervisor environment

5. Which of the following changes can be made in the Fabric Policies view?
   a. Configuration of interface-level policies
   b. AAA configurations
   c. Configuration of policies that impact large numbers of switches in the fabric
   d. Integration of L4–L7 services into a tenant

6. Which of the following tools can be used to query the ACI object hierarchy? (Choose all that apply.)

    a. MOQuery

    b. Find

    c. Grep

    d. Visore

7. Which fault state suggests that some type of user intervention will definitively be required for the underlying fault condition to be resolved?

    a. Soaking

    b. Raised

    c. Retaining

    d. Raised-Clearing

8. An administrator has resolved the underlying condition for a fault, but the fault has not been deleted from the Faults view. Which of the following steps need to take place for the fault to be deleted? (Choose all that apply.)

    a. The administrator acknowledges the fault.

    b. The fault is deleted after the clearing interval.

    c. Faults are immutable and never deleted from the system.

    d. The fault is deleted after the retention interval.

9. Which of the following classes governs fabricwide monitoring policies when no corresponding policy exists under the more specific infra or tenant scopes?

    a. monEPGPol

    b. monFabricPol

    c. monInfraPol

    d. monCommonPol

10. Which of the following objects can be used for periodic reporting of the operational status of a tenant, a pod, or an entire fabric to management teams?

    a. Faults

    b. Health scores

    c. Events

    d. Audit logs

Foundation Topics

ACI Access Methods

ACI provides three methods for managing an ACI fabric. For programmatic management and data collection, an administrator can use the ACI representational state transfer (REST) application programming interface (API). For more manual configuration, an administrator can use the built-in graphical user interface (GUI) or the command-line interface (CLI). These management access methods are shown in Figure 4-1.

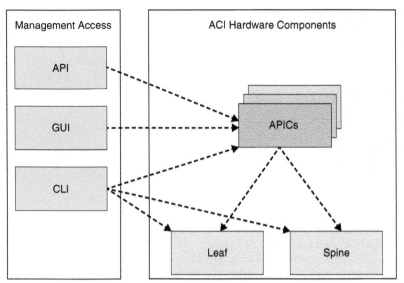

Figure 4-1   *Management Access to an ACI Fabric*

Administrators configure APICs through one of the three access methods, and all configuration changes are eventually resolved to the API. The GUI and the CLI are basically interfaces into the API.

The process of configuring a fabric involves administrators sending configuration changes to the APICs. The APICs, in turn, deploy necessary configuration changes to leaf and spine switches through an in-band management channel between the APICs and the switches.

GUI

The ACI GUI is an HTML5 application rich with wizards and configuration tools that also enables administrators to verify and monitor an ACI fabric. It is the primary starting point for most newcomers to ACI.

By default, the GUI can only be accessed via HTTPS, but HTTP can be enabled manually, if desired, in lab and low-security environments or in situations in which a backup communication channel to ACI is needed due to HTTPS port changes.

When logging in to the ACI GUI right after fabric initialization, you use the local admin user. However, if you are using a brownfield fabric to familiarize yourself with ACI, chances are that TACACS or some other method for authenticating to the fabric may have been implemented. In this case, the APIC GUI login screen reflects the existence of multiple login domains using a Domain drop-down box like the one shown in Figure 4-2. Sometimes AAA administrators change the default authentication method to reflect the most commonly used authentication domain. In such a case, selecting an explicit login domain from the list may not be necessary. In Figure 4-2, the user explicitly selects the authentication domain named tacacs_domain to authenticate to a domain other than the default authentication domain.

Chapter 15, "Implementing AAA and RBAC," provides a more thorough review of authentication methods and AAA implementation.

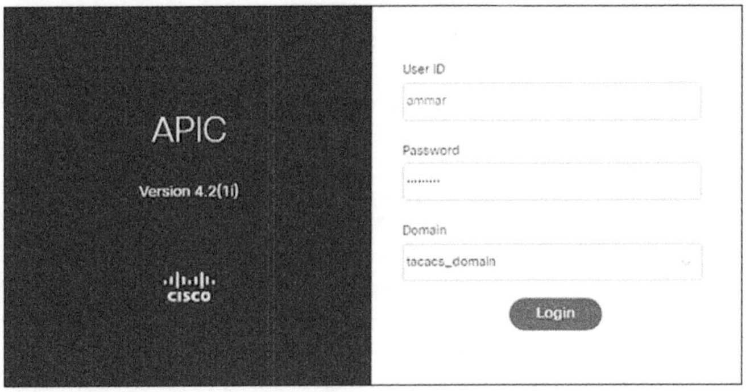

Figure 4-2   *Selecting the Right Login Domain in the GUI*

CLI

Both APICs and ACI switches offer feature-rich CLIs. The APIC CLI can be used to perform configuration changes in an ACI fabric, but ACI switches cannot be configured directly via the switch CLI. The primary function of the switch CLI is to confirm that intended configurations have been accurately deployed to switches in a fabric and to verify that necessary changes have been programmed into hardware. For these reasons, the switch CLI is an ideal tool for troubleshooting.

> **NOTE**   Some configuration changes can be made within an ACI switch CLI. For example, a switch configuration can be restored to its factory defaults by using the script **setup-clean-config.sh** and then reloaded via the **reload** command. Hence, the switch CLI should not be interpreted as a read-only access vector into ACI.

APIC CLI

Administrators can access the APIC CLI directly through the console or by using SSH, Telnet, or the Cisco Integrated Management Console (IMC) Keyboard Video Mouse (KVM) interface with administrative credentials. However, Telnet is disabled by default.

Just as when logging in to an ACI GUI, the local admin user can be used to log in to the APIC CLI after initializing a fabric or if local authentication remains the default authentication avenue configured. However, if AAA settings have been modified and you need to use a non-default domain for authentication, CLI access requires use of a special login format. Example 4-1 shows how the CLI-based username format **apic#***domain******username* can be used to explicitly authenticate by using the desired domain.

Example 4-1   *Specifying an Explicit Login Domain for APIC CLI Access*

```
login as: apic#tacacs_domain\\ammar
Pre-authentication banner message from server:
| Application Policy Infrastructure Controller
End of banner message from server
apic#tacacs-domain\\dcaci@10.100.5.21's password: <Enter Password >
apic1#
```

Like other Cisco operating systems, the APIC CLI has multiple configuration modes, as highlighted in Table 4-2.

Table 4-2   Configuration Modes for APIC CLI

Mode	How to Access	Prompt	Exit Method
Exec	Log in to APIC.	apic1#	exit closes session
Global configuration	From EXEC mode, enter **configure**.	apic1(config)#	exit moves back to EXEC mode
Configuration submode	From global configuration mode, enter an acceptable command (such as **dns**).	apic1(config-dns)#	exit moves to the parent end moves to EXEC mode

When logging in to the APIC CLI, the APIC drops administrators into EXEC mode. The command **configure** or **configure terminal** places administrators into global configuration mode. Execution of certain commands may move the user into a configuration submode.

Example 4-2 shows these concepts. The command **dns** places the user into the DNS configuration submode. The APIC CLI supports the use of question marks to find acceptable commands and arguments for a command. To see a list of commands that begin with a particular character sequence, use a question mark without spaces. Like the majority of other Cisco CLIs, both the APIC and switch CLIs support tab completion. To remove a line from the configuration, use the **no** form of the command in the APIC CLI. The command **end** drops a user into EXEC mode, and **exit** drops the user down one configuration mode or submode.

Example 4-2   *Basic Navigation in the APIC CLI*

```
apic1# configure
apic1(config)# dns
apic1(config-dns)# show ?
 aaa            Show AAA information
 access-list    Show Access-list Information
(...output truncated for brevity...)
apic1(config-dns)# e?
 end            Exit to the exec mode
 exit           Exit from current mode
 export-config  Export Configuration
apic1(config-dns)# show dns <TAB>
dns-address  dns-domain
apic1(config-dns)# show dns-address
 Address                      Preferred
 ----------------------------  ---------
 10.100.1.72                  no
 10.100.1.71                  yes
apic1(config-dns)# no address 10.100.1.72
apic1(config-dns)# end
apic1# configure t
apic1(config)# dns
apic1(config-dns)# exit
apic1(config)#
```

Just like NX-OS, the APIC CLI allows users to see a context-based view of the current configuration. Example 4-3 shows a user limiting running configuration output to commands pertinent to DNS.

Example 4-3 *Viewing a Specific Portion of the Running Configuration*

```
apic1# show running-config dns
# Command: show running-config dns
# Time: Mon Oct 28 14:36:08 2019
  dns
    address 10.100.1.71 preferred
    domain aci.networksreimagined.com
    use-vrf oob-default
    exit
```

NOTE Unlike with NX-OS, IOS, and IOS XE, configuration changes in ACI are automatically saved without user intervention.

Both the APIC and ACI operating systems are highly customized distributions of Linux and therefore support certain Linux functionalities and commands, such as **grep**. In addition, both have a Bash shell that can be used to script and automate tasks. Example 4-4 shows that the Bash shell can be accessed via the **bash** command. You can use the syntax **bash -c** *'command'* to execute a Bash-based command while outside the Bash shell.

Example 4-4 *Basic Interactions with the Bash Shell*

```
apic1# bash
admin@apic1:~>
Display all 1898 possibilities? (y or n)
:                                   mkmanifest
!                                   mknbi-dos
  (...output truncated for brevity...)
admin@apic1:~> exit
apic1# bash -c 'uname -ro'
4.14.119atom-3 GNU/Linux
```

Every so often, an ACI user may try to use SSH to access a switch CLI just to find that a management port cable has failed. In such instances, the APIC CLI is your friend. Log in to the APIC CLI and use the **ssh** command followed by the name of the switch in question to establish an SSH session with the switch. This works regardless of the status of the out-of-band management cables to the switches because these SSH sessions flow over the VICs between the APICs and the switches.

Switch CLI

Unlike the APIC CLI, ACI switches do not support the **show running-config** command. However, a wealth of **show** and **debug** commands is available in the ACI switch CLI.

Unlike the APIC CLI, the ACI switch CLI does not support use of question marks. Instead, you can press the keyboard Tab key twice to leverage tab completion.

> **NOTE**   ACI switches have several additional CLI shells, such as Bash, that are beyond the scope of the DCACI 300-620 exam. These shells are sometimes beneficial in troubleshooting ACI. They include the following:
>
> - **Virtual Shell (VSH):** The output provided in this CLI mode can sometimes be inaccurate, and this mode has been deprecated.
> - **vsh_lc:** This is a line card shell and can be used to check line card processes and hardware forwarding tables.
> - **Broadcom shell:** This shell is used to view information on a Broadcom ASIC.

API

Administrators can establish REST API connections with an APIC via HTTP or HTTPS to rapidly configure ACI fabrics via Extensible Markup Language (XML) and JavaScript Object Notation (JSON) documents. The API can also be used to pull data from an ACI system.

A Python software development kit (SDK) and Python adapter are available for those who want to configure ACI via Python. Ansible can also be used to establish REST API connections and configure ACI via playbooks.

Programmatic configuration and verification of ACI is beyond the scope of the DCACI 300-620 exam and is therefore not covered in this book.

Management Access Modifications

An administrator can enable or disable supported management protocols or change the ports associated with the enabled management access methods. To do so, the administrator needs to edit the active pod management access policy or policies.

To find out which management access policy is active, navigate to the Fabric menu, select Fabric Policies, double-click Pods, select Policy Groups, and then review the available pod policy groups. Figure 4-3 shows a screenshot from an ACI fabric in which only a single pod policy group has been configured. In this figure you can see that Resolved Management Access Policy is set to default. Therefore, to modify enabled management access methods for the pod, you can either navigate to the object or click on the blue link in front of the Management Access Policy pull-down to directly modify the management access methods.

If multiple pod policy groups have been configured and each one points to a different management access policy, you can click on the Show Usage button in each pod policy group to review the nodes grouped into that pod policy group. Figure 4-4 shows that nodes 301, 302, 401, and 402 have been associated with a pod policy group named Pod-PolGrp.

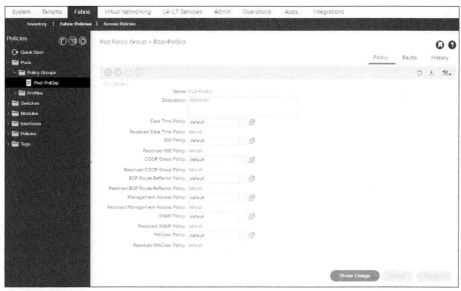

Figure 4-3 *Identifying an Active Management Access Policy from the Pod Policy Group Page*

Figure 4-4 *Auditing Associated Objects and Nodes via Show Usage*

To edit a management access policy, navigate to Fabric Policies under the Fabric menu, double-click on Policies, double-click on Pod, open Management Access, and select the desired policy. Figure 4-5 shows that a user has toggled the Telnet Admin State parameter to Enabled and is ready to click Submit.

Notice the SSH Access via WEB option in Figure 4-5. This feature allows you to use the GUI to establish SSH sessions into the APIC over port 4200. This might help in the rare case that port 22 access to APICs has been erroneously blocked by firewalls.

Figure 4-5 *Modifying Enabled Management Access Methods in ACI*

NOTE As discussed in Chapter 3, "Initializing an ACI Fabric," ACI allows a few default protocols, such as HTTPS and SSH, to access the OOB management interfaces in the fabric. Enabling Telnet as shown in Figure 4-5, however, necessitates that a contract allowing Telnet access as well as its association with an external management network instance profile and the out-of-band or in-band EPG also be defined.

In Chapter 8, "Implementing Tenant Policies," you will learn more about contract implementation and how to create custom contracts that lock down management access to specified management systems and subnets. For now, the procedure covered in Chapter 3 using the default contract in the common tenant and a 0.0.0.0/0 subnet will suffice in allowing any changes to management access protocols and ports through management access policies.

Understanding the ACI Object Model

An ACI fabric is built using both physical and logical components. These components can be represented in an object hierarchy that is managed by and stored on the APICs and is called the *Management Information Model (MIM)*. The MIM forms a hierarchical tree. The top portion of the tree that represents the bulk of user-configurable policies is called the *Policy Universe*, as shown in Figure 4-6.

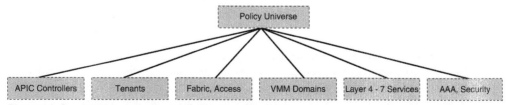

Figure 4-6 *ACI Management Information Model Overview*

Some of the most important branches in the hierarchical tree are the following items:

- **APIC controllers:** An APIC cluster is a clustered set of (usually three) controllers that attaches directly to a leaf switch and provides management, policy programming, application deployment, and health monitoring for an ACI fabric.

- **Tenants:** A tenant is a container for policies that enables an administrator to exercise access control and ensure a level of configuration fault isolation. ACI fabrics come with three predefined tenants. Administrators can create new tenants that are referred to as *user tenants*. Applications as well as Layer 2 and Layer 3 constructs are deployed inside tenants.

- **Fabric policies:** *Fabric policies* govern configurations that apply more holistically at the switch or pod level. Fabric policies also include the operation and configuration of switch fabric ports. Some of the parameters that are configured in the fabric policies branch of the MIM include switch Network Time Protocol (NTP) synchronization, Intermediate System-to-Intermediate System (IS-IS) protocol peering within the fabric, Border Gateway Protocol (BGP) route reflector functionality, and Domain Name System (DNS).

- **Access policies:** *Access policies* primarily govern the configuration and operation of non-fabric (access) ports. Configuration of parameters such as link speed, Cisco Discovery Protocol (CDP), Link Layer Discovery Protocol (LLDP), and Link Aggregation Control Protocol (LACP) for connectivity to downstream servers, appliances, or non-ACI switches, as well as routers all fall into the realm of access policies. Access policies also include mechanisms to allow or block the flow of tenant traffic on access ports.

- **Virtual networking:** ACI integrations with hypervisor environments referred to as VMM domains as well as integrations with container environments called container domains fall under the umbrella of virtual networking. These types of integrations enable deeper network visibility into virtual environments and policy automation.

- **Layer 4 to Layer 7 Services:** L4–L7 services such as firewalls and load balancers can be integrated to selectively steer traffic to L4–L7 appliances and to enable ACI to dynamically respond when a service comes online or goes offline. L4–L7 services integrations also enable ACI to automatically push configuration changes to devices such as firewalls if they are configured in managed mode.

- **Access, authentication, and accounting (AAA):** AAA policies govern user privileges, roles, and security domains in a Cisco ACI fabric. AAA is a key component of management plane multitenancy in ACI.

NOTE The Policy Universe is not the true root in the ACI hierarchy, but it is the portion of the ACI object hierarchy that you are most directly manipulating when you do everyday configuration changes within ACI. Examples of other branches under the real root (topRoot) that reside at the same level as the Policy Universe include topology and compUni.

Figure 4-7 shows several major branches of the ACI object hierarchy that reside directly under topRoot.

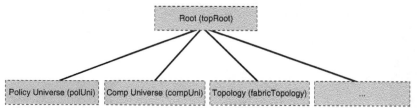

Figure 4-7   *Several Branches of the topRoot Object*

Learning ACI Through the Graphical User Interface

The menus in ACI have a level of correlation to the branches of the management information tree (MIT). This makes it possible to learn the high-level aspects of the ACI object hierarchy just by configuring ACI. Figure 4-8 shows the System submenus, which include the APIC Controllers view.

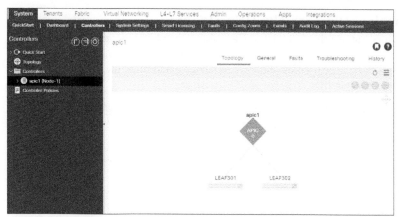

Figure 4-8   *APIC Controllers as a System Submenu*

The Fabric menu includes the ACI Inventory, Fabric Policies, and Access Policies submenus (see Figure 4-9).

Figure 4-9   *Fabric Submenus*

Figure 4-10 shows that AAA is a submenu of the Admin menu.

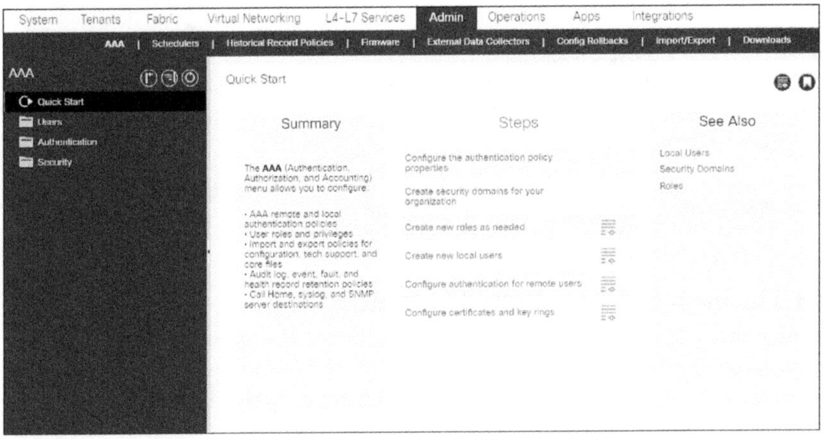

Figure 4-10   *Admin Submenus*

Exploring the Object Hierarchy by Using Visore

While administrators can use the ACI GUI to learn about the object hierarchy, the menus in the GUI do not translate literally to how objects are placed in the hierarchical tree. In reality, the ACI GUI strives to be user-friendly and easy to navigate and therefore cannot align with the actual object hierarchy.

A tool that can be used to gain a better understanding of the object hierarchy in ACI is *Visore*. Visore can be accessed by navigating to https://*apic-ip-address*/visore.html, as shown in Figure 4-11.

Figure 4-11   *Accessing Visore*

Once in Visore, you can enter the term **uni** and click the Run Query button to the right of the screen, as shown in Figure 4-12. The object titled polUni appears with the distinguished name uni.

Figure 4-12   *Navigating the Policy Universe in Visore*

A *distinguished name (DN)* is a unique name that describes an ACI managed object and locates its place in the ACI object hierarchy. Using a DN to search for a specific object is considered an object-level query. A DN query yields zero matches or one match.

To view objects that form direct branches of the policy universe, hover over the arrow pointing to the right and click to examine any direct child objects.

As indicated in Figure 4-12, besides DNs, parameters that can be used in Visore queries are object classes. A *class* refers to one or more objects in the MIM that are of a similar type. For example, the class *fabricNode* refers to all switches and APICs in a fabric. A query of this class, therefore, could help to quickly glean important information across multiple devices, such as serial numbers. Class-based queries are useful in searching for a specific type of information without knowing any or all of the details. A class-based query yields zero or many results.

An object or a group of objects within the hierarchical tree is called a *managed object (MO)*. MOs are abstractions of fabric resources. An MO can represent a physical object, such as a switch, an interface, or a logical object, such as an application profile, an endpoint group, or a fault.

By navigating the hierarchical tree, you may find that each individual tenant forms its own branch directly under the Policy Universe object. This may not be obvious to engineers who only use the GUI because the GUI places each tenant under a dedicated menu called Tenants.

You can also explore and query the ACI object hierarchy by using an APIC command-line tool called *MOQuery*. You can access help for this tool by using the **moquery -h** command. The -c option can be used with **moquery** to query the object model for all objects of a specific class. The **-d** option enables queries based on DN.

Why Understand Object Hierarchy Basics for DCACI?

The purpose of introducing you to the object hierarchy within ACI at this point in the book is more or less to convey how ACI uses a tree structure to enable programmability, to abstract configurations, and to reduce the impact of configuration mistakes.

> **NOTE**   The separation of tenant configurations from access policy configurations by placing them into separate branches within the hierarchical object tree lowers the scope of impact when making tenant-level configuration changes.

While gaining a detailed understanding of the ACI object hierarchy is important for troubleshooting and automating ACI, it is not necessarily essential for the DCACI 300-620 exam. A rudimentary understanding of the object hierarchy and configuration of ACI via the GUI and the APIC CLI should be sufficient for the DCACI 300-620 exam.

Policy in Context

The word *policy* is used very often in the context of ACI. The term can mean different things in different situations. Because ACI is a policy-driven system, *policy* can refer to almost anything in ACI. In this book, however, if the word *policy* is used independently of any other qualifying words and without further context, it should be interpreted to primarily refer to security policies, forwarding policies, QoS policies, and any other types of policies that specifically center around applications.

Integrated Health Monitoring and Enhanced Visibility

As discussed in Chapter 1, "The Big Picture: Why ACI?" one of the shortcomings of traditional networks is related to network management, including the difficulty of correlating information across multiple devices in data centers and identifying problems and associated root causes quickly and efficiently.

In traditional data centers, switches typically have no mechanisms for fault management. Ideally, traditional switches are configured to forward syslog messages to one or more syslog servers. Switches and other devices in the data center are then polled by monitoring servers via protocols like SNMP and ICMP. An ideal outcome for most companies is that one or more applications in the network are able to accurately aggregate and correlate available data from all managed endpoints, identify problems in the network, and open a ticket in an IT service management (ITSM) platform to enable troubleshooting. The best-case end result would be for automated mechanisms to resolve problems without human intervention.

The challenge with this approach is that current-day network management tools do not always provide the level of data needed to identify the root causes of issues, and they are also generally not designed with the deep solution-specific data needed to be used as effective proactive monitoring tools.

In addition to enabling standard monitoring capabilities such as syslog and SNMP, ACI introduces integrated health monitoring and enhanced visibility into the data center network, allowing network operators to identify problems faster when they occur and potentially become more proactive in their approach toward network management.

Some of the features in ACI that enable integrated health monitoring and enhanced visibility include health scores, faults, event logs, and audit logs. The inclusion of these concepts here in this chapter is intentional. Understanding some of the monitoring capabilities of ACI helps to better convey the flexibility of the ACI object model, the methods with which ACI provides feedback to users, and the ease of troubleshooting the system.

Understanding Faults

A *fault* indicates a potential problem in an ACI fabric or the lack of required connectivity outside the fabric. Each fault has a weight and a severity and is registered into the ACI object hierarchy as a child object to the MO primarily associated with the fault.

Faults in ACI can be created as a result of the following four triggers:

- The failure of a task or finite state machine (FSM) sequence

- Counters crossing defined thresholds, which may, for example, indicate packet loss in the fabric

- Fault rules

- Object resolution failures, which typically result from the deletion of objects referenced by other objects in the fabric

Figure 4-13 shows how active faults in a fabric can be viewed by navigating to **System > Faults**. The leftmost column indicates the faults in order of severity, with red indicating the severity level Critical and green indicating the severity level Warning.

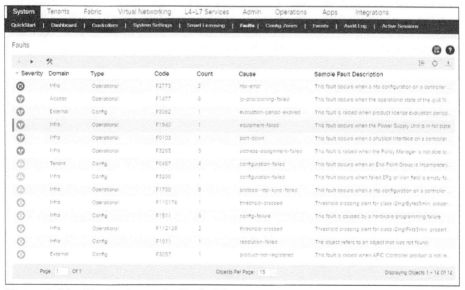

Figure 4-13 *Navigating to the Faults View*

Table 4-3 shows the available severity levels for faults.

Table 4-3   Fault Severity Levels Users May See in the Faults Page

Mode	Description
Critical	A service-affecting condition that requires immediate corrective action. For example, this severity could indicate that the managed object is out of service, and its capability must be restored.
Major	A service-affecting condition that requires urgent corrective action. For example, this severity could indicate a severe degradation in the capability of the managed object and that its full capability must be restored.
Minor	A non-service-affecting fault condition that requires corrective action to prevent a more serious fault from occurring. For example, this severity could indicate that the detected alarm condition is not currently degrading the capacity of the managed object.
Warning	A potential or impending service-affecting fault that currently has no significant effects in the system. An action should be taken to further diagnose, if necessary, and correct the problem to prevent it from becoming a more serious service-affecting fault.
Info	A basic notification or informational message that is possibly independently insignificant.
Cleared	A notification that the underlying condition for a fault has been removed from the system and that the fault will be deleted after a defined interval or after being acknowledged by an administrator.

When a fault is generated, it is assigned a fault code, which helps to categorize and identify different types of faults. Users can use fault codes to research the fault and possible resolutions for the fault. Codes for each fault are shown in the fourth column of Figure 4-13.

Double-clicking on an individual fault within the Faults view allows a user to drill down further into the details of each fault. Figure 4-14 shows the detailed Fault Properties view for the fault highlighted in Figure 4-13. In this case, the fault correctly reflects the fact that a power supply on an APIC has failed or has been removed.

Figure 4-14   *Fault Properties View in the GUI*

Notice that in addition to severities levels, the faults depicted in Figure 4-13 have been categorized into fault types and fault domains. Table 4-4 details the categories of faults that exist in ACI as of Release 4.2.

Table 4-4 Fault Types

Fault Type	Description
Configuration	The system is unable to configure a component as requested by a user.
Environmental	The system has detected a power issue, a thermal issue, a voltage issue, or a loss of CMOS settings.
Communication	The system has detected a serious management issue. For example, critical services cannot be started or components within a fabric might have incompatible firmware versions.
Operational	The system has detected an operational issue, such as a log capacity limit having been hit, a link failure, or a component discovery failure.

Domain, in the context of faults, refers to the aspect of the fabric that may be impacted by a fault. For instance, the domain named Security would categorize security-related issues such as lack of connectivity to configured TACACS servers. The domain named Tenant might include faults generated within a specific user tenant. Figure 4-15 shows a view of the GUI dashboard in which faults have been categorized by domain for quick administrator review.

Figure 4-15 *Fault Count by Domain*

Aside from the GUI, administrators are also able to query the APICs from the CLI or via the REST API and view all faults.

The Life of a Fault

Faults follow a lifecycle and transition between the phases shown in Figure 4-16.

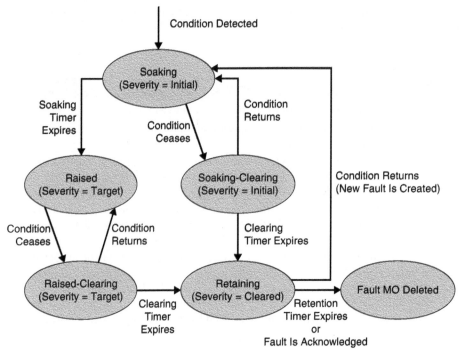

Figure 4-16 *Fault Lifecycle*

NOTE The severity levels initial and target are not included in Table 4-3 earlier in this chapter. The severity level target shown in Figure 4-16 should be understood more as a variable that refers to any severity between Critical and Info. The exact severity for a fault is determined by the default or custom monitoring policies applied to the object experiencing a fault condition.

Table 4-5 provides additional context for Figure 4-16 and details the transitions between fault phases.

Table 4-5 Fault Lifecycle Phases

State	Description
Soaking	The initial state of a fault, when a problematic condition is first detected. When a fault is created, the soaking interval begins.
Soaking-Clearing	If a fault condition in the Soaking state is resolved at the end of the soaking interval, the fault enters the Soaking-Clearing state. The fault then stays in this state for the clearing interval. During the clearing interval, if the condition reoccurs, the fault transitions back to Soaking. If not, the fault transitions to the Retaining state.
Raised	If a fault condition in the Soaking state is not resolved by the end of the soaking interval, it transitions to the Raised state and can have its severity raised. This state suggests the existence of an active problem in the network. Faults in the Raised state remain in this state until the condition is resolved.

State	Description
Raised-Clearing	When an administrator addresses a fault condition in the Raised state or when a condition is somehow removed from the system, the fault transitions to the Raised-Clearing state. The clearing interval then begins, and if the condition does not reoccur within this interval, the fault transitions to the Retaining state. If the condition does return within the clearing interval, the fault transitions back to the Raised state.
Retaining	A fault in the Raised-Clearing or Soaking-Clearing state pertaining to a condition that has been absent within the system for the duration of the clearing interval transitions to the Retaining state with the severity level cleared. The retention interval then begins, and the fault remains in the Retaining state for the length of the interval. The fault is deleted either if the condition does not reoccur in this interval or if an administrator acknowledges the fault. If the fault condition reoccurs during the retention interval, a new fault is generated and placed in the Soaking state. The retention interval is generally lengthy, and the goal of this timer is to ensure that administrators are aware of fault conditions that occur in ACI.

Three timers play key roles in the process of transitioning between fault states (see Table 4-6). These timers can be modified and are defined in fault lifecycle policies.

Table 4-6   Fault Lifecycle Timers

Timer	Description
Clearing Interval	This timer counts the period of time between the system detecting the resolution of a fault condition and the time when the fault severity is set to cleared. This interval refers to the time between the Soaking-Clearing and Retaining fault states. The range for this setting is 0 to 3600 seconds. The default is 120 seconds.
Retention Interval	This timer counts the period of time between the system setting the fault severity to cleared and the time when the fault object is deleted. This interval refers to the time between the Retaining fault state and when the fault is deleted. The range for this setting is 0 to 31536000 seconds. The default is 3600 seconds.
Soaking Interval	This timer counts the period of time between ACI creating a fault with the initial severity and the time when it sets the fault to the target severity. This interval refers to the time between the Soaking and Raised fault states. The range for this setting is 0 to 3600 seconds. The default is 120 seconds.

Acknowledging Faults

An administrator can acknowledge a fault when the intent is to delete a fault whose underlying condition has been addressed. To do so, an administrator right-clicks on a given fault and selects Acknowledge Fault, as shown in Figure 4-17.

Figure 4-17   *Acknowledging a Fault*

ACI then asks the user to confirm the acknowledgment, as shown in Figure 4-18.

Figure 4-18   *Confirming Fault Acknowledgment*

It is important to understand that the act of acknowledging a fault in ACI may sometimes lead to an instantaneous removal of a fault from the system. However, this is true only when the fault condition has also been removed from the system, and the fault has already transitioned to the Retaining state. In this sense, the acknowledgment is just meant to clear the fault without requiring the Retention Interval to transition to 0.

Acknowledging a fault when the underlying condition remains within the system does not prompt the deletion of the fault. In the case of the fault depicted in Figures 4-17 and 4-18, the underlying condition has not been removed from the system. This is proven by the fact that ACI sees this as an active condition in the Raised state. Although ACI allows the administrator to acknowledge this fault, it does not delete the fault MO until the underlying condition is removed.

Faults in the Object Model

A fault is included in the ACI object hierarchy as an MO of class faultInst or faultDelegate. Fault MOs are usually generated by parent objects. Not all objects can create faults. Objects that *can* generate faults have an attribute called ***monPolDn*** that points to a monitoring policy object. Figure 4-19 shows an administrator query via Visore of the affected power supply object depicted earlier in this chapter, in Figure 4-14. As shown in Figure 4-19, the monPolDn attribute for this object references the DN uni/fabric/monfab-default. This distinguished name refers to the monitoring policies governing all aspects of fault generation for this object.

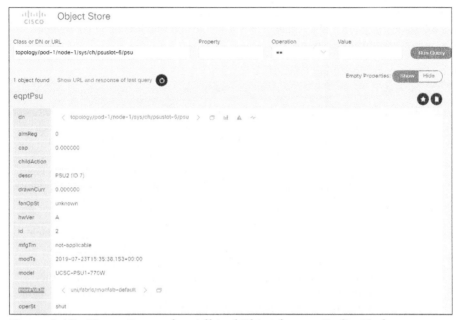

Figure 4-19   *Visore Query of an Affected Object from an Earlier Fault*

Using this type of exploration of the policy model, an administrator can begin to gain a deep understanding of how ACI works. Further exploration might lead the administrator to click the link referencing the object uni/fabric/monfab-default in Visore. As shown in Figure 4-20, this object is actually of a specific class called monFabricPol and has the name default.

Figure 4-20   *Fabric Monitoring Policy Object in Visore*

It turns out that there are four different classes of monitoring policies in ACI that govern aspects of fault and event generation within the fabric. The following section describes them.

Monitoring Policies in ACI

There are four classes of monitoring policies in ACI. You can use the classnames presented in Table 4-7 to query the ACI object hierarchy via Visore and find lists of all configured monitoring policies of the desired class.

Table 4-7   Classes of Monitoring Policies

Monitoring Policy Class Name	Description
monInfraPol	A class of policies that deals with monitoring of infra objects, which includes monitoring of VMM domains, access ports, and external fabric connectivity. Navigate to **Fabric > Access Policies > Policies > Monitoring** to configure monitoring policies of the monInfraPol class. By default, all infra objects point to the monInfraPol monitoring policy called default. The DN for this default infra monitoring object is uni/infra/moninfra-default.
monFabricPol	A class of policies that deals with monitoring of fabric objects, which includes monitoring of fabric uplinks. Navigate to **Fabric > Fabric Policies > Policies > Monitoring** to configure monitoring policies of the monFabricPol class. By default, all fabric objects point to the monFabricPol monitoring policy called default. The DN for this default fabric monitoring policy is uni/fabric/monfab-default.
monCommonPol	A policy class that has a global fabricwide scope and deals with monitoring of objects such as the APIC controllers and fabric nodes. The policies configured in this class are also used when there is no corresponding policy under the more specific infra or tenant scopes. Navigate to **Fabric > Fabric Policies > Policies > Monitoring > Common Policy** to modify the common monitoring policy. The DN for the common monitoring policy is uni/fabric/moncommon.
monEPGPol	A class of policies that deals with monitoring of tenant objects. Navigate to Tenants, select a tenant, and double-click Policies and then Monitoring to configure monitoring policies of the monEPGPol class. By default, all tenant objects point to the monEPGPol monitoring policy called default. The DN for this default tenant monitoring policy is uni/tn-common/monepg-default. This DN refers to a monitoring policy that resides in a tenant called common. Custom tenant-specific monitoring policies can be created and assigned to tenant objects, if desired.

Note that each of the four classes of monitoring policies outlined in Table 4-7 references a default policy that monitors pertinent objects out of the box. Default monitoring policies can be overridden by specific policies. For example, a user might create a specific monitoring policy within a tenant and associate this new custom policy at the tenant level to override the default policy for the tenant. Customizing the monitoring policy for a specific tenant does not delete the default policy that resides at uni/tn-common/monepg-default. Other tenants still reference this default monitoring policy.

One key reason monitoring policies have been introduced in this chapter is to complete the subject of the ACI object model and the use of Visore for developing a better understanding of how ACI works. Figure 4-21, for example, shows how you can right-click almost any object in the GUI and then select Open in Object Store Browser to determine the DN of the object and how other objects may be associated with the object in question. By digging into details like these, you can start to grasp the bigger picture of how policies link together. This figure shows the user trying to find the object representing a fabric port in Visore.

Figure 4-21   *Using the GUI to Find an Object in Visore*

Figure 4-22 shows that the fabric port in question has the monitoring policy uni/fabric/ monfab-default associated with it. This should reinforce the fact that the monitoring class monFabricPol is what determines the monitoring policy for fabric ports.

id	eth1/50
inhBw	unspecified
isReflectiveRelayCfgSupported	Supported
layer	Layer3
lcOwn	local
linkDebounce	100
linkLog	default
mdix	auto
medium	broadcast
modTs	2019-10-29T04:39:01.033+00:00
mode	trunk
monPolDn	< uni/fabric/monfab-default >
mtu	9366

Figure 4-22   *Finding the Monitoring Policy (monPolDn) Associated with a Port*

If the DN being displayed is not enough of a hint, you can navigate to the actual DN and determine the class of the specified DN and correlate that with the various monitoring policies in the fabric.

> **NOTE** Some of the concepts in this chapter may seem overwhelming. However, the goal is for you to be able to understand the more theoretical concepts of the object model. By the end of this chapter, you should also be able to identify the various types of monitoring policies and the high-level purposes of each. In addition, you should be able to edit the default monitoring policies and make minor changes. Another important skill you should have developed by the end of this chapter is to be able to use Visore to figure out which monitoring policy applies to any given object.

Customizing Fault Management Policies

A *fault lifecycle policy* specifies the timer intervals that govern fault transitions between states in the lifecycle. Fault lifecycle policies can be specified in the Common policy, within default policies, or in a custom monitoring policy.

To change the timer values configured in the fabricwide Common policy, navigate to Fabric, select Fabric Policies, open up the Policies folder, double-click Monitoring, double-click Common Policy, and select Fault Lifecycle Policy, as shown in Figure 4-23. Then select the new interval values and click Submit.

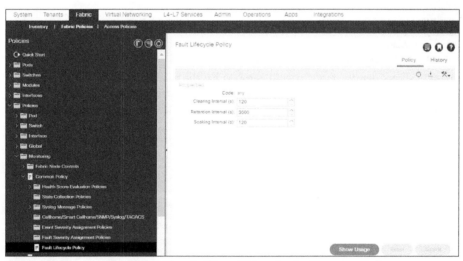

Figure 4-23 *Modify Fault Lifecycle Timer Values in the Common Policy*

To customize fault lifecycle timer values for default or custom monitoring policies, navigate to the intended monitoring policy, right-click it, and select Create Fault Lifecycle Policy, as shown in Figure 4-24.

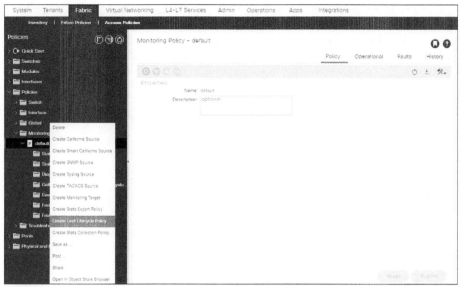

Figure 4-24 *Creating a Fault Lifecycle Policy for a Default or Custom Monitoring Policy*

Finally, select the desired timer values and click Submit, as shown in Figure 4-25.

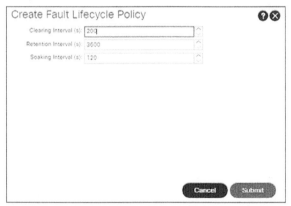

Figure 4-25 *Entering the Desired Timer Values*

NOTE When specifying timer intervals in a lifecycle policy, remember that each type of monitoring policy applies to a different set of objects within the object hierarchy.

Squelching Faults and Changing Fault Severity

There are times when a specific fault generated in an environment may be reported incorrectly. Sometimes false positives result from software defects; other times, there may be certain faults a company wants to ignore due to certain conditions within the network. The process of suppressing, or *squelching*, faults with a specific fault code helps reduce the noise from a monitoring perspective and allows a company to focus on the faults that really matter.

To squelch a fault, navigate to the Faults view, right-click the fault that should no longer be reported, and select Ignore Fault. Then, in the Ignore Fault window, confirm that the fault code shown should indeed be suppressed, as shown in Figure 4-26. Note that the confirmation window also shows the monitoring policy that will be modified to squelch the fault code.

Figure 4-26   *Squelching a Fault from the Faults View*

If you decide that the fault code should no longer be squelched, you can navigate to the affected monitoring policy and delete the fault code from the Fault Severity Assignment Policies folder, as shown in Figure 4-27.

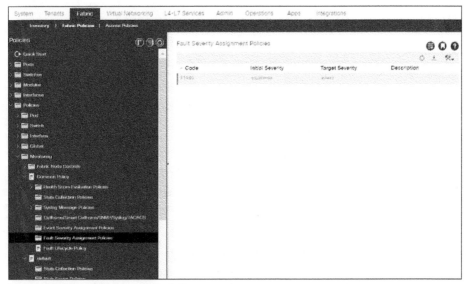

Figure 4-27   *Reversing a Fault Suppression*

To squelch a fault within the scope of a specific monitoring policy, you can navigate to the monitoring policy in question, open the Fault Severity Assignment Policies folder, open the pull-down menu on the right, and select Modify Fault Severity Assignment Policies, as shown in Figure 4-28.

Figure 4-28 *Squelching a Fault Code Under a Specific Monitoring Policy*

Figure 4-29 shows all faults with fault code F2409 pertinent to Bridge Domain objects being squelched. The monitoring policy under modification in this case is the default monitoring policy in the common tenant. Notice that for squelching to take place, the initial severity of the fault needs to be set to squelched, but the target severity does not need to be modified from inherit.

Remember that the default monitoring policy in the common tenant also serves as the default monitoring policy for all other tenants. Be aware of the scope of impact for any monitoring policy changes.

Figure 4-29 *Setting the Initial Severity of an Object to Squelched*

This last example involves fault suppression and also introduces fault severity modification. What else can fault severity modification be used for? Let's say that a fault of little significance shows up in an environment with a higher severity than what the monitoring team deems reasonable. In such a case, the target severity for the fault code can be lowered slightly to reflect the desired severity.

Understanding Health Scores

By using *health scores*, an organization can evaluate and report on the health and operation of managed objects, switches, tenants, pods, or the entire ACI fabric. By associating a weight with each fault, ACI provides a means for allocating health scores to objects. An object whose children and associated objects are not impacted by faults has a health score of 100. As faults occur, the health score of an object diminishes until it trends toward 0. With the resolution of all related faults, the health score returns to 100.

Figure 4-30 shows three health score panels in the System dashboard. The System Health panel presents the health score of the entire fabric over time. The Nodes panel provides a view of all switches in the fabric whose health scores are less than 100. The Tenants panel lists all tenants whose health scores are less than 100.

Figure 4-30   *View of Health Score Panels from the System Dashboard*

The highlighted leaf switch named LEAF301 in Figure 4-30 has a health score of 98. Double-clicking a node or tenant from the health panels opens the object in the GUI. By navigating to the Health tab of the object in question, as shown in Figure 4-31, you can drill down into the details of why the object has a degraded health score. In this case, it might make the most sense to begin the troubleshooting process by investigating the child objects that are impacted by faults and that have the most degraded health scores.

Figure 4-31 *The Health Tab for an Object*

> **NOTE** The companies with the best operations teams make a point of addressing faults and identifying the underlying causes of health score degradation in ACI fabrics as much as possible. Health score analysis can be used not only for reactive monitoring but as an ideal tool for proactive monitoring. If health degradation occurs frequently, for example, it may point to issues such as packet loss or oversubscription, knowledge of which can greatly assist in capacity planning and proactive mitigation of performance issues.

To modify the weights or percentage of health degradation associated with each fault of a given severity, navigate to the common monitoring policy, as shown in Figure 4-32, and edit the Health Score Evaluation policy. Figure 4-32 shows the default values associated with each fault severity in ACI Release 4.2. To remove acknowledged faults from the health score calculation, you can enable the Ignore Acknowledged Faults option.

Figure 4-32 *Modifying Health Score Calculation Weights for Each Fault Severity*

Understanding Events

Event records are objects that are created by a system to log the occurrence of a specific condition that might be of interest to ACI administrators. An event record contains the fully qualified domain name (FQDN) of the affected object, a timestamp, and a description of the condition. Examples of events logged by ACI include link-state transitions, starting and stopping of protocols, and detection of new hardware components. Event records are never modified after creation and are deleted only when their number exceeds the maximum value specified in the event retention policy.

To view a list of events in a system, navigate to System and click on Events, as shown in Figure 4-33.

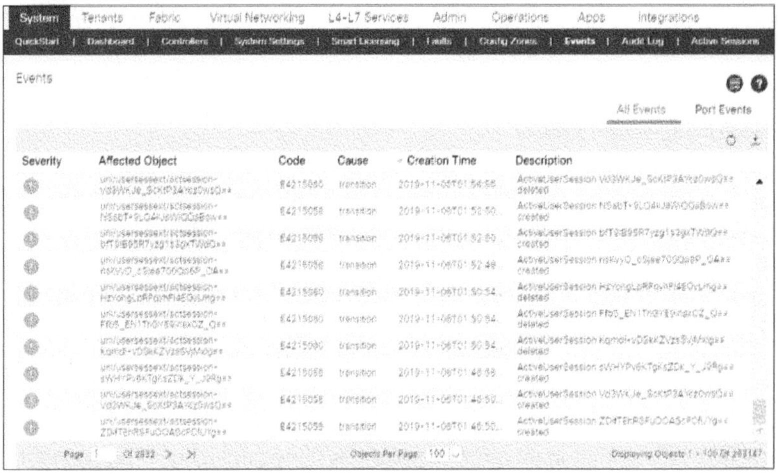

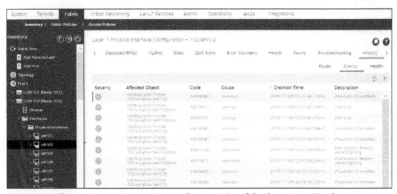

Figure 4-33   *Viewing Events Under the System Menu*

When using event records to troubleshoot specific issues, it is usually most beneficial to navigate to the object most relevant to the problem at hand. Say that an administrator has been asked to troubleshoot a server outage. She navigates to the event record view for the switch port that connects to the server and finds that the switch interface has transitioned out of the up state. Figure 4-34 shows the port Events view under the object History tab. Oftentimes, the Description column provides a hint about the cause of the event. In this case, the description "Physif eth 1/2 modified" suggests that a user may have disabled the interface intentionally, but the event record provides no indication which user disabled the port.

Figure 4-34   *Using Event Records as a Troubleshooting Tool*

Squelching Events

Events can be squelched in a similar way to faults. The easiest way to squelch events of a specific event code is to right-click an event of a specific type and select Ignore Event. This method of squelching events was introduced in ACI Release 4.2(1).

To manually squelch an event of a particular event code, navigate to the pertinent monitoring class object, click Event Severity Assignment Policies, select an object from the Monitoring Object pull-down, select the event code of interest, and set Severity to Squelched, as shown in Figure 4-35.

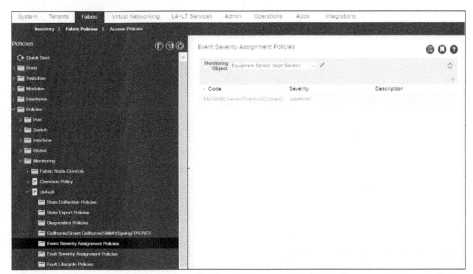

Figure 4-35 *Squelching Events of a Specific Event Code Under Monitoring Policies*

To un-squelch the event code, delete the squelch entry from the Event Severity Assignment policy.

Understanding Audit Logs

Audit logs are records of user actions in ACI, such as logins, logouts, object creations, object deletions, and any other configuration changes (object attribute changes).

Figure 4-34, earlier in this chapter, shows that port 1/2 on a leaf switch was likely shut down intentionally by another ACI user. You can use the audit log to try to find more data on this event. Figure 4-36 shows how you can navigate to **System > Audit Log**. After exploring the audit logs, you might find that the admin user initiated the configuration change that led to the port shutdown. After following up with the one user who has access to the admin user credentials, you might find that the admin user shut down the wrong port. You could then reenable the port to restore service.

There are a lot of objects in ACI that have a History menu, under which audit logs for the object can be accessed. When troubleshooting faults pertinent to a specific object, it is sometimes a good idea to see if any configuration changes were made to the object. The ability to quickly review audit logs helps troubleshoot issues faster.

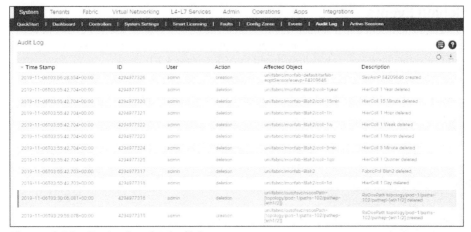

Figure 4-36 *Reviewing the Audit Logs*

NOTE   The class aaaSessionLR represents fabric logins and logouts. The class aaaModLR represents a configuration change within the fabric. Use the commands **moquery -c aaaSessionLR** and **moquery -c aaaModLR** to query the object model and understand user actions.

Exam Preparation Tasks

As mentioned in the section "How to Use This Book" in the Introduction, you have a couple of choices for exam preparation: Chapter 17, "Final Preparation," and the exam simulation questions on the companion website.

Review All Key Topics

Review the most important topics in this chapter, noted with the Key Topic icon in the outer margin of the page. Table 4-8 lists these key topics and the page number on which each is found.

Table 4-8   Key Topics for Chapter 4

Key Topic Element	Description	Page Number
Paragraph	Explains the MIM and Policy Universe	105
Paragraph	Defines Visore	108
Paragraph	Defines distinguished name	109
Paragraph	Defines class	109
Paragraph	Defines MO	109
Paragraph	Describes MOQuery and most rudimentary options	110

Key Topic Element	Description	Page Number
Paragraph	Describes faults	111
Table 4-3	Lists fault severity levels users may see in the Faults page	112
Table 4-4	Lists fault types	113
Table 4-5	Lists fault lifecycle phases	114
Table 4-6	Lists fault lifecycle intervals	115
Paragraph	Provides an example of an MO attribute and describes monPolDn	116
Table 4-7	Lists classes of monitoring policies	118
Paragraph	Explains the use case and definition of fault squelching	121
Paragraph	Describes health scores	124
Paragraph	Describes event records	126
Paragraph	Describes audit logs	127

Complete Tables and Lists from Memory

Print a copy of Appendix C, "Memory Tables" (found on the companion website), or at least the section for this chapter, and complete the tables and lists from memory. Appendix D, "Memory Tables Answer Key" (also on the companion website), includes completed tables and lists you can use to check your work.

Define Key Terms

Define the following key terms from this chapter and check your answers in the glossary:

Management Information Model (MIM), Policy Universe, user tenant, fabric policy, access policy, managed object (MO), Visore, MOQuery, distinguished name (DN), fault, monPolDn, fault lifecycle policy, squelching, health scores, event record, audit log

## CHAPTER 5

Tenant Building Blocks

This chapter covers the following topics:

Understanding the Basic Objects in Tenants: This section describes the key logical constructs in tenants, including bridge domains and EPGs.

Contract Security Enforcement Basics: This section details how ACI uses contracts, subjects, filters, and filter entries to enforce whitelisting.

Objects Enabling Connectivity Outside the Fabric: This section describes how L3Outs and external EPGs fit in the bigger picture of tenants.

Tenant Hierarchy Review: This section covers the relationships between tenant objects.

This chapter covers the following exam topics:

- 1.6 Implement ACI logical constructs

  - 1.6.a tenant

  - 1.6.b application profile

  - 1.6.c VRF

  - 1.6.d bridge domain (unicast routing, Layer 2 unknown hardware proxy, ARP flooding)

  - 1.6.e endpoint groups (EPG)

  - 1.6.f contracts (filter, provider, consumer, reverse port filter, VRF enforced)

Because ACI functions are based on objects, it is reasonable to expect that a book introducing ACI as a multitenant solution would include detailed coverage of the theory around objects that make up tenants. This chapter begins with an overview of key tenant constructs that all ACI engineers need to know. It provides a basic understanding of how contracts enforce security in ACI. Because ACI needs to also enable communication with the outside world, this chapter also discusses the role of tenant L3Outs and related objects.

"Do I Know This Already?" Quiz

The "Do I Know This Already?" quiz allows you to assess whether you should read this entire chapter thoroughly or jump to the "Exam Preparation Tasks" section. If you are in doubt about your answers to these questions or your own assessment of your knowledge of the topics, read the entire chapter. Table 5-1 lists the major headings in this chapter and their corresponding "Do I Know This Already?" quiz questions. You can find the answers in Appendix A, "Answers to the 'Do I Know This Already?' Questions."

Table 5-1 "Do I Know This Already?" Section-to-Question Mapping

Foundation Topics Section	Questions
Understanding the Basic Objects in Tenants	1–5
Contract Security Enforcement Basics	6–8
Objects Enabling Connectivity Outside the Fabric	9
Tenant Hierarchy Review	10

CAUTION The goal of self-assessment is to gauge your mastery of the topics in this chapter. If you do not know the answer to a question or are only partially sure of the answer, you should mark that question as wrong for purposes of the self-assessment. Giving yourself credit for an answer you correctly guess skews your self-assessment results and might provide you with a false sense of security.

1. Which tenant does ACI use to push configurations to switches in-band?

    a. Mgmt

    b. User

    c. Infra

    d. Common

2. Which tenant allows deployment of a shared L3Out?

    a. Mgmt

    b. User

    c. Infra

    d. Common

3. Which of the following most accurately describes an EPG?

    a. An EPG defines a broadcast domain in ACI.

    b. An EPG is a logical grouping of IP-based endpoints that reside inside an ACI fabric.

    c. An EPG is the equivalent of a VLAN in ACI.

    d. An EPG is a logical grouping of endpoints, IP-based or otherwise, that have similar policy-handling requirements and are bound to a single bridge domain.

4. Which of the following statements about application profiles is true?

    a. EPGs tied to different bridge domains cannot be grouped into a single application profile.

    b. An application profile is typically a grouping of EPGs that together form a multi-tiered application.

    c. An application profile is bound to a VRF instance.

    d. The function of application profiles is to differentiate between DMZ and inside zones of a firewall.

5. Which of the following commands displays all routes in a VRF instance called DCACI?

   a.   show ip route DCACI:CCNP

   b.   show route DCACI

   c.   show ip route

   d.   show ip route CCNP:DCACI

6. Which of the following defines the action that should be taken on interesting traffic?

   a.   Filter

   b.   Filter entry

   c.   Subject

   d.   Contract

7. True or false: There is no way to isolate traffic between endpoints that reside in the same EPG.

   a.   True

   b.   False

8. An administrator has defined constructs that match traffic based on destination ports 80 and 443, allowing such traffic along with return traffic through the ports. The contract is expected to be applied to communication between a client EPG and a web EPG. How should the contract be applied to the two EPGs to allow the clients to establish communication with the web EPG?

   a.   In the consumer direction on both EPGs

   b.   In the provider direction on both EPGs

   c.   In the provider direction on the client EPG and in the consumer direction on the web EPG

   d.   In the consumer direction on the client EPG and in the provider direction on the web EPG

9. True or false: An external EPG represents endpoints outside ACI and behind an L3Out.

   a.   True

   b.   False

10. True or false: Large numbers of filters can be created in any given tenant.

   a.   True

   b.   False

Foundation Topics

Understanding the Basic Objects in Tenants

ACI has multiple tenants enabled out of the box. There is little reason not to deploy multiple user tenants to achieve fault isolation and tighter administrative control. However, to fully leverage ACI multitenancy, you must first master the tenant hierarchy.

In true multitenancy environments where roles are heavily delineated, tenant policies are typically configured by a user who has been assigned either the tenant-admin role or a role with similar privileges. (For more on implementation of roles, see Chapter 15, "Implementing AAA and RBAC.")

Tenants

An ACI *tenant* is a secure and exclusive virtual computing environment that forms a unit of isolation from a policy perspective but does not represent a private network.

If you investigate further into use cases for tenants in the real world, you will find that tenants are often deployed in order to achieve these two technical controls:

- **Administrative separation:** When a business acquires other entities and needs to allow outside administrators access into its data centers, tenants are often used as a unit of administrative separation. This is accomplished through role-based access control (RBAC). Other instances where administrative separation may be important are when business units or application owners want to be involved in the process of defining network and security policies for applications. In this case, each relevant business unit can be provided its own tenants, or a tenant can be defined and dedicated to a specific application. Another instance in which administrative separation is vital is in service provider environments, where customers sometimes have access and visibility into the endpoints and systems they own.

- **Configuration fault isolation:** An application is a collection of tightly integrated endpoints that need to communicate with one another to achieve a particular business objective. Some applications have low business relevance and some have high business relevance. The networking, security, and QoS handling required for applications are defined in tenants. A hospital, for example, will likely consider its electronic medical record system to be business critical, with very well-defined dependencies, and may want any network or security policy changes around such an environment to be bound by change control. In such a case, it might make sense to place such an application and its dependencies in its own tenant. The same hospital may see a host of other applications as having very little business relevance and may therefore lump such applications into another tenant. The idea here is that configuration changes made in one tenant should have very limited or no impact on endpoints and applications in other tenants.

Figure 5-1 shows how you can navigate to the Tenants menu in the APIC GUI and execute the tenant creation wizard by clicking Add Tenant.

Figure 5-1 *Navigating to the Tenants Menu and Clicking Add Tenant*

In the Create Tenant wizard, you can enter the name of the desired tenant and click Submit to create the tenant, as shown in Figure 5-2. Note in this figure that one of the items you can create simultaneously while in the Create Tenant wizard is a VRF instance (VRFs are discussed later in this chapter.)

Figure 5-2   *Create Tenant Wizard*

NOTE   This chapter does not cover all configuration items depicted in the figures. Chapters 7, "Implementing Access Policies," through 15 address additional configurations and features that are within the scope of the Implementing Cisco Application Centric Infrastructure DCACI 300-620.

NOTE   Tenants cannot be nested within each other.

Predefined Tenants in ACI

ACI comes preconfigured with three tenants:

- **Infra:** The infra tenant is for internal communication between ACI switches and APICs in an ACI fabric. When APICs push policy to leaf switches, they are communicating into the infra tenant. Likewise, when leaf and spine switches communicate with one another, they do so in the infra tenant. The infra tenant is the underlay that connects ACI switches together and does not get exposed to the user space (user-created tenants). In essence, the infra tenant has its own private network space and bridge domains. Fabric discovery, image management, and DHCP for fabric functions are all handled within this tenant. Note also that an Application Virtual Switch (AVS) software switch can be considered an extension of an ACI fabric into virtualized infrastructure. When AVS is deployed, it also communicates with other ACI components in the infra tenant.

- **Mgmt:** APICs configure switches in a fabric via the infra tenant, but it is likely that administrators at some point will want APIC GUI access or CLI access to nodes within a fabric to validate that a policy has been pushed or to troubleshoot issues. Administrator SSH access to ACI switches and any contracts limiting communication with switch management IP addresses are configured in the mgmt tenant. Both out-of-band and in-band management options are configured in this tenant.

- **Common:** The common tenant is a special tenant for providing common services to other tenants in an ACI fabric. The common tenant is most beneficial for placement of services that are consumed by multiple tenants. Such services typically include DNS, DHCP, and Active Directory. The common tenant also allows the creation of shared Layer 3 connections outside the fabric, shared bridge domains, and shared VRF instances.

NOTE   This section refers to the infra tenant as the underlay in ACI. The term *underlay* can technically be used to refer not just to the tenant itself but also to the protocols that enable interswitch connectivity within the fabric. That said, user traffic typically resides in either user-created tenants or the common tenant. Therefore, user tenants and the common tenant can be considered the overlay in ACI.

VRF Instances

A *virtual routing and forwarding (VRF)* instance is a mechanism used to partition a routing table into multiple routing tables for the purpose of enabling Layer 3 segmentation over common hardware. In ACI, each tenant can contain multiple VRF instances.

IP addresses within a VRF need to be unique, or traffic can be black-holed. IP address overlap between different VRFs, on the other hand, is not an issue. Where subnet overlap does exist within ACI VRFs, the overlapping subnets *cannot* be leaked between the VRFs to allow communication.

VRF instances are sometimes also referred to as *private networks*, or *contexts*.

Figure 5-3 provides a view from within the newly created tenant DCACI. To create a VRF instance, navigate to the tenant in which you intend to create the VRF, open Networking, right-click on VRFs, and select Create VRF.

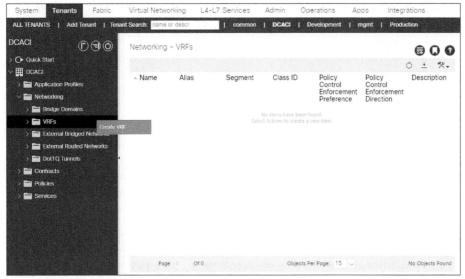

Figure 5-3 *Navigating to the Create VRF Wizard*

Figure 5-4 displays the Create VRF wizard, in which you enter the name of the desired VRF and click Finish to create the VRF. Note in this figure that you can create bridge domains simultaneously when creating a VRF. (Bridge domains are covered later in this chapter.)

Figure 5-4 *Create VRF Wizard*

Example 5-1 illustrates that routing tables in ACI find meaning only in the context of VRF instances. There is no concept of a default VRF in ACI. As you can see, the command **show ip route** is invalid in ACI. A reference to a tenant and VRF using the syntax **show ip route** vrf {*tenant-name:vrf-name*} is required when verifying the routing table of user-created VRFs within ACI. The list of VRFs that have been activated on a leaf and the references needed to pull further output can be identified using the **show vrf** command.

Example 5-1 *Routing Table Output in ACI*

```
DC1-LEAF101# show ip route
Incorrect command "show ip route"
DC1-LEAF101# show vrf
 VRF-Name         VRF-I State     Reason
 black-hole       3 Up            --
 DCACI:Chapter5   6 Up            --
 management       2 Up            --
 overlay-1        4 Up            --


DC1-LEAF101# show ip route vrf DCACI:Chapter5
IP Route Table for VRF "DCACI: Chapter5"
'*' denotes best ucast next-hop
'**' denotes best mcast next-hop
'[x/y]' denotes [preference/metric]
'%<string>' in via output denotes VRF <string>


10.233.52.0/24, ubest/mbest: 1/0, attached, direct, pervasive
 *via 10.233.47.66%overlay-1, [1/0], 09w05d, static
10.233.52.1/32, ubest/mbest: 1/0, attached, pervasive
 *via 10.233.52.1, vlan12, [0/0], 09w05d, local, local
```

Note that the subnet and IP addresses shown in Example 5-1 were not created as a result of the VRF instance creation process demonstrated in Figure 5-3 and Figure 5-4.

Bridge Domains (BDs)

Official ACI documentation describes a *bridge domain (BD)* as a Layer 2 forwarding construct that is somewhat analogous to a VLAN and has to be associated with a VRF instance.

The official definition, presumably, explains why the term *bridge* has been used in the name of this construct since a bridge domain is the true boundary of any server-flooded traffic.

Although this definition is technically accurate and must be understood for the purpose of the DCACI 300-620 exam, it is a great source of confusion for newcomers to ACI. So, let's first explore endpoint groups and application profiles and then revisit bridge domains to get a better understanding of the role these two constructs play in the greater picture of ACI.

Endpoint Groups (EPGs)

An *endpoint group (EPG)* is a grouping of physical or virtual network endpoints that reside within a single bridge domain and have similar policy requirements. Endpoints within an EPG may be directly or indirectly attached to ACI leaf switches but communicate in some fashion over an ACI fabric. ACI can classify both IP-based and non-IP-based endpoints into EPGs.

Some examples of endpoints that can be classified into EPGs include virtual machines, physical servers, appliance ports, Kubernetes namespaces, and users accessing ACI.

Application Profiles

An *application profile* is a container that allows EPGs to be grouped according to their relationship with one another to simplify configuration and auditing of relevant policies and to enable a level of policy reuse.

Many modern applications contain multiple components (tiers). For instance, an e-commerce application could require one or more web servers, backend database servers, storage, and access to outside resources that enable financial transactions. In ACI deployments, especially if whitelisting is desired, each one of these component types (for example, web servers) would be classified into a separate EPG. An important benefit of organizing interrelated component EPGs of a multitiered application into an application profile container is that the allowed communication between these application tiers can then be easily audited by exploring the resulting application profile topology. Figure 5-5 presents a sample application profile topology comprising a web tier and a database tier rendered by ACI.

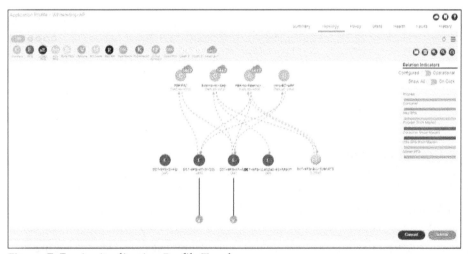

Figure 5-5   *An Application Profile Topology*

Another advantage of application profiles is that they allow application policy requirements to be modeled to accommodate policy standardization and future reuse. For example, let's say an IT department finds itself spinning up new instances of a very specific multitiered application very often. It understands the communication protocols that should be allowed between various tiers of these standardized deployments because it has already had to implement whitelisting policies for a previous multitiered instance of this same application. By limiting the scope of policies that have already been created to that of an application profile, the IT department can apply the same policies to new instances of this multitiered application without having the various instances of the application communicating with one another. This requires that the new instance of the application be placed in a new application profile. This type of policy reuse can cut down on the time needed to deploy applications and ensures that when policy changes are needed (for example, when a new port needs to be opened between application tiers), they can be applied to all instances at once.

> **NOTE**   Scope-limiting policies and creating new application profiles for each application instance is not the only way to take advantage of policy reuse for standardized applications in ACI. In many cases with ACI, you can achieve desired business or technical objectives in multiple ways.

EPGs can be organized into application profiles according to one of the following:

- The application they provide, such as a DNS server, a LAMP stack, or SAP

- The function they provide (such as infrastructure)

- Where they are in the structure of the data center (such as the DMZ)

- Any organizing principle that a tenant administrator chooses to use

EPGs that are placed in an application profile do not need to be bound to the same bridge domain. In addition, application profiles are not tied to VRF instances.

The Pain of Designing Around Subnet Boundaries

In traditional data centers, security policy in particular is usually applied at subnet boundaries. Access lists are rarely used to drop traffic flows within traditional data centers, but when they are, they are almost always used for isolated use cases that do not involve very granular control at the individual IP address level.

For example, technical controls such as access lists and route maps may be used in traditional data centers to prevent non-production server traffic from reaching a production server block *if* production and non-production server blocks have very well-defined subnets and no interdependencies. However, it is very unlikely that an organization that uses traditional networking capabilities would leverage its data center network to set up controls and define policy for limiting communications to and from every single server.

Where application-level firewalling is needed for an endpoint or set of endpoints within a traditionally built data center, careful engineering is applied to ensure that traffic is pushed through a firewall. The common traditional solution to a requirement like this may be to build out a new security zone on a firewall and move the default gateway for the subnet in question onto the firewall to guarantee that the firewall has control over traffic flowing into and out of the subnet. This type of solution, shown in Figure 5-6, forces engineers to think a lot about subnet boundaries when designing networks.

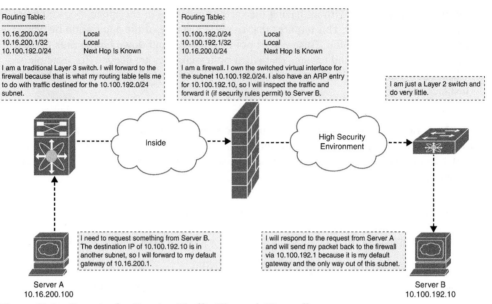

Figure 5-6　*Security by Routing Traffic Through Firewalls*

Sometimes engineers may decide to enforce security by leveraging a firewall in transparent mode in conjunction with an isolation VLAN. This solution ensures that certain critical endpoints are firewalled off from other endpoints within a subnet and allows for limited policy control within a subnet boundary. Figure 5-7 demonstrates how a transparent firewall attached to a traditional network can be placed between endpoints within a subnet to segment the subnet into two VLANs (VLAN 100 and 200 in this case) to enforce security policies between the VLANs.

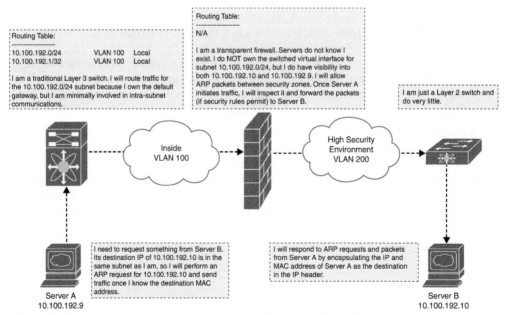

Figure 5-7　*Security Through Transparent Bridging via Firewalls*

There are several challenges associated with both of these security solutions when implemented using traditional networking capabilities. First, if the servers are already in production, dropping a firewall into the traffic path after the fact almost always necessitates an outage of the servers that are firewalled off. This is particularly true when segmenting the subnet in which the server resides. Second, granular east–west traffic filtering using these methods is nearly impossible. (For instance, what happens if a subnet needs to be subdivided into 10 sets of servers and security zones?) Finally, even with these methods, there is very little that can be done to specifically direct only the desired traffic through security devices. In other words, engineers may find that it requires a lot more planning to design a solution that sends all traffic from certain servers to firewalls if a required secondary objective were for traffic from these servers to completely bypass said firewalls when the traffic is found to be destined toward backup appliances.

The complexity of enforcing solutions to security challenges using traditional data center networks underscores the basic point that subnet boundaries play an important role in the average data center. Even though security policy has been the main focus in this discussion, the reality is that the challenge and rigidity involved in designing networks with subnet boundaries in mind also extend to other aspects of policy enforcement.

BDs and EPGs in Practice

Unlike traditional networks, ACI breaks the shackles and endless limitations imposed by subnet boundaries to eliminate the need for overengineered designs. It does so by decoupling Layer 3 boundaries from security and forwarding policies.

For the purpose of gaining a fuller picture, let's redefine bridge domains and EPGs based on their practical application.

As a construct that is directly associated with a VRF instance, a bridge domain serves as the subnet boundary for any number of associated EPGs. One or more subnets can be assigned to a bridge domain. General forwarding aspects of the associated subnets—such as whether flooding and multicast are enabled or whether the subnets should be advertised out of an ACI fabric or not—are governed by the bridge domain.

Endpoints that live within a bridge domain subnet need to be associated with an EPG to be able to forward traffic within ACI. An EPG serves as an endpoint identity from a policy perspective. EPGs are the point of security policy enforcement within ACI. Traffic flowing between EPGs can be selectively filtered through the use of contracts. Policies not necessarily related to security, such as QoS, can also be applied at the EPG level. If traffic from a set of endpoints may need to be selectively punted to a firewall or any other stateful services device, a policy-based redirect (PBR) operation can be applied to the EPG to bypass the default forwarding rules. In a sense, therefore, EPG boundaries also have a hand in the application of forwarding policies.

Figure 5-8 demonstrates how ACI decouples policy from forwarding by using bridge domains as the subnet definition point and EPGs as the policy application point.

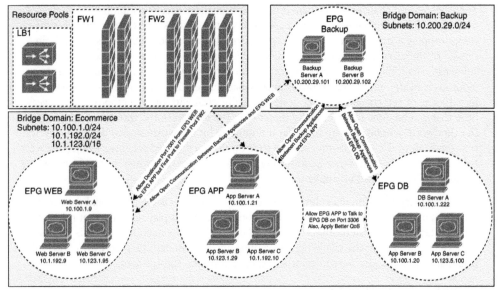

Figure 5-8 *Selective Policy Application at the EPG Boundary*

NOTE Endpoints within an EPG can reside in different subnets as long as all the subnets are associated with the same bridge domain to which the EPG is associated.

Configuring Bridge Domains, Application Profiles, and EPGs

Because EPGs need to be associated with bridge domains and application profiles need to be created before EPGs, the ideal order of operation is to first create bridge domains, then application profiles, and finally EPGs.

Figure 5-9 shows how to navigate to the Create Bridge Domain wizard. Within the Tenants view, open Networking, right-click Bridge Domains, and select Create Bridge Domain.

Figure 5-9 *Navigating to the Create Bridge Domain Wizard*

In the first page of the Create Bridge Domain wizard, which relates to general aspects of the bridge domain, enter a name for the bridge domain and associate the bridge domain to a VRF instance, as shown in Figure 5-10. Then click Next.

Figure 5-10   *Create Bridge Domain Wizard, Page 1*

Figure 5-11 shows the second page of the Create Bridge Domain wizard, where you enter Layer 3 configurations for the bridge domain. Click the + sign in the Subnets section to open the Create Subnet page.

Figure 5-11   *Create Bridge Domain Wizard, Page 2*

In the Create Subnet page, enter the default gateway IP address of the desired subnet, using CIDR notion (see Figure 5-12). This gateway IP address will be created in ACI when certain conditions are met. Click OK to return to page 2 of the Create Bridge Domain wizard. Then click Next to move to the last page of the Create Bridge Domain wizard. Note that you can assign multiple subnet IP addresses to each bridge domain.

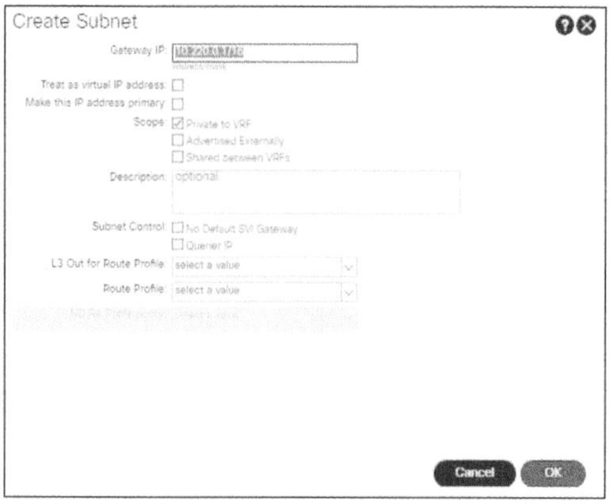

Figure 5-12 *Creating a Subnet for the Bridge Domain*

Figure 5-13 shows the final page of the Create Bridge Domain wizard, which provides advanced bridge domain settings. Click Finish.

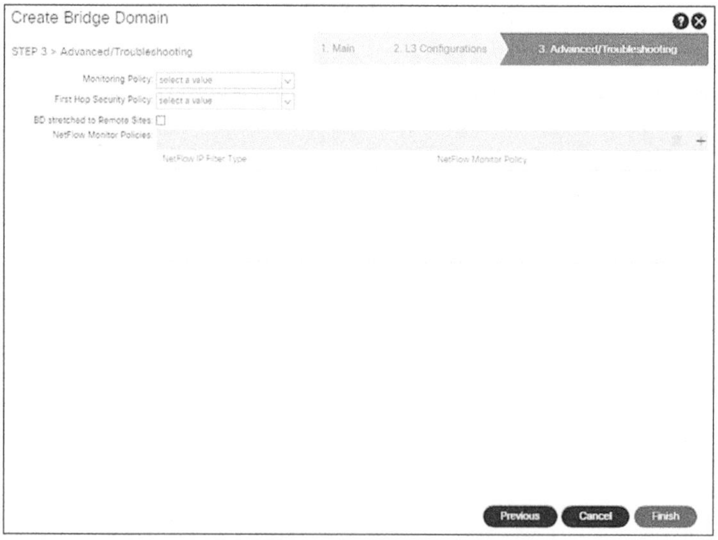

Figure 5-13 *Create Bridge Domain Wizard, Page 3*

After you create bridge domains, you can create application profiles. Figure 5-14 shows how to navigate to a tenant, right-click Application Profile, and select Create Application Profile.

Figure 5-14 *Navigating to the Create Application Profile Wizard*

In the Create Application Profile wizard, enter a name for the application profile and click Submit, as shown in Figure 5-15.

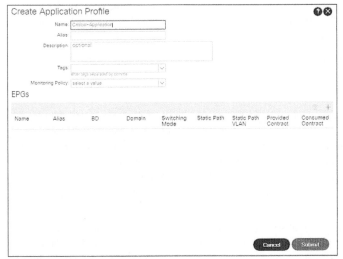

Figure 5-15 *Creating an Application Profile*

Once an application profile has been created, you can create EPGs within the application profile. Navigate to the Tenants view, right-click the desired application profile under which EPGs should be created, and select Create Application EPG to access the Create Application EPG wizard. As shown in Figure 5-16, you enter a name for an EPG and click Finish.

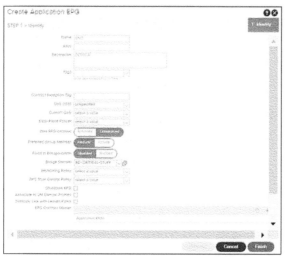

Figure 5-16 *Create Application EPG Wizard*

Classifying Endpoints into EPGs

In the backend, EPGs and bridge domains each correlate to VXLAN IDs, which are not supported on most server operating systems. ACI needs a mechanism to classify or place endpoint traffic it receives on switch ports into the proper EPGs. ACI most often classifies endpoints and associated traffic into EPGs through the encapsulations that have been mapped to the leaf interfaces on which traffic arrives.

VLAN IDs and VXLAN IDs are forms of encapsulation that ACI uses to classify Ethernet traffic into EPGs.

> **NOTE** A uSeg EPG is a specific type of endpoint group that uses endpoint attributes as opposed to encapsulations to classify endpoints. For instance, if you wanted to dynamically classify all virtual machines that run a specific operating system (OS) into an EPG, you could use uEPGs. Classifying endpoints into uSeg EPGs is particularly useful when there is a need to leverage endpoint attributes defined outside ACI (for example, VMware vCenter) to whitelist communication. Use of uSeg EPGs for whitelisting is called *microsegmentation.*

Figure 5-17 provides a simple but realistic depiction of a tenant, a VRF instance, bridge domains, EPGs, and subnets, and it shows how VLAN encapsulations are used to classify endpoints into a given EPG. The encapsulation configurations shown are commonly configured within tenants and at the EPG level. In this case, the tenant administrator has decided to map the EPG named DNS to port channel 1 on Leaf 101 using the VLAN 101 encapsulation. Likewise, the same encapsulation has been mapped to port 1 (Eth1/1) on Leaf 102 to classify server traffic in VLAN 101 into the DNS EPG. Encapsulations can also be mapped to virtual port channels.

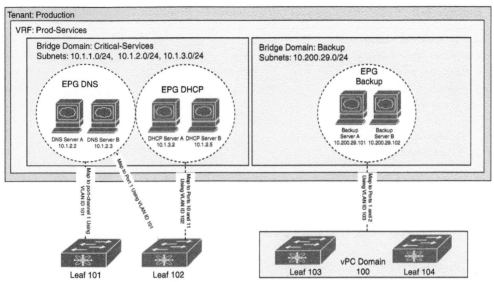

Figure 5-17 *Mapping EPGs to Encapsulations*

There is no hard requirement for an EPG to be mapped to a single encapsulation across all leaf switches within an ACI fabric. However, it is common practice, and most companies do it to promote standardization.

> **NOTE** If you do a cursory review of the ACI GUI, you might wonder why there is a subnet definition section under the EPG view if bridge domains are the construct that defines subnets. Although you can define a subnet under an EPG (and definition of subnets under EPGs is required in some cases), it is still the switch virtual interface (SVI) associated with the bridge domain and not the EPG that handles routing. Later chapters expand on this simplistic explanation.

APIC CLI Configuration of Tenant Objects

The GUI-based configurations performed in this section can be completed using the CLI commands depicted in Example 5-2.

As a review, the command **tenant DCACI** in Example 5-2 creates a tenant named DCACI. Under the tenant, the ACI engineer creates a VRF instance called Chapter5 by using the **vrf context Chapter5** command. The **exit** command that follows is required because a bridge domain is not a VRF subtree but a tenant child object. The command **bridge-domain BD-CRTICAL-STUFF** creates a bridge domain named BD-CRITICAL-STUFF under the tenant, and **vrf member Chapter5** associates the bridge domain with the Chapter5 VRF. The command **interface bridge-domain BD-CRITICAL-STUFF** is used to signal the intent to create one or more SVIs under the bridge domain BD-CRITICAL-STUFF. The **ip address** subcommand creates an SVI with the address 10.220.0.1/16 as the default gateway. Although the subnet has been created as a secondary subnet, it could as well have been defined as the primary IP address with the **secondary** keyword omitted from the command.

Example 5-2   *CLI Equivalents for Configurations Performed in This Section*

```
apic1# show run tenant DCACI
# Command: show running-config tenant DCACI
# Time: Sat Sep 21 21:12:14 2019
    tenant DCACI
    vrf context Chapter5
      exit
    bridge-domain BD-CRITICAL-STUFF
      vrf member Chapter5
      exit
    application Critical-Application
      exit
    interface bridge-domain BD-CRITICAL-STUFF
      ip address 10.220.0.1/16 secondary
      exit
    exit
```

Contract Security Enforcement Basics

ACI performs whitelisting out of the box. This means that, by default, ACI acts as a firewall and drops all communication between EPGs unless security rules (most commonly contracts) are put in place to allow communication.

ACI security policy enforcement generally involves the implementation of contracts, subjects, and filters.

Contracts, Subjects, and Filters

In the ACI whitelisting model, all inter-EPG communication is blocked by default unless explicitly permitted. Contracts, subjects, and filters complement each other to specify the level of communication allowed to take place between EPGs. These constructs can be described as follows:

- **Filter:** The job of a *filter* is to match interesting traffic flows. The EtherType, the Layer 3 protocol type, and Layer 4 ports involved in communication flows can all be used to match interesting traffic using *filter entries*. Filters can be defined to be relatively generic to enable extensive reuse.

- **Subject:** Once filters are defined, they are linked to one or more *subjects*. A subject determines the actions that are taken on the interesting traffic. Should matching traffic be forwarded, dropped, or punted to a firewall or load balancer? Should the traffic that has been matched by filters be reclassified into a different QoS bucket? These can all be defined by subjects. A subject can also define whether corresponding ports for return traffic should be opened up.

- **Contract:** A *contract* references one or more subjects and is associated directionally to EPGs to determine which traffic flows are bound by the contract. Contracts are scope limited and can also be configured to modify traffic QoS markings.

Because the concept of ACI contracts can be difficult to grasp, some examples are in order. Figure 5-18 shows an example of how you might set up filters, subjects, and contracts to lock down a basic multitier application. Applications also require connectivity to critical services such as DNS and some method to enable connectivity for outside users. This figure does not show contracts beyond those needed for the various tiers of the application to communicate.

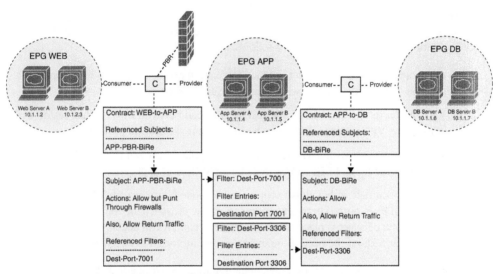

Figure 5-18 *Filters, Subjects, and Contracts*

For now, do not worry about implementation procedures for contracts, subjects, and filters. Implementation of these objects is covered in Chapter 8, "Implementing Tenant Policies."

ACI allows open communication between endpoints residing in a single EPG (intra-EPG) by default without the need for contracts, but intra-EPG communication can also be locked down. Figure 5-16, presented earlier in this chapter, shows the Intra EPG Isolation configuration option, which is set to Unenforced by default. There are very compelling use cases for setting Intra EPG Isolation to Enforced. For example, management stations that would reside either outside an ACI fabric or in a separate EPG may need to communicate with server CIMC out-of-band connections, but CIMC ports across multiple servers have no need to cross-communicate. Where there is no need for endpoints within an EPG to communicate with one another, intra-EPG isolation can be implemented on the given EPG. This feature uses private VLAN functionality without the headache of administrators having to define primary and secondary VLANs for bare-metal connections.

Contract Direction

ACI contracts are directional because TCP/IP communication is inherently directional. A client service initiates communication with a server. The server is a *provider* of a service to the client machine, and the client is a *consumer* of a service. (A sample directional application of contracts is presented in Figure 5-18.)

All communication within data centers conforms to this provider/consumer model. Although a web server provides services to users, it is also consuming services itself. For example, it may attempt to initiate communication with a backend database server, NTP servers, and

DNS servers. In these cases, the web server acts as a client machine. Any contracts that allow outside users to access web services on the web server should be applied to the web server EPG in the provider direction. However, any contracts that allow the web server to communicate with other servers for NTP, DNS, and backend database access need to be applied to the web EPG in the consumer direction and to the database server, NTP servers, and DNS servers in the provider direction.

Contract Scope

A *contract scope* is a condition that determines whether a contract can be enforced between EPGs. Options for contract scope are as follows:

- **Application profile:** A contract with an application profile scope can be enforced between EPGs if they reside within the same application profile.

- **VRF:** A contract with a VRF scope can be enforced between EPGs if they reside within the same VRF instance. EPGs can be in different application profiles.

- **Tenant:** A contract with a tenant scope can be applied between EPGs if they are all in the same tenant. The EPGs can be in different VRFs and application profiles.

- **Global:** A contract with a global scope can be applied between any EPGs within a fabric and can be exported between tenants to enable cross-tenant communication. If a global scope contract is placed in the common tenant, it can enable cross-tenant communication without the need to be exported and imported between tenants.

To better understand contract scopes, reexamine Figure 5-18. Notice that Web Server A and Web Server B can communicate with one another without contracts because they are in the same EPG. An administrator who wanted to prevent all communication between endpoints within an EPG could block all intra-EPG traffic at the EPG level. However, this is not always desirable. Sometimes, a subset of endpoints within an EPG might be in a clustered setup and need to communicate, while others should not be allowed to communicate. Moreover, the contracts shown in Figure 5-18 enable open communication between Web Server A and App Server B, with the hope that the firewall blocks such communication if it is not desired. If the suffixes A and B denote different applications, the contracts depicted would be considered suboptimal because ACI would allow communication across different applications.

As an alternative, consider Figure 5-19. All endpoints suffixed with the letter A form a LAMP stack and have been placed into an application profile called LAMP1. Similarly, endpoints suffixed with the letter B form a separate three-tier application and have been placed into LAMP2. Moreover, the scope of the contracts, which was unclear from the previous example, has been clarified to be Application Profile. With this modification, even if a slight configuration mistake were to occur in contract configuration and its application to the EPGs (for example, if all ports were erroneously opened), the mistake would be scope limited to each application profile. In other words, various tiers of different application profiles would still be unable to communicate. Therefore, you can translate the logic applied by the contract scope to mean "apply this contract between EPGs only if they are all in the same application profile."

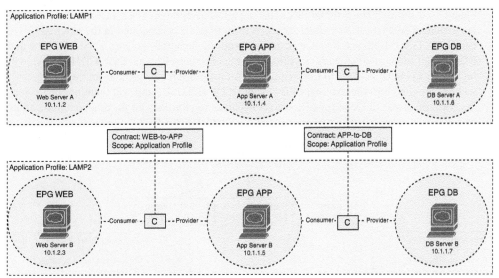

Figure 5-19 *Contract Scope Example*

As an extension of this example, what scope would you need to use in a new contract applied to all of the depicted EPGs, assuming that the contract seeks to allow them to communicate with an NTP server that is in a separate VRF instance within the same tenant? If you answered that the scope needs to be Tenant, you would be right. What scope would have to be defined if the NTP server were in a different tenant? The answer in that case would be Global.

Zero-Trust Using EPGs and Contracts

A zero-trust network architecture is an information security framework originally proposed by research and advisory firm Forrester that addresses the inherent weakness of a perimeter-focused approach to security by assuming no default trust between entities.

Attainment of a zero-trust data center is the primary security objective of EPGs and contracts. As noted earlier, ACI assumes no trust by default between EPGs unless the desired communication has been whitelisted.

Objects Enabling Connectivity Outside the Fabric

Whereas bridge domains, EPGs, and other constructs introduced in this chapter enable the deployment of applications and communication of application tiers, at some point, tenant endpoints need to communicate with the outside world. External EPGs and L3Out objects play a key role in enabling such communication.

External EPGs

An *external EPG* is a special type of EPG that represents endpoints outside an ACI fabric, such as user laptops, campus IoT devices, or Internet users. There are many reasons you might want to classify traffic outside ACI. One reason to do so is to be able to apply different security policies to different sets of users. External EPGs classify outside traffic using subnets, but the subnets can be as granular and numerous as needed.

Figure 5-20 shows three external EPGs that are allowed different levels of access to servers within an ACI fabric. Any traffic sourced from IP addresses defined in the external EPG named EXT-ADMINS will be allowed access to all the depicted servers via SSH, HTTPS, and RDP, but all other internal users classified into the external EPG called EXT-INTERNAL will be limited to HTTPS access to the web server. All users sourcing traffic from the Internet will be classified into the external EPG called EXT-INTERNET and will therefore be denied any form of access to these specific servers because no contracts permitting communication have been associated between the servers and EXT-INTERNET.

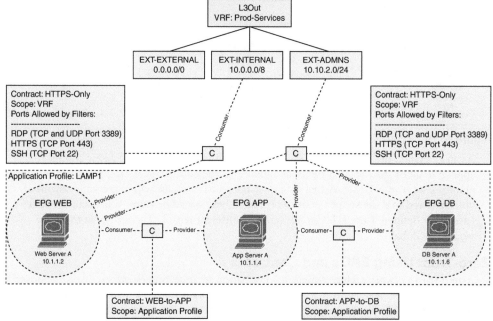

Figure 5-20 *Controlling Access to ACI Fabrics by Using External EPGs*

One point that is important to clarify here is that external EPG subnets are longest prefix-match subnets. Therefore, EXT-INTERNET, which consists of the 0.0.0.0/0 subnet, classifies all endpoints out on the Internet but not internal subnets in the more specific 10.0.0.0/8 range allocated to EXT-INTERNAL.

Expanding on this concept, it is important to understand that any given outside endpoint will be classified to one and only one external EPG. Just because the administrator group defined by EXT-ADMINS at 10.10.2.0/24 also falls within the 10.0.0.0/8 range does *not* mean that administrators will have some of their access removed to reflect the access levels of the 10.0.0.0/8 range. Likewise, if EXT-INTERNAL were allocated more access than EXT-ADMINS, the 10.10.2.0/24 administrator subnet would not inherit expanded access.

So, what happens if an administrator associates a particular subnet with multiple external EPGs? ACI triggers a fault, and the second subnet allocation to an external EPG is invalidated. The only exception to this rule is the 0.0.0.0/0 subnet. Regardless of this exception, deployment of multiple external EPGs that reference the same subnet is bad practice.

External EPGs, sometimes referred to as *outside EPGs*, classify traffic based on a longest-prefix match, and any given outside endpoint will be classified into the most specific applicable external EPG that has been defined.

> **NOTE**   Other types of external EPGs exist. The type of external EPG used for classification of external traffic that is described here is configured with the Scope value External Subnets for the External EPG. Chapter 9, "L3Outs," addresses the other Scope settings that are available.

Also, as shown in Figure 5-20, external EPGs associate with objects called Layer 3 Outs, which in turn bind to VRF instances.

Layer 3 Outside (L3Out)

An *L3Out* is an object that defines a route peering or a series of route peerings to allow route propagation between ACI and an external Layer 3 switch, router, or appliance. BGP, OSPF, and EIGRP are all supported protocols for use on L3Outs. Static routes pointing outside ACI can also be configured on L3Outs.

A regular L3Out is configured within a tenant and is bound to a single VRF instance. A number of specialized L3Outs can be created in the infra tenant, which can advertise routes from multiple ACI VRF instances to the outside world. This book focuses on regular L3Outs.

Tenant Hierarchy Review

Figure 5-21 provides an overview of the tenant hierarchy and the relationship between the objects outlined so far in this chapter. Each relationship between tenant objects is shown to be either a 1:*n* (one-to-many) relationship or an *n*:*n* (many-to-many) relationship. Figure 5-21 shows, for example, that any one bridge domain can be associated with one and only one VRF instance. However, any one bridge domain can also have many subnets associated with it, so a bridge domain can have a 1:*n* relationship with subnets.

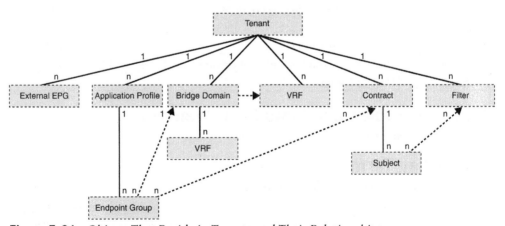

Figure 5-21   *Objects That Reside in Tenants and Their Relationships*

Exam Preparation Tasks

As mentioned in the section "How to Use This Book" in the Introduction, you have a couple of choices for exam preparation: Chapter 17, "Final Preparation," and the exam simulation questions in the Pearson Test Prep Software Online.

Review All Key Topics

Review the most important topics in this chapter, noted with the Key Topic icon in the outer margin of the page. Table 5-2 lists these key topics and the page number on which each is found.

Table 5-2 Key Topics for Chapter 5

Key Topic Element	Description	Page Number
Paragraph	Defines tenants	133
List	Describes predefined tenants in ACI	134
Paragraph	Defines VRF instances	135
Paragraph	Defines bridge domains	137
Paragraph	Defines EPGs	137
Paragraph	Defines application profiles	138
Paragraph	Describes associations between application profiles, bridge domains, and EPGs	139
Paragraph	Describes practical bridge domain functions	141
Paragraph	Describes practical EPG functions	141
Paragraph	Lists encapsulations in ACI for Ethernet traffic	146
List	Defines contracts, subjects, filters, and filter entries	148
Paragraph	Defines and provides a sample use case for intra-EPG isolation	149
Paragraph	Defines contract direction options	149
List	Lists and describes contract scopes	150
Paragraph	Defines external EPGs	151
Paragraph	Describes method of endpoint classification by external EPGs	153
Paragraph	Defines L3Outs	153

Complete Tables and Lists from Memory

There are no memory tables or lists in this chapter.

Define Key Terms

Define the following key terms from this chapter and check your answers in the glossary:

tenant, fabric policy, fabric port, access policy, Virtual Machine Manager (VMM) domain, virtual routing and forwarding (VRF) instance, application profile, bridge domain (BD), endpoint group (EPG), filter, subject, contract, contract scope, consumer, provider, external EPG, L3Out

## CHAPTER 6

Access Policies

This chapter covers the following topics:

Pools, Domains, and AAEPs: This section outlines the significance of multitenancy-centric objects in the Access Policies view.

Policies and Policy Groups: This section addresses the grouping of interface policies and switch policies into reusable policy groups.

Profiles and Selectors: This section explains the role of profiles and selector objects in configuring ports and enabling stateless networking.

Bringing It All Together: This section summarizes how the critical objects detailed in this chapter link tenancy to the underlying infrastructure.

This chapter covers the following exam topics:

- 1.5 Implement ACI policies

  - 1.5.a access

Aside from tenant objects, the most important objects ACI administrators deal with on a regular basis are those that relate to access policies.

The objects detailed in this chapter are critical to the configuration of switch ports. They enable service providers and central IT to control the encapsulations, the types of external devices, and the switch ports to which tenant administrators are allowed to deploy endpoints.

"Do I Know This Already?" Quiz

The "Do I Know This Already?" quiz allows you to assess whether you should read this entire chapter thoroughly or jump to the "Exam Preparation Tasks" section. If you are in doubt about your answers to these questions or your own assessment of your knowledge of the topics, read the entire chapter. Table 6-1 lists the major headings in this chapter and their corresponding "Do I Know This Already?" quiz questions. You can find the answers in Appendix A, "Answers to the 'Do I Know This Already?' Questions."

Table 6-1 "Do I Know This Already?" Section-to-Question Mapping

Foundation Topics Section	Questions
Pools, Domains, and AAEPs	1–5
Policies and Policy Groups	6–8
Profiles and Selectors	9, 10

1. Which of the following objects is used when attaching a bare-metal server to an ACI fabric?
   a. External bridge domain
   b. VMM domain
   c. Routed domain
   d. Physical domain

2. True or false: When an administrator assigns a VLAN pool to a domain that is associated with an AAEP and the administrator then assigns the AAEP to switch interfaces, the VLANs in the VLAN pool become trunked on all the specified ports.
   a. True
   b. False

3. True or false: A VMM domain allows dynamic binding of EPGs into virtualized infrastructure.
   a. True
   b. False

4. Before a tenant administrator maps an EPG to ports and encapsulations, he or she should first bind the EPG to one or more _____.
   a. endpoints
   b. VRF instances
   c. AAEPs
   d. domains

5. Which of the following statements is correct?
   a. An EPG cannot be assigned to more than one domain.
   b. An EPG can be bound to multiple domains, but the domains ideally should not reference overlapping VLAN pools.
   c. An EPG cannot have static mappings to physical ports.
   d. An EPG can be directly associated with a VRF instance.

6. Which of the following protocols does ACI use for loop prevention?
   a. Spanning Tree Protocol
   b. LACP
   c. MCP
   b. DWDM

7. A port channel interface policy group configuration has been assigned to a switch. An engineer has been tasked with creating a second port channel with equivalent configurations on the same switch. He decides to reuse the interface policy group and make a new port assignment using a new access selector name. Which of the following statements is accurate?

   a. ACI creates a new port channel because a new access selector is being used.

   b. ACI adds the ports assigned to the new access selector to the previously created port channel bundle.

   c. ACI triggers a fault and does not deploy the configuration.

   d. ACI does not trigger a fault or deploy the configuration.

8. True or false: Access (non-aggregated) interface policy groups are fully reusable.

   a. True

   b. False

9. True or false: Multiple interface profiles can be assigned to a switch.

   a. True

   b. False

10. Which of the following need to be directly associated with node IDs?

   a. Interface profiles

   b. AAEPs

   c. Switch profiles

   d. Interface policies

Foundation Topics

Pools, Domains, and AAEPs

While tenant network policies are configured separately from access policies, tenant policies are *not* activated unless their underlying access policies are in place. Therefore, tenants depend on access policies.

Access policies govern the configuration of any non-fabric (access) ports. The term *access policies* in the context of ACI, therefore, should not be understood as the access versus trunking state of a port. In fact, the trunking state of ports is usually determined by encapsulation mappings and is often configured within tenants and not in the access policies view.

Regardless of whether a non-fabric port is expected to function as a trunk port or an access port, configuration of parameters such as interface speed and the protocols to be enabled on the interface are still made under the umbrella of access policies.

In true multitenancy environments with tight role delineation, access policies are configured either by an admin user or a user who has been assigned the access-admin role or a role with equivalent privileges. A user who has been assigned the access-admin role can create the majority of objects in this chapter but would need expanded privileges to create domains.

VLAN Pools

A *VLAN pool* defines the range of VLAN IDs that are acceptable for application to ACI access (non-fabric) ports for a particular function or use. Allocation of VLAN IDs can be performed either statically or dynamically.

With a *static VLAN allocation*, or *static binding*, an administrator statically maps a specific EPG to a VLAN ID on a port, a port channel, a virtual port channel, or all ports on a switch. With *dynamic VLAN allocation*, ACI automatically picks a VLAN ID out of a range of VLANs and maps it to an EPG.

Static VLAN allocation is required when configuring access or trunk ports connecting to bare-metal servers and appliances. Dynamic allocation is beneficial in deployments that rely on automated service insertion or VMM integration, where ACI is able to automatically push EPGs into virtualized environments to allow virtualization administrators to assign virtual machines directly to EPGs.

Other forms of pools do exist in ACI, such as VXLAN pools. However, VLAN IDs are the most common form of encapsulation used on ports connecting to servers and appliances as well as outside switches and routers.

> **NOTE** Cisco Application Virtual Switch (AVS) and the Cisco ACI Virtual Edge (AVE) support both VLAN and VXLAN as acceptable encapsulations for EPG mappings.

To create a VLAN pool, select **Fabric > Access Policies > Pools** and right-click VLANs. Finally, select Create VLAN Pool, as shown in Figure 6-1.

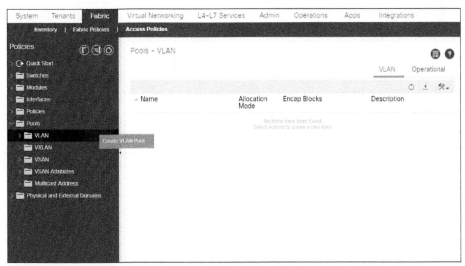

Figure 6-1 *Opening the Create VLAN Pool Wizard*

In the wizard, type a name for the VLAN pool, select the allocation mode, and then click on the + sign, as shown in Figure 6-2, to open the Create Ranges window.

Figure 6-2   *Entering the VLAN Pool Name and Allocation Mode*

In the Create Ranges window, enter an acceptable range of encapsulations and the role of the range and click OK, as shown in Figure 6-3. A range of VLANs consists of a set of one or more subsequent VLANs. Note that you can create additional ranges and add them to the VLAN pool by navigating to the Create Range window and repeating the process.

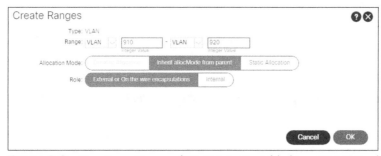

Figure 6-3   *Creating a Range of VLANs to Be Added to a VLAN Pool*

VLAN ranges created in VLAN pools can take one of two roles:

- **External, or on-the-wire, encapsulation:** Any range of encapsulations used for bare-metal servers or hypervisor uplinks where traffic is trunked outside an ACI fabric is considered to be external or on the wire.

- **Internal:** Private VLAN allocations within very specific virtual switching solutions such as AVE require internal VLAN ranges. Internal VLAN encapsulation ranges reside inside hypervisors and do *not* extend outside hypervisors and onto the wire.

Domains

Domains are the central link between the access policies hierarchy and the tenant hierarchy. A *domain* is the glue that binds tenant EPGs to access and virtual networking policies. With the help of pools, domains determine whether a tenant administrator is even allowed to map an EPG to a certain encapsulation and underlying infrastructure. Each domain points to and consumes a single VLAN pool.

Note that the word *allowed* in the above definition is key. In environments with management multitenancy, an ACI administrator assigns domains to security domains, thereby determining which tenant administrators can bind EPGs to the domain and consume the VLAN IDs defined in the associated VLAN pool. Chapter 15, "Implementing AAA and RBAC," covers ACI role-based access control in detail.

The following types of domains within ACI fall within the scope of the Implementing Cisco Application Centric Infrastructure DCACI 300-620 exam:

- **Physical domain:** A *physical domain* governs the attachment of bare-metal servers and appliances that need static VLAN allocations.

- **External bridge domains:** An *external bridge domain* is a type of domain used in attachments to switches outside ACI for Layer 2 connectivity.

- **External routed domains:** An *external routed domain* is a type of domain used in attachments to switches and routers outside ACI for Layer 3 connectivity.

- **Fibre Channel domains:** This type of domain is used in attachments to servers and storage area networks (SANs) outside ACI for FC or FCoE traffic. In addition to referencing a VLAN pool, a Fibre Channel domain also references a VSAN pool.

- **Virtual Machine Manager (VMM) domain:** A *Virtual Machine Manager (VMM) domain* is a type of domain that enables ACI to deploy EPGs and corresponding encapsulations into virtualized environments.

If you find it difficult to remember the function of domains and why there are numerous types of domains, you can think of the word *how*. The association of domains with objects like bridge domains, AAEPs, and L3Outs tells ACI how a given endpoint is allowed to connect to the fabric.

Keep in mind that a domain, by itself, does not determine whether a tenant administrator can actually map an EPG to an individual server. It just determines the list of VLAN IDs or other forms of encapsulation a tenant administrator has been approved to use for any given type of connectivity (for example, type of domain).

Common Designs for VLAN Pools and Domains

There are many ways to lay out VLAN pools and domains, but three methods are most prevalent in the industry.

For the first type of VLAN pool and domain layout described here, central IT manages everything in ACI. Even though multiple user tenants may have been created, role-based access control may not be a desired goal of multitenancy in such environments, and all network administrators have full permission to make any changes in ACI. For this reason, a single VLAN pool and domain is created for each device attachment type. Table 6-2 shows an example of this type of design.

Table 6-2 Single VLAN Pool for Each Type of Domain

Domain Name	VLAN Range	Allocation Mode	Use Case
physical-domain	1–1000	static	Bare metal, appliances, firewalls
VMM-domain	2001–3000	dynamic	Virtual environment
L3-domain	3091–3100	static	L3Outs

While this layout minimizes the number of VLAN pools and domains in ACI, it lacks granularity.

With the second type of VLAN pool and domain layout, central IT still manages everything in ACI, and management plane multitenancy is not seen as a business objective. However, there may be an orientation toward aligning VLAN pools and domains with function. Table 6-3 shows an example of a layout that takes function into consideration.

Table 6-3   Single VLAN Pool per Function

Domain Name	VLAN Range	Allocation Mode	Use Case
physical-domain	1–900	static	Bare metal
firewall-domain	901–910	static	Trunks to firewalls
VMM-PROD	2001–2400	dynamic	vSphere production
VMM-NONPROD	2401–2800	dynamic	vSphere non-production
VMM-VOICE	2801–3000	dynamic	vSphere voice
L3core-domain	3091–3095	static	L3Outs to core layer
L3partner-domain	3096–3100	static	L3Outs to partner network

The layout illustrated in Table 6-3 offers a lot more flexibility than the design outlined in Table 6-2. For example, by separating VMM domains into the three separate vSphere environments, the organization has decided to align its domains with the function of each set of vCenter instances within the environment. This approach to domain definition provides administrators more flexibility in deploying EPGs solely to the desired vCenter environments.

NOTE   Chapter 11, "Integrating ACI into vSphere Using VDS," covers vCenter and vSphere networking in detail. If the concepts presented on VMM domains in this chapter seem intimidating, come back and review this chapter once more after studying Chapter 11.

As shown in Table 6-3, a company may also want to allocate critical traffic such as firewalls and each L3Out into its own domain to reduce the impact of minor configuration mistakes.

Table 6-4 shows an example of a granular layout that takes into consideration both function and tenancy. By creating dedicated domains for each tenant, the administrator defining the domains and pools is basically allocating certain VLAN ID ranges for dedicated use by specific tenants. Also, it is worth noting that VMM domains do not change in this example. This is because the dynamic VLAN allocation mode ensures that ACI itself (and not tenant administrators) is responsible for mapping VLANs to EPGs. This means separate per-tenant VLAN pools are not desired for VMM domains.

Table 6-4   A Hybrid Approach Oriented Toward Both Function and Tenancy

Domain Name	VLAN Range	Allocation Mode	Use Case
tenant-a-pdomain	1–280	static	Bare metal in Tenant A
tenant-a-l3domain	281–300	static	L3Outs in Tenant A
tenant-b-pdomain	301–580	static	Bare metal in Tenant B
tenant-b-l3domain	581–600	static	L3Outs in Tenant B
tenant-c-pdomain	601–880	static	Bare metal in Tenant C
tenant-c-l3domain	881–900	static	L3Outs in Tenant C
firewall-domain	901–910	static	Trunks to firewalls
VMM-PROD	2001–2400	dynamic	vSphere production

Domain Name	VLAN Range	Allocation Mode	Use Case
VMM-NONPROD	2401–2800	dynamic	vSphere non-production
VMM-VOICE	2801–3000	dynamic	vSphere voice

To create a domain, navigate to the **Fabric > Access Policies > Physical and External Domains** and select the folder related to the desired domain type. As shown in Figure 6-4, you can right-click the Physical Domain folder and select Create Physical Domain to start the Create Physical Domain wizard.

Figure 6-4 *Opening the Create Physical Domain Wizard*

In the Create Physical Domain wizard, type a name for the physical domain and select the VLAN pool that you want to associate with the new domain (see Figure 6-5). As a result of this configuration, any EPG that is able to bind to the domain called DCACI-Domain can potentially use VLAN IDs 910 through 920 as acceptable on-the-wire encapsulations.

Figure 6-5 *Associating a VLAN Pool with a Domain*

> **NOTE** VMM domains cannot be created under Access Policies and need to be created under the Virtual Networking tab. The process for creating VMM domains is covered in Chapter 11.

Challenges with Overlap Between VLAN Pools

Overlapping VLAN pools in ACI is not a problem in and of itself. It can become a problem, however, if an EPG has associations with multiple domains and the domains reference overlapping VLAN pools.

Navigating the CLI to troubleshoot the resulting performance problems and traffic blackholing is beyond the scope of the DCACI 300-620 exam. However, it is still important to understand how you can sidestep this type of issue in the first place.

So how should VLAN pools and domains be created? In an ideal world, you should not need to overlap VLAN pools at all (as demonstrated in the examples of VLAN pools presented in the previous section).

In large environments, however, you may have or expect to have more than 4000 VLANs after all data center traffic is whitelisted. In such cases, you may have to plan for a lot more VLAN IDs than the number of VLANs currently in production. In such a case, you may want to dedicate switches for specific purposes so that overlapping VLAN pools and domains never fall onto the same set of leaf switches in the first place. Table 6-5 presents an example of this type of VLAN pool and domain design.

Table 6-5 Optimizing VLAN Pools and Domains in Large Environments

Domain Name	VLAN Range	Allocation Mode	Leaf Node IDs
tenant-a-pdomain	1–900	static	101–110
tenant-a-l3domain	901–1000	static	101–110
tenant-b-pdomain	1001–1900	static	101–110
tenant-b-l3domain	1901–2000	static	101–110
tenant-c-pdomain	2001–2900	static	101–110
tenant-c-l3domain	2901–3000	static	101–110
firewall-domain	3001–3100	static	101–110
VMM-VOICE	3101–4000	dynamic	101–110
VMM-PROD	1–4000	dynamic	111–120
VMM-NONPROD	1–4000	dynamic	121–130

The design in Table 6-5 makes several assumptions. First, it assumes that the environment in question has a very large virtual footprint consisting of a set of production vCenter instances and a set of non-production vCenter instances. Second, it assumes that the customer will not be pushing EPGs that are dedicated to production uses into vCenter instances that are meant for non-production use cases. Finally, it assumes that any given EPG will be assigned solely to a single domain.

NOTE Despite the reasoning in the previous paragraph, multiple VMM domains can be linked to a single vCenter instance. The reason for this is that VMM domains are bound to data center objects in vCenter. Therefore, a vCenter instance that has multiple data center folders can have multiple VMM domain associations.

Can VXLAN be used instead of a VLAN to scale the number of segments in an environment beyond the 4094 usable VLAN limit that is common in traditional networks? The answer is yes! Certain virtual switches, such as AVS and AVE, leverage VXLAN. However, it is not very common for companies to want to install specialized drivers or specialized virtual switches in each server to enable support for VXLAN. That is why encapsulating traffic down to hypervisors and servers using VLAN IDs is still the norm with ACI. Table 6-5 already showed how you can use good design practice to scale beyond the number of usable VLAN IDs within a single fabric. Another way ACI is able to use VXLAN internally to scale the number of segments in a fabric beyond what is possible with VLANs is through use of a feature called Port Local Scope, which is discussed in Chapter 10, "Extending Layer 2 Outside ACI."

NOTE The concepts in this section are not documented best practices. The examples are meant solely to convey core concepts related to VLAN pools and domains. Furthermore, names of any objects should not be misconstrued as recommendations for naming best practices.

Attachable Access Entity Profiles (AAEPs)

So far, you have learned how to limit the VLAN IDs that can be used to encapsulate EPG traffic coming into and leaving an ACI fabric for each function and each endpoint attachment type. But how can a fabric administrator control where (for example, behind which switch ports, behind which vSphere servers) endpoints within each tenant can be deployed?

An *attachable access entity profile (AAEP)*, also referred to as an AEP, is a construct that fabric administrators use to authorize the placement of endpoint traffic on external entities, such as bare-metal servers, virtual machine hypervisors, switches, and routers. ACI can connect to external entities by using individual ports, port channels, or even vPCs.

To make this authorization possible, a user with the access-admin role or a role with equivalent privileges associates any number of domains, as needed, to an AAEP. Because any one port, port channel, or vPC configuration can reference only a single AAEP, tenant administrators with access to a domain assigned to that AAEP are authorized to deploy endpoints behind the specified ports.

Just because a tenant administrator is authorized to deploy a server, a virtual machine, or another endpoint behind a switch port does not mean that the administrator is required to do so. Furthermore, the authorization provided by an AAEP does not actually provision VLANs on ports. Traffic for an EPG does not flow on ports until a tenant administrator maps the EPG to an encapsulation. The goal of an AAEP, therefore, is just to specify the potential scope of where endpoints associated with a domain are allowed to be deployed in the first place.

NOTE   An AAEP EPG enables users with the access-admin role to map tenant EPGs to AAEPs directly from the Access Policies menu. AAEP EPGs are addressed in Chapter 7, "Implementing Access Policies."

A tenant administrator who wants to map an EPG to a port needs to first bind the EPG to a domain. Through this domain association, the tenant administrator tells ACI how EPG endpoints are intended to connect to the fabric. Based on the VLAN pool the domain references, ACI knows which VLAN IDs are potential encapsulation options for the EPG. In any case, the tenant administrator is still limited to mapping the EPG to switch ports, port channels, or vPCs that reference an AAEP associated with the domain or domains bound to the EPG.

NOTE   A tenant administrator has visibility (access) to a domain only if the tenant administrator and domain have been assigned to the same security domain.

Figure 6-6 illustrates the relationship between pools, domains, and AAEPs. In the first sample configuration in this figure, an engineer creates an AAEP called Infrastructure-AAEP with the domains Infra-Physical-Domain and Infra-VMM-Domain associated to it. The domain called Infra-Physical-Domain allows the attachment of bare-metal servers and appliances using any desired encapsulations between VLAN IDs 100 through 199. The VMM domain enables deployment of EPGs into a virtualized environment using any VLAN IDs between 2000 and 2999. The second example depicted provides a common configuration for L3Out domains where Layer 3 peerings may be established with adjacent devices over multiple VRFs or L3Outs via switch virtual interfaces (SVIs) over a single subset of physical ports. In this case, assume that Prod-L3Domain will be used for an L3Out in a VRF instance called Production, and NonProd-L3Domain will be used for an L3Out in a VRF called NonProduction. The Production L3Out SVIs in this case can use VLAN IDs 800 through 809, while the NonProduction L3Out SVIs can use VLAN IDs 810 through 819.

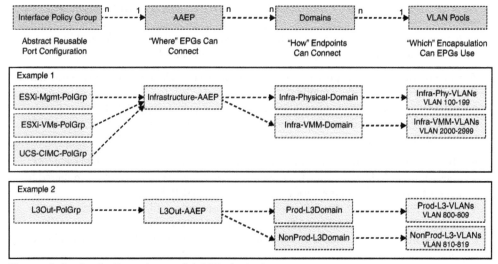

Figure 6-6   *Pools, Domains, and AAEPs in Action*

In Figure 6-6, ESXi-Mgmt-PolGrp, ESXi-VMs-PolGrp, and UCS-CIMC-PolGrp point to AAEPs. (These objects are called *interface policy groups*, which have yet to be introduced.)

To configure an AAEP, navigate to **Fabric > Access Policies > Policies > Global > Attachable Access Entity Profiles.** Right-click and select Create Attachable Access Entity Profile, as shown in Figure 6-7.

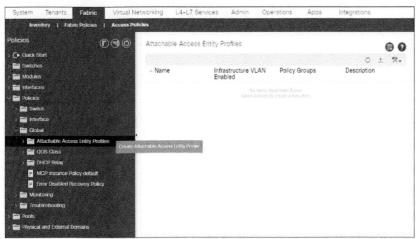

Figure 6-7   *Navigating to the Create Attachable Access Entity Profile Wizard*

In the Create Attachable Access Entity Profile wizard, type the desired AAEP name and select the domains you intend to associate with the AAEP. As domains are added to the AAEP, the acceptable encapsulation ranges dictated by the VLAN pools bound to each domain are displayed in the right column. When all the desired domains are selected and added to the AAEP, click Next. Figure 6-8 shows the configuration of an AAEP named DCACI-AAEP with a physical domain association that allows the mapping of VLAN encapsulations 910 through 920.

Figure 6-8   *Creating an AAEP and Binding One or More Domains*

If desired and if an interface policy group has been created, you can associate an AAEP with an interface policy group in the Create Attachable Access Entity Profile wizard. Figure 6-9 shows the Association to Interfaces page of the wizard, but no interface policy groups have yet been configured. Note that it is more common to associate AAEPs to interface policy groups through the interface policy group configuration wizard. Click Finish to execute the AAEP creation.

Figure 6-9   *Associating an AAEP to One or More Interface Policy Groups*

Note in Figure 6-5, shown earlier in this chapter, that an AAEP was intentionally left unselected. From an object hierarchy perspective, a child object of a domain needs to reference an AAEP, and a child object of the AAEP needs to reference the domain to establish a bidirectional relationship. However, the configuration process shown in Figures 6-7 through 6-9 creates all the required cross-references. Figure 6-10 shows that DCACI-AAEP has been automatically associated with DCACI-Domain as a result of the AAEP to domain association shown earlier.

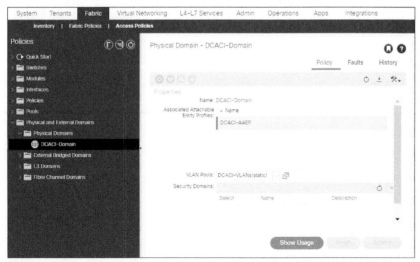

Figure 6-10   *Domain View Updated Automatically with AAEP Association*

Example 6-1 shows the APIC CLI equivalents for the configurations outlined in this section.

Example 6-1   *CLI Equivalents for VLAN Pool, Domain, and AAEP Configurations*

```
apic1# show running-config vlan-domain DCACI-Domain
  vlan-domain DCACI-Domain type phys
    vlan-pool DCACI-VLANs
    vlan 910-920
    exit
```

NOTE   AAEP configuration cannot be performed via the APIC CLI, but the existence of AAEP objects can be verified via MOQuery.

Policies and Policy Groups

This chapter has made multiple references to the configuration of individual ports, port channels, and vPCs, but it has not discussed the objects and relationships that enable policy assignment to switch ports.

Some of the most important constructs of interest in configuring a switch port are interface policies, interface policy groups, switch policies, and switch policy groups.

Interface Policies and Interface Policy Groups

In ACI, configuration parameters that dictate interface behavior are called *interface policies*. Examples of interface policies include port speeds, enabled or disabled protocols or port level features, and monitoring settings.

It is common for interface policies to be defined when an ACI fabric is initialized unless automation is employed to dynamically create objects that define desired interface policies as part of an interface configuration script.

For instance, when an ACI fabric is initialized, an administrator may create an interface policy called LLDP-Enable, which enables the LLDP protocol. The administrator may also create another interface policy called LACP-Active to enable link aggregation via LACP. Interface policies do not take effect by themselves; they need to be assigned to an interface policy group to be applicable to switch ports. When the two interface policies LLDP-Enable and LACP-Active are applied together to an interface policy group and assigned to a set of ports, the newly configured ports then enable LLDP and attempt to form an LACP port channel.

An *interface policy* group is a port configuration template that aligns with link types. Each individual physical interface or link aggregation within ACI derives two critical configuration components from an interface policy group: The first is a collection of interface policies, and the second is an AAEP. Some types of interface policy groups are fully reusable, and others are semi-reusable.

Figure 6-11 illustrates the relationships between and functions of interface policies and interface policy groups.

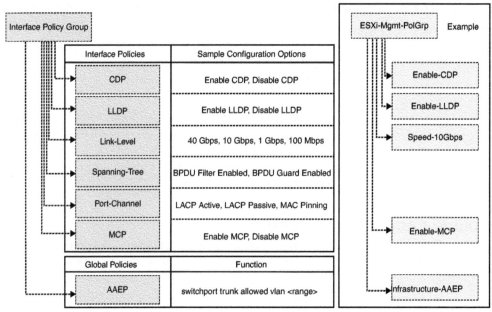

Figure 6-11 *Interface Policies and Interface Policy Groups*

As illustrated in this figure, you can think of an interface policy group as having two components. The first component is the collection or grouping of interface policies applicable to a set of ports that therefore dictates the features (for example, control plane policing, storm control), protocols (for example, Cisco Discovery Protocol, Link Layer Discovery Protocol), and other link aspects (for example, speed) applied to relevant ports. The second component of an interface policy group is the AAEP, which dictates the domains associated with the interface policy group and therefore determines the tenants and VLAN IDs that can be encapsulated on the relevant ports.

In NX-OS, interface configuration lines related to Cisco Discovery Protocol (CDP) and storm control would be considered interface policies. An NX-OS configuration line like **switchport trunk allowed vlan 100-200** dictates the range of acceptable VLANs and therefore would be equivalent in function to an AAEP.

Table 6-6 describes the types of interface policy groups available for ACI leaf switches at the time of this writing.

Table 6-6 Types of Interface Policy Groups in ACI

Interface Policy Group Type	Description
Leaf access port policy group	Fully reusable interface configuration templates used for individual (non-aggregated) non-fabric ports on a leaf switch.
Port channel interface policy group	A single-switch port channel configuration template that can be applied to non-fabric ports on a leaf switch.
VPC interface policy group	A vPC configuration template used to create a port aggregation across two switches that are in the same vPC domain.

Interface Policy Group Type	Description
PC/VPC override policy group	Where an administrator reuses PC or VPC interface policy groups across multiple leafs or vPC domains, an override policy group can override the settings applied on an individual leaf or vPC domain.
Leaf breakout port group	Some ACI switches support breaking out high-bandwidth ports into lower-bandwidth ports using breakout cabling. This enables configuration of high-bandwidth ports for breakouts.
Fibre Channel (FC) interface policy group	A fully reusable interface policy group that allows the selection of an FC interface policy and AAEP for connectivity to SAN-accessing servers or a Fibre Channel Forwarder (FCF).
FC port channel interface policy group	A pseudo-reusable FC port channel interface policy group that allows the selection of an FC interface policy, a port channel policy, and an AAEP for connectivity to SAN-accessing servers or an FCF.

Not all interface policy groups are fully reusable. Leaf access port policy groups and FC interface policy groups are reusable without caveats because they do not necessitate link aggregation.

If a port channel interface policy group has already been used to deploy a port channel on a leaf switch, reuse of the PC interface policy group on that leaf results in the newly configured ports being added to the previously created bundle. A similar situation occurs when a vPC interface policy group is used to create a vPC and the interface policy group is reused across the same vPC domain.

Therefore, if a port channel interface policy group has already been deployed to a leaf and the intent is to create a new port channel on the leaf, you can create and deploy a new PC interface policy group to the leaf. Likewise, if a vPC interface policy group has been deployed to a vPC switch pair, you should not reuse the vPC interface policy group unless the intent is to join new links to the previously created vPC.

Table 6-7 presents the most commonly used types of interface policies available in ACI.

Table 6-7   Types of Interface Policies Available in ACI

Interface Policy Type	Description of Settings
Link level	Determines a port link speed, auto-negotiation status, forward error correction (FEC), and link debounce interval.
CDP	Allows the creation of policies that enable or disable CDP.
LLDP	Allows the creation of policies that enable or disable LLDP.
NetFlow	Allows the creation of NetFlow monitors, NetFlow records, or NetFlow exporters for traffic and flow data collection at the interface level.
Port channel	Enables the creation of policies involving port aggregations, such as Link Aggregation Control Protocol (LACP) and static port channels. Additional options, including MAC pinning and explicit failover order, are available for virtual environments.

6

Interface Policy Type	Description of Settings
Spanning Tree	Allows the creation of policies that enable BPDU Guard, BPDU Filtering, or both.
Storm control	Enables the creation of policies that can prevent traffic disruptions on physical interfaces caused by a broadcast, multicast, or unknown unicast traffic storm.
MCP	Allows the creation of policies that enable or disable *MisCabling Protocol (MCP)*, which is a loop-prevention protocol in ACI. MCP can be applied on both physical Ethernet interfaces and port channel interfaces. MCP needs to be enabled globally for MCP interface policies to be applied.
CoPP (Control Plane Policing)	Control Plane Policing (CoPP) interface policies protect ACI switches by setting limits on the number of packets per second the switch may process in CPU when received on a link. CoPP policies are applied on a per-protocol basis.
L2 interface policy	L2 interface policies govern policies related to VLAN scopes, Q-in-Q encapsulation, and Reflexive Relay functionality. Later chapters address these policies.

As a supplement to the previous list, Table 6-8 describes some of the less commonly used interface policy types available in ACI as of the time of this writing. Even though these interface policy types are not used as often, they still technically fall under the umbrella of access policies and therefore may be considered within the scope of the DCACI 300-620 exam.

Table 6-8 Additional Interface Policy Types Available in ACI

Interface Policy Type	Description of Settings
Priority flow control	Enables or disables priority-based flow control (PFC) or sets it to automatic. PFC is a QoS PAUSE mechanism often used to ensure lossless Fibre Channel forwarding over an Ethernet medium.
Fibre Channel interface	Sets the port speed, mode (F or NP), trunking status, and receive buffer credit size for Fibre Channel interfaces.
PoE	Sets a Power over Ethernet (PoE) policy that can be applied to switch ports for direct phone or wireless attachment to an ACI fabric. Use of PoE in ACI fabrics is not very common.
Port channel member	Defines a common policy that applies to one or more member interfaces within a port channel bundle. For example, LACP port priorities can be configured in a port channel member policy to help determine which ports should be put in standby mode when not all ports configured in the bundle can be moved into a forwarding state. LACP fast timers are also configured in a port channel member interface policy.
Data plane policing	Data plane policing (DPP) policies manage bandwidth consumption on ACI fabric access interfaces. DPP policies can apply to egress traffic, ingress traffic, or both. DPP monitors the data rates for a particular interface. When traffic exceeds user-configured values, marking or dropping of packets occurs immediately.

Interface Policy Type	Description of Settings
Port security	Port security policies protects the ACI fabric from being flooded with unknown MAC addresses by limiting the number of MAC addresses per port.
MACsec	MACsec is an IEEE 802.1AE standards-based Layer 2 hop-by-hop encryption that provides data confidentiality and integrity for media access independent protocols. MACsec interface policies can be used on host-facing links to secure switch-to-endpoint communication via MACsec.
DWDM	When a DWDM optic is inserted into an ACI switch, the port defaults to DWDM channel 32 and the corresponding frequency and wavelength. Using a DWDM interface policy, an administrator can change the DWDM channel used on a port.
Firewall	An interface policy used for implementation of the ACI Distributed Firewall in an ACI Virtual Edge environment.
802.1X port authentication	801.1X port authentication interface policies allow administrators to restrict unauthorized endpoints from connecting to the network through ACI switch ports.
Slow drain	Slow drain interface policies manage FCoE traffic congestion by specifying the actions ACI should take if congestion is detected on an interface.

NOTE   Although some types of interface policies do have default values, it is highly recommended that you create and use explicit interface policies as much as possible.

Chapter 7 covers the configuration of interface policies and interface policy groups.

Planning Deployment of Interface Policies

Remember that all interface policies are reusable. While administrators usually deploy interface policy groups when new physical infrastructure is introduced into the data center, they tend to plan and configure a large set of interface policies at the time of initial fabric deployment. If a specific use arises for additional interface policies, the administrator can add the new interface policy to the deployment.

Table 6-9 shows a basic sample collection of interface policies an administrator might configure at the time of fabric initialization. The data in this table is for learning purposes only and should not be interpreted as a recommendation for policy naming.

Table 6-9   Sample Interface Policies Configured During Fabric Initialization

Interface Policy Name	Configuration Settings Selected for Policy
CDP-Enable	Sets CDP to enabled
CDP-Disable	Sets CDP to disabled
LLDP-Enable	Sets LLDP to enabled
LLDP-Disable	Sets LLDP to disabled
MCP-Enable	Sets MCP to enabled

Interface Policy Name	Configuration Settings Selected for Policy
MCP-Disable	Sets MCP to disabled
40-Gbps	A link-level policy that sets the port speed to 40 Gbps. All other settings may remain set to the defaults.
10-Gbps	A link-level policy that sets the port speed to 10 Gbps. All other settings may remain set to the defaults.
1-Gbps	A link-level policy that sets the port speed to 1 Gbps. All other settings may remain set to the defaults.
100-Mbps-Full	A link-level policy that sets the port speed to 100 Mbps, with auto-negotiation set to full.
LACP-Active	A port channel policy that sets LACP to active with suspend individual port, graceful convergence, and fast select hot standby ports enabled.
Static-On	A port channel policy used for the creation of static port channels.

Switch Policies and Switch Policy Groups

Just like interfaces, switches at times require custom policies. An example of a custom policy might be specific CoPP settings or a vPC domain peer dead interval modification. Custom switch policies are defined using switch policies and are grouped together for allocation via switch policy groups.

ACI does not require that custom switch policies be defined and allocated to switches.

Configuration parameters that dictate switch behavior are called *switch policies*. A *switch policy group* is a switch configuration template that includes a set of switch policies for allocation to one or more switches in an ACI fabric. Switch policies and switch policy groups are usually configured during fabric initialization and are fully reusable.

Table 6-10 outlines the most commonly deployed switch policies available in ACI as of the time of writing.

Table 6-10 Most Commonly Deployed Switch Policies in ACI

Switch Policy	Description of Settings
CoPP (leaf and spine)	Enables the modification of switch Control Plane Policing (CoPP) profiles to allow a more lenient or more strict profile compared to the default CoPP switch profile. If the predefined CoPP profiles are not sufficient, a custom CoPP switch profile can be configured and allocated to switches.
BFD	Enables the configuration of global IPv4 and IPv6 Bidirectional Forwarding Detection (BFD) policies in the fabric to provide subsecond failure detection times in the forwarding path between ACI switches.
NetFlow node	Allows the configuration of NetFlow timers that specify the rate at which flow records are sent to the external collector.

Switch Policy	Description of Settings
Forwarding scale profile	This policy provides different scalability options, including the following: ■ **Dual Stack:** Provides scalability of up to 12,000 endpoints for IPv6 configurations and up to 24,000 endpoints for IPv4 configurations. ■ **High LPM:** Provides scalability similar to Dual Stack except that the longest prefix match (LPM) scale is 128,000, and the policy scale is 8000. ■ **IPv4 Scale:** Enables systems with no IPv6 configurations to increase scalability to 48,000 IPv4 endpoints. ■ **High Dual Stack:** Provides scalability of up to 64,000 MAC endpoints and 64,000 IPv4 endpoints. IPv6 endpoint scale can be 24,000/48,000, depending on the switch hardware model.

Table 6-11 describes some less commonly modified ACI switch policies.

Table 6-11   Additional Switch Policies in ACI

Switch Policy	Description of Settings
Spanning Tree	Enables configuration of certain spanning-tree policies, such as MST region policies.
Fibre Channel node	Sets parameters related to the FCoE functionality of the switch, including disruptive load balancing and FIP keepalive intervals.
Fibre Channel SAN	Specifies FC map values, Error Detect Timeout (EDT) values, and Resource Allocation Timeout (RAT) values for an NPV leaf switch targeted to support FCoE connectivity.
PoE node	Controls the overall default power consumption of a switch, in milliwatts. Further interface-level policies, such as the PoE VLAN, need to also be configured to enable PoE power delivery to devices such as IP phones.
Fast link failover	Reduces the data plane outage resulting from a fabric link failure to less than 200 milliseconds. This feature requires EX leaf switches or newer switches. Enabling this feature on leaf uplinks prevents the use of these links for port mirroring.
CoPP prefilter	To protect against DDoS attacks, a CoPP prefilter profile can filter access to authentication services based on specified sources and TCP ports. When a CoPP prefilter profile is deployed on a switch, control plane traffic is denied by default. Only the traffic specified in the CoPP prefilter profile is permitted.
802.1X node authentication	802.1X authentication allows administrators to restrict unauthorized endpoints from connecting to the network through ACI switch ports. By default, leaf switches use the OOB (out-of-band) management IP address to source packets to a RADIUS server for 802.1X authentication. If you wish to use an in-band management IP address for communication with the 802.1X server, you need to configure an 802.1X node authentication policy and associate the RADIUS provider group to it.

6

Switch Policy	Description of Settings
Equipment flash configuration policies	The SSD monitoring feature enables administrators to override the preconfigured thresholds for the SSD lifetime parameters. Faults are generated in ACI when the SSD reaches some percentage of the configured thresholds. These faults enable network operators to monitor and proactively replace any switch before the switch fails due to SSD lifetime parameter values becoming exceeded.

NOTE As demonstrated in Chapter 4, "Exploring ACI," administrators assign vPC domain IDs and vPC domain policies to leaf switch pairs from the switch policies folder. These two switch policies cannot be allocated to switches using switch policy groups and are therefore not discussed here.

Chapter 7 includes configuration examples for switch policies and switch policy groups.

Profiles and Selectors

Once administrators create interface policy groups, they need to assign them to one or more ports. The port mapping occurs under an interface profile using an object called an *interface selector*, as shown in Figure 6-12. The interface profile contains port mappings but not switch mappings. The switch mappings are determined through associations between interface profiles and switch profiles.

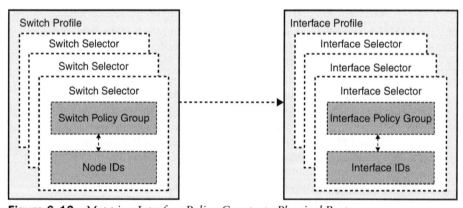

Figure 6-12 *Mapping Interface Policy Groups to Physical Ports*

Figure 6-13 provides some context for how this might be deployed in practice.

Figure 6-13 shows that an administrator creates an interface selector called ESXi-Mgmt under an interface profile named Leaf101-IntProfile and maps an interface policy group named ESXi-Mgmt-PolGrp to Ports 1, 2, and 3. The administrator creates a separate interface selector with the same name and port assignments under an interface profile called Leaf102-IntProfile. The administrator then associates Leaf101-IntProfile and Leaf102-IntProfile to switch profiles Leaf101-SwitchProfile and Leaf102-SwitchProfile, respectively.

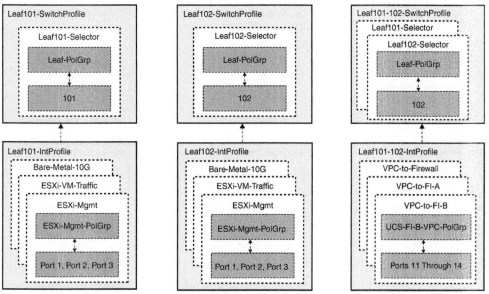

Figure 6-13 *A Sample Port Configuration Design in ACI*

The administrator has also created an interface profile named Leaf101-102-IntProfile. She makes several interface selector mappings on the interface profile. The interface selector VPC-to-FI-B maps an VPC interface policy group called UCS-FI-B-VPC-PolGrp to Ports 11 through 14. The administrator associates the interface profile with a single switch profile named Leaf101-102-SwitchProfile, which has switch selectors referencing both node IDs 101 and 102. This configures Ports 11 through 14 on both (leaf) Node 101 and Node 102 into a vPC. The use of a switch profile referencing both vPC peers is not the only way this type of configuration can be accomplished. The administrator could have just as well mapped the VPC interface policy group to both Leaf101-SwitchProfile and Leaf102-SwitchProfile to attain the same result.

Note that in this example, all eight ports are collectively bundled into a single virtual port channel because a single vPC interface policy group has been used. If the intent were for four separate vPCs to be created, four separate vPC interface policy groups would be needed. For the eight ports to be correctly aggregated into a vPC, it is important that the switches also be configured in the same vPC domain.

Figure 6-14 shows a slightly different interpretation of interface profiles compared to the example in Figure 6-13. With the interpretation depicted earlier, a single interface profile needs to be created for each individual switch, and a separate interface profile needs to be created for each vPC switch pair. Such an approach enables the creation of interface profiles at the time of switch deployment; there is then no need to create interface profiles when port assignments are being made. Under the interpretation shown in Figure 6-14, however, separate interface profiles may be used for each interface configuration use case.

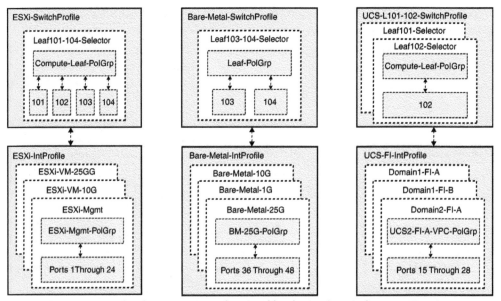

Figure 6-14 *Example of Separate Interface Profiles for Each Interface Use Case*

The interface profile presented in Figure 6-14 assumes that all port assignments for all ESXi hypervisors in the network will be allocated to a single interface profile called ESXi-IntProfile. Multiple switch profiles reference the interface profile. With this approach, exactly the same port assignments are made on all switches whose switch profiles reference the given interface profile.

NOTE   The examples presented in this section are just that: examples. There is no recommended approach for interface and switch profile design. An important benefit of profiles is their flexibility. You need to understand what an interface profile does and consider the benefits and drawbacks of any given approach and decide which approach will work best in any given environment. Although the approaches outlined are not mutually exclusive, it usually makes sense to stick to a single approach in a given environment. For example, if a defined set of switch ports will always be dedicated to a given use case across large numbers of switches and if ports can be preconfigured, it might make sense to consider an approach similar to the one outlined in Figure 6-14. This also enables quick audits of all port assignments related to the specific platform for which the interface profiles were defined. On the other hand, if quick auditability of port assignments on any given switch in the environment is most important and the use of scripting is not desirable, it might be more feasible to reach this goal by using an approach similar to the one outlined in Figure 6-13.

NOTE   Note that even though ACI allows multiple switch profiles to reference a given switch node ID, ACI does not allow the assignment of different switch policy groups to a given switch.

Table 6-12 summarizes the types of profiles and selectors covered in this section.

Table 6-12   Access Policy Profiles and Selectors

Object Name	Definition
Interface profile	An interface profile is a collection of interface mappings that gets bound to switch IDs through its association with one or more switch profiles.
Interface selector	An interface selector is a child object of an interface profile that ties an interface policy group to one or more port IDs. Since switch associations are determined by switch profiles and not interface profiles, interface selectors only determine port ID associations and not the list of switches to which the interface policy groups should be assigned.
Switch profile	A switch profile is a collection of switch policy group-to-node ID mappings that binds policy to switch IDs using switch selectors. Switch profiles reference interface profiles and deploy the port configurations defined in the interface profiles to switches to which the switch profile is bound. There are two types of switch profiles: leaf profiles and spine profiles.
Switch selector	A switch selector is a child object of a switch profile that associates a switch policy group to one or more node IDs.

Configuring Switch Profiles and Interface Profiles

To configure an interface profile, navigate to the Access Policies menu, double-click Interfaces, open Leaf Interfaces, right-click Profiles, and select Create Leaf Interface Profile, as shown in Figure 6-15.

Figure 6-15   *Navigating to the Leaf Interface Profile Creation Wizard*

In the Create Leaf Interface Profile wizard, type in an object name and click Submit, as illustrated in Figure 6-16. Note that interface selectors can be directly configured from within this wizard if desired.

Figure 6-16 *Configuring a Leaf Interface Profile*

To create a switch profile, navigate to the Access Policies menu, double-click Switches, open Leaf Switches, right-click Profiles, and select Create Leaf Profile, as shown in Figure 6-17.

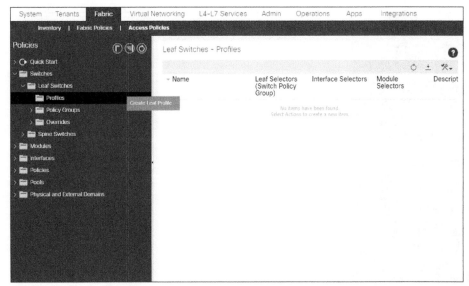

Figure 6-17 *Navigating to the Leaf Switch Profile Creation Wizard*

In the Create Leaf Profile wizard, type in the switch profile name and associate the switch profile with node IDs through the configuration of switch selectors, which are shown with the label Leaf Selectors in Figure 6-18. Then click Next.

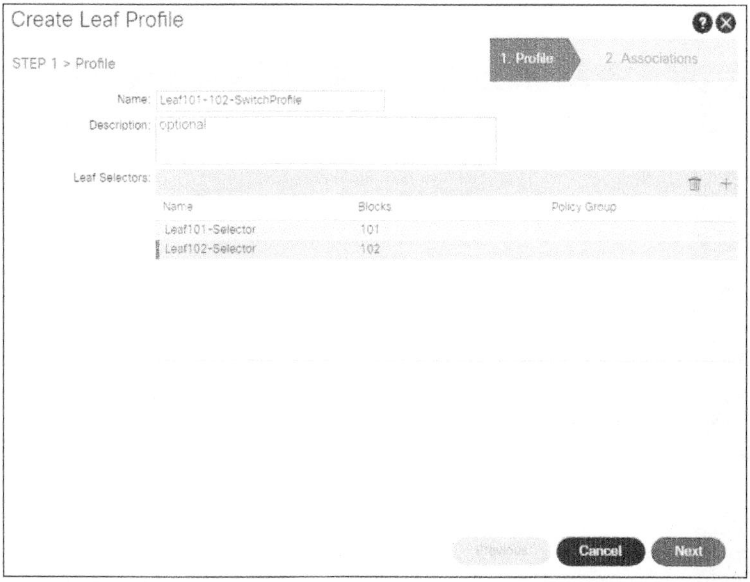

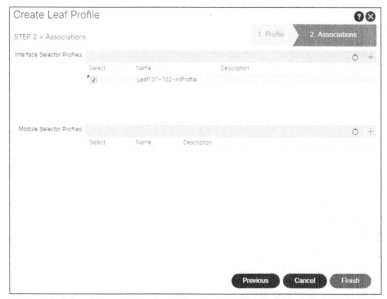

Figure 6-18 *Associating a Switch Profile to Node IDs Using Switch Selectors*

Finally, associate interface profiles to the new switch profile. In the window displayed in Figure 6-19, interface profiles are referred to as "leaf interface selectors." Click Finish after selecting the proper interface profile(s) from the list.

Figure 6-19 *Associating Interface Profiles to the New Switch Profile*

The screens shown in Figures 6-15 through 6-19 show configuration of the objects also presented on the right side of Figure 6-13. After switch profiles and interface profiles have been created, their association can be confirmed under **Fabric > Access Policies > Switches > Leaf Switches > Profiles**, as shown in Figure 6-20.

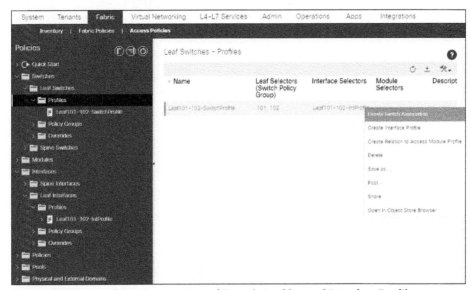

Figure 6-20 *Verifying Association of Switch Profiles and Interface Profiles*

These configurations can also be done via the APIC CLI, using the commands shown in Example 6-2.

Example 6-2 *CLI Equivalents for Interface and Switch Configurations*

```
apic1# show running-config leaf-interface-profile Leaf101-102-IntProfile
  leaf-interface-profile Leaf101-102-IntProfile
apic1# show running-config leaf-profile Leaf101-102-SwitchProfile
  leaf-profile Leaf101-102-SwitchProfile
    leaf-group Leaf101-Selector
      leaf 101
    leaf-group Leaf102-Selector
      leaf 102
    exit
    leaf-interface-profile Leaf101-102-IntProfile
```

Stateless Networking in ACI

The approach of using node IDs, switch profiles, and interface profiles and not tying configurations to physical hardware is called *stateless networking*.

Stateless networking has the benefit of minimizing the time to recover from hardware issues. Sometimes, it also enables expedited data center network migrations.

If a switch needs to be returned to Cisco due to hardware issues, an administrator can easily migrate the switch configurations to a new switch by decommissioning the switch from the

Fabric Membership view and commissioning a replacement switch using the previous node ID. All old optics can be reseated into the same port IDs to which they were earlier attached. Cables can then be connected to the previously assigned ports.

Alternatively, switch profiles assigned to the leaf in question can be assigned to a new node ID, and all port configurations carry over to the new node ID, ensuring that administrators do not have to modify port configurations. There are caveats to this approach when virtual port channels are deployed, but a strategy can almost always be identified to expedite the overall process.

If a data center network migration needs to take place and an ACI fabric needs to be upgraded to new hardware, it is most likely that a process can be identified to allow for re-allocation of switch profiles to new node IDs or re-association of interface profiles to new switch profiles to speed up the migration process.

Bringing It All Together

When learning new concepts, it sometimes helps to have a visual summary of the concepts to aid in learning. This section provides such a visual aid and also aims to draw a bigger picture of how the concepts in this chapter and Chapter 5, "Tenant Building Blocks," relate to one another.

Access Policies Hierarchy in Review

Figure 6-21 provides a visual representation of the objects covered in this chapter and how they relate with one another.

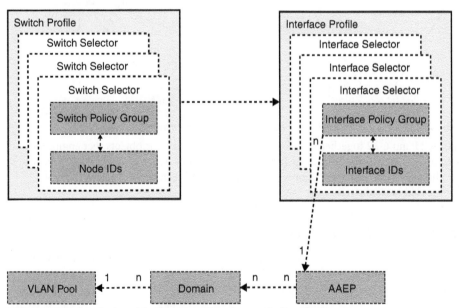

Figure 6-21 *Relationship Between Key Access Policy Objects*

Keep in mind that administrators are not limited in the number of times they can instanti-ate any of the types of objects depicted in Figure 6-21. The one-to-one relationships and one-to-many relationships shown only apply to the relationships between these subobjects in the access policies hierarchy.

One of the key things to remember from this diagram is that multiple interface policy groups can reference a single AAEP. However, any given interface policy group can reference one and only one AAEP. Also remember that a domain can reference no more than one VLAN pool, even though multiple domains can technically share a VLAN pool.

Access Policies and Tenancy in Review

Figure 6-22 summarizes the critical relationships between the access policies and tenant logical policy model subtrees. It illustrates how domains serve as the central object that tenant administrators use to map EPGs to the underlying physical infrastructure.

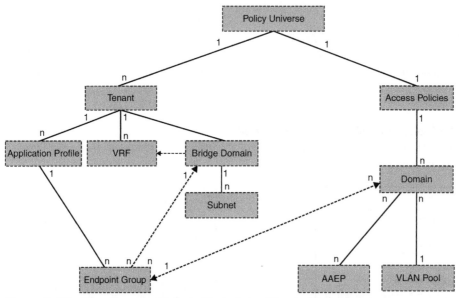

Figure 6-22 *How Tenancy Links to Underlying Physical Infrastructure*

Figures 6-21 and 6-22 together show some of the most important objects that engineers deal with on a day-to-day basis in ACI. More often than not, when port configuration issues occur, the objects in these two figures and the configured relationships between these objects should be evaluated first.

Exam Preparation Tasks

As mentioned in the section "How to Use This Book" in the Introduction, you have a couple of choices for exam preparation: Chapter 17, "Final Preparation," and the exam simulation questions in the Pearson Test Prep Software Online.

Review All Key Topics

Review the most important topics in this chapter, noted with the Key Topic icon in the outer margin of the page. Table 6-13 lists these key topics and the page number on which each is found.

Table 6-13   Key Topics for Chapter 6

Key Topic Element	Description	Page Number
Paragraph	Defines VLAN pools	159
Paragraph	Describes static and dynamic VLAN allocation	159
Paragraph	Describes domains	160
List	Outlines the types of domains in ACI	161
Paragraph	Touches on challenges related to VLAN pool overlap across multiple domains	164
Paragraph	Defines AAEPs	165
Paragraph	Defines interface policies	169
Paragraph	Defines interface policy groups	169
Table 6-6	Describes the types of interface policy groups in ACI	170
Paragraph	Calls out which types of interface policy groups are fully reusable	171
Table 6-7	Describes the types of interface policies available in ACI	171
Paragraph	Defines switch policies and switch policy groups	174
Table 6-10	Describes the most commonly deployed switch policies in ACI	174
Table 6-12	Describes access policy profiles and selectors	179

Complete Tables and Lists from Memory

Print a copy of Appendix C, "Memory Tables" (found on the companion website), or at least the section for this chapter, and complete the tables and lists from memory. Appendix D, "Memory Tables Answer Key" (also on the companion website), includes completed tables and lists you can use to check your work.

Define Key Terms

Define the following key terms from this chapter and check your answers in the glossary:

VLAN pool, static VLAN allocation, dynamic VLAN allocation, domain, physical domain, external bridge domain, external routed domain, Virtual Machine Manager (VMM) domain, attachable access entity profile (AAEP), interface policy, MisCabling Protocol (MCP), interface policy group, interface profile, interface selector, switch profile, switch selector, leaf selector, spine selector

CHAPTER 7

Implementing Access Policies

This chapter covers the following topics:

Configuring ACI Switch Ports: This section addresses practical implementation of ACI switch port configurations.

Configuring Access Policies Using Quick Start Wizards: This section shows how to configure access policies using quick start wizards.

Additional Access Policy Configurations: This section reviews implementation procedures for a handful of other less common access policies.

This chapter covers the following exam topics:

- 1.5 Implement ACI policies

  - 1.5.a access

  - 1.5.b fabric

Chapter 6, "Access Policies," covers the theory around access policies and the configuration of a limited number of objects available under the Access Policies menu. This chapter completes the topic of access policies by covering the configuration of all forms of Ethernet-based switch port connectivity available in ACI.

"Do I Know This Already?" Quiz

The "Do I Know This Already?" quiz allows you to assess whether you should read this entire chapter thoroughly or jump to the "Exam Preparation Tasks" section. If you are in doubt about your answers to these questions or your own assessment of your knowledge of the topics, read the entire chapter. Table 7-1 lists the major headings in this chapter and their corresponding "Do I Know This Already?" quiz questions. You can find the answers in Appendix A, "Answers to the 'Do I Know This Already?' Questions."

Table 7-1 "Do I Know This Already?" Section-to-Question Mapping

Foundation Topics Section	Questions
Configuring ACI Switch Ports	1–5
Configuring Access Policies Using Quick Start Wizards	6
Additional Access Policy Configurations	7–10

1. An administrator has configured a leaf interface, but it appears to have the status out-of-service. What does this mean?

    a.   The port has a bad transceiver installed.

    b.   The server behind the port has failed to PXE boot, and the port has been shut down.

    c.   This status reflects the fact that access policies have been successfully deployed.

    d.   The port has been administratively disabled.

2. Where would you go to configure a vPC domain in ACI?

    a.   Fabric > Access Policies > Policies > Switch > Virtual Port Channel default

    b.   Fabric > Access Policies > Interfaces > Leaf Interfaces > Policy Groups

    c.   Fabric > Access Policies > Policies > Switch > VPC Domain

    d.   Fabric > Fabric Policies > Policies > Switch > Virtual Port Channel default

3. True or false: To configure an LACP port channel, first create a leaf access port policy group and then add a port channel policy to the interface policy group.

    a.   True

    b.   False

4. True or false: To forward traffic destined to an endpoint behind a vPC, switches within the fabric encapsulate each packet twice and forward a copy separately to the loopback 0 tunnel endpoint of each vPC peer.

    a.   True

    b.   False

5. True or false: The only way to enable CDP in ACI is through the use of interface overrides.

    a.   True

    b.   False

6. True or false: The Configure Interface wizard in ACI can be used to make new port assignments using preconfigured interface policy groups.

    a.   True

    b.   False

7. True or false: To configure a fabric extender (FEX), you first create a FEX profile and then configure an access port selector from the parent leaf down to the FEX with the Connected to FEX checkbox enabled.

    a.   True

    b.   False

8. Which of the following are valid steps in implementing MCP on all 20 VLANs on a switch? (Choose all that apply.)

   a. Enable MCP at the switch level.

   b. Ensure that MCP has been enabled on all desired interfaces through interface policies.

   c. Select the Enable MCP PDU per VLAN checkbox.

   d. Enable MCP globally by toggling the Admin State to Enabled and defining a key.

9. True or false: With dynamic port breakouts, a port speed can be lowered, but a dramatic loss occurs in the forwarding capacity of the switch.

   a. True

   b. False

10. True or false: ACI preserves dot1q CoS bits within packets by default.

   a. True

   b. False

Foundation Topics

Configuring ACI Switch Ports

Put yourself in the shoes of an engineer working at a company that has decided to deploy all new applications into ACI. Looking at a platform with an initial focus on greenfield deployments as opposed to the intricacies of migrations can often lead to better logical designs that fully leverage the capabilities of the solution.

Imagine as part of this exercise that you have been asked to accommodate a newly formed business unit within your company, focusing on multiplayer gaming. This business unit would like to be able to patch its server operating systems independently and outside of regular IT processes and to have full autonomy over its applications with close to zero IT oversight beyond coordination of basic security policies. The business unit thinks it can achieve better agility if it is not bound by processes dictated by IT. Aside from whether deploying a shadow environment alongside a production environment is even desirable, is a setup like this even feasible with ACI? By thinking about this question while reading through the following sections, you may gain insights into how access policies can be used to share underlying infrastructure among tenants in ACI.

Configuring Individual Ports

This section shows how to deploy access policies for two new multiplayer gaming servers. Assume that each of these new servers has a single 10 Gbps network card and does not support port channeling. Let's say that the network engineers configuring switch ports for connectivity to these servers want to enable LLDP and CDP to have visibility into host names, if advertised by the servers. They also decide to auto-detect speed and duplex settings to reduce the need for their team to have to coordinate network card upgrades with the business unit.

NOTE   This chapter demonstrates a wide variety of common port configurations through examples. The examples are not meant to imply that implementation of auto-negotiation, LLDP, and CDP toward servers outside an organization's administrative control is a best practice. Where the intent is to convey that something is a best practice, this book explicitly says so.

To configure an interface policy with LLDP enabled, navigate to **Fabric > Access Policies > Policies > Interface**, right-click LLDP Interface, and select Create LLDP Interface Policy. Figure 7-1 shows an interface policy with LLDP enabled bidirectionally.

It is often good practice to use explicit policies. Auto-negotiation of port speed and duplex settings can be achieved by using a link level policy. To create a link level policy, navigate to **Fabric > Access Policies > Policies > Interface**, right-click Link Level, and select Create Link Level Policy.

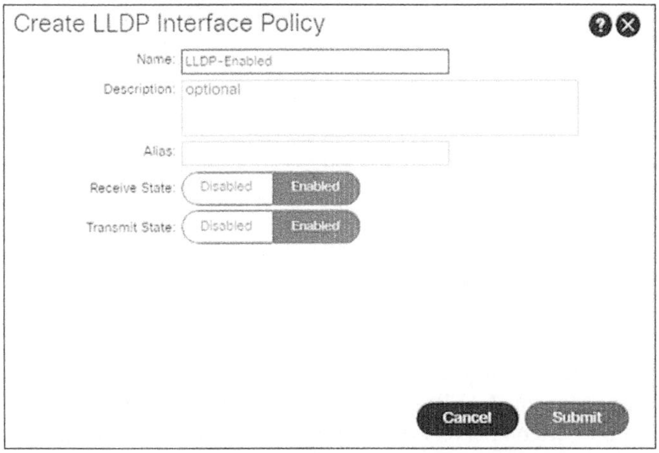

Figure 7-1   *Configuring an LLDP Interface Policy*

Figure 7-2 shows the settings for a link level policy. By default, Speed is set to Inherit, and Auto Negotiation is set to On to allow the link speed to be determined by the transceiver, medium, and capabilities of the connecting server. The ***Link Debounce Interval*** setting delays reporting of a link-down event to the switch supervisor. The Forwarding Error Correction (FEC) setting determines the error correction technique used to detect and correct errors in transmitted data without the need for data retransmission.

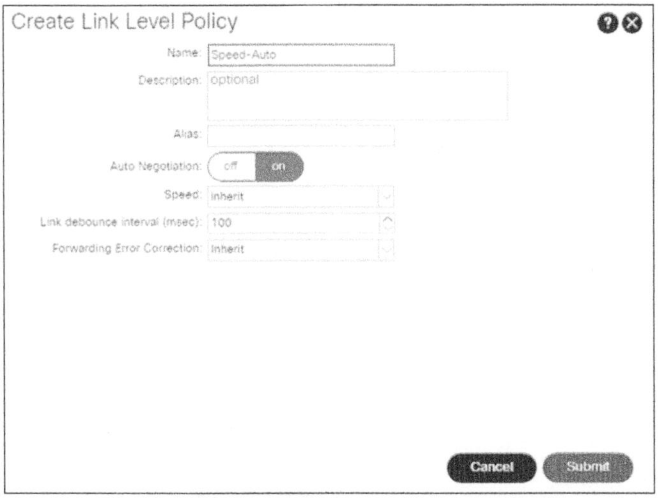

Figure 7-2   *Configuring a Link Level Interface Policy*

To create a policy with CDP enabled, navigate to **Fabric > Access Policies > Policies > Interface**, right-click CDP Interface, and select CDP Interface Policy. Figure 7-3 shows an interface policy with CDP enabled.

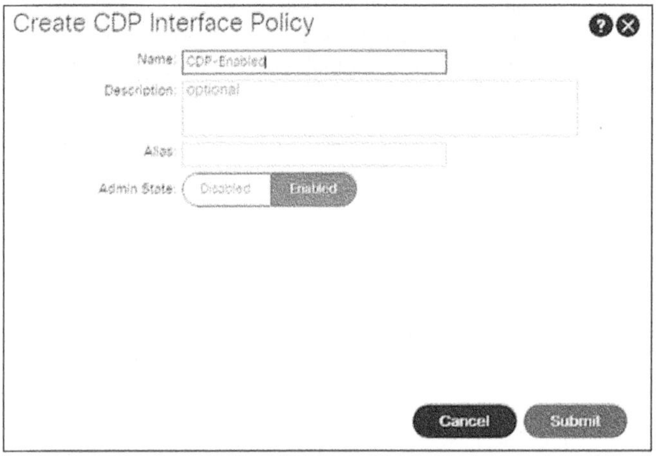

Figure 7-3   *Configuring a CDP Interface Policy*

In addition to interface policies, interface policy groups need to reference a global access policy (an AAEP) for interface deployment. AAEPs can often be reused. Figure 7-4 shows the creation of an AAEP named Bare-Metal-Servers-AAEP. By associating the domain phys as shown in Figure 7-4, you enable any servers configured with the noted AAEP to map EPGs to switch ports using VLAN IDs 300 through 499.

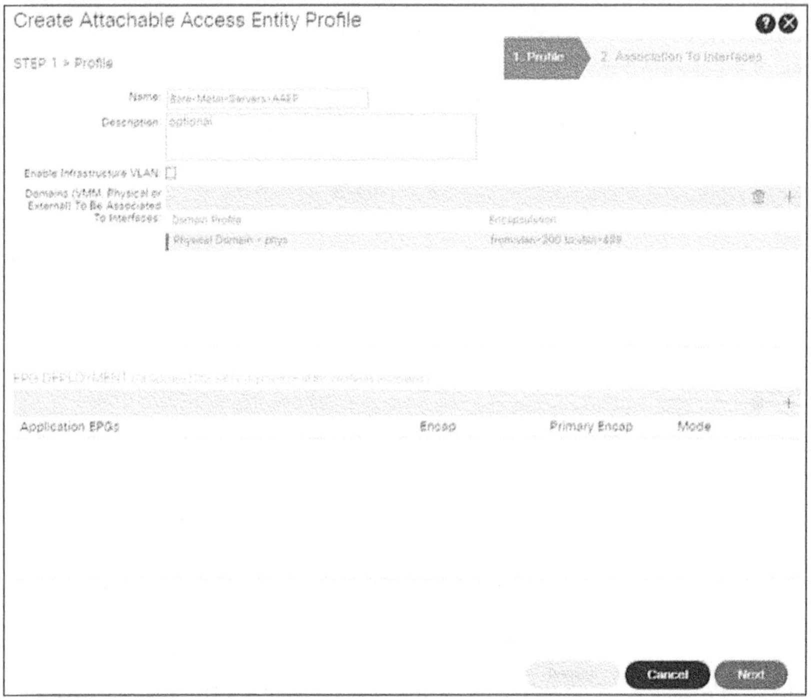

Figure 7-4   *Configuring an AAEP*

With interface policies and global policies created, it is time to create an interface policy group to be applied to ports.

To create an interface policy group for individual (non-aggregated) switch ports, navigate to **Fabric > Access Policies > Interfaces > Leaf Interfaces > Policy Groups**, right-click the Leaf Access Port option, and select Create Leaf Access Port Policy Group.

Figure 7-5 shows the association of the interface policies and AAEP created earlier with an interface policy group. Because policy groups for individual ports are fully reusable, a generic name not associated with any one server might be most beneficial for the interface policy group.

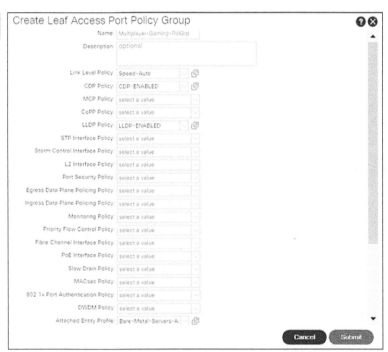

Figure 7-5 *Configuring a Leaf Access Port Policy Group*

Next, the interface policy group needs to be mapped to switch ports. Let's say a new switch has been procured and will be dedicated to multiplayer gaming servers for the business unit. The switch, which has already been commissioned, has node ID 101 and a switch profile. An interface profile has also been linked with the switch profile.

To associate an interface policy with ports, navigate to the desired interface profile, click on the Tools menu, and select Create Access Port Selector, as shown in Figure 7-6.

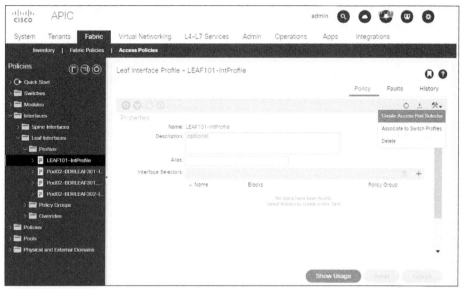

Figure 7-6 *Navigating to the Create Access Port Selector Window*

Figure 7-7 demonstrates the association of the new interface policy group with ports 1/45 and 1/46. Since this is a contiguous block of ports, you can use a hyphen to list the ports. After you click Submit, the interface policy group is deployed on the selected switch ports on all switches referenced by the interface profile.

Figure 7-7 *Mapping Ports to an Interface Policy Group*

Back under the leaf interface profile, notice that an entry should be added in the Interface Selectors view (see Figure 7-8).

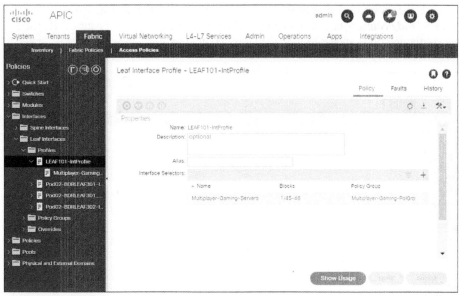

Figure 7-8 *Port Mappings Added to the Interface Selector View*

Double-click the entry to view the Access Port Selector page. As shown in Figure 7-9, ports that are mapped to an interface policy group as a contiguous block cannot be individually deleted from the port block. This might pose a problem if a single port that is part of a port block needs to be deleted and repurposed at some point in the future. Therefore, use of hyphens to group ports together is not always suitable.

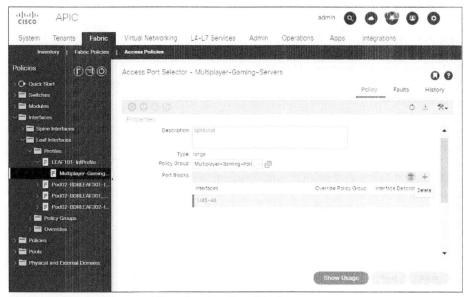

Figure 7-9 *Ports Lumped Together in a Port Block*

In the GUI, the operational state of ports can be verified under **Fabric > Inventory > Pod number > Node Name > Interfaces > Physical Interfaces**. According to Figure 7-10, the newly configured ports appear to have the Usage column set to Discovery.

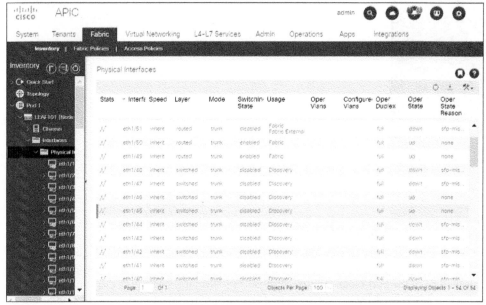

Figure 7-10 *Verifying the Status of Physical Interfaces in the ACI GUI*

Example 7-1 shows how to verify the operational status of ports in the switch CLI.

Example 7-1 *Verifying Port Status via the ACI Switch CLI*

```
LEAF101# show interface ethernet 1/45-46 status
-----------------------------------------------------------------------------
Port         Name         Status       Vlan     Duplex   Speed    Type
-----------------------------------------------------------------------------
Eth1/45      --           out-of-ser trunk      full     10G      10Gbase-SR
Eth1/46      --           out-of-ser trunk      full     10G      10Gbase-SR
```

What does the status "out-of-service" actually mean? When this status appears for operational fabric downlink ports, it simply means that tenant policies have not yet been layered on top of the configured access policies.

Table 7-2 summarizes port usage types that may appear in the GUI.

Table 7-2 Port Usages

Port Usage	Description
Blacklist	Blacklist indicates that a port has been disabled either by an administrator or by an APIC having detected anomalies with the port. Anomalies can include wiring errors or switches with nonmatching fabric IDs connecting to the fabric.
Controller	ACI detects an APIC controller attached to the port.
Discovery	The port is not forwarding user traffic because no tenant policies have been enabled over the port. This can be due to the lack of an EPG mapping or routing configuration on the port. This is the default state for all fabric downlinks.
EPG	At least one EPG has been correctly associated with the port. This is a valid state even if the port is disabled.
Fabric	Fabric indicates that a port functions or can potentially function as a fabric uplink for connectivity between leaf and spine switches. By default, fabric ports have Usage set to both Fabric and Fabric External until cabling is attached or a configuration change takes place.
Fabric External	Fabric External indicates that a port functions as an L3Out, peering with some switch or router outside the fabric. By default, fabric ports have Usage set to both Fabric and Fabric External until cabling is attached or a configuration change takes place.
Infra	Infra indicates that a port is trunking the overlay VLAN.

The APIC CLI commands shown in Example 7-2 are the equivalent of the configurations completed via the GUI. Notice that the LLDP setting does not appear in the output. This is because not all commands appear in the output of the APIC CLI running configuration. Use the command **show running-config all** to see all policy settings, including those that deviate for default values for a parameter.

Example 7-2 *APIC CLI Configurations Equivalent to the GUI Configurations Demonstrated*

```
APIC1# show run
(...output truncated for brevity...)
template policy-group Multiplayer-Gaming-PolGrp
    cdp enable
    vlan-domain member phys type phys
    exit
leaf-interface-profile LEAF101-IntProfile
    leaf-interface-group Multiplayer-Gaming-Servers
      interface ethernet 1/45-46
      policy-group Multiplayer-Gaming-PolGrp
      exit
    exit
```

> **NOTE** Switch port configurations, like all other configurations in ACI, can be scripted or automated using Python, Ansible, Postman, or Terraform or using workflow orchestration solutions such as UCS Director.

Configuring Port Channels

Let's say that the business unit running the multiplayer project wants a server deployed using LACP, but it has purchased only a single leaf switch, so dual-homing the server to a pair of leaf switches is not an option. Before LACP port channels can be deployed in ACI, you need to configure an interface policy with LACP enabled. To do so, navigate to **Fabric > Access Policies > Policies > Interface**, right-click Port Channel, and select Create Port Channel Policy. The window shown in Figure 7-11 appears.

Figure 7-11 *Configuring a Port Channel Interface Policy with LACP Enabled*

The function of the Mode setting LACP Active should be easy to understand. Table 7-3 details the most commonly used Control settings available for ACI port channels.

Table 7-3 Common Control Settings for ACI Port Channel Configuration

Control Setting	Description
Fast Select Hot Standby Ports	This setting enables fast select for hot standby ports. Enabling this feature makes possible the faster selection of a hot standby port when the last active port in the port channel is going down.
Graceful Convergence	This setting ensures optimal failover of links in an LACP port channel if the port channel or virtual port channel configured with this setting connects to Nexus devices.

Control Setting	Description
Suspend Individual Port	With this setting configured, LACP suspends a bundled port if it does not receive LACP packets from its peer port. When this setting is not enabled, LACP moves such ports into the Individual state.
Symmetric Hashing	With this setting enabled, bidirectional traffic is forced to use the same physical interface, and each physical interface in the port channel is effectively mapped to a set of flows. When an administrator creates a policy with Symmetric Hashing enabled, ACI exposes a new field for selection of a hashing algorithm.

After you create a port channel interface policy, you can create a port channel interface policy group for each individual port channel by navigating to **Fabric > Access Policies > Policies > Interface > Leaf Interfaces > Policy Groups**, right-clicking PC Interface, and selecting Create PC Interface Policy Group. Figure 7-12 shows the grouping of several policies to create a basic port channel interface policy group.

Figure 7-12 *Configuring a Port Channel Interface Policy Group*

You use an access selector to associate the interface policy group with the desired ports. If the intent is to configure ports 1/31 and 1/32 without lumping these ports into a single port block, it might make sense to first associate a single port with the port channel interface policy group and then add the next port as a separate port block. Figure 7-13 demonstrates the association of port 1/31 on Leaf 101 with the interface policy group.

Figure 7-13   *Mapping Ports to a Port Channel Interface Policy Group*

To add the second port to the port channel, click on the **+** sign in the Port Blocks section, as shown in Figure 7-14, to create a new port block.

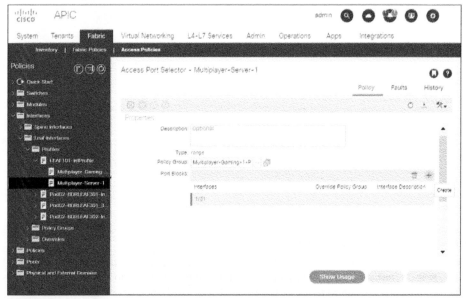

Figure 7-14   *Navigating to the Create Access Port Block Page*

Finally, you can add port 1/32 as a new port block, as shown in Figure 7-15.

Figure 7-15 *Adding a New Port Block to an Access Port Selector*

Example 7-3, taken from the Leaf 101 CLI, verifies that Ethernet ports 1/31 and 1/32 have indeed been bundled into an LACP port channel and that they are up. Why was there no need to assign an ID to the port channel? The answer is that ACI itself assigns port channel IDs to interface bundles.

Example 7-3 *Switch CLI-Based Verification of Port Channel Configuration*

```
LEAF101# show port-channel summary
Flags:  D - Down          P - Up in port-channel (members)
        I - Individual   H - Hot-standby (LACP only)
        s - Suspended    r - Module-removed
        S - Switched     R - Routed
        U - Up (port-channel)
        M - Not in use. Min-links not met
        F - Configuration failed
--------------------------------------------------------------------------------
Group Port-         Type    Protocol  Member Ports
      Channel
--------------------------------------------------------------------------------
1     Po1(SU)       Eth     LACP      Eth1/6(P)       Eth1/8(P)
2     Po2(SU)       Eth     LACP      Eth1/31(P)      Eth1/32(P)
```

You have already learned that port channel interface policy groups should ideally not be reused, especially on a single switch. But why is this the case? Figure 7-16 shows that an administrator has created a new interface selector and has mistakenly associated the same port channel interface policy group with ports 1/35 and 1/36. Note in this figure that using commas to separate the interface IDs leads to the creation of separate port blocks.

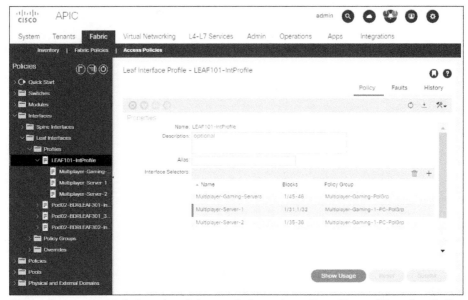

Figure 7-16 *Multiple Interface Selectors Referencing a Port Channel Interface Policy Group*

The setup in Figure 7-16 would lead to the switch CLI output presented in Example 7-4.

Example 7-4 *Interfaces Bundled Incorrectly Due to PC Interface Policy Group Reuse*

```
LEAF101# show port-channel summary
Flags:  D - Down        P - Up in port-channel (members)
        I - Individual  H - Hot-standby (LACP only)
        s - Suspended   r - Module-removed
        S - Switched    R - Routed
        U - Up (port-channel)
        M - Not in use. Min-links not met
        F - Configuration failed
--------------------------------------------------------------------------------
Group Port-        Type      Protocol    Member Ports
      Channel
--------------------------------------------------------------------------------
1     Po1(SU)      Eth       LACP        Eth1/6(P)     Eth1/8(P)
2     Po2(SU)      Eth       LACP        Eth1/31(P)    Eth1/32(P)    Eth1/35(D)
                                         Eth1/36(D)
```

To the administrator's surprise, ports 1/35 and 1/36 have been added to the previously created port channel. The initial assumption may have been that because a different interface selector name was selected, a new port channel would be created. This is not the case.

Example 7-5 shows the CLI-equivalent configuration of the port channel interface policy group and the assignment of the policy group to ports on Leaf 101.

Example 7-5 *APIC CLI Configuration for the Port Channel Interfaces*

```
template port-channel Multiplayer-Gaming-1-PC-PolGrp
    cdp enable
    vlan-domain member phys type phys
    channel-mode active
    speed 10G
    no negotiate auto
    exit
  leaf-interface-profile LEAF101-IntProfile
    leaf-interface-group Multiplayer-Server-1
      interface ethernet 1/31
      interface ethernet 1/32
      channel-group Multiplayer-Gaming-1-PC-PolGrp
      exit
    exit
```

There is nothing that says you cannot reuse port channel or virtual port channel interface policy groups in new interface selector configurations if the intent truly is to bundle the new interfaces into a previously created port channel or virtual port channel. You may still question whether a port channel interface policy group or a vPC interface policy group can be reused on a different switch or vPC domain. As a best practice, you should avoid reuse of port channel and vPC interface policy groups when creating new port channels and vPCs to minimize the possibility of configuration mistakes.

NOTE You may not have noticed it, but the Control settings selected in the port channel interface policy shown earlier are Suspend Individual Ports, Graceful Convergence, and Fast Select Hot Standby Ports (refer to Figure 7.11). These settings are the default Control settings for LACP port channel interface policy groups in ACI. Unfortunately, these default Control settings are not always ideal. For example, LACP graceful convergence can lead to packet drops during port channel bringup and teardown when used to connect ACI switches to servers or non-Cisco switches that are not closely compliant with the LACP specification. As a general best practice, Cisco recommends keeping LACP graceful convergence enabled on port channels connecting to Nexus switches but disabling this setting when connecting to servers and non-Nexus switches.

Configuring Virtual Port Channel (vPC) Domains

When configuring switch ports to servers and appliances, it is best to dual-home devices to switches to prevent total loss of traffic if a northbound switch fails. Some servers can handle failover at the operating system level very well and may be configured using individual ports from a switch point of view, despite being dual-homed. Where a server intends to hash traffic across links dual-homed across a pair of switches, virtual port channeling needs to be configured.

vPC technology allows links that are physically connected to two different Cisco switches to appear to a downstream device as coming from a single device and part of a single port channel. The downstream device can be a switch, a server, or any other networking device that supports Link Aggregation Control Protocol (LACP) or static port channels.

Standalone Nexus NX-OS software does support vPCs, but there are fewer caveats to deal with in ACI because ACI does not leverage peer links. In ACI, the keepalives and cross-switch communication needed for forming vPC domains all traverse the fabric.

> **NOTE**   One limitation around vPC domain configuration in ACI that you should be aware of is that two vPC peer switches joined into a vPC domain must be of the same switch generation. This means you cannot form a vPC domain between a first-generation switch suffixed with TX and a newer-generation switch suffixed with EX, FX, or FX2. ACI does allow migration of first-generation switches that are in a vPC domain to higher-generation switches, but it typically requires 10 to 20 seconds of downtime for vPC-attached servers.

The business unit running the multiplayer gaming project has purchased three additional switches and can now make use of vPCs in ACI. Before configuring virtual port channels, vPC domains need to be identified.

To configure a vPC domain, navigate to **Fabric > Access Policies > Policies > Switch**, right-click Virtual Port Channel Default, and select Create VPC Explicit Protection Group. Figure 7-17 shows how to navigate to the Create VPC Explicit Protection Group wizard.

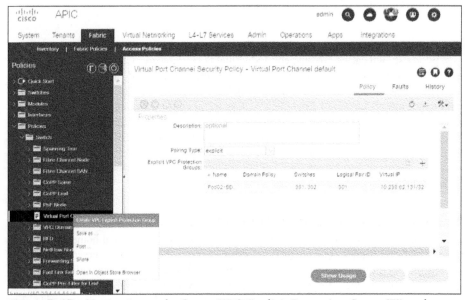

Figure 7-17   *Navigating to the Create VPC Explicit Protection Group Wizard*

Figure 7-18 shows how you can pair together two switches with node IDs 101 and 102 into vPC domain 21 by populating the Name, ID, Switch 1, and Switch 2 fields. Even though populating the Name field is mandatory, it has little impact on the configuration.

Figure 7-18 *Configuring a vPC Domain*

The only vPC failover parameter that can be tweaked in ACI at the time of writing is the *vPC peer dead interval*, which is the amount of time a leaf switch with a vPC secondary role waits following a vPC peer switch failure before assuming the role of vPC master. The default peer dead interval in ACI is 200 seconds. This value can be tuned between 5 and 600 seconds through configuration of a vPC domain policy, which can then be applied to the vPC explicit protection group.

NOTE   As a best practice, vPC domain IDs should be unique across each Layer 2 network. Problems can arise when more than one pair of vPC peer switches attached to a common Layer 2 network have the same vPC domain ID. This is because vPC domain IDs are a component in the generation of LACP system IDs.

The CLI-based equivalent of the vPC domain definition completed in this section is the command **vpc domain explicit 21 leaf 101 102**. Example 7-6 shows CLI verification of Leaf 101 and Leaf 102 having joined vPC domain ID 21. Note that the vPC peer status indicates that the peer adjacency with Leaf 102 has been formed, but the vPC keepalive status displays as Disabled. This is expected output from an operational vPC peering in ACI.

Example 7-6 *Verifying a vPC Peering Between Two Switches*

```
LEAF101# show vpc
Legend:
                (*) - local vPC is down, forwarding via vPC peer-link

vPC domain id                                   : 21
Peer status                                     : peer adjacency formed ok
vPC keep-alive status                           : Disabled
Configuration consistency status                : success
Per-vlan consistency status                     : success
Type-2 consistency status                       : success
vPC role                                        : primary, operational secondary
Number of vPCs configured                       : 1
Peer Gateway                                    : Disabled
Dual-active excluded VLANs                      : -
Graceful Consistency Check                      : Enabled
Auto-recovery status                            : Enabled (timeout = 240 seconds)
Operational Layer3 Peer                         : Disabled


vPC Peer-link status
---------------------------------------------------------------------------------
id    Port    Status Active vlans
--    ----    ------ ----------------------------------------------------------
1             up         -


vPC status
---------------------------------------------------------------------------------
id    Port    Status  Consistency   Reason              Active vlans
--    ------  ------- ------------- ---------            ----------------
```

 From a forwarding perspective, the result of creating a vPC explicit protection group is that ACI assigns a common virtual IP address to the loopback 1 interface on the two vPC peers. This new IP address functions as a tunnel endpoint within the fabric, enabling all other switches in the fabric to forward traffic to either of the two switches via equal-cost multipathing. For this to work, the two vPC switches advertise reachability of vPC-attached endpoints using the loopback 1 interface, and traffic toward all endpoints that are not vPC attached continues to be forwarded to the tunnel IP addresses of the loopback 0 interfaces.

NOTE A vPC domain is a Layer 2 construct. ACI spine switches do not function as connection points for servers and non-ACI switches at Layer 2. Therefore, vPC is not a supported function for spine switches.

Configuring Virtual Port Channels

Let's say you want to configure a resilient connection to a new multiplayer gaming server that does not support LACP but does support static port channeling. The first thing you need to do is to create a new interface policy that enables static port channeling. Figure 7-19 shows such a policy.

Create Port Channel Policy ❓❌

Name: Static-On

Description: optional

Alias:

Mode: Static Channel - Mode On
Not Applicable for FC PC

Control: Suspend Individual Port ×   Fast Select Hot Standby Ports ×

Minimum Number of Links: 1
Not Applicable for FEX PC/VPC and FC PC

Maximum Number of Links: 16
Not Applicable for FEX PC/VPC and FC PC

Cancel   Submit

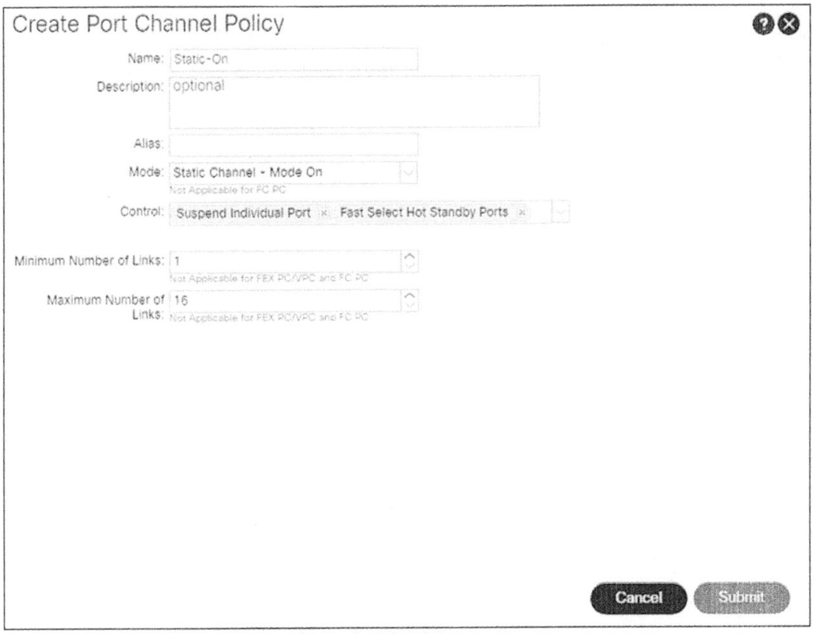

Figure 7-19 *Configuring an Interface Policy for Static Port Channeling*

Next, you can move onto the configuration of a vPC interface policy group by navigating to **Fabric > Access Policies > Policies > Interface > Leaf Interfaces > Policy Groups**, right-clicking VPC Interface, and selecting Create VPC Interface Policy Group. Figure 7-20 shows the configuration of a vPC interface policy group.

7

Create VPC Interface Policy Group ❓❌

Name: Multiplayer-Gaming-3-VPC-PolGr

Description: optional

Link Level Policy: 10Gbps

CDP Policy: CDP-ENABLED

MCP Policy: select a value

CoPP Policy: select a value

LLDP Policy: LLDP-ENABLED

STP Interface Policy: select a value

L2 Interface Policy: select a value

Port Security Policy: select a value

Egress Data Plane Policing Policy: select a value

Ingress Data Plane Policing Policy: select a value

Priority Flow Control Policy: select a value

Fibre Channel Interface Policy: select a value

Slow Drain Policy: select a value

MACsec Policy: select a value

Attached Entity Profile: Bare-Metal-Servers-AAEP

Port Channel Policy: Static-On

Monitoring Policy: select a value

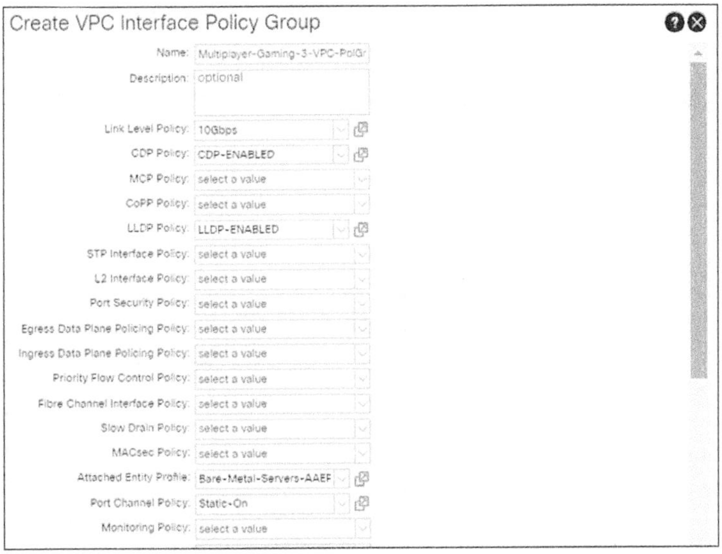

Figure 7-20 *Configuring a vPC Interface Policy Group*

Next, you need to associate the vPC interface policy group with interfaces on both vPC peers. The best way to associate policy to multiple switches simultaneously is to create an interface profile that points to all the desired switches.

Figure 7-21 shows that the process of creating an access port selector for a vPC is the same as the process of configuring access port selectors for individual ports and port channels.

Figure 7-21 *Applying vPC Access Port Selectors to an Interface Profile for vPC Peers*

The **show vpc** and **show port-channel summary** commands verify that the vPC has been created. As indicated in Example 7-7, vPC IDs are also auto-generated by ACI.

Example 7-7 *Verifying the vPC Configuration from the Switch CLI*

```
LEAF101# show vpc
Legend:
                (*) - local vPC is down, forwarding via vPC peer-link

vPC domain id                          : 21
Peer status                            : peer adjacency formed ok
vPC keep-alive status                  : Disabled
Configuration consistency status       : success
Per-vlan consistency status            : success
Type-2 consistency status              : success
vPC role                               : primary, operational secondary
Number of vPCs configured              : 2
Peer Gateway                           : Disabled
Dual-active excluded VLANs             : -
Graceful Consistency Check             : Enabled
Auto-recovery status                   : Enabled (timeout = 240 seconds)
Operational Layer3 Peer                : Disabled
```

```
vPC Peer-link status
------------------------------------------------------------------------------
id    Port    Status  Active vlans
--    ----    ------  ------------------------------------------------------
1             up      -

vPC status
------------------------------------------------------------------------------
id    Port    Status      Consistency     Reason        Active vlans
--    ----    ------      -------------   --------       ---------------
685   Po3     up          success         success        -

LEAF101# show port-channel summary
Flags:  D - Down        P - Up in port-channel (members)
        I - Individual  H - Hot-standby (LACP only)
        s - Suspended   r - Module-removed
        S - Switched    R - Routed
        U - Up (port-channel)
        M - Not in use. Min-links not met
        F - Configuration failed
--------------------------------------------------------------------------------
Group   Port-         Type     Protocol   Member Ports
        Channel
--------------------------------------------------------------------------------
1       Po1(SU)       Eth      LACP       Eth1/6(P)    Eth1/8(P)
2       Po2(SU)       Eth      LACP       Eth1/31(P)   Eth1/32(P)
3       Po3(SU)       Eth      NONE       Eth1/38(P)
```

Example 7-8 shows the APIC CLI configurations equivalent to the GUI-based vPC configuration performed in this section.

Example 7-8 *Configuring a vPC Using the APIC CLI*

```
template port-channel Multiplayer-Gaming-3-VPC-PolGrp
  cdp enable
  vlan-domain member phys type phys
  speed 10G
  no negotiate auto
  exit
leaf-interface-profile LEAF101-102-vPC-IntProfile
  leaf-interface-group Multiplayer-Server-3
    interface ethernet 1/38
    channel-group Multiplayer-Gaming-3-VPC-PolGrp vpc
    exit
  exit
```

The static port channel policy setting does not show up in the configuration. As shown in Example 7-9, by adding the keyword **all** to the command, you can confirm that the setting has been applied.

Example 7-9   *Using* **all** *to Include Defaults Not Otherwise Shown in the APIC CLI*

```
APIC1(config)# show running-config all template port-channel
Multiplayer-Gaming-3-VPC-PolGrp
(...output truncated for brevity...)
  template port-channel Multiplayer-Gaming-3-VPC-PolGrp
    no description
    lldp receive
    lldp transmit
    cdp enable
    vlan-domain member phys type phys
    channel-mode on
    lacp min-links 1
    lacp max-links 16
    no lacp symmetric-hash
      exit
    mcp enable
    spanning-tree bpdu-filter disable
    spanning-tree bpdu-guard disable
    speed 10G
    no negotiate auto
    exit
```

Configuring Ports Using AAEP EPGs

Even seasoned ACI engineers are often under the impression that EPG assignments can only be made under the Tenants menu. This is not true. Figure 7-22 shows the mapping of an EPG to VLAN 302. The mappings in this view require that users prefix the VLAN ID with **vlan-**.

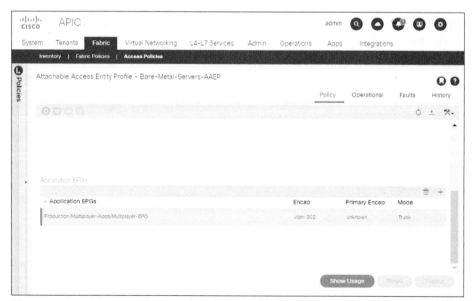

Figure 7-22   *Mapping One or More EPGs to All Ports Leveraging a Specific AAEP*

Figure 7-23 shows that after making this change, the newly configured ports, which all referenced the AAEP, transition out of the Usage status Discovery to EPG.

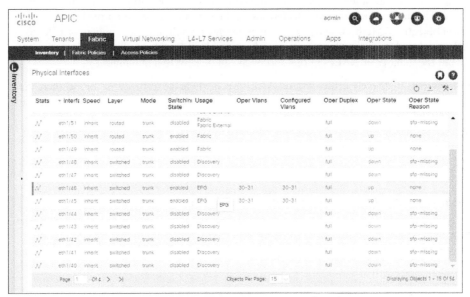

Figure 7-23 *Ports with AAEP Assignment Transitioned to the EPG State*

As shown in Example 7-10, the ports are no longer out of service. This indicates that tenant policies have successfully been layered on the access policies by using the AAEP.

Example 7-10 *Operational Ports with an Associated EPG Transition to Connected Status*

```
LEAF101# show interface ethernet 1/45-46, ethernet 1/31-32, ethernet 1/38 status
--------------------------------------------------------------------------------

Port         Name        Status       Vlan      Duplex    Speed    Type
--------------------------------------------------------------------------------

Eth1/31      --          connected    trunk     full      10G      10Gbase-SR
Eth1/32      --          connected    trunk     full      10G      10Gbase-SR
Eth1/38      --          connected    trunk     full      10G      10Gbase-SR
Eth1/45      --          connected    trunk     full      10G      10Gbase-SR
Eth1/46      --          connected    trunk     full      10G      10Gbase-SR
```

So, what are AAEP EPGs, and why use this method of EPG-to-VLAN assignment? Static path mappings in the Tenants view associate an EPG with a single port, port channel, or vPC. If a set of 10 EPGs need to be associated with 10 servers, a sum total of 100 static path assignments are needed. On the other hand, if exactly the same EPG-to-VLAN mappings are required for the 10 servers, the 10 assignments can be made once to an AAEP, allowing all switch ports referencing the AAEP to inherit the EPG-to-VLAN mappings. This reduces administrative overhead in some environments and eliminates configuration drift in terms of EPG assignments across the servers.

NOTE   Some engineers strictly stick with EPG-to-VLAN mappings that are applied under the Tenants menu, and others focus solely on AAEP EPGs. These options are not mutually exclusive. The method or methods selected should be determined based on the business and technical objectives. Methods like static path assignment result in large numbers of EPG-to-VLAN mappings because each port needs to be individually assigned all the desired mappings, but the number of AAEPs in this approach can be kept to a minimum.

In environments that solely center around AAEP EPGs, there are as many AAEPs as there are combinations of EPG-to-VLAN mappings. Therefore, the number of AAEPs in such environments is higher, but tenant-level mappings are not necessary. In environments in which automation scripts handle the task of assigning EPGs to hundreds of ports simultaneously, there may be little reason to even consider AAEP EPGs. However, not all environments center around scripting.

Implications of Initial Access Policy Design on Capabilities

What are some of the implications of the configurations covered so far in this chapter? The EPG trunked onto the object Bare-Metal-Servers-AAEP resides in the tenant Production. This particular customer wants to manage its own servers, so would it make more sense to isolate the customer's servers and applications in a dedicated tenant? The answer most likely is yes.

If a new tenant were built for the multiplayer gaming applications, the business unit could be provided not just visibility but configuration access to its tenant. Tasks like creating new EPGs and EPG-to-port mappings could then be offloaded to the business unit.

In addition, what happens if this particular customer wants to open up communication between the tenant and a specific subnet within the campus? In this case, a new external EPG may be needed to classify traffic originating from the campus subnet. Creating a new external EPG for L3Outs in already available VRF instances in the Production tenant could force a reevaluation of policies to ensure continuity of connectivity for other applications to the destination subnet. Sometimes, use of a new tenant can simplify the external EPG design and the enforcement of security policies.

Finally, what are the implications of the AAEP and domain design? If central IT manages ACI, there's really nothing to worry about. However, if all bare-metal servers in a fabric indeed leverage a common AAEP object as well as a common domain, how would central IT be able to prevent the gaming business unit from mistakenly mapping an EPG to a corporate IT server? How could central IT ensure that an unintended VLAN ID is not used for the mapping? The answer is that it cannot. This highlights the importance of good AAEP and domain design.

In summary, where there is a requirement for the configuration of a server environment within ACI to be offloaded to a customer or an alternate internal organization or even when there are requirements for complete segmentation of traffic in one environment (for example, production) and a new server environment, it often makes sense to use separate tenants, separate physical domains, and separate non-overlapping VLAN pools. Through enforce-ment of proper role-based access control (RBAC) and scope-limiting customer configuration changes to a specific tenant and relevant domains, central IT is then able to ensure that any configuration changes within the tenant do not impact existing operations in other server environments (tenants).

Configuring Access Policies Using Quick Start Wizards

All the configurations performed in the previous section can also be done using quick start wizards. There are two such wizards under the Access Policies view: the Configure Interface, PC, and vPC Wizard and the Configure Interface Wizard.

The Configure Interface, PC, and VPC Wizard

Under **Fabric > Access Policies > Quick Start,** click on Configure Interface, PC, and VPC. The page shown in Figure 7-24 appears. Everything from a switch profile-to-node ID associa-tion to interface policies and mapping configurations can be done in this simple view.

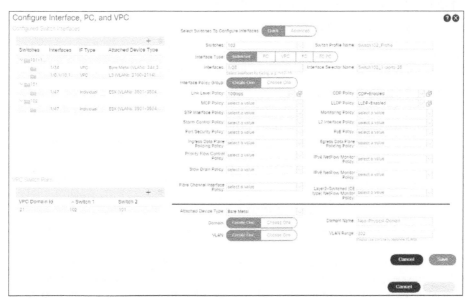

Figure 7-24 *The Configure Interface, PC, and VPC Wizard*

The Configure Interface Wizard

Under **Fabric > Access Policies > Quick Start,** notice the Configure Interface wizard. Click it to see the page shown in Figure 7-25. This page provides a convenient view for double-checking previously configured interface policy group settings before making port assignments.

Figure 7-25 *View of the Configure Interface Wizard*

Additional Access Policy Configurations

The access policies covered so far in this chapter apply to all businesses and ACI deployments. The sections that follow address the implementation of less common access policies.

Configuring Fabric Extenders

Fabric extenders (FEX) are a low-cost solution for low-bandwidth port attachment to a parent switch. Fabric extenders are less than ideal for high-bandwidth and low-latency use cases and do not have a lot of appeal in ACI due to feature deficiencies, such as analytics capabilities.

> **NOTE** Ideally, new ACI deployments should not leverage fabric extenders. This book includes coverage of FEX because it is a topic that can appear on the Implementing Cisco Application Centric Infrastructure DCACI 300-620 exam and because not all companies are fortunate enough to be able to remove fabric extenders from their data centers when first migrating to ACI.

Fabric extenders attach to ACI fabrics in much the same way they attach to NX-OS mode switches. However, ACI does not support dual-homing of fabric extenders to leaf switch pairs in an active/active FEX design. Instead, to make FEX-attached servers resilient to the loss of a single server uplink in ACI, you need to dual-home the servers to a pair of fabric extenders. Ideally, these fabric extenders connect to different upstream leaf switches that form a vPC domain. In such a situation, you can configure vPCs from the servers up to the fabric extenders to also protect server traffic against the failure of a single leaf switch.

There are two steps involved in implementing a fabric extender:

Step 1. Configure a FEX profile.

Step 2. Associate the FEX profile with the parent switch by configuring access policies down to the fabric extender.

After these two steps have been completed, you can configure FEX downlinks to servers by configuring access port selectors on the newly deployed FEX profile.

Let's say you want to deploy a fabric extender to enable low-bandwidth CIMC connections down to servers. To do so, navigate to **Fabric > Access Policies > Interfaces > Leaf Interfaces**, right-click Profiles, and select Create FEX Profile. The page shown in Figure 7-26 appears. The FEX Access Interface Selectors section is where the CIMC port mappings need to be implemented. Enter an appropriate name for the FEX interface profile and click Submit.

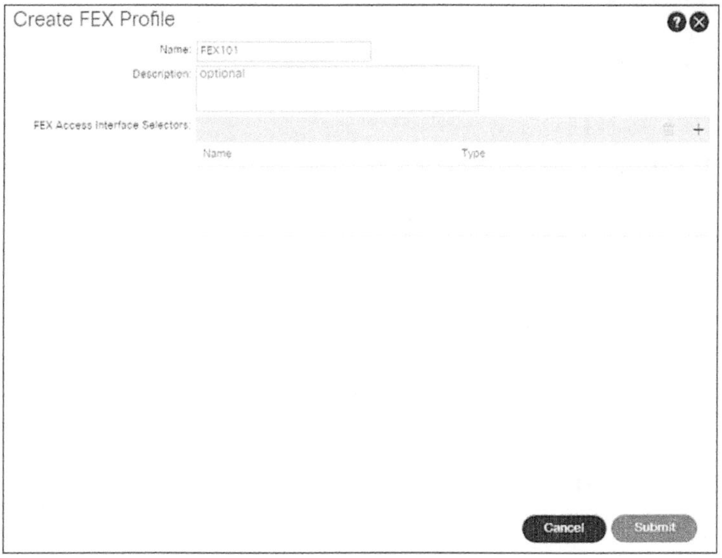

Figure 7-26   *Configuring a FEX Profile*

Next, navigate to the interface profile of the parent leaf and configure an interface selector. In Figure 7-27, ports 1/11 and 1/12 on Leaf 101 connect to uplink ports on the new fabric extender. To expose the list of available FEX profiles, enable the Connected to FEX checkbox and select the profile of the FEX connecting to the leaf ports.

Figure 7-27   *Associating a FEX Profile with a Parent Switch*

After you click Submit, ACI bundles the selected ports into a static port channel, as indicated by the output NONE in the Protocol column in Example 7-11. The FEX eventually transitions through several states before moving to the Online state.

Example 7-11 *Verifying FEX Association with a Parent Leaf Switch*

```
LEAF101# show port-channel summary
Flags:  D - Down         P - Up in port-channel (members)
        I - Individual   H - Hot-standby (LACP only)
        s - Suspended    r - Module-removed
        S - Switched     R - Routed
        U - Up (port-channel)
        M - Not in use. Min-links not met
        F - Configuration failed
--------------------------------------------------------------------------------
Group   Port-        Type    Protocol   Member Ports
        Channel
--------------------------------------------------------------------------------
1       Po1(SU)      Eth     LACP       Eth1/6(P)      Eth1/8(P)
2       Po2(SU)      Eth     LACP       Eth1/31(P)     Eth1/32(P)
3       Po3(SU)      Eth     NONE       Eth1/38(P)
4       Po4(SU)      Eth     NONE       Eth1/11(P)     Eth1/12(P)


LEAF101# show fex
 FEX            FEX            FEX            FEX
Number      Description       State          Model                 Serial
--------------------------------------------------------------------------------
 101           FEX0101        Online     N2K-C2248TP-1GE           XXXXX
```

When the FEX has been operationalized, access policies are still needed for FEX port connectivity down to CIMC ports. You can navigate to the FEX profile and configure an interface selector for these ports. Figure 7-28 shows connectivity for 24 FEX ports being prestaged using a newly created interface policy group for non-aggregated ports.

Figure 7-28 *Configuring FEX Downlinks to Servers via FEX Interface Profiles*

Example 7-12 shows how fabric extenders might be implemented via the APIC CLI.

Example 7-12   *Configuring a FEX and Downstream Connectivity via the APIC CLI*

```
APIC1# show running-config leaf-interface-profile LEAF101-IntProfile
(...output truncated for brevity...)
  leaf-interface-profile LEAF101-IntProfile
    leaf-interface-group Port-Channel-to-FEX101
      interface ethernet 1/11-12
      fex associate 101 template FEX101
      exit
    exit

APIC1# show running-config fex-profile FEX101
  fex-profile FEX101
    fex-interface-group Multiplayer-Gaming-CIMC
      interface ethernet 1/1-24
      policy-group Server-CIMC-PolGrp
      exit
    exit
```

NOTE   Not all ACI leaf switches can function as FEX parents.

Configuring Dynamic Breakout Ports

Cisco sells ACI leaf switches like the Nexus 93180YC-FX that are optimized for 10 Gbps/ 25 Gbps compute attachment use cases. It also offers switch models like the Nexus 9336C-FX2, whose 36 ports each support speeds of up to 100 Gbps.

Port speeds on platforms like the Nexus 9336C-FX2 can be lowered by seating a CVR-QSFP-10G adapter into a port, along with a supported 10 Gbps or 1 Gbps transceiver. Purchasing a platform like this and using CVR adapters to lower port speeds, however, could turn out to be an expensive approach when calculating the per-port cost because this approach makes suboptimal use of the forwarding capacity of the switch. This approach may still be deemed economical, however, if only a fraction of ports are "burned" this way.

Another approach is to dynamically split ports into multiple lower-speed connections. With *dynamic breakout ports*, a 40 Gbps switch port can be split into four independent and logical 10 Gbps ports. Likewise, a 100 Gbps port can be split into four independent and logical 25 Gbps ports. This does require special breakout cabling, but it allows customers to use a greater amount of the forwarding capacity of high-bandwidth ports.

Let's say you have just initialized two new high-density Nexus switches with node IDs 103 and 104. These two switches both support dynamic breakout ports. Imagine that you have been asked to deploy 12 new servers, and each server needs to be dual-homed to these new switches using 25 Gbps network cards. Since the ports on these particular switches are optimized for 100 Gbps connectivity, implementation of dynamic breakout ports can help. Splitting three 100 Gbps ports on each switch, in this case, yields the desired 12 25 Gbps connections from each leaf to the servers.

To deploy dynamic breakout ports, create a new interface selector on the interface profiles bound to each switch and select Create Leaf Breakout Port Group from the Interface Policy Group drop-down box, as shown in Figure 7-29.

Figure 7-29   *Navigating to the Create Leaf Breakout Port Group Page*

On the Create Leaf Breakout Port Group page, select a name for the new interface selector and select an option from the Breakout Map drop-down box. Figure 7-30 shows the option 25g-4x being selected, which implies that a 100 Gbps port will be broken out into four 25 Gbps ports.

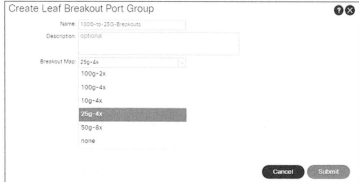

Figure 7-30   *Configuring Dynamic Port Breakouts*

When implementing the equivalent breakouts for any additional nodes, you may find that you can reuse the interface policy group that references the breakout map.

Once breakouts have been implemented on the desired ports on the switches, you can configure the desired access policies for the resulting subports. These subports resulting from dynamic breakouts need to be referenced using the numbering *module/port/subport*. Figure 7-31 illustrates access policies being applied to subports of interface 1/1—namely, logical ports 1/1/1, 1/1/2, 1/1/3, and 1/1/4.

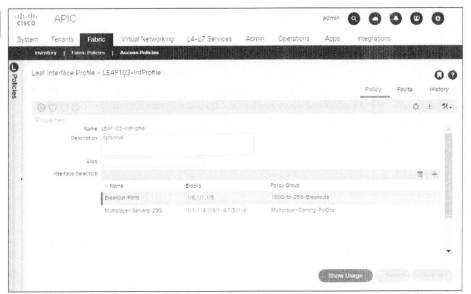

Figure 7-31 *Implementing Access Policies for Subports Within a Breakout Port*

Example 7-13 shows the APIC CLI commands that are equivalent to the GUI-based dynamic breakout port configurations implemented in this section.

Example 7-13 *Implementing Dynamic Breakout Ports via the APIC CLI*

```
leaf-interface-profile LEAF103-IntProfile
  leaf-interface-group Breakout-Ports
    interface ethernet 1/1
    interface ethernet 1/5
    interface ethernet 1/6
    breakout 25g-4x
    exit
  leaf-interface-group Multiplayer-Servers-25G
    interface ethernet 1/1/1-4
    interface ethernet 1/5/1-4
    interface ethernet 1/6/1-4
    policy-group Multiplayer-Gaming-PolGrp
    exit
  exit
```

Configuring Global QoS Class Settings

Quality of service (QoS) allows administrators to classify network traffic and prioritize and police the traffic flow to help avoid congestion in the network.

To gain an understanding of QoS in ACI, the behavior of the platform can be analyzed in four key areas:

- **Traffic classification:** *Traffic classification* refers to the method used for grouping traffic into different categories or classes. ACI classifies traffic into *priority levels*. Current ACI code has six user-configurable priority levels and several reserved QoS groups. ACI allows administrators to classify traffic by trusting ingress packet headers, such as Differentiated Services Code Point (DSCP) or Class of Service (CoS). Administrators can also assign a priority level to traffic via contracts or by manually assigning an EPG to a priority level.

- **Policing:** The term *policing* refers to enforcement of controls on traffic based on classification. Even though there should be no oversubscription concerns in ACI fabrics, there is still a need for policing. Suppose backup traffic has been trunked on the same link to a server as data traffic. In such cases, administrators can police traffic to enforce bandwidth limits on the link for the backup EPG. ACI policing can be enforced on an interface or on an EPG. If traffic exceeds prespecified limits, packets can be either marked or dropped. Policing applies both in the inbound direction and in the outbound direction.

- **Marking:** Once a switch classifies traffic, it can also *mark* traffic by setting certain values in the Layer 3 header (DSCP) or in the Layer 2 header (Class of Service [CoS]) to notify other switches in the traffic path of the desired QoS treatment. Under default ACI settings, marking takes place on ingress leaf switches only.

- **Queuing and scheduling:** Once a platform assigns packets to a QoS group, outbound packets are queued for transmission. Multiple queues can be used based on packet priority. A scheduling algorithm determines which queue's packet should be transmitted next. Scheduling and queuing, therefore, collectively refer to the process of prioritization of network packets and scheduling their transmission outbound on the wire. ACI uses the Deficit Weighted Round Robin (DWRR) scheduling algorithm.

Which aspects of QoS relate to access policies? Global QoS class settings govern priority levels and other fabricwide aspects of QoS applicable to treatment of server and other endpoint traffic and therefore fall under access policies.

To review the global QoS class settings or make changes, navigate to **Fabric > Access Policies > Policies > Global > QoS Class.**

Let's say that at some point in the future, your company intends to connect its Cisco Unified Computing System (UCS) domains to the ACI fabric in an effort to gradually migrate all workloads into ACI. Default gateways will move into the fabric at a later time, and legacy data center infrastructure is expected to remain in the network for a long time. UCS server converged network adapters (CNA) tag certain critical traffic with CoS values, and the production network currently honors markings from UCS servers. The IT organization wants to ensure that ACI preserves these CoS values and restores them as these packets leave the fabric so that the legacy network can act on these markings. After reviewing the settings in the Global - QoS Class page, you might learn that ACI preserves DSCP markings by default but does not preserve CoS markings. You can enable the Dot1p Preserve setting to address this requirement, as shown in Figure 7-32.

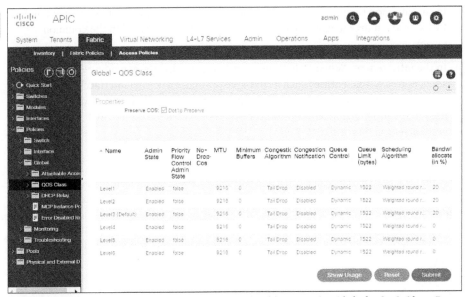

Figure 7-32 *Enabling the Dot1p Preserve Checkbox on the Global - QoS Class Page*

Notice in the figure the six user-configurable QoS priority levels in ACI and the bandwidth allocation for each of them. Any traffic that cannot be otherwise classified into a priority level gets assigned to the default class (Level 3).

NOTE Reserved QoS groups in ACI consist of APIC controller traffic, control plane protocol traffic, Switched Port Analyzer (SPAN) traffic, and traceroute traffic. ACI places APIC and control plane protocol traffic in a strict priority queue; SPAN and traceroute traffic are considered best-effort traffic.

Configuring DHCP Relay

In ACI, if a bridge domain has been configured to allow flooding of traffic and a DHCP server resides within an EPG associated with the bridge domain, any endpoints within the same EPG can communicate with the DHCP server without needing DHCP relay functionality.

When flooding is not enabled on the bridge domain or when the DHCP server resides in a different subnet or EPG than endpoints requesting dynamic IP assignment, DHCP relay functionality is required.

To define a list of DHCP servers to which ACI should relay DHCP traffic, a DHCP relay policy needs to be configured. There are three locations where a DHCP relay policy can be configured in ACI:

- **In the Access Policies view:** When bridge domains are placed in user tenants and one or more DHCP servers are expected to be used across these tenants, DHCP relay policies should be configured in the Access Policies view.

- **In the common tenant:** When bridge domains are placed in the common tenant and EPGs reside in user tenants, DHCP relay policies are best placed in the common tenant.

- **In the infra tenant:** When DHCP functionality is needed for extending ACI fabric services to external entities such as hypervisors and VMkernel interfaces need to be assigned IP addresses from the infra tenant, DHCP relay policies need to be configured in the infra tenant. This option is beyond the scope of the DCACI 300-620 exam and, therefore, this book.

Once DHCP relay policies have been configured, bridge domains can reference these policies.

Let's say that you need to configure a DHCP relay policy referencing all DHCP servers within the enterprise network. In your environment, your team has decided that bridge domains will all be configured in user tenants. For this reason, DHCP relay policies should be configured under **Fabric > Access Policies > Policies > Global > DHCP Relay**. Figure 7-33 shows how you create a new DHCP policy by entering a name and adding providers (DHCP servers) to the policy.

Figure 7-33 *Configuring a New DHCP Relay Policy in the Access Policies View*

Define each DHCP server by adding its address and the location where it resides. Where a DHCP server resides within the fabric, select Application EPG and define the tenant, application profile, and EPG in which the server resides and then click OK. Then add any redundant DHCP servers to the policy and click Submit.

Figure 7-34 *Configuring a Provider Within a DHCP Relay Policy*

Chapter 8, "Implementing Tenant Policies," covers assignment of DHCP relay policies to EPGs and DHCP relay caveats in ACI.

Configuring MCP

A Layer 2 loop does not impact the stability of an ACI fabric because ACI can broadcast traffic at line rate with little need to process the individual packets. Layer 2 loops, however, can impact the ability of endpoints to process important traffic. For this reason, mechanisms are needed to detect loops resulting from miscabling and misconfiguration. One of the protocols ACI uses to detect such externally generated Layer 2 loops is MisCabling Protocol (MCP).

MCP is disabled in ACI by default. To enable MCP, you must first enable MCP globally and then ensure that it is also enabled at the interface policy level. As part of the global enablement of MCP, you define a key that ACI includes in MCP packets sent out on access ports. If ACI later receives an MCP packet with the same key on any other port, it knows that there is a Layer 2 loop in the topology. In response, ACI can either attempt to mitigate the loop by disabling the port on which the MCP protocol data unit was received or it can generate a system message to notify administrators of the issue.

To enable MCP globally, navigate to **Fabric > Access Policies > Policies > Global > MCP Instance Policy Default**. As shown in Figure 7-35, you can then enter a value in the Key field, toggle Admin State to Enabled, check the Enable MCP PDU per VLAN checkbox, select the desired Loop Prevention Action setting, and click Submit.

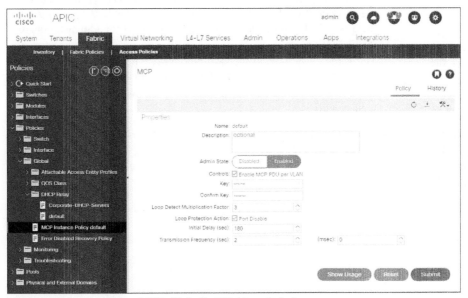

Figure 7-35 *Enabling MCP Globally Within a Fabric*

Table 7-4 describes these settings.

Table 7-4 Settings Available in Global MCP Policy

Setting	Description
Admin State	This setting determines whether MCP is globally enabled or disabled. The default setting for this field is Disabled.
Enable MCP PDU per VLAN	By default, ACI only sends MCP packets on the native VLAN on a port. This tends to be useless in detecting Layer 2 loops when an EPG has been trunked over a port. To ensure that loops behind tagged ports can also be detected, the Enable MCP PDU per VLAN option needs to be checked. If this option is checked, ACI sends MCP packets on up to 256 VLANs per interface. If more than 256 VLANs have been mapped to EPGs on a port, the first 256 VLAN IDs are chosen.
Key	This is a string that ACI includes in MCP packets to uniquely identify the fabric with the intent to be able to later validate whether it has been the originator of a given MCP packet.
Loop Detect Multiplication Factor	This is the number of self-originated continuous MCP packets ACI needs to receive before it declares a loop. The default value for this setting is 3. With default settings, it takes ACI approximately 7 seconds to detect a loop.
Loop Protection Action	This is the response ACI takes after receiving a number of self-originated MCP packets on a port. If the Port Disable option is checked, ACI disables the port on which the MCP packets have been received and logs the incident. If the Port Disabled checkbox is disabled, ACI just logs the incident, which can be forwarded to a syslog server for administrators to take action.
Initial Delay	This is the delay time, in seconds, before MCP begins taking action. By default, the option is set to 180 seconds, but it can be tuned down.
Transmission Frequency	This is the frequency for transmission of MCP packets, in seconds or milliseconds.

To enable MCP on a port-by-port basis, create an explicit MCP interface policy by navigating to **Fabric > Access Policies > Policies > Interface**, right-clicking MCP Interface, and selecting Create MisCabling Protocol Interface Policy. Assign a name to the policy and toggle Admin State to Enabled, as shown in Figure 7-36.

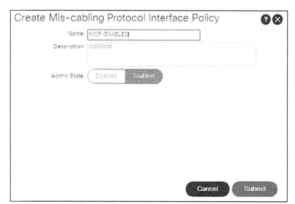

Figure 7-36 *Creating an Interface Policy with MCP Enabled*

Then you can apply the policy on relevant interface policy groups, as shown in Figure 7-37.

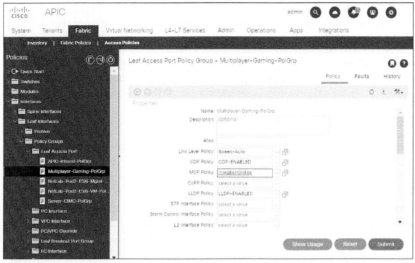

Figure 7-37 *Applying an MCP Interface Policy to an Interface Policy Group*

Configuring Storm Control

Storm control is a feature that enables ACI administrators to set thresholds for broadcast, unknown unicast, and multicast (BUM) traffic so that traffic exceeding user-defined thresholds within a 1-second interval can be suppressed. Storm control is disabled in ACI by default.

Say that for the multiplayer gaming business unit, you would like to treat all multiplayer servers with suspicion due to lack of IT visibility beyond the physical interfaces of these servers. Perhaps these servers may someday have malfunctioning network interface cards and might possibly trigger traffic storms. If the servers never need to push more than 30% of the bandwidth available to them in the form of multicast and broadcast traffic, you can enforce a maximum threshold for multicast and broadcast traffic equivalent to 30% of the bandwidth of the server interfaces. Figure 7-38 shows the settings for such a storm control interface policy, configured by navigating to **Fabric > Access Policies > Policies > Interface**, right-clicking Storm Control, and selecting Create Storm Control Interface Policy.

Figure 7-38 *Configuring a Storm Control Interface Policy*

As indicated in Figure 7-38, thresholds can be defined using bandwidth percentages or the number of packets traversing a switch interface (or aggregates of interfaces) per second.

The Rate parameter determines either the percentage of total port bandwidth or number of packets allowed to ingress associated ports during each 1-second interval. The Max Burst Rate, also expressed as a percentage of total port bandwidth or the number of packets entering a switch port, is the maximum accumulation of rate that is allowed when no traffic passes. When traffic starts, all the traffic up to the accumulated rate is allowed in the first interval. In subsequent intervals, traffic is allowed only up to the configured rate.

The Storm Control Action setting determines the action ACI takes if packets continue to exceed the configured threshold for the number of intervals specified in the Storm Control Soak Count setting. In the configuration shown in Figure 7-38, the Storm Control Soak Count has been kept at its default value of 3, but Storm Control Action has been set to Shut-down. This ensures that any port or port channel configured with the specified interface policy is shut down on the third second it continues to receive BUM traffic exceeding the configured rate. Storm Control Soak Count can be configured to between 3 and 10 seconds.

Figure 7-39 shows that once created, a storm control interface policy needs to be applied to an interface policy group before it can be enforced at the switch interface level.

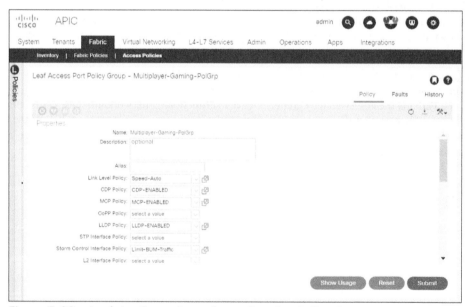

Figure 7-39 *Applying Storm Control to an Interface Policy Group*

NOTE In the configurations presented in Figure 7-38 and Figure 7-39, the assumption is that the L2 Unknown Unicast setting on the bridge domains associated with the servers will be configured using the Hardware Proxy setting, which enables use of spine-proxy addresses for forwarding within a fabric when a destination is unknown to leaf switches. If the L2 Unknown Unicast setting for relevant bridge domains were configured to Flood, it would be wise to also set a threshold for unicast traffic. This example shows how the storm control threshold for unicast traffic does not really come into play when Hardware Proxy is enabled on pertinent bridge domains.

Configuring CoPP

Control Plane Policing (CoPP) protects switch control planes by limiting the amount of traffic for each protocol that can reach the control processors. A switch applies CoPP to all traffic destined to the switch itself as well as exception traffic that, for any reason, needs to be handled by control processors. CoPP helps safeguard switches against denial-of-service (DoS) attacks perpetrated either inadvertently or maliciously, thereby ensuring that switches are able to continue to process critical traffic, such as routing updates.

ACI enforces CoPP by default but also allows for tuning of policing parameters both at the switch level and at the interface level. Supported protocols for per-interface CoPP are ARP, ICMP, CDP, LLDP, LACP, BGP, Spanning Tree Protocol, BFD, and OSPF. CoPP interface policies apply to leaf ports only. Switch-level CoPP can be defined for both leaf switches and spine switches and supports a wider number of protocols.

Let's say you need to ensure that multiplayer gaming servers can send only a limited number of ICMP packets to their default gateways. They should also be allowed to send only a limited number of ARP packets. This can be accomplished via a CoPP interface policy. As indicated in Figure 7-40, the relevant interface policy wizard can be accessed by navigating to **Fabric > Access Policies > Interface**, right-clicking CoPP Interface, and selecting Create per Interface per Protocol CoPP Policy.

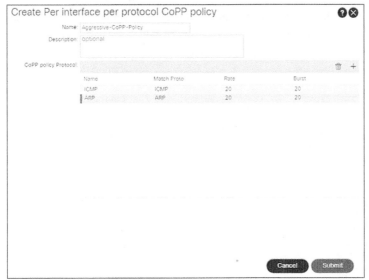

Figure 7-40 *Configuring a CoPP Interface Policy*

The columns Rate and Burst in Figure 7-40 refer to Committed Information Rate (CIR) and Committed Burst (BC), respectively. The Committed Information Rate indicates the desired bandwidth allocation for a protocol, specified as a bit rate or a percentage of the link rate. The Committed Burst is the size of a traffic burst that can exceed the CIR within a given unit of time and not impact scheduling.

For the CoPP interface policy to take effect, it needs to be applied to the interface policy groups of the multiplayer gaming servers, as shown in Figure 7-41.

Figure 7-41   *Applying a CoPP Interface Policy to Interface Policy Groups*

What do the default settings for CoPP on leaf switches look like? Example 7-14 displays the result of the command **show copp policy** on a specific leaf switch.

Example 7-14   *Default CoPP Settings on a Leaf Switch*

```
LEAF101# show copp policy
COPP Class          COPP proto          COPP Rate           COPP Burst
lldp                lldp                1000                1000
traceroute          traceroute          500                 500
permitlog           permitlog           300                 300
nd                  nd                  1000                1000
icmp                icmp                500                 500
isis                isis                1500                5000
eigrp               eigrp               2000                2000
arp                 arp                 1360                340
cdp                 cdp                 1000                1000
ifcspan             ifcspan             2000                2000
ospf                ospf                2000                2000
bgp                 bgp                 5000                5000
tor-glean           tor-glean           100                 100
acllog              acllog              500                 500
```

mcp	mcp	1500	1500
pim	pim	500	500
igmp	igmp	1500	1500
ifc	ifc	7000	7000
coop	coop	5000	5000
dhcp	dhcp	1360	340
ifcother	ifcother	332800	5000
infraarp	infraarp	300	300
lacp	lacp	1000	1000
glean	glean	100	100
stp	stp	1000	1000

To modify the CoPP settings applied on a leaf, navigate to **Fabric > Access Policies > Policies > Switch**, right-click Leaf CoPP, and select Create Profiles for CoPP to be Applied at the Leaf Level. Notice that there are options to define custom values for each protocol, apply default CoPP values on a per-platform basis, apply permissive CoPP values, enforce strict CoPP values, and apply values between permissive and strict. Figure 7-42 shows the selection of strict CoPP settings. Strict values can potentially impact certain operations, such as upgrades.

Figure 7-42   *Creating a CoPP Switch Policy That Uses Aggressively Low Values*

Switch CoPP policies need to be applied to a switch policy group before they can be associated with switch profiles. Figure 7-43 shows the creation and application of switch CoPP policies to a new switch policy group.

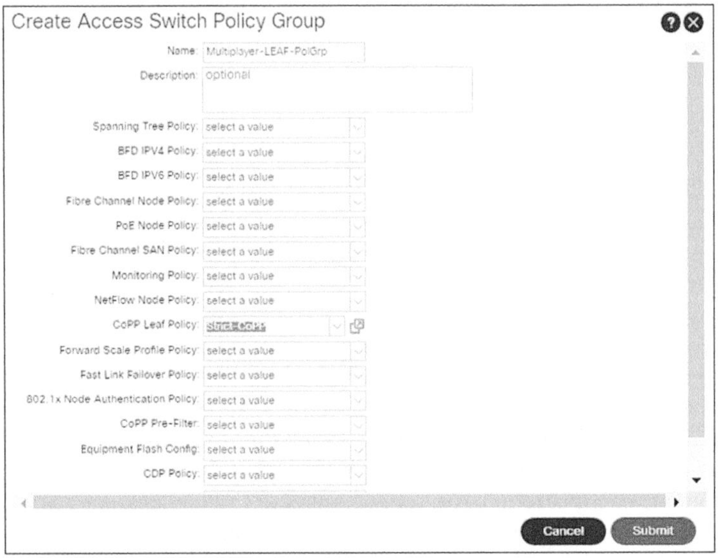

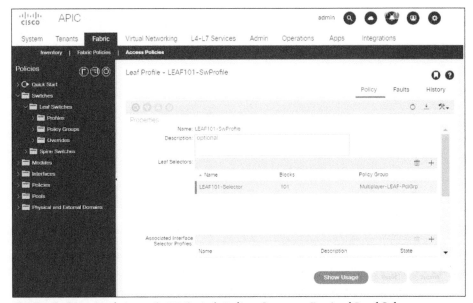

Figure 7-43   *Applying of a CoPP Switch Policy to a Switch Policy Group*

Finally, you can allocate the CoPP switch policy group to leaf selectors referencing the intended switches as shown in Figure 7-44.

Figure 7-44   *Applying a CoPP Switch Policy Group to Desired Leaf Selectors*

Verification of the current CoPP settings indicates that the application of the strict CoPP policy has dramatically lowered the CoPP values to those that appear in Example 7-15.

Example 7-15 *Switch CoPP Settings Following Application of Strict CoPP Values*

```
LEAF101# show copp policy
COPP Class                  COPP proto              COPP Rate        COPP Burst
lldp                        lldp                    10               10
traceroute                  traceroute              10               10
permitlog                   permitlog               10               10
nd                          nd                      10               10
icmp                        icmp                    10               10
isis                        isis                    10               10
eigrp                       eigrp                   10               10
arp                         arp                     10               10
cdp                         cdp                     10               10
ifcspan                     ifcspan                 10               10
ospf                        ospf                    10               10
bgp                         bgp                     10               10
tor-glean                   tor-glean               10               10
acllog                      acllog                  10               10
mcp                         mcp                     10               10
pim                         pim                     10               10
igmp                        igmp                    10               10
ifc                         ifc                     7000             7000
coop                        coop                    10               10
dhcp                        dhcp                    10               10
ifcother                    ifcother                10               10
infraarp                    infraarp                10               10
lacp                        lacp                    10               10
glean                       glean                   10               10
stp                         stp                     10               10
```

NOTE IFC stands for Insieme Fabric Controller. Even strict CoPP policies keep IFC values relatively high. This is important because IFC governs APIC communication with leaf and spine switches.

Another CoPP configuration option in ACI is to implement CoPP leaf and spine prefilters. CoPP prefilter switch policies are used on spine and leaf switches to filter access to authentication services based on specified sources and TCP ports with the intention of protecting against DDoS attacks. When these policies are deployed on a switch, control plane traffic is denied by default, and only the traffic specified by CoPP prefilters is permitted. Misconfiguration of CoPP prefilters, therefore, can impact connectivity within multipod configurations, to remote leaf switches, and in Cisco ACI Multi-Site deployments. For these reasons, CoPP prefilter entries are not commonly modified.

Modifying BPDU Guard and BPDU Filter Settings

Spanning Tree Protocol bridge protocol data units (BPDUs) are critical to establishing loop-free topologies between switches. However, there is little reason for servers and appliances that do not have legitimate reasons for participating in Spanning Tree Protocol to be sending BPDUs into an ACI fabric or receiving BPDUs from the network. It is therefore best to implement BPDU Guard and BPDU Filter on all server-facing and appliance-facing ports unless there is a legitimate reason for such devices to be participating in Spanning Tree Protocol. Although ACI does not itself participate in Spanning Tree Protocol, this idea still applies to ACI. When a BPDU arrives on a leaf port, the fabric forwards it on all ports mapped to the same EPG on which the BPDU arrived. This behavior ensures that non-ACI switches connecting to ACI at Layer 2 are able to maintain a loop-free topology.

When applied on a switch port, BPDU Filter prevents Spanning Tree Protocol BPDUs from being sent outbound on the port. BPDU Guard, on the other hand, disables a port if a Spanning Tree Protocol BPDU arrives on the port.

If you were concerned that a group of servers might one day be hacked and used to inject Spanning Tree Protocol BPDUs into the network with the intent of triggering changes in the Spanning Tree Protocol topology outside ACI, it would make a lot of sense to implement BPDU Filter and BPDU Guard on all ACI interfaces facing such servers.

To implement BPDU Filter and BPDU Guard, you first create a Spanning Tree Protocol interface policy with these features enabled (see Figure 7-45).

Figure 7-45   *Creating a Spanning Tree Interface Policy*

The policy should then be associated with interface policy groups for the intended servers (see Figure 7-46).

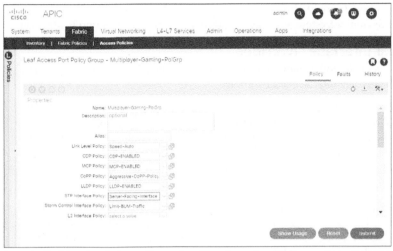

Figure 7-46 *Applying a Spanning Tree Interface Policy to Interface Policy Groups*

Note that FEX ports enable BPDU Guard by default, and this behavior cannot be changed.

Modifying the Error Disabled Recovery Policy

When administrators set up features like MCP and BPDU Guard and determine that ports should be error disabled as a result of ACI loop-detection events, the error disabled recovery policy can be used to control whether the fabric automatically reenables such ports after a recovery interval.

ACI can also move a port into an error-disabled state if an endpoint behind the port moves to other ports at a high frequency with low intervals between moves. The reasoning in such cases is that high numbers of endpoint moves can be symptomatic of loops.

To modify the error disabled recovery policy in a fabric, navigate to **Fabric > Access Policies > Policies > Global > Error Disabled Recovery Policy**. Figure 7-47 shows a configuration with automatic recovery of ports that have been disabled by MCP after a 300-second recovery interval.

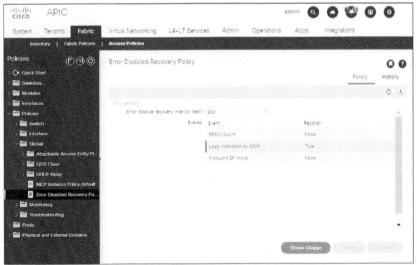

Figure 7-47 *Editing the Error Disabled Recovery Policy*

To configure whether ACI should disable ports due to frequent endpoint moves in the first place, navigate to **System > System Settings > Endpoint Controls > Ep Loop Protection**.

Configuring Leaf Interface Overrides

A *leaf interface override* policy allows interfaces that have interface policy group assignments to apply an alternate interface policy group.

Imagine that a group of ports have been configured on Node 101, using a specific interface policy group. One of the interfaces connects to a firewall, and security policies dictate that LLDP and CDP toward the firewall need to be disabled on all firewall-facing interfaces. It might be impossible to modify the interface policy group associated with the port because it might be part of a port block. In this case, a leaf interface override can be used to assign an alternative interface policy group to the port of interest.

To implement such a leaf interface override, you create a new interface policy group with the desired settings. Then you navigate to **Fabric > Access Policies > Interfaces > Leaf Interfaces**, right-click Overrides, and select Create Leaf Interface Overrides. Set Path Type and Path to identify the desired switch interface and the new policy group that needs to be applied to the interface. Figure 7-48 shows a leaf interface override configuration.

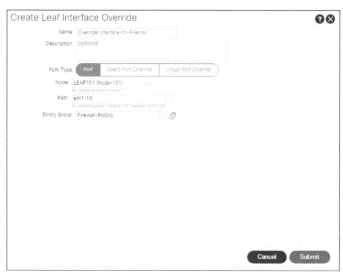

Figure 7-48 *Configuring a Leaf Interface Override*

With this configuration, LLDP and CDP have been disabled on firewall-facing interface 1/16.

Configuring Port Channel Member Overrides

When an override needs to be applied to one or more links that are part of a port channel or vPC but not necessarily the entire port channel or vPC, a *port channel member override* can be used. Examples of port channel member overrides include the implementation of LACP fast timers and the modification of LACP port priorities.

To configure a port channel member override, first configure an interface policy that will be used to override the configuration of one or more member ports. Create a port channel member policy by navigating to **Fabric > Access Policies > Policies > Interface**, right-clicking Port Channel Member, and selecting Create Port Channel Member Policy. Figure 7-49 shows a policy that enables LACP fast timers.

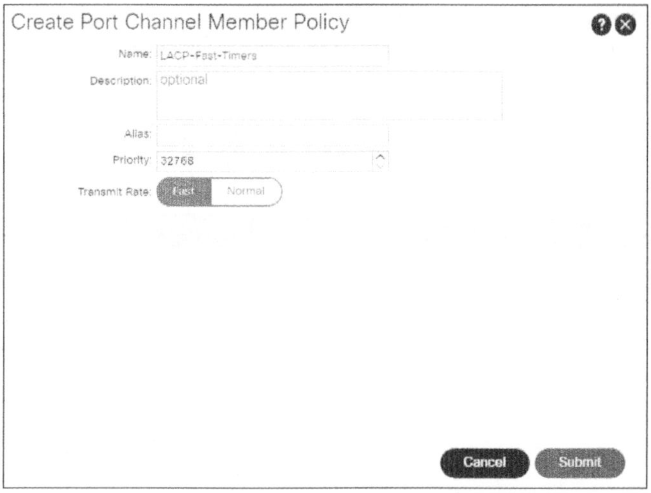

Create Port Channel Member Policy

Field	Value
Name:	LACP-Fast-Timers
Description:	optional
Alias:	
Priority:	32768
Transmit Rate:	Fast Normal

Cancel   Submit

Figure 7-49 *Configuring a Port Channel Member Policy*

Note that the port priority setting in this policy has not been modified from its default. The Priority setting can be used to determine which ports should be put in standby mode and which should be active when there is a limitation preventing all compatible ports from aggregating. A higher port priority value means a lower priority for LACP.

Example 7-16 shows the current timer configuration for port 1/32 on Node 101. This port has been configured as part of a port channel along with port 1/31.

Example 7-16 *Ports 1/31 and 1/32 Both Default to Normal LACP Timers*

```
LEAF101# show port-channel summary interface port-channel 2
Flags:  D - Down         P - Up in port-channel (members)
        I - Individual   H - Hot-standby (LACP only)
        s - Suspended    r - Module-removed
        S - Switched     R - Routed
        U - Up (port-channel)
        M - Not in use. Min-links not met
        F - Configuration failed
-------------------------------------------------------------------------------
Group Port-       Type     Protocol  Member Ports
      Channel
-------------------------------------------------------------------------------
2    Po2(SD)     Eth      LACP      Eth1/31(P)    Eth1/32(P)
LEAF101# show lacp interface  ethernet 1/31 | egrep -A8  "Local" | egrep "Local|LACP"
Local Port: Eth1/31   MAC Address= 00-27-e3-15-bd-e3
  LACP _ Activity=active
  LACP _ Timeout=Long Timeout (30s)
LEAF101# show lacp interface  ethernet 1/32 | egrep -A8  "Local" | egrep "Local|LACP"
Local Port: Eth1/32   MAC Address= 00-27-e3-15-bd-e3
  LACP _ Activity=active
  LACP _ Timeout=Long Timeout (30s)
```

7

To apply the port channel member policy, you first associate the policy to the desired port channel or vPC interface policy group in the form of an override policy group (see Figure 7-50).

Figure 7-50   *Adding a Port Channel Member Policy to an Interface Policy Group*

Next, you determine specifically which ports the override policy applies to. Figure 7-51 shows the application of the policy to port 1/32. After you shut down and reenable the port, it appears to have LACP fast timers implemented. This can be confirmed in the output displayed in Example 7-17.

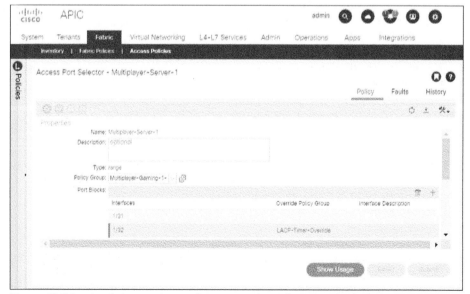

Figure 7-51   *Applying an Override to a Member of a Port Channel*

Example 7-17 *Port 1/32 Overridden Using Fast LACP Timers*

```
LEAF101# show lacp interface  ethernet 1/31 | egrep -A8  "Local" | egrep
"Local|LACP"
Local Port: Eth1/31    MAC Address= 00-27-e3-15-bd-e3
  LACP_Activity=active
  LACP_Timeout=Long Timeout (30s)
LEAF101# show lacp interface  ethernet 1/32 | egrep -A8  "Local" | egrep
"Local|LACP"
Local Port: Eth1/32    MAC Address= 00-27-e3-15-bd-e3
  LACP_Activity=active
  LACP_Timeout=Short Timeout (1s)
```

Exam Preparation Tasks

As mentioned in the section "How to Use This Book" in the Introduction, you have a couple of choices for exam preparation: Chapter 17, "Final Preparation," and the exam simulation questions in the Pearson Test Prep Software Online.

Review All Key Topics

Review the most important topics in this chapter, noted with the Key Topic icon in the outer margin of the page. Table 7-5 lists these key topics and the page number on which each is found.

Table 7-5 Key Topics for Chapter 7

Key Topic Element	Description	Page Number
Figure 7-1	Shows the settings that are available when configuring an LLDP interface policy	189
Figure 7-2	Shows the settings that are available when configuring a link level interface policy	189
Paragraph	Clarifies that the leaf access port policy group needs to be used when configuring non-aggregated ports	191
Figure 7-5	Shows a sample configuration of a leaf access port policy group	191
Figure 7-7	Shows how to map an interface policy group to switch ports via switch access port selectors	192
Figure 7-11	Shows a sample configuration of an interface policy group with LACP enabled	196
Table 7-3	Details the common control options available for configuration of port channel interface policies	196
Paragraph	Addresses the extent of reusability of port channel and vPC interface policy groups	201
Figure 7-18	Shows how to configure vPC domains in ACI	203
Paragraph	Describes the result of defining a vPC explicit protection group from a forwarding perspective	204
Figure 7-19	Shows the configuration of a port channel interface policy with static port channeling enabled	205

7

Key Topic Element	Description	Page Number
Figure 7-20	Shows the creation of a vPC interface policy group	205
Paragraph	Describes the use case and benefits of AAEP EPGs	209
List	Lists the steps necessary for deploying a new fabric extender in ACI	212
Paragraph	Explains the function of dynamic breakout ports	215
Figure 7-30	Shows a sample configuration of a leaf port breakout group	216
Figure 7-31	Depicts the implementation of access policies for dynamic breakout subports and the resulting port numbering convention	217
Paragraph	Describes a common use case for implementing the Dot1p Preserve setting	218
Figure 7-32	Shows how to enable the Dot1p Preserve setting	219
Figure 7-33	Shows configuration of a DHCP relay policy in the Access Policies view	220
Figure 7-34	Shows the addition of a DHCP server to a DHCP relay policy in the Access Policies view	220
Paragraph	Provides an understanding of the steps needed to implement MCP	221
Paragraph	Explains where MCP can be globally enabled	221
Table 7-4	Describes the configuration settings available when implementing MCP globally	222
Paragraph	Reinforces the idea that MCP needs to be enabled both globally and at the interface level	222
Paragraph	Describes the use case for storm control and its default configuration state in ACI	223
Paragraph	Describes CoPP in ACI and how CoPP can be configured	225
Figure 7-47	Shows how to edit the error disabled recovery policy	231

Complete Tables and Lists from Memory

Print a copy of Appendix C, "Memory Tables" (found on the companion website), or at least the section for this chapter, and complete the tables and lists from memory. Appendix D, "Memory Tables Answer Key" (also on the companion website), includes completed tables and lists you can use to check your work.

Define Key Terms

Define the following key terms from this chapter and check your answers in the glossary:

link debounce interval, vPC peer dead interval, dynamic breakout port, leaf interface override, port channel member override

CHAPTER 8

Implementing Tenant Policies

This chapter covers the following topics:

ACI Endpoint Learning: This section describes the various lookup tables available in ACI and details how ACI learns endpoints attached to the fabric.

Packet Forwarding in ACI: This section complements the topic of endpoint learning by examining the four major packet forwarding scenarios in ACI.

Deploying a Multi-Tier Application: This section walks through the deployment of tenant policies for a hypothetical application to the point of endpoint learning.

Whitelisting Intra-VRF Communications via Contracts: This section covers whitelisting of components of a hypothetical application using contracts.

This chapter covers the following exam topics:

- 1.6 Implement ACI logical constructs

  - 1.6.b application profile

  - 1.6.d bridge domain (unicast routing, Layer 2 unknown hardware proxy, ARP flooding)

  - 1.6.e endpoint groups (EPG)

  - 1.6.f contracts (filter, provider, consumer, reverse port filter, VRF enforced)

- 2.1 Describe endpoint learning

- 2.2 Implement bridge domain configuration knob (unicast routing, Layer 2 unknown hardware proxy, ARP flooding)

Thus far in the book, you have learned how to configure switch ports for connectivity to servers and appliances. Next, you need to learn how to deploy the policies that enable these attached devices to communicate with one another.

The goal of this chapter is not simply to show you what buttons to push when configuring tenant objects. Rather, the objective is to convey some of the logic behind decisions that enable you to deploy applications and associated whitelisting policies more effectively. In the process, you will also learn how to verify endpoint learning and proper traffic forwarding at a basic level.

"Do I Know This Already?" Quiz

The "Do I Know This Already?" quiz allows you to assess whether you should read this entire chapter thoroughly or jump to the "Exam Preparation Tasks" section. If you are in doubt about your answers to these questions or your own assessment of your knowledge of the topics, read the entire chapter. Table 8-1 lists the major headings in this chapter and their corresponding "Do I Know This Already?" quiz questions. You can find the answers in Appendix A, "Answers to the 'Do I Know This Already?' Questions."

Table 8-1 "Do I Know This Already?" Section-to-Question Mapping

Foundation Topics Section	Questions
ACI Endpoint Learning	1–4
Packet Forwarding in ACI	5–7
Deploying a Multi-Tier Application	8
Whitelisting Intra-Tenant Communications via Contracts	9, 10

CAUTION The goal of self-assessment is to gauge your mastery of the topics in this chapter. If you do not know the answer to a question or are only partially sure of the answer, you should mark that question as wrong for purposes of the self-assessment. Giving yourself credit for an answer you correctly guess skews your self-assessment results and might provide you with a false sense of security.

1. Which of the following statements about endpoint learning is correct?

   a. ACI learns devices behind L3Outs as remote endpoints.

   b. An ACI leaf prevents the need for flooding by learning all endpoints, including remote endpoints to which no local devices seek to communicate.

   c. An ACI leaf learns both the MAC address and any IP addresses of any local endpoint.

   d. An ACI leaf notifies the spine of any remote endpoints it has learned.

2. An ACI fabric has problems learning a silent host. Which of the following best explains why ACI cannot learn this endpoint?

   a. ACI has trouble detecting silent hosts.

   b. The silent host is in an L2 BD, which has been configured for hardware proxy.

   c. Unicast Routing has been enabled for the BD.

   d. An SVI has been deployed for the BD.

3. Which of the following may signal endpoint flapping?

   a. Non-transient output in ACI suggesting that a MAC address has more than one IP address association

   b. Non-transient output in ACI suggesting that an IP address has more than one MAC address association

   c. Transient output in ACI suggesting that a MAC address has more than one IP address association

   d. Transient output in ACI suggesting that an IP address has more than one MAC address association

4. True or false: An endpoint learned locally by a leaf becomes the single source of truth for the entire fabric.

   a. True

   b. False

5. True or false: With hardware proxy configured, a leaf forwards L2 unknown unicast traffic to the spine. If the spine does not know the destination, it drops the traffic and initiates silent host detection.

   a. True

   b. False

6. True or false: When hardware proxy is enabled, ACI no longer needs to forward ARP traffic.

   a. True

   b. False

7. True or false: An ACI leaf that needs to perform flooding forwards the traffic out all uplinks, and spines, likewise, forward the traffic on all the fabric links as well until the traffic has flowed over all fabric links within the topology.

   a. True

   b. False

8. There appears to be a delay in forwarding when a port with a static binding comes up. Which of the following could potentially explain the reason behind this delay?

   a. The Deployment Immediacy parameter for the static binding has been set to Immediate.

   b. The Port Encap parameter was set incorrectly, and ACI had to dynamically correct the issue.

   c. ACI has trouble learning endpoints because it has to wait for ARP packets.

   d. The Deployment Immediacy parameter for the static binding has been set to On Demand.

9. An administrator has created a restrictive filter to allow any source to reach destination port 22. She now wants to create a contract using this single filter. Which setting or settings should she use to enable ACI to automatically generate a rule for return traffic from the server to client?

   a. Apply Both Directions

   b. Established

   c. Apply Both Directions and Reverse Filter Ports

   d. Reverse Filter Ports

10. An engineer wants to log traffic if it matches a particular criterion. How can this be achieved?

   a. Specify Log in the Actions column of the relevant filter within a contract subject.

   b. Specify Log in the Directives column of the relevant filter within a contract subject.

   c. Specify Log in the filter itself.

   d. Specify Log on the Create Contract page.

Foundation Topics

ACI Endpoint Learning

Traditional networks rely heavily on control plane mechanisms such as Address Resolution Protocol (ARP), Gratuitous ARP (GARP), and IPv6 Neighbor Discovery (ND) to populate switch and router forwarding tables. Because of reliance on protocols like these, traffic flooding remains a cornerstone of address resolution in most networks.

ACI takes a different approach to endpoint learning. In ACI, the emphasis is on learning all endpoint information through the data plane and in hardware. It does so through analysis of both the source MAC address and source IP address included in packets it receives. ACI still takes action based on information in address resolution packets (such as ARP requests) because reliance on the data plane alone can sometimes create an unrealistic picture of endpoint locations. But when analyzing address resolution packets, ACI does so in the data plane, without the need to use switch CPU resources.

In addition to learning endpoint information from the data plane, ACI introduces various enhancements to greatly reduce unknown devices. The idea is that if there are ways to detect unknown endpoints in a fabric, the need for flooding can be minimized.

There are three primary benefits to how ACI learns endpoints. First, data plane–focused endpoint learning is less resource intensive and therefore enables greater fabric scalability. Second, ACI fabrics are able to react to endpoint movements and update endpoint information faster than traditional networks because ACI does *not* need to wait for GARP packets. Third, the emphasis on eliminating unknown endpoints enables ACI to optimize traffic forwarding and greatly reduce packet flooding. This last benefit has a direct impact on endpoint performance.

This section describes how ACI optimizes endpoint learning.

Lookup Tables in ACI

ACI uses endpoint data to forward traffic within the fabric. In ACI, an *endpoint* is defined as one MAC address and zero or more IP addresses associated with the MAC address.

In a traditional network, three forwarding tables are used to track devices. Table 8-2 documents these tables and their purposes.

Table 8-2 Traditional Switch Lookup Tables and Their Purposes

Table	Purpose
Routing Information Base (RIB)	Stores IPv4 and IPv6 routes to known destinations as well as the next-hop IP address to reach each destination. The RIB in traditional networks may include /32 host routes for certain interfaces, such as loopback interfaces.
MAC address table	Stores MAC addresses of Layer 2–adjacent devices and the local switch interface that needs to be used to reach the destination MAC address.
ARP table	Stores MAC-to-IP associations, allowing a switch or router to look up the MAC address it needs to encapsulate in a packet destination MAC field for receipt by a destination or next-hop device.

ACI also uses three tables to maintain network addresses, but these tables have different purposes and store different information compared to traditional networks. Table 8-3 details the lookup tables in ACI and the function each serves.

Table 8-3 ACI Lookup Tables and Their Purposes

Table	Purpose
Endpoint table	Stores MAC addresses and/or IP addresses (only /32 addresses for IPv4 and /128 addresses for IPv6). The endpoint table is the primary lookup table used by ACI leaf switches in determining how to forward traffic to other endpoints within the fabric.
Routing Information Base (RIB)	Stores IPv4 and IPv6 routes to destination subnets beyond an L3Out or within the Layer 3 domain inside the fabric. If advertised to ACI, this may also include external /32 host routes for IPv4 or /128 host routes for IPv6. For destinations within the fabric, the RIB stores bridge domain subnets. ACI routing tables do not store host routes (/32 for IPv4 or /128 for IPv6) pointing to endpoints within the fabric, but they do include host routes pointing to anycast subnet default gateways. ACI leaf switches consult the routing table if a destination endpoint is not found to be in the endpoint table.
ARP table	Stores IP-to-MAC relationships for direct neighbors sitting behind L3Out connections. ACI switches do not perform ARP table lookups when forwarding traffic to endpoints within the fabric.

When a leaf switch needs to make a decision on how to forward a packet, it first consults its endpoint table. If the destination is not in the endpoint table, it then consults the routing table. The ARP table is examined only if the destination is outside the fabric and behind an L3Out.

Local Endpoints and Remote Endpoints

If an ACI leaf learns an endpoint from an access (non-fabric) port, it considers the endpoint a *local endpoint*. With this definition, an ACI leaf that learns an endpoint from a Layer 2 extension to a traditional switch would also consider the new endpoint to be a local endpoint even though the endpoint is not directly attached to the leaf. Some ACI documentation refers to non-fabric ports as front-panel ports.

If, on the other hand, a leaf learns an endpoint over a fabric port (that is, over tunnel interfaces), the leaf considers the endpoint a *remote endpoint*.

The distinction between local and remote endpoints is important first and foremost because ACI leafs store different information for endpoints depending on whether the endpoints are local or remote. If an endpoint is local to a leaf, the leaf needs to store as much information about the endpoint as possible. If an endpoint is remote, it is not always necessary for a switch to learn both its MAC address and associated IP addresses. Therefore, if local endpoints on a leaf need only intra-subnet communication with a remote endpoint, the leaf only stores the MAC address of the remote endpoint. If local endpoints need traffic routed to the remote endpoint, the leaf stores the remote endpoint's IP information. If endpoints on a leaf require both intra-subnet and inter-subnet communication with a remote endpoint, the leaf then stores both the MAC address and any IP addresses of the remote endpoint. Having leaf switches store the minimum amount of information they need enables a substantial amount of endpoint table scalability.

Another important difference between local and remote endpoints is the role each plays in the overall learning process. A leaf communicates endpoint information to the spine Council of Oracle Protocol (COOP) database only if the endpoint is local.

Finally, an additional difference between these endpoint types is the amount of time a leaf retains relevant endpoint information. If an endpoint moves to a different leaf switch, the new leaf advertises the endpoint as a local endpoint to the spine COOP database, which triggers an immediate notification to the previous leaf and the creation of a bounce entry. Remote endpoint information, on the other hand, is more susceptible to becoming stale. Therefore, it is reasonable for leaf switches to retain local endpoint information for a longer period of time compared to remote endpoints.

Table 8-4 summarizes the key differences between local and remote endpoints.

Table 8-4 Differences Between Local and Remote Endpoints

Feature	Local Endpoint	Remote Endpoint
One endpoint	1 MAC address and n IP addresses	1 MAC address or 1 IP address
Learning scope	Communicated to spine COOP database	Learned on leafs as a cache of the actual endpoint information
Endpoint retention timer	900 seconds (by default)	300 seconds (by default)

Understanding Local Endpoint Learning

An ACI leaf follows a simple process to learn a local endpoint MAC and its associated IP addresses:

Step 1. The leaf receives a packet with source MAC address X and source IP address Y.

Step 2. The leaf learns MAC address X as a local endpoint.

Step 3. The leaf learns IP address Y and ties it to MAC address X only if the packet is either an ARP packet or a routed packet.

Once a leaf learns a local endpoint, it communicates the endpoint information to spines via a protocol called ZeroMQ. The spine switches receive endpoint data using COOP.

It should be apparent by now that one major difference between ACI and traditional endpoint learning is that ACI can also learn source IP addresses from the data plane, even if the packets are not ARP packets. In traditional networks, switches trust only specific packet types, such as ARP and GARP, when learning device IP information.

Unicast Routing and Its Impact on Endpoint Learning

The ACI local endpoint learning process requires that a packet entering a switch port be either a routed packet or an ARP packet for ACI to learn the IP address of the transmitting system. However, there are multiple configuration knobs that may prevent ACI from learning IP addresses.

One such BD configuration knob is the Unicast Routing setting. If this setting has been disabled for a bridge domain, ACI does not learn IP addresses for endpoints within EPGs associated with the BD. The reason for this is that if ACI is not expected to route traffic for a BD, there should be no need for ACI to analyze ARP packets for their source IP addresses in the first place.

Unicast Routing is also cornerstone to some other endpoint learning optimizations concerning silent hosts that are covered later in this chapter.

Note that Unicast Routing is not the only ACI configuration setting that can prevent IP learning. Other BD configuration knobs that can impact IP address learning include Limit IP Learning to Subnet and Endpoint Data Plane Learning. There are further fabric-level and VRF instance–level configuration options that can also impact endpoint IP learning.

Understanding Remote Endpoint Learning

Like local endpoint learning, remote endpoint learning occurs in the data plane.

When an ACI leaf switch needs to forward traffic to spines or other leafs in the fabric, it encapsulates the packet in VXLAN. Figure 8-1 provides a high-level view of the ACI VXLAN packet format. Only the fields most significant for understanding how ACI forwards traffic are depicted; headers shown are not meant to represent realistic sizes.

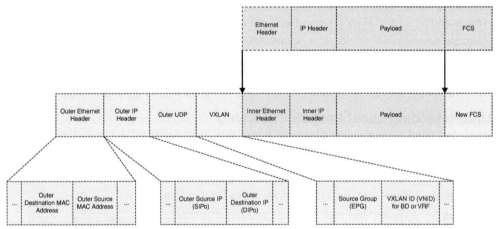

Figure 8-1   *ACI VXLAN Packet Format*

The top portion of the figure represents the original Ethernet frame sent by an endpoint. Once the local leaf makes the decision to forward the traffic across the fabric, it adds a VXLAN header, an outer UDP header, an outer IP header, and an outer MAC header to the packet and calculates a new frame check sequence (FCS). The middle portion of the figure reflects the frame after VXLAN encapsulation.

The ACI VXLAN header includes fields for a VXLAN network identifier (VNID) and a source EPG identifier so that a receiving switch can determine the EPG to which a packet belongs. Details about the UDP header are not significant for the purpose of understanding endpoint learning and basic forwarding. The outer IP header includes fields for the source TEP and destination TEP addresses for the traffic. The outer MAC header contains fields for a source MAC address and a destination MAC address, among other data. (This book places no further emphasis on the MAC header since its analysis would contribute very little to understanding forwarding in a routed fabric.)

NOTE   In addition to TEP addresses covered in Chapter 3, "Initializing an ACI Fabric," this chapter introduces a type of VTEP called vPC VIP addresses. These tunnel endpoint IP addresses also reside in the infra tenant in the overlay-1 VRF instance and are also sometimes placed in the source and destination outer IP address fields for cross-fabric forwarding.

If the leaf sending traffic into the fabric knows which leaf the traffic needs to be sent to, it can forward the traffic directly to the destination leaf by populating the destination leaf PTEP in the outer destination IP header. If the leaf does not know where to forward the traffic, it can either flood the traffic or forward it to one of the anycast spine proxy TEP addresses. When forwarding to the spine proxy, the COOP database determines where the traffic needs to be sent next. The L2 Unknown Unicast setting and a host of other settings on the respective bridge domain determine whether traffic should be flooded or forwarded to the spine proxy TEP.

Once the traffic arrives at the destination leaf, the leaf verifies that it is the intended destination leaf by checking the value in the outer destination IP field. It then decapsulates the extra headers. From the outer source IP field, the destination leaf knows which leaf is local to the source endpoint because it has a record of all tunnel IP addresses in the fabric. From the source EPG field, it knows to which EPG the source endpoint belongs. It then uses data in the VNID field to determine whether to cache the endpoint MAC address or IP address.

ACI allocates VNIDs to VRF instances, bridge domains, and EPGs. Because each VRF instance represents a Layer 3 domain, inclusion of a VRF instance VNID in the VXLAN header communicates to the destination leaf that the forwarding represents a routing operation. If the VNID included in the VXLAN header is a bridge domain VNID, the destination leaf understands that the forwarding represents a switching operation.

In summary, an ACI leaf follows these steps to learn a remote endpoint's MAC or IP address:

Step 1.   The leaf receives a packet with source MAC address X and source IP address Y on a fabric port.

Step 2.   If the forwarding represents a switching operation, the leaf learns source MAC address X as a remote endpoint.

Step 3.   If the forwarding represents a routing operation, the leaf learns IP address Y as a remote endpoint.

NOTE   One benefit of ACI remote endpoint learning is that once a leaf learns a remote endpoint, it can address packets directly to the destination leaf TEP. This ensures that ACI does not use spine processor resources for forwarding between known endpoints.

Understanding the Use of VLAN IDs and VNIDs in ACI

Look under the hood in ACI, and you will find a range of VLAN types. Add VXLAN to the mix, and you have a recipe for ultimate confusion. Figure 8-2 addresses some common VLAN types in ACI and how they correlate with VXLAN.

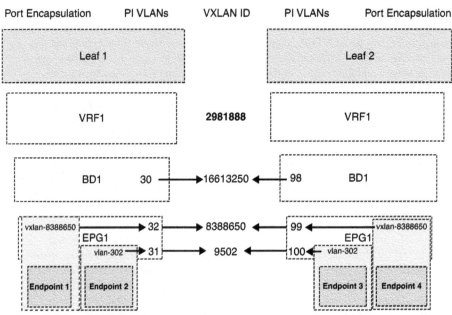

Figure 8-2 *Basic VLAN Types in ACI*

One type of VLAN depicted in this figure is *port encapsulation VLANs*, sometimes called access encapsulation VLANs. These are the VLAN IDs an administrator uses when mapping an EPG to a switch port. Both static path mapping and AAEP EPG assignments are of this VLAN type. The term *port encapsulation* implies that the VLAN encapsulation used appears on the wire. Of course, ACI does not include the encapsulation on the wire when mapping an EPG to a port untagged.

In truth, the term *port encapsulation* does not only refer to VLANs. ACI can encapsulate VNIDs on the wire over trunk links to certain virtual switching environments to further extend the fabric. This is why VXLAN ID 8388650 also appears as a port encapsulation VLAN in Figure 8-2.

The second type of VLAN called out in the figure is *platform-independent VLANs (PI VLANs)*. These are VLAN IDs that are locally significant to each leaf switch and represent a bridge domain or EPG for internal operations. Each PI VLAN maps to a VNID, although not all VNIDs map to PI VLANs. Because PI VLANs are locally significant, they cannot be used in the forwarding of traffic.

Finally, *VNIDs*, or VXLAN IDs, are allocated by APICs for VRF instances, BDs, and EPGs. The VNIDs are globally unique within a fabric and are used for forwarding purposes.

Example 8-1 illustrates some of these concepts using output of a slight variation of the **show vlan extended** command. The leftmost column that includes VLAN IDs 30 and 31 lists PI VLANs. The column titled Encap shows port encapsulation VLAN IDs or VNIDs. Each line in the output represents a mapping between internal VLANs and VNIDs. Finally, multiple commands enable verification of VRF instance VNIDs, such as the **show vrf** *<tenant:vrf>* **detail extended** command.

Example 8-1 *Leaf Output Showing PI VLANs, Port Encapsulations, and VRF Instance VNIDs*

```
LEAF102# show vlan id 30,31 extended

VLAN     Name                                        Encap             Ports
-------- ------------------------------------        ----------------  ----------
30       Production:Multiplayer-Servers-BD           vxlan-16613250    Eth1/38, Po2
31       Production:3rd-Party:Servers-EPG            vlan-302          Eth1/38, Po2


LEAF102# show vrf Production:MP detail extended | grep vxlan
    Encap: vxlan-2981888
```

> **NOTE**   There are several additional VLAN ID terms you may come across in ACI that may be important for advanced troubleshooting purposes but that are not covered on the DCACI 300-620 exam.

Endpoint Movements Within an ACI Fabric

Endpoints may move between Cisco ACI leaf switches as a result of a failover event or a virtual machine migration in a hypervisor environment.

When a new local endpoint is detected on a leaf, the leaf updates the COOP database on spine switches with its new local endpoint information. If the COOP database already learned the same endpoint from another leaf, COOP recognizes this event as an endpoint move and reports this move to the original leaf that advertised the old endpoint information. The old leaf that receives this notification deletes its old endpoint entry and creates a *bounce entry* pointing to the new leaf. A bounce entry is basically a remote endpoint created by COOP communication instead of data plane learning. With a bounce entry in place, a leaf is able to swap the outer destination IP address of packets destined to the endpoint that moved without having to notify the sending leaf via control plane mechanisms.

The advantage of this approach is scalability. No matter how many leaf switches have learned the endpoint, only three components need to be updated after an endpoint moves: the COOP database, the endpoint table on the new leaf switch to which the endpoint has moved, and the endpoint table on the old leaf switch from which the endpoint has moved. Eventually, all other leaf switches in the fabric update their information about the location of the endpoint through data plane learning.

Understanding Hardware Proxy and Spine Proxy

One of the major benefits of ACI that this book has alluded to is the use of the bridge domain L2 Unknown Unicast Hardware Proxy setting as a means for optimizing forwarding and minimizing flooding within ACI fabrics. This setting can be configured in the General tab under bridge domains, as shown in Figure 8-3.

Figure 8-3 *Hardware Proxy and Flood as Possible L2 Unknown Unicast Settings*

Under this optimized forwarding scheme, a leaf that receives a packet intended for an unknown destination in the fabric can populate the outer destination IP header with a spine proxy TEP address to allow the spine COOP database to forward the traffic onto its destination. This behavior on the part of leaf switches is sometimes called a *zero-penalty forwarding decision* because the leaf has nothing to lose by sending traffic to the spine, given that the spines are the best candidates for forwarding the traffic onward to its destination anyway.

When a spine receives a packet destined to its spine proxy address, it knows it needs to perform some action on the traffic. It checks the destination against its COOP database. If the spine also acknowledges the destination to be unknown, it then drops the traffic.

> **NOTE** Do not let placement of hardware proxy in this section on endpoint learning become a source of confusion. Hardware proxy relates to forwarding, not endpoint learning. However, there are endpoint learning considerations when configuring bridge domains for hardware proxy.

Endpoint Learning Considerations for Silent Hosts

One problem with hardware proxy logic becomes apparent in the analysis of silent hosts.

A *silent host* is a server or virtual machine that prefers to remain silent until called upon. Because silent hosts, by definition, do not initiate data plane communication, ACI may not be able to learn such endpoints through data plane mechanisms alone. If ACI is to be able to eliminate unknown endpoints, it needs to have methods to detect silent hosts—and that it does.

To detect a silent host, ACI attempts to "tickle" it into sending traffic to then learn it in the data plane. Upon dropping traffic toward an IP address that is not found in the COOP database, spines trigger this tickle effect by prompting leaf nodes that have programmed SVIs for the destination bridge domain to send ARP requests toward the unknown IP address. This process is called **ARP gleaning**, or *silent host detection*.

ARP gleaning works best when there is a BD SVI from which to generate ARP requests. This means that the destination subnet should be defined, and Unicast Routing should be enabled on the destination BD.

If the default gateway for a bridge domain is outside ACI, the bridge domain's L2 Unknown Unicast parameter should not be set to Hardware Proxy. Instead, it should be set to Flood to ensure that the network can learn about potential silent hosts through regular ARP flooding.

Where Data Plane IP Learning Breaks Down

Optimized endpoint learning in ACI works perfectly when all the endpoints in an ACI fabric are servers and do not perform any routing. Problems sometimes occur when devices that route traffic between subnets are placed into an ACI fabric in ways that were not originally intended.

The next few subsections deal with instances in which data plane learning can lead to suboptimal situations.

Endpoint Learning on L3Outs

If ACI were to use data plane IP learning to record each MAC address that lives directly behind an L3Out and associate with these MAC addresses all the external IP addresses that communicate into the fabric, the ACI endpoint table would conceivably grow exponentially to encompass all IP addresses in the Internet. However, this would never actually happen because ACI places a cap on the number of IP addresses that can be associated with a MAC address. Even so, it is likely that the endpoint table would quickly grow beyond the capabilities of the physical switch hardware.

To optimize the endpoint table size, ACI learns only the source MAC addresses (and not source IP addresses) from data plane packets that arrive on an L3Out. ACI then uses ARP to resolve next-hop IP-to-MAC address information it needs to send traffic out L3Outs.

In summary, information in the ACI routing table and ARP table are all ACI needs to forward traffic out an ACI fabric. There is no technical benefit for ACI to learn /32 IP addresses for all endpoints outside the fabric.

Limiting IP Learning to a Subnet

There might be times when a device is placed in an EPG as a result of a misconfiguration. ACI may then learn the endpoint in the data plane, even if the endpoint has an IP address in a different subnet than that of the EPG and bridge domain in which it has been configured. The Limit IP Learning to Subnet bridge domain setting prevents unnecessary learning of IP addresses when an endpoint IP address does not fall into a subnet that has been defined on the bridge domain (see Figure 8-4).

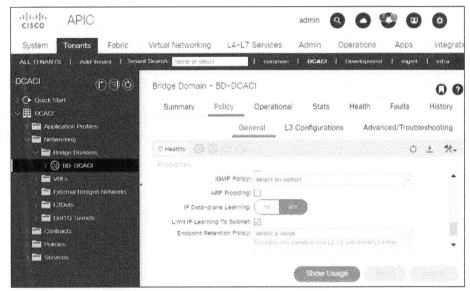

Figure 8-4   *Enabling the Limit IP Learning to Subnet Feature*

NOTE   Limit IP Learning to Subnet does not prevent the learning of MAC addresses.

Understanding Enforce Subnet Check

The Limit IP Learning to Subnet BD setting prevents the local learning of endpoint IP addresses if the endpoint is in a subnet other than those configured on a bridge domain, but it does *not* prevent potential erroneous learning of the endpoint MAC address.

The Enforce Subnet Check feature, on the other hand, ensures that an IP address and MAC address are learned as a new local endpoint *only if* the source IP address of the incoming packet belongs to one of the ingress bridge domain subnets.

NOTE   Regardless of the source IP range, the Cisco ACI leaf still learns the MAC address if the forwarding represents a switching operation.

Enforce Subnet Check, which is enabled at the VRF instance level, to an extent supersedes Limit IP Learning to Subnet and enables slightly stronger checks against bridge domain subnets. It is, therefore, a beneficial tool in preventing IP spoofing.

Disabling Data Plane Endpoint Learning on a Bridge Domain

In general, there is very little downside to ACI data plane learning behavior. There *are* times, however, when it may be valid to turn off data plane learning altogether for a particular bridge domain. There are also times when it makes sense to dumb down ACI a little to accommodate devices with special forwarding or failover needs.

For example, say that you have connected a pair of firewalls to the fabric and have created service graphs. You have created a bridge domain for IP connectivity between the firewalls and the fabric and wish to punt specific traffic to these firewalls. This is the definition of a service graph with policy-based redirect (PBR). But what happens if the firewalls send the traffic back to ACI, and the recipient leaf connecting to the firewalls thinks it has now locally learned the endpoint that generated the traffic?

For this PBR use case, the Endpoint Data Plane Learning setting (shown in Figure 8-4) can be disabled on the bridge domain connecting the leaf and firewalls together to signal to the leaf not to learn any endpoints in this special-use bridge domain. Note that, as of the time of writing, the PBR use case is the only valid instance for disabling data plane learning at the bridge domain level. This configuration setting prevents both MAC and IP address learning.

Disabling IP Data Plane Learning at the VRF Level

In some environments, there may be challenges with alternative vendor solutions that indirectly impact data plane endpoint learning in ACI. For example, some load-balancer platforms tend to send TCP resets after an active/standby failover has taken place under certain conditions. If these TCP resets are sent by the formerly active node using the source IP address of the then-active node, ACI data plane learning interprets the erroneously sourced TCP reset as an endpoint move. In such cases, this could lead to service disruption.

The best way to approach problems like these is to attach offending devices like load balancers and firewalls to ACI by using service graphs. But if a customer has concerns about service graphs, IP Data Plane Learning can be set to Disabled at the VRF level. With this setting, ACI acts like a traditional network in terms of endpoint learning: ACI continues to learn MAC addresses via the data plane, but it learn IP addresses only via traditional mechanisms, such as ARP, GARP, and ND.

Packet Forwarding in ACI

Even though traffic forwarding is not called out on the Implementing Cisco Application Centric Infrastructure DCACI 300-620 exam blueprint, bridge domain configuration knobs such as L2 Unknown Unicast Flood and Hardware Proxy as well as Unicast Routing and ARP Flooding do appear on the blueprint.

The four major ACI forwarding scenarios in this section help you better understand the difference between these settings and, more generally, better grasp how ACI works.

Forwarding Scenario 1: Both Endpoints Attach to the Same Leaf

If both the source and destination endpoints attempting to communicate with one another attach to the same leaf switch, the leaf considers the two endpoints to be local endpoints.

In this scenario, the forwarding is very similar to how Layer 2 and Layer 3 forwarding takes place in traditional networks. With ACI, the leaf performs a lookup in the endpoint table and forwards the traffic to the destination switch port. This, of course, assumes that the destination endpoint has been learned properly and that the traffic flow has been whitelisted.

Note that an ACI leaf does not need to encapsulate packets in VXLAN if the destination is local. Packets need to be encapsulated in VXLAN only if they need to be forwarded to a VTEP associated with another fabric node.

Example 8-2 shows that two endpoints with IP addresses 10.233.58.20 and 10.233.58.32 have been learned locally on LEAF102. This is evident because the endpoints appear with the letter L in the fourth column. The output also shows that they have different port encapsulation and PI VLANs, implying that they are likely to be in different EPGs. As long as the necessary contracts have been applied to the respective EPGs, these two endpoints should have no problem communicating with one another.

Example 8-2   *Verifying Endpoint Learning and the Path Between Locally Attached Endpoints*

```
LEAF102# show endpoint ip 10.233.58.20
Legend:
 s - arp                 H - vtep             V - vpc-attached     p - peer-aged
 R - peer-attached-rl    B - bounce           S - static           M - span
 D - bounce-to-proxy     O - peer-attached    a - local-aged       m - svc-mgr
 L - local                                    E - shared-service
+---------------------+---------------+-----------------+--------------+-----------+
        VLAN/            Encap           MAC Address       MAC Info/      Interface
        Domain           VLAN            IP Address        IP Info
+---------------------+---------------+-----------------+--------------+-----------+
76                       vlan-3171       0050.56b7.c60a    L              eth1/46
Prod:Temp                vlan-3171       10.233.58.20      L              eth1/46


LEAF102# show endpoint ip 10.233.58.32
Legend:
 s - arp                 H - vtep             V - vpc-attached     p - peer-aged
 R - peer-attached-rl    B - bounce           S - static           M - span
 D - bounce-to-proxy     O - peer-attached    a - local-aged       m - svc-mgr
 L - local                                    E - shared-service
+---------------------+---------------+-----------------+--------------+-----------+
        VLAN/            Encap           MAC Address       MAC Info/      Interface
        Domain           VLAN            IP Address        IP Info
+---------------------+---------------+-----------------+--------------+-----------+
73                       vlan-3169       0050.56b7.751d    L              eth1/45
Prod:Temp                vlan-3169       10.233.58.32      L              eth1/45
```

Understanding Pervasive Gateways

Sometimes you might find that ACI has not learned a local endpoint or the IP address associated with the endpoint. If this is the case and the default gateway for the relevant bridge domain is in the fabric, it helps to verify that ACI has programmed a pervasive gateway for the endpoint subnet on the intended leaf. When you deploy a static path mapping to a switch port on a leaf, this action should be sufficient for the leaf to deploy a pervasive gateway for the bridge domain subnet unless the EPG domain assignment or underlying access policies for the port have been misconfigured.

A *pervasive gateway* is an anycast default gateway that ACI leaf switches install to allow local endpoints to communicate beyond their local subnets. The benefit of this anycast function is that each top-of-rack leaf switch is able to serve as the default gateway for all locally attached endpoints. A pervasive gateway is deployed as a bridge domain SVI and appears in the leaf routing table as a local host route.

Example 8-3 shows pervasive gateways for a particular bridge domain deployed on two switches with hostnames LEAF101 and LEAF102. The distributed nature of pervasive gateways is a key component of how ACI is optimized for east–west traffic flows.

Example 8-3 *Output Reflecting Installation of Pervasive Gateway on Relevant Leafs*

```
LEAF101# show ip int brief vrf Prod:Temp
IP Interface Status for VRF " Prod:Temp"(23)
Interface            Address              Interface Status
vlan72               10.233.58.1/24       protocol-up/link-up/admin-up


LEAF101# show ip route 10.233.58.1 vrf Prod:Temp
10.233.58.1/32, ubest/mbest: 1/0, attached, pervasive
    *via 10.233.58.1, vlan72, [0/0], 05w01d, local, local


LEAF102# show ip int brief vrf Prod:Temp
IP Interface Status for VRF "Prod:Temp"(25)
Interface            Address              Interface Status
vlan65               10.233.58.1/24       protocol-up/link-up/admin-up


LEAF102# show ip route 10.233.58.1 vrf Prod:Temp
10.233.58.1/32, ubest/mbest: 1/0, attached, pervasive
    *via 10.233.58.1, vlan65, [0/0], 05w01d, local, local
```

In case the reference to VLANs 72 and 65 seems confusing, take a look at Example 8-4, which shows output from both switches. These two VLAN IDs are PI VLANs for a bridge domain deployed on LEAF101 and LEAF102, respectively. You know that both of these PI VLANs reference the same global object because the VNIDs are the same.

Example 8-4 *Verifying the Relationship Between PI VLANs and VNIDs*

```
LEAF101# show vlan id 72 extended

VLAN      Name                          Encap                Ports
--------  ----------------------------  -------------------  ----------------------
72        Prod:BD-Temp                  vxlan-15826916       Eth1/45,Eth1/46

LEAF102# show vlan id 65 extended
VLAN      Name                          Encap                Ports
--------  ----------------------------  -------------------  ----------------------
65        Prod:BD-Temp                  vxlan-15826916       Eth1/45, Eth1/46
```

It is important to reiterate that a pervasive gateway for a bridge domain can be installed on any number of leaf switches within a fabric as long as relevant EPG mappings exist on the leaf. Scalability dictates that ACI does not deploy policy where it is not needed.

NOTE Pervasive gateways are never deployed on spines; they are only deployed on leaf switches.

8

If a bridge domain has more than one subnet assignment, additional subnet gateways appear as secondary IP addresses associated with the same BD SVI.

Forwarding Scenario 2: Known Destination Behind Another Leaf

Suppose endpoint EP1 local to LEAF102 wants to communicate with EP2 on LEAF101, as shown in Figure 8-5. To make this forwarding possible, LEAF102 needs to place a tunnel endpoint IP address corresponding to LEAF101 in the Outer Destination IP field of the VXLAN encapsulation and send it on its way. Because EP1 only connects to LEAF102, the Outer Source IP field would contain the LEAF102 PTEP and not a vPC VIP.

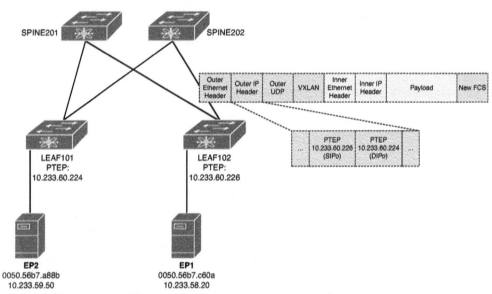

Figure 8-5   *Cross-Leaf Communication Between Known Endpoints*

Verifying the Traffic Path Between Known Endpoints

Let's use the switch CLI to verify the traffic path shown in Figure 8-5. ACI forwarding logic dictates that in determining where to send traffic, the endpoint table is consulted before anything else. Example 8-5 shows that LEAF102 needs to send the traffic out logical interface tunnel2 toward PTEP address 10.233.60.224 for traffic to reach 10.233.59.50. The fact that a tunnel is shown as the egress interface in the **show endpoint** output is confirmation that LEAF102 considers the endpoint to be a remote endpoint.

Example 8-5   *CLI Output Showing a Remote Endpoint*

```
LEAF102# show endpoint ip 10.233.59.50
Legend:
  s - arp                 H - vtep          V - vpc-attached   p - peer-aged
  R - peer-attached-rl    B - bounce        S - static         M - span
  D - bounce-to-proxy     O - peer-attached a - local-aged     m - svc-mgr
  L - local                                 E - shared-service
```

```
+--------------------+----------------+-----------------+---------------+-------------+
      VLAN/               Encap           MAC Address       MAC Info/     Interface
      Domain              VLAN            IP Address        IP Info
+--------------------+----------------+-----------------+---------------+-------------+
66                       vlan-3172       0050.56b7.a88b       0            tunnel2

Prod:Temp                vlan-3172       10.233.59.50         0            tunnel2


LEAF102# show interface tunnel 2
Tunnel2 is up
    MTU 9000 bytes, BW 0 Kbit
    Transport protocol is in VRF "overlay-1"
    Tunnel protocol/transport is ivxlan
    Tunnel source 10.233.60.226/32 (lo0)
    Tunnel destination 10.233.60.224
    Last clearing of "show interface" counters never
    Tx
    0 packets output, 1 minute output rate 0 packets/sec
    Rx
    0 packets input, 1 minute input rate 0 packets/sec
```

What leaf corresponds to 10.233.60.224? As indicated in Example 8-6, 10.233.60.224 is the PTEP for LEAF101. Note that the command **acidiag fnvread** can be run on either APICs or fabric nodes.

Example 8-6   *Identifying the Node Corresponding to a Tunnel Destination*

```
APIC1# acidiag fnvread
ID    Pod ID    Name      Serial Number   IP Address         Role    State LastUpdMsgId
-------------------------------------------------------------------------------------
101      1       LEAF101   FDOXXXXXA       10.233.60.224/32   leaf    active    0
102      1       LEAF102   FDOXXXXXB       10.233.60.226/32   leaf    active    0
103      1       LEAF103   FDOXXXXXC       10.233.60.228/32   leaf    active    0
104      1       LEAF104   FDOXXXXXD       10.233.60.229/32   leaf    active    0
201      1       SPINE201  FDOXXXXXE       10.233.60.225/32   spine   active    0
202      1       SPINE202  FDOXXXXXF       10.233.60.227/32   spine   active    0
Total 4 nodes
```

When LEAF101 receives the encapsulated packet, it sees that the outer destination IP address is its PTEP. It therefore decapsulates the packet, sees that it is destined to one of its local endpoints, and forwards it on to 10.233.59.50.

At this point, if LEAF101 does not have entries for remote endpoint EP1, it adds the necessary remote endpoint entry to its endpoint table. In this case, it only needs to learn the IP address because the two communicating endpoints are in different subnets. It populates its local tunnel interface corresponding with PTEP 10.233.60.226 as the egress interface toward this remote endpoint.

Before we move on to the next topic, there is one more point to reflect on. The output in Example 8-5 shows that LEAF102 learned both the MAC address and IP address 10.233.59.50. While a leaf may learn both the MAC address and any IP addresses for a remote endpoint if the switch is performing both switching and routing operations to a destination endpoint, this is not the case in this example. In fact, EP2 is the only endpoint in this particular BD and EPG at the moment; therefore, no Layer 2 operation with endpoints behind LEAF102 could have possibly occurred. Clues to why LEAF102 learned both the MAC address and IP address in this instance can be found by reviewing the type of endpoint registered. The endpoint table logs 10.233.59.50 with the letter O, implying that LEAF102 and LEAF101 have a vPC peering with one another. Even though EP2 is not itself behind a virtual port channel, leaf switches in a vPC domain do synchronize entries. This synchronization includes both MAC addresses and IP addresses.

Behind the scenes, let's break the vPC peering by deleting the explicit vPC protection group. Example 8-7 shows that, as expected, LEAF102 now only learns the IP address of EP2 since all of its local endpoints only have inter-subnet communication with this particular remote endpoint.

Example 8-7   *No Intra-Subnet Communication Means the Remote Endpoint MAC Address Is Not Learned*

```
LEAF102# show system internal epm endpoint ip 10.233.59.50


MAC : 0000.0000.0000 ::: Num IPs : 1
IP# 0 : 10.233.59.50 ::: IP# 0 flags :  ::: l3-sw-hit: No
Vlan id : 0 ::: Vlan vnid : 0 ::: VRF name : Prod:Temp
BD vnid : 0 ::: VRF vnid : 2228225
Phy If : 0 ::: Tunnel If : 0x18010002
Interface : Tunnel2
Flags : 0x80004400 ::: sclass : 49161 ::: Ref count : 3
EP Create Timestamp : 06/02/2020 06:07:58.418861
EP Update Timestamp : 06/02/2020 06:07:58.418861
EP Flags : IP|sclass|timer|
```

Understanding Learning and Forwarding for vPCs

Sometimes a tunnel may correspond to a logical switch representing two vPC peers. This is the case when an endpoint is behind a vPC. Figure 8-6 shows EP1 vPC attached to LEAF101 and LEAF102. If EP1 were to send traffic to known remote endpoint EP2, the recipient leaf (either LEAF101 or LEAF102) would encapsulate the traffic in VXLAN to send it to LEAF103. But the PTEP addresses would not be used to source this traffic. Instead, these vPC peers would place a special TEP address called a *vPC VIP* or (*virtual IP*) in the Outer Source IP Address field.

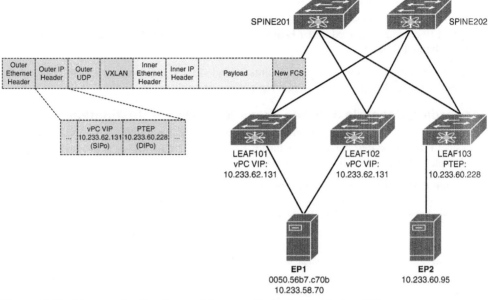

Figure 8-6 *Communication Sourced from an Endpoint Behind a vPC*

This behavior ensures that LEAF103 learns the endpoint from the vPC VIP and not LEAF101 and LEAF102 PTEP addresses. If ACI did not employ this approach, remote switches would see endpoint entries for EP1 bouncing between LEAF101 and LEAF102. Use of vPC VIPs, therefore, ensures that endpoint learning always remains stable and that Layer 3 equal-cost multipathing can be used for forwarding to and from vPC-attached endpoints.

Example 8-8 shows how you can identify the vPC VIP assigned to a leaf switch that is part of a vPC domain. This command shows only the vPC VIP for the local vPC domain.

Example 8-8 *Identifying the VTEP Assigned to a vPC Domain*

```
LEAF101# show system internal epm vpc
(...output truncated for brevity...)
Local TEP IP                      : 10.233.60.224
Peer TEP IP                       : 10.233.60.226
vPC configured                    : Yes
vPC VIP                           : 10.233.62.131
MCT link status                   : Up
Local vPC version bitmap          : 0x7
Peer vPC version bitmap           : 0x7
Negotiated vPC version            : 3
Peer advertisement received       : Yes
Tunnel to vPC peer                : Up
```

An alternative way to identify all the vPC VIPs in a fabric is to log in to the APICs instead and run the command **show vpc map**. Similar output can be obtained from the GUI in the Virtual IP column displayed under **Fabric > Access Policies > Policies > Switch > Virtual Port Channel Default.**

In light of how ACI learns remote endpoints behind vPCs, it is important for switches to be paired into vPC domains before deploying vPC interfaces.

Forwarding Scenario 3: Spine Proxy to Unknown Destination

Imagine that an ACI leaf has performed a lookup in its endpoint table and finds that it has not learned the destination endpoint for a particular traffic flow, as is the case in Example 8-9. What does the leaf do next?

Example 8-9   *Endpoint Not Found in Leaf Endpoint Table*

```
LEAF102# show endpoint ip 10.233.59.100
Legend:
 s - arp                 H - vtep              V - vpc-attached       p - peer-aged
 R - peer-attached-rl    B - bounce            S - static             M - span
 D - bounce-to-proxy     O - peer-attached     a - local-aged         m - svc-mgr
 L - local               E - shared-service
+--------------------+---------------+----------------+---------------+-------------+
      VLAN/                Encap          MAC Address      MAC Info/      Interface
      Domain               VLAN           IP Address       IP Info
+--------------------+---------------+----------------+---------------+-------------+
```

Once destination endpoint 10.233.59.100 has been confirmed to *not* be in the endpoint table, LEAF102 consults its routing table. Example 8-10 shows what the specific route lookup on LEAF102 might yield.

Example 8-10   *Pervasive Route for a Bridge Domain Subnet*

```
LEAF102# show ip route 10.233.59.100 vrf Prod:Temp
IP Route Table for VRF "Prod:Temp"
'*' denotes best ucast next-hop
'**' denotes best mcast next-hop
'[x/y]' denotes [preference/metric]
'%<string>' in via output denotes VRF <string>

10.233.59.0/24, ubest/mbest: 1/0, attached, direct, pervasive
    *via 10.233.62.130%overlay-1, [1/0], 06:50:59, static, tag 4294967294
         recursive next hop: 10.233.62.130/32%overlay-1
```

As indicated by the keyword **pervasive** in Example 8-10, the lookup yields a special route called a *pervasive route*. Pervasive routes and pervasive gateways are two different things with different purposes. To better understand the function of a pervasive route, it helps to identify its next hop. For this purpose, examine Example 8-11.

Example 8-11 *Anycast TEP Address Used for Forwarding to the Spine Proxy*

```
LEAF102# show isis dteps vrf overlay-1
IS-IS Dynamic Tunnel End Point (DTEP) database:
DTEP-Address      Role    Encapsulation    Type
10.233.60.224     LEAF    N/A              PHYSICAL
10.233.60.225     SPINE   N/A              PHYSICAL
10.233.62.130     SPINE   N/A              PHYSICAL,PROXY-ACAST-V4
10.233.62.129     SPINE   N/A              PHYSICAL,PROXY-ACAST-MAC
10.233.62.128     SPINE   N/A              PHYSICAL,PROXY-ACAST-V6
10.233.60.227     SPINE   N/A              PHYSICAL
10.233.62.131     LEAF    N/A              PHYSICAL
```

It should be clear from the output in Example 8-11 that the pervasive route references the anycast spine proxy address for IPv4 forwarding as the next hop. This is because traffic toward unknown destinations can potentially be sent to one of the spines to allow the spine COOP database to then determine how to forward the traffic onward to its destination.

To summarize, a *pervasive route* is a route to a BD subnet that points to the spine proxy TEP as its next-hop IP address. Because each leaf consults its endpoint table first, a pervasive route does not come into play unless an endpoint is deemed to be unknown. The function of a pervasive route, therefore, is to ensure that a leaf switch knows that a particular destination is expected to be inside the fabric. If a pervasive route were not deployed for a BD subnet, a leaf might think that a default route learned via an L3Out is the best way to get the traffic to its destination. If so, it could decide to either drop the traffic or forward it to the border leaf TEP addresses instead of the spine proxy address. Pervasive routes help prevent this suboptimal forwarding scenario.

NOTE A pervasive route is installed on a leaf if at least one EPG on the leaf is allowed through contracts or another whitelisting mechanism to communicate with at least one EPG associated with the destination bridge domain. This is in line with ACI deploying policies only where they are needed.

8

Just because a pervasive route exists and the spine proxy function can potentially be used for forwarding to an unknown destination does not mean that the leaf will choose to forward traffic to the spine proxy. Bridge domain settings dictate what happens next. If, for example, the traffic is L2 unknown unicast traffic and hardware proxy has been configured for the bridge domain, the leaf forwards the traffic destined to an unknown endpoint to the spine proxy function.

When a leaf decides to forward traffic to a spine proxy TEP, it does so by placing its own PTEP or vPC VIP as the outer source IP address in the VXLAN encapsulation. The intended spine proxy TEP gets populated as the outer destination IP address.

Figure 8-7 recaps how spine proxy forwarding works. In this case, EP1 needs to get traffic to EP2. Both endpoints are in the same bridge domain, and the default gateway (10.233.59.1/24) is in the fabric. Let's suppose that EP1 has never communicated with EP2. If that were the case, EP1 would first send an ARP request out to EP2 because it is in the same subnet as EP2. LEAF102 would consult its endpoint table and not find an entry. It would then do a routing table lookup and see a pervasive route. Regardless of the pervasive route, it knows the default gateway is in the fabric. This is because it, too, has deployed a pervasive gateway for the bridge domain. It then needs to decide whether to use flooding or hardware proxy. It decides to send the traffic to the spine proxy because the L2 Unknown Unicast setting on the bridge domain was set to Hardware Proxy, and ARP flooding has been disabled. Next, it needs to decide which spine proxy TEP to place in the Outer Destination IP Header field. It selects the spine proxy PROXY-ACAST-V4 IP address. Because EP1 is single-homed, LEAF102 places its PTEP in the Outer Source IP Address field. In this example, LEAF101 and LEAF102 are not vPC peers anyway.

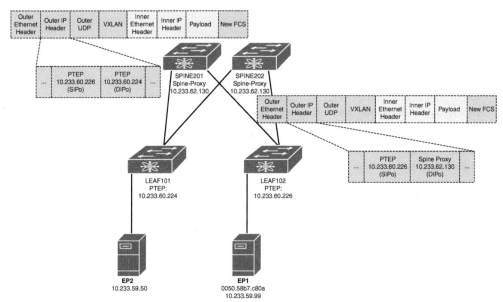

Figure 8-7   *LEAF102 Using Spine Proxy to Send EP1 Traffic to an Unknown Destination*

Once a spine receives a frame with the spine proxy TEP as the outer destination IP address, it knows it needs to perform a COOP lookup on the destination. If it *does* know the destination, it updates the outer destination IP address to that of the recipient leaf PTEP or vPC VIP and sends the traffic onward. This DIPo update at the spine is demonstrated in Figure 8-7. If the spine *does not* know the destination and the destination is in a routed bridge domain, it drops the traffic and then kicks off the ARP gleaning process, with the assumption that the destination may be a silent host. If the destination *is* a silent host, it is likely to be learned in time for future spine proxy operations to succeed.

After the spine updates the outer destination IP address and the traffic eventually reaches its destination, the response from the destination endpoint leads to the source leaf learning the remote destination. Future traffic is then sent directly between the leaf switches without spine proxy involvement.

Note that in this entire process, there is no need to flood traffic across the fabric. By minimizing flooding, the hardware proxy forwarding behavior reduces the impact of endpoint learning on switch resources and safeguards the stability of the network.

NOTE   The discussion around Figure 8-7 makes reference to the PROXY-ACAST-V4 address. Recall from Example 8-11 that ACI assigns three separate IP addresses to spine proxy functions. PROXY-ACAST-V4 concerns spine proxy forwarding for IPv4 traffic, which also includes ARP requests when ARP flooding has been disabled. The PROXY-ACAST-MAC address is used for L2 unknown unicast traffic when the L2 Unknown Unicast parameter is set to Hardware Proxy. Finally, PROXY-ACAST-V6 is used when spine proxy forwarding IPv6 traffic to an unknown destination.

Forwarding Scenario 4: Flooding to Unknown Destination

There are multiple forwarding scenarios for which ACI may need to flood traffic instead of using the spine proxy. For example, if there are silent hosts in an L2 bridge domain, ACI silent host detection would not work, and spine proxy forwarding might black-hole traffic. Also, when extending a VLAN into an ACI fabric and the default gateway remains outside ACI, flooding can help prevent certain traffic black holes. Chapter 10, "Extending Layer 2 Outside ACI," discusses Layer 2 extension in detail and addresses the logic behind flooding during network migrations. For now, let's dive into the details of how flooding and multi-destination forwarding work in ACI.

When a leaf switch receives traffic that needs to be flooded in a bridge domain, it takes the BD multicast address, selects one of several predefined loop-free topologies, and adds bits corresponding with the selected topology to the BD multicast address. The resulting IP address becomes the outer multicast Group IP outer (GIPo) address, which the source leaf places in the Outer Destination IP Address field when encapsulating the original payload in VXLAN.

The predefined topologies based on which ACI forwards multi-destination traffic are called *forwarding tag (FTag) trees*. Each FTag tree does not necessarily use all fabric uplinks. That is why ACI creates multiple FTag trees and load balances multi-destination traffic across them. All switches in a fabric understand based on the FTag bits in the GIPo address how to forward the traffic they receive further along the specified FTag tree. Four bits are used to identify FTag IDs; ACI fabrics support up to 12 FTag trees.

For example, Figure 8-8 depicts intra-subnet communication between EP1 and EP2 at a time when LEAF101 has not learned EP2. Say that LEAF101 has either not yet learned EP2 and L2 Unknown Unicast has been set to Flood, or the ARP Flooding setting has been enabled on the respective bridge domain. Either of these two settings would force ARP requests to be flooded. In this case, when LEAF101 determines through an endpoint table lookup that the endpoint is unknown, it needs to decide whether to send the ARP request to the spine proxy or to flood the ARP request. Because the ARP Flooding setting has been enabled, it floods the ARP request by adding the GIPo address as the destination outer IP address and adding its PTEP as the source outer IP address. Let's say that it selected FTag ID 0 when determining the GIPo address. That is why the GIPo address depicted appears to be a /28 subnet ID. In this case, the BD multicast address is the same as the GIPo address. This is not always the case.

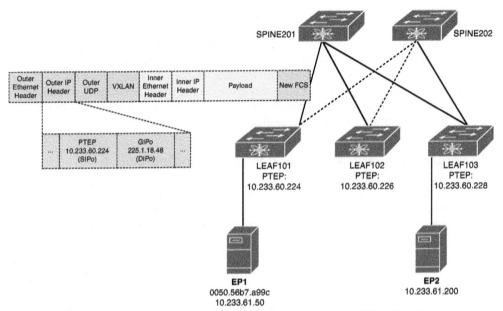

Figure 8-8 *Flooding Traffic to an Unknown Destination over an FTag Topology*

When determining where to forward the ARP request, LEAF101 follows the FTag 0 tree and sends the packet to SPINE201. As root of the FTag 0 tree, this spine then forwards the packet to all other leaf switches. Finally, LEAF103 forwards the packet to SPINE202. This last forwarding operation to SPINE202 is not really required for single-pod fabrics because spines do not themselves house endpoints. However, ACI ensures that flooded traffic reaches all leaf and spine switches anyway. This approach addresses specific use cases like multi-destination forwarding in multipod environments.

Note that even though both of these last two forwarding scenarios involved ARP requests, it is not just ARP traffic that may be flooded or spine proxied in ACI.

Understanding ARP Flooding

By now, it should be clear that ACI has ways to learn *almost all endpoints*, regardless of the L2 Unknown Unicast setting chosen.

If the Hardware Proxy setting is enabled, the ARP Flooding setting is disabled, and COOP knows of the endpoint, the fabric unicasts ARP requests to the intended destination. If the spine COOP database does not know the destination endpoint, the spines drop the ARP traffic and trigger ARP gleaning.

If, on the other hand, the ARP Flooding setting is enabled, the leaf switch receiving ARP traffic floods the traffic based on an FTag tree. The source leaf then learns the destination endpoint in response packets if the destination endpoint actually exists.

A tangible difference between enabling and disabling ARP flooding occurs with silent host movements. Suppose that hardware proxy has been enabled on a bridge domain, ARP flooding has been disabled, and ACI has already learned a silent host in the BD through ARP gleaning. If the silent host moves from one location to another without notifying the new ACI leaf via GARP or some other mechanism, ACI switches continue to forward traffic intended for the silent IP address to the previous location until retention timers clear the endpoint from COOP. Until that point, if an endpoint sends ARP requests toward this silent host, ARP gleaning is not triggered because COOP considers the destination endpoint to be known. On the other hand, with ARP flooding enabled on the BD, ARP requests are flooded, and the silent host responds at its new location, enabling the new local leaf to learn the silent host and update COOP.

Just because ARP flooding can help in endpoint learning in situations like these does *not* mean ARP flooding should be enabled on all bridge domains. But in environments in which silent hosts with low-latency communication requirements can move between leaf switches, enabling ARP flooding on the bridge domains housing such endpoints can minimize the potential for traffic disruption.

Note a caveat related to ARP flooding: If Unicast Routing has been disabled on a bridge domain, ARP traffic is always flooded, even if the ARP Flooding setting is not enabled.

Deploying a Multi-Tier Application

In this section, we put into practice the information provided so far in this chapter. Suppose the business unit involved in gaming products from Chapter 7, "Implementing Access Policies," wants to deploy an application consisting of multiple component tiers. One of the first things engineers typically consider is the number of bridge domains and EPGs needed.

For the sake of argument, say that the engineers involved in the project know that none of the servers that are part of the solution will be silent hosts. All default gateways will reside inside ACI since the desire is to implement granular whitelisting for the application and leverage pervasive gateways for east–west traffic optimization.

With the data already available, the ACI engineers know that flooding for this application can be kept at an absolute minimum. For this reason, they decide to deploy only a single bridge domain; each tier of this application will be a separate EPG.

Figure 8-9 shows a hypothetical BD/EPG design for such an application that is simple yet effective. If the application ever scales beyond a single /24 subnet, the engineers know they can easily add additional subnets to the BD.

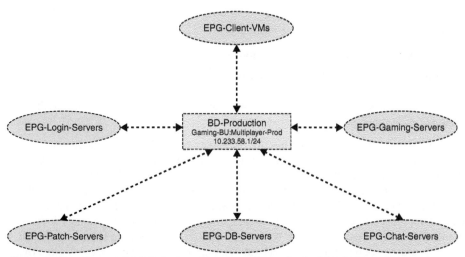

Figure 8-9   *BD and EPG Relationships for a Hypothetical Multi-Tier Application*

Configuring Application Profiles, BDs, and EPGs

Because bridge domains and EPGs for the gaming business unit application are known, it is time to implement the required objects.

To create the bridge domain in line with the diagram shown in Figure 8-9, navigate to **Tenants > Gaming-BU > Networking**, right-click Bridge Domains, and select Create Bridge Domain. Figure 8-10 shows optimal settings for the first page of the Create Bridge Domain wizard.

Figure 8-10 *Configuring a Bridge Domain Using Optimize Forwarding Parameters*

The default Optimize forwarding settings depicted in the Create Bridge Domain wizard are as follows:

- **L2 Unknown Unicast:** Hardware Proxy

- **L3 Unknown Multicast Flooding:** Flood

- **Multi-destination Flooding:** Flood in BD

If any of these settings need to be modified, you can select the Custom option from the Forwarding drop-down box to view these three settings.

Click Next to move on to the second page of the Create Bridge Domain wizard, which allows you to adjust Layer 3 settings. Leave Unicast Routing enabled because ACI will be performing routing for the BD and will be expected to learn endpoint IP addresses in the BD. ARP Flooding is enabled by default in some ACI code versions. However, it can be disabled for this BD because the subnet default gateway will reside in the fabric, and none of the endpoints are anticipated to be silent hosts. Finally, under the Subnets view, click the + sign and add the specified BD subnet. When defining a BD subnet, always enter the default gateway IP address followed by the subnet CIDR notation and *not* the subnet ID. The Private to VRF Scope setting shown in Figure 8-11 suggests that subnet 10.233.58.0/24 will not be advertised out the fabric for the time being. Click Next on the L3 Configurations page and then click Finish on the final page of the Create Bridge Domain wizard to create the BD.

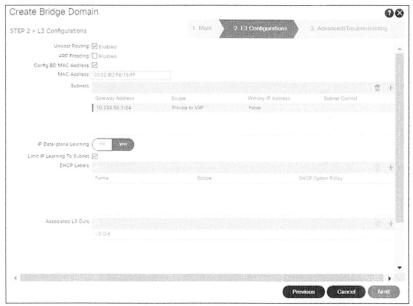

Figure 8-11 *Configuring Layer 3 Settings for a Bridge Domain*

Note that once the BD is created, the APIC assigns a BD multicast address to the bridge domain, as shown in Figure 8-12. This is the address used as the basis for the GIPo address for traffic flooding.

Figure 8-12 *Multicast Address Assigned to a Bridge Domain*

With the BD created, it is now time to create the required EPGs. Before creating EPGs, an application profile needs to be created to house the EPGs. Anticipating that further instances of the application may be needed in the future, the ACI engineers decide to name this application container Multiplayer-App1. To create this EPG, you navigate to **Tenants > Gaming-BU > Application Profiles > Multiplayer-App1**, right-click Application EPGs, and select Create Application EPG.

Figure 8-13 shows that the most important settings for an EPG at this point are the name and bridge domain association. All other settings shown here have been left at their defaults.

Note that if traffic from endpoints in this EPG should be assigned to a specific QoS level, this can be accomplished via the QoS Class drop-down box. Click Finish to create the EPG.

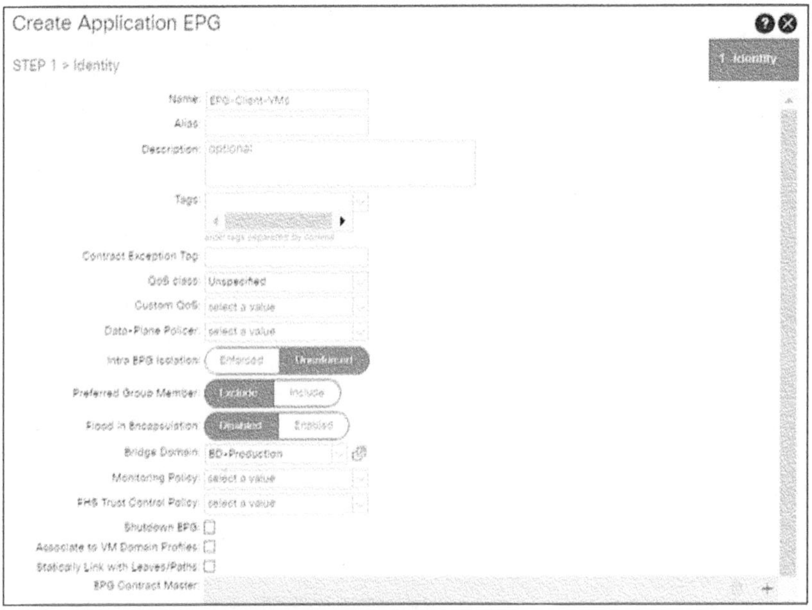

Figure 8-13 *The Create Application EPG Wizard*

By navigating to the Application EPGs subfolder of an application profile, you can view the list of all EPGs in the application profile. Figure 8-14 lists all the EPGs under the Multi-player-App1 application profile. Note that the APICs have assigned a Class ID to each EPG. This parameter is used in the application of contracts between EPGs.

Figure 8-14 *Verifying EPGs Under a Specific Application Profile*

In Figure 8-14, notice the In Shutdown column. Shutting down an EPG is an easy way to isolate a set of endpoints without having to make any changes to policy if at any point they are compromised.

Assigning Domains to EPGs

Before you can map an EPG to physical switch ports, you need to assign a domain to the EPG. Figure 8-15 shows a physical domain named GamingBU-Physical associated with EPG-Client-VMs.

Figure 8-15 *Assigning a Domain to an EPG*

Recall that assigning a domain to an EPG is a tenant-side confirmation that an EPG has endpoints of a particular type. It also links the Tenants view with the Access Policies view by enabling certain ACI users to deploy an EPG to certain switch ports using encapsulations specified in the VLAN pool referenced by the added domain.

Policy Deployment Following BD and EPG Setup

It would be natural but incorrect to assume that the configurations performed so far in this section would lead to the deployment of pervasive gateways, pervasive routes, or even PI VLANs on any leaf switches in the fabric. This goes back to the concept discussed earlier of ACI not deploying policy that is not needed on the switches. In this case, no policy is needed on switches because no form of EPG-to-port mapping has yet been implemented.

Mapping EPGs to Ports Using Static Bindings

Chapter 7 covers the creation of a number of access policies. One of the access policies created there is a vPC named Multiplayer-Server-3, which is assigned to Nodes 101 and 102 on port 1/38. This section shows how to assign one of the newly created EPGs to this vPC and how to get traffic flowing to the Multiplayer-Server-3 server. To do so, navigate to the EPG in question and expose its subfolders, right-click the Static Ports folder, and select Deploy Static EPG on PC, vPC, or Interface.

Figure 8-16 shows the subsequent mapping of the EPG to the access policy Multiplayer-Server-3 using the VLAN Port Encap setting 271. Static binding path types include ports, port channels, and vPCs. Note that two of the critical settings shown require further explanation: Mode and Deployment Immediacy.

Figure 8-16 *Statically Mapping an EPG to an Encapsulation on a vPC*

The static binding Mode is concerned with how ACI deploys an EPG on a given port. Three port binding modes are available in ACI:

- **Trunk:** Traffic for the EPG is sourced by the leaf switch with the specified VLAN tag. The leaf switch also expects to receive traffic tagged with that VLAN to be able to associate it with the EPG. Traffic received untagged is discarded.

- **Access (Untagged):** Traffic for the EPG is sourced by the leaf as untagged. Traffic received by the leaf switch as untagged or with the tag specified during the static binding configuration is associated with the EPG.

- **Access (802.1P):** When only a single EPG is bound to an interface using this setting, the behavior is identical as that of the untagged case. If additional EPGs are associated with the same interface, traffic for the EPG is sourced with an IEEE 802.1Q tag using VLAN 0 (IEEE 802.1P tag) or is sourced as untagged in the case of EX switches.

In general, the Deployment Immediacy setting governs when policy CAM resources are allocated for EPG-to-EPG communications. (Think whitelisting policies.) The Deployment Immediacy parameter can be set to either of the following:

- **On Demand:** Specifies that the policy should be programmed in hardware only when the first packet is received through the data path. This setting helps optimize the hardware space.

- **Immediate:** Specifies that the policy should be programmed in hardware as soon as the policy is downloaded in the leaf software.

For static bindings, a leaf policy download occurs at the time the binding is correctly configured. Chapter 13, "Implementing Management," addresses policy download in further detail.

> **NOTE** In small and medium-sized fabrics that have limited any-to-any contracts and where there is little fear of policy CAM exhaustion, implementing static path bindings with Deployment Immediacy set to Immediate is most common. Chapters 9, "L3Outs," and 10, "Extending Layer 2 Outside ACI," address any-to-any contracts and policy CAM utilization in more detail.

There is a key configuration difference between mapping an EPG to port channels and vPCs and mapping it to individual ports. When mapping an EPG to a link aggregation, you select the desired vPC or port channel interface policy group in the Path drop-down box and are not necessarily concerned with physical port assignments. This is clear in Figure 8-16. When mapping an EPG to an individual port, however, the desired leaf and physical port associated with the mapping need to be selected using the Node and Path drop-downs, respectively. Compare Figure 8-17 with Figure 8-16 for context.

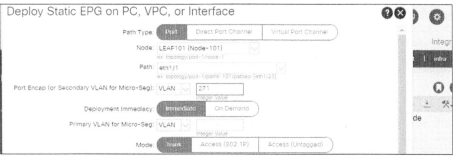

Figure 8-17 *Statically Mapping an EPG to an Encapsulation on an Individual Port*

Verifying EPG-to-Port Assignments

Static path bindings for an EPG can be verified under the Static Ports subfolder of the EPG. Although Figure 8-18 shows that static path bindings have been configured, it does not verify whether the configuration has taken effect. It helps to check faults to rule out the possibility of underlying configuration problems preventing the deployment of the policy.

Figure 8-18 *Verifying a Static Path Binding for an EPG*

A more valid way to verify an EPG-to-port mapping is to check the status of its deployment on the switch itself. Example 8-12 shows that EPG-Client-VMs has indeed been mapped to port Eth1/38 using the desired encapsulation. Note that Eth1/38 is a member of Po3, and it shows up in the output because the static binding being verified is for a vPC.

Example 8-12 *CLI Output Indicating EPG-to-Port Mapping Deployed to a Leaf Switch*

```
LEAF101# show vlan extended
(...output truncated for brevity...)

VLAN Name                                             Encap            Ports
-------- -------------------------------------------  ------------     ----------------
69       Gaming-BU:BD-Production                       vxlan-16285613   Eth1/38, Po3
70       Gaming-BU:Multiplayer-App1:EPG-Client-VMs    vlan-271         Eth1/38, Po3
```

Policy Deployment Following EPG-to-Port Assignment

When a leaf deploys EPG-to-port bindings, it also enables any other associated policies, such as BD subnet pervasive gateways and pervasive routes. Example 8-13 verifies the deployment of additional policies on LEAF101.

Example 8-13 *Verifying Deployment of a Pervasive Gateway and a Pervasive Route*

```
LEAF101# show ip int brief vrf Gaming-BU:Multiplayer-Prod
IP Interface Status for VRF "Gaming-BU:Multiplayer-Prod"(23)

Interface           Address              Interface Status
vlan69              10.233.58.1/24       protocol-up/link-up/admin-up


LEAF101# show ip route vrf Gaming-BU:Multiplayer-Prod
IP Route Table for VRF "Gaming-BU:Multiplayer-Prod"
'*' denotes best ucast next-hop
'**' denotes best mcast next-hop
'[x/y]' denotes [preference/metric]
'%<string>' in via output denotes VRF <string>

10.233.58.0/24, ubest/mbest: 1/0, attached, direct, pervasive
    *via 10.233.62.130%overlay-1, [1/0], 09:16:13, static, tag 4294967294
10.233.58.1/32, ubest/mbest: 1/0, attached, pervasive
    *via 10.233.58.1, vlan69, [0/0], 09:16:13, local, local
```

Mapping an EPG to All Ports on a Leaf

Sometimes, a company procures a leaf for a particular function and requires that a handful of EPGs be deployed to all non-fabric ports on the leaf. This might be the case when attaching CIMC connections to a dedicated low-bandwidth copper leaf, for instance. In cases like these, use of the Static Leafs feature can reduce the number of clicks necessary to deploy EPG-to-port mappings.

To map an EPG to all non-fabric ports on a leaf, double-click the desired EPG to expose its subfolders. Then right-click Static Leafs and select Statically Link with Node. Figure 8-19 shows the binding of an EPG to all non-fabric ports on a leaf with node ID 102 using the Port Encap setting 272.

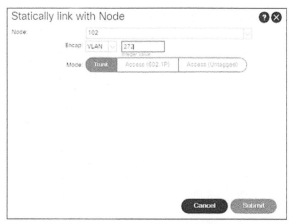

Figure 8-19 *Mapping an EPG to All Non-Fabric Ports on a Leaf Switch*

Enabling DHCP Relay for a Bridge Domain

Chapter 7 addresses the creation of DHCP relay policies under the Access Policies menu. These policies can then be consumed by bridge domains in any tenant to allow the BD to relay DHCP traffic to servers in different subnets.

To launch the Create DHCP Relay Label wizard, double-click the bridge domain in question to expose its subfolders, right-click DHCP Relay Labels, and select Create DHCP Relay Labels.

Figure 8-20 illustrates the deployment of DHCP relay functionality for BD-Production using a DHCP relay policy created in Chapter 7. The Scope setting shown in this figure refers to whether the DHCP relay policy that will be consumed resides within a tenant (tenant) or under the Access Policies menu (infra). You can select a DHCP relay policy under the Name drop-down or create a new one and then click Submit.

Figure 8-20 *Enabling DHCP Relay Functionality for a Bridge Domain*

You can configure a DHCP option policy to provide DHCP clients with configuration parameters such as the domain, name servers, subnet, and IP addresses. Once the policy is deployed, you can verify the DHCP relay configuration on leaf switches via the **show ip dhcp relay** command.

Whitelisting Intra-VRF Communications via Contracts

ACI being able to learn endpoints is not the same as endpoints being able to communicate with one another. Administrators still need to define valid traffic flows and whitelist them.

Chapter 5, "Tenant Building Blocks," provides a primer on contract theory. The remainder of this chapter puts that theory into practice by covering the implementation of contracts for a hypothetical multitier application.

> **NOTE**   While Cisco calls out contracts and filters as DCACI 300-620 exam topics, it does not cover route leaking (which is instead covered on the DCACIA 300-630 exam). This implies that DCACI candidates should not be tested on whitelisting inter-VRF communications. Therefore, this section limits its focus to enabling intra-VRF communication among EPGs.

Planning Contract Enforcement

Before enforcing contracts between endpoints, it is important to compile some form of data outlining valid and approved traffic flows. Solutions such as Cisco Tetration can help visualize all traffic flows in a data center. After you list the traffic flows that should be allowed, contracts can be put in place.

On the other hand, deploying a new application does not have to be very complex. Imagine that Figure 8-21 represents traffic flows that an applications team says should be allowed between EPGs that will together form a very basic in-house application.

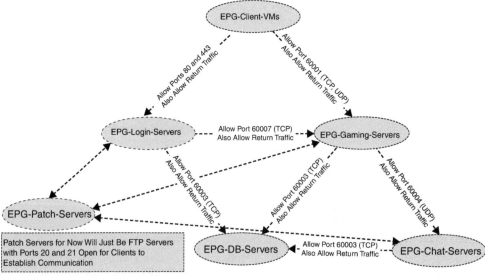

Figure 8-21   *Valid Traffic Flows for a Hypothetical Multi-Tier Application*

NOTE Figure 8-21 is not intended to represent a real-world application, nor is it meant to represent the network architecture of an actual game. It is meant only to provide a conceptual understanding of contracts. That is why the majority of ports shown are in the dynamic port range.

Say that the team deploying this application wants to keep the environment isolated for the time being. All application tiers reside in a VRF instance that has no Layer 3 connectivity with the outside world. For this reason, the deployment team has decided to stage a set of client virtual machines that can connect to the frontend components of the overall solution and mimic customer systems.

The first set of requirements, therefore, relates to client virtual machine connectivity into the environment. EPG-Client-VMs will serve as the EPG for such endpoints and should be able to communicate with EPG-Login-Servers on ports 80 and 443 and also with EPG-Gaming-Servers on port 60001. Both TCP and UDP traffic from EPG-Client-VMs to EPG-Gaming-Servers should be allowed.

The second set of requirements relates to bidirectional communications between servers that are part of the gaming infrastructure. Endpoints in EPG-Gaming-Servers, for example, need to be able to communicate with EPG-Chat-Servers via UDP port 60004. Likewise, EPG-Login-Servers, EPG-Gaming-Servers, and EPG-Chat-Servers need to be able to communicate with a number of database servers in EPG-DB-Servers via port 60003. Only TCP communication with database servers should be allowed. Finally, endpoints in EPG-Login-Servers should be able to connect to those in EPG-Gaming-Servers bidirectionally via TCP port 60007.

The final set of requirements relates to patch management. EPG-Login-Servers, EPG-Gaming-Servers, and EPG-Chat-Servers should all be allowed to initiate bidirectional communication with EPG-Patch-Servers via TCP on port 60006. UDP port 60005 to EPG-Patch-Servers and UDP port 60010 from EPG-Patch-Servers to the three noted endpoint groups also need to be opened.

Configuring Filters for Bidirectional Application

The first set of requirements listed is quite basic. To create a filter for HTTP and HTTPS traffic, navigate to the tenant in question, double-click the Contracts menu, right-click Filters, and select Create Filter.

NOTE Filters and contracts can also be created in the common tenant for reuse across all tenants, but using the common tenant and associated caveats are beyond the scope of the DCACI 300-620 exam.

Figure 8-22 shows the configuration of a single filter with two filter entries: one for HTTP traffic and the other for HTTPS. Recall that filters are only for matching traffic. They do *not* determine what to do with traffic.

Figure 8-22 *A Unidirectional Filter Whose Return Traffic Will Be Allowed via Subject*

Various columns can be populated for a filter entry. When you do not populate a column, ACI does not verify the associated part or parts of the packet. Some of the most important columns are as follows:

- **Name:** This is the (mandatory) name for the filter entry.

- **EtherType:** This field allows you to filter on EtherType. Available EtherType options include IP, IPv4, IPv6, ARP, FCoE, and Unspecified. For example, you might want to classify FCoE traffic in a filter to be able to drop such traffic to a server but at the same time allow ARP and IP traffic.

- **ARP Flag:** This field allows matching of ARP traffic, using the options ARP Reply, ARP Request, or Unspecified.

- **IP Protocol:** Available protocol options include TCP, UDP, ICMP, EIGRP, PIM, and Unspecified.

- **Match Only Fragments:** This field allows you to match only packet fragments. When it is enabled, the rule applies to any IP fragment, except the first.

- **Stateful:** This setting takes effect only when ACI is extended into hypervisors using Cisco AVE or Cisco AVS. By itself, ACI hardware performs stateless filtering. (Stateful filtering is described in more detail later in the chapter.)

- **Source Port/Range and Destination Port/Range:** These fields allow you to define a single port by specifying the same value in the From and To fields, or you can define a range of ports from 0 to 65535 by specifying different values in the From and To fields.

- **TCP Session Rules:** This field allows you to specify that ACI should match the traffic only if certain TCP flags are present in the packet. The available options for matching are Synchronize, Established, Acknowledgment, Unspecified, Reset, and Finish.

If you select the most generic EtherType option, Unspecified, all other fields are grayed out, and the resulting filter matches all traffic. To be able to match on specific TCP or UDP ports, it is crucial to first set EtherType to IP, IPv4, or IPv6. Otherwise, the IP Protocol and Match Only Fragments fields are grayed out because they do not apply to the other EtherType options. The same concept holds for ARP traffic. It is only when EtherType is set to ARP that a user can specify an ARP flag on which to match traffic. Likewise, the Stateful checkbox and the TCP Session Rules field appear grayed out until TCP is selected in the IP Protocol field.

To understand Source Port/Range and Destination Port/Range, you need to put these fields into the context of traffic flow. For instance, when looking at traffic from a consumer (client) to a provider (server), the Source Port/Range field refers to the port or range of ports on the client side that should be matched to allow the clients to talk to servers. Because client-side port selection is almost always dynamic, selection of the option Unspecified for this field makes the most sense for filters applied in the consumer-to-provider direction. With this same traffic direction in mind, the Destination Port/Range field refers to ports that need to remain open on the provider side. Selection of separate entries for HTTP and HTTPS in Figure 8-22 is based on the fact that ports 80 and 443 are not subsequent ports and therefore do not fall into a range.

Thinking about that logic, it may be clear that the filter depicted is just one side of the equation. What happens to return traffic from the server? The answer is that ACI *is* able to create an equivalent rule to also allow traffic in the reverse direction. This is why filters created for bidirectional application to contracts often only specify destination ports.

Configuring Subjects for Bidirectional Application of Filters

Subjects are bound to contracts and are not reusable, even though the contracts to which they are bound are reusable. You create subjects as part of the contract creation process. To create a contract, navigate to the tenant in question, double-click Contracts, right-click Standard, and select Create Contract.

Figure 8-23 shows the Create Contract page. On this page, you select a name for the contract, select a scope, and click the + sign next to Subjects to create a subject.

Figure 8-23   *The Create Contract Page*

Figure 8-24 shows the Create Contract Subject page. Here, you add all relevant filters in the Filters section. When you add multiple filters to a subject, you are telling ACI to take the same actions on traffic matched by any of the filters.

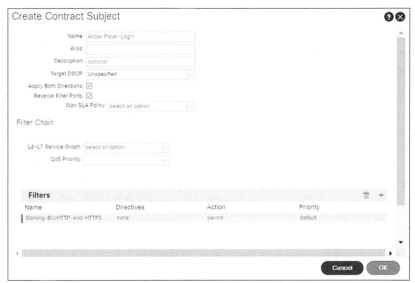

Figure 8-24 *Creating a Subject for a Contract*

The following four columns appear in the Filters view at the bottom of the Create Contract Subject page:

■ **Name:** This is the name of the filter added to the subject.

■ **Directives:** As of ACI Release 4.2, available options for this column are Log, Enable Policy Compression, and None. The Log directive enables rate-limited logging of traffic that matches the filter. This is only supported on Generation 2 and later switches. The Enable Policy Compression directive potentially reduces leaf policy CAM utilization by allowing identical filter rules to share a single TCAM entry even if applied to multiple different pairs of provider and consumer EPGs. This comes at the expense of logging data granularity and is supported only on Nexus 9300 series FX and later switches. If you do not select any of the noted directives, the filter shows up with the default setting None.

■ **Action:** Available options are Permit and Deny. The Permit option allows matched traffic through. The Deny option drops traffic matched by the filter.

■ **Priority:** When a Deny action has been selected for a filter, the Priority field defines the level of the precedence of the specific filter action. The Priority field for a filter is grayed out when the action is Permit.

Aside from the Filters section, you may have noticed two critical checkboxes in Figure 8-24: Apply Both Directions and Reverse Filter Ports. These two checkboxes determine whether the selected filter actions are applied bidirectionally.

Understanding Apply Both Directions and Reverse Filter Ports

There have been many instances of engineers disabling the Reverse Filter Ports checkbox and inadvertently breaking connectivity between EPGs. The reason usually turns out to be misinterpretation. Undeniably, it is easy to misinterpret the text Apply Both Directions to mean that communication in the return direction should also be allowed. However, this does *not* align with how ACI applies contracts.

Consider the filter entries created in Figure 8-22, earlier in the chapter. These filter entries allow traffic sourced from any port to reach port 80 or 443 on the destination side in one direction. If this same filter were to be applied in both the consumer-to-provider direction as well as the provider-to-consumer direction on two EPGs, both EPGs could communicate with one another on destination ports 80 and 443 unidirectionally. This is what happens when you keep the Apply Both Directions checkbox enabled but disable the Reverse Filter Ports checkbox. Figure 8-25 illustrates the resulting communication.

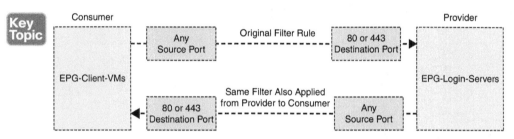

Figure 8-25 *Apply Both Directions Enabled and Reverse Filter Ports Disabled*

Although some applications benefit from unidirectional flows, there are not many realistic use cases for applying a single unidirectional filter toward a destination port bidirectionally across multiple EPGs.

Reverse Filter Ports complements the Apply Both Directions feature by swapping the ports in the Source Port/Range and Destination Port/Range fields with one another in the return direction, thus truly enabling return traffic to flow. Figure 8-26 illustrates what ACI does when Apply Both Directions and Reverse Filter Ports are both enabled.

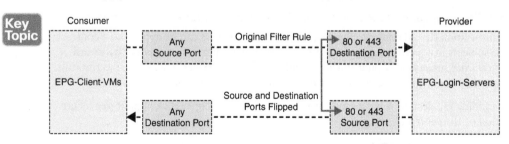

Figure 8-26 *Apply Both Directions and Reverse Filter Ports Enabled*

The bottom line is that you should exercise caution when disabling Reverse Filter Ports.

NOTE   If you are struggling to put these concepts into words, it helps to interpret Apply Both Directions as "apply these filters as is both in the consumer-to-provider and provider-to-consumer directions." Translate Reverse Filter Ports as "reverse the filter source and destination ports for return traffic."

Because there is no reason for Reverse Filter Ports to be used without first applying a filter bidirectionally, this option is grayed out when Apply Both Directions is disabled.

Verifying Subject Allocation to a Contract

After you define one or more contract subjects, these subjects should appear in the Subjects section of the contract. Figure 8-27 shows that the subject Allow-Player-Login from Figure 8-24 has been added to a contract called Players-to-Login-Servers.

Figure 8-27   *Confirming That a Subject Has Been Created and Added to a Contract*

This illustration should reinforce the idea that multiple subjects can be applied to a contract. Some subjects may permit forwarding of particular traffic, and others may deny forwarding. Yet other subjects may punt traffic via PBR to stateful services devices such as firewalls, change QoS markings, or perform some other function on the traffic.

After adding the desired subjects and verifying the contract scope, click Submit to execute creation of the contract.

Assigning Contracts to EPGs

After you create a contract, you need to assign the contract to relevant EPGs. Based on the example in Figure 8-21, the contract Players-to-Login-Servers should be applied to EPG-Login-Servers as a provided contract and to EPG-Client-VMs as a consumed contract.

Figure 8-28 shows the contract being added as a provided contract to EPG-Login-Servers. To allocate a contract to an EPG in the provider/provided direction, double-click on the EPG to expose its subfolders, right-click Contracts, and select Add Provided Contract. Then, select the contract and click Submit.

Figure 8-28 *Adding a Contract to an EPG in the Provided Direction*

The contract then needs to be consumed by one or more EPGs. Figure 8-29 shows the contract being consumed by EPG-Client-VMs. To accomplish this, you double-click the EPG, right-click on the Contracts subfolder, select Add Consumed Contract, select the desired contract, and click Submit.

Figure 8-29 *An EPG Functioning as Consumer of a Contract*

Understanding the TCP Established Session Rule

The contract just applied does whitelist client to server communication to destination ports 80 and 443. However, some engineers may find that the provider will also be able to initiate communication back to the consumer if it sources its communication from port 80 or 443.

This could be considered an issue if the system is ever compromised because ACI is a stateless firewall.

To ensure that a provider is not able to initiate TCP communication toward a consumer by sourcing the session from a port intended to be opened as a destination port, one thing you can do is to allow return traffic only on the condition that the session has already been established or is in the process of being established. This can be done using a filter that has Established configured in the TCP Session Rules column.

The Established keyword adds the extra condition of matching traffic based on the control bits in the TCP header. Established matches TCP control bits ACK and RST.

Creating Filters for Unidirectional Application

Let's take a more in-depth look at applying a contract to specific EPGs using the Established TCP Session Rules using the requirements for EPG-Client-VMs communication with EPG-Login-Servers. It is clear that the filter for consumer-to-provider communication would be the same as what is shown in Figure 8-22.

Figure 8-30 shows the complementary filter to that shown in Figure 8-22, matching the desired return traffic from EPG-Login-Servers.

Figure 8-30 *Filter for Established Return Traffic from the EPG-Login-Servers*

Notice that the source and destination ports for each entry in Figure 8-30 have been reversed. This is a very important point when applying a filter unidirectionally as ACI does not reverse source and destination ports.

Configuring Subjects for Unidirectional Application of Filters

Use of the new filter created in the previous section requires a new contract but with Apply Both Directions and Reverse Filter Ports disabled. Figure 8-31 shows that once these two checkboxes are disabled, separate filters can be applied in the consumer-to-provider direction versus the provider-to-consumer direction.

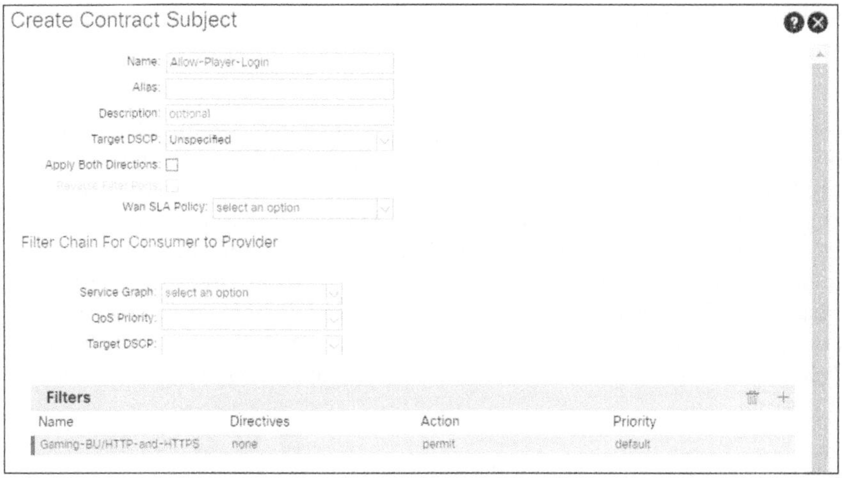

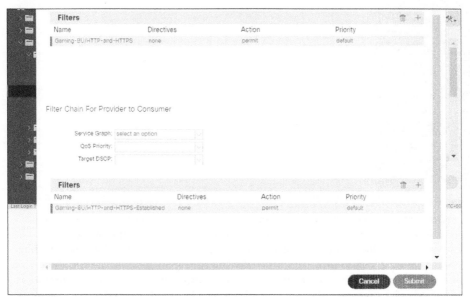

Figure 8-31 *New Contract with Filter in the Consumer-to-Provider Direction*

Whereas Figure 8-31 shows the filter that ACI applies in the consumer-to-provider direction, Figure 8-32 shows the filter with the Established keyword applied in the reverse direction.

Figure 8-32 *A Separate Filter Applied in the Provider-to-Consumer Direction*

Once applied as a provided contract to EPG-Login-Servers and as a consumed contract to EPG-Client-VMs, this contract prevents servers in EPG-Login-Servers from initiating any form of communication with the outside world. This, of course, does not hold if the system is someday compromised by somebody who is able to craft packets with either the TCP ACK or RST flags set and knows to source them from port 80 or 443.

Additional Whitelisting Examples

Let's take a look at the remaining requirements from Figure 8-21, shown earlier in this chapter.

To complete the set of requirements dealing with communication from and to EPG-Client-VMs, this book needs to address how you can allow both TCP and UDP traffic from EPG-Client-VMs to EPG-Gaming-Servers on destination port 60001 as well as relevant return traffic. There is nothing unique about this requirement. Let's say, however, that you want to use a bidirectional contract using Apply Both Directions and Reverse Filter Ports to achieve this. It is important to understand that just because ACI stateless filtering would allow return traffic for a port as a result of a TCP filter that doesn't have the Established TCP Sessions Rules parameter set doesn't mean that the filter would also allow UDP traffic over the same port. Hence, Figure 8-33 shows that both TCP and UDP filter entries would be needed if both are desired.

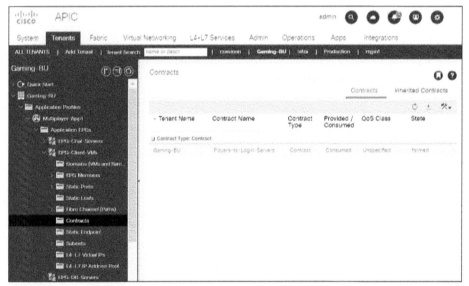

Figure 8-33   *Both TCP and UDP Filter Entries Needed If EPG Talks on Both for a Port*

The second set of requirements for communication between EPG-Login-Servers, EPG-Gaming-Servers, and EPG-DB-Servers is very basic. However, one point to make here is that, in practice, engineers often enable this type of TCP communication by creating a filter addressing the consumer-to-provider traffic flow and then apply it to the relevant EPGs via a unidirectional subject. TCP return traffic for all EPGs within the associated VRF instance is then enabled using a separate filter with the Established keyword. To do this, you can use a construct called vzAny, which is discussed in Chapter 10.

The next requirement relates to UDP communication from EPG-Gaming-Servers to EPG-Chat-Servers on port 60004. This would most likely be implemented using a bidirectional contract. It is important to note that provider EPG-Chat-Servers would still be able to initiate communication with endpoints in EPG-Client-VMs as a result of the required bidirectional contract. But there is nothing that can be done with the Established parameter since UDP is connectionless.

Finally, let's look at the glorified patch server that needs to be able to communicate on ports 20 and 21. Without going into the details of how FTP works, it is important to understand that some types of communication greatly benefit from stateful firewalling. If a stateful firewall were placed between ACI and these FTP servers, the stateful firewall could snoop the FTP control connection (TCP port 21) and get the data connection details. It could then prevent any connection to port 20 unless it is an authentic data connection. Either way, the filter to make this communication possible would look something like the one in Figure 8-34.

Figure 8-34   *Filter Matching on TCP Ports 20 and 21*

If ACI were to place a firewall in front of the traffic, it would be in the form of PBR. This would be possible using a service graph associated with the subject.

Verifying Contract Enforcement

Through the GUI, you can verify contract allocation to EPGs within an application profile by simply navigating to the Topology menu, as shown in Figure 8-35.

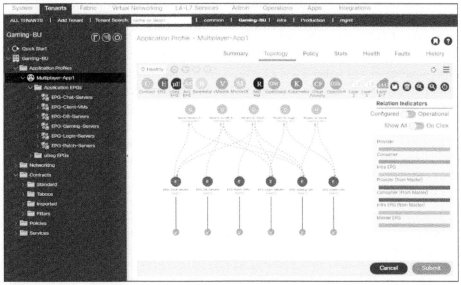

Figure 8-35   *Viewing Contracts Applied to EPGs Within an Application Profile*

Unfortunately, this view does not actually indicate whether contracts are applied in hardware on a particular leaf switch. The switch CLI **show zoning-rule** command does, however. Example 8-14 shows a variation of this command. (Several relatively insignificant columns have been removed from the output in order to fit it on a printed page.)

Example 8-14 *Verifying Hardware Enforcement of a Contract on a Leaf Switch*

```
LEAF101# show zoning-rule contract Players-to-Login-Servers
+---------+----------+---------+-----------+-----------+-------------- ----------+----------+
| SrcEPG | DstEPG | Dir    | operSt   | Scope   |      Name        | Action  |
+------ --+----------+---------+-----------+-----------+------------------------+----------+
| 16389  | 32780  | uni-dir | enabled  | 2228225 | Players-to-Login-Servers | permit |
| 32780  | 16389  | uni-dir | enabled  | 2228225 | Players-to-Login-Servers | permit |
+----------+----------+---------+-----------+-----------+----------------+----------------+
```

In this output, SrcEPG and DstEPG represent the sclass or pcTag of the source and destination EPGs, respectively. The scope is the VRF instance VNID. In this case, the administrator could have verified application of all contracts within the VRF instance by using the **show zoning-rule scope 2228225** command.

Understanding the Stateful Checkbox in Filter Entries

Just as it is important to understand what ACI is, it is also important to understand what it is not. ACI, by itself, is *not* a stateful firewall. At best, you can consider it semi-stateful if you associate TCP control bit checking with connection state. Most often, though, it is termed *stateless*. This should not be a surprise because ACI does not track TCP sequence numbers and other aspects of TCP sessions.

So, what is the Stateful checkbox that can be enabled when creating filters? This feature takes effect only in conjunction with Cisco AVS and AVE. When ACI is extended into one of these stateful firewalling hypervisor solutions, AVS and AVE can use server resources to enable a connection-tracking capability. Not only is the overall solution then able to track TCP handshake state and sequence numbers, it is also able to inspect traffic and dynamically open negotiated TCP ports. In the case of FTP traffic, for example, this would enable port 20 to be usable for only valid data communication between the server and client.

Another point about ACI is that it is not intended to do application layer inspection. If you whitelist port 80 to a provider EPG, ACI would not care to drop traffic destined to the provider just because the consumer EPG was found to be sending a payload other than HTTP.

At the end of the day, ACI is here to do line-rate packet filtering. Its EPG architecture is a basic zone-based firewall of sorts. It can be configured to forward flows that require inspection to next-generation firewalls. It can also integrate with other solutions, such as AVS and AVE, to improve the overall data center security posture. But it is not here to replace firewalls.

Contract Scopes in Review

Let's revisit contract scopes in light of the implementation examples covered in this chapter. The contracts shown in this chapter were all created using the VRF scope. But what if the business unit deploying this new application actually intends to deploy multiple instances of this same application? Maybe it intends to deploy one for development, one for customer testing, and one or more for production. Would the company be able to reuse the EPGs and contracts, or would it need to do all this work over again?

Practically, customers that want to deploy an application multiple times could automate the policy deployment. There are very easy ways to generate a script based on an application profile and all the EPGs under it. The script could then deploy the same objects with different application profile names. (Yes, EPGs under different application profiles can have the same name.)

But what about contract reuse? The answer lies in the contract scope. When you change the contract scope to Application Profile, the contracts are only enforced between EPGs that are in a common application profile. This approach helps ensure that security rules only need to be put in place once and can be updated (for example, by adding a new subject to a contract) across all relevant application profiles simultaneously. This approach underscores why contract scopes are so important.

Exam Preparation Tasks

As mentioned in the section "How to Use This Book" in the Introduction, you have a couple of choices for exam preparation: Chapter 17, "Final Preparation," and the exam simulation questions in the Pearson Test Prep Software Online.

Review All Key Topics

Review the most important topics in this chapter, noted with the Key Topic icon in the outer margin of the page. Table 8-5 lists these key topics and the page number on which each is found.

Table 8-5   Key Topics for Chapter 8

Key Topic Element	Description	Page Number
Paragraph	Describes the key benefits of ACI endpoint learning	241
Paragraph	Provides the official definition of an endpoint in ACI	241
Table 8-3	Lists and describes the forwarding tables used in ACI	242
Paragraph	Defines a local endpoint	242
Paragraph	Defines a remote endpoint	242
Table 8-4	Summarizes the differences between local endpoints and remote endpoints	243
Paragraph	Explains why Unicast Routing must be enabled for ACI to learn IP addresses of relevant endpoints	243
List	Details the logic an ACI leaf uses to figure out whether to learn a remote endpoint MAC address or IP address	245
Paragraph	Defines port encapsulation VLANs	246
Paragraph	Describes hardware proxy logic from the perspective of spines	248
Paragraph	Describes why ACI uses the ARP table in conjunction with the routing table for learning devices outside ACI behind L3Outs	249
Paragraph	Describes pervasive gateways and how they are deployed	252

8

Key Topic Element	Description	Page Number
Paragraph	Describes pervasive routes and their significance in spine proxy forwarding	259
Paragraph	Explains how bridge domain settings such as L2 Unknown Unicast determine whether spine proxy forwarding can be used for a given communication	259
Paragraph	Details the spine proxy destination lookup process and what happens to traffic next	260
Paragraph	Describes ACI ARP forwarding behavior with the Hardware Proxy parameter enabled and the ARP Flooding parameter disabled	262
Paragraph	Describes ACI ARP forwarding behavior with the ARP Flooding parameter enabled	262
Paragraph	Describes ACI ARP forwarding behavior when unicast routing has been disabled on a bridge domain	263
List	Lists the settings impacted when Optimize is selected in a bridge domain's Forwarding drop-down	264
Figure 8-15	Shows how to verify domain assignment to an EPG	267
Figure 8-16	Shows how to map an encapsulation to an EPG by using static paths	268
List	Lists and describes the static binding mode options for EPGs	268
List	Lists and describes the Deployment Immediacy options	268
Figure 8-17	Shows how to statically map an EPG to an encapsulation on an individual port	269
Figure 8-18	Shows how to verify the static path bindings for an EPG	269
Figure 8-22	Shows how to create a unidirectional filter when return traffic will be allowed via subject settings	274
List	Describes the columns available in the filter configuration view	274
Paragraph	Describes how the filter configuration view disables selection of certain settings based on selected options	274
Paragraph	Describes how to fill out the Source Port/Range and Destination Port/Range columns during filter configuration	275
List	Describes the various columns that appear in the Create Contract Subject page	276
Figure 8-25	Illustrates ACI behavior with Apply Both Directions enabled and Reverse Filter Ports disabled for a subject	277
Figure 8-26	Illustrates ACI behavior with both Apply Both Directions and Reverse Filter Ports enabled for a subject	277
Figure 8-28	Shows how to associate a contract with an EPG in the provider direction	279
Figure 8-29	Shows a contract associated with an EPG in the consumer direction	279

Key Topic Element	Description	Page Number
Paragraph	Explains how to further lock down communication on the provider end of communication by using the established TCP session rule	280
Paragraph	Explains what the Established keyword does	280
Paragraph	Reiterates that ports in the source and destination columns need to be reversed when creating an additional filter for return traffic	280
Paragraph	Reiterates that Apply Both Directions and Reverse Filter Ports need to be disabled when applying two different filters for consumer-to-provider versus provider-to-consumer traffic	280
Paragraph	Explains the function of the Stateful checkbox within filters	284

Complete Tables and Lists from Memory

There are no memory tables or lists in this chapter.

Define Key Terms

Define the following key terms from this chapter and check your answers in the glossary:

endpoint, local endpoint, remote endpoint, port encapsulation VLAN, platform-independent VLAN (PI VLAN), ARP gleaning, pervasive gateway, pervasive route, FTag tree

8

CHAPTER 9

L3Outs

This chapter covers the following topics:

L3Out Fundamentals: This section covers concepts related to L3Outs, the subobjects that make up L3Outs, interface types, and BGP route reflection.

Deploying L3Outs: This section details the process of establishing routing to the outside world via user tenant L3Outs.

Implementing Route Control: This section covers the basics of route profiles and some use cases for route profiles in ACI.

This chapter covers the following exam topic:

- 3.2 Implement Layer 3 Out

Previous chapters address how ACI access policies control the configuration of switch downlink ports and the level of tenant access to such ports. This chapter expands on that information by addressing the implementation of L3Outs on switch downlinks to communicate subnet reachability into and out of ACI user VRF instances.

This chapter tackles a number of issues related to L3Outs, such as classifying external endpoints for contract enforcement, implementing BGP route reflection, and basic route filtering and route manipulation.

"Do I Know This Already?" Quiz

The "Do I Know This Already?" quiz allows you to assess whether you should read this entire chapter thoroughly or jump to the "Exam Preparation Tasks" section. If you are in doubt about your answers to these questions or your own assessment of your knowledge of the topics, read the entire chapter. Table 9-1 lists the major headings in this chapter and their corresponding "Do I Know This Already?" quiz questions. You can find the answers in Appendix A, "Answers to the 'Do I Know This Already?' Questions."

Table 9-1 "Do I Know This Already?" Section-to-Question Mapping

Foundation Topics Section	Questions
L3Out Fundamentals	1–4
Deploying L3Outs	5–9
Implementing Route Control	10

1. An ACI administrator wants to deploy an L3Out to ASR 1000 Series routers in a user VRF while ensuring that future L3Outs in other tenants can also reuse the same physical connectivity to the outside routers. Which interface type should be used?

    a. Routed subinterfaces

    b. Routed interfaces

    c. SVIs

    d. Floating SVIs

2. An L3Out has been created in a user VRF and border leaf switches have learned external subnet 10.0.0.0/8 via dynamic routing and added it to their routing tables. Which of the following explains why a compute leaf that has deployed the same user VRF instance has not received that route?

    a. A user has configured a route profile for interleak and applied it to the L3Out.

    b. A default import route profile has been added to the L3Out.

    c. Routing protocol adjacencies between ACI and external routers never formed.

    d. BGP route reflection has not been configured for the fabric.

3. Which interface type is ideal for L3Out deployment when a physical firewall appliance needs to be dual-homed to a pair of leaf switches and establish routing protocol adjacencies directly with an ACI fabric?

    a. Routed subinterfaces

    b. Routed interfaces

    c. SVIs

    d. Floating SVIs

4. When configuring BGP route reflection in ACI, what are the two critical parameters that administrators need to define?

    a. BGP ASN and cluster ID

    b. Border leaf switches and L3Outs from which ACI should import routes

    c. BGP ASN and the spines in each pod that should function as route reflectors

    d. BGP ASN and border leafs in each pod that should function as a route reflector client

5. An administrator learns that when she modifies a bridge domain subnet scope to Advertised Externally and adds the bridge domain for advertisement to an OSPF L3Out, the subnet also gets advertised out an EIGRP L3Out. Which of the following options would allow advertisement of the BD subnet out a single L3Out? (Choose all that apply.)

   a. Remove the bridge domain from the EIGRP L3Out.

   b. Move one of the L3Outs to a different switch or set of switches.

   c. Switch the bridge domain back to Private to VRF.

   d. Use BGP for a dedicated route map per L3Out.

6. True or false: The same infra MP-BGP ASN used for route reflectors is also used to establish connectivity out of BGP L3Outs unless ACI uses a *local-as* configuration.

   a. True

   b. False

7. Regarding configuration of BGP L3Outs, which of the following statements are true? (Choose all that apply.)

   a. When establishing BGP connectivity via loopbacks, BGP peer connectivity profiles should be configured under the node profile.

   b. ACI allows EIGRP to be configured on a BGP L3Out for BGP peer reachability in multihop scenarios.

   c. ACI tries to initiate BGP sessions with all IP addresses in a subnet as a result of the dynamic neighbor establishment feature involving prefix peers.

   d. ACI implements BGP subnet advertisement to outside as a redistribution.

8. Which statements about OSPF support and configuration in ACI are correct? (Choose all that apply.)

   a. The administrative distance for OSPF can be modified at the node profile level.

   b. OSPF authentication is supported in ACI and can be configured under an OSPF interface profile.

   c. Border leaf L3Outs support VRF-lite connectivity to external routers.

   d. ACI does not support OSPFv3 for IPv6.

9. Which statements are correct regarding ACI support for BFD? (Choose all that apply.)

   a. BFD is supported for EIGRP, OSPF, and BGP in ACI.

   b. BFD is supported on L3Out loopback interfaces.

   c. BFD is supported for BGP prefix peers (dynamic neighbors).

   d. BFD is supported on routed interfaces, routed subinterfaces, and SVIs.

10. True or false: Route profiles are a little different from route maps on NX-OS and IOS switches and routers because they may merge configurations between implicit route maps and explicitly configured route profile match statements.

   a. True

   b. False

Foundation Topics

L3Out Fundamentals

An ACI Layer 3 Out (L3Out) is the set of configurations that defines connectivity into and out of an ACI fabric via routing. The following sections discuss the key functions other than routing that an L3Out provides and the objects that comprise an L3Out.

Stub Network and Transit Routing

To better understand L3Outs, it helps to first understand the difference between a stub network and a transit network. ACI was originally built to function as a stub network. As a stub, the intent was for ACI to house all data center endpoints but to not be used to aggregate various routing domains (for example, core layer, firewalls, WAN, campus, mainframe) within a data center.

The community of network engineers then banded together and told Cisco that ACI as a stub was not enough. Shortly afterward, Cisco began to support ACI as a transit. The idea is that ACI performs route redistribution, mostly behind the scenes, to interconnect multiple routing domains (L3Outs) and transit routes as well as traffic between L3Outs.

Figure 9-1 compares ACI as a stub and ACI as a transit. On the left-hand side, ACI is depicted as a stub. The fabric has only a single L3Out. In this case, ACI does not need to do anything to campus subnet 10.10.0.0/16 except to learn it. On the right-hand side, however, the campus core layer has been depicted connecting directly into ACI using an L3Out. Data center core and edge infrastructure connect to a separate L3Out. Because the data center core and campus layers do not have any direct connectivity with one another, ACI needs to be configured to transit routes between the L3Outs for machines in the 10.10.0.0/16 subnet to be able to reach the Internet. It is important to understand that it is not the existence of multiple L3Outs that implies transit routing; it is the expectation that ACI functions as a hub and routes traffic from one L3Out to another that necessitates transit routing.

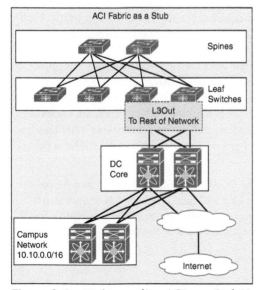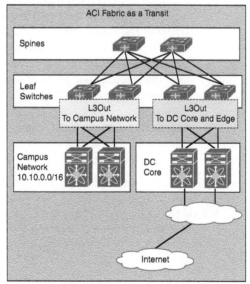

Figure 9-1   *Understanding ACI as a Stub Versus ACI as a Transit*

> **NOTE** Route redistribution between Layer 3 domains is a large topic, and it is not something that the majority of ACI engineers deal with on a day-to-day basis. Therefore, transit routing is beyond the scope of the Implementing Cisco Application Centric Infrastructure DCACI 300-620 exam.

Types of L3Outs

Chapter 5, "Tenant Building Blocks," provides a basic definition of L3Outs. It may be possible to interpret that definition as suggesting that each L3Out is only able to advertise subnets that exist within a single VRF. The following points expand on the previous definition by describing the numerous categories of L3Outs you can create in ACI:

- **L3Outs in the infra tenant:** This type of L3Out is actually more of a family of L3Outs that typically associate with the overlay-1 VRF instance and enable either integration of an ACI fabric with other fabrics that are part of a larger ACI Multi-Site solution or expansion of a fabric into additional pods as part of an ACI Multi-Pod or vPod solution. The overlay-1 VRF can also be used to interconnect a fabric with its Remote Leaf switches. These solutions should all be familiar from Chapter 2, "Understanding ACI Hardware and Topologies." One particular infra tenant L3Out, however, has not been mentioned before. A GOLF L3Out uses a single BGP session to extend any number of VRF instances out an ACI fabric to certain OpFlex-capable platforms, such as Cisco ASR 1000 Series routers, Cisco ASR 9000 Series routers, and Nexus 7000 Series switches. One common theme across the infra tenant family of L3Outs is that traffic for multiple VRFs can potentially flow over these types of L3Outs. Another common theme is that routing adjacencies for these L3Outs are sourced from the spines.

- **User VRF L3Outs (VRF-lite):** This type of L3Out extends Layer 3 connectivity out one or more border leaf switches. It is the most commonly deployed L3Out in ACI. Administrators typically deploy these L3Outs in user tenants, but they can also be deployed in VRFs in the common tenant or any other VRF used for user traffic. Each L3Out of this type is bound to a single user VRF and supports a VRF-lite implementation. Through the miracle of subinterfaces, a border leaf can provide Layer 3 outside connections for multiple VRFs over a single physical interface. This VRF-lite implementation requires one protocol session per tenant. A *shared service L3Out* is the name given to any user VRF L3Out that has additional configuration to leak routes learned from external routers into a VRF other than the VRF to which the L3Out is bound. This allows external routes to be consumed by EPGs in another VRF. This feature is also referred to as *shared L3Out* because a service behind the L3Out is being shared with another VRF.

If all this seems overwhelming, don't worry. The DCACI 300-620 exam only focuses on implementation of user VRF L3Outs. Route leaking and shared service L3Outs are also beyond the scope of the exam. Nonetheless, you need to be aware of the different types of L3Outs so you can better recognize which configuration knobs are relevant or irrelevant to the type of L3Out being deployed.

NOTE   The term *shared service* is used here to refer to a user tenant using a component from the common tenant. This term can also apply to consumption of common tenant objects by other tenants, but use of the term to imply route leaking is now more prevalent.

Key Functions of an L3Out

For an L3Out to be effective in connecting an ACI fabric to outside Layer 3 domains, it needs to be able to perform the following five critical functions:

- **Learn external routes:** This entails one or more border leafs running a routing protocol and peering with one or more external devices to exchange routes dynamically. Alternatively, static routes pointing to a next-hop device outside the fabric can be configured on an L3Out.

- **Distribute external routes:** This involves ACI distributing external routes learned on an L3Out (or static routes) to other switches in the fabric using Multiprotocol BGP (MP-BGP) with VPNv4 configured in the overlay-1 VRF (tenant infra). ACI automates this distribution of external routes in the background. This distribution requires BGP route reflection.

- **Advertise ACI bridge domain subnets out an L3Out:** For external devices to have reachability to servers in the fabric, an ACI administrator needs to determine which BD subnets should be advertised out of an L3Out. ACI then automates creation of route maps in the background to allow the advertisement of the specified BD subnets via the selected L3Outs.

- **Perform transit routing:** Advertising external routes between Layer 3 domains can be achieved by using the L3Out EPG subnet scope Export Route Control Subnet. (The DCACI 300-620 exam does not cover transit routing, so neither does this book.)

- **Allow or deny traffic based on security policy:** Even with ACI exchanging routes with the outside world, there still needs to be some mechanism in place for ACI to classify traffic beyond an L3Out and determine whether a given source should be allowed to reach a particular destination. L3Outs accomplish this by using special EPGs referred to as external EPGs. EPGs classifying traffic beyond an L3Out are configured on the L3Outs themselves using the L3EPG scope External Subnets for External EPG.

The Anatomy of an L3Out

Each L3Out is structured to include several categories of configuration. Figure 9-2 shows a sample L3Out and its subobjects.

Figure 9-2   *The Anatomy of an ACI L3Out*

The following points summarize the structure and objects within an L3Out:

- **L3Out root:** As shown in Figure 9-2, the most critical L3Out configurations that are of a global nature can be found under the **Policy > Main** page at the root of the L3Out. Configurations you apply here include the routing protocol to enable on the L3Out, the external routed domain (L3 domain) linking the L3Out with the underlying access policies, the VRF where the L3Out should be deployed, the autonomous system number in the case of EIGRP, and the area type and area ID to be used for OSPF.

- **Logical node profiles:** The main function of a *logical node profile* is to specify which switches should establish routed connectivity to external devices for a given L3Out. ACI creates two subfolders under each logical node profile: Logical Interface Profiles and Configured Nodes.

- **Logical interface profiles:** An administrator can configure one or more *logical interface profiles* for each set of interface configurations. It is under logical interface profiles that interface IP addresses and MTU values for routing protocol peering can be configured. Protocol-specific policies such as authentication and timers for EIGRP, OSPF, and BGP can also be configured under logical interface profiles. Bidirectional Forwarding Detection (BFD) and custom policies for QoS, data plane policing, NetFlow, and IGMP can also be applied at the logical interface profile level.

- **Configured nodes:** The Configured Nodes folder includes a single node association entry for each switch node that is part of an L3Out. Static routes, router IDs, and loopback IP addresses are all configured in node association entries in this folder.

- **External EPGs:** Any EPG that is defined directly on an L3Out can be called an external EPG. The only external EPGs of concern for the DCACI 300-620 exam are those used to classify traffic from external endpoints.

■ **Route map for import and export route control:** These special route maps are applied on the entire L3Out and associated bridge domains. The two route maps that can be applied are default-import and default-export.

Planning Deployment of L3Out Node and Interface Profiles

As mentioned earlier in this chapter, logical node profiles and logical interface profiles for user VRF L3Outs together define which switches are border leaf switches and what interface-level configurations and policies the L3Out should use for route peering with the outside world. But how are these two object types deployed side-by-side?

The first thing to remember is that logical interface profiles fall under the Logical Node Profiles folder. On the left-hand side of Figure 9-3, an administrator has configured two leaf switches with node IDs 101 and 102 as border leaf switches using a single logical node profile. A single logical interface profile under the logical node profile then defines configurations for interfaces on both of these nodes. In the second design pattern, the administrator has created a single node profile but then deployed one interface profile for each switch. In the iteration on the right, separate logical node profiles and interface profiles have been created for each individual border leaf switch. All three of these design patterns are correct.

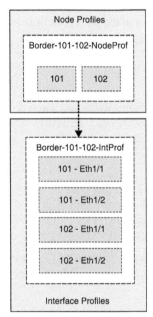 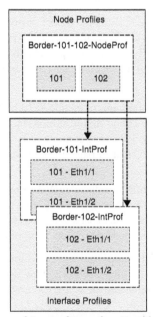 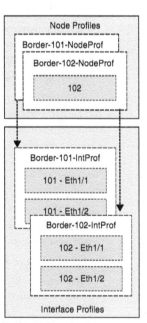

Figure 9-3 *Logical Node Profile and Logical Interface Profile Design Patterns*

Some of the confusion that occurs for engineers when deciding between these options is due to the fact that most engineers think in terms of design patterns for access policies. Deployment of an interface configuration under an interface profile that is bound to multiple switches under the Access Policies menu can lead to the simultaneous deployment of interface configurations on multiple switches. In contrast, each interface or port channel added under an L3Out configuration requires explicit configuration before routing can be enabled on the port. Therefore, logical node profiles and logical interface profiles are used more to achieve organizational hierarchy than for automating simultaneous interface configuration.

Understanding L3Out Interface Types

The following types of interfaces can be part of an L3Out:

- Routed subinterfaces

- Routed interfaces

- Switch virtual interfaces (SVIs)

- Floating SVIs

The design considerations for the first three options listed here are mostly the same as what you would expect when configuring connectivity between any set of Layer 3 devices.

Use of routed subinterfaces is very common in multitenancy environments because one VLAN ID and subinterface can be allocated for each user VRF L3Out, enabling multiple tenant L3Outs to flow over a single set of physical ports.

Use of router interfaces is most common in single-tenant environments or in instances when the fabric is expected to have dedicated physical connectivity to a specific switch block or segregated environment via a single L3Out.

If an administrator has trunked an EPG out a port or port aggregation, the same port or port channel cannot be used as for a routed subinterface or routed interface because the port has already been configured as a (Layer 2) switchport. Such a port or port aggregation can still be configured as part of an L3Out that leverages SVIs or floating SVIs.

> **NOTE** It is has become very common for engineers to build ACI L3Outs using pure Layer 3 solutions such as routed interfaces and routed subinterfaces, but there are many great use cases for building L3Outs using SVIs. One common use case is establishing a redundant peering with firewalls over a vPC from a pair of border leaf switches.

The new *floating SVI* option, first introduced in ACI Release 4.2(1), with further enhancements in ACI Release 5.0(1), enables users to configure an L3Out without locking down the L3Out to specific physical interfaces. This feature enables ACI to establish routing adjacencies with virtual machines without having to build multiple L3Outs to accommodate potential VM movements.

The floating SVI feature is only supported for VMM integrated environments in ACI Release 4.2(1) code. Enhancements in ACI Release 5.0(1) allow floating SVIs to be used with physical domains, eliminating the requirement for VMM integration.

Understanding L3Out Bridge Domains

When instantiating an L3Out SVI, ACI creates an *L3Out bridge domain (BD)* internally for the SVI to provide a Layer 2 flooding domain. This BD is called an *L3Out BD* or *external BD* and is not visible to ACI administrators.

ACI creates a different L3Out BD for each encapsulation used in an SVI-based L3Out. If an administrator uses a common VLAN encapsulation for SVIs on multiple border leaf nodes in a single L3Out, ACI spans the L3Out BD and the associated flooding domain across the switches. In Figure 9-4, L3Out SVI encapsulation 10, deployed to both border leafs 101 and 102, prompts ACI to place all interfaces associated with the SVI in a common flooding domain. Meanwhile, selection of encapsulation 20 for another SVI on the same L3Out triggers ACI to create a new L3Out BD with a different Layer 2 flooding domain.

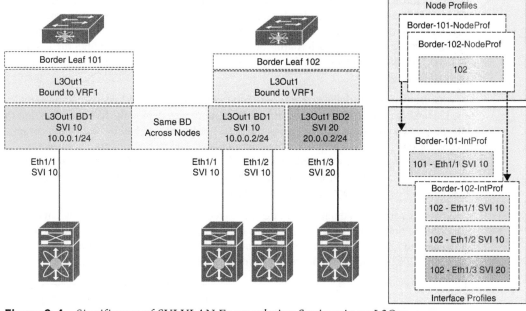

Figure 9-4 *Significance of SVI VLAN Encapsulation Settings in an L3Out*

Effectively, what happens as a result of this configuration is that the border leaf switches and any other routers in the stretched flooding domain establish somewhat of a full mesh of routing protocol adjacencies with one another (in the case of OSPF or EIGRP). Figure 9-5 shows the neighbor adjacencies established for the VLAN 10 L3Out BD. Meanwhile, the single router connecting to the L3Out via encapsulation 20 forms only a single adjacency with ACI.

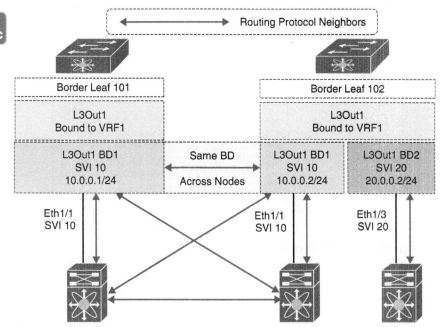

Figure 9-5 *Impact of L3Out BD Flooding Domains on Neighbor Relationships*

While this full mesh of adjacencies is generally a good thing, in some cases it can lead to ACI unintentionally transiting traffic between external routers. This is especially true when the routers connecting to ACI each have different routes in their routing tables. Because these routers are able to establish routing adjacencies with one another through the L3Out BD Layer 2 flooding domain, they are then able to use ACI as a transit to forward data plane traffic to each other.

But what happens if an administrator tries to instantiate a common SVI encapsulation in multiple L3Outs? It depends. If the administrator is attempting to deploy the SVI encapsulation to different ports across different L3Outs on the same border leaf, ACI allows use of the encapsulation for one L3Out but generates a fault when the second instance of the encapsulation is used, indicating that the encapsulation is already in use. Because of this, multiple L3Outs that need to use the same encapsulation cannot coexist on the same border leaf. However, this behavior can be changed with the SVI Encap Scope option under the L3Out SVI.

If, on the other hand, an administrator attempts to reuse an encapsulation in a new L3Out and on a different border leaf switch, ACI accepts the configuration and deploys a new L3Out BD for the second L3Out. This is the case in Figure 9-6. The assumption, of course, is that the two L3Out BDs are intended to represent different subnets if deployed in the same VRF.

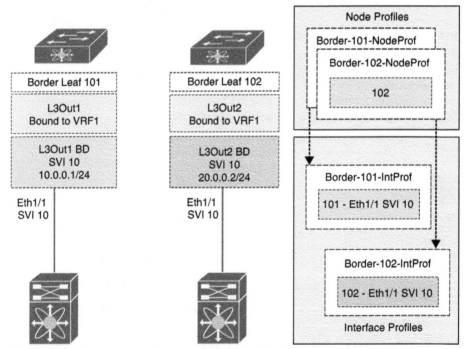

Figure 9-6 *Common SVI Encapsulation Used for L3Outs on Different Switches*

Understanding SVI Encap Scope

When configuring L3Outs using SVIs, one important setting is the Encap Scope. The acceptable values for this setting are VRF and Local.

The only reason to modify this setting from its default value of Local is to be able to reuse an SVI in other L3Outs within a VRF. There are two specific use cases for this:

- Establishing adjacencies using multiple routing protocols from a single leaf using a common SVI

- Establishing granular route control over each BGP peer on the same leaf by using a dedicated L3Out for each BGP peer

Figure 9-7 compares the two values for this setting. Let's say that an engineer needed to run both OSPF and EIGRP to an external device. In ACI, each L3Out can be configured for only one routing protocol; therefore, two L3Outs are needed to fulfill this requirement. The engineer determines that it would not be feasible to run multiple physical connections between ACI and the external device and that routed subinterfaces cannot be used in this design. In this case, an SVI encapsulation and IP address on a border leaf needs to be shared between the two L3Outs. If Encap Scope is set to Local for the SVI, ACI expects a unique external SVI for each L3Out and generates a fault when an L3Out SVI encapsulation is reused for a secondary L3Out on the switch. On the other hand, setting Encap Scope to VRF for an SVI tells ACI to expect a unique SVI encapsulation for each VRF and the two L3Outs are therefore allowed to share the encapsulation.

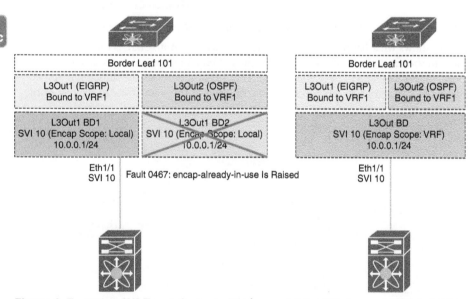

Figure 9-7 *Using SVI Encap Scope to Deploy an L3Out BD Across Multiple L3Outs*

There is one exception to the aforementioned rule that each L3Out enable only a single routing protocol: OSPF can be enabled on a BGP L3Out to provide IGP reachability for BGP. When OSPF is enabled in the same L3Out as BGP, OSPF is programmed to only advertise logical node profile loopback addresses and interface subnets.

Understanding SVI Auto State

Under default configurations, SVIs on an ACI leaf are always up, even if associated physical ports are down. Although this is typically not a problem, it could pose a problem when using static routes.

Figure 9-8 illustrates that a static route pointing out an L3Out SVI will remain in the routing tables of the border leaf switches and will continue to be distributed to other switches in the fabric if SVI Auto State is set at its default value, Disabled.

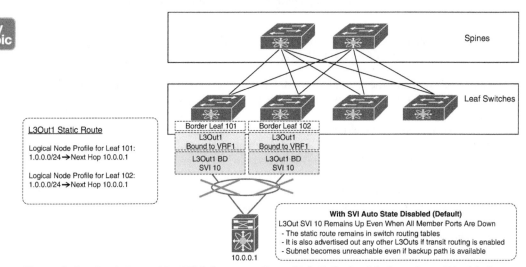

Figure 9-8 *Static Route Not Withdrawn on Downlink Failure with Auto State Disabled*

Figure 9-9 shows what happens to the static route when SVI Auto State is toggled to Enabled. In this case, the border leaf disables the L3Out SVI once it detects that all member ports for the L3Out SVI have gone down. This, in turn, prompts the static route to be withdrawn from the routing table and halts distribution of the static route to the rest of the fabric.

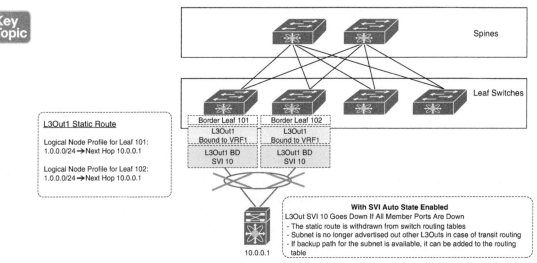

Figure 9-9 *Static Route Withdrawn on Downlink Failure with Auto State Set to Enabled*

Note that the implementation of BFD for the static route could also resolve this problem.

Understanding Prerequisites for Deployment of L3Outs

Before going into a tenant and creating an L3Out, access policies should be implemented for any physical switch ports that will be part of the L3Out. This includes assignment of an AAEP to an interface policy group and assignment of the interface policy group to an interface profile. The interface profile needs to be bound to the intended border leaf node IDs for the access policies to work. If access policies for the underlying physical ports are not in place to begin with, Layer 3 adjacencies will never be established.

Let's say that you have created several L3 domains and have already associated a VLAN pool with each of them. It is also important to ensure that an L3 domain is associated with the AAEP controlling connectivity to the underlying physical ports. It is the L3 domain that an L3Out references. If an L3 domain has not been associated with the AAEP that governs connectivity for the intended L3Out ports, you may be unable to deploy the L3Out.

L3 Domain Implementation Examples

Say that the business unit (BU) from earlier chapters wants to deploy three L3Outs in its tenant, as shown in Figure 9-10. One of the L3Outs uses EIGRP and connects to a dedicated switch on the floor where most of the BU employees work. An OSPF connection to a firewall and a BGP connection to a router toward a partner network are also needed.

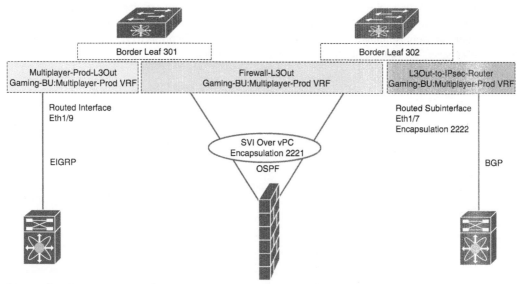

Figure 9-10 *Hypothetical L3Out Connectivity Desired for a VRF*

Before deploying these L3Outs, the L3 domain objects would need to be configured. Figure 9-11 shows how an L3 domain for connectivity to the firewall might be configured. Because the firewall will peer with ACI using an SVI, a VLAN pool *does* need to be defined.

Figure 9-11 *Sample L3 Domain Configuration That Includes VLAN Pool Assignment*

Figure 9-12 shows the configuration of an L3 domain for connectivity to a router via subinterfaces. Notice that a VLAN pool has *not* been assigned to the L3 domain. This is a valid configuration. Administrators do not need to assign VLAN pools to L3 domains that will be used solely for routed interfaces or routed subinterfaces.

Figure 9-12 *Creation of an L3 Domain Without VLAN Pool Assignment*

Finally, Figure 9-13 shows the AAEP for connectivity to all appliances owned by the gaming BU. There was no need for the AAEP to be specific to the gaming BU systems since AAEP objects are designed with multitenancy in mind. Note here that a physical domain has also been associated with this AAEP. This makes sense if there is a need for the firewall to simply trunk some VLANs down to ACI using its port channel.

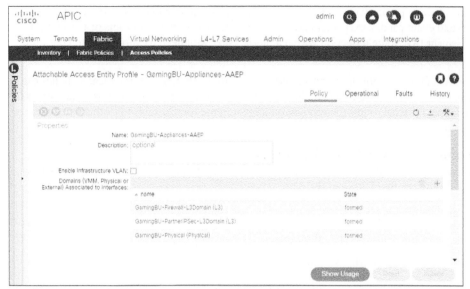

Figure 9-13 *Associating Physical Domains and L3 Domains Simultaneously with an AAEP*

Understanding the Need for BGP Route Reflection

To distribute external routes across the fabric, ACI leaf and spine switches establish iBGP peerings with one another within a user-defined BGP autonomous system number (ASN).

Whenever iBGP peerings are involved, BGP split-horizon rules apply. These rules state that a BGP router that receives a BGP route from an iBGP peer shall not advertise that route to another router that is an iBGP peer.

While BGP split horizon works wonders in preventing intra-ASN route loops, it requires that all routers in a BGP ASN form a full mesh to ensure that all routes propagate correctly between all iBGP peers. This can impact scalability given that a full-mesh design involves $N(N-1)/2$ unique iBGP sessions, where N is the number of routers. Imagine an ACI fabric with 50 switches, all having to form BGP relationships with one another. The fabric would need to manage $50(49)/2 = 1225$ BGP sessions to make this possible. Full-mesh iBGP is not scalable and therefore is not used in ACI fabrics.

The scalable alternative to an iBGP full mesh is the deployment of *route reflectors*. A route reflector is a BGP speaker that is allowed to advertise iBGP-learned routes to certain iBGP peers. Route reflection bends the rules of BGP split horizon just a little by introducing a new set of BGP attributes for route loop prevention. In modern Clos fabrics such as ACI, spines make ideal route reflectors because they often have direct connections with all leaf switches.

Using BGP route reflection, the number of unique iBGP peerings in a single-pod ACI fabric drops down to $RR \times RRC$, where RR is the number of route reflectors and RRC is the number of route reflector clients. In a hypothetical 50-switch single-pod ACI fabric consisting of 2 spines that have been configured as route reflectors and 48 leaf switches (route reflector clients), the sum total number of unique iBGP sessions needed stands at 96.

9

None of these points may be critical DCACI trivia. What should be important for DCACI 300-620 exam candidates is first and foremost to recognize the symptoms of forgetting to implement BGP route reflection within a fabric. Next, you need to know how to configure BGP route reflection in the first place.

If an ACI fabric has not been configured for BGP route reflection, border leaf switches can learn routes from external routers, but ACI does not distribute such routes to other nodes in the fabric. External routes therefore never appear in the routing tables of other leaf switches in the fabric.

Implementing BGP Route Reflectors

Administrators usually configure BGP route reflection during fabric initialization or when they deploy the first L3Out in the fabric.

An administrator needs to do two things for BGP route reflection to work in ACI:

- Enter the BGP ASN the fabric should use internally.

- Select the spines that will function as route reflectors.

Not all spines need to be configured as route reflectors, but it usually makes sense to have at least two for redundancy.

To configure route reflection in ACI, navigate to **System > System Settings > BGP Route Reflector**. Figure 9-14 shows the selection of two spines with node IDs 201 and 202 as BGP route reflectors for Pod 1. The fabric uses BGP ASN 65000 in this example. Note that route reflectors for additional pods can also be configured on this page.

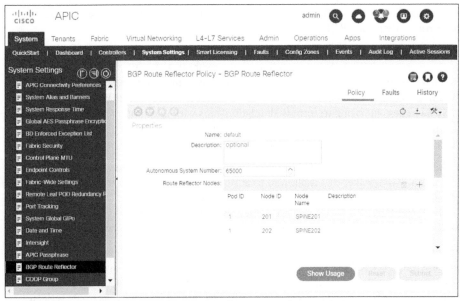

Figure 9-14 *Configuring BGP Route Reflectors Within a Fabric*

You might be wondering whether you can deploy an alternative BGP route reflector policy. The answer is that you cannot do so in ACI Release 4.2. Figure 9-15 indicates that even when creating a new pod policy group, ACI does not allow modification of the BGP route reflector policy named default shown earlier, in Figure 9-14.

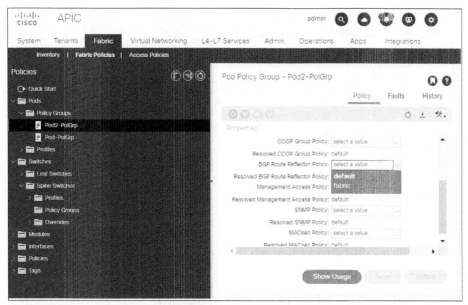

Figure 9-15 *Assigning a BGP Route Reflector Policy to a Pod Policy Group*

Understanding Infra MP-BGP Route Distribution

Once BGP route reflection has been configured, ACI deploys MP-BGP on all leaf and spine switches. The following steps summarize what takes place for external routes to propagate from border leaf switches to all other switches in the fabric:

Step 1.   The BGP IPv4/IPv6 address family (AF) is deployed on all leaf switches (both border and non-border leaf switches) in all user VRF instances.

Step 2.   The BGP VPNv4/VPNv6 AF is also deployed on all leaf and route reflector spine switches in the infra VRF (overlay-1 VRF). All leaf switches establish iBGP sessions with route reflector spine switches in the infra VRF and are then able to exchange their VPNv4/VPNv6 routes.

Step 3.   Once an L3Out is deployed on a leaf, the BGP IPv4/IPv6 AF on the same border leaf automatically creates a redistribution rule for all the routes from the routing protocol of the L3Out within the same user VRF. This redistribution is called *interleak*. If the L3Out is using BGP, no redistribution (interleak) is required for routes learned via BGP because the BGP process for the L3Out and for the infra MP-BGP is the same.

Step 4.   The redistributed IPv4/IPv6 routes are exported from the user VRF to the infra VRF as VPNv4/VPNv6.

Step 5.   On other leaf switches, the VPNv4/VPNv6 routes distributed through route reflector spines are imported from the infra VRF to the user VRF as IPv4/IPv6.

Figure 9-16 recaps this route distribution process.

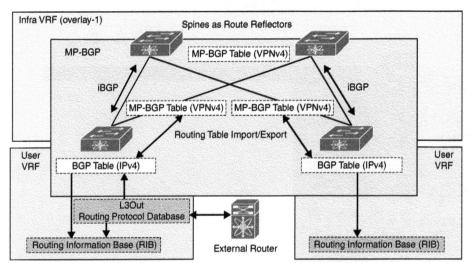

Figure 9-16 *Infra MP-BGP Architecture and Route Distribution*

Those interested in learning more about the MP-BGP route distribution process can begin their exploration process using the commands **show bgp process detail vrf all**, **show bgp ipv4 unicast vrf all**, and **show bgp vpnv4 unicast vrf overlay-1**.

For those not interested in the route distribution process, perhaps the only thing of importance on this issue is to be able to verify spine-to-leaf BGP peerings. Example 9-1 shows how to verify the number of BGP adjacencies on a leaf switch. It also demonstrates how you can correlate neighbor router IDs with their hostnames, node IDs, and TEP addresses.

Example 9-1 *Validating BGP Peerings Between a Leaf and Route Reflector Spines*

```
LEAF101# show bgp sessions vrf overlay-1
Total peers 5, established peers 5
ASN 65000
VRF overlay-1, local ASN 65000
peers 2, established peers 2, local router-id 10.233.46.32
State: I-Idle, A-Active, O-Open, E-Established, C-Closing, S-Shutdown


Neighbor        ASN    Flaps LastUpDn|LastRead|LastWrit St Port(L/R)  Notif(S/R)
10.233.46.33    65000 0     16w06d  |never   |never    E  60631/179  0/0
10.233.46.35    65000 0     16w06d  |never   |never    E  44567/179  0/0
LEAF101# acidiag fnvread | grep spine
     201       1     SPINE201    FDOXXXX1    10.233.46.33/32    spine   active    0
     202       1     SPINE202    FDOXXXX2    10.233.46.35/32    spine   active    0
```

The external route distribution process in ACI is extremely reliable. If all expected BGP peerings appear to be in an *established* state, you should see external routes pop up in the routing table of all leaf switches where the relevant user VRF has been deployed.

Deploying L3Outs

ACI Release 4.2 has a streamlined wizard for setting up L3Outs. While use of the wizard is required when configuring an L3Out via the GUI, administrators can make modifications to L3Outs afterward.

This section demonstrates the process of going through the streamlined wizard to create L3Outs for each routing protocol and interface type. It also touches on deployment of external EPGs on L3Outs and some configuration changes you might want to make manually.

Configuring an L3Out for EIGRP Peering

To launch the L3Out creation wizard, navigate to Tenants, select the tenant in question, open the Networking folder, right-click L3Outs, and select Create L3Out.

Figure 9-17 shows the first page of the wizard. Following completion of the wizard, the settings on this page all appear at the root of the L3Out on the Main subtab of the Policy page. Enter a name for the L3Out, select the VRF instance with which the L3Out should be associated, and select the L3 domain created for this individual L3Out. Then select the routing protocol. When EIGRP has been selected as the protocol of choice, the wizard disables the OSPF and BGP checkboxes, and the Autonomous System Number text box appears. Entry of an autonomous system number is mandatory. Click Next to continue.

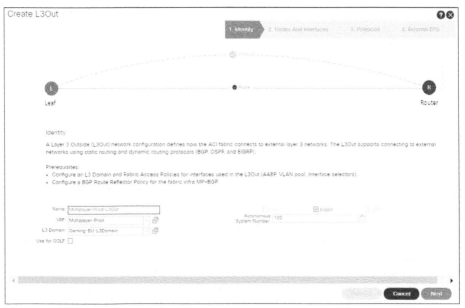

Figure 9-17 *Entering the EIGRP and ASN Configuration in the L3Out Creation Wizard*

> **NOTE** If you are unfamiliar with domains in general, see Chapter 6, "Access Policies." For coverage of VRF configuration, see Chapter 5.

In Figure 9-17, notice the checkbox Use for GOLF. Selecting the Use for GOLF checkbox on a user VRF L3Outs tells ACI that the L3Out will be a mere placeholder for external EPGs and other policies for a GOLF L3Out. There is no reason to select this option when the intent is to establish Layer 3 peerings for border leaf switches.

The next page in the wizard pertains to logical node profiles and logical interface profiles. The wizard selects a node profile name by default. Deselect Use Defaults, as shown in Figure 9-18, if you need to customize the logical node profile name. Next, select an interface type. This example shows a routed interface selected with the port option in line with the L3Out designs presented in Figure 9-10, earlier in this chapter. Select a node ID and enter a router ID for this border leaf switch. Do not use CIDR notation for router IDs. Entering a loopback address is required only if you expect to implement BGP Multihop by sourcing a loopback address. Finally, enter information for the interfaces on the border leaf that need to be enabled for EIGRP. CIDR notation for these interfaces is required. Click Next to move on to the next page.

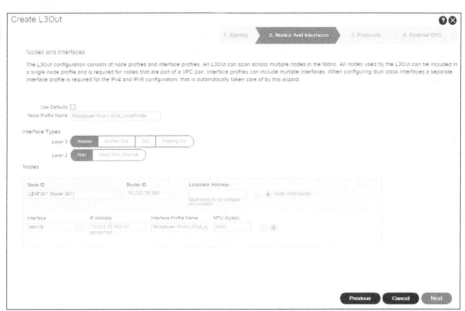

Figure 9-18 *Entering Node and Interface Information for an EIGRP L3Out*

The Protocol Associations page, shown in Figure 9-19, allows association of a custom EIGRP interface policy with the EIGRP interface profile for this L3Out. By default, ACI selects an EIGRP interface policy called default from the common tenant. New protocol interface policies cannot currently be created in the L3Out creation wizard. Custom EIGRP interface policies are discussed and applied to L3Outs later in this chapter. Click Next to continue.

Figure 9-20 shows the final page of the L3Out creation wizard. This page allows you to define external EPGs for the L3Out. When the Default EPG for All External Networks checkbox is enabled, ACI automatically generates an EPG that matches all traffic not matched by a more specific external EPG. Disable this checkbox if you want to manually create external EPGs after the L3Out has been deployed. Click Finish to deploy the L3Out.

Figure 9-19 *Associating an EIGRP Interface Policy with the EIGRP Interface Profile*

Figure 9-20 *External EPG Creation Page in the L3Out Creation Wizard*

Once the L3Out is deployed, if you check to see whether EIGRP adjacencies have been established, you will find that they have not. ACI does not attempt to establish route peerings out an L3Out until at least one external EPG has been deployed on the L3Out.

Deploying External EPGs

Chapter 5 describes the significance of external EPGs in classifying traffic behind L3Outs, and Chapter 8, "Implementing Tenant Policies," covers contract implementation. These topics are not repeated here, but Figure 9-21 outlines hypothetical connectivity that needs to be whitelisted between external endpoints and internal EPGs. In this figure, Public-Access, Internal-Access, and Admin-Access are external EPGs.

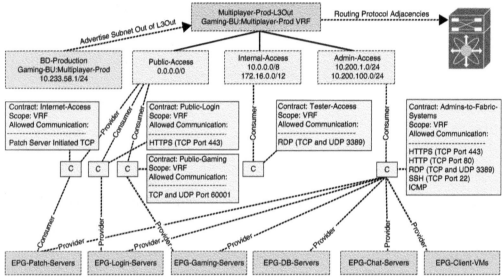

Figure 9-21 *External EPG Design in a Specific VRF*

To create an external EPG on an L3Out, drill down into the subfolders of the L3Out and select the External EPG folder. Then right-click the Tools menu and select Create External EPG (see Figure 9-22).

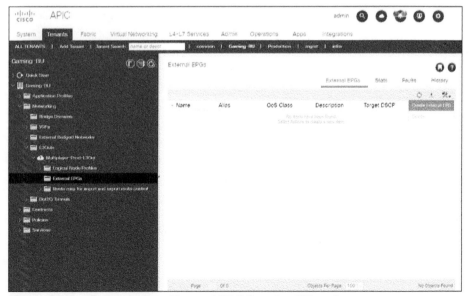

Figure 9-22 *Kicking Off the External EPG Creation Wizard*

Enter a name for the external EPG. Chapter 10, "Extending Layer 2 Outside ACI," briefly touches on the idea of the preferred group member. When contracts are used to allow communication, the Preferred Group Member parameter can be left at the default value, Exclude. To define subnets for the external EPG, click the **+** sign in the Subnet part of the screen shown in Figure 9-23.

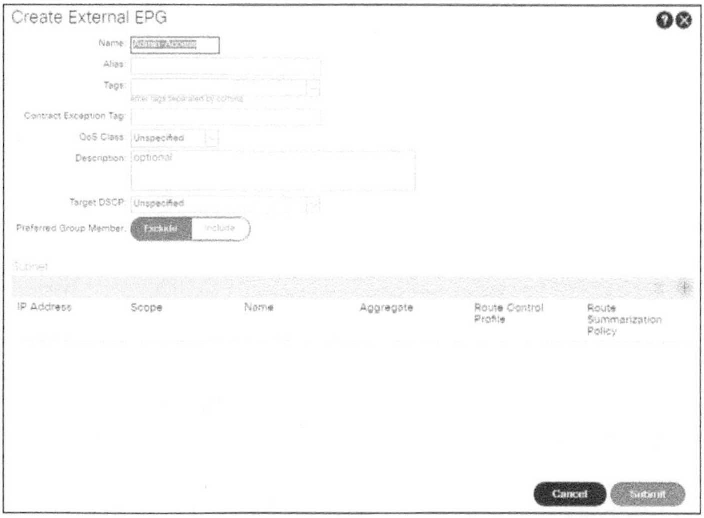

Figure 9-23   *Main Page of the Create External EPG Wizard*

Note that this figure shows configuration of the Admin-Access external EPG. Two subnets have been called out for association with this particular external EPG: 10.200.1.0/24 and 10.200.100.0/24.

Figure 9-24 shows the addition of the subnet 10.200.100.0/24 to Admin-Access. The Name field on this page reflects the function of the particular subnet being added. Several groups of checkboxes exist on this page. These checkboxes are called *Scope* options, and they determine the function(s) of each external EPG. The checkboxes in the Route Control section predominantly relate to transit routing scenarios. The Shared Security Import Subnet checkbox relates to shared service L3Outs. The only checkbox of interest for DCACI candidates is External Subnets for External EPG. When enabled, this checkbox tells ACI that this external EPG should be used to classify external traffic matching the subnet for contract enforcement. Enable this checkbox and click Submit.

After you add a subnet to an external EPG, the Create External EPG page reappears so you can assign additional subnets to the external EPG. When you finish this, click Submit. Figure 9-25 shows the General tab for an external EPG that has been created. Notice in this figure that the external EPGs Internal-Access and Public-Access have been created in the background. This view is particularly useful because it verifies that the external EPG has been deployed and also that all intended subnets have been assigned to it, using the proper scope.

Figure 9-24 *Adding Subnets as External Subnets for an External EPG*

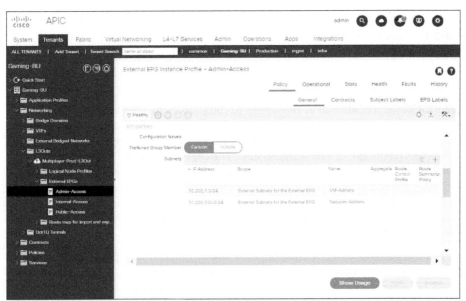

Figure 9-25 *The General Tab of an External EPG*

Now that at least one external EPG has been deployed on the L3Out, ACI should attempt to establish routing adjacencies with external routers.

Verifying Forwarding Out an L3Out

Example 9-2 shows how to verify that an EIGRP adjacency has been established in a VRF.

Example 9-2 *Verifying EIGRP Adjacencies Resulting from L3Out Configuration*

```
LEAF301# show ip eigrp neighbors vrf Gaming-BU:Multiplayer-Prod
EIGRP neighbors for process 100 VRF Gaming-BU:Multiplayer-Prod
H   Address             Interface     Hold    Uptime    SRTT  RTO  Q    Seq
                                      (sec)             (ms)       Cnt  Num
0   10.233.75.161       eth1/9        13      07:30:37  1     50   0    19
```

NOTE Keep in mind that you have not seen any switch ports configured in this chapter. L3Out adjacencies cannot form unless access policies for underlying switch ports have been configured.

Following adjacency verification, it makes sense to confirm whether ACI has learned any routes. Example 9-3 shows the routing table of node 301 and node 302. Notice the highlighted routes learned by node ID 301, where the L3Out has been deployed. These all appear to have been learned via EIGRP. This is expected because the L3Out runs EIGRP. Node 302, on the other hand, has learned these same routes from bgp-65000. This is because node 302 learned these routes from MP-BGP route distribution, and route reflectors in this particular fabric have been configured with BGP ASN 65000. Notice that these route entries on node 302 all have next-hop addresses pointing to the TEP address of node 301. This is expected behavior.

Example 9-3 *Verifying the Routing Table for a Specific VRF*

```
LEAF301# show ip route vrf Gaming-BU:Multiplayer-Prod
IP Route Table for VRF "Gaming-BU:Multiplayer-Prod"
(...output truncated for brevity...)
10.199.90.0/24, ubest/mbest: 1/0
    *via 10.233.75.161, eth1/9, [90/128576], 22:35:22, eigrp-default, internal
10.200.1.0/24, ubest/mbest: 1/0
    *via 10.233.75.161, eth1/9, [90/128576], 22:43:09, eigrp-default, internal
10.200.100.0/24, ubest/mbest: 1/0
    *via 10.233.75.161, eth1/9, [90/128576], 23:01:31, eigrp-default, internal


LEAF302# show ip route vrf Gaming-BU:Multiplayer-Prod
IP Route Table for VRF "Gaming-BU:Multiplayer-Prod"
(...output truncated for brevity...)
10.199.90.0/24, ubest/mbest: 1/0
    *via 10.233.60.234%overlay-1, [200/128576], 22:43:13, bgp-65000, internal, tag 65000
10.200.1.0/24, ubest/mbest: 1/0
    *via 10.233.60.234%overlay-1, [200/128576], 22:51:01, bgp-65000, internal, tag 65000
10.200.100.0/24, ubest/mbest: 1/0
    *via 10.233.60.234%overlay-1, [200/128576], 23:09:23, bgp-65000, internal, tag 65000
```

Finally, recall from Chapter 8 that ACI does not store information about external endpoints learned via an L3Out in endpoint tables. ARP is used to keep track of next-hop MAC-to-IP address bindings for endpoints behind L3Outs. Example 9-4 shows the ARP table for the VRF from the perspective of border leaf 301.

Example 9-4   *Checking the ARP Table for Next-Hop MAC-to-IP Address Binding*

```
LEAF301# show ip arp vrf Gaming-BU:Multiplayer-Prod

Flags: * - Adjacencies learnt on non-active FHRP router
       + - Adjacencies synced via CFSoE
       # - Adjacencies Throttled for Glean
       D - Static Adjacencies attached to down interface


IP ARP Table for context Gaming-BU:Multiplayer-Prod
Total number of entries: 1
Address          Age        MAC Address      Interface
10.233.75.161    00:02:30   a0e0.af66.c5a1   eth1/9
```

Unless data in one of these tables is inaccurate, ACI should be able to forward traffic to external devices without issue.

Advertising Subnets Assigned to Bridge Domains via an L3Out

When ACI is learning subnets behind an L3Out, it is time to advertise ACI subnets out of the fabric. The most basic and yet common form of bridge domain subnet advertisement involves a two-step process. First, navigate to the desired BD and add one or more L3Out in the Associated L3Outs view. Then, drill down into an individual subnet that needs to be advertised and update its scope to Advertised Externally. These two configurations do not need to be done in the order specified, but together, they tell ACI to internally create a route map rule on the border leaf switches to redistribute the desired BD subnets into the routing protocol of the associated L3Out.

Figure 9-26 shows the addition of a bridge domain named BD-Production to the L3Out named Multiplayer-Prod-L3Out.

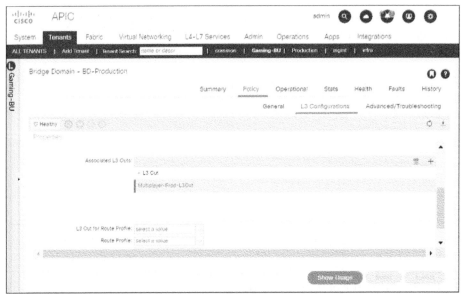

Figure 9-26   *Marking a BD as a Candidate for Subnet Redistribution into an L3Out*

Figure 9-27 shows a BD subnet scope with Advertised Externally selected.

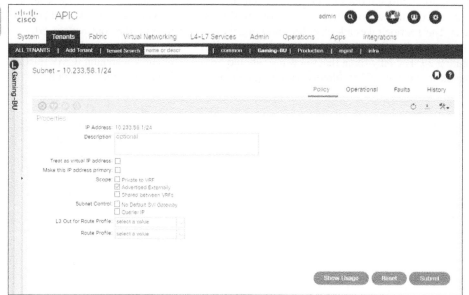

Figure 9-27 *Marking a BD Subnet for Redistribution into One or More L3Outs*

Figure 9-28 shows the L3 Configuration tab for a BD after an associated subnet has been marked for advertisement out an L3Out. Notice that this view shows not only the scope of associated subnets but also the fact that Unicast Routing has been enabled. One issue that prevents advertisement of a subnet out an L3Out is Unicast Routing being disabled in the first place.

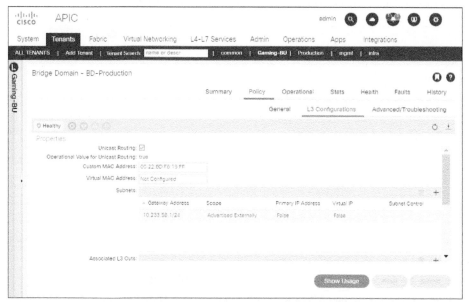

Figure 9-28 *Verifying That Unicast Routing Is Enabled for BDs with Subnets Advertised Out an L3Out*

Enabling Communications over L3Outs Using Contracts

Once routing into and out of a fabric has been enabled, the next step is to whitelist desired endpoint communication. Figure 9-21 earlier in this chapter provides a list of desired contracts. This section takes a look at how you might go about creating the contract named Admins-to-Fabric-Systems. To match interesting traffic, first create a filter, as shown in Figure 9-29. The only thing that's new here should be the filter entry matching ICMP traffic. As indicated earlier, ICMP filters do not require definition of ports in either direction.

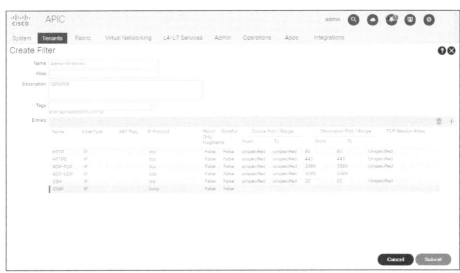

Figure 9-29 *A Filter That Matches Interesting Traffic*

Figure 9-30 shows that the filter has been added to a subject under the desired contract that permits forwarding of all matched traffic as well as all return traffic.

Figure 9-30 *Contract Subject Allowing Traffic Matching the Previous Filter*

Finally, you see that the contract Admins-to-Fabric-Access is ready to be created. Note that the default value, VRF, has been selected as the contract scope in Figure 9-31. It is important to understand that even though this contract is between devices external to the fabric and internal devices, no route leaking between ACI user VRFs is taking place. This is why the scope of VRF is sufficient when the L3Out is not being used as a shared service L3Out.

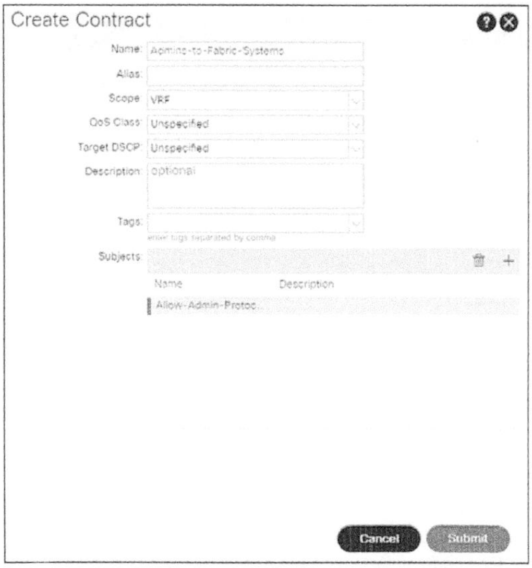

Figure 9-31 *Contract Scope Shown in the Create Contract Wizard*

Next, the contract needs to be assigned between external EPGs and internal EPGs. The easiest way to understand provider and consumer directionality for external EPGs is to first realize that external EPGs represent external systems. Will these external systems be initiating requests, or will they be waiting for data center systems to send traffic? Because administrators need to initiate connections such as SSH and HTTPS, Admin-Access should be configured as a consumer of the contract, as indicated in Figure 9-32.

Figure 9-32 *An External EPG Consuming a Contract*

Meanwhile, internal EPGs need to be configured as providers of services to the administrators. Figure 9-33 shows the Admins-to-Fabric-Systems being added to an internal EPG in the provided direction.

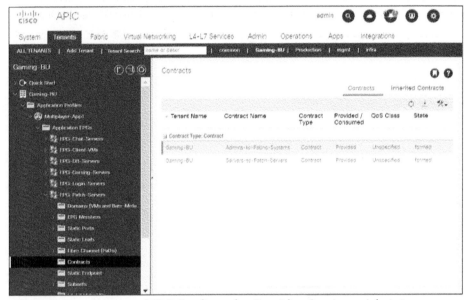

Figure 9-33   *An Internal EPG Configured to Provide a Service to Administrators*

After the desired contracts are put in place, all endpoints should have the desired connectivity.

Before moving on to the next section, revisit Figure 9-21. An internal EPG called EPG-Patch-Servers is shown consuming a service from the Internet. Basically, for the only EPG with access to initiate communication with Internet systems, the desire is to ensure that endpoints in this EPG can initiate TCP sessions destined to any port, but Internet systems cannot initiate sessions to these patch servers. This is a good example of where you might avoid use of bidirectional filter application and instead use a return filter matching the TCP established bits.

Deploying a Blacklist EPG with Logging

Sometimes, IT teams identify the need to block or log certain traffic that should be able to enter the data center but should not be allowed to reach servers within ACI. In such cases, you can deploy an external EPG that either has no contracts associated or has a contract that denies and perhaps logs the traffic.

Because external EPGs use a longest-prefix match, all you need to do to classify the intended traffic is to add the relevant subnets or host routes to the blacklist EPG and make sure more specific IP addresses in the blacklisted range(s) have not been allocated to other external EPGs.

Figure 9-34 shows creation of an external EPG for this purpose. Note that one particular host, 10.200.1.5/32, falls within the administrator subnet range. This is completely valid. In this case, ACI would always classify traffic from 10.200.1.5 into this new EPG and not into the Admin-Access external EPG.

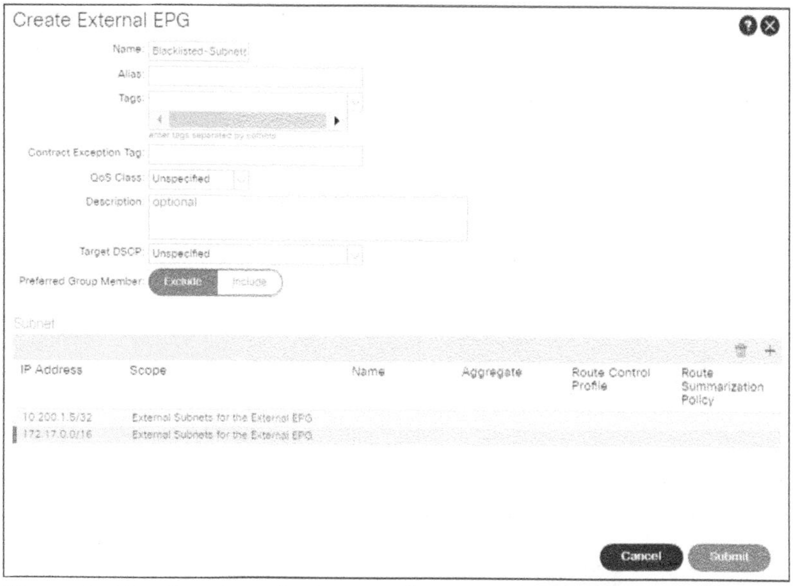

Figure 9-34 *Creation of an External EPG to Classify Specific Endpoints and Ranges*

If all you want is to drop traffic from these ranges, you have already succeeded because no contracts have been enforced on this external EPG. However, if you also want to log the traffic, you can create a specific contract that has a subject whose filter matches all traffic. The directive in this case should be Log, and the action should be Deny, as shown in Figure 9-35.

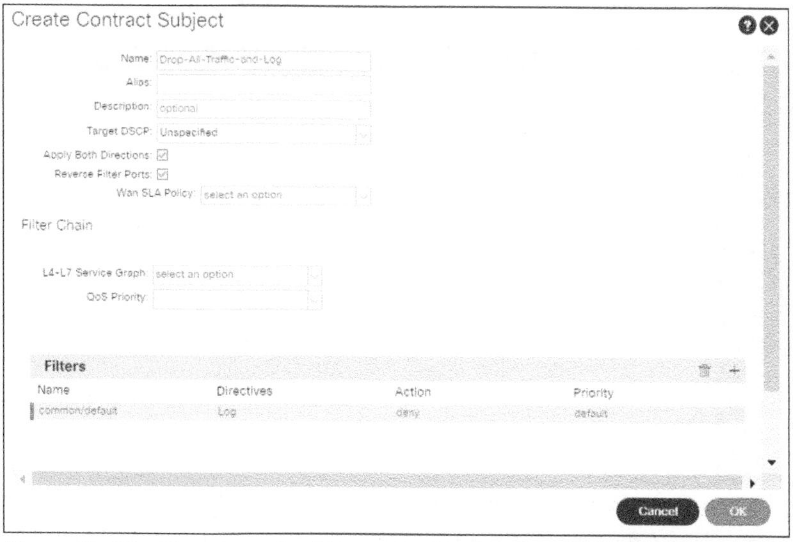

Figure 9-35 *Creation of a Contract Subject to Log and Drop All Traffic*

As indicated in Figure 9-36, the contract scope VRF is sufficient for this contract.

Figure 9-36 *Contract for Blacklisting Traffic from and to Certain External Sources*

Next, you need to apply the contract on the new external EPG in both the consumed and provided directions. Figure 9-37 shows its application as a consumed contract.

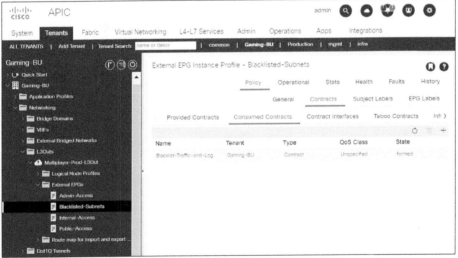

Figure 9-37 *Applying a Contract to an External EPG to Blacklist Traffic*

Navigate to Tenants and open the tenant in question. Go to the tenant's Operational tab, select Flows, and select L3 Drop. As shown in Figure 9-38, if traffic has been initiated by any of the blacklisted external devices or if any traffic in the VRF was destined to the black-listed devices, ACI should have a deny log for the traffic flow. Note that contract logging uses processor resources and is rate limited in ACI.

Figure 9-38 *Verifying Dropped Traffic Logged as a Result of a Contract*

Advertising Host Routes Out an ACI Fabric

One of the configuration knobs under bridge domains in recent ACI code revisions is Advertise Host Routes. When this option is enabled, ACI advertises not only BD subnets but also any host routes that ACI has learned within any BD subnet ranges selected for external advertisement. Figure 9-39 shows this configuration checkbox.

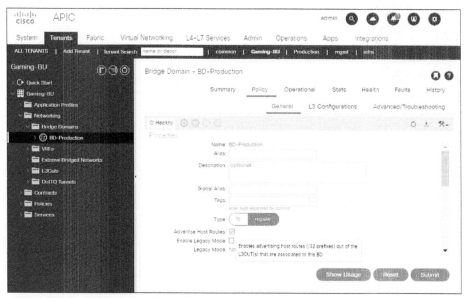

Figure 9-39 *Advertising Host Routes Out an L3Out*

Implementing BFD on an EIGRP L3Out

A common desire in modern data centers is to implement BFD to enable subsecond routing failover capabilities. To implement BFD on an EIGRP L3Out, enable BFD under the associated EIGRP interface policy. If further customization of BFD settings and timers is required, you can create a BFD interface policy and associate it with the EIGRP L3Out.

Figure 9-40 shows an EIGRP interface policy that is active on an L3Out. This particular L3Out has the default EIGRP interface policy from the common tenant set. If BFD were to be enabled on this particular EIGRP interface policy, all L3Out interfaces in other tenants that consume this policy would also attempt to establish BFD neighbor relationships out their respective L3Outs. This is likely not what you want to do if you are configuring this in a production fabric. Instead, you can create and associate a new EIGRP interface policy with the L3Out EIGRP interface profile.

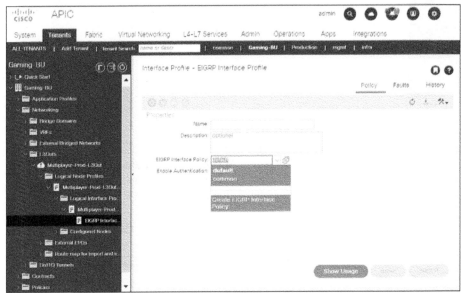

Figure 9-40   *Verifying an Operational EIGRP Interface Policy on an L3Out*

Figure 9-41 shows the Create EIGRP Interface Policy page. Notice that this page also allows tuning of EIGRP hello and hold intervals as well as tuning of bandwidth and delay for route metric manipulation. Enable the BFD checkbox and click Submit.

Figure 9-41   *Configuring a New EIGRP Interface Policy with BFD Enabled*

ACI comes preconfigured with a default global BFD policy located under **Fabric > Access Policies > Policies > Switch > BFD > BFD IPv4/v6 > default**. To customize timers or to enable subinterface optimization for BFD for an individual L3Out, navigate to a logical interface profile on the L3Out and select Create BFD Interface Profile. The Create BFD Interface Profile window shown in Figure 9-42 appears. Select Create BFD Interface Policy.

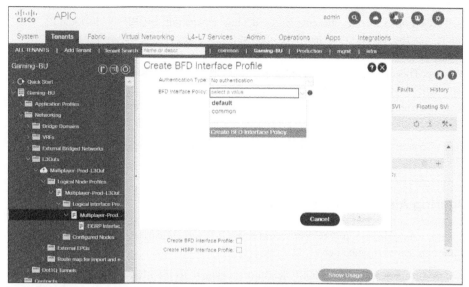

Figure 9-42 *Launching the BFD Interface Profile Creation Wizard*

Then, on the Create BFD Interface Policy page, shown in Figure 9-43, select the desired settings and click Submit. If neighboring devices that peer with ACI over the L3Out also have BFD enabled, BFD should become fully operational.

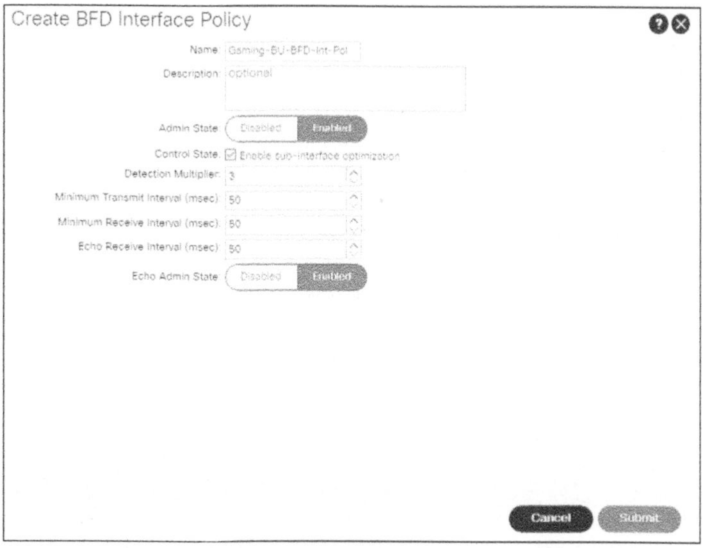

Figure 9-43 *L3Out BFD Timer and Policy Customization*

BFD interface policies are not protocol specific and so are not revisited in future sections.

NOTE   In addition to BFD, the following EIGRP interface policy Control State options are available:

- **Self Nexthop:** This option is enabled by default. By default, EIGRP sets its local IP address as the next hop when advertising routes. When you disable this option, the border leaf does not overwrite the next hop and keeps the original next-hop IP address.

- **Passive:** This option is used to configure the interfaces as an EIGRP passive interface. This option is disabled by default.

- **Split Horizon:** Split horizon is a feature that helps prevent routing loops by not sending EIGRP updates or queries to the interface where it was learned. This option is enabled by default.

It is very uncommon for engineers to need to modify any of these three settings from their defaults.

Configuring Authentication for EIGRP

ACI supports authentication of EIGRP peers using MD5, but routing protocol authentication is not very common in data centers today. EIGRP authentication, therefore, does not warrant extensive coverage here.

To enable authentication with EIGRP neighbors, navigate to the EIGRP interface profile under the EIGRP L3Out and select Enable Authentication. Then either select the default keychain policy from the common tenant from the EIGRP KeyChain Policy drop-down or define a new one.

You can define EIGRP keychain policies by navigating to **Tenant > Policies > Protocol > EIGRP > EIGRP KeyChains**.

A keychain policy is a collection of key policies. Each key policy consists of a key ID, a key name, a pre-shared key, a start time, and an end time.

The only caveat to point out is that because EIGRP authentication is implemented at the logical interface profile level, the use of multiple logical interface profiles becomes necessary if some EIGRP peers are required to authenticate over the L3Out while others are not.

EIGRP Customizations Applied at the VRF Level

If you select a VRF within a tenant and click the Policy menu, one of the configuration sections you see on the Policy page is EIGRP Context per Address Family. This is where you can modify certain VRF-wide settings for EIGRP by deploying a custom EIGRP address family context policy for IPv4 or IPv6. The configuration settings that together form an EIGRP address family context policy are described in Table 9-2.

Table 9-2   Customizable Settings for an EIGRP Address Family Context Policy

Configuration Parameter	Description
Active Interval (min)	The interval the border leaf waits after an EIGRP query is sent before declaring a stuck in active (SIA) situation and resetting the neighborship. The default is 3 minutes.
External Distance	The administrative distance (AD) for external EIGRP routes. The default AD for external routes is 170.

Configuration Parameter	Description
Internal Distance	The AD for internal EIGRP routes. The default AD for internal routes is 90.
Maximum Path Limit	The maximum number of equal-cost multipathing (ECMP) next-hop addresses EIGRP can install into the routing table for a prefix. The default is eight paths.
Metric Style	EIGRP calculates its metric based on bandwidth and delay along with default K values. However, the original 32-bit implementation cannot differentiate interfaces faster than 10 Gigabit Ethernet. This original implementation is called the classic, or narrow, metric. To solve this problem, a 64-bit value with an improved formula was introduced for EIGRP; this is called the wide metric. Valid values for metric style are narrow metric and wide metric. The default is the narrow metric.

Configuring an L3Out for OSPF Peering

Let's revisit the requirements from Figure 9-10. The next L3Out that needs to be provisioned is Firewall-L3Out, which will leverage SVIs over a vPC to peer with a firewall via OSPF. Figure 9-44 shows the first page of the L3Out creation wizard. Enter parameters for name, VRF, and L3 domain. Enable OSPF by selecting the OSPF checkbox. In this example, the OSPF area ID 1 has been selected, and NSSA Area is selected for OSPF Area Type. Select the parameters that meet your requirements and click Next. Note that each OSPF L3Out can place interfaces in a single area. If peerings in multiple areas are required, you need to deploy additional L3Outs.

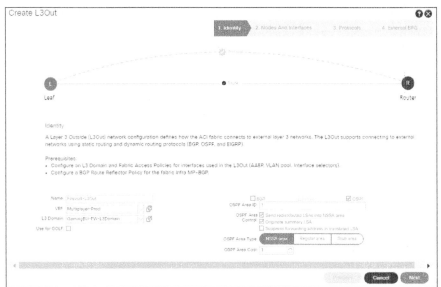

Figure 9-44 *Select Global Routing Protocol Parameters for OSPF L3Out*

On the Nodes and Interfaces page, shown in Figure 9-45, select the interface type that will be deployed for the L3Out. In this case, SVIs will be used. When deploying SVIs on a vPC in ACI, select different primary IP addresses for each vPC peer. If the external device behind the L3Out needs to point to a common IP address that both border leaf switches respond to, you can define a *secondary IP address* by using the IP Address: Secondary field. That is not required in this case due to the reliance on OSPF, but this same L3Out will also be used to demonstrate static routing in ACI. Also, note the Encap field. Enter the VLAN ID that needs to be trunked out the L3Out to the external device here. The VLAN ID selected here must be in the VLAN pool associated with the L3 domain for the L3Out. Click Next when you're finished making selections.

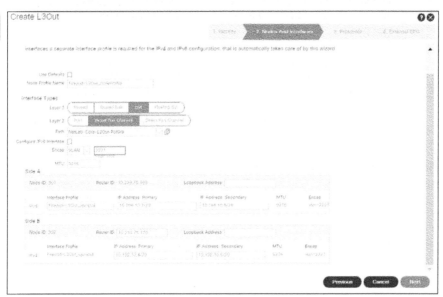

Figure 9-45 *Configuring L3Out SVIs Trunked onto a vPC with Secondary IP Addresses*

The Protocol Associations page for OSPF, shown in Figure 9-46, allows you to associate an OSPF interface policy to the L3Out OSPF interface profile. The default OSPF interface policy resides in the common tenant. Click Next.

Figure 9-46 *Associating an OSPF Interface Policy with the OSPF Interface Profile*

Key Topic

The final step in creating the L3Out is to configure an external EPG. A critical thing to understand about external EPGs used for traffic classification is that their scope is VRF-wide. This means that if you have already configured all your desired subnets for classification using the scope External Subnets for External EPG on another L3Out associated with a VRF, there is no need to duplicate these configurations on a secondary L3Out in the same VRF. In fact, if you try to add a subnet previously classified by another external EPG in the VRF to an external EPG on a second L3Out, ACI raises an error and does not deploy the erroneous configuration. However, one problem remains. ACI L3Out still expects to see at least one external EPG before it attempts to form routing protocol adjacencies with external devices. Figure 9-47 shows the creation of a dummy external EPG called Placeholder. No subnets need to be associated with this external EPG, whose only function is to ensure that ACI enables the L3Out. Click Finish to deploy the L3Out.

Figure 9-47 *Configuring a Dummy External EPG to Enable the L3Out*

To verify OSPF adjacency establishment via the leaf CLI, you can execute the command **show ip ospf neighbors vrf** *<vrf name>*. Example 9-5 shows that ACI has learned a default route from the adjacent firewall.

Example 9-5 *Verifying Routes Learned via OSPF*

```
LEAF301# show ip route ospf vrf Gaming-BU:Multiplayer-Prod
IP Route Table for VRF "Gaming-BU:Multiplayer-Prod"
'*' denotes best ucast next-hop
'**' denotes best mcast next-hop
'[x/y]' denotes [preference/metric]
'%<string>' in via output denotes VRF <string>

0.0.0.0/0, ubest/mbest: 1/0
    *via 10.198.10.2, vlan76, [110/5], 00:01:02, ospf-default, inter
```

9

A Route Advertisement Problem for OSPF and EIGRP L3Outs

One problem commonly experienced by engineers who dedicate a pair of switches to border leaf functions and need to create both OSPF and EIGRP L3Outs on these switches within the same VRF is that any BD subnets marked for advertisement out one L3Out also gets advertised out the other L3Out.

The reason for this behavior is that the route map ACI automatically generates as a result of BD subnet advertisements is common across OSPF and EIGRP. There are two common and recommended solutions for avoiding this behavior:

■ Deploy OSPF and EIGRP L3Outs for a given VRF on different border leaf switches.

■ Use BGP instead of OSPF and EIGRP. This recommendation is due to the fact that ACI generates route maps for BGP on a per-L3Out basis.

Implementing BFD on an OSPF L3Out

To enable BFD on an OSPF L3Out, select the OSPF interface profile for the L3Out. Either edit the default interface policy associated with the common tenant or create a new OSPF interface policy to associate with the L3Out OSPF interface profile. Figure 9-48 shows creation of a new OSPF interface policy that enables BFD.

Figure 9-48 *Enabling BFD on a Custom OSPF Interface Policy*

NOTE In addition to BFD, the following OSPF interface policy Control State options are available:

- **Advertise Subnet:** This allows OSPF to advertise a loopback IP address with its subnet instead of /32 without requiring that the network type be changed from loopback to point-to-point. However, in ACI, a loopback IP address is always configured with /32. Hence, at the time of writing, this option does not do anything in particular.

- **MTU Ignore:** This option allows the OSPF neighborship to form even with a mismatching MTU. This option is intended to be enabled on an OSPF interface with a lower MTU. Use of this option is not recommended in general.

- **Passive Participation:** This option configures the interfaces as OSPF passive interfaces.

Modifying any of these settings from their defaults is very uncommon in ACI.

OSPF Customizations Applied at the VRF Level

Just as with EIGRP, there are some VRF-wide settings for OSPF. A number of these settings are documented in Table 9-3. All OSPF timer values have been removed to limit coverage. A custom OSPF timer policy can be applied either to all address families within a VRF using the OSPF Timers drop-down box on the VRF Profile menu or to an individual address family (IPv4 or IPv6).

Table 9-3 Customizable Settings Besides Timers in an OSPF Timer Policy

Configuration Parameter	Description
Bandwidth Reference (Mbps)	Specifies the reference bandwidth used to calculate the default metrics for an OSPF interface. The default is 40,000 Mbps (40 Gbps).
Admin Distance Preference	Specifies the administrative distance (AD) for OSPF routes. The default is 110.
Maximum ECMP	Specifies the maximum number of ECMP that OSPF can install into the routing table. The default is 8 paths.
Enable Name Lookup for Router IDs	Prompts ACI to display router IDs as DNS names in OSPF show commands. This is disabled by default.
Prefix Suppression	Reduces the number of Type 1 (router) and Type 2 (network) LSAs installed in the routing table. This option is disabled by default.
Graceful Restart Helper	Keeps all the LSAs that originated from the restarting router during the graceful restart period. ACI border leaf switches do not themselves perform OSPF graceful restarts. ACI enables this option by default.

9

Adding Static Routes on an L3Out

Say that members of an IT team think that a firewall or an appliance they have procured and enabled for dynamic routing is not very reliable and that the routing protocol in the current appliance code may crash. Or say that they want to disable an appliance altogether and just leverage static routing. Sometimes, an appliance may lack the capability to leak a default route into a specific dynamic routing protocol. In such cases, static routes can be deployed on an L3Out either alongside a dynamic routing protocol or by themselves, and they can be distributed throughout the fabric via MP-BGP.

If an L3Out does not require dynamic routing, you can leave the checkboxes for EIGRP, OSPF, and BGP within the L3Out unchecked. Static routing does not need to be configured alongside dynamic routing protocols.

Static routes in ACI are configured on individual fabric nodes. Select the node of interest under the Configured Nodes folder and click the + sign under the Static Routes view. Figure 9-49 shows the configuration of a static default route. The Preference value ultimately determines the administrative distance of the static route. There are two places where such values can be defined. Each next hop can assign its own preference. If next-hop preference values are left at 0, the base Preference setting in the Prefix field takes effect. Configure the Prefix, Preference, and Next Hop IP settings for a static route and click Submit. If you create a route without setting a next-hop IP address, ACI assigns the NULL interface as the next hop.

Figure 9-49 *Adding a Static Route on an L3Out*

Note the BFD checkbox. Enabling BFD for a static route leads to the subsecond withdrawal of the static route from the routing table in the event that the BFD session on the egress interface for the static route goes down.

Implementing IP SLA Tracking for Static Routes

With IP service-level agreement (SLA) tracking for static routes, introduced in ACI Release 4.1(1), you have the option to collect information about network performance in real time by tracking an IP address using ICMP or TCP probes; you can influence routing tables by allowing a static route to be removed when tracking results are negative and returning the routes to the table when the results become positive again. IP addresses tracked can be next-hop IP addresses, external addresses several hops away, or internal endpoints.

To implement IP SLA tracking for static routes, perform the following steps:

Step 1. Create an IP SLA monitoring policy if custom probe frequency and multipliers are desired.

Step 2.   Define the IP addresses to be probed. These are called track members.

Step 3.   Create and associate a track list with either an individual static route or a next-hop address for the static route.

To create an IP SLA monitoring policy, navigate to the tenant in which the policy should be created, double-click the Policies folder, double-click the Protocol folder, right-click the IP SLA folder, and select Create IP SLA Monitoring Policy. Figure 9-50 shows creation of an IP SLA policy using default settings. The SLA Frequency field specifies the frequency, in seconds, to probe the track member IP address. Acceptable values range from 1 second to 300 seconds. The Detect Multiplier setting defines the number of missed probes in a row that moves the track object into a down state. The SLA Type setting defines which protocol is used for probing the track member IP. For L3Out static routes, the supported options are either ICMP or TCP with a specified destination port.

Figure 9-50   *Creating an IP SLA Monitoring Policy*

Define each IP address that needs to be probed in a track member object by right-clicking the Track Members or IP SLA folder and selecting Create Track Member. Figure 9-51 shows the track member IP address entered in the Destination IP field. The Scope of Track Member drop-down allows you to define the component (L3Out or BD) on which the destination IP address should exist. The IP SLA monitoring policy should also be specified in the IP SLA Policy drop-down unless the default IP SLA policy in the common tenant is desired.

Figure 9-51   *Creating a Track Member*

Create a track list by right-clicking either the IP SLA folder or the Track Lists folder and selecting Create Track List. Alternatively, you can create a new track list and simultaneously associate it with a static route or next-hop address on the Static Route page. The Type of Track List field has Threshold Percentage and Threshold Weight as options. Use the percentage option if all track members are at the same level of importance. Use the weight option to assign a different weight to each track member for more granular threshold conditions. With Threshold Percentage selected, ACI removes the associated static route(s) from the routing table when probes to the percentage of track members specified by the Percentage Down field become unreachable. ACI then reenables the static route(s) only when probes to the percentage of track members specified by Percentage Up become reachable. Similarly, the Weight Up Value and Weight Down Value fields, which are exposed when Threshold Weights is selected, determine the overall weight that needs to be reached for associated static routes to be removed or re-introduced into the routing table.

Figure 9-52 shows a track list which demands that probes be sent against two track member IP addresses. Because two objects have been included in the track list, reachability to each destination contributes 50% to the overall threshold of the track list. The Percentage Up value 51 indicates that both track members need to be up for the static route to be added to the routing table. In this example, ACI withdraws the associated route(s) even if one track member becomes unreachable due to the Percentage Down value 50.

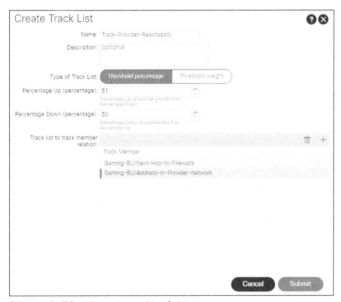

Figure 9-52 *Creating a Track List*

Example 9-6 shows that when this track list is assigned to the static default route created earlier, ACI implements a track object for each track member and track list. The overall status of the track list is *down* because the Percentage Down condition has been hit due to lack of reachability to one track member. This prompts the associated route prefix to be withdrawn from the routing tables of all ACI switches.

Example 9-6   *Verifying Tracking of Static Routes*

```
LEAF301# show track

Track 2
    IP SLA 2256
    reachability is down
    1 changes, last change 2020-07-11T19:23:25.179+00:00
    Tracked by:
        Track List 1

Track 3
    IP SLA 2288
    reachability is up
    2 changes, last change 2020-07-11T19:23:25.181+00:00
    Tracked by:
        Track List 1

Track 1
    List Threshold percentage
    Threshold percentage is down
    1 changes, last change 2020-07-11T19:23:25.176+00:00
    Threshold percentage up 51% down 50%
    Tracked List Members:
        Object 3 (50)% up
        Object 2 (50)% down
    Attached to:
        Route prefix 0.0.0.0/0
```

As noted earlier, track lists can also be associated with a next-hop IP address for a static route. Figure 9-53 shows configurable options besides the next-hop IP address that are available on the Next Hop Profile page. Next Hop Type can be set to None or Prefix. None is used to reference the NULL interface as the next hop of a static route. ACI accepts None as a valid next-hop type only if 0.0.0.0/0 is entered as the prefix. Alternatively, a static route without a next-hop entry is essentially a route to the NULL interface. Prefix is the default option for Next Hop Type and allows users to specify the actual next-hop IP address.

Applying an IP SLA policy on a next-hop entry for a static route is functionally equivalent to creating a track list with the next-hop address as its only track member and applying the resulting track list to the next-hop entry. In other words, referencing an IP SLA policy on a next-hop entry provides a shortcut whereby the APIC internally creates a track list with the next-hop IP address as the probe IP address.

9

Figure 9-53 *Options Available on the Next Hop Profile Page*

NOTE One difference between applying a track list to a static route and applying it to a next-hop entry is apparent when a backup floating static route for the same prefix exists on the same leaf switch(es) even when configured on a different L3Out. In this case, a track list applied to the primary static route (lower preference value) prevents the floating static route (higher preference value) from being added to the routing table. This behavior is not experienced when the track list is applied to the next-hop entry of the primary static route.

Configuring an L3Out for BGP Peering

ACI supports both iBGP and eBGP peerings with external routers. A BGP-enabled L3Out automatically belongs to the same BGP ASN configured for route reflection. You need to define each BGP peering under a BGP peer connectivity profile. If there is a need for the fabric to appear as an ASN other than the one configured for route reflection, you can tweak the *local-as* settings in the BGP peer connectivity profile for the intended BGP neighbor.

Given that BGP designs often require peering with neighbors that may be several hops away, an important topic with BGP is establishing IP reachability to potential neighbor peering addresses. Supported methods for BGP peering IP reachability in ACI are direct connections, static routes, and OSPF.

Figure 9-54 shows that the first step in creating a BGP L3Out via the GUI is to enable the BGP checkbox. Notice that this does not disable the OSPF checkbox. Enter the L3Out name, VRF instance, and L3 domain and click Next.

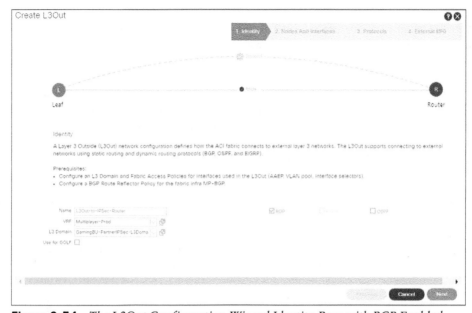

Figure 9-54 *The L3Out Configuration Wizard Identity Page with BGP Enabled*

Figure 9-55 indicates that the Use Defaults checkbox has been enabled for this L3Out. Because of this checkbox, ACI does not show the logical node profile or logical interface profile names it intends to create. Even though there is little benefit in creating a loopback for EIGRP and OSPF L3Outs, the Loopback Address field in this case has been populated. This is recommended for BGP because a design change at any time may require the addition of redundant multihop peerings. Enter interface configuration parameters and click Next to continue.

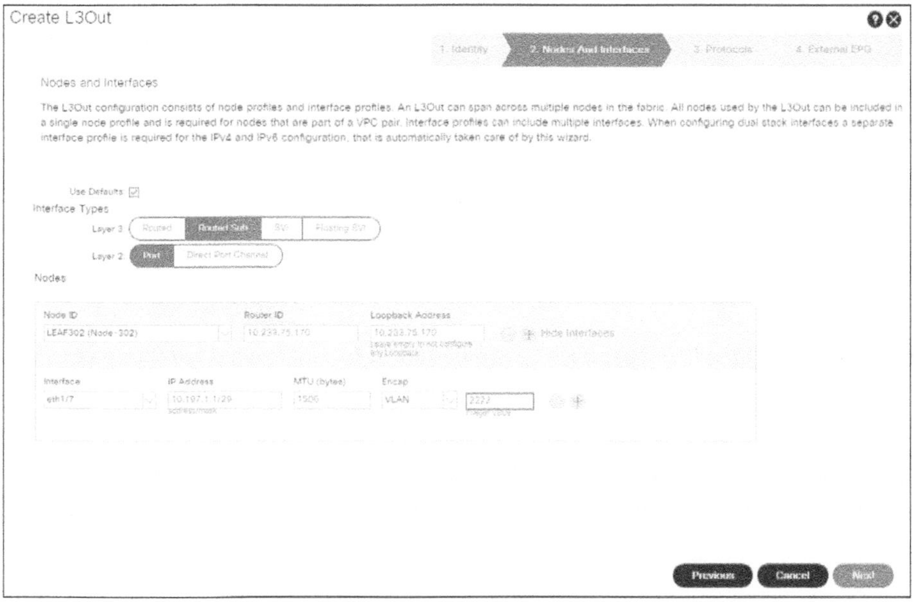

Figure 9-55 *Configuration Options on the Nodes and Interfaces Page*

NOTE   In L3Outs with interface type SVI, configuration of secondary addresses is an option. However, BGP sessions can only be sourced from the primary IP address of each interface.

For BGP L3Outs, the Protocol Association page is where all the action is. Each row completed on this page leads to the creation of a BGP peer connectivity profile. While BGP peer connectivity profiles contain many options, the wizard allows configuration of only the minimum number of required settings, which in the case of eBGP consist of the neighbor IP address (Peer Address parameter), the remote ASN, and the maximum number of hops to the intended peer (EBGP Multihop TTL parameter). BGP peers need to be defined either under logical interface profiles or under logical node profiles. When the intent is to source a BGP session from the node loopback interface, you can configure the BGP peer under a logical node profile. The first row in Figure 9-56 represents a configuration that will be placed under the logical node profile. BGP peers whose sessions should be sourced from non-loopback interfaces need to be configured under a logical interface profile. The second row in this figure represents a configuration object that will be deployed under a logical interface profile sourcing the subinterface earlier defined for interface Ethernet1/7. Click Next to continue.

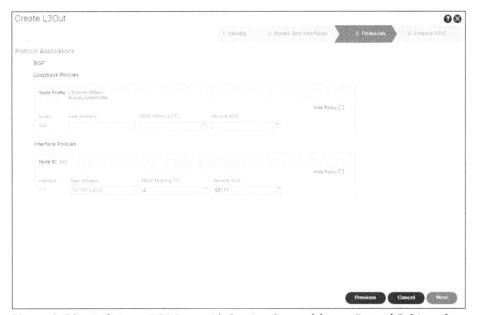

Figure 9-56   *Defining a BGP Peer with Session Sourced from a Routed Subinterface*

NOTE   If you decide to populate only the Peer Address field, ACI builds a BGP peer connectivity profile suitable for a directly attached iBGP peer.

NOTE   Instead of creating multiple BGP peer connectivity profiles for neighbors that are all in a single subnet and that require the same set of policies, you can use a feature called Dynamic Neighbor. With this feature, you can have ACI dynamically establish BGP peerings with multiple neighbors by configuring a subnet instead of an individual IP address in the Peer Address field. When BGP is configured with dynamic neighbor configuration, ACI does not attempt to initiate sessions to IP addresses in the peer subnet. The other side needs to explicitly configure the ACI border leaf IP address to start the BGP session. The Dynamic Neighbor feature was called Prefix Peers in standalone NX-OS, and this term is also used in some Cisco ACI documentation.

Finally, Figure 9-57 shows how to create a new external EPG straight from the L3Out creation wizard. In this case, the external EPG has the scope External Subnets for External EPG set, which means the external EPG can be used for classification of outside traffic. Because in this example remote testers need to log in to systems in EPG-Client-VMs, created in Chapter 8, the external EPG is consuming a contract that grants such access. Click Finish to deploy the BGP L3Out. BGP peerings should come up if equivalent configuration has been deployed on the peer router.

Figure 9-57   *Creating an External EPG Classifying External Traffic in the L3Out Wizard*

Implementing BGP Customizations at the Node Level

Once a BGP L3Out has been created, you may want to customize certain BGP settings at the border leaf level. Assuming that different logical node profiles have been used for each border leaf, different node-specific policies such as BGP timers can be applied to each switch.

To configure a node-specific BGP protocol profile, right-click the node profile of interest and select Create BGP Protocol Profile. The Create Node Specific BGP Protocol Profile page contains two drop-downs at the time of writing. One is for BGP timer customization, and the other is for AS_PATH policy customizations. Recent versions of ACI code no longer support AS_PATH policy customizations to enable ECMP across eBGP peers in different AS_PATHs; therefore, this second set of policies is not addressed in this book. Figure 9-58 shows the creation of a custom BGP timer policy.

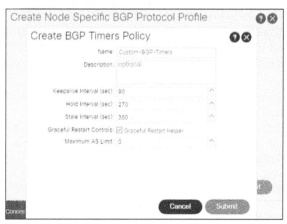

Figure 9-58   *Creating a Custom BGP Timer Policy*

None of the settings in Figure 9-58 should be new for you if you deal with BGP on a regular basis, but Table 9-4 provides a review of the options.

Table 9-4   Configuration Parameters for BGP Timer Policies

Configuration Parameter	Description
Keepalive Interval (sec)	Specifies the interval at which keepalive messages are sent after a BGP peer is established. The default value for this setting is 60 seconds.
Hold Interval (sec)	Specifies the interval at which keepalive messages must be received for ACI to consider the BGP peer operational. The default value for this setting is 180 seconds.
Stale Interval (sec)	Specifies when to delete stale routes in case a session is not reestablished within the established interval. When a graceful restart is in progress, the routes previously received from the peer are still used for forwarding but marked as stale. Once the session between two routers is reestablished and route information is synced again, all the stale routes are deleted and the routes from the latest exchange are used. This interval is applied locally. The default value is 300 seconds.
Graceful Restart Helper	Specifies the restarting router triggered when a graceful restart is in progress. The peer is likely simply helping the graceful restart operation with the restarting router. Cisco ACI provides only graceful restart helper capability because ACI does not support stateful supervisor switchover within each individual switch node. Only a cold reboot is available. Instead, routing protocol high availability (HA) should be achieved by using multiple switch nodes.
Maximum AS Limit	When nonzero, prompts ACI to discard eBGP routes received if the number of AS_PATH segments exceeds the stated limit. The default value of zero implies no maximum AS limit.

Note that configured intervals take effect only after a new BGP session is established.

BGP timer policies can also be applied at the VRF level.

Implementing Per-Neighbor BGP Customizations

Figure 9-59 shows the majority of settings that can be customized on a per-BGP-neighbor basis. Two additional settings, Admin State and Route Control Profile, have been left out of this screenshot. Depicted customizations include modification of the Local-AS Number setting 65600 for establishing an eBGP session to a router in remote ASN 65700. The Local-AS Number Config parameter has been left blank, prompting ACI to advertise routes to this external neighbor by appending 65600 to the fabric route reflector ASN.

Figure 9-59 *Customization of the Local AS Number for a Specific BGP Peer*

Table 9-5 describes the customization options available in BGP peer connectivity profiles.

Table 9-5 Configuration Parameters in BGP Peer Connectivity Profiles

Configuration Parameter	Description
Allow Self AS	Allows ACI to receive routes from eBGP neighbors when the routes have the ACI BGP AS number in the AS_PATH. This option is valid only for eBGP peers.
AS override	Allows ACI to overwrite a remote AS in the AS_PATH with the ACI BGP AS. This is typically used when performing Transit Routing from an eBGP L3Out to another eBGP L3Out with the same AS number. Otherwise, an eBGP peer device may not accept the route from ACI because of AS_PATH loop prevention. When this option is enabled, Disable Peer AS Check also needs to be enabled. This option is valid only for eBGP peers.

9

Configuration Parameter	Description
Disable Peer AS Check	Allows ACI to advertise a route to the eBGP peer even if the most recent AS in the AS_PATH of the route is the same as the remote AS for the eBGP peer. This option is valid only for eBGP peers.
Next-hop Self	Allows ACI to update the next-hop address when advertising a route from an eBGP peer to an iBGP peer. By default, route advertisement between iBGP peers keeps the original next-hop address of the route, and the one between eBGP peers always updates the next-hop address with a self IP address.
Send Community	When enabled, allows ACI L3Out to advertise routes with a BGP Community attribute, such as AS2:*NN* format. Otherwise, the BGP Community attribute is stripped when routes are advertised to the outside.
Send Extended Community	When enabled, allows ACI L3Out to advertise routes along with the BGP Extended Community attribute, such as RT:AS2:NN, RT:AS4:NN, and so on. Otherwise, the BGP Extended Community attribute is stripped when routes are advertised to the outside.
Password/Confirm Password	When configured, allows the BGP peering to use MD5 authentication on the BGP TCP session. The password can be reset by right-clicking the BGP peer connectivity profile and selecting Reset Password.
Allowed Self AS Count	Sets the maximum count for the Allow Self AS option under BGP controls.
Bidirectional Forwarding Detection	Enables BFD on the BGP neighbor.
Disable Connected Check	Provides an alternative to increasing the eBGP multihop TTL in cases where there is a security concern about increasing TTL unnecessarily. For eBGP peering, BGP checks whether the neighbor IP is on the same subnet as any of its local interfaces to see if the neighbor IP is directly connected. If it is not, BGP automatically assumes that the TTL needs to be larger than 1. Hence, when BGP is peering via loopbacks with directly connected routers, the BGP peering is rejected without the eBGP Multihop TTL being set to 2 or larger, even though TTL 1 is technically enough.
Weight for routes from this neighbor	Sets the default value of a Cisco proprietary BGP path attribute weight on all the routes learned from the border leaf by the configured peer.
Remove Private AS	In outgoing eBGP route updates to this neighbor, removes all private AS numbers from the AS_PATH when the AS_PATH has only private AS numbers. This option is not applied if the neighbor remote AS is in the AS_PATH.
Remove All Private AS	In outgoing eBGP route updates to this neighbor, removes all private AS numbers from the AS_PATH, regardless of whether a public AS number is included in the AS_PATH. This feature does not apply if the neighbor remote AS is in the AS_PATH. To enable this option, Remove Private AS needs to be enabled.

Configuration Parameter	Description
Replace Private AS with Local AS	In outgoing eBGP route updates to this neighbor, replaces all private AS numbers in the AS_PATH with ACI local AS, regardless of whether a public AS or the neighbor remote AS is included in the AS_PATH. To enable this option, Remove All Private AS needs to be enabled.
BGP Peer Prefix Policy	Defines an action to take when the number of received prefixes from this neighbor exceeds the configured maximum number. This option is activated by attaching a BGP peer prefix policy to the BGP peer connectivity profile.
Local-AS Number	Disguises the ACI BGP ASN with the configured local ASN to peer with a particular neighbor. When this feature is used, it looks like there is one more ASN (local AS) between the ACI BGP AS and the external neighbor. Hence, the neighbor peers with the configured local ASN instead of the real ACI BGP ASN. In such situations, both the local ASN and the real ACI BGP ASN are added to the AS_PATH of routes advertised to the neighbor. The local ASN is also prepended to routes learned from the neighbor.
Local-AS Number Config	Allows granular control over how the local ASN and the fabric ASN appear in the AS_PATHs of routes advertised to external routers or received by the fabric.
	The no-prepend option prevents ACI from prepending the local ASN in the AS_PATHs of routes learned from this neighbor.
	The no-prepend, replace-as option allows ACI to add only a local ASN, instead of both a local ASN and a real ACI BGP ASN, to the AS_PATHs of routes advertised to this neighbor on top of the no-prepend option effect.
	The no-prepend, replace-as, dual-as option allows the neighbor to peer with both a local ASN and a real ACI BGP ASN on top of the no-prepend and replace-as option effect.
Admin State	Enables a BGP session with a peer to be turned off or on.
Route Control Profile	Allows application of a route profile to a specific BGP neighbor.

Implementing BFD on a BGP L3Out

One of the most common tweaks in BGP peer connectivity profiles is to implement BFD with neighbors. BFD is not supported on loopback interfaces since there is no support for BFD multihop in ACI at the time of writing. BFD is also not supported for dynamic neighbors (prefix peers).

To enable BFD on a BGP L3Out, navigate to the desired BGP peer connectivity profile and enable the Bidirectional Forwarding Detection checkbox, which is visible in the Peer Controls section of Figure 9-59, shown earlier.

Customization of BFD timers on a BGP L3Out requires application of a custom BFD policy and BFD interface profile. To apply a previously created BFD interface policy or to create a new one, right-click the desired logical interface profile under the L3Out and select Create BFD Interface Profile. Then select or create a BFD interface policy.

Implementing BGP Customizations at the VRF Level

Aside from assigning a BGP timer policy at the VRF level, you can create a custom BGP address family context policy for VRF-wide application to the IPv4 unicast address family or the IPv6 unicast address family. Figure 9-60 shows options that can be tweaked for a BGP address family context policy.

Figure 9-60 *Creating a BGP Address Family Context Policy*

Table 9-6 explains these configuration options.

Table 9-6 Configuration Parameters for BGP Timer Policies

Configuration Parameter	Description
eBGP Distance	Specifies the administrative distance for eBGP-learned routes. The default AD for such routes is 20.
iBGP Distance	Specifies the administrative distance for eBGP-learned routes. The default AD for such routes is 200.
Local Distance	Is used for aggregate discard routes. The default AD for such routes is 220.
eBGP/iBGP Max ECMP	Configures the maximum number of equal-cost paths a switch adds to the routing table for eBGP-learned and iBGP-learned routes. The default value in ACI for this setting is 16.
Enable Host Route Leak	Is used only for the GOLF feature and is therefore beyond the scope of the DCACI 300-620 exam.

Once it is configured, a BGP address family context policy needs to be applied to an address family for the policy to take effect. Figure 9-61 shows a BGP timer policy being applied VRF-wide to Multiplayer-Prod and a BGP address family context policy being applied to the IPv4 unicast address family for the VRF.

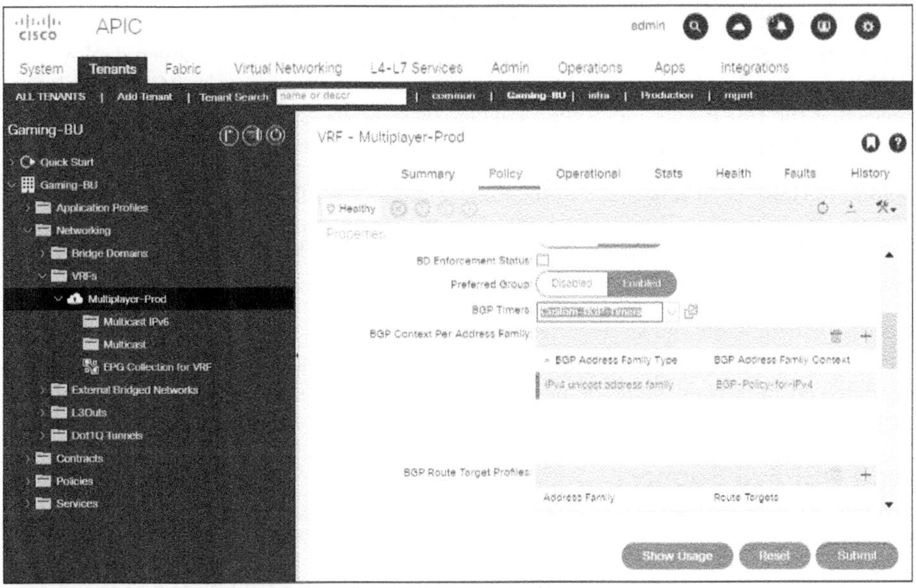

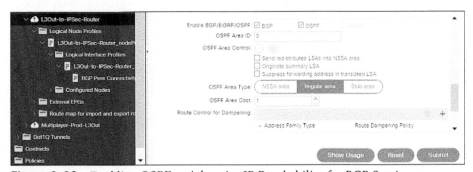

Figure 9-61   *Applying BGP Policies at the VRF Level*

> **NOTE**   Although it is not impossible, it *is* improbable that DCACI candidates will need to know the name of a setting that modifies the administrative distance of routes learned by a specific routing protocol. DCACI 300-620 exam candidates should, however, know that enforcement of policies around protocol timers and administrative distances often take place at the VRF level.

Implementing OSPF for IP Reachability on a BGP L3Out

To use OSPF for dynamic IP reachability advertisement on a BGP L3Out, select the root of the L3Out, click the Policy menu, and navigate to the Main submenu. Toward the bottom of the page, you see options for enabling OSPF. The available configuration options, as indicated in Figure 9-62, are exactly the same as those available for OSPF L3Outs. But when OSPF and BGP are enabled side-by-side in the same L3Out, OSPF is programmed only to advertise its L3Out loopback and interfaces IP addresses.

Figure 9-62   *Enabling OSPF to Advertise IP Reachability for BGP Sessions*

Implementing Hot Standby Router Protocol (HSRP)

ACI supports HSRP on L3Out routed interfaces and routed subinterfaces. When deploying HSRP, external devices must provide Layer 2 connectivity between the ACI border leaf switches that run HSRP. This allows the exchange of Hello messages over external Layer 2 connections. HSRP Hello messages do not pass through spine switches.

To configure HSRP in ACI, navigate to the logical interface profile of interest and select the Create HSRP Interface Profile checkbox. The process of configuring an HSRP interface policy should be straightforward for those familiar with HSRP. Note that the HSRP virtual IP address must be in the same subnet as the interface IP address.

Because SVIs on L3Outs can leverage secondary addresses, use of HSRP in ACI L3Outs for connectivity to appliances that only support static routing is not common. In such cases, static routes on appliances should point to the secondary addresses configured in the L3Out to enable next-hop high availability.

IPv6 and OSPFv3 Support

IPv6 is not discussed in this book because ACI attempts to make the transition to IPv6 natural by not delineating between IPv6 and IPv4.

To enable OSPFv3 on an L3Out, enable the OSPF checkbox on the L3Out Main page and assign an IPv6 address to the L3Out and witness the border leaf bring up the OSPFv3 process.

Implementing Route Control

Sometimes it may be necessary to filter certain routes or make changes to metrics and other attributes of routes advertised out of a fabric or learned by a fabric. Where granular route control is a requirement, ACI route profiles can help.

Route Profile Basics

As you have seen, ACI creates route maps behind the scenes to accomplish certain tasks. For example, when an administrator associates a bridge domain with an L3Out and updates the scope of a BD subnet to Advertised Externally, ACI creates a route map to redistribute the subnet out the specified L3Out.

ACI uses route maps internally for quite a few different purposes, such as infra MP-BGP route distribution, BD subnet advertisement to the outside world, and transit routing.

Route profiles give users the ability to add user-defined match rules or set rules for route filtering or route manipulation. Route profiles can alternatively be referred to as *route control profiles*. The term *route map* is also sometimes used interchangeably with *route profile*, but in terms of implementation, each route profile is more a collection of implicit and explicit route maps.

Some of the use cases for this feature that are inside the scope of the DCACI 300-620 exam are as follows:

- A route profile to allow advertisement (export) of BD subnets to the outside world via L3Outs

- A route profile to limit learning (importing) of external routes from the outside world via L3Outs

- A route profile to set certain attributes on routes exiting or entering the fabric if they meet a certain criterion

A route profile can be associated with any of the following objects/components:

- A bridge domain

- A bridge domain subnet

- An EPG on an L3Out

- A subnet of an EPG on an L3Out

- A route peering neighbor

- An entire L3Out

Table 9-7 defines the various components of a route profile in ACI.

Table 9-7   Components of a Route Profile

Component	Description
Route Profile Type	The route profile type is specific to ACI. There are two route profile types. One type, Match Prefix AND Routing Policy, combines prefixes from the component that the route profile is associated with and the match criteria configured in the route profile. Components that route profiles can be associated to include bridge domains, bridge domain subnets, L3Outs, L3Out EPGs, and L3Out EPG subnets. The other type, Match Routing Policy Only, only matches routes based on criteria configured in the route profile and ignores prefixes from the components with which the route profile is associated.
Context	In a sense, each entry in a route profile includes two context options: Order and Action. Order is equivalent to a sequence number in a normal route map with the caveat that some route profiles merge internal route maps of components with statements explicitly entered by administrators, changing the actual applicable sequence of rules. Action consists of permit or deny and is equivalent in function to permit or deny in a normal route map.
Match Rules	Route profile match rules are similar to match clauses in route maps. Clauses ACI can match against include prefixes, community attributes, and regular expressions.
Set Rule	Set rules are equivalent to set clauses in a route map. ACI can set parameters such as community attributes, weight, OSPF types, and AS_PATH.

The next few subsections provide examples of route profile implementation.

NOTE   The coverage of route profiles in this book is just the tip of the iceberg when it comes to route control in ACI. The content and examples in this chapter reflect the scope of the DCACI 300-620 exam. Where deploying these solutions in environments with route leaking or transit routing, additional caveats may apply.

Modifying Route Attributes to All Peers Behind an L3Out

One of the most prevalent use cases for route maps in traditional routers and Layer 3 switches is to manipulate route metrics or to add attributes to routes. Let's take a look at an example of how route profiles address this use case. Say that a fabric has multiple L3Outs, and an IT team wants to assign different BGP communities to routes advertised out of each L3Out. The idea is that the BGP communities could then be used by the external devices for traffic engineering or any type of policy enforcement.

To address any route profile requirement, the implementation team needs to fully understand the required match rules and set rules. Since the idea is that the interesting prefixes are any ACI routes egressing a specific L3Out, and routes advertised have already been marked with the scope Advertised Externally and have been associated with the relevant L3Out, there should be an easy way to match such prefixes. It turns out there is. Application of a route profile at the default export level of an L3Out automatically satisfies this requirement without the need for Match statements.

The next part of the equation is configuration of set rules. To configure a set rule, go to the tenant in question, double-click Policies, double-click Protocol, right-click Set Rules, and select Create Set Rules for a Route Map. Figure 9-63 shows a set rule that assigns BGP community 65000:100 to any matched routes. Note also the other potential options for set rules.

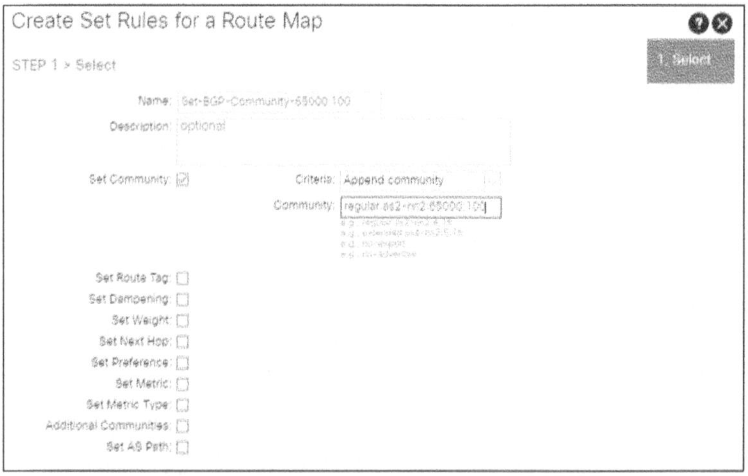

Figure 9-63 *Creating Set Rules for a Route Profile*

By default, ACI strips BGP communities in route advertisements to external peers. To address this, as shown in Figure 9-64, you can enable the Send Community checkbox in the BGP peer connectivity profile for the single BGP neighbor currently attached to the L3Out. If advertising extended BGP communities, you need to enable the Send Extended Community.

The next step is to actually configure the route profile on the L3Out. At a minimum, each route profile requires at least one context. Each context is similar to a sequence number in a traditional route map. As indicated in Figure 9-65, creation of a context requires entry of a numeric value indicating the priority or order of the context, whether to permit (advertise) or deny (drop) the route, any match criteria (Match Rule drop-down) to determine prefixes of interest, and any modifications (Set Rule drop-down) ACI should apply to matched routes.

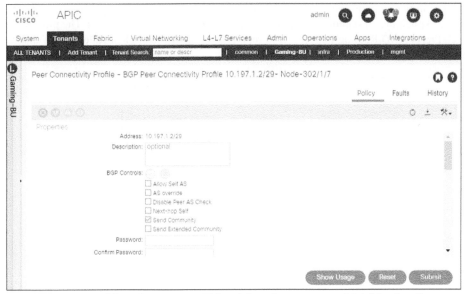

Figure 9-64   *Enabling Community Value Advertisements to a Neighboring Router*

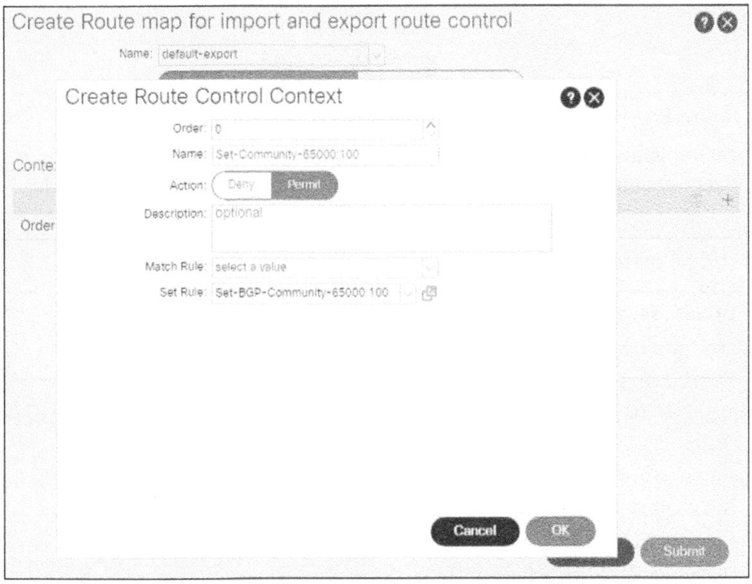

Figure 9-65   *Creating a Context Within a Route Profile*

Note in Figure 9-65 that a match rule, in this instance, was not required. This is specifically because the route profile type Match Prefix AND Routing Policy has been selected, as indicated in Figure 9-66. The term Match Prefix Policy can be understood as a directive for ACI to consider any prefixes associated with the object(s) to which the route profile is associated to be implicit match rules. In this case, the default-export route profile is associated with the entire L3Out. Therefore, Match Prefix Policy implicitly matches all BD subnets associated with the L3Out with the scope Advertised Externally, even though there is no explicit match statement in the route profile. You can read the term Match Routing Policy to refer to the type of explicit match statements engineers are used to adding to route maps. The phrase Match Prefix AND Routing Policy, therefore, is a merging of the implicit route map(s) and match rules explicitly configured in the route profile.

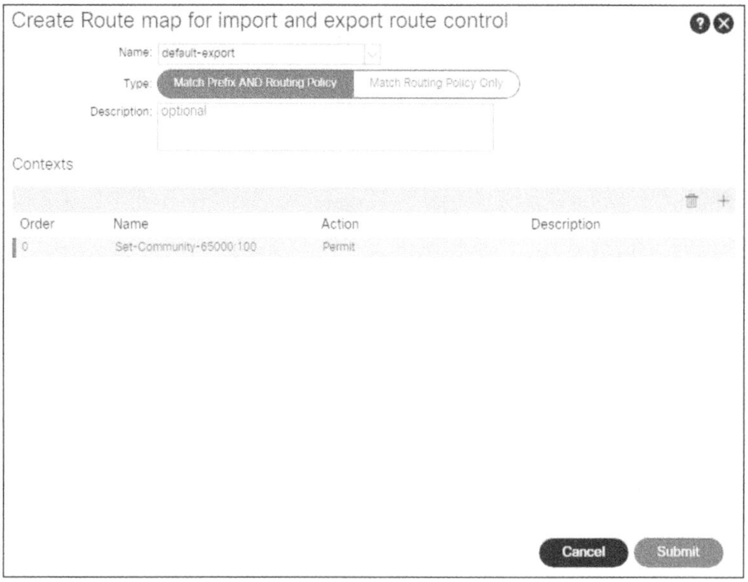

Figure 9-66   *Setting Route Profile Type to Match Prefix AND Routing Policy*

Once these settings are implemented, all routes out of the specified L3Out should be advertised out to all peers behind the L3Out using the community 65000:100, as shown in Example 9-7.

Example 9-7   *Validating Community Values on a Route on Nexus Platforms*

```
Router# show ip bgp 10.233.58.0/24 vrf LAB-BGP
(...output truncated for brevity...)
BGP routing table information for VRF LAB-BGP, address family IPv4 Unicast
BGP routing table entry for 10.233.58.0/24, version 14
Paths: (1 available, best #1)
  AS-Path: 65000 , path sourced external to AS
    10.197.1.1 (metric 0) from 10.197.1.1 (10.233.75.170)
      Origin incomplete, MED 0, localpref 100, weight 0
      Community: 65000:100

  Path-id 1 not advertised to any peer
```

Earlier in this example configuration, the text indicated that the Deny action drops matched routes and does not advertise them out the L3Out. This is not always true, especially when using route profiles of the type Match Prefix AND Routing Policy. Because this particular type of route profile merges multiple route maps together, it can sometimes be difficult to determine whether an implicit route map has already permitted advertisement of the prefix.

Modifying Route Attributes to a Specific Peer Behind an L3Out

Now let's say that the objective is a little different from the objective we've been considering. Assume that multiple BGP peers have been deployed behind an L3Out, and different community values need to be applied to outbound routes to each peer behind the L3Out. In such a scenario, the default-export route profile would be of little help. Instead, route profiles would need to be applied to the BGP peer connectivity profiles. But, in addition, explicit match rules would be needed to specify the prefixes of interest. This is because BD subnets do not have a direct association with BGP peers.

Figure 9-67 shows an explicit match statement for the subnet assigned to BD-Production. Note that the Aggregate flag has been set to False, indicating that this rule matches only 10.233.58.0/24 and not host routes within that range.

Figure 9-67 *An Example of a Match Rule Determining an Explicit Prefix as the Only Match*

If the expectation is that several conditions need to be met for a prefix to be matched, all the conditions can be specified under a single Match Rule object. For example, if the requirement for a match is for a prefix to be in the 10.5.0.0/16 range AND have a community value of 65600:100, these two conditions should both be included in a single match rule. On the other hand, if the goal is to say that either prefixes under 10.5.0.0/16 OR community value 65600:100 matches the criteria for advertisement with a particular set rule, separate route map sequences (separate context policies) should be configured for these two requirements, each referencing a different match rule.

Once the match rule has been defined, a route profile needs to be created under **Tenants >** *the tenant in question* **> Policies > Protocol > Route Maps for Route Control**. As indicated in the background in Figure 9-68, tenant-level route profiles do not display the route profile type because route profiles defined here are for use cases such as MP-BGP interleak and

BGP route dampening, which do not benefit from Match Prefix AND Routing Policy. Notice in Figure 9-68 that both a match rule and a set rule have been assigned to the route profile context.

Figure 9-68 *Creating a Route Profile with an Explicit Prefix List Assigned*

After the route profile has been created, it needs to be assigned to the desired BGP peer. Figure 9-69 shows that the route has been assigned to a BGP peer connectivity profile in the export direction. In traditional route map terms, this should be understood as the *out* direction.

Figure 9-69 *Applying a Custom Route Profile in the Outbound (Export) Direction*

With this change, the defined community values should only be applied to the one BGP peer.

One thing that might not be apparent from the configuration shown here is that the act of matching 10.233.58.0/24 in a custom outbound route profile or default-export route map is an alternative method to redistribute BD subnets outside the fabric. In other words, as long as BD subnet 10.233.58.0/24 has been marked Advertised Externally, this configuration would work to advertise the subnet out of the fabric, even without a BD association with the L3Out.

> **NOTE**   At the time of writing, there is no mechanism to assign a route profile on a per-neighbor basis for OSPF and EIGRP.

Assigning Different Policies to Routes at the L3Out Level

Let's say there is a need to be more granular and assign different community values to routes as they leave the fabric on an L3Out. Figure 9-70 shows that a new match rule and a new set rule have been associated with one another under a route profile context. Notice that the order 1 has been assigned, given that multiple requirements exist.

Figure 9-70   *Configuring Multiple Route Profile Contexts*

Figure 9-71 shows how contexts can be used together to match different subnets with community values or other set rules. One very important question here is whether it makes sense to use Match Prefix AND Routing Policy in instances like this. The problem with using this particular route profile type is that the merging of the explicit route profile rules with implicit route maps may place implicit matches into the route map sequence specified with the order 0. This, in turn, could assign 65000:100 to all BD subnets, even though this might not be the intention. In any instance, where the intention is to only apply explicit policy, the route profile type can be toggled to Match Routing Policy Only. In this example, subnets in the 10.233.58.0/23 supernet range are assigned the BGP community 65000:100, while subnets in the 10.233.60.0/23 supernet range are assigned to 65000:101. Any subnets not in the ranges specified by match rules hit an implicit deny rule and are not advertised.

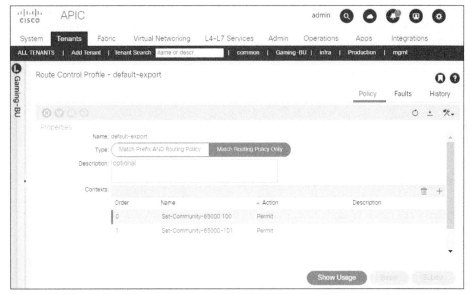

Figure 9-71 *Reliance on Explicit Match Rules Using Match Routing Policy Only*

> **NOTE**　Although not apparent in this case, the policy type depicted here blocks exit of any routes not matched with an explicit Permit action. Can this be useful if a border leaf needs to deploy OSPF and EIGRP L3Outs side-by-side within a VRF? If there is a requirement to advertise different subnets out of each L3Out and sidestep the issue discussed earlier in this chapter, the answer is yes. Use of a route profile with Match Routing Policy Only on one L3Out and leveraging regular BD subnet advertisement mechanisms for the second L3Out is a valid (but probably not recommended) way to overcome limitations related to OSPF and EIGRP L3Outs in the same VRF on the same border leaf advertising the same subnets due to application of common implicit route maps.

Configuring Inbound Route Filtering in ACI

ACI learns all routes inbound by default. If this behavior is not desired, navigate to **Policy > Main** for an L3Out and enable the Route Control Enforcement Import checkbox, as shown in Figure 9-72. This setting enables administrators to enforce inbound route profiles.

Figure 9-72 *Enabling Route Control in the Inbound Direction on an L3Out*

As shown in Figure 9-73, the default-import route profile on the L3Out can be used in conjunction with explicit prefix lists and match rules to determine what routes can be imported into the fabric.

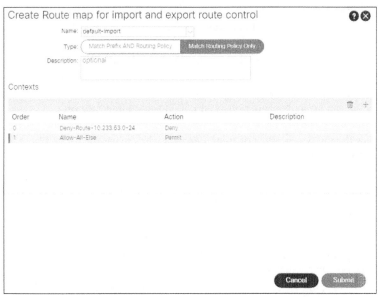

Figure 9-73   *Creating a default-import Route Profile to Filter Specific Inbound Routes*

NOTE   The goal of this section on route profiles was not to provide step-by-step guidance on configuring route profiles but to demonstrate route profiles and route profile types in context. The coverage is by no means complete but shows that what is within the scope of DCACI is very limited.

Exam Preparation Tasks

As mentioned in the section "How to Use This Book" in the Introduction, you have a couple of choices for exam preparation: Chapter 17, "Final Preparation," and the exam simulation questions in the Pearson Test Prep Software Online.

Review All Key Topics

Review the most important topics in this chapter, noted with the Key Topic icon in the outer margin of the page. Table 9-8 lists a reference of these key topics and the page numbers on which each is found.

Table 9-8   Key Topics for Chapter 9

Key Topic Element	Description	Page Number
List	Details the five critical functions of an L3Out	293
List	Describes the anatomy and important components of a typical L3Out	294
List	Lists the types of interfaces that can be configured under an L3Out logical interface profile	296
Paragraph	Describes why a port or port aggregation with an EPG mapping can no longer function as an L3Out routed interface or routed subinterface	296
Figure 9-5	Details the impact in terms of route peerings when using the same SVI encapsulation across interfaces than when different encapsulations are used	297
Paragraph	Describes ACI behavior when an SVI with a particular encapsulation is deployed on a second L3Out on a different border leaf switch	298
Paragraph	Describes the significance of the SVI Encap Scope setting	299
Figure 9-7	Compares use of SVI Encap Scope of a VRF versus Local on L3Outs on a particular leaf switch	299
Paragraph	Describes default ACI behavior with SVI Auto State set to Disabled	299
Figure 9-8	Illustrates the impact on static routes during failover with ACI Auto State set to Disabled	300
Figure 9-9	Illustrates the impact on static routes during failover with ACI Auto State set to Enabled	300
Paragraph	Details what happens if no BGP route reflector has been configured in an ACI fabric	304
List	Lists the two configuration parameters needed for implementing BGP route reflection in ACI	304
Figure 9-14	Shows configuration of BGP route reflection under the BGP route reflector policy object	304
Figure 9-17	Shows enablement of EIGRP and entry of autonomous system	307
Figure 9-18	Illustrates entry of node and interface information using routed interfaces	308
Figure 9-20	Shows the external EPG creation page of the L3Out wizard	309
Paragraph	Describes the significance of the External Subnets for External EPG subnet scope	311
Figure 9-25	Shows the General tab in an external EPG, which provides a quick view into subnets and scopes	312
Figure 9-26	Shows how to mark a BD as a candidate for subnet redistribution	314
Figure 9-27	Shows toggling a BD subnet with Advertised Externally	315
Figure 9-29	Illustrates a filter for communication over an L3Out	316
Figure 9-30	Illustrates a contract subject for filter	316

Key Topic Element	Description	Page Number
Paragraph	Explains contract directionality in the context of external EPGs	317
Paragraph	Describes the Advertise Host Routes setting	321
Paragraph	Describes implementation of BFD on an EIGRP L3Out	321
Table 9-2	Details customizable settings for EIGRP applied at the VRF level	324
Figure 9-44	Shows OSPF configuration options and area types supported in ACI	325
Paragraph	Describes a use case for secondary IP addresses on L3Out SVIs	325
Figure 9-45	Illustrates configuration of L3Out SVIs with secondary IP addresses	326
Paragraph	Describes some scope implications for external EPGs that classify traffic	327
Paragraph	Describes a common problem related to deployment of OSPF and EIGRP L3Outs side-by-side within a VRF on the same leaf switches	328
List	Calls out the most common and recommended solutions where OSPF and EIGRP need to be deployed on the same border leaf while advertising different subnets	328
Table 9-3	Details customizable parameters under OSPF timer policies	329
Paragraph	Explains that static routing L3Outs do not need to deploy any dynamic routing protocols	330
Paragraph	Explains the Preference field for static routes	330
Figure 9-49	Demonstrates adding a static route to an L3Out	330
List	Describes the process for implementing IP SLA tracking for static routes	330
Paragraph	Describes the various fields in the IP SLA configuration wizard	331
Paragraph	Describes the process of creating a track member	331
Paragraph	Describes the significance of configuration options for track lists	332
Paragraph	Explains the difference between deploying BGP configurations at the node profile level versus the interface profile level	336
Figure 9-58	Shows the custom BGP timer policy page	338
Paragraph	Explains that BGP timer policies can be applied not just at the node level but at the VRF level	339
Table 9-5	Defines configuration parameters in BGP peer connectivity profiles	339
Table 9-7	Describes the various configuration components that make up a route profile	345

9

Complete Tables and Lists from Memory

Print a copy of Appendix C, "Memory Tables" (found on the companion website), or at least the section for this chapter, and complete the tables and lists from memory. Appendix D, "Memory Tables Answer Key" (also on the companion website), includes completed tables and lists you can use to check your work.

Define Key Terms

Define the following key terms from this chapter and check your answers in the glossary:

logical node profile, logical interface profile, floating SVI, L3Out bridge domain (BD), route reflector, interleak, secondary IP address, route profile

## CHAPTER 10

Extending Layer 2 Outside ACI

This chapter covers the following topics:

Understanding Network Migrations into ACI: This section describes the network-centric approach to ACI and settings significant to network migrations.

Implementing Layer 2 Connectivity to Non-ACI Switches: This section covers the implementation of bridge domain and EPG extensions out an ACI fabric.

Understanding ACI Interaction with Spanning Tree Protocol: This section addresses how ACI reacts when it receives Spanning Tree Protocol BPDUs from a traditional network.

This chapter covers the following exam topics:

- 1.6 Implement ACI logical constructs

  - 1.6.d bridge domain (unicast routing, Layer 2 unknown hardware proxy, ARP flooding)

  - 1.6.e endpoint groups (EPG)

  - 1.6.f contracts (filter, provider, consumer, reverse port filter, VRF enforced)

- 3.1 Implement Layer 2 out (STP/MCP basics)

In the current world of routed Clos fabrics, Layer 2 connectivity to traditional switches is often intended to be an interim state adopted either to enable workload migrations into the fabric or to prolong the life of non-supported hardware.

Sometimes Layer 2 connectivity to traditional switches is used to keep a specific device outside a fabric indefinitely. This is seldom an approach engineers use to deploy high-availability appliances whose failover procedures or selected settings conflict with ACI endpoint learning and where there is no desire to mitigate the issue through IP learning customizations.

Because migrations into ACI fabrics are the most prominent use case for Layer 2 extension to non-ACI switches, this chapter first addresses bridge domain, EPG, and contract configuration settings significant to network migrations. Next, it details the implementation of the two current flavors of Layer 2 connectivity to traditional switches. Finally, it covers ACI interaction with Spanning Tree Protocol.

"Do I Know This Already?" Quiz

The "Do I Know This Already?" quiz allows you to assess whether you should read this entire chapter thoroughly or jump to the "Exam Preparation Tasks" section. If you are in doubt about your answers to these questions or your own assessment of your knowledge of the topics, read the entire chapter. Table 10-1 lists the major headings in this chapter and their corresponding "Do I Know This Already?" quiz questions. You can find the answers in Appendix A, "Answers to the 'Do I Know This Already?' Questions."

Table 10-1 "Do I Know This Already?" Section-to-Question Mapping

Foundation Topics Section	Questions
Understanding Network Migrations into ACI	1–4
Implementing Layer 2 Connectivity to Non-ACI Switches	5–8
Understanding ACI Interaction with Spanning Tree Protocol	9, 10

CAUTION The goal of self-assessment is to gauge your mastery of the topics in this chapter. If you do not know the answer to a question or are only partially sure of the answer, you should mark that question as wrong for purposes of the self-assessment. Giving yourself credit for an answer you correctly guess skews your self-assessment results and might provide you with a false sense of security.

1. True or false: When trunking a VLAN to ACI and the default gateway is outside the fabric, it is best to set L2 Unknown Unicast to Hardware Proxy.
   a. True
   b. False

2. An any-to-any contract that allows open communication between a large number of EPGs for the purpose of migration into ACI can heavily constrain which of the following resources?
   a. Contract database
   b. VLAN encapsulations
   c. Endpoint table scalability
   d. Policy CAM

3. Which of the following solutions can best optimize hardware resources on leaf switches if the only whitelisting requirement is to allow SSH access to all endpoints in a VRF instance?
   a. Standard contracts provided and consumed by all EPGs
   b. Preferred group member
   c. vzAny
   d. Policy Control Enforcement Preference set to Unenforced

4. Which of the following BD configuration knobs governs how Layer 2 multicast traffic is forwarded in an ACI fabric?
   a. Multi Destination Flooding
   b. ARP Flooding
   c. GARP Based Detection
   d. L3 Unknown Multicast Flooding

5. Which of the following statements about implementation of bridge domain extension is accurate?

   a. ACI runs all variants of Spanning Tree Protocol.

   b. No more than one Layer 2 EPG can be associated with a given bridge domain extension.

   c. Bridge domain extension requires use of a physical domain.

   d. The same VLAN ID used to extend a bridge domain out a border leaf can be reused for border leaf downstream connectivity to servers via EPG extension.

6. Which of the following are valid forms of Layer 2 extension to outside switches in ACI? (Choose all that apply.)

   a. Remote Leaf Layer 2 domain extension

   b. AAEP extension

   c. BD extension

   d. EPG extension

7. Using EPG extension, an engineer has moved all endpoints in a VLAN into an ACI fabric. When he moves the default gateway from traditional switches into the fabric, he suddenly loses all connectivity to the endpoints from outside the fabric. Which of the following are possible reasons this has taken place? (Choose all that apply.)

   a. The Layer 2 connection between ACI switches and non-ACI switches has been disconnected.

   b. The bridge domain does not have an associated L3Out configured.

   c. The subnet Scope parameter on the BD needs to be set to Advertised Externally.

   d. No contracts have been associated with the EPG.

8. A customer has deployed a fabric using two ACI switches. Two overlapping VLANs exist in the customer environment in the DMZ and in the Inside network zone. Both need to be moved into the fabric using a vPC to the two switches. Is this possible? If so, what feature enables this capability? If not, why?

   a. Yes. Use the VLAN scope setting Port Local Scope.

   b. No. ACI rejects use of an encapsulation for more than a single EPG on a switch.

   c. Yes. Use a feature called Global Scope.

   d. No. Spanning Tree Protocol in ACI disables any ports to which overlapping VLAN IDs are deployed.

9. An ACI deployment was functioning perfectly when an EPG was extended to two different pairs of external switches. Then the ACI administrator extended the EPG to another external switch, and the performance of all endpoints in the bridge domain degraded to a crawl. By investigating event logs, the administrator finds that ACI never blocked any ports to external switches. What is a possible reason for the performance degradation?

   a. The ACI administrator enabled MCP on all ports, and MCP blocked redundant connections.

   b. ACI does not support connectivity to switches with Rapid PVST+.

   c. The ACI administrator forgot to enable Rapid PVST+ on the leaf interfaces facing external switches.

   d. External switches connect to ACI with a point-to-point Spanning Tree Protocol port, which has led to premature Spanning Tree Protocol convergence causing a Layer 2 loop.

10. Which one of the following statements is correct?

    a. Without special configuration, ACI may drop MST BPDUs on ingress.

    b. ACI runs Spanning Tree Protocol and participates in the Spanning Tree Protocol topology.

    c. Cisco ACI drops Spanning Tree Protocol BPDUs arriving in EPGs associated with a bridge domain if unicast routing has been enabled at the bridge domain level and a default gateway has been deployed to the bridge domain.

    d. It is important to enable BPDU filtering on ACI leaf ports facing all external switches to ensure that ACI no longer receives Spanning Tree Protocol BPDUs and becomes loop free.

Foundation Topics

Understanding Network Migrations into ACI

On paper, the topic of network migrations is beyond the scope of the Implementing Cisco Application Centric Infrastructure DCACI 300-620 exam and is addressed by the DCACIA 300-630 exam. However, effectively, all of the configuration knobs required for network migrations have actually been included in the DCACI 300-620 exam blueprint. Therefore, this chapter goes a bit beyond the scope of the DCACI 300-620 to provide the additional theoretical coverage necessary for successful Layer 2 extension and basic migration into ACI.

You do not need to memorize every single detail included in this chapter, but you should try to understand the logic behind and use cases for the most important settings related to bridge domains. You should also try to understand the information called out with Key Topic icons for the exam. You should also definitely master the configuration steps needed for EPG and bridge domain extension.

The following section dives into the network-centric approach to ACI, which is the basis for most network migrations into ACI.

Understanding Network-Centric Deployments

This book has so far emphasized application centricity in the sense that previous chapters divide each sample bridge domain (or the majority of bridge domains) into multiple EPGs and focus on whitelisting of traffic flows via contracts.

However, the assumption that traffic flows can be whitelisted at the moment they are moved into ACI is often unrealistic. The most significant reason for this is that companies often lack a detailed understanding of their application traffic flows and interdependencies. This is *not* meant to suggest that ACI cannot be used for zero-trust security enforcement at the moment endpoints are moved into the fabric. Indeed, ACI *can* be used this way.

The polar opposite of the application-centric model described in earlier chapters is the network-centric approach to ACI. The *network-centric approach* is more of a mindset than any specific ACI feature. It allows network teams to move endpoints into ACI without necessarily changing the network architecture. This ensures that they can achieve some of the benefits of ACI while familiarizing themselves with the platform.

10

In essence, you can think of the network-centric approach as a way to dumb down ACI to the level of traditional networks, whose security relies mostly on VLANs, VRF instances, and rudimentary access list enforcement.

The most fundamental aspect of the network-centric approach is that each VLAN in traditional networking needs to be mapped to a single bridge domain and a single EPG. In other words:

Network-centric approach: Each VLAN = 1 bridge domain = 1 EPG = 1 subnet

Adoption of the network-centric approach does not necessarily mean that security mechanisms such as contracts are not used. However, it does imply that there will be minimal security enforcement within subnet boundaries. For the most part, the network-centric mode, when seen in the context of how traditional data centers are built, assumes that the ACI fabric needs to be configured to perform blacklisting. Therefore, network-centric deployment often starts out with all traffic flows being allowed unless denied through explicit security enforcement. That said, network-centric deployment is often seen as a stepping stone toward application-centric deployment.

Understanding Full-Mesh Network-Centric Contracts

One way for ACI to mimic a traditional network is through assignment of a contract allowing any-to-any communication between all EPGs. Because this any-to-any contract needs to be applied to all EPGs, it can be understood as a sort of full mesh of contract relationships.

The only real drawback to this approach is that with any full mesh, the number of relationships between participants grows exponentially. Translated into ACI terminology, any-to-any communication using contracts can consume a large amount of policy content-addressable memory (CAM) resources.

The thought process with full-mesh any-to-any contracts is that VLANs will be migrated into ACI in network-centric mode, and IT will later move endpoints into application-centric EPGs dedicated to endpoint functions. Once the original EPGs have the endpoints removed, they can be deleted. The resulting deployment is application-centric.

If an eventual evolution from a network-centric design to a more application-centric approach is not one of the drivers for migration to an ACI fabric, use of a full-mesh network-centric contract may not be the most ideal migration approach.

Let's examine what an any-to-any contract might look like. Figure 10-1 shows the creation of a filter that matches all traffic. The single entry in the filter has the EtherType value Unspecified. No other tweaks have been made from the default entry settings.

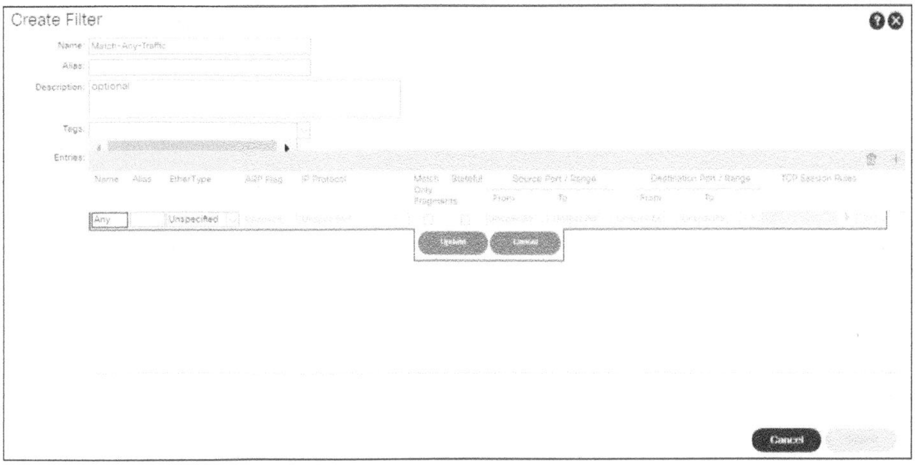

Figure 10-1   *Creating a Filter Matching All Traffic*

This contract is pretty basic. Figure 10-2 shows creation of a contract named Permit-Any with Scope set to VRF. To create a subject for the contract, you click the + sign next to Subjects.

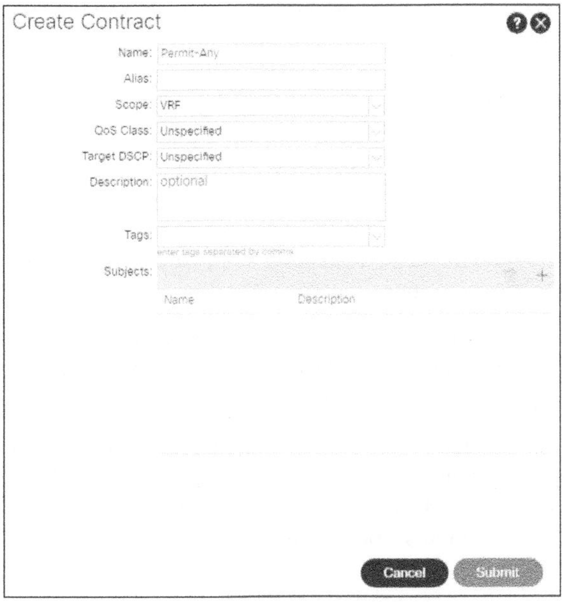

Figure 10-2   *Creating an Any-to-Any Contract*

Finally, you can associate the filter with the contract by adding it to the subject and enabling the Apply Both Directions and Reverse Filter Ports settings (see Figure 10-3). Click OK and then click Submit to complete the process.

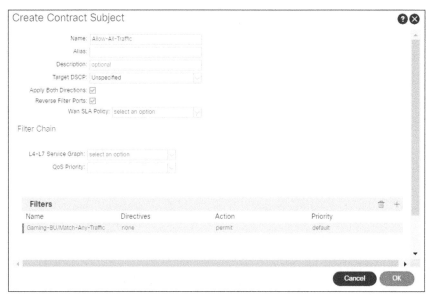

Figure 10-3 *Associating a Filter Matching All Traffic to a Contract Subject*

The contract should then be allocated as both consumed and provided on all network-centric EPGs as well as any external EPGs that should be able to access the EPGs.

> **NOTE** A contract with no filter applied also enables the any-to-any communication necessary for open network-centric communication.

Understanding Any EPG

Any EPG, more commonly called *vzAny*, provides a convenient way of associating all endpoint groups (EPGs) in a VRF instance with one or more contracts.

Whereas a contract applied bidirectionally to tens of EPGs forms a many-to-many relationship, vzAny creates a one-to-all contract relationship and is thus considered an optimization of policy CAM space more than anything else.

The ideal use case for vzAny is permitting common services. For example, if all endpoints in all EPGs within a specific VRF instance should be able to respond to **ping**, a contract allowing ICMP traffic can be associated with vzAny in the given VRF instance in the provided direction. All EPGs that need to ping these endpoints would then need to consume the contract.

Likewise, if all endpoints within a VRF should be able to query a set of DNS servers, a contract allowing DNS queries can be configured and consumed by vzAny within the VRF. The same contract would then be allocated to the DNS server EPG as a provided contract.

Figure 10-4 shows how vzAny can be used to enable open communication among all EPGs within a VRF when the any-to-any contract defined previously is instead associated with vzAny in both the provided and consumed directions.

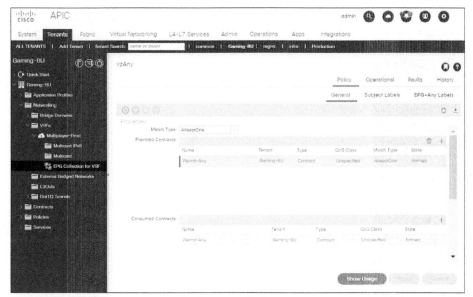

Figure 10-4   *Using vzAny as the Contract Enforcement Point for Open Communication*

As shown in the figure, you can associate contracts with vzAny by navigating to the VRF in question and opening the EPG Collection for VRF subfolder.

> **NOTE**   The advent of preferred group members has dramatically reduced the utility of vzAny as a mechanism for establishing open communication among EPGs.

Understanding Preferred Group Members

Whereas vzAny is great for opening specific ports and services to all endpoints in a VRF instance, it poses a new challenge when used as a network-centric implementation tool. If open communication is enforced between all EPGs in a VRF, how can companies transition to a whitelisting model? This is exactly the question that preferred group members address.

Select EPGs within a VRF instance, called ***preferred group members***, can be afforded open communication, while others can be locked down with contracts. Basically, this enables all EPGs to be moved into a fabric with open communication, and once contracts are fully defined for an EPG, the EPG can then be excluded as a preferred group member to allow for full contract enforcement.

Figure 10-5 shows that the Preferred Group setting needs to be first toggled to Enabled at the VRF level to confirm that the VRF is a candidate for open communication among EPGs.

10

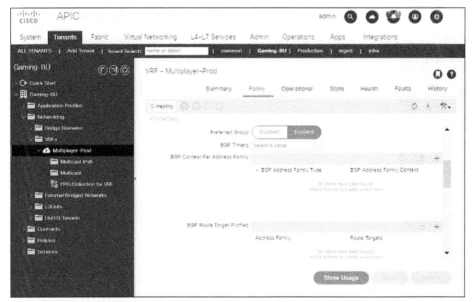

Figure 10-5 *Enabling Preferred Group at the VRF Level*

Once Preferred Group is enabled at the VRF level, you can navigate to each individual EPG that is a candidate for open communication and toggle the Preferred Group Member setting to Include under **Policy > General**, as shown in Figure 10-6.

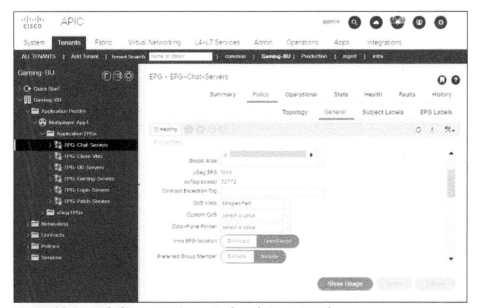

Figure 10-6 *Including an EPG as a Preferred Group Member*

If outside endpoints also need open communication with all EPGs configured as preferred group members within the VRF instance, you need to also enable the Include setting for the external EPG (see Figure 10-7).

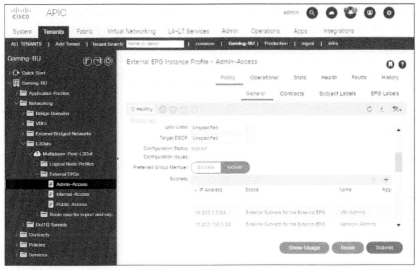

Figure 10-7 *Including an External EPG as a Preferred Group Member*

If at any point contracts are defined for an EPG that is part of the preferred group, the Preferred Group Member setting on the EPG can be toggled back to Exclude, which is the default value.

Disabling Contract Enforcement at the VRF Instance Level

Although it is very uncommon to deploy new fabrics with contract enforcement disabled, use of the Policy Control Enforcement Preference setting is feasible if the deployment is not expected to ever make use of contracts. It is also a useful feature for troubleshooting whether the loss of expected connectivity is a result of a contract misconfiguration.

Figure 10-8 shows how contract enforcement can be disabled for a VRF instance by setting Policy Control Enforcement Preference to Unenforced under the VRF instance.

Figure 10-8 *Disabling Contract Enforcement Altogether for an Individual VRF Instance*

Flooding Requirements for L2 Extension to Outside Switches

Figure 10-9 shows the best practice bridge domain configurations around forwarding that must be in place for proper Layer 2 extension between ACI and external switches. The use of these settings is not mandatory in every setup. However, these settings help ensure that ACI behaves as much like traditional switches as possible, without data plane learning being disabled, thereby resolving some forwarding issues that may be experienced when migrating endpoints and subnets into ACI. Note that use of these settings is especially important when the default gateway for a subnet is outside ACI.

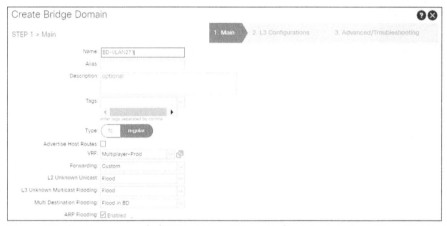

Figure 10-9   *Recommended BD Settings When Endpoints Attach to Non-ACI Switches*

Table 10-2 explains what these settings do and the logic behind their use.

Key Topic

Table 10-2   Bridge Domain Settings for ACI Layer 2 Extension to Non-ACI Switches

BD Property	Required Setting for Property and Justification
Forwarding	The Forwarding field only appears when a bridge domain is first configured. Its default value, Optimized, automatically sets the Unicast and ARP parameters. To enable customization of forwarding settings to values that enable Layer 2 extension, select the Custom option.
L2 Unknown Unicast	This field applies to unicast traffic destined to an endpoint whose MAC address cannot be found in the ACI endpoint table.
	The forwarding options available for the L2 Unknown Unicast parameter are Flood and Hardware Proxy. When endpoints directly attach to leaf switches and ACI is the default gateway for the BD, hardware proxy forwarding is preferred because it allows for a reduction in flooding within the fabric. However, when some endpoints associated with a bridge domain as well as the default gateway for the BD subnet(s) reside outside the fabric, the ACI spine proxy forwarding behavior can lead to suboptimal learning on non-ACI switches outside the fabric. For this reason, the L2 Unknown Unicast setting needs to be set to Flood to accommodate any endpoints behind the Layer 2 extension until default gateways are moved into the fabric and unicast routing is enabled on the BD.

BD Property	Required Setting for Property and Justification
L3 Unknown Multicast Flooding	By default, IGMP snooping is enabled on bridge domains. The IGMP snooping feature snoops the IGMP membership reports and leave messages and forwards them to the IGMP router function only when necessary. When a leaf receives traffic for a multicast group that is unknown, this traffic is considered unknown Layer 3 multicast, and the L3 Unknown Multicast Flooding setting determines how the traffic is forwarded. The two options for this setting are Flood and Optimized Flood. When Flood is selected, traffic destined to unknown multicast groups is flooded on the ingress switch and any border leafs on which the BD is active. When Optimized Flood is selected, traffic for the unknown multicast group is forwarded to the multicast router ports only.
ARP Flooding	When the ARP Flooding parameter is enabled, ARP requests with a broadcast destination MAC address are flooded in the bridge domain. If this option is disabled and the fabric has already learned the destination endpoint, it unicasts the ARP request to the destination. If this option is disabled and the fabric has *not* learned the destination endpoint, it uses ARP gleaning to identify the destination endpoint. When unicast routing is disabled, ARP traffic is always flooded, even if the ARP Flooding parameter has been disabled on the BD.
	Enabling ARP Flooding ensures that ACI behaves much like traditional networks and allows non-ACI switches behind a Layer 2 extension to proactively learn endpoints residing in the fabric. This, by itself, should be sufficient justification for its use during migrations into ACI. There is one other compelling use case for enabling the ARP Flooding parameter that relates to silent hosts. Remember from Chapter 8, "Implementing Tenant Policies," that ARP gleaning detects silent hosts by prodding them into communicating on the network, but in the rare case that the silent host moves elsewhere without sending a GARP packet into the network, ACI continues to think that the endpoint details it learned prior to the endpoint move are accurate. In this case, if ARP Flooding has been disabled, the ACI leaf continues to unicast ARP requests that are destined to the silent host to the old location until the IP endpoint ages out. On the other hand, with ARP Flooding enabled, ACI floods all ARP requests with broadcast destination MAC addresses. When the silent host receives the ARP request, it responds to the ARP request, prompting ACI nodes to update the endpoint table accordingly. Even though the issue of silent hosts is not specifically related to Layer 2 extension, this example should help illuminate why the ARP Flooding parameter can help alleviate some corner-case endpoint learning issues.

10

BD Property	Required Setting for Property and Justification
Multi Destination Flooding	This parameter primarily addresses forwarding of traffic types not covered by the other settings mentioned in this table, such as broadcast, L2 multicast, and link-local traffic. There are three configuration options for the Multi Destination Flooding property: ■ **Flood in BD:** Sends a packet to all ports in the same bridge domain. ■ **Drop:** Drops a packet and never sends it to any other ports. ■ **Flood in Encapsulation:** Sends a packet to all ports in the same VLAN encapsulation. If there is a one-to-one relationship between encapsulations and EPGs, this setting effectively limits flooding to each EPG. Note that while Flood in Encapsulation does enable Layer 2 extension and is an option in some deployments, there are more caveats that require careful consideration when using this option for migrations. The Flood in BD option, which is the default setting for the L3 Unknown Multicast Flooding bridge domain property, remains the most ideal setting for Layer 2 extension.

Understanding GARP-Based Detection

GARP-based detection helps in a variety of scenarios in both first- and second-generation Cisco ACI leaf switches.

Although ACI can detect MAC and IP address movement between leaf switch ports, leaf switches, bridge domains, and EPGs, first-generation leaf switches cannot detect the movement of an IP address to a new MAC address if the new MAC address resides behind the same switch interface and the same EPG as the old MAC address. Enabling GARP-based detection addresses this caveat related to first-generation switches as long as the ARP Flooding parameter has also been enabled on the relevant bridge domain (see Figure 10-10).

Figure 10-10   *GARP-Based Detection Enabled in the L3 Configurations Subtab of a BD*

When might an IP address reasonably move to a new MAC address, and what is the probability that the IP address will remain behind a single interface, port channel, or vPC? A common example of an IP address moving to a different MAC address is a high-availability cluster failover, as with some load balancer and firewall cluster setups. When the failover takes place with non-ACI switches behind a Layer 2 extension, the failover in essence stays behind a single interface, port channel, or vPC. If unicast routing has been enabled on the BD and the switch connecting to the non-ACI switch(es) is a first-generation leaf, ACI communication with the cluster IP is, in effect, black-holed.

Note that GARP-based detection is also a significant configuration item in second-generation leaf switches. If there is ever a need to disable ACI data plane learning for a bridge domain or VRF, GARP-based detection along with ARP flooding enable the network to perform endpoint learning using traditional control plane–oriented methods.

That said, you should never disable data plane learning without first consulting the latest Cisco documentation! The only valid use case for disabling data plane learning is to do so in conjunction with service graphs. If there is a valid technical driver for disabling data plane learning outside of service graphs, it should only be done at the VRF level.

NOTE You may have noticed in Figure 10-10 that the Unicast Routing checkbox has been disabled for the BD. It is a common misconception that this feature can be enabled on bridge domains whose default gateways are outside the fabric to force ACI to learn endpoint IP addresses. The problem with this approach, as well intentioned as it may be, is that it may also cause ACI to directly forward traffic to other endpoints in the Layer 3 domain if ACI also happens to have learned the destination endpoint IP address. This behavior can lead to asynchronous routing and can inadvertently change traffic flows in the data center. If the default gateway for a subnet is outside ACI and the fabric should not be performing routing for the bridge domain, you should save yourself the headache and disable the Unicast Routing checkbox for the bridge domain.

Understanding Legacy Mode

One feature you can use to increase the number of VLAN IDs available for encapsulating traffic out of leaf switch ports is the Legacy mode bridge domain subconfiguration. Use of this feature makes sense only for network-centric bridge domains in environments in which thousands of VLANs need to be deployed to a given switch. This feature locks the bridge domain and its corresponding EPG into a single encapsulation, freeing up the encapsulation that would have been used by the bridge domain.

Because there are quite a few caveats associated with Legacy mode and due to the fact that it reduces the ease of migrating to an application-centric model, it is not used very often. But you need to be aware of this feature and why it exists.

You can find the Legacy Mode checkbox to enable this feature by navigating to the desired bridge domain, selecting the Policy tab, and then selecting the General subtab.

Endpoint Learning Considerations for Layer 2 Extension

An important consideration for Layer 2 extension is the number of endpoints that an ACI leaf may be expected to learn from external switches.

10

You can review the Verified Scalability Guide for your target ACI code release to understand the number of endpoints each leaf platform can learn based on its ASICs.

In larger environments, it helps to distribute Layer 2 extensions among multiple leafs and to trunk VLANs to different leafs to reduce the likelihood of filling up the local station table on the leafs.

Preparing for Network-Centric Migrations

There are certainly tenant design and endpoint placement considerations that you need to think about that are beyond the scope of this book. But if all endpoints moving into the fabric are expected to be placed in a single user tenant and VRF instance, you may be able to simply create a basic table. This table would need to include each VLAN that needs to be migrated and its equivalent network-centric bridge domain, EPG, and subnet. It should also include ideal target state settings for the bridge domain, including whether hardware proxy, ARP flooding, and/or GARP-based detection should be enabled following the move of the subnet default gateway into the fabric.

If there is a need for multiple Layer 2 or Layer 3 connections between an ACI fabric and non-ACI switches, this prep work should also detail the Layer 2 connections through which a bridge domain or EPG needs to be extended or the L3Out(s) through which bridge domain subnets need to be advertised after the migration.

Implementing Layer 2 Connectivity to Non-ACI Switches

There are three primary methods for extending Layer 2 outside an ACI fabric:

- **Extend the EPG out the ACI fabric:** In this method, an ACI administrator extends an EPG out an ACI fabric by statically mapping the EPG to a VLAN ID on a given port, port channel, or vPC. Extending an EPG outside a fabric allows endpoints both within and outside ACI to be classified into the same EPG.

- **Extend the bridge domain out the ACI fabric:** Technically, the term *L2Out* refers to bridge domain extension even though the term may be used colloquially for both bridge domain and EPG extensions. In the ACI GUI, bridge domain extensions are also referred to as *external bridged networks*. When extending a bridge domain, ACI classifies endpoints residing in a VLAN outside the fabric into a Layer 2 EPG (an external EPG used in a bridge domain extension). Administrators can create additional EPGs and associate them with the bridge domain to enable policy enforcement between the external Layer 2 EPG and any other EPGs in the fabric. This can essentially enable enforcement of a zero-trust architecture at the moment endpoints are fully moved into a fabric, but it still requires that traffic flows between endpoints be well understood.

- **Extend the Layer 2 domain with remote VTEP:** The remote VTEP feature can be used to implement either EPG extension or bridge domain extension. Remote VTEP is beyond the scope of the DCACI 300-620 exam and is not discussed further in this book.

Understanding EPG Extensions

If you have followed along and read this book chapter by chapter, EPG extension should not be new to you. Statically mapping an EPG to a VLAN on a switch port connecting to a server *is* EPG extension.

Figure 10-11 illustrates the extension of an EPG to non-ACI switches. Note three significant points regarding EPG extension in this figure. First, EPG extension does not necessitate use of a new VLAN ID for server connections. Second, endpoints within the EPG, regardless of location (inside or outside the fabric), are considered part of the same EPG. This means there is no need for contracts to allow these endpoints to communicate. Finally, for EPG extension with the recommended flooding settings described in the previous section to work seamlessly, no more than one EPG associated with each bridge domain should ever be extended.

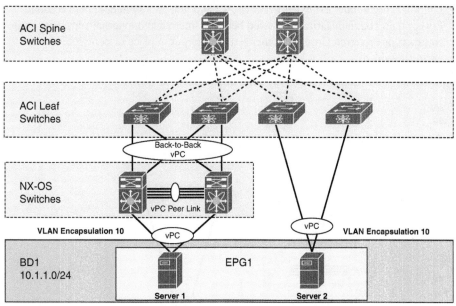

Figure 10-11 *Extending an EPG out a Fabric*

NOTE   Quite a few engineers have asked whether multiple EPGs associated with a single bridge domain can be extended to non-ACI switches outside a fabric. The answer is yes. Among the options for Multi Destination Flooding, administrators can choose Flood in Encapsulation at the bridge domain level to isolate flooding to each associated EPG.

In the context of migrations, the use case many proponents of this feature have in mind is to consolidate multiple VLANs and subnets into a small number of bridge domains. This way, when migrating to an application-centric model, endpoints dedicated to a particular function that live across several subnets but are bound to a common bridge domain can be placed into a single EPG as opposed to having the number of EPGs aligned with the number of network-centric bridge domains.

The challenge with this feature is that not all hardware supports it, and it is riddled with caveats. For instance, ACI Multi-Site does not currently support the stretching of objects that have this feature enabled. Therefore, use of this feature is not suitable in all environments. If you decide to use this feature to migrate multiple VLANs into a single bridge domain, make sure you understand all the caveats.

10

Understanding Bridge Domain Extensions

Bridge domain extensions are dramatically different from EPG extensions. Figure 10-12 demonstrates two of the main differences:

■ Bridge domain extensions necessitate use of a separate encapsulation for EPGs inside the fabric compared to the Layer 2 EPG encapsulation used to bridge the traffic to non-ACI switches.

■ Endpoints in a subnet extended between ACI and non-ACI switches are in separate EPGs, so no communication is allowed between internal and external endpoints until contracts or Preferred Group Member settings are put in place or contract enforcement is disabled.

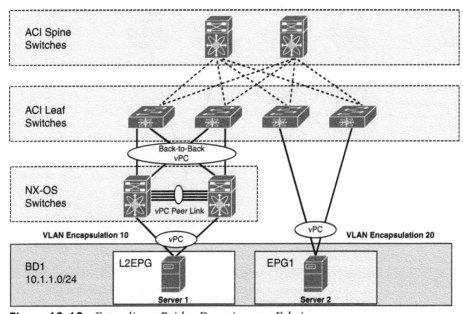

Figure 10-12 *Extending a Bridge Domain out a Fabric*

Comparing EPG Extensions and BD Extensions

Table 10-3 recaps the points already made and compares EPG extensions with BD extensions based on a number of criteria.

Table 10-3   Comparison Between Bridge Domain Extension and EPG Extension

Comparison Criteria	Extend EPG	Extend Bridge Domain
Use cases	Extend EPG beyond an ACI fabric; migrate VLANs into ACI in network-centric mode with Flood in BD; consolidate multiple VLANs and subnets into a single bridge domain at the time of migration to ACI by using Flood in Encapsulation	Extend a bridge domain out the fabric or extend a tenant subnet of the bridge domain out the fabric; migrate VLANs into ACI with intra-VLAN policy enforcement applied at the time of migration
Configuration	Statically assign a port to an EPG (static binding under EPG or direct assignment to an AAEP)	Create external bridged networks (L2Out) in a tenant where a bridge domain resides
Domain type applicable	Physical domain	External bridged domain
External endpoint placement	Endpoints connected to non-ACI switches placed in the same EPG (VLAN) as directly attached endpoints	Endpoints connected to non-ACI switches in a different EPG (VLAN) but the same bridge domain as directly attached endpoints
Policy model	External endpoints are seen as an internal EPG, and the same principles apply.	An external endpoint is placed under an external EPG (Layer 2 EPG). Policy is applied between internal EPGs and a Layer 2 EPG.
Endpoint learning	ACI learns both MAC and IP addresses. (IP addresses are only learned if unicast routing is enabled at the BD level.)	ACI learns both MAC and IP addresses. (IP addresses are only learned if unicast routing is enabled at the BD level.)

NOTE   EPG extensions are by far the most popular method for migrating VLANs into ACI.

Implementing EPG Extensions

Just as with any other type of switch port configuration in ACI, the first thing you need to do when implementing an EPG extension is to configure access policies. Figure 10-13 shows the configuration of a vPC interface policy group toward a non-ACI switch. Note that in this case, a Spanning Tree Protocol interface policy called Switch-Facing-Interface is created to ensure that BPDU Filter and BPDU Guard are not enabled on this particular vPC interface policy group. In the Attached Entity Profile field, a newly created AAEP called L2-to-Legacy-Network-AAEP is selected. The figure does not show it, but this AAEP has a physical domain named GamingBU-Physical as its domain association, enabling use of a range of static VLAN IDs assigned to the VLAN pool associated with GamingBU-Physical as potential encapsulations for the EPG extension.

10

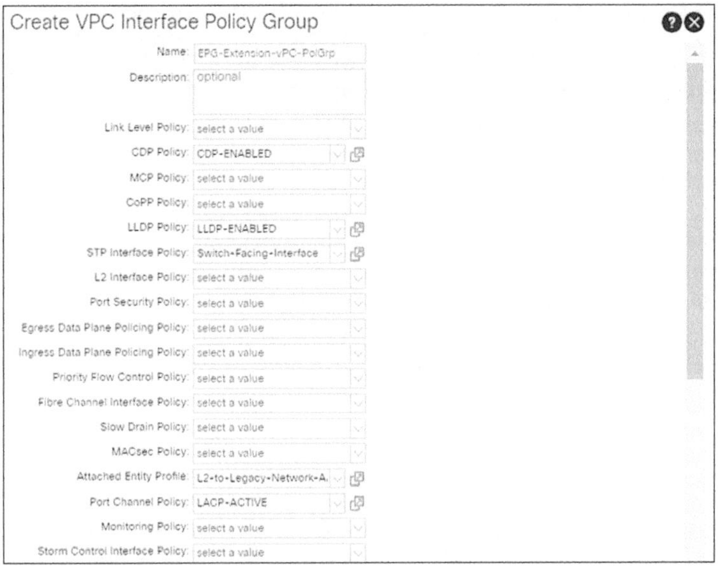

Figure 10-13 *Configuring an Interface Policy Group as a Prelude to EPG Extension*

Next, you need to map the interface policy group to switch ports. Figure 10-14 shows the vPC interface policy group being mapped to port 1/6 on two switches that have been bound to a single interface profile.

Figure 10-14 *Implementing Access Policies as a Prerequisite to EPG Extension*

After verifying that the vPC has come online, you navigate to the Tenants view to extend the desired EPGs out the fabric. Figure 10-15 shows a new EPG called EPG-VLAN271 being associated with the physical domain GamingBU-Physical, so that VLAN encapsulations allowed by the physical domain and port assignments associated with the relevant AAEP can be used to extend the given EPG.

Figure 10-15 *Associating a Physical Domain with an EPG*

With the physical domain assignment in place, the stage has been set to map the EPG to an allowed encapsulation on the vPC. To do this mapping, you navigate to the desired EPG and expand its subfolders, right-click the Static Ports subfolder, and select Deploy Static EPG on PC, VPC, or Interface. Figure 10-16 shows the resulting wizard. In this wizard, you enter the vPC interface policy group created earlier as the path and enter the VLAN ID used to encapsulate the traffic in the Port Encap field. Notice the options in the Mode field and that the port does not necessarily need to be configured as a trunk. Finally, review the Deployment Immediacy setting. (Deployment Immediacy settings are covered in Chapter 8. They are further covered in Chapter 12, "Implementing Service Graphs.") The Deployment Immediacy setting Immediate is often the best choice for EPG extensions to non-ACI switches because it commits the configuration (and any relevant contracts, if applicable) to hardware immediately.

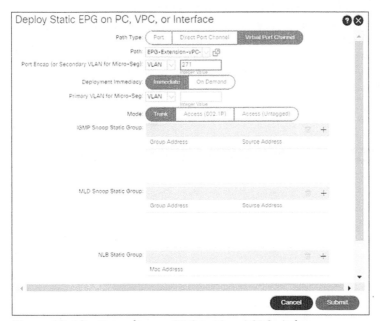

Figure 10-16 *Extending an EPG to Non-ACI Switches*

After clicking Submit, navigate to the Operational tab for the EPG. Figure 10-17 shows that ACI has learned five endpoints over the EPG extension. Notice in the figure that MAC addresses have been learned, but no IP addresses have been learned. With the assumption that this is part of a VLAN migration into ACI, this would be normal. The reason ACI has not learned the endpoint IP addresses in this case is that unicast routing has been intentionally disabled on the associated bridge domain to eliminate the possibility of asynchronous routing.

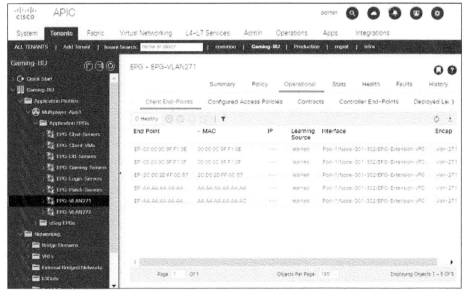

Figure 10-17 *Verifying Endpoint Learning over EPG Extension to Non-ACI Switches*

Note that there is no requirement that says that all endpoints in a VLAN need to be moved into ACI before the VLAN default gateway can be migrated into the fabric. Figure 10-18 shows how you can move the default gateway into the fabric by assigning the subnet default gateway to the bridge domain and enabling unicast routing. The default gateway assignment needs to be simultaneously removed from non-ACI devices to reduce the length of the accompanying outage.

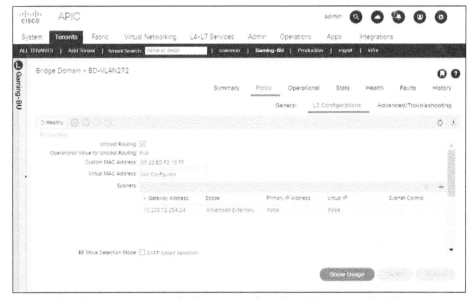

Figure 10-18 *Moving the Default Gateway for a VLAN into an ACI Fabric*

Once these settings have been applied, ACI learns the endpoint IP addresses and can route traffic to other subnets within the fabric. Notice in Figure 10-18 that the subnet has been defined with the Scope setting Advertise Externally. This implies that the bridge domain is also intended to be advertised out an L3Out. Figure 10-19 shows Multiplayer-Prod-L3Out selected as the L3Out from which the subnet should be advertised to the rest of the enterprise network.

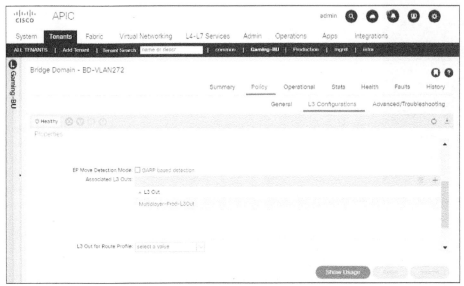

Figure 10-19 *Advertising the Subnet out ACI via an L3Out*

> **NOTE**   Even though you can move a default gateway into ACI before moving endpoints into the fabric, doing so changes traffic patterns because all cross-subnet traffic between outside endpoints needs to flow over the Layer 2 links between the fabric and non-ACI switches twice. Therefore, you should ensure beforehand that you have sized the Layer 2 connection appropriately.

Although migrating subnets into an ACI fabric is not explicitly within the scope of the DCACI 300-620 exam, the final part of this implementation example illustrates that default gateways can be moved into ACI or out of ACI with relative ease.

Figure 10-20 completes coverage of EPG extensions by showing endpoint information for EPG-VLAN272, which has also been extended over the newly created vPC. This output shows an endpoint off the legacy switch whose IP address has been learned in addition to another endpoint internal to the fabric off node ID 301 port 1/46. Because they are in the same EPG, these endpoints are allowed to communicate with one another without contracts by default. Because the default gateway has been migrated into ACI, however, the endpoints within the EPG cannot communicate with other EPGs or outside the ACI fabric until proper contracts have been put in place. Also, note in Figure 10-20 that a single MAC address is shown without an IP assignment. In this case, this is the MAC address of a deleted switch virtual interface (SVI) on a switch outside ACI and will eventually time out and be removed from ACI endpoint tables.

10

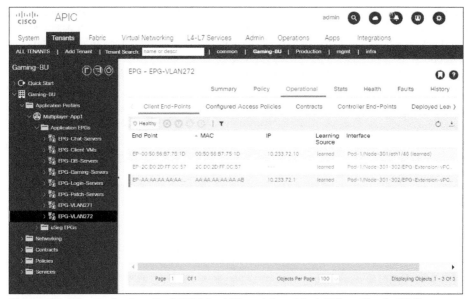

Figure 10-20 *Endpoints Both Within ACI and Outside ACI in a Single EPG*

> **NOTE** You may be wondering at this point when it might be an ideal time to change the L2 Unknown Unicast setting from Flood to Hardware Proxy and to disable ARP Flooding for VLANs that have been migrated into ACI. Eliminating flooding, after all, increases stability in the network and reduces the control plane impact of endpoint learning. The ideal time depends! Flooding helps enable non-ACI switches to learn endpoints residing in the fabric because it ensures that non-ACI switches receive all ARP packets. Therefore, this flooding behavior should remain in place until all endpoints within a given VLAN as well as the default gateway have been fully migrated into the ACI fabric.

Implementing L2Outs

In the previous subsection, you may have noticed that multiple EPG extensions can be implemented by trunking EPGs over a single interface, port channel, or vPC. L2Outs are no different. One configuration difference between EPG extension and bridge domain extension that you do need to remember is that L2Outs do not use physical domains. They require a special type of domain called an *external bridged domain*. Because the implementation of access policies beyond the domain is the same across both Layer 2 extension methods, the implementation of an interface policy group and its assignment to ports is not repeated here. Assume for the following example that an AAEP has been assigned to the interface policy group, and the interface policy group has been assigned to physical ports via an interface profile, but the domain assignment to the AAEP is still outstanding.

To create an L2Out, after configuring access policies, you can navigate to the Tenants view, expose the Networking folder in the tenant, right-click External Bridged Networks, and select Create Bridged Outside. The Create Bridged Outside wizard appears, as shown in Figure 10-21.

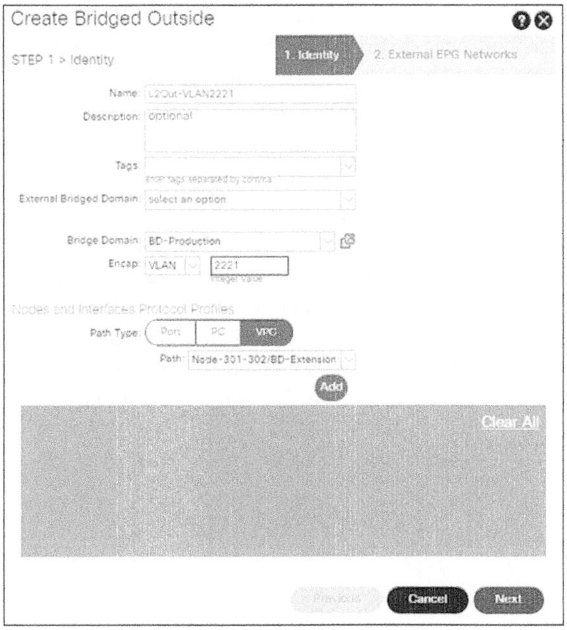

Figure 10-21 *The Create Bridged Outside Wizard*

In the Create Bridged Outside wizard, enter a descriptive name in the Name field, specify the internal bridge domain to extend in the Bridge Domain field, and enter an encapsulation to use for the Layer 2 EPG in the Encap field. The External Bridge Domain drop-down box allows you to select an existing domain to use for the L2Out or to create a new one. From the options in the drop-down box, select Create External Bridge Domain to open the page shown in Figure 10-22.

Figure 10-22 *Creating an External Bridge Domain*

10

From in Figure 10-22, it is clear that the external bridged domain will be named L2Out-Domain, and it will be bound to the attachable access entity profile (AAEP) created in the "Implementing EPG Extensions" section of this chapter. Note that whatever AAEP you select must be the same AAEP you assign to the interface policy group you use for bridge domain extension. It is best to dedicate a new VLAN pool for bridge domain extension purposes when first implementing this feature. Click Submit to create the external bridged domain.

Back in the Create Bridged Outside wizard, you need to validate that ACI has populated the External Bridged Domain drop-down and that the information in all other required fields is correct. Then you can reference each interface, port channel, and vPC over which the bridge domain should be trunked by selecting the correct path type and path information and clicking Add. Figure 10-23 shows that the full path of the port, port channel, or vPC appears at the bottom of the window. Click Next when you are ready to define the Layer 2 EPG.

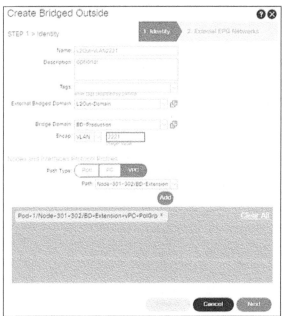

Figure 10-23 *Confirming BD Extension Ports, Port Channels, or vPCs at the Bottom of the Window*

On the External EPG Networks page of the Create Bridged Outside wizard, click the + sign to create a Layer 2 EPG. As shown in Figure 10-24, the wizard allows configuration of Preferred Group Member settings at the time of external EPG creation, but it does not allow assignment of contracts. Populate the Name field and click OK.

Figure 10-24 *Creating a Layer 2 EPG When Implementing Bridge Domain Extension*

Once you have configured the Layer 2 EPG (yes, you can only configure one per bridge domain), click Finish to create the bridge extension. Figure 10-25 shows the newly created Layer 2 EPG. In this view, contracts can be assigned in the desired direction(s). Notice that a contract named Permit-LB-to-Login-Servers has been assigned bidirectionally to the Layer 2 EPG. In this case, this contract has a subject that allows any-to-any communication, ensuring that any internal EPGs to which this contract is assigned can communicate with the Layer 2 EPG.

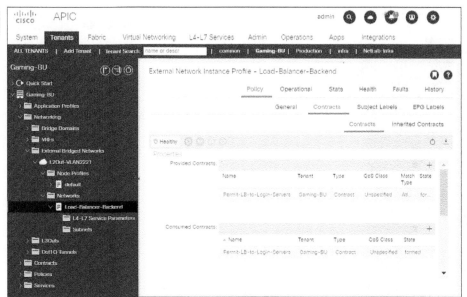

Figure 10-25 *Applying Contracts on a Layer 2 EPG After Implementing BD Extension*

A single internal EPG, EPG-Login-Servers, has been selected for communication with the Layer 2 EPG. Figure 10-26 shows the contract shown earlier applied to this EPG. When the contract is applied as both Provided and Consumed, the communication can be initiated either by endpoints in the Layer 2 EPG or endpoints in the internal EPG.

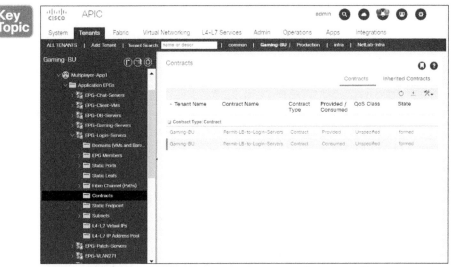

Figure 10-26 *Applying Contracts on an Internal EPG to Allow Layer 2 EPG Communication*

As a result of the bridge domain extension, the endpoint depicted in Figure 10-27 and residing behind the L2Out has been learned. Notice that this view does not and should not show endpoints learned in EPG-Login-Servers. With the contract application in place, this endpoint has open communication with any endpoints in EPG-Login-Servers.

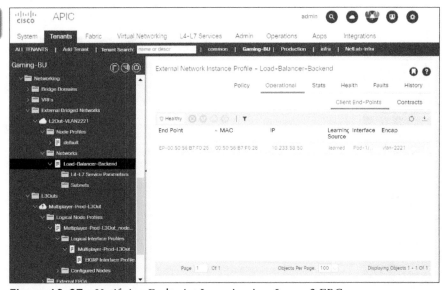

Figure 10-27 *Verifying Endpoint Learning in a Layer 2 EPG*

Be very careful when using any-to-any contracts, especially when applying them in both the consumed and provided directions. In the previous example, if the contract Permit-LB-to-Login-Servers were also applied to a tertiary EPG, it would allow this new EPG to communicate not just with the Layer 2 EPG but also with EPG-Login-Servers. If this is not the intent, and full contract-based communication is expected, either dedicated contracts can be created between each pair of EPGs requiring full communication or more thought needs to be put into the contract design.

> **NOTE**   When the Legacy Mode checkbox has been enabled for a bridge domain, the BD can no longer be extended out of the fabric. But why? The reason is that Legacy mode does not allow allocation of an additional encapsulation for any EPGs that are bound to it. This includes the Layer 2 EPG.

Migrating Overlapping VLANs into ACI

Under ACI default behavior, each VLAN ID used to encapsulate Layer 2 traffic to and from external switches and servers can be mapped to only a single EPG on each leaf switch. If you deploy a second EPG with an encapsulation that has already been used on the leaf, ACI raises a fault and does not encapsulate the traffic for the second EPG. This behavior is governed by the VLAN scope setting, which defaults to Global.

During network migrations into ACI, it sometimes happens that a company has multiple switch blocks that have overlapping VLAN IDs. Suppose that these overlapping VLAN IDs need to be migrated into ACI. Ideally, they would be migrated onto separate Layer 2 extensions terminating on different sets of leaf switches. In such a case, the VLAN overlap would not even matter. But what if both Layer 2 extensions need to terminate on the same leaf switch(es)? In that case, the VLAN Scope setting Port Local Scope can assist.

To implement the Port Local Scope capability, you navigate to **Fabric > Access Policies > Policies > Interface**, right-click L2 Interface, and select Create L2 Interface Policy. Then, as shown in Figure 10-28, you can enter a value in the Name field, set VLAN Scope to Port Local Scope, and click Submit.

Figure 10-28   *Creating an L2 Interface Policy*

Once this new L2 interface policy has been assigned to all interface policy groups on which overlapping VLANs will flow, the overlapping VLANs can then be trunked to the intended leaf using EPG extension. Separate VLAN pools and thus separate physical domains are required for EPG extension to successfully deploy this feature.

Example 10-1 verifies that EPG-VLAN272 bound to BD-VLAN272 and EPG-Client-VMs bound to BD-Production have both been successfully extended from LEAF102 to outside switches via the encapsulation vlan-272 after deployment of Port Local Scope.

Example 10-1 *Single Encapsulation Across Multiple EPGs with Port Local Scope*

```
LEAF102# show vlan extended


VLAN Name                            Encap            Ports
---- ------------------------------- ---------------- -----------------------

27   Gaming-BU:Multiplayer-App1:EPG- vlan-272         Eth1/6, Po5
     VLAN272

28   Gaming-BU:Multiplayer-App1:EPG- vlan-272         Eth1/33
     Client-VMs

54   Gaming-BU:BD-VLAN272            vxlan-15040469    Eth1/6, Eth1/45,
                                                      Eth1/46, Po5

61   Gaming-BU:Multiplayer-App1:EPG- vlan-2508        Eth1/45, Eth1/46
     VLAN272

65   Gaming-BU:BD-Production         vxlan-15826916    Eth1/33, Eth1/45,
                                                      Eth1/46

73   Gaming-BU:Multiplayer-App1:EPG- vlan-3169        Eth1/45, Eth1/46
     Client-VMs
```

NOTE Use of the Port Local Scope feature does have an impact on leaf scalability. Review the Verified Scalability Guide and Cisco APIC Layer 2 Networking Configuration Guide for your ACI release to understand scalability impact and additional caveats.

Understanding ACI Interaction with Spanning Tree Protocol

There is not much to know about ACI interaction with Spanning Tree Protocol aside from the fact that ACI does not run Spanning Tree Protocol and does not participate in building the overall Spanning Tree Protocol topology. ACI does, however, flood Spanning Tree Protocol bridge protocol data units (BPDUs) that it receives in an EPG to all other ports with the same VLAN encapsulation within the EPG. From this perspective, ACI acts like a hub for Spanning Tree Protocol BPDUs. It provides external switches the data they need to be able to prevent a Layer 2 loop—but that is about all it does.

Remediating Against Excessive Spanning Tree Protocol TCNs

When a Spanning Tree Protocol topology change occurs, the root bridge sends a special BPDU called a topology change notification (TCN) out its ports. Something as simple as a server-facing port bouncing can trigger a TCN. Because ACI does not process Spanning

Tree Protocol packets, the fabric needs to assume that the change may have impacted end-point locations and must therefore respond by flushing all endpoint table entries in the EPG encapsulation in which the TCN arrived.

If external switches send an excessive number of TCNs into the fabric, this can cause ACI to be constantly flushing endpoint entries. This problem manifests as intermittent packet loss, which can be detrimental to production traffic.

Note that a healthy network should not transmit large numbers of TCNs. This, therefore, is not an ACI problem. Where excessive TCNs occur, it is often the result of a lack of attention to Spanning Tree Protocol optimizations. For instance, a server NIC hardware or driver problem that causes a port to bounce tens of times per second would cause a flurry of TCNs. Preventing servers and other devices that do not bridge traffic from impacting the Spanning Tree Protocol topology would therefore ensure a more stable Spanning Tree Protocol topology with a minimal number of TCNs.

In networks in which excessive TCNs impact production traffic within ACI, the following actions can be taken to remediate the situation:

- Optimize the Spanning Tree Protocol topology by implementing PortFast (**spanning-tree port type edge** or **spanning-tree port type edge trunk** in NX-OS) and BPDU Guard on all switch interfaces that face non-bridging devices such as servers.

- Use a bridge domain extension to non-ACI switches. Because internal EPGs use different encapsulations compared to the Layer 2 EPG configured for bridge domain extension, ACI does not need to flush entries for the internal EPGs if it receives a TCN on the Layer 2 EPG. This limits the number of entries that need to be relearned.

- Extend EPGs or BDs that need to be extended out of the fabric only for legitimate purposes. When all endpoints and the default gateway for a VLAN have been migrated into ACI, prune the VLAN/EPG/BD off the Layer 2 extension.

- Implement BPDU Filter on non-ACI switch interfaces that face ACI to prevent all BPDUs from entering the fabric in the first place. Note that this should be done only if there is no more than one point of entry (single interface, port channel, or vPC) for external Layer 2 traffic for each VLAN into the ACI fabric. If this not the case, BPDU Filter could trigger a Layer 2 loop.

Configuring MST Instance Mappings in ACI

Per-VLAN Spanning Tree (PVST+) and Rapid Per-VLAN Spanning Tree (Rapid PVST+) BPDUs include VLAN tags. ACI can therefore easily identify the encapsulation and EPG associated with the BPDUs and flood the BPDUs out other ports that have the same EPG and encapsulation combination without any further user action.

Multiple Spanning Tree (MST) BPDUs, on the other hand, do not carry VLAN tags and are sent between switches untagged over any interswitch trunk links. Because ACI does not process traffic received on downlink ports unless there is an EPG assigned to it, there is a possibility that MST BPDUs will be dropped on ingress. Furthermore, MST relies on region names, revisions, and instance-to-VLAN mappings to build the Spanning Tree Protocol topology. Because ACI receives MST BPDUs untagged, it has no way to determine which VLAN IDs and therefore EPGs to flush upon TCN receipt.

10

For the reasons noted here, administrators need to take the following actions to safely connect legacy networks that run MST with ACI:

1. Create a special MST EPG and map it to all ports facing non-ACI switches that run MST. This ensures that ACI does not drop MST BPDUs.

2. Navigate to **Fabric > Access Policies > Policies > Switch > Spanning-Tree > default** and create MST region policies that include the MST region names, MST instance IDs, revision IDs, and relevant VLAN encapsulations. This ensures that ACI knows which EPGs to flush when it receives a TCN and also out of which ports it should forward MST BPDUs.

> **NOTE**   The VLAN Scope setting Port Local Scope is not supported on interfaces configured with MST.

Understanding Spanning Tree Protocol Link Types

When two Spanning Tree Protocol-speaking switches have a direct connection with one another, the default **spanning-tree link type point-to-point** interface subcommand on IOS and NX-OS switch platforms helps expedite Spanning Tree Protocol convergence. This is because when two switches are the only switches on a link or port aggregation, they are able to use basic proposals and agreements to safely negotiate an immediate transition from the Spanning Tree Protocol blocking state to the forwarding state.

Because ACI can transmit Layer 2 traffic between multiple external switches, an immediate transition to a forwarding state upon receipt of a single agreement can cause Layer 2 loops.

Therefore, when connecting multiple external switches to ACI, you can configure ACI-facing interfaces, port channels, and vPCs with the **spanning-tree link type shared** interface subcommand. This slows down Spanning Tree Protocol convergence if ACI ever becomes a transit point for Spanning Tree Protocol BPDUs between external switches and prevents external switches from negotiating expedited Spanning Tree Protocol state transitions.

Using MCP to Detect Layer 2 Loops

As discussed in Chapter 7, "Implementing Access Policies," MisCabling Protocol (MCP) can detect loops. In response, it can either log an incident or take action by blocking an offending port or link aggregation to break the loop.

While having MCP shut down ports is not always recommended, some customers do implement BPDU Filter on external switch interfaces facing ACI to prevent excessive TCNs from impacting ACI. In such cases, it is important to use MCP to block external Layer 2 connections and break any potential Layer 2 loops if at any point they do occur.

When used, MCP should ideally be enabled on all leaf downlinks, regardless of whether a server or switch connects to the port.

Exam Preparation Tasks

As mentioned in the section "How to Use This Book" in the Introduction, you have a couple of choices for exam preparation: Chapter 17, "Final Preparation," and the exam simulation questions in the Pearson Test Prep Software Online.

Review All Key Topics

Review the most important topics in this chapter, noted with the Key Topic icon in the outer margin of the page. Table 10-4 lists these key topics and the page number on which each is found.

Table 10-4   Key Topics for Chapter 10

Key Topic Element	Description	Page Number
Paragraph	Calls out the most important criteria for network-centric deployments	362
Paragraph	Define vzAny (Any EPG)	364
Table 10-2	Describes the bridge domain settings that should be used when extending Layer 2 out an ACI fabric and some of the logic behind these settings	368
List	Lists the three primary methods for extending Layer 2 outside an ACI fabric	372
Table 10-3	Compares bridge domain extension and EPG extension	375
Paragraph	Describes how to launch the Create Bridged Outside wizard	380
Figure 10-21	Shows the Create Bridged Outside wizard	381
Figure 10-22	Shows how to create an external bridge domain for BD extension	381
Figure 10-23	Emphasizes the need to verify that ports, port channels, or vPCs used to extend a BD have been added as candidates for extension in the wizard	382
Figure 10-24	Shows how to create a Layer 2 EPG when implementing bridge domain extension	383
Figure 10-25	Shows how to apply contracts on a Layer 2 EPG after implementing a BD extension	383
Figure 10-26	Shows how to apply contracts on an internal EPG to allow communication with a Layer 2 EPG	384
Figure 10-27	Shows how to verify endpoint learning in a Layer 2 EPG	384
Paragraph	Describes a common pitfall of any-to-any contract use and how to avoid this pitfall	385
Paragraph	Describes the default VLAN scope setting Global Scope	385
Paragraph	Describes how to implement the Port Local Scope capability	385
Paragraph	Emphasizes the need for separate VLAN pools and physical domains when deploying Port Local Scope	386

10

Key Topic Element	Description	Page Number
Paragraph	Emphasizes the fact that ACI does not run Spanning Tree Protocol or participate in the Spanning Tree Protocol topology and simply transits Spanning Tree Protocol BPDUs	386
List	Calls out two important measures ACI administrators should take if external switches running MST connect to an ACI fabric	388
Paragraph	Describes why it is necessary to configure external switch interfaces that face ACI with the **spanning-tree link type shared** interface subcommand	388
Paragraph	Describes a use case in which it is sometimes vital to run MCP as an ACI-side loop-detection and mitigation mechanism	388

Complete Tables and Lists from Memory

Print a copy of Appendix C, "Memory Tables" (found on the companion website), or at least the section for this chapter, and complete the tables and lists from memory. Appendix D, "Memory Tables Answer Key" (also on the companion website), includes completed tables and lists you can use to check your work.

Define Key Terms

Define the following key terms from this chapter and check your answers in the glossary:

Any EPG (vzAny), preferred group member, L2 Unknown Unicast, L3 Unknown Multicast Flooding, Multi Destination Flooding, external bridged network

## CHAPTER 11

Integrating ACI into vSphere Using VDS

This chapter covers the following topics:

Understanding Networking in VMware vSphere: This section provides a primer on networking in ESXi hypervisors.

Understanding VMM Integration: This section covers VMM integration concepts and prerequisites for successful integration using a VDS.

Integrating ACI into vSphere Using VDS: This section walks through the implementation of the most common and simple form of VMM integration.

This chapter covers the following exam topics:

- 4.1 Implement VMware vCenter DVS integration
- 4.2 Describe resolution immediacy in VMM

APIC controllers can integrate into hypervisor and container environments to extend the benefits of ACI—such as whitelisting and network automation—into virtualized infrastructure.

vSphere is an ecosystem of server virtualization products from VMware. ACI has multiple ways to integrate with vSphere, the most common of which is by using a vSphere distributed switch (VDS).

When APICs integrate with a virtualized environment, they generally do so by integrating with Virtual Machine Manager (VMM). The term VMM can refer to any system or application that manages virtual machines. In the case of vSphere, the APICs integrate with the VMM component called vCenter. ACI integrations of this type are called *VMM integrations*.

This chapter addresses the Implementing Cisco Application Centric Infrastructure DCACI 300-620 exam objectives related to VMM integration using the VMware VDS and also builds the context that ACI engineers need to better understand basic networking in vSphere environments.

"Do I Know This Already?" Quiz

The "Do I Know This Already?" quiz allows you to assess whether you should read this entire chapter thoroughly or jump to the "Exam Preparation Tasks" section. If you are in doubt about your answers to these questions or your own assessment of your knowledge of the topics, read the entire chapter. Table 11-1 lists the major headings in this chapter and their corresponding "Do I Know This Already?" quiz questions. You can find the answers in Appendix A, "Answers to the 'Do I Know This Already?' Questions."

Table 11-1 "Do I Know This Already?" Section-to-Question Mapping

Foundation Topics Section	Questions
Understanding Networking in VMware vSphere	1–3
Understanding VMM Integration	4, 5
Integrating ACI into vSphere Using VDS	6–10

CAUTION The goal of self-assessment is to gauge your mastery of the topics in this chapter. If you do not know the answer to a question or are only partially sure of the answer, you should mark that question as wrong for purposes of the self-assessment. Giving yourself credit for an answer you correctly guess skews your self-assessment results and might provide you with a false sense of security.

1. A vSphere administrator has placed the vCenter instance that manages a VDS on the same VDS. What port binding setting can ensure optimal recoverability of the vSphere environment?

   a. Dynamic binding

   b. Static binding

   c. Default

   d. Ephemeral

2. Which of the following virtual switch options allows more advanced features but is still owned and managed by VMware?

   a. vSphere standard switch

   b. vSphere distributed switch

   c. Nexus 1000v

   d. Application Virtual Switch

3. Which of the following vSphere constructs receives and processes system traffic?

   a. VMkernel adapter

   b. Port group

   c. Data center

   d. vMotion

4. An ACI administrator creates three non-overlapping dynamic VLAN pools and associates a VLAN pool with each of three separate VMM domains. A vSphere administrator notices that port groups across the VMM domains have different VLAN IDs associated with them and asks for feedback on why this is the case. Which responses together are the most accurate responses? (Choose all that apply.)

   a. The automatic assignment of VLAN IDs increases operational efficiency.

   b. Port group VLAN assignments are not important.

   c. There is no way to control VLAN assignments when implementing VMM integration.

   d. ESXi servers from multiple vCenter instances connect to the same set of leaf switches. Therefore, overlapping VLANs to ensure that VLAN IDs match can cause performance issues.

5. Which objects do vSphere distributed switches tie to in vCenter?

   a. vCenter

   b. Cluster

   c. Data center

   d. EPG

6. True or false: A vSphere administrator can associate ESXi hosts to an ACI-generated VDS before an ACI administrator configures a VMM domain profile.

   a. True

   b. False

7. Which steps need to be completed before a VM can be reassigned to an ACI-generated VDS? (Choose all that apply.)

   a. A vSphere administrator needs to add the host on which the VM resides to the VDS.

   b. An ACI administrator performs a VMM domain association for the EPG needed to be pushed into ACI.

   c. ACI pushes a bridge domain into vCenter.

   d. ACI generates a VDS through configuration of a VMM domain profile.

8. Which of the following resolution immediacy and deployment immediacy settings should be used for ESXi VMkernel interfaces with management services enabled, assuming that the VMkernel will reside on an ACI-generated VDS?

   a. Immediate, Immediate

   b. On Demand, On Demand

   c. Pre-Provision, Immediate

   d. Immediate, On Demand

9. True or false: ACI should not be used to deploy multiple virtual distributed switches that use the same name into a vCenter instance.

   a. True

   b. False

10. True or false: ACI can be used to create multiple LACP port channels on a VDS.

   a. True

   b. False

Foundation Topics

Understanding Networking in VMware vSphere

With the movement of servers into hypervisors, the need arises for certain switching functions to be performed within hypervisors. For example, a hypervisor with several virtual machines (VMs) in a particular VLAN needs to know how to forward unicast traffic between the VMs or to a destination on the physical network and how to forward broadcast traffic.

Additional services that virtual switches need to provide include control over network bandwidth allocations for virtual machines and visibility and monitoring functions such as NetFlow.

In the vSphere ecosystem, hypervisors are referred to as *ESXi servers* or *ESXi hosts*. The two traditional flavors of virtual switches within this ecosystem are the vSphere standard switch (vSwitch) and the vSphere distributed switch (VDS).

NOTE   VMware has additional virtual switch solutions that can be implemented in vSphere, such as the N-VDS and the NSX-T VDS. Earlier versions of vSphere supported Cisco Nexus 1000v. Cisco also has hypervisor-agnostic solutions that can be deployed in vSphere. These solutions, however, are all beyond the scope of the DCACI 300-620 exam.

Understanding vSphere Standard Switches

A *vSphere standard switch (vSwitch)* is a basic Layer 2 virtual switch instantiated by and limited in scope to a single hypervisor. It can be used to enable ESXi host IP connectivity with other hosts or endpoints. It can also enable basic connectivity for virtual machines.

When an administrator creates a vSphere standard switch, the system defaults to label such switches with the prefix vSwitch. The term *vmnic* describes a physical network interface card connecting an ESXi server to a physical switch. You can think of vmnic as a string used in the naming of virtual switch uplinks within ESXi hypervisors. To enable network connectivity for VMs, administrators configure virtual network adapters (vNICs) within them and associate those vNICs with port groups. A *port group* is a group of ports with similar policy requirements. For example, a user might create a port group for endpoints in VLAN 10. *VMkernel adapters* are logical interfaces that enable transmission, receipt, or processing of hypervisor system traffic. Examples of ESXi system traffic include management, vMotion, IP storage, fault tolerance, and vSAN. Like virtual machines, VMkernel adapters need to be associated with port groups.

A lot of the terminology presented in the previous paragraph can be best understood through analysis of Figure 11-1, which provides an overview of the vSphere standard switch architecture using two ESXi hosts. In this example, the ESXi hosts are not part of a vCenter server cluster. VM1 on ESXi-Host-1 is in VLAN 20 because its vNIC has been associated with the VLAN 20 port group. Because VM3 has been associated with the same port group as VM1, ESXi-Host-1 can locally switch traffic between the two virtual machines using vSwitch1. By default, all port groups leverage the interface teaming and failover policies of their parent virtual switch. However, these teaming and failover policies can be overridden at the port group level. For example, Figure 11-1 shows that the port group for VLAN 20 within ESXi-Host-1 has an active path through vmnic2 to a top-of-rack switch named Nexus-Switch-1 and a standby path to Nexus-Switch-2. The standby path becomes active only if vmnic2 fails. Meanwhile, the VLAN 10 port group on the same host has both uplinks always active. Another point worthy of note from Figure 11-1 is that ESXi-Host-1 has two standard switches deployed, while ESXi-Host-2 has only one. The nature of vSphere standard switches and the fact that they can be configured differently across hosts means that configuration drift across ESXi hosts that leverage these types of virtual switches is a serious possibility.

NOTE   Figure 11-1 may suggest that the number of VLAN IDs in an environment determines the number of port groups. In reality, multiple port groups can be created to accommodate different policies for endpoints within a given VLAN.

11

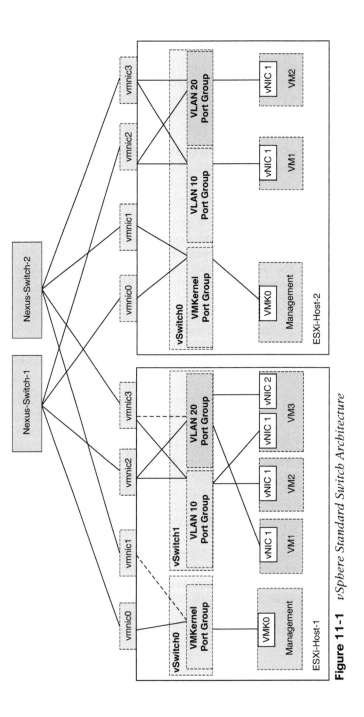

Figure 11-1 *vSphere Standard Switch Architecture*

Understanding vSphere Distributed Switches

ESXi servers can be standalone hypervisors or can be centrally managed by vCenter. Since the overwhelming majority of ESXi hypervisor deployments are centrally managed, it stands to reason that there should be a way to also manage virtual switches through vCenter. And that is exactly what a vSphere distributed switch does. A *vSphere distributed switch (VDS)* is a virtual switch that is created and centrally managed by vCenter with the switch data plane residing within the ESXi hypervisors. When an administrator updates a setting on a VDS, the change is propagated to all hosts associated with the VDS. This approach to virtual switching eases management and minimizes the possibility of configuration drift across hosts in the environment.

Figure 11-2 presents the conceptual (not literal) architecture of a VDS. Note that the majority of concepts are the same as those covered in the previous section on vSphere standard switches. One notable difference between the two switch types beyond the fact that a VDS is managed by vCenter is that port groups on a VDS are called *distributed port groups*. Another difference reinforced by Figure 11-2 is that a distributed port group whose teaming and failover setting has been modified will have the same setting across all hosts. Finally, one difference not depicted here but that is still significant is that the vSphere distributed switch supports more advanced functionality, such as private VLANs, LACP, and NetFlow.

> **NOTE**   As of the time of writing, the DCACI 300-620 exam blueprint calls out DVS and not VDS as an exam topic. For the purpose of the exam, both terms refer to the same thing.

Understanding vSphere System Traffic

The DCACI 300-620 exam does not really test your expertise with vSphere. Nonetheless, it seems a reasonable expectation that candidates who push VDS configuration changes from ACI to vCenter understand how to build the minimum ESXi server connectivity necessary for hypervisors to be able to communicate with vCenter. Without basic IP connectivity, ESXi servers have no way to receive updates on VDS configuration changes.

To enable ESXi communication with vCenter, ESXi servers need a VMkernel interface with management services enabled. This typically (but not always) is an interface named vmk0, which is created at the time of host deployment. Figure 11-3 shows the settings of a VMkernel interface used for management of an ESXi host. One of the settings shown is the TCP/IP Stack parameter. If you need multiple VMkernel adapters for various services and different default gateways for each VMkernel adapter, the adapters with such requirements need to be assigned to different TCP/IP stacks. On the left side of the image is a link that allows navigation to the IPv4 Settings page, which is where you allocate an IP address and default gateway to the interface.

11

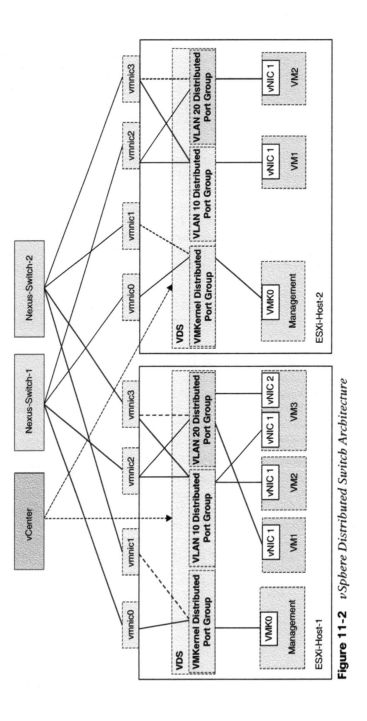

Figure 11-2 *vSphere Distributed Switch Architecture*

Figure 11-3 *A VMkernel Adapter with Management Services Enabled*

Aside from the management service, the only other VMkernel service that all (or very close to all) vCenter-managed ESXi environments have enabled is vMotion. With vMotion, servers are able to migrate virtual machines between one another. The vMotion service can be enabled on the same VMkernel interface as management traffic or on a separate VMkernel interface. A detailed analysis of requirements for vMotion is beyond the scope of this book.

NOTE All images that depict vCenter and ESXi settings in this book have been taken with vCenter Release 6.7.

Impact of vCenter Failure on Production Traffic

A failure of vCenter does not impact IP connectivity for endpoints behind vSphere standard switches since these types of virtual switches are local to each hypervisor and have no dependency on vCenter.

A failure of vCenter also does not halt IP connectivity of operational virtual machines and VMkernel interfaces on distributed virtual switches. It does, however, impact certain hypervisor services, such as vMotion and Distributed Resource Scheduler (DRS), that rely on vCenter.

When the vCenter server gets its network access through a VDS that it manages, a chicken-or-egg conundrum has been created that may impact the recoverability of the environment under very specific failure scenarios. An analysis of vSphere virtual port bindings can help illuminate how this type of challenge can be addressed.

Understanding Port Bindings in vSphere

Just like physical switches, distributed switches have the concept of ports—although in the case of distributed switches, the ports are virtual. *Port bindings* determine when virtual machines in a port group get allocated to a virtual port on a VDS. There are three different types of port bindings in vSphere:

- **Static binding:** A virtual port is immediately assigned and reserved for a VM the moment it is assigned to a distributed port group if the distributed port group is configured with a static binding. This virtual port assignment remains valid unless the VM is removed from the distributed port group, even if the VM is migrated between servers. Note that VMs cannot be associated with a distributed port group configured for static bindings unless the vCenter instance managing the relevant VDS is operational. Static binding is the default binding type for new distributed port groups and is ideal for general use.

- **Dynamic binding:** With dynamic bindings configured on a port group, a virtual port is assigned to a virtual machine only after the VM powers on and its vNIC moves to an operational status. This port binding type has been deprecated since ESXi Version 5.0.

- **Ephemeral binding:** If a distributed port group has been configured with an ephemeral binding, a virtual port is created and assigned to a virtual machine by the ESXi host on which the VM resides (not by vCenter) once the VM powers on and its vNIC moves to an operational state.

As a best practice, all general use VMs placed on a VDS should be assigned to port groups configured for static bindings. Critical VMs such as vCenter itself can also be assigned to a distributed port group configured for static bindings. But if vCenter lives on a VDS it itself manages, administrators should consider assigning it and other critical VMs that vCenter relies on to a distributed port group configured for ephemeral bindings. At the very least, a distributed port group can be created for vCenter purely for recovery operations and can be left without VM assignments.

> **NOTE**   In some environments, vCenter and management VMs may be placed on vSphere standard switches. Port groups on vSphere standard switches have ephemeral bindings.

As shown in Figure 11-4, you can configure an ephemeral port group in vSphere by selecting Ephemeral - No Binding as the port binding type. You can access the New Distributed Port Group wizard shown in this figure by right-clicking a VDS under the Network tab in the vSphere web client, selecting Distributed Port Group, and clicking New Distributed Port Group.

Understanding Teaming and Failover Policies

Some of the most important aspects of port group deployments are the teaming and failover policies. Figure 11-5 shows some of the teaming and failover settings available for configuring a distributed port group on a VDS.

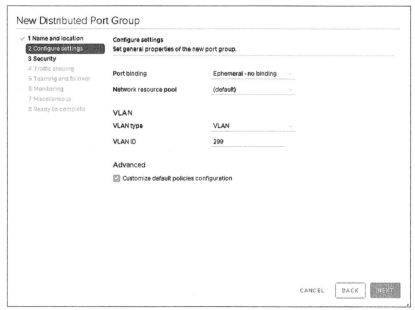

Figure 11-4 *Selecting Ephemeral - No Binding as the Port Binding Type*

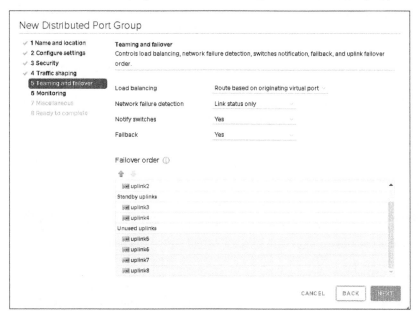

Figure 11-5 *Teaming and Failover Settings for Port Groups*

vSphere load balancing enables you to choose how uplink ports on the virtual switch are used to distribute network traffic originating from virtual machines and VMkernel interfaces. As of the time of this writing, there are five load-balancing methods to choose from:

■ **Route based on originating virtual port:** With this load-balancing method, each VM or VMkernel interface is pinned to a single uplink, based on the virtual port assigned to it. If a switch uplink fails, all virtual machines and VMkernel interfaces associated with it are then repinned to an alternate operational uplink. This is the default load-balancing method in vSphere and is preferred in most environments. With this method configured across port groups, physical network switches do not need to configure ports facing ESXi servers in a port channel, even though this load-balancing method can lead to active/active forwarding of traffic across uplinks due to endpoints being pinned to different uplinks.

■ **Route based on IP hash:** When you think of the word *hash*, you should automatically think of port channeling. That is exactly what this load-balancing option is. When used on port groups in a vSphere standard switch, this option results in the deployment of a static port channel. LACP port channeling, on the other hand, *is* supported on virtual distributed switches.

■ **Route based on source MAC hash:** With this option, the virtual machine MAC address determines the uplink over which network-bound traffic should be forwarded. Compared to routing based on originating virtual port, this load-balancing option is rarely used because it is resource intensive and requires that the virtual switch calculate an uplink for each packet received from virtual machines.

■ **Use explicit failover order:** This option is actually not a load-balancing method. When this method is selected, the virtual switch uses the failover order and sends traffic out the first uplink in the Active adapters list. If all interfaces in the Active adapters list are down, the virtual switch can use uplinks in the Standby adapters list, in order of priority.

■ **Route based on physical NIC load:** This is a slight variation of routing based on originating virtual port, in which the virtual switch also tests the load on uplinks every 30 seconds and repins traffic to an alternate uplink if the load exceeds 75% of uplink bandwidth of the physical interface. This load-balancing option is only available with vSphere distributed switches.

Other teaming and failover settings that can be configured for a vSwitch or DVS and that are shown in Figure 11-5 are detailed in Table 11-2.

Table 11-2 vSphere Teaming and Failover Settings

Setting	Description
Network Failure Detection	Specifies one of two ways with which a virtual switch can detect network uplink failures. The first, Link Status Only, relies on the operational state of the link. The second option, Beacon Probing, sends probes into the network through its uplinks to see if other uplinks receive the probes. If an uplink is unable to receive the transmitted probes, it is deemed to have suboptimal connectivity. Use of beacon probing is very uncommon because it requires at least three uplinks to allow the virtual switch to effectively determine which of the uplinks has failed. The beacon probing option should never be used in combination with port channeling.

Setting	Description
Notify Switches	When set to Yes, prompts the virtual switch repinning a virtual machine to a different uplink following an uplink failure to send a Reverse ARP (RARP) packet into the network in the hope that upstream switches update their CAM tables faster.
Fallback	When all interfaces in the Active Uplinks list have been determined to be non-operational and virtual machines and VMkernel interfaces have been pinned to interfaces in the Standby list, a fallback setting of Yes specifies whether the virtual switch should fall back to interfaces in the Active uplinks list if they become available.
Failover Order	Specifies how traffic should be rerouted when an adapter fails. There are three possible adapter states that can be configured in the teaming and failover page: Active Uplinks, Standby Uplinks, and Unused Uplinks. Active uplinks actively forward traffic, while standby uplinks are only used if all active uplinks fail. An uplink that has been added to the Unused Uplinks list is never used for traffic in a port group, even if both the active and standby uplinks fail.

Understanding VMM Integration

Why bother with VMM integration? For companies that intend to focus heavily on whitelisting, the splitting of traditional VLANs into EPGs necessitates the creation of more and more port groups within vSphere, thereby increasing the operational burden for vSphere administrators. VMM integration not only minimizes this burden but introduces a level of network policy automation that enables vSphere administrators to delegate the task of vSphere networking to network engineers.

But there is also another argument that can be made in favor of VMM integration. At the end of the day, the vSphere ecosystem relies on the network to get server traffic from point A to point B. If end-to-end connectivity relies on the network in the first place, there really is no reason to define network policy twice (once in the physical network and once in the virtual network). The end results of VMM integration for companies that don't seek to implement whitelisting are less duplication of effort, better end-to-end visibility into connectivity issues, faster policy deployment, and more involvement of network teams in virtual networking.

Planning vCenter VMM Integrations

This section looks at some of the things ACI administrators should take into account when planning VMM integrations.

First, it is important to understand that ACI treats each VMM integration definition as a domain object. This does not necessarily mean that any time ACI integrates with a separate vCenter instance, a separate VMM domain is required. ACI does allow multiple vCenter instances to be grouped under a single VMM domain. Creating a single VMM domain and configuring multiple vCenter instances under the VMM domain makes a lot of sense if all vCenter instances require the same distributed port groups.

For instance, say that you have 10 instances of vCenter that have ESXi hosts in a fabric. Five of these instances are dedicated to production applications, and 5 are dedicated to development purposes. In this case, it might make sense to deploy 2 VMM domains: one for the production environment and one for the development environment. Each VMM domain would have 5 associated vCenter instances. A design like this ensures that when an ACI administrator adds the VMM domain association to an EPG, distributed port groups are pushed to 5 separate vCenter instances simultaneously. Alternatively, if 5 separate VMM domains had been defined for the production environment, the administrator might find that 5 different VMM domains need to be associated with each EPG that needs to be pushed into the production vCenter instances.

On the topic of domains, remember that an administrator needs to allocate one (and only one) VLAN pool to each VMM domain. In the case of VMM domains, it makes a lot of sense to use dynamic VLAN pools. This approach allows ACI to determine what VLAN ID to allocate to each distributed port group it creates within vSphere and therefore dramatically reduces the time spent implementing network policy. By default, ACI dynamically allocates VLANs to distributed port groups, but this behavior can be modified if administrators need to statically allocate a specific VLAN ID to a distributed port group.

It should be clear by now that a single VMM domain can span multiple vCenter instances, but can a single vCenter instance have multiple VMM domain integrations? The answer to this question is yes! To understand why someone might want to perform multiple VMM integrations into a vCenter instance, let's take a look at the vSphere object hierarchy.

In vSphere, each virtual distributed switch is actually tied directly to a data center object, not to a vCenter instance. A data center object is itself a child object of a vCenter instance. Under each data center object, various clusters of ESXi hosts may exist. Figure 11-6 shows a data center object named DC2, which has been selected by a user. DC2 appears below its parent vCenter instance, dc2-vcenter. A host cluster named Production appears under DC2. A new data center object named Gaming-BU is also shown under dc2-vcenter. Two new clusters and several hosts have also been staged for this new data center object.

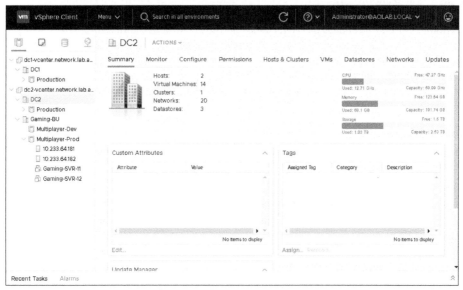

Figure 11-6 *Data Center, Cluster, and ESXi Host Hierarchy in vCenter*

As noted earlier, a VDS is tied directly to a data center object. If both the DC2 and Gaming-BU data centers shown in Figure 11-6 required access to exactly the same EPGs, on the surface it would seem reasonable to think that you could create two references to the vCenter instance dc2-vcenter, each pointing to separate data centers within a single VMM domain. However, this would not work because vCenter expects each VDS to have a unique name across vCenter. This, therefore, would be a case in which at least two VMM integrations within the vCenter instance would be required in spite of the requirement for access to the same EPGs.

So, if an ACI fabric can integrate into a vCenter instance using multiple VMM domains, is the earlier example in which five production vCenter integrations were made possible using a single VMM domain always accurate? The answer is no. The example assumes that each vCenter instance has only a single data center object that requires VMM integration in the first place.

What Happens After VDS Deployment?

Once an ACI administrator creates a VMM domain and associates one or more vCenter instances with the VMM domain, ACI leverages vSphere APIs to execute the creation of a VDS in each of the specified vCenter instances.

Just because a VMM domain and therefore a VDS have been created does not mean that EPGs will be available for consumption within vSphere. To create distributed port groups, an ACI administrator needs to first add VMM domain associations to the desired EPGs.

Eventually, a vSphere administrator needs to log in to vCenter and add a number of ESXi hosts to the VDS. The process of adding ESXi hosts to the VDS involves specifying VDS uplinks for each host and possibly migrating VMkernel adapters, or *VM VNICs*, to distributed port groups on the VDS.

Once a vSphere administrator adds a virtual machine or VMkernel interface to an ACI-generated distributed port group, ACI classifies the endpoint as part of the EPG, ensuring that the endpoint inherits the network access specified by any associated contracts.

Understanding Immediacy Settings

ACI is built for extreme scalability. Some ACI fabrics are home to hundreds (and others thousands) of ESXi servers. For ACI to be able to support such large environments, policies should be deployed where they are needed—not everywhere.

Imagine an environment with 1000 physical servers and 10,000 EPGs spread across 50 leaf switches. Do all 50 of these leaf switches need to know about every single VRF, bridge domain, EPG, and contract detail associated with these 10,000 EPGs? Do all leaf switches need to push all these policies into hardware? The answer to both of these questions is no! To better understand why, let's take a look at resolution immediacy and deployment immediacy.

In ACI *resolution immediacy* defines when policies, such as VLANs, VXLAN bindings, contracts, and filters, are downloaded to leaf switches. Three resolution immediacy options are available in ACI:

Key Topic

- **Pre-Provision:** This resolution immediacy option specifically relates to VMM integration. In the context of ACI integrations with vSphere, Pre-Provision prompts policies

11

to be downloaded to leaf switches even if a vCenter instance has not been defined within the VMM domain configuration. Only leaf switches with access policies referencing an AAEP associated with a VMM domain download policies as a result of EPG pre-provisioning.

- **Immediate:** This resolution immediacy option specifies that EPG policies are downloaded to a leaf switch once an ESXi host has been added to a VDS created by the APIC and the VDS has been verified via LLDP or CDP to be adjacent to the leaf switch.

- **On Demand:** This resolution immediacy option specifies that policies are downloaded to a leaf switch only when an ESXi host has been validated via LLDP or CDP to be attached to a VDS created by the APICs and at least one VM VNIC has been assigned to a distributed port group on the VDS.

NOTE When there is a single layer of intermediary devices between a leaf switch and an APIC-generated VDS and the resolution immediacy settings used are Immediate and On Demand, ACI can sometimes use LLDP and CDP neighborships reported by the VDS as well as data in LLDP and CDP packets arriving on leaf ports to reverse engineer the data path and determine whether policies should be downloaded to the leaf.

Note that the Immediate and On Demand resolution immediacy options both rely on ESXi host VMkernel adapters being operational and ACI trunking the VMkernel management VLAN down to the hypervisors. Otherwise, ACI would never receive LLDP or CDP information from the hypervisor to begin with. This chicken-and-egg headache necessitates use of the resolution immediacy Pre-Provision option for the VMM domain association for the hypervisor management EPG.

Use the resolution immediacy setting Pre-Provision for critical EPGs to which hypervisors require access in order to reach a fully operational state. This rule also applies to EPGs that are home to critical vSphere servers such as vCenter, LDAP, and any vCenter database servers.

NOTE In small-scale deployments in which hardware resource utilization requirements are never expected to surpass the capabilities of deployed leaf switches, there is little reason not to use the resolution immediacy option Pre-Provision for all EPGs. Also, if hypervisors connect indirectly to ACI leaf switches through an intermediate device and the LLDP and CDP capabilities of the intermediate device are suspect, consider using the resolution immediacy option Pre-Provision.

Whereas resolution immediacy determines whether policies should be downloaded to a leaf, *deployment immediacy* governs whether policies should be pushed into hardware.

When policies, such as VLANs, VXLAN bindings, contracts, and filters, have been downloaded to a leaf switch, deployment immediacy specifies when the policy is actually pushed into the hardware policy content-addressable memory (CAM). There are two deployment immediacy configuration options:

- **Immediate:** This deployment immediacy option specifies that the policy is programmed in the hardware policy CAM as soon as the policy is downloaded in the leaf software.

■ **On Demand:** This deployment immediacy option specifies that the policy should be programmed in the hardware policy CAM only after the switch receives a packet through the data path. This setting helps optimize the hardware space.

Connecting ESXi Servers to the Fabric

It is critical for DCACI candidates to understand that VMM integration does not eliminate the need for ACI access policies. Without access policies, ACI has no way to know to which leaf switches it needs to deploy policy. Based on the load-balancing algorithm configured, ACI downlinks to ESXi servers may be port channels. They may be non-aggregated ports. Whatever the case may be, access policies need to be deployed.

If a leaf downlink connects to a vSphere standard switch or a VDS that will not be managed by ACI, it does not need to have an AAEP association that provides access to a VMM domain. If, on the other hand, a leaf downlink connects to an ESXi uplink that will be associated with an ACI-generated VDS, the VMM domain triggering the creation of the VDS creation needs to have also been associated with the AAEP.

To sum up, it is important to understand that it is distributed port group generation and deployment assignments (and not deployment of access policies) that is automated by VMM integration.

Configuring Connectivity to ESXi in UCS Domains

Engineers sometimes find the task of selecting optimal load-balancing settings for virtual standard switch or VDS uplinks to be mystifying. The Cisco Unified Computing System (UCS) B-Series server architecture offers a good Cisco-centric case in point.

Say that an engineer has been asked to provide guidance on virtual switch load balancing prior to deployment of VMM integration. The hypervisors housing the virtual switches reside within a UCS domain. The engineer has studied the basics of UCS B-Series architecture and learns that fabric interconnect links northbound to the network attach to leaf switches via vPCs. He or she also learns about port channeling within the system and may then incorrectly assume that routing based on IP hash should be selected as the virtual switch load-balancing algorithm. What is being misinterpreted in this case is that the port channeling that occurs within UCS domains is between the I/O modules and fabric interconnects, not the server vNICs northbound. In addition, the fabric interconnect vPC connectivity with leaf switches has no direct relationship with the virtual switch load-balancing capabilities.

To avoid these types of pitfalls, engineers should only analyze the port channeling capabilities between hypervisor uplinks and the directly connected device, even if the hypervisor uplinks do not directly connect to ACI leaf switches.

When in doubt, routing based on originating virtual port is often the best load-balancing method for ESXi virtual switches.

Integrating ACI into vSphere Using VDS

Now that we have covered the basics of vSphere networking and VMM integration, let's take a look at how VMM integration works in practice.

11

Prerequisites for VMM Integration with vSphere VDS

The following items are basic prerequisites for VMM integration with a VMware VDS and should be addressed before you configure VMM integration:

- Either in-band or out-of-band management should have been configured for the APICs.

- The APICs need to be able to reach vCenter from their out-of-band or in-band management connections.

- All leaf switches to which ESXi servers connect should have been discovered and should be fully operational.

Configuring a VMM Domain Profile

To create a VMM domain profile, navigate to **Virtual Networking > Inventory > VMM Domains**, right-click VMware, and select Create vCenter Domain.

In the Create vCenter Domain wizard, populate the Virtual Switch Name field with a VDS name, select VMware vSphere Distributed Switch as the virtual switch type, create an AAEP or select a pre-created AAEP from the Associated Attachable Entity Profile drop-down box, and select the access mode and VLAN pool. Then click on the + symbol in front of the vCenter Credentials section. Figure 11-7 shows a sample configuration of these parameters. Note that the Access Mode parameter defines whether ACI will be making configuration changes to the VDS. The Read Only Mode setting enables ACI to gain visibility into a VDS it does not manage as well as the hypervisors and VMs associated with it.

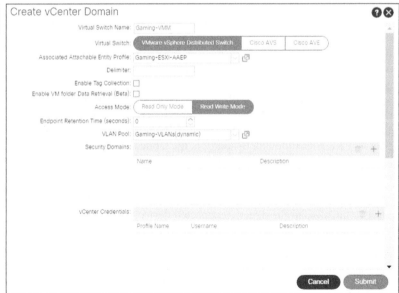

Figure 11-7 *vCenter Domain Creation Wizard*

On the Create vCenter Credential page, shown in Figure 11-8, populate the Username, Password, and Confirm Password fields with credentials that allow ACI to log in to vCenter and conduct networking tasks. Enter a descriptive name describing the credentials or differentiating it from other saved credentials if multiple integrations have been implemented and click OK. Ideally, vCenter credentials used should be for an account that does not expire.

Figure 11-8   *The Create vCenter Credentials Page*

NOTE   VMM integration with vSphere does not require full admin privileges. However, the list of privileges required is long enough that it is not suited for coverage on an exam like the DCACI 300-620 exam. Review the latest Cisco ACI Virtualization Guide to get an idea of the minimum privileges required for the tasks relevant to a given environment.

Back in the Create vCenter Domain page, scroll further down and click the + symbol in front of the section titled vCenter. In the Add vCenter Controller page, shown in Figure 11-9, enter a descriptive name for the vCenter instance being added and provide either the DNS name or IP address of the vCenter instance, select a VDS version from the DVS Version drop-down box, enter the case-sensitive data center name in the Datacenter field (exactly as it appears in vCenter), select a management EPG if in-band management should be used for APIC connectivity to this vCenter instance, and then select the previously created credentials from the Associated Credential drop-down box and click OK.

Figure 11-9 *The Add vCenter Controller Page*

Back in the Create vCenter Domain page, populate the Number of Uplinks field with the maximum number of uplinks. If no value is entered, a default value of 8 uplinks is assumed. Select a value for Port Channel Mode if port channeling or MAC pinning will be used. In the vSwitch Policy field, select whether LLDP or CDP should be enabled on the VDS, and finally create a NetFlow exporter policy if you want the VDS to send NetFlow data to a NetFlow collector. Then click Submit to execute the necessary API calls to generate the VDS within the vCenter instances selected, as shown in Figure 11-10.

Figure 11-10 *vCenter Domain Creation Wizard, Continued*

In the Networking tab in each configured vCenter instance, a VDS with the name specified earlier can be validated as having been created, as shown in Figure 11-11. No hypervisors or VMs should be associated with the VDS at this point. By default, the VDS should have two distributed port groups: one called quarantine and the other dedicated to hypervisor uplinks.

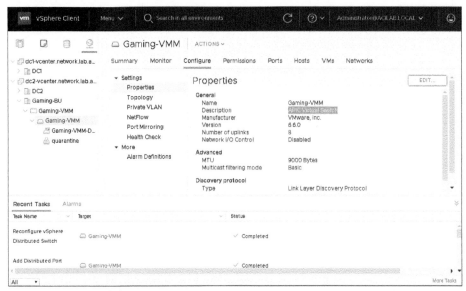

Figure 11-11 *Validating VDS Creation in vCenter*

Adding ESXi Hosts to a VDS

Once ACI has generated a VDS in vCenter, you can right-click on the VDS and select Add and Manage Hosts, as shown in Figure 11-12.

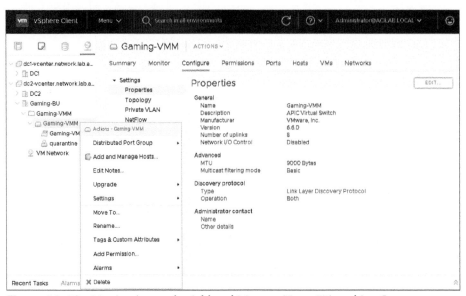

Figure 11-12 *Navigating to the Add and Manage Hosts Wizard in vCenter*

As indicated in Figure 11-13, select the Add Hosts option and click Next.

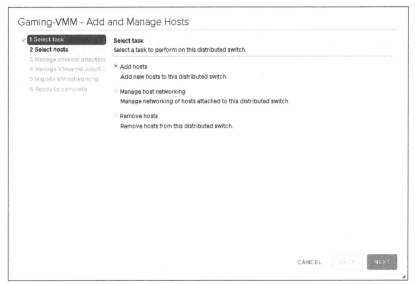

Figure 11-13   *Selecting Add Hosts*

Click New Hosts to select available hosts to add to the VDS, as shown in Figure 11-14.

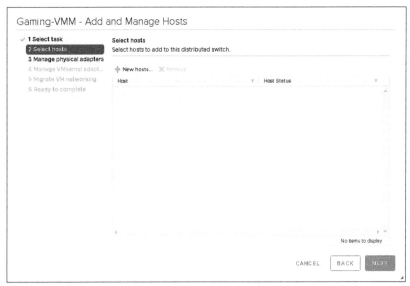

Figure 11-14   *Clicking New Hosts*

In the Select New Hosts page, enable the checkbox in front of each ESXi host that should be added to the VDS, as shown in Figure 11-15, and click OK.

Figure 11-15   *Choosing the Hosts to Add on the Select New Hosts Page*

Next, click the Assign Uplink command button to define which vmnics should be assigned to the VDS. Note in Figure 11-16 that vmnic interfaces previously assigned to another virtual switch can be reassigned in this window. Just make sure not to reassign interfaces governing VMkernel connectivity for management or any other critical services. To move on to the next step, click Next.

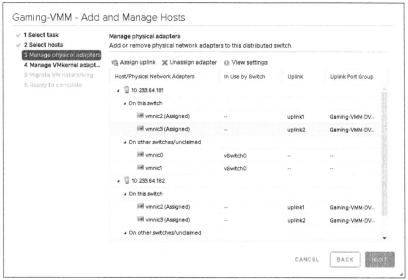

Figure 11-16   *Assigning Uplinks to a VDS*

In the Manage VMkernel Adapters page, shown in Figure 11-17, VMkernel interfaces can be migrated to the new VDS. It is sometimes best to first assign uplinks, push port groups, and validate connectivity before migrating VMkernel adapters, but if proper access policies are

11

in place, migration of VMkernel adapters can take place at this stage without issue. When you are ready to move on to the next step, click Next.

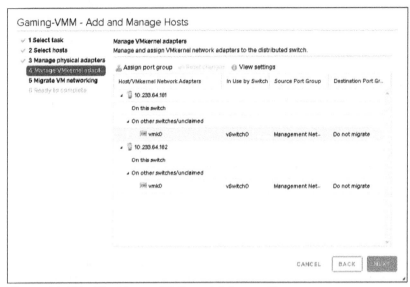

Figure 11-17　*The Manage VMkernel Adapters Page*

The Migrate VM Networking page is shown in Figure 11-18. If any VM vNICs should be migrated to VDS distributed port groups, you can select the target port groups. Because ACI has not yet pushed any EPGs into vCenter, you can move on to the next step for now.

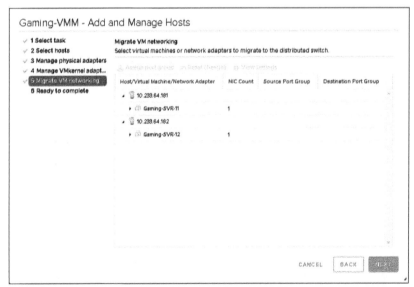

Figure 11-18　*The Manage VM Networking Page*

Figure 11-19 shows the changes the wizard is making. Click Finish to confirm and add the ESXi hosts to the VDS.

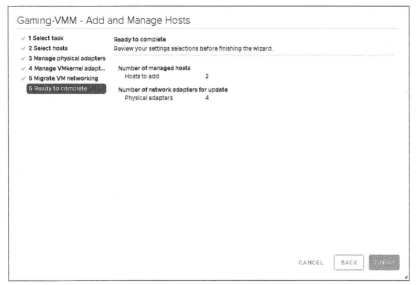

Figure 11-19 *Confirming the Addition of ESXi Hosts to the VDS*

Pushing EPGs to vCenter as Distributed Port Groups

Before VM traffic can be placed in EPGs through VMM integration, ACI needs to push desired EPGs into any vCenter instances defined by the VMM domain.

To push an EPG into vCenter, navigate to the desired EPG and expose its subfolders. In the Domains folder, right-click the Tools menu and select Add VMM Domain Association (see Figure 11-20).

Figure 11-20 *Navigating to the Add VMM Domain Association Page*

From the VMM Domain Profile drop-down, select the desired VMM domain with which the EPG should be associated, select Deploy Immediacy and Resolution Immediacy settings, select the VLAN mode (Dynamic indicates dynamic VLAN ID allocation), configure the port binding (the ACI default value for VDS integration is Static Binding, which is suitable for general-use virtual machines), and click Submit. Figure 11-21 shows settings entered to enable the deployment of an EPG named EPG-Gaming-Servers into vCenter as a distributed port group.

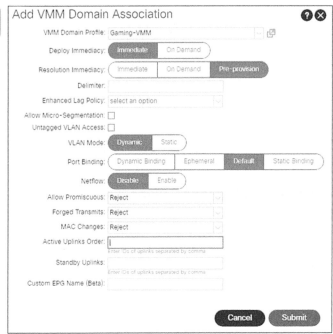

Figure 11-21 *Pushing an EPG with Basic Settings into vCenter*

Back in vCenter, you can expect to see a distributed port group created for the EPG. Figure 11-22 shows that the EPG has indeed been pushed to vCenter and uses VLAN ID 3500. By selecting the distributed port group, you can verify the number of uplinks that can potentially be associated with the distributed port group. Because the Active uplinks and Standby uplink settings were left untouched, the first eight possible uplinks have been chosen as candidates for active/active forwarding of traffic over hypervisor uplinks. You may notice that virtual machines have not yet been associated with the distributed port group.

NOTE By default, ACI names the distributed port group using the format *tenant/application/epg*. The character separating the parameters is called a *delimiter* character. In recent versions of ACI code, the naming can be customized using the Custom EPG Name field.

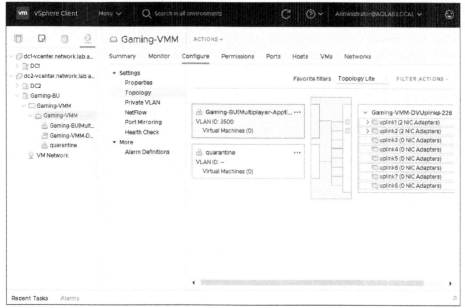

Figure 11-22   *Verifying Distributed Port Group Generation in vCenter*

Assigning VMs to Distributed Port Groups

In vCenter, navigate to the leftmost tab, called Hosts and Clusters, select a VM whose vNIC needs to be reassigned to the new distributed port group, click on the Actions menu, and select Edit Settings. Then, as shown in Figure 11-23, select the ACI-generated distributed port group under the desired network adapter configuration, and click OK.

Figure 11-23   *Reassigning a VM vNIC to a Distributed Port Group*

If the VM has a valid IP address for the associated EPG, it should become available on the network and become visible in ACI. For validation of proper learning, navigate to the EPG, select the Operational tab, and review the list of detected endpoints in the Client End-Points subtab. If troubleshooting is required, first evaluate any faults at the VMM domain and EPG levels.

Less Common VMM Domain Association Settings

Let's take a look at some more VMM domain association settings by pushing another EPG into vCenter. On the Add VMM Domain Association page shown in Figure 11-24, enter an explicit delimiter character in the Delimiter field. By default, eight uplinks can potentially be active for each distributed port group if the Active Uplinks and Standby Uplinks settings remain unchanged. Selecting the comma-separated values 1,2 for Active Uplinks Order and 3,4 for Standby Uplinks ensures that the remaining uplinks (5 through 8) are unavailable to this particular distributed port group. Finally, select a value for the custom EPG name and click Submit.

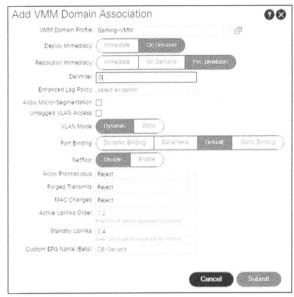

Figure 11-24 *Tweaking VMM Domain Association Settings*

Figure 11-25 shows the result of these changes. The resulting distributed port group generated in vCenter has a custom name. The attribute ACI_IFC_EPG_Name in the Custom Attributes view, however, continues to show the EPG name (using the new delimiter value) that would have been selected if the Custom EPG Name field had not been populated.

When editing the settings of the distributed port group, it is clear that the first two uplinks have been set as Active and appear in the order entered in ACI. The next two uplinks appear in the Standby uplinks list, and any further uplinks remain unused for this distributed port group (see Figure 11-26).

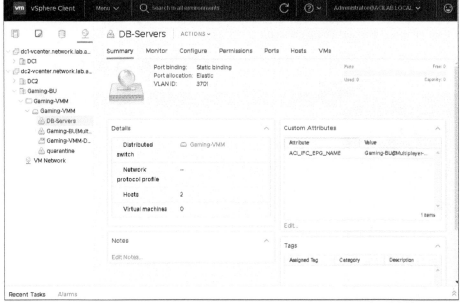

Figure 11-25 *Verifying the Result of Custom EPG Naming and Delimiter Modification*

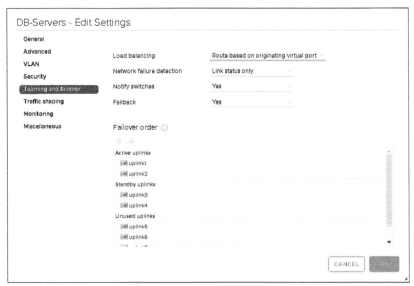

Figure 11-26 *Verifying the Result of Active Uplinks and Standby Uplinks Settings*

Enhanced LACP Policy Support

Let's say that you want an ACI-generated VDS to have multiple sets of uplink port channels and want to allow some traffic to flow over one port channel and other traffic to flow over a separate port channel. This capability involves enhanced LACP policy support.

To implement enhanced LACP policy support, navigate to Virtual Networking, select the desired VMM domain, click Policy, and select vSwitch Policy. Then select a port channel policy that enables LACP. Next, define a name and load-balancing mode for each logical LACP port channel that should be created on the VDS. Figure 11-27 shows two sets of LACP uplink port channels being created.

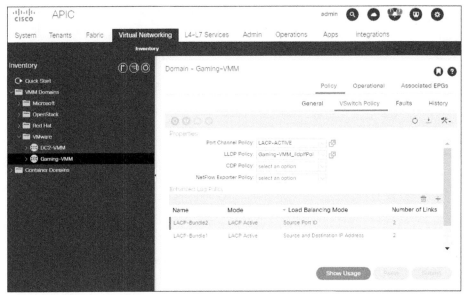

Figure 11-27 *Configuring an Enhanced LAG Policy*

This is more likely a policy you would deploy before hosts are added to the VDS. When hosts are being added to the VDS, you can assign hypervisor uplinks to the uplink port groups that resemble the logical port channel name configured earlier. Figure 11-28 shows two ports on each hypervisor being added to the port channel named LACP-Bundle1.

Gaming-VMM - Add and Manage Hosts

✓ 1 Select task
✓ 2 Select hosts
3 Manage physical adapters
4 Manage VMkernel adapt...
5 Migrate VM networking
6 Ready to complete

Manage physical adapters
Add or remove physical network adapters to this distributed switch.

📇 Assign uplink   ✕ Unassign adapter   ⓘ View settings

Host/Physical Network Adapters	In Use by Swi...	Uplink	Uplink Port Group
▲ 🖥 10.233.64.181			
▲ On this switch			
🔲 vmnic2 (Assigned)	--	LACP-Bundle1-0	Gaming-VMM-DV...
🔲 vmnic3 (Assigned)	--	LACP-Bundle1-1	Gaming-VMM-DV...
▲ On other switches/unclaimed			
🔲 vmnic0	vSwitch0	--	--
🔲 vmnic1	vSwitch0	--	--
▲ 🖥 10.233.64.182			
▲ On this switch			
🔲 vmnic2 (Assigned)	--	LACP-Bundle1-0	Gaming-VMM-DV...
🔲 vmnic3 (Assigned)	--	LACP-Bundle1-1	Gaming-VMM-DV...
▲ On other switches/unclaimed			

CANCEL   BACK   NEXT

Figure 11-28 *Assigning ESXi Host Uplinks to a Link Aggregation Group*

After ESXi hosts have been added to the VDS, navigate to an EPG that has been pushed to vCenter and edit its VMM domain association. Figure 11-29 shows an EPG being associated with an enhanced LAG policy named LACP-Bundle1.

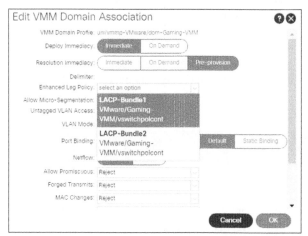

Figure 11-29 *Assigning an Enhanced LAG Policy to an EPG VMM Domain Association*

As a result of this change, traffic in the distributed port group begins to flow solely over the selected uplink port channel, as shown in Figure 11-30.

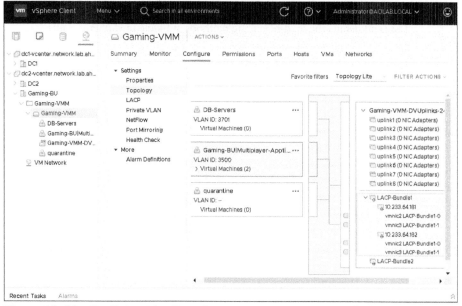

Figure 11-30 *Verifying Distributed Port Group Mapping to Uplinks*

Exam Preparation Tasks

As mentioned in the section "How to Use This Book" in the Introduction, you have a couple of choices for exam preparation: Chapter 17, "Final Preparation," and the exam simulation questions in the Pearson Test Prep Software Online.

Review All Key Topics

Review the most important topics in this chapter, noted with the Key Topic icon in the outer margin of the page. Table 11-3 lists these key topics and the page number on which each is found.

Table 11-3 Key Topics for Chapter 11

Key Topic Element	Description	Page Number
Paragraph	Defines some basic terminology important to understanding vSphere networking	395
Paragraph	Describes vSphere distributed switches	397
Paragraph	Describes the significance of VMkernel adapters with management services enabled	397
List	Describes port binding types in vSphere and lists the significance of each	400
Paragraph	Details best practices around use of static binding and ephemeral settings	400
List	Lists and details the load-balancing methods available in vSphere	401
Table 11-2	Describes vSphere teaming and failover settings	402
Paragraph	Describes the significance of the data center object in vSphere in VDS deployment and therefore VMM integration	404
List	Describes resolution immediacy and details relevant configuration options	405
Paragraph	Describes a key use case for the Pre-Provision resolution immediacy setting	406
List	Describes deployment immediacy and details the two configuration options involving deployment immediacy	406
Figure 11-7	Demonstrates steps to configure a basic VMM domain profile	408
Figure 11-8	Shows how to enter credentials into ACI to allow APICs to generate API calls against vCenter instances	409
Figure 11-9	Demonstrates how to enter vCenter access information in a VMM domain profile	410
Figure 11-10	Demonstrates further steps to configure a basic VMM domain profile	410
Figure 11-21	Demonstrates how an administrator can push an EPG into vCenter as a distributed port group	416
Paragraph	Calls out the location in the ACI GUI where VMM-learned endpoints in an EPG should appear	418

Complete Tables and Lists from Memory

Print a copy of Appendix C, "Memory Tables" (found on the companion website), or at least the section for this chapter, and complete the tables and lists from memory. Appendix D, "Memory Tables Answer Key" (also on the companion website), includes completed tables and lists you can use to check your work.

Define Key Terms

Define the following key terms from this chapter and check your answers in the glossary:

vSphere standard switch (vSwitch), vmnic, VM vNIC, port group, VMkernel adapter, vSphere distributed switch (VDS), port binding, vSphere load balancing, resolution immediacy, deployment immediacy

11

## CHAPTER 12

Implementing Service Graphs

This chapter covers the following topics:

Service Graph Fundamentals: This section covers service graph theory, including the management models, benefits, and bridge domain configurations.

Service Graph Implementation Workflow: This section provides a high-level overview of the steps necessary to deploy service graphs.

Service Graph Implementation Examples: This section goes through several service graph deployment examples step by step to solidify the concepts.

This chapter covers the following exam topic:

- 4.3 Implement service graph (managed and unmanaged)

Traditional methods of inserting services devices such as firewalls and load balancers between endpoints often involve architecting the network to ensure that basic routing and switching rules guide traffic through firewalls. It is also typical to have no integration between traditional networks and stateful services devices.

ACI supports all the traditional methods of inserting Layer 4 through Layer 7 services between endpoints, but with service graphs, it also introduces new management models for L4–L7 services. These new management models enable deeper integration between the network and services devices, aligning the network with the ongoing industry shifts toward automation and cross-platform integration.

With service graphs, ACI can also enable selective redirection of traffic to services devices, even if services devices are outside the normal forwarding path.

This chapter does not go into traditional methods of attaching firewalls and load balancers to networks. Rather, it provides implementation guidance on how some of the most commonly deployed traditional services attachment designs can be translated into service graphs.

"Do I Know This Already?" Quiz

The "Do I Know This Already?" quiz allows you to assess whether you should read this entire chapter thoroughly or jump to the "Exam Preparation Tasks" section. If you are in doubt about your answers to these questions or your own assessment of your knowledge of the topics, read the entire chapter. Table 12-1 lists the major headings in this chapter and their corresponding "Do I Know This Already?" quiz questions. You can find the answers in Appendix A, "Answers to the 'Do I Know This Already?' Questions."

Table 12-1 "Do I Know This Already?" Section-to-Question Mapping

Foundation Topics Section	Questions
Service Graph Fundamentals	1–5
Service Graph Implementation Workflow	6–8
Service Graph Implementation Examples	9, 10

CAUTION The goal of self-assessment is to gauge your mastery of the topics in this chapter. If you do not know the answer to a question or are only partially sure of the answer, you should mark that question as wrong for purposes of the self-assessment. Giving yourself credit for an answer you correctly guess skews your self-assessment results and might provide you with a false sense of security.

1. Which service insertion model enables ACI to manage the entire configuration of an L4–L7 services device?

    a. Manual service insertion

    b. Network policy mode

    c. Service manager mode

    d. Service policy mode

2. True or false: A device package should be used only when configuring L4–L7 devices in service policy mode.

    a. True

    b. False

3. True or false: When deploying a service graph without PBR, ACI effectively steers the desired traffic to the L4–L7 devices, even if they are outside the normal routing and switching path for interesting traffic.

    a. True

    b. False

4. What is the name for the process APICs go through to translate user intentions expressed in service graph configurations into a path through the services devices?

    a. Rendering

    b. Connector configuration

    c. Template instantiation

    d. Device selection policies

5. When using non-PBR service graphs to deploy a transparent firewall that bridges traffic between endpoints in a single subnet, which deployment mode should be used, and how many bridge domains are needed?

    a. One-arm mode and one bridge domain

    b. GoTo mode and two bridge domains

    c. GoThrough mode and two bridge domains

    d. GoThrough mode and one bridge domain

6. Which policy associates one or more L4–L7 devices to a service graph template and contract?

   a. Device package

   b. Function profile

   c. L4–L7 service graph policy

   d. Device selection policy

7. In a service policy mode environment that has granular role-based access control implemented, how can a services administrator dictate that only specified configuration settings be deployed to services appliances?

   a. Create a function profile and mark parameters of interest with the mandatory attribute.

   b. There is no need. L4–L7 devices are not managed by ACI in service policy mode.

   c. Prevent any users who may want to change firewall configurations from ACI from having access to the fabric in the first place.

   d. Create a function profile, set values for the parameters that should not change, and set the Locked attribute to True.

8. True or false: A service graph template determines which EPGs communicate indirectly through L4–L7 services devices.

   a. True

   b. False

9. True or false: Selecting Virtual as the L4–L7 services device attachment method necessitates VMM integration.

   a. True

   b. False

10. Which of the following items refers to a series of appliance interfaces that require common interface configurations and map directly to physical or virtual interfaces?

   a. Concrete interfaces

   b. Consumer connector interface

   c. Provider connector interface

   d. Cluster interfaces

Foundation Topics

Service Graph Fundamentals

Common Layer 4 through Layer 7 services include firewalls, load balancers, traffic inspection appliances, SSL offload functions, and application flow acceleration functions.

Traditionally, inserting these types of services required a highly complicated and manual process of VLAN or VRF stitching between network devices and services appliances. In addition to the fact that deployment of services may necessitate weeks of cross-team coordination and planning, it was difficult to scale services up or down based on load. And, once an application was retired, there was no automated way to remove associated service appliance configurations.

ACI addresses these types of issues by providing customers with a plethora of options in addition to traditional VRF and VLAN stitching methods to automate service insertion tasks based on their comfortability level and technical requirements. This service insertion automation is accomplished through deployment of service graphs.

Service Graphs as Concatenation of Functions

A *service graph* is a variation on the concept of a contract. In ACI, a contract whitelists communication between two endpoint groups (EPGs). This same whitelisting concept can also be extended to functions such as traffic filtering, traffic load balancing, and SSL offloading. When a contract has been associated with a service graph policy, ACI locates the devices that provide the functions defined by the policy and inserts them into the path. A service graph is, therefore, a concatenation of functions (and not of network devices).

The significance of using contracts as a tool for implementing service functions is not limited to just inserting services devices into the path. Each subject within a contract allows association of a different service graph to matched traffic. Figure 12-1 shows how the allocation of different service graphs to different subjects within a contract can enable very granular control over the flow of traffic through L4–L7 services functions.

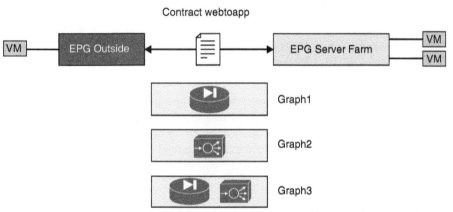

Figure 12-1 *Associating Different Service Graphs to Different Subjects Within a Contract*

Note that not all service graphs are created equally. The phrase "inserting services devices into the path" can be interpreted in two different ways from a traffic flow perspective:

- **Service graph with policy-based redirect (PBR):** The service graph effectively steers traffic to the L4–L7 device, redirecting traffic to the proper services devices even if they are outside the regular routing and switching path between the source and destination EPGs.

- **Service graph without PBR:** The service graph does not steer traffic to the L4–L7 device, but it does dictate that traffic flowing between the source and destination EPGs must pass through the functions identified by the service graph or be dropped. Only traffic that flows through the specified functions and is permitted by intermediate appliances is allowed to reach the intended destination EPG.

Effectively, service graphs without PBR necessitate that normal routing and switching rules steer traffic to services devices. That said, the enforcement of different functions between two EPGs through diversification of contract subjects, as indicated in Figure 12-1, typically requires some form of policy-based routing.

Because PBR is outside the scope of the DCACI 300-620 exam, this chapter focuses on the more basic service graph deployments.

Service Graph Management Models

In a large company, a network team typically manages the network, a security team manages the firewalls, and application delivery engineers manage load balancers. While this trend still exists, the desire for agility tends to push IT teams to become more aggregated. For ACI to align with these trends and to begin to bring teams together, Cisco has enabled integrations that use different operational models within the data center.

ACI has three management models for deploying service graphs:

- *Network policy mode* (**unmanaged mode**): This operational model aligns with the traditional approach of network engineers configuring network connectivity to L4–L7 devices without implementing any configurations on the L4–L7 devices themselves.

- *Service policy mode* (**managed mode**): In this operational model, the APICs handle not just the configuration of network connectivity to the L4–L7 devices but also the configuration of the L4–L7 devices. This approach is geared toward end-to-end infrastructure automation.

- *Service manager mode* (**hybrid mode**): With this operational model, the firewall and load balancer administrators define L4–L7 policies using traditional L4–L7 management tools. Network administrators apply a limited set of L4–L7 policies to service graphs. These policies are often limited to interface-level configurations. ACI automates networking to the L4–L7 devices and pushes only basic configurations to the L4–L7 devices.

> **NOTE**   ACI can trigger the instantiation of L4–L7 services devices using a feature called *service VM orchestration*. However, it is not very common for ACI to be the platform used to orchestrate the deployment of new services appliances. For ACI to integrate with an L4–L7 device via managed or hybrid mode and be able to push configurations, the services device needs to be bootstrapped with a minimum level of configuration that includes a management interface IP address and default gateway as well as enablement of any programmatic interface that allows the APIC to configure the appliance.

Understanding Network Policy Mode

When deploying service graphs in network policy mode, ACI automates the configuration of network connectivity to L4–L7 services appliances. This involves ACI potentially modifying bridge domain settings to bring BDs into compatibility with the associated service graph, creating shadow EPGs, mapping shadow EPGs to physical switch ports, whitelisting communication between shadow EPGs and the pertinent consumer or provider EPG(s), and finally associating the service graph policy with the relevant contract(s). In the event that the L4–L7 device is a virtual machine associated with an ACI-generated VDS, ACI also pushes the shadow EPGs into vCenter as VDS port groups and associates them with services appliance virtual network adapters.

NOTE A *shadow EPG* is any form of EPG automatically generated by ACI, typically for the purpose of automating enforcement of contracts between two components. To mandate that traffic flow from a consumer EPG through a services appliance, ACI creates a shadow EPG and assigns it to the consumer-side interface of the L4–L7 services device. A contract is then applied between this shadow EPG and the consumer EPG, and ACI needs to create another shadow EPG to associate with the egress interface of the appliance. These shadow EPGs are effectively placeholders for the application of additional contracts to enforce the desired traffic flow. Service graphs are *not* the only use case for shadow objects in ACI.

To better understand network policy mode, take a look at Figure 12-2, which provides a reminder of the central tenet of network policy mode that network administrators are responsible for configuring the network but not services appliances.

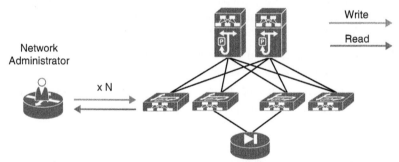

Figure 12-2 *Network Admins Only Configure the Network in Network Policy Mode*

Meanwhile, security and load balancer administrators continue to configure firewalls and load balancers either directly or by using the L4–L7 management tools they have always used, as shown in Figure 12-3.

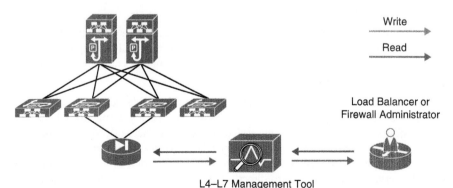

L4–L7 Management Tool

Figure 12-3 *Services Admins Experience No Change with Network Policy Mode*

Network policy mode service graphs are ideal when there is no need for firewalls to be decommissioned and provisioned again periodically (for example, with perimeter firewalls controlling access to the data center), there is no desire to change how teams manage data center infrastructure, or there is no support from an L4–L7 services device vendor for deployment of the device in service policy mode or service manager mode.

Understanding Service Policy Mode

In environments in which there is a desire for deep integration between all infrastructure components in the data center and IT expects all configurations to be scripted, the APICs can be used as the central point of automating not just the network but also L4–L7 services device configurations. Full automation of L4–L7 services device configuration through ACI requires that services devices be identified to ACI in service policy mode.

Before ACI can configure a load balancer or firewall, an administrator needs to upload or import a device package for the appliance to the APICs. This is what enables ACI to speak to its APIs.

A *device package* is a zip file that an ACI administrator obtains from an L4–L7 services appliance vendor and imports into the APICs. It includes a description of the device, the functions it performs, and a laundry list of parameters exposed to the APIC. When a device package is uploaded/imported to the APICs, ACI gains a full understanding of what a services device can do, how it connects to the fabric, how to deliver traffic to the device, how to receive return traffic from it, and how to translate user intent to the device.

The Cisco Adaptive Security Appliance (ASA) is an example of a L4–L7 services device that can run in service policy mode and that supports feature-rich device packages.

Device packages designed for service policy mode often expose a large amount of information to ACI, sometimes allowing the L4–L7 device to be configured almost entirely from the APIC.

The main mechanism L4–L7 services device administrators use to define configuration parameters in ACI to feed back to services devices is *function profiles*. Configurations defined in function profiles may be amended at the time of service graph deployment. When a vendor creates a device package, it defines a number of function profiles corresponding with the various functions provided by the services device. The vendor populates default values for some parameters within function profiles. Administrators can then modify the bulk of the default values to suit their needs.

Figure 12-4 shows the creation of a custom function profile for a device that will operate in service policy mode. Notice that the range of configurations that ACI can deploy to the type of firewall for which this function profile is being created includes not only interface configurations but also access lists and NAT.

Figure 12-5 illustrates the change in the data center management model achieved with service policy mode. Notice that ACI function profiles are the primary avenue for L4–L7 services administrators to dictate policies in service policy mode. Network administrators typically leverage function profiles preconfigured by L4–L7 services administrators when deploying service graphs. With this model, role-based access control is often implemented to enable L4–L7 services administrators to directly log in to APICs and configure function profiles and perhaps service graph templates. Monitoring of L4–L7 services appliances continues to take place within the L4–L7 management tool or services devices themselves. The integration between ACI and L4–L7 services devices also ensures that ACI is able to query services devices for health and to ensure that configurations have not been modified. In service policy mode, ACI may take corrective action and update L4–L7 device configurations if configurations are modified locally on L4–L7 services devices.

Figure 12-4   *Function Profile for Configuration of L4–L7 Devices in Service Policy Mode*

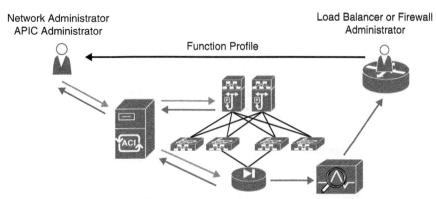

Figure 12-5   *Service Policy Mode Management Model in Review*

One difference between service policy mode and traditional service insertion methods is that this mode forces IT teams to configure security and load-balancing rules at the same time the network configurations for the service graph are applied.

A differentiator for this management model is that it automates and manages the lifecycle of security rules, load-balancing rules, and network connectivity and aligns them with one another. When a service graph is deleted, ACI automatically removes relevant configurations within ACI and on associated L4–L7 services devices.

At the same time, a negative aspect of service policy mode is that it creates a dependency between the ACI code versions, L4–L7 services device software versions, and associated device packages.

Understanding Service Manager Mode

One positive aspect of network policy mode is that it is easy to deploy and has very few associated caveats. Furthermore, configuration changes at the firewall or load balancer level very seldom bring about the need for a service graph redeployment when network policy mode is used.

Compared to network policy mode, service policy mode is more difficult to operationalize and support unless careful consideration is given to ensuring optimal object reuse. Because service policy mode ties firewall configuration to service graphs, it is common to need to redeploy service graphs for firewall changes to take effect. Also, the sheer number of parameters exposed to APICs through device packages makes the APIC GUI less user-friendly than native firewall and load balancer management applications for implementing configuration changes on L4–L7 services devices.

Service manager mode sits at the intersection between network policy mode and service policy mode and is often acknowledged as the best of both worlds. The idea behind service manager mode is that the APICs should be able to automate network policy and stitch traffic all the way to the L4–L7 services devices but also have the ability to automate certain basic configurations on the L4–L7 devices themselves. The most important facet of this hybrid approach is that function profiles within ACI do not serve as the primary tool for L4–L7 services device configuration. Instead, services administrators deploy the bulk of L4–L7 configurations independently of ACI in the L4–L7 management tool produced by the associated services device vendors.

Figure 12-6 illustrates the management model achieved via service manager mode. Firewall and load balancer administrators define L4–L7 policies within the L4–L7 management tool supported by the L4–L7 device vendor. Example L4–L7 management solutions that support service manager mode include Cisco Firepower Management Center (FMC) and Citrix NetScaler Management and Analytics System (MAS). The service graph deployment process in this case merely references the names of policies created within the L4–L7 management tool to ensure that appliance interfaces as well as ACI endpoints get assigned to the correct policies within the L4–L7 services management tool.

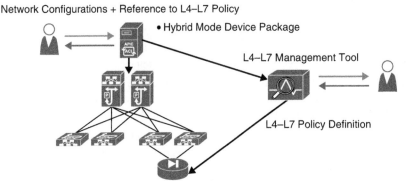

Figure 12-6 *Service Manager Mode Management Model*

Even though the diagram omits any reference of function profiles, it is important to under-stand that service manager mode uses function profiles. However, fewer parameters can actu-ally be configured in ACI through function profiles. Figure 12-7 shows a function profile for FMC-integrated Firepower Threat Defense firewalls that will be deployed in service manager mode. Notice that most of the configuration parameters that the device package allows ACI to deploy to FMC are limited to the configuration of interfaces and the association of pre-created policies to these interfaces. Now, contrast this with Figure 12-4, shown earlier in the chapter.

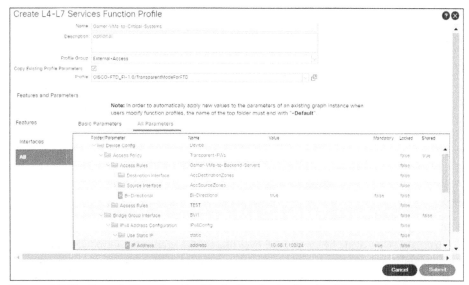

Figure 12-7 *Sample Function Profile for Device in Service Manager Mode*

There are three minor implementation differences between service policy mode and service manager mode:

- The APIC administrator needs to import a special device package that supports service manager mode.

- The APIC administrator needs to define a ***device manager***, which calls out the IP address, communication protocol, and credentials for APIC access to the L4–L7 man-agement solution.

- When the APIC administrator identifies L4–L7 devices to the fabric, the associated device manager configuration needs to be referenced.

NOTE Note that the implementation differences outlined are generalizations rather than firm rules.

Figure 12-8 shows a sample configuration of a device manager in ACI. Note that a management EPG needs to be defined only if ACI in-band management is used to access the L4–L7 management application. Device managers can be defined under **Services > L4–L7 > Device Managers** within each tenant.

Figure 12-8   *Configuration of a Device Manager Within a Tenant*

When to Use Service Graphs

Few concepts in ACI boggle heads and roll eyes like service graphs do. Opponents of service graphs sometimes like to point to the complexities involved with service policy mode and argue that the caveats associated with service graphs far outweigh the benefits. This argument misses the central point that this management model is most useful for creating elastic environments with rapid scale-out capabilities.

Furthermore, unmanaged mode provides benefits over manual service insertion, which makes it very useful in most environments. One such benefit is use of PBR.

Service graphs were never intended to be used in all ACI deployments. Service graphs should be deployed when there are tangible benefits to their use when compared to manual service insertion.

Service graphs offer the following advantages, among others.

- A service graph with PBR can redirect traffic to L4–L7 devices, eliminating the need for more complex designs.

- Service graphs automatically manage VLAN assignments.

- Service graphs automatically connect virtual network interface cards (vNICs).

- Associated configuration templates can be reused multiple times.

- A service graph provides a logical view of the network and offers an application-related view of services.

■ A service graph provides a good model for sharing a device across multiple departments.

■ A service graph collects health scores from a device or service.

■ A service graph collects statistics from the services devices.

■ Service graphs can update firewall ACLs and load balancer server pools automatically using endpoint discovery.

It is only when an IT team sees tangible benefits in service graphs for a given environment that service graphs should be embraced over manual insertion methods. Otherwise, there is a risk that IT may be introducing capabilities that operations teams do not comprehend or that they are reluctant to support.

Choosing an L4–L7 Services Integration Method

Cisco has created the flowchart shown in Figure 12-9 to provide very high-level guidance in deciding how to integrate L4–L7 services, given very general requirements.

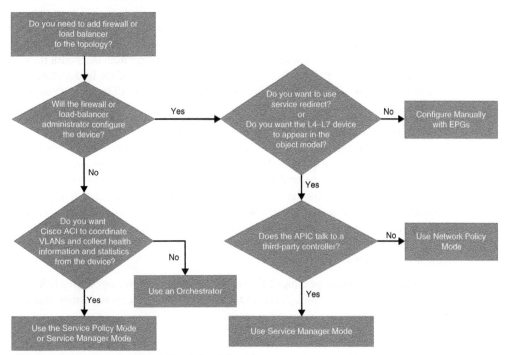

Figure 12-9 *Service Graph Decision Flowchart*

Understanding Deployment Modes and the Number of BDs Required

ACI supports the following device deployment modes for non-PBR L4–L7 devices with a service graph:

■ **GoTo:** In this mode, the default gateway for servers is the L4–L7 device. This mode requires use of separate bridge domains for consumer-side and provider-side interfaces unless PBR is used. This mode is also known as *routed* mode.

- **GoThrough:** This mode requires use of two separate bridge domains. In this mode, the default gateway for the servers is the consumer-side bridge domain. The provider-side bridge domain should *not* be configured to perform routing. The L4–L7 device bridges the consumer-side bridge domain and the provider-side bridge domain. This mode is also known as *transparent* mode, or bridged mode.

- **One-arm:** In this mode, the default gateway for any servers is the server-side bridge domain. The load balancer connects to the fabric using a single bridge domain that serves as the default gateway for the load balancer itself. The services device is inserted into the topology using source NAT (SNAT), which ensures receipt of the return traffic.

Deploying Service Graphs for Devices in GoTo Mode

Three designs are valid and can be used for deployment of non-PBR service graphs with devices in routed mode:

- **Routed mode with outside Layer 2 bridge domain:** In this implementation, ACI may function as a Layer 2 transit for endpoints behind an L4–L7 services device. In this design, it is the job of an external router to direct traffic to the services device. This is a common design for companies that need to move a firewall containing DMZ subnets into ACI but that do not want to rearchitect their DMZ environments until they gain more familiarity with ACI. From an ACI perspective, none of the bridge domains connecting to the L4–L7 services devices or extending the firewall traffic outside the fabric have routing enabled.

- **Routed mode with L3Out and NAT:** In this case, a services device external interface, for instance, may connect to ACI using a bridge domain that has a subnet defined with routing enabled. The services device internal interface connects to another bridge domain. If routing were to be enabled on this internal bridge domain without NAT, there would be no reason for the fabric to send traffic to the L4–L7 device; routing to the destination could happen directly. With NAT enabled, client machines need to go to the services device. Because NAT ranges fall into the external bridge domain subnet range, it is possible to advertise the NAT range outside the fabric over an L3Out using regular bridge domain advertisements.

- **Routed mode with route peering:** This basically involves ACI learning routes behind an L4–L7 services device through an L3Out. (This option is discussed further later in this chapter.)

Figure 12-10 illustrates use of ACI as a Layer 2 network with an external router directing traffic to the L4–L7 services device(s).

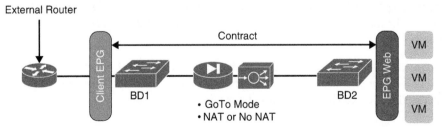

Figure 12-10 *Routed Mode with an Outside Layer 2 Bridge Domain*

Figure 12-11 illustrates the use of NAT and a routable external bridge domain to direct traffic to the services device(s).

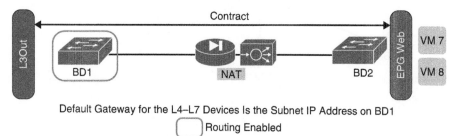

Figure 12-11   *Routed Mode with L3Out and NAT*

Deploying Service Graphs for Devices in GoThrough Mode

Two common non-PBR implementations allow transparent devices to leverage service graphs:

■ **Transparent mode with an outside Layer 2 bridge domain:** In this design, ACI functions as a Layer 2 transit because both the outside and inside of the service graph connect to Layer 2 bridge domains. It is the job of an external routing device to direct traffic to the services device.

■ **Transparent mode with L3Out:** In this design, the outside bridge domain of a service graph connects to the outside network through routing provided by the Cisco ACI fabric.

Use of ACI as a Layer 2 transit is typically straightforward. Figure 12-12 shows a transparent mode deployment with an L3Out and required bridge domain settings.

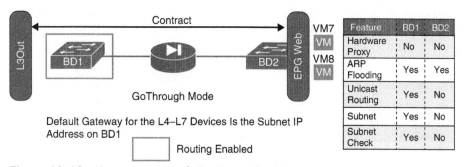

Feature	BD1	BD2
Hardware Proxy	No	No
ARP Flooding	Yes	Yes
Unicast Routing	Yes	No
Subnet	Yes	No
Subnet Check	Yes	No

Figure 12-12   *Transparent Mode Design with L3Out*

Deploying Service Graphs for One-Arm Load Balancers

Figure 12-13 illustrates a one-arm load balancer deployment using SNAT. This design leverages one bridge domain for ACI to connect to the load balancer, and the server and client sides of the communication are likely to each be in bridge domains of their own.

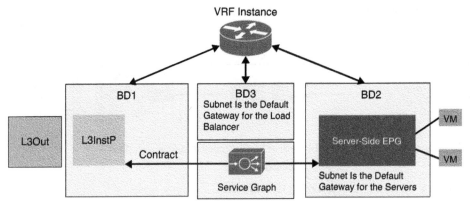

Figure 12-13   *Load Balancer Deployed in One-Arm Mode in ACI*

Understanding Route Peering

Not all of the designs mentioned in the previous sections allow use of ACI anycast default gateways for east–west traffic optimization. From a contract application perspective, the majority of design options covered are less flexible than alternate design options that move the default gateways for all subnets into ACI and attempt to eliminate the need for NAT.

Figure 12-14 shows a VRF sandwich design. This design places each interface of an L4–L7 services device and therefore each associated bridge domain in a different VRF. Because of this, there is no potential for endpoints behind different subnets to communicate with one another directly in the absence of transit routing. ACI then establishes a separate L3Out with the L4–L7 services device in each VRF. This design is highly recommended when PBR is not an option because it forces traffic through services devices due to the existence of different IP spaces in each VRF. It also enables administrators to move server default gateways in all VRFs into ACI to fully leverage ACI anycast default gateways. Either static routing or dynamic routing can be used to advertise any subnets behind the services device.

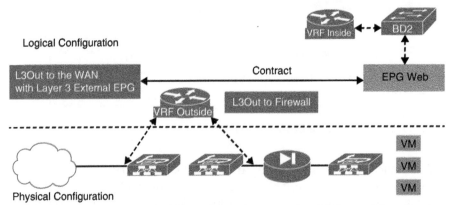

Figure 12-14   *Route Peering Through Deployment of an L3Out and Interface in Each VRF*

12

NOTE It is good to understand this design, but is not very likely to be a DCACI 300-620 exam topic because most route peering use cases fall into the gray area of transit routing.

Understanding Dynamic Endpoint Attach

One popular capability with service graphs and a good case in point for harmonious cross-platform integrations within ACI is the *dynamic endpoint attach* feature.

Let's take a look at the benefits of this feature for application delivery controllers as an example. An application delivery engineer defines a virtual server using an IP address and port. The virtual server is typically a frontend IP address provided via DNS to client machines that load balances traffic across multiple backend servers. When integrated with ACI through service manager mode or service policy mode, an EPG can be created to identify the backend servers that correspond with the virtual server. Through this type of integration, ACI is able to communicate endpoint attachment and detachment events to load balancers, thereby dynamically increasing or decreasing the size of the backend server pool without the need for manual configuration or scripting.

The beauty of this feature and this type of integration using service manager mode is that it does not require a drastic management model change but provides many benefits that reduce the need for manual changes in the network.

The dynamic endpoint attach feature can also be used to communicate EPG names and update EPG members on firewalls dynamically to help security administrators in the creation of firewall rules based on EPGs as objects.

Understanding Bridge Domain Settings for Service Graphs

When guiding traffic to or through services devices without PBR, it is often necessary to modify the following settings to accommodate various designs:

- L2 Unknown Unicast

- ARP Flooding

- Unicast Routing

- Subnets

When a device is deployed in routed mode, the goal is to place default gateways on L4–L7 services devices and not in ACI. Therefore, the following BD settings should be used (unless PBR is being used in conjunction with default gateways in the fabric):

- **L2 Unknown Unicast:** Flood

- **ARP Flooding:** Enabled

- **Unicast Routing:** Disabled

- **Subnets:** N/A

Generally speaking, it is highly recommended to use flooding and enable ARP for bridge domains that connect to L4–L7 services devices. Two reasons for this are as follows:

- Some L4–L7 devices in transparent (GoThrough) mode rely on flooding to build the forwarding tables, just like a transparent bridge does.

- When an L4–L7 device fails over, the IP address of that device may or may not change the MAC address as well. If it does change the MAC address, the Gratuitous ARP (GARP) traffic generated by the L4–L7 device must reach the ARP cache of the adjacent devices. For this to happen, ARP flooding must be enabled.

To accommodate transparent firewall deployments, you should enable ARP flooding and set L2 Unknown Unicast to Flood. If these two settings are not pre-selected, ACI modifies bridge domain settings to conform with these requirements.

In spite of the general recommendations provided on bridge domain settings, there are instances when a bridge domain connecting a service graph can be set to Hardware Proxy to minimize flooding. Figure 12-15 shows an example. Because GoThrough mode does not allow use of Hardware Proxy, we can assume that devices in this figure are in GoTo mode.

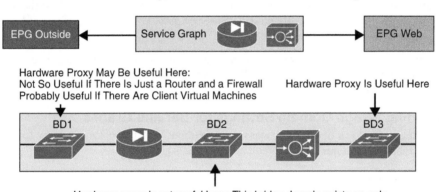

Figure 12-15 *Service Chain with Use Case for Hardware Proxy in BD3*

This illustration depicts a multimode service chain. A ***service chain*** is merely a succession of functions. Here, traffic from Outside to Web flows through a firewall and then a load balancer. BD2 is an intermediary bridge domain that connects the two appliances. There is very little to optimize in terms of flooding in BD2 since the only devices in it are the two services devices. Assuming that BD1 connects the firewall to an L3Out, there is also likely to be little benefit in moving away from flooding in this bridge domain. However, if BD3 connects to servers, use of Hardware Proxy can help server performance by minimizing flooding.

Understanding Service Graph Rendering

Once users define a service graph, the APICs translate the user intentions expressed in the service graph into a path through the services devices. This translation of intent is called *rendering*.

Depending on the service graph management model, the process of rendering can involve configuration of network policies or potentially even deployment of configurations on services appliances.

The end goal of the rendering process is to make sure that the only acceptable path between EPGs is the path defined in the service graph.

Service Graph Implementation Workflow

The following high-level steps are required to implement service graphs:

Step 1. Import device packages (if L4–L7 services devices are deployed in managed or hybrid mode).

Step 2. Identify L4–L7 devices to the fabric.

Step 3. (Optional) Create custom function profiles.

Step 4. Configure a service graph template.

Step 5. (Optional) Configure device selection policies.

Step 6. Apply the service graph template.

Step 7. (Optional) Configure additional service graph parameters.

Step 8. Monitor the service graph and devices to confirm proper implementation.

The following sections describe these steps.

Importing Device Packages

You import device packages into ACI by selecting **L4–L7 Services > Packages**. Figure 12-16 shows the General tab for a sample device package.

Figure 12-16 *General Information Page for a Device Package Imported into ACI*

A device package contains the components described in Table 12-2.

Table 12-2 Components of a Device Package

Device Package Component	Description

Device specification	An XML file that defines the following:
	
	■ Device properties:
	  ■ **Model:** Model of the device
	  ■ **Vendor:** Vendor of the device
	  ■ **Version:** Software version of the device
	■ Functions provided by the device
	■ Interfaces and network connectivity information for each function
	■ Device configuration parameters
	■ Configuration parameters for each function

Device script	A Python script that allows the APICs to interact with the device. The device script maps APIC events to function calls. A device package can contain multiple device scripts. A device script can interface with services devices via REST, SSH, or any similar mechanism.
Function Profile	An L4–L7 configuration template that includes configuration values for deployment to L4–L7 services devices. When a vendor creates a device package, it typically defines a number of function profiles corresponding with the various functions provided by the services device. The vendor populates default values for a number of parameters within each function profile. Administrators can modify most of the default values to suit their requirements.
Device-level configuration parameters	A configuration file that specifies parameters that are required by a device. This configuration can be shared by one or more service graphs.

When an administrator imports a device package to the APICs, various subfolders appear under the installed device package. Figure 12-17 shows the L4–L7 Services Function Profiles page for a sample device package. Function profiles may differ dramatically based on the profiles' purposes. For instance, a function profile used to configure a transparent firewall may include parameters to configure a BVI, while a function profile for a firewall in routed mode may require that IP addresses be assigned to each firewall interface configured.

A vendor may include multiple function profiles for a given use case with only minor differences in the parameters included. (For example, there are multiple routed mode function profiles in Figure 12-17.) This ensures that services administrators have a wide range of templates to choose from when deciding which function profiles are best suited to an environment.

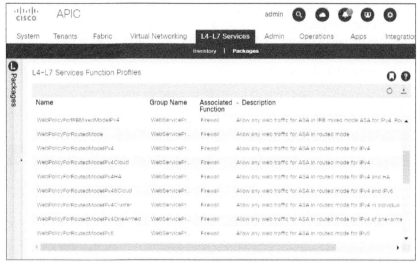

Figure 12-17 *Function Profiles Included in a Sample Device Package*

Identifying L4–L7 Devices to the Fabric

You configure L4–L7 services by opening the tenant where they will be used and navigating to **Services > L4–L7 > Create L4–L7 Devices.** Any services devices that need to be shared across multiple tenants need to be exported to the other tenants. This is true even for L4–L7 services devices defined in the common tenant.

Figure 12-18 shows two L4–L7 devices being identified to ACI as a high-availability pair. A configuration that enables the Managed checkbox and has an L4–L7 service manager defined under the Device Manager pull-down usually points to service manager mode. On the other hand, a device definition that enables only the Managed checkbox usually suggests a service policy mode deployment.

Figure 12-18 *Configuring a Firewall Pair to ACI in Service Manager Mode*

An L4–L7 services appliance that will be used in a service graph template is called a *concrete device*. Services appliances are often deployed as a pair of active/active or active/standby devices. Concrete devices clustered together form a *logical device*. In Figure 12-18, the Devices section defines concrete devices, and the Cluster section maps concrete device interfaces to logical device interfaces.

Most of the configurations you have seen so far in the chapter are straightforward. Table 12-3 describes some of the items that may require additional information.

Table 12-3   Configuration Options in the Create L4–L7 Devices Page

Configuration	Description
Service Type	Three options are available in this drop-down box: ■ ADC ■ Firewall ■ Other
Device Type	Possible options available for this parameter include the following: ■ **Physical:** Bare-metal servers, physical appliances, or non-VMM integrated virtual environments ■ **Virtual:** A VM integrated using a VMM integration
VM Instantiation Policy	This configuration option is part of the service VM orchestration solution and enables APICs to trigger an instantiation of a VM template in vCenter.
Context Aware	This option specifies the context-awareness of the device, which can be one of the following: ■ **Single:** The device cluster cannot be shared across multiple tenants of a given type that are hosted on the provider network. You must give the device cluster to a specific tenant for a given user. ■ **Multiple:** The device cluster can be shared across multiple tenants of a given type that you are hosting on the provider network. For example, two hosting companies might share the same device. When defining a load balancer as a Layer 4 to Layer 7 services device, the Context Aware parameter is not used and can be ignored.
Function Type	This option refers to deployment modes, including GoThrough and GoTo for routed firewalls and transparent firewalls, respectively.

Creating Custom Function Profiles

With a function profile, a services administrator can create a collection of L4–L7 configuration templates that can be reused across service graphs.

To organize customized function profiles, administrators often group these policies for various purposes (for example, organizational hierarchy, purpose, environment). To create a function grouping, select **Services > L4–L7**, right-click Function Profiles, and select Create L4–L7 Services Function Group.

To create a function profile, right-click the Function Profiles folder and select Create L4–L7 Services Function Profile to launch the page shown in Figure 12-7, earlier in this chapter. Notice that Figure 12-7 shows the checkbox Copy Existing Profile Parameters enabled, and a profile included in a device package is selected from the Profile drop-down box. This indicates that the administrator would like to leverage a built-in function profile from the device package to create a more custom function profile.

On the Create L4–L7 Services Function Profile page, there are three columns to the right:

- **Mandatory:** If a parameter has this attribute set to true, the configuration item is mandatory. This attribute offers a way for vendors or L4–L7 services administrators to ensure entry of a value for certain parameters as a prerequisite for deployment of the service graph. If a parameter has been set as mandatory in a device package, custom function profiles cannot override this mandatory setting. In Figure 12-7, the L4–L7 services administrator mandates entry of an IP address to the BVI1 interface and enters a default value for this attribute.

- **Locked:** L4–L7 parameters used by a service graph can be stored under the provider EPG, bridge domain, application profile, or tenant. When a graph is instantiated, the APIC resolves the needed configuration for a service graph by looking up the parameters in various places. If Locked has been set to true for a given parameter, parameter values set under the associated provider EPG, bridge domain, application profile, or tenant will be ignored when applying the service graph. If an administrator wants to ensure a specific value is used for a parameter within a function profile at all times, this option should be set to true.

- **Shared:** If this option is set to true, the parameter value in the function profile will be used unless a parameter value is set under a provider EPG, a bridge domain, an application profile, or a tenant. Therefore, setting the value in the Shared column for a parameter to true basically sets the value within the function profile as a modifiable default.

Configuring a Service Graph Template

A service graph template defines the desired functions through which certain traffic should flow without actually specifying the traffic (EPGs) to which it applies. Service graph templates are intended to be generic, so that they can be ported to multiple contracts between different EPGs when feasible. This generic nature also means that equivalent service graph templates calling the same functions can be deployed in different data centers and rendered with locally available services appliances.

Figure 12-19 shows a service graph template that chains a firewall and load balancer between a consumer and a provider EPG. To create a service graph template like this, you drag select device clusters (logical devices) from the left-hand column into the work pane in the middle of the screen. Each function is represented as a node. N1 and N2 are *function node* names. Service graph template subconfiguration gets tied to these function node names. Note also the consumer connectors and provider connectors represented by C and P, respectively. These represent connection points for shadow EPGs and application of traffic filters. As shown, service graph templates do not include a dramatic amount of information for each node. Primarily, the configuration includes the firewall or load balancer configuration type, the function profile (Profile) used for deployment of managed or hybrid mode devices, and whether the Route Redirect setting or PBR should be used.

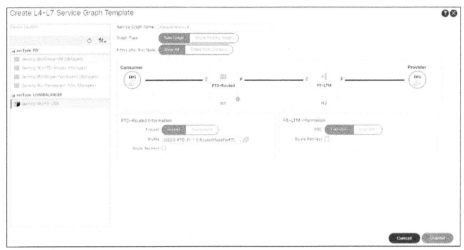

Figure 12-19   *Creating a Service Graph Template*

Configuring Device Selection Policies

As explained earlier in this chapter, service graphs insert L4–L7 devices into the traffic path. Device selection policies determine which L4–L7 devices are inserted.

In short, a *device selection policy*, or *logical device context*, is a policy that associates or ties one or more L4–L7 devices to a graph template and contract.

Among the benefits of separating device selection from service graphs is that if you have an existing firewall deployed in a graph and you want to replace it, you simply need to define where the new firewall is connected and how it should be managed. Then you reference the newly introduced firewall in the device selection policy, and the associated graph(s) then points to the new firewall. As part of rendering, ACI then configures the new firewall just like the existing one if the firewall has been configured in managed or hybrid mode.

Applying a Service Graph Template

Creation of a service graph template does not trigger a rendering of service graphs. A service graph template needs to first be instantiated. This can be done by right-clicking a service graph template and selecting Apply L4–L7 Service Graph Template. This launches a wizard that enables users to apply the service graph template to a consumer and a provider EPG by defining a new contract or adding the L4–L7 service policy to an existing contract. This wizard also requests user input regarding consumer connector and provider connector configurations. These connector configurations also include administrators specifying the consumer and provider bridge domains.

What is not evident in the service graph template application wizard is that this same process also prompts ACI to create a device selection policy behind the scenes.

An auto-generated device selection policy is bound to a single contract. For this reason, each time an administrator needs to reuse the service graph template for a new set of EPGs, the service graph template needs to be reapplied using the same wizard.

An alternative to this approach is to manually create a device selection policy that includes Any as the associated contract. Then, any application of the associated L4–L7 services policy in a new contract enables automatic reuse of the service graph template without having to go through the wizard again.

Configuring Additional Service Graph Parameters

When a graph is instantiated, the APIC resolves the needed configuration for a service graph by looking up the parameters in various places. These parameters are commonly placed at the provider EPG level or the tenant level.

For service graphs that have been instantiated and require configuration updates, it is sometimes easiest to make changes by navigating to **Services > L4–L7 > Service Parameters** in the desired tenant and updating the desired service graph parameters.

Monitoring Service Graphs and Devices

After a service graph has been instantiated, the best way to monitor it is to navigate to **Services > L4–L7 > Deployed Graph Instances** within the tenant where a service graph has been deployed and find the service graph instance in the list. The state applied means the graph has been applied and is active in the fabric and the services device.

To monitor devices, navigate to **Services > L4–L7 > Deployed Devices** in the tenant. You should be trying to achieve the operational state stable.

Any object directly or indirectly related to service graphs showing fault can be problematic for service graphs. Verify that there are no relevant faults and that the desired data plane forwarding is in place before announcing that the mission has been accomplished.

Service Graph Implementation Examples

It can be difficult to take in all the details of the service graph implementation workflow without an example, so this section solidifies the concepts covered so far in this chapter by showing how to configure some basic service graphs. These examples address a diversity of configuration options while also remaining as straightforward as possible.

Deploying an Unmanaged Firewall Pair in a Service Graph

In the example shown in Figure 12-20, two ASA transparent firewalls need to be integrated into a tenant named Gaming-BU to provide application inspection and segment two different EPGs. Base configurations and prohibitive firewall rules have already been put in place on the firewalls, and they have formed a high-availability pair. The firewalls are physical appliances and connect directly to the ACI fabric on ports 1/13 and 1/14 on leafs 301 and 302. The transparent firewalls need to be able to bridge traffic between an EPG called Frontend-Servers and another EPG called Backend-Servers.

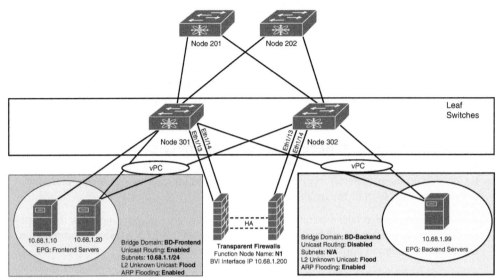

Figure 12-20 *Example for Unmanaged Transparent Firewall Insertion via Service Graphs*

Notice that two bridge domains are needed for this design. The subnet IP 10.68.1.1/24 assigned to BD-Frontend serves as the default gateway for endpoints in both EPGs. Removal of unicast routing capabilities together with the enablement of L2 unknown unicast flooding and ARP flooding on BD-Backend is required for insertion of the firewalls in the natural forwarding path between the EPGs.

Because devices outside the subnet beyond an L3Out may also at some point need access to endpoints in this subnet, one of these bridge domains needs to have unicast routing enabled—but which one? Service graphs that include transparent firewalls trigger faults when the provider-side bridge domain in the service graph enables IP routing. Hence, BD-Frontend has been selected as the routable bridge domain.

Given the requirements, there is no need to import device packages because the firewalls will be deployed in network policy mode.

Next, therefore, you need to identify the L4–L7 devices to the fabric. Open the tenant in which the L4–L7 device will be deployed and navigate to **Services > L4–L7**, right-click Devices, and select Create L4–L7 Devices to launch the wizard shown in Figure 12-21.

Because the firewalls are physical appliances, select Physical as the device type and select the physical domain to be used. Note that ACI deploys VLANs and stitches traffic for L4–L7 services devices. It is usually best to ensure that the VLAN pool associated with the selected physical domain has a dynamic VLAN range for ACI to choose from. In this example, Single has been selected to communicate to the system that the devices being defined will not be shared across tenants and will have no context awareness. Finally, select GoThrough as the function type to indicate that the devices are transparent firewalls.

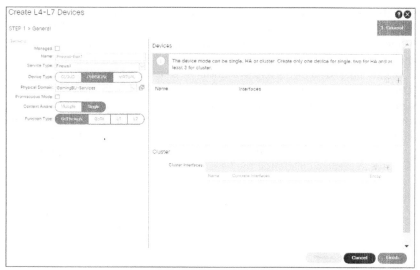

Figure 12-21   *Providing General Information About an L4–L7 Device to ACI*

NOTE   Starting from APIC Release 4.1, PBR can be used with L4–L7 services devices operating in L1 or L2 mode. Function type options L1 and L2 shown in Figure 12-21 refer to L1/L2 PBR.

When you are ready to configure concrete devices, click the + symbol in the Devices section to launch the page shown in Figure 12-22. Enter a name in the Name field to identify the first transparent firewall to ACI. Then enter interface names along with path information, one line at a time. Note that Figure 12-22 shows information entered only for the data interfaces because failover and state links are irrelevant when deploying service graphs for unmanaged devices. Click OK when you're finished making selections and then repeat the process to identify the standby firewall as an additional concrete device.

Figure 12-22   *Defining a Concrete Device to an ACI Fabric*

After you define the concrete devices, you need to define cluster interfaces. As opposed to concrete interfaces, cluster or logical interfaces are basically logical mappings to the interfaces on each concrete device. Put in a slightly different way, defining logical interfaces is like putting a label on interfaces that require similar policy assignment. Notice that Figure 12-23 uses the label Backend-Servers as a cluster interface name; as shown earlier, the concrete interface name for the interfaces is Backend. You can see through this example that the names assigned in the Name columns are truly arbitrary. The cluster interfaces need to accurately reference the concrete interface names, but beyond that, concrete interface names are barely used in any other ACI configuration. The cluster interfaces in particular are what other objects reference; therefore, user-friendly names for the cluster interfaces are recommended. Click Finish to execute creation of the L4–L7 device definitions.

Figure 12-23   *Mapping Cluster Interfaces to Concrete Interfaces on Each Device in a Pair*

With devices defined, it is time to create a service graph template. To do so, navigate to **Services > L4–L7** within the tenant, right-click Service Graph Templates, and select Create Service Graph Template.

Figure 12-24 shows an example with a service graph name and the transparent firewall pair just defined dropped into the work pane. By default, a node is assigned a function node name. This example uses the default function node name N1. This is the name the service graph uses to identify the first function of interest. If additional functions are added to form a service chain, these new functions are assigned different node names. Notice that the wizard has disabled all options for the firewall that has been dropped into the graph. This is because the devices have already been identified as transparent firewalls, and PBR is not an acceptable option for GoThrough devices. Finally, recall that service graph templates are intended to be reusable. Therefore, they focus on flow and functions and not on specific EPGs.

Next, you need to decide whether to configure device selection policies manually. In terms of non-PBR service graphs, this decision often depends on how many contracts need to leverage the service graph template. If a large number of contracts are needed, it is often most practical to define device selection policies with an any contract. Otherwise, the Apply

L4–L7 Service Graph Template to EPG(s) wizard automatically creates device selection policies, but the wizard then needs to be run again for each new contract. Because these firewalls are not expected to require any additional contracts, in this case you can apply the service graph template by using the wizard.

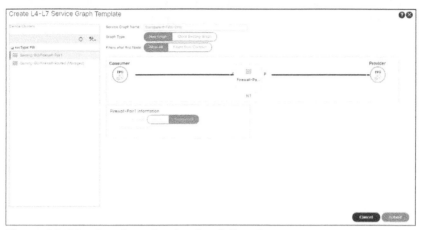

Figure 12-24 *Creating a Service Graph Template*

Another decision an implementation engineer needs to make is whether to deploy a custom function profile. This decision does not apply to the current deployment because function profiles are specific to managed and hybrid mode devices.

To instantiate a service graph template, right-click it and select Apply L4–L7 Service Graph Template to EPG(s). Figure 12-25 shows the wizard that appears. Identify the client-side EPG or external EPG in the Consumer EPG/External Network drop-down on the left. Select the server-side EPG in the Provider EPG/Internal Network drop-down. Then determine if the service graph policy should be attached to an already existing contract or whether the system should create one. When you ask ACI to create a contract by using the No Filter (Allow All Traffic) checkbox, ACI creates a subject using a filter in the common tenant that matches all traffic. Disable this checkbox if you want to match specific protocols only. Click Next to move on to the next step of the wizard.

Figure 12-25 *Applying a Service Graph Between Two EPGs Using the Wizard*

The second page in the wizard, shown in Figure 12-26, is where you configure provider connector and consumer connector interfaces. Based on the EPGs selected in the previous step, ACI attempts to intelligently populate the BD drop-down boxes. It is not always successful, but in this case, the EPGs are in the same subnet as the firewall interfaces. Therefore, the bridge domains ACI has selected are correct. Ensure that the correct cluster interface has been chosen for both the provider connector and the consumer connector and click Finish.

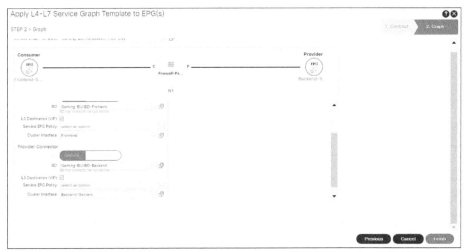

Figure 12-26 *Configuring Consumer Connector and Provider Connector Interfaces*

NOTE The L3 Destination (VIP) checkbox identifies nodes that do not require redirection when both PBR and non-PBR nodes are deployed in a service chain. Therefore, this checkbox is of no significance in the non-PBR service graph examples presented in this chapter. In addition, at the time of writing, the only thing that can be configured within a service EPG policy is preferred group membership.

As a result of instantiating the service graph template, ACI creates a device selection policy and applies a contract whose subject references the L4–L7 service policy to the consumer and provider EPGs selected by the user. ACI is then ready to render the newly created service graph. If any issues are identified during rendering, faults should appear. If you resolve the faults, forwarding should work as expected.

Sometimes there is a need to tell ACI that a given connector interface on a service graph template enables unicast routing. Figure 12-27 shows how to do so. A *terminal node* enables input and output through a service graph. In this case, terminal node T1 has been indicated to be the consumer. This terminal node correlates with connection C1. A connection represents an input or output point for a node. You can see that the Unicast Route parameter is set to True. Note that the Adjacency Type column has not been modified manually. If a connector is associated with a bridge domain that provides an L3Out interface function, however, the adjacency needs to be set to L3. In this example, this setting is insignificant.

The ultimate test of a service graph is whether traffic is forwarded correctly through the desired functions.

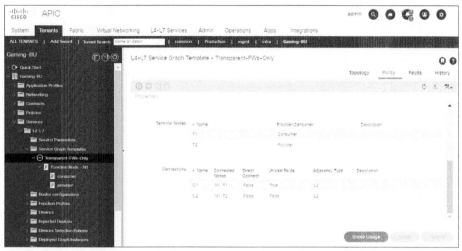

Figure 12-27 *Checking Whether Service Graph Template Connector Settings Are Correct*

NOTE Another valid design for non-PBR service graphs consisting of transparent firewalls is to have an external router function as the default gateway for the bridged subnet and provide routing functionality.

Deploying Service Graphs for a Firewall in Managed Mode

The example in this section involves service graphs for managed devices. Figure 12-28 shows the topology used for this example. In this case, the firewall is a virtual firewall within a VMM-integrated environment. This makes things easier because there is less concern about tracking physical interfaces. Both bridge domains have unicast routing disabled because the firewall serves as default gateway for endpoints within the two bridge domains.

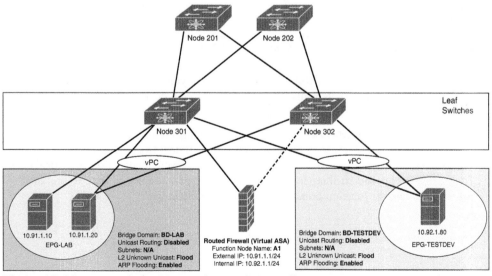

Figure 12-28 *Example for Managed Routed Firewall Insertion via Service Graphs*

A device package has already been imported for the appliance. Figure 12-29 shows creation of the L4–L7 device. The Managed checkbox is selected to signal to the system that the device should be deployed in service policy or service manager mode. The device package settings determine which of these two modes is supported. When device type Virtual is selected, ACI exposes the VMM Domain drop-down, and you can select the VMM domain where the virtual L4–L7 services device(s) have been deployed. Notice that selection of a device package and model is mandatory during managed mode device definition. Also notice the concrete device portion of the screen. The Interfaces column shows interface identifiers that match those on an ASA virtual firewall. ACI is able to provide valid interface names as configurable options thanks to information it obtained from the device package. When managing L4–L7 devices through ACI, it is important to understand that these same interface names are used for configuration deployment. If incorrect interface names are entered, configuration deployment to the appliance can fail. Click Next to continue.

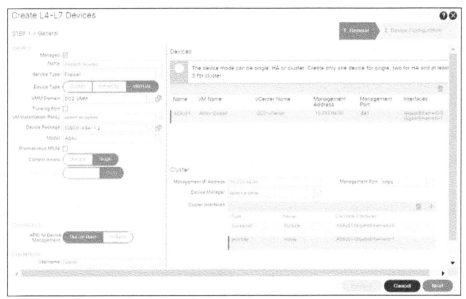

Figure 12-29   *Creation of an ACI-Managed L4–L7 Device Definition*

During managed mode device definition, the APICs give you the option to define certain parameters in line with requirements dictated in the selected device package. Figure 12-30 shows that high availability can be configured during device definition, if desired.

In parallel with defining L4–L7 devices, a services administrator may want to define a function profile to encourage reuse or prevent other administrators from making certain changes. Figure 12-31 shows configuration of a function profile to avoid repeat entry of critical data. Notice that the Locked attribute for interface IP addresses is toggled to True, to prevent users consuming the function profile from making modifications.

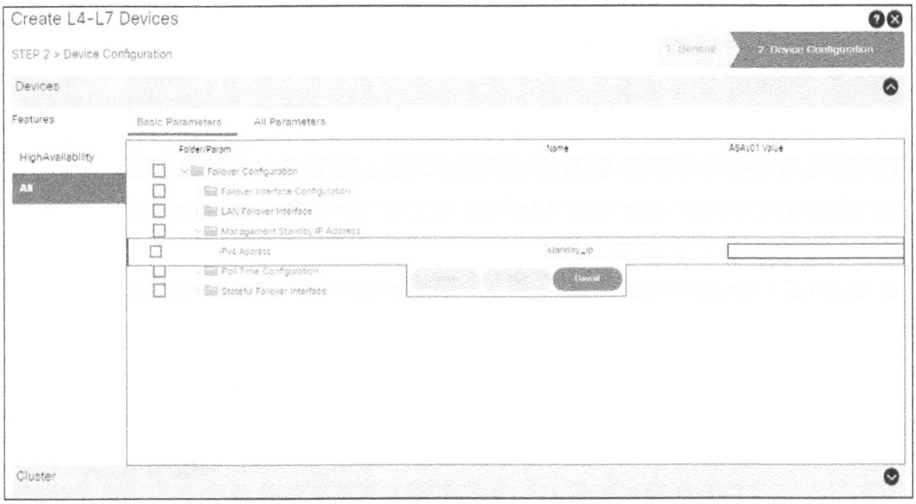

Figure 12-30 *High-Availability Configuration Options If Needed*

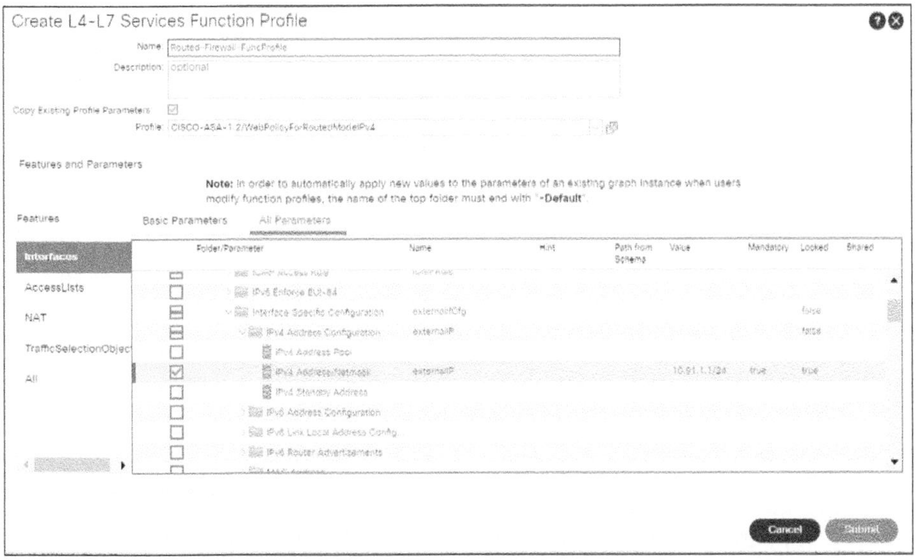

Figure 12-31 *Defining a Function Profile for Configuring an L4–L7 Services Device*

Next, a service graph template needs to be created. You can select the newly created function profile from the Profile drop-down box as shown in Figure 12-32.

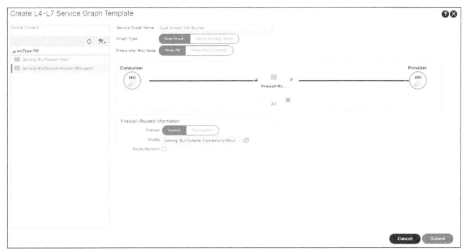

Figure 12-32 *Associating a Function Profile with a Service Graph Template*

Next, you define the consumer and provider EPGs and create a contract for assignment to the EPGs and allocation of the L4–L7 service graph, as shown in Figure 12-33.

Figure 12-33 *Applying a Contract and Service Graph to Provider and Consumer EPGs*

The next step is to configure the consumer connector and the provider connector interfaces for the node. This involves configuring interfaces connecting to the appliance(s) and not configuring ports within the services appliance operation system. The process, shown in Figure 12-34, is very similar to the preceding example.

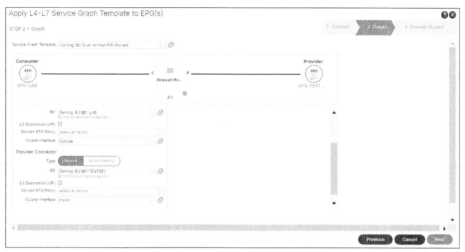

Figure 12-34 *Configuring Consumer and Provider Connector Interfaces*

Finally, it is time to define configurations for deployment to the services device(s). Notice that Figure 12-35 suggests that no parameters are required for deployment. This is not because no parameters have been set as mandatory. The reason nothing is shown actually is that all mandatory parameters have already been entered into the associated function profile. Click Finish to have ACI render the service graph.

Figure 12-35 *Services Device Configuration Parameters*

As part of rendering, ACI pushes port groups into vCenter based on the number of interfaces defined in the device configuration and the graph configuration. These new port groups are shadow EPGs and follow a naming convention that includes the VRF instance name. Figure 12-36 shows two shadow EPGs assigned to the VM interfaces as port groups. This automation takes place without any further user interaction.

Figure 12-36 *ACI Assigns Port Groups to Relevant Network Adapters on a Virtual Appliance*

The status of instantiated service graphs can be reviewed in the Deployed Graph Instances folder, as shown in Figure 12-37. The state applied indicates a successfully rendered graph.

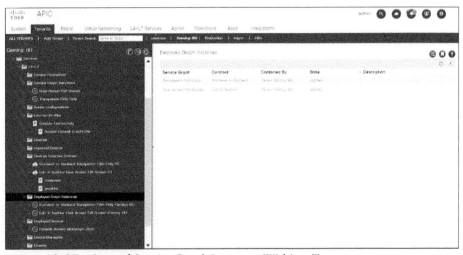

Figure 12-37 *State of Service Graph Instances Within a Tenant*

As a result of the rendering process, ACI has configured the ASA. Example 12-1 shows some lines of interest that are directly related to this configuration.

Example 12-1 *Sample Configuration Deployed by ACI to a Virtual ASA in Managed Mode*

```
interface GigabitEthernet0/0
 nameif externalIf
 security-level 50
 ip address 10.91.1.1 255.255.255.0
!
interface GigabitEthernet0/1
 nameif internalIf
 security-level 100
 ip address 10.92.1.1 255.255.255.0
!
object network web_server
 subnet 10.92.1.0 255.255.255.0
access-list access-list-inbound extended permit tcp any object web_server eq www
access-list access-list-inbound extended permit tcp any object web_server eq https
access-group access-list-inbound in interface externalIf
```

Once a graph involving managed devices has been rendered, it is often best to edit the graph parameters if changes need to be made to the services device configuration. As shown in Figure 12-38, you can navigate to **Services > L4–L7 > Services Parameters** within the tenant and click Switch to Edit Mode to modify the deployed service parameters or to add new device configurations.

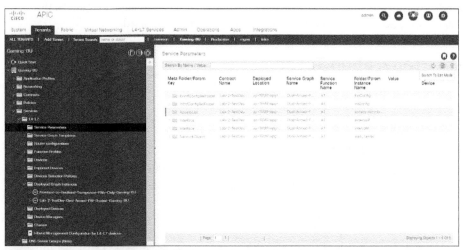

Figure 12-38 *Editing L4–L7 Services Parameters*

Device configurations can be applied at the provider EPG level or at the tenant level, as shown in Figure 12-39. Select the relevant configurations from the drop-down boxes to expose current configurations. Figure 12-39 shows configurations being added for ICMP.

Figure 12-39   *Configuring L4–L7 Services Parameters for Deployment to Services Devices*

As a result of these configurations, ACI adds the command **access-list access-list-inbound extended permit icmp any any** to the firewall configuration. Although it is simple, this example shows how function profiles and service parameters are used.

Exam Preparation Tasks

As mentioned in the section "How to Use This Book" in the Introduction, you have a couple of choices for exam preparation: Chapter 17, "Final Preparation," and the exam simulation questions in the Pearson Test Prep Software Online.

Review All Key Topics

Review the most important topics in this chapter, noted with the Key Topic icon in the outer margin of the page. Table 12-4 lists these key topics and the page number on which each is found.

Table 12-4   Key Topics for Chapter 12

Key Topic Element	Description	Page Number
Paragraph	Defines service graphs	427
List	Describes the different management models achieved through service graphs	428
Paragraph	Describes the scope of configuration automated for services devices deployed in network policy mode	428
Paragraph	Describes device packages	430

Key Topic Element	Description	Page Number
Paragraph	Describes function profiles and their use in feeding configuration data to L4–L7 services devices	430
Paragraph	Summarizes some key aspects regarding the deployment of L4–L7 services devices in service policy mode	430
Paragraph	Describes the function of a device manager	433
List	Explains device deployment modes and the number of bridge domains needed for typical designs using each deployment mode	435
List	Describes service graph designs for GoTo devices	436
List	Describes service graph designs for GoThrough devices	437
List	Lists the most common bridge domain settings for non-PBR service graph connector interfaces	439
Paragraph	Explains the absolute requirement for Layer 2 Unknown Unicast Flooding and ARP Flooding for transparent firewalls	440
Paragraph	Defines rendering	440
List	Lists the service graph implementation workflow	441
Table 12-2	Describes the components included in a device package	442
Figure 12-18	Provides an example of defining L4–L7 devices for deployment in service manager mode	443
Paragraph	Defines concrete devices and logical devices and their associated interfaces	444
Table 12-3	Describes some configuration options available in the Create L4–L7 Devices page	444
List	Describes the function profile attributes mandatory, locked, and shared	445
Paragraph	Describes service graph templates	445
Paragraph	Describes device selection policies	446
Paragraph	Describes the purpose of the Apply L4–L7 Service Graph Template wizard	446

Complete Tables and Lists from Memory

Print a copy of Appendix C, "Memory Tables" (found on the companion website), or at least the section for this chapter, and complete the tables and lists from memory. Appendix D, "Memory Tables Answer Key" (also on the companion website), includes completed tables and lists you can use to check your work.

Define Key Terms

Define the following key terms from this chapter and check your answers in the glossary:

service graph, network policy mode, shadow EPG, service policy mode, service manager mode, function profile, device manager, service chain, concrete device, logical device

Implementing Management

This chapter covers the following topic:

> **Configuring Management in ACI:** This section compares in-band and out-of-band management and covers the deployment of in-band management.

This chapter covers the following exam topic:

- 5.1 Implement out-of-band and in-band

ACI offers two avenues for management and monitoring as well as cross-platform communications such as VMM integration and managed service graphs: in-band management and out-of-band management.

Chapter 3, "Initializing an ACI Fabric," covers the implementation of out-of-band (OOB) management. This chapter revisits out-of-band management to uncover some of the reasons in-band management is sometimes desirable. It also covers the deployment of contracts for management access.

"Do I Know This Already?" Quiz

The "Do I Know This Already?" quiz allows you to assess whether you should read this entire chapter thoroughly or jump to the "Exam Preparation Tasks" section. If you are in doubt about your answers to these questions or your own assessment of your knowledge of the topics, read the entire chapter. Table 13-1 lists the major heading in this chapter and its corresponding "Do I Know This Already?" quiz questions. You can find the answers in Appendix A, "Answers to the 'Do I Know This Already?' Questions."

Table 13-1 "Do I Know This Already?" Section-to-Question Mapping

Foundation Topics Section	Questions
Configuring Management in ACI	1–10

CAUTION The goal of self-assessment is to gauge your mastery of the topics in this chapter. If you do not know the answer to a question or are only partially sure of the answer, you should mark that question as wrong for purposes of the self-assessment. Giving yourself credit for an answer you correctly guess skews your self-assessment results and might provide you with a false sense of security.

1. True or false: Changes to ACI access policies cannot directly affect out-of-band management connectivity.
   a. True
   b. False

2. True or false: Changes to ACI access policies cannot directly affect in-band management connectivity.
   a. True
   b. False

3. True or false: One solution for enabling management system connectivity to out-of-band interfaces is to leak data plane traffic to the out-of-band network.
   a. True
   b. False

4. True or false: When deploying in-band and out-of-band management side by side, Cisco recommends that either static IP addressing or dynamic IP addressing be used for both communication avenues.
   a. True
   b. False

5. True or false: An administrator can create an L3Out to advertise out-of-band subnets out an ACI fabric.
   a. True
   b. False

6. Which of the following steps cannot possibly be part of an in-band management deployment process?
   a. Assign in-band IP addresses to switches and APICs.
   b. Configure a gateway IP address on the inb subnet.
   c. Enable NTP under the Fabric Policies menu.
   d. Configure access policies and assign them to switch ports.

7. True or false: The configuration of a managed node connectivity group is mandatory when using dynamic IP addressing.
   a. True
   b. False

8. True or false: APICs are VRF aware and have separate routing tables for segmentation of traffic into in-band and out-of-band VRFs.
   a. True
   b. False

9. True or false: All ACI management contracts offer the same features and functionality.
   a. True
   b. False

10. True or false: APIC default route metrics can be modified by using the APIC Connectivity Preferences setting.
    a. True
    b. False

Foundation Topics

Configuring Management in ACI

An ACI fabric allows management access in the form of out-of-band management, in-band management, or both. This section helps you gain an understanding of some of the benefits and caveats of each option before going through the implementation of in-band management.

Understanding Out-of-Band Management Connectivity

When deploying OOB management, network engineers often dedicate a set of low-cost non-ACI copper switches to the out-of-band function and attach all out-of-band links to these switches.

Sometimes terminal servers are also deployed alongside OOB switches to ensure that a misconfigured or inaccessible switch can be remotely restored. The APIC Cisco IMC in a sense functions like a terminal server, enabling KVM access to the APIC operating system. For this reason, terminal servers are not usually necessary for the recoverability of APICs, as long as administrators are able to maintain IP connectivity to the APIC Cisco IMC. This is why administrators commonly allocate APIC Cisco IMC addressing from OOB subnet ranges.

Generally speaking, out-of-band environments are perfect for network recoverability. This is also the case in ACI. In fact, misconfigurations of ACI access policies or fabric policies most likely *cannot* affect core connectivity to OOB interfaces. Furthermore, the design of out-of-band interfaces in ACI is such that ACI does not even handle routing for such interfaces, keeping connectivity into the out-of-band network as simple as possible.

It is very common for network engineers to connect OOB switches directly to firewalls so that administrators can VPN into the network and ensure rapid network recovery in the event of an outage.

Figure 13-1 shows OOB network deployment for an ACI fabric. Notice that switch mgmt0 interfaces as well as selected APIC LOM ports should connect to the OOB environment. Connecting Cisco IMC interfaces to this network is optional but highly advised.

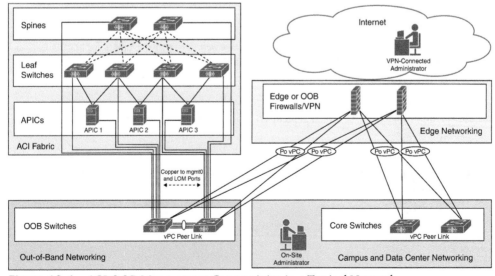

Figure 13-1   *ACI OOB Management Connectivity in a Typical Network*

In case an ACI deployment relies solely on OOB management, a mechanism may be needed to ensure that the IP connectivity required for monitoring, VMM integration, and other cross-platform integrations is also available. To establish such IP connectivity, Figure 13-1 shows that the firewalls to which the out-of-band network connects has a secondary connection back to the data center core switching layer. The core switching layer can then direct traffic to vCenter instances for VMM integration or to management or monitoring stations within the network.

The requirement to establish physical connectivity back to the in-band network in OOB-only ACI deployments illuminates a key aspect of out-of-band management in ACI: ACI does not allow users to leak traffic from the out-of-band VRF into other tenants and VRFs within ACI.

Aside from recoverability, a key use case for out-of-band management is to ensure full management plane and data plane separation. For this reason, there is no configuration available to leak the out-of-band management plane into the data plane within ACI.

Understanding In-Band Management Connectivity

In stark contrast with out-of-band management, in-band management enables a range of connectivity options, including use of EPG extensions, L2Outs, and L3Outs. Administrators can also add additional virtual network interface cards (vNICs) to VMs that may be used for monitoring and assign them to VMM-integrated port groups for direct IP assignment within the in-band management subnet. In-band management also allows administrators to leak traffic from the in-band VRF denoted by inb into user-created VRFs. If monitoring systems reside within an ACI fabric, direct leaking of traffic to and from the in-band environment can enable monitoring of an ACI fabric to persist even when northbound non-ACI switches suffer an outage.

Figure 13-2 demonstrates how an L3Out can be used to advertise an in-band management subnet to the rest of the network. In-band management deployments are likely to incorporate designs that drop connectivity directly onto core switches or a layer that has more direct connectivity to data center interconnects. This puts the in-band network in closer proximity to monitoring systems that may reside in an adjacent data center compared to connectivity models that feature firewall-based segmentation.

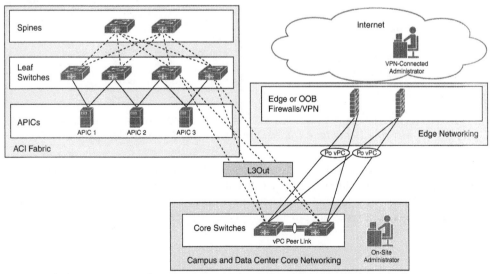

Figure 13-2 *ACI In-Band Management Connectivity in a Typical Network*

Figure 13-3 provides a reminder that L3Outs are not the only connectivity mechanism available to administrators who want to extend in-band connectivity out of an ACI fabric. From a tenancy perspective, the in-band management VRF provides the majority of the bells and whistles of user VRFs. In this example, the out-of-the-box bridge domain inb has been configured to serve as the default gateway for in-band traffic via the address 10.100.1.1/24. The in-band management EPG, shown here generically with the text EPG In-Band, has been assigned a dynamic IP address pool that ranges from 10.100.1.2 to 10.100.1.200. With a dynamic IP address pool assignment, ACI is able to automatically allocate IP addresses to APICs and ACI switches. The in-band management EPG also requires an encapsulation to enable end-to-end in-band connectivity across all ACI switches and APICs. After all, in-band connectivity flows over the same physical interfaces as the infrastructure VLAN and data plane traffic. To enable the desired communication with management stations, administrators can assign contracts to this in-band EPG. To place servers in the mgmt tenant, administrators need to create additional EPGs. The same in-band EPG used for switch and APIC connectivity cannot be reused for this purpose. These new server-mapped EPGs *can* be associated with the inb bridge domain. Hence, a number of syslog and SNMP servers have been depicted in the same subnet as the inb bridge domain. To establish connectivity between these types of server EPGs and the in-band EPG, a contract with the scope VRF is sufficient. For cross-tenant communication through route leaking, the contract scope should be set to Global.

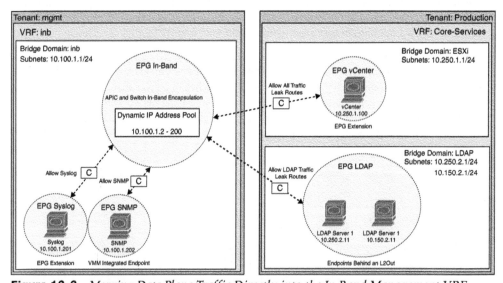

Figure 13-3 *Merging Data Plane Traffic Directly into the In-Band Management VRF*

NOTE   The implementation of route leaking is beyond the scope of the Implementing Cisco Application Centric Infrastructure DCACI 300-620 exam and is therefore not covered here. Moreover, this book has already addressed the implementation of EPG extensions and L2Outs, and this chapter does not provide additional coverage.

Although in-band management is powerful, not everything about in-band management in ACI is rosy. In-band management does depend on access policies, tenant-level policies, and sometimes cross-tenant contracts to enable connectivity. You would be correct in assuming that in-band management has greater dependency on fabric configuration and that it is also more susceptible to software defects than OOB management—and therein lies its fundamental challenge.

13

Deploying In-Band and OOB Management Side by Side

Because ACI out-of-band management is optimized for recoverability and ACI in-band management can enable more direct connectivity into the data plane, a marriage between the two can be a beautiful thing.

In instances in which a company decides to deploy in-band and OOB management alongside each other, Cisco recommends that you not combine static and dynamic IP addressing with one another. Rely on either dynamic IP addressing or static IP addressing for both in-band and out-of-band communication.

Configuring In-Band Management

It is difficult to come up with a specific set of steps that applies to all in-band management deployments. But the following steps provide an understanding of the high-level thinking necessary to effectively deploy in-band management:

Step 1. **Configure access policies for APIC in-band interfaces:** When implementing in-band management, it is important to understand that access policies need to be configured and assigned to all switch ports to which APICs connect. At the very least, these access policies need to enable LLDP, trunk the infrastructure VLAN, and allow one additional encapsulation over APIC-facing switch ports.

Step 2. **Configure the in-band management bridge domain:** If ACI will handle routing for the in-band management subnet, ensure at the very least that unicast routing has been enabled and that a default gateway has been configured on the bridge domain. Note that multiple subnets can be assigned to the in-band bridge domain.

Step 3. **Configure in-band management IP addressing:** Deploy either static IP addressing or dynamic IP addressing to switches and APICs, based on the intended target state design.

Step 4. **Optionally extend the in-band network out of the fabric:** If in-band subnets are expected to be advertised across the network, administrators can deploy an L3Out in the mgmt tenant. For basic connectivity requirements, L2Outs and EPG extensions usually suffice.

Step 5. **Optionally set up additional connectivity within the fabric:** If management and monitoring endpoints reside in the fabric and there is a preference to do route leaking or place new endpoints directly in the inb VRF, this can be easily done at this point to enable communication with in-band ACI addresses.

Step 6. **Whitelist desired connectivity to and from in-band EPGs:** While each ACI node should be able to ping its default gateway within the in-band VRF without issue, all inter-EPG communication requires contract enforcement. Configure and assign the contracts necessary to enable your desired communication.

Step 7. Evaluate APIC connectivity preferences: By default, APICs prefer in-band connectivity for outbound traffic unless specific routes are available in the APIC routing table. If, for example, out-of-band connectivity is being decommissioned in favor of in-band management due to lack of out-of-band infrastructure, it makes sense to ensure that once in-band communication has been fully tested, the APIC Connectivity Preferences setting is set to inband.

Configuring Access Policies for APIC In-Band Interfaces

The first step in implementing in-band management is to assign access policies to APIC-facing switch ports. To do so, configuration of a dedicated AAEP is highly advised. In the configuration shown in Figure 13-4, VLAN 260 is the infrastructure VLAN, and VLAN 266 will be used to encapsulate in-band traffic. Notice that a new VLAN pool has been created for this configuration. The Enable Infrastructure VLAN checkbox should be enabled for this AAEP.

Figure 13-4 *In-Band Management AAEP Configuration*

Next, an interface policy group that enables LLDP and includes the newly created AAEP needs to be configured. Figure 13-5 indicates that an access port policy group (non-aggregated) should be used for this configuration.

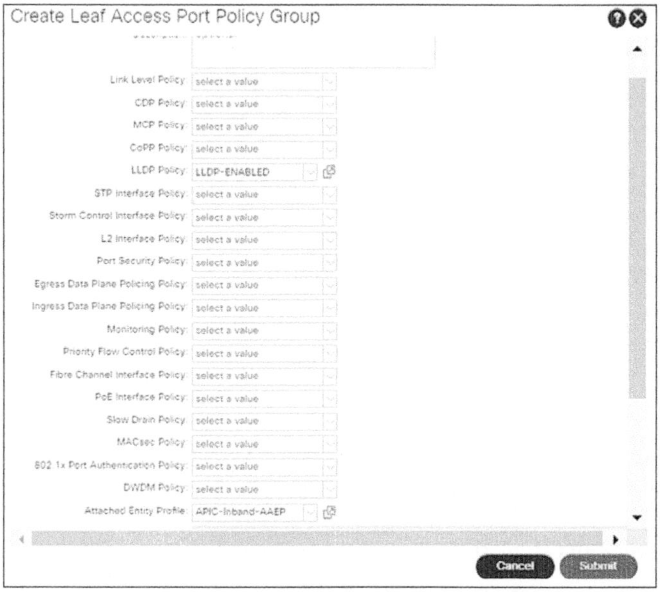

Figure 13-5 *In-Band Management Interface Policy Group Configuration*

Once the interface policy group has been configured, you can assign it to all switch ports that connect to APICs. Figure 13-6 shows the interface policy group being assigned to ports 1, 2, and 3 on a single-module switch.

Figure 13-6 *Assigning New Interface Policy Group to Switch Ports*

Configuring the In-Band Management Bridge Domain

An important step in in-band management configuration is to assign a default gateway to the inb bridge domain. Figure 13-7 shows that configuration of the in-band management bridge domain is trivial and like any other bridge domain configuration. If the in-band subnet is not expected to be advertised out the VRF instance, you can keep the Scope setting Private to VRF.

Figure 13-7   *Assigning a Subnet and Gateway for In-Band Management*

Configuring In-Band Management IP Addressing

As noted earlier in this chapter, two options exist for IP addressing. Figure 13-8 shows that the process for configuring static in-band management addresses is almost identical to the process for configuring static out-of-band IP addresses covered in Chapter 3, minus the exception that ACI does not come preconfigured with an in-band management EPG.

Figure 13-8   *Configuring Static Addresses for In-Band Management*

To enable creation of static in-band node management addresses, configure an in-band management EPG either through the pull-down menu on the Create Static Node Management

Addresses page or by navigating to Tenants > mgmt > Node Management EPGs. Figure 13-9 shows that the Create In-Band Management EPG page requires assignment of an encapsulation to the in-band EPG.

Figure 13-9   *Configuring an In-Band Management EPG*

Creation of an in-band EPG and assignment of IP addresses to it can trigger a warning message, as shown in Figure 13-10, suggesting that a communication outage can be expected. If out-of-band connectivity is fully in place, manually toggling the APIC Connectivity Preferences parameter to ooband can prevent an outage and render the warning invalid.

Figure 13-10   *Confirming Warning Message*

Static IP assignments, whether in-band or out-of-band, can be validated by navigating to **Tenants > mgmt > Node Management Addresses > Static Node Management Addresses,** as shown in Figure 13-11.

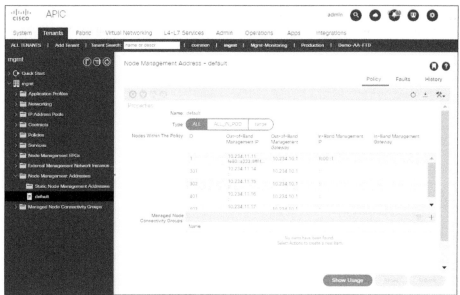

Figure 13-11 *Verifying Static IP Address Assignments*

Now, let's take a look at how you might go about configuring dynamic IP addressing instead. Figure 13-12 shows the default node management policy. In this example, because all nodes are part of a single fabric and will be placed into a single subnet, you select ALL in the Type field and add all nodes to the default node management policy. The page then displays any configured out-of-band or in-band IP addressing in the fabric. From Figure 13-12, it is clear that all nodes have been assigned static out-of-band addresses.

Figure 13-12 *Configuring the Default Node Management Policy*

> **NOTE**   If an administrator has deleted the default node management policy that comes with ACI, a new one can be created and automatically gets assigned to all selected nodes.

Assuming that the intention here is to migrate to dynamic IP addressing in both the in-band and out-of-band networks, you would need to navigate to the Tools menu and select Add a Managed Node Connectivity Group. The majority of configuration objects shown in Figure 13-13 should be familiar by now. An IP address pool needs to be configured for dynamic IP addressing to work, so you need to select Create IP Address Pool and configure an IP pool for in-band connectivity.

Figure 13-13   *Configuring a Node Management Connectivity Group*

As indicated in Figure 13-14, the pool configuration enables you to determine the range of addresses to use for ACI nodes that are part of the node management address policy config-uration. It also enables you to select the default gateway for nodes assigned to the specified pool. By default, ICMP probes are executed against the specified default gateway to enable default route failover for APICs. This behavior can be changed through the Skip Gateway Validation checkbox. After selecting your desired settings, click Submit on each of the open windows to execute the changes.

Figure 13-14   *Creating a Dynamic IP Address Pool*

Figure 13-15 shows that the node management policy just configured can also be used to verify IP assignment from the dynamic pool.

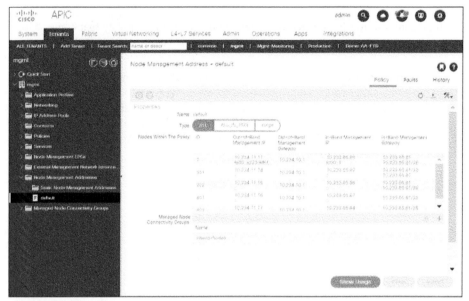

Figure 13-15 *Verifying Dynamic IP Address Assignments*

After in-band IP addresses have been assigned to all nodes within the fabric, the modes should be able to ping one another within the mgmt:inb VRF instance. As explained earlier and indicated in Example 13-1, the APIC is not VRF aware and does not need a VRF reference to ping in-band addresses.

Example 13-1 *Testing Connectivity in the In-Band Network*

```
APIC1# ping 10.233.65.81 -c 2
PING 10.233.65.81 (10.233.65.81) 56(84) bytes of data.
64 bytes from 10.233.65.81: icmp_seq=1 ttl=64 time=0.140 ms
64 bytes from 10.233.65.81: icmp_seq=2 ttl=64 time=0.152 ms

--- 10.233.65.81 ping statistics ---
2 packets transmitted, 2 received, 0% packet loss, time 2010ms
rtt min/avg/max/mdev = 0.140/0.155/0.173/0.013 ms
```

NOTE Pinging spine switches from other ACI nodes can sometimes lead to unexpected results. The inability to ping spine nodes should not be interpreted as meaning that the in-band IP addressing configuration has failed.

Optionally Extending the In-Band Network Out of the Fabric

As noted earlier in this chapter, for the most part, the in-band VRF functions just like any other VRF. In anticipation of advertising the in-band management subnets over an L3Out, you can update the inb bridge domain scope setting to Advertised Externally, as shown in Figure 13-16.

Figure 13-16 *Enabling External Advertisement of the inb Bridge Domain*

Figure 13-17 shows that a typical L3Out has been created within the mgmt tenant. Dynamic routing is not necessarily needed, but if it is deployed, remember that neighbor adjacencies do not form until at least one external EPG is created.

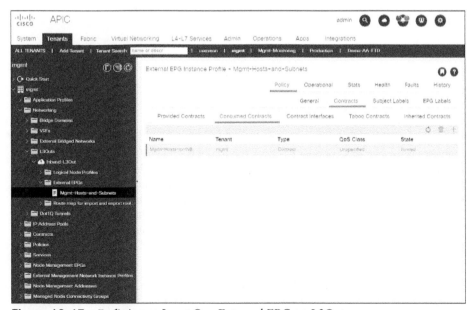

Figure 13-17 *Defining at Least One External EPG on L3Out*

After adjacencies form over the L3Out, the in-band subnet should be advertised out of the fabric, and ACI should learn routes advertised from outside neighbors.

Optionally Setting Up Additional Connectivity

At this point, you might decide to establish cross-tenant communications with the in-band subnet or create server EPGs within the in-band environment. There is nothing new to cover on this subject. All the relevant constructs, except for route leaking, function the same as in any other tenant.

Whitelisting Desired Connectivity to and from an In-Band EPG

Even though end-to-end routing may have been established, ACI still expects contracts to enable management communication. Figure 13-17 shows a contract applied in the consumed direction to the external EPG. Another look at the details of the contract allocation suggests that in-band contracts are very similar to any other contracts. Figure 13-18 shows the same contract from Figure 13-17 configured with the scope VRF and a single subject.

Figure 13-18 *Contract Enabling Access to In-Band Management via Basic Protocols*

The subject created for this contract has both the Apply Both Directions and Reverse Filter Ports checkboxes enabled, as shown in Figure 13-19. This ensures that return traffic from ports specified by associated filters from ACI back to any management endpoints is also allowed by the contract. While a review of the filter name implies that in-band management will only be used for SSH and HTTPS access in this particular fabric, you could very easily add new filters to the depicted subject or, alternatively, add additional protocols to the permitted filter.

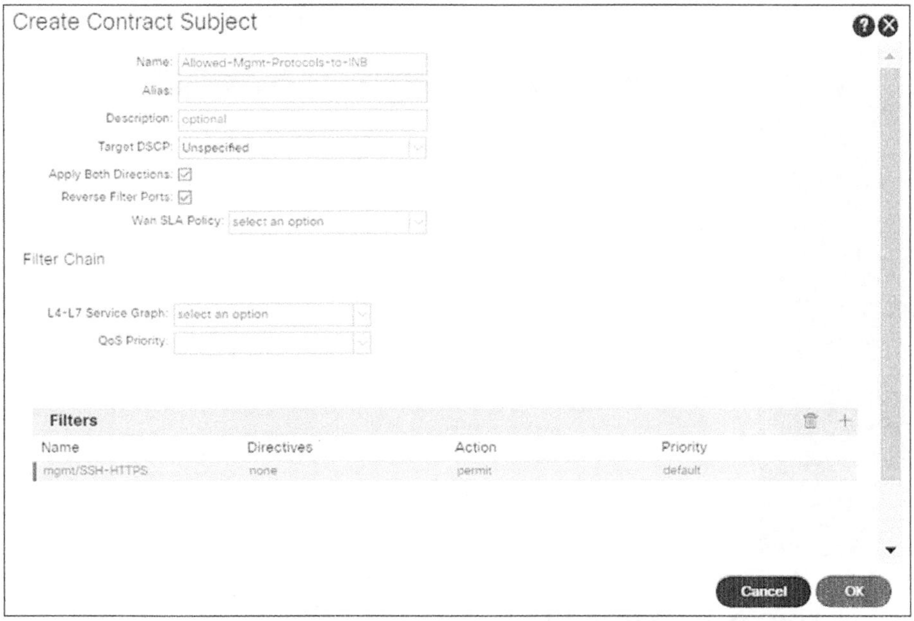

Figure 13-19 *Subject Configuration for a Sample Management Contract*

Figure 13-20 shows the filter associated with this contract. This filter classifies SSH and HTTPS traffic as interesting traffic.

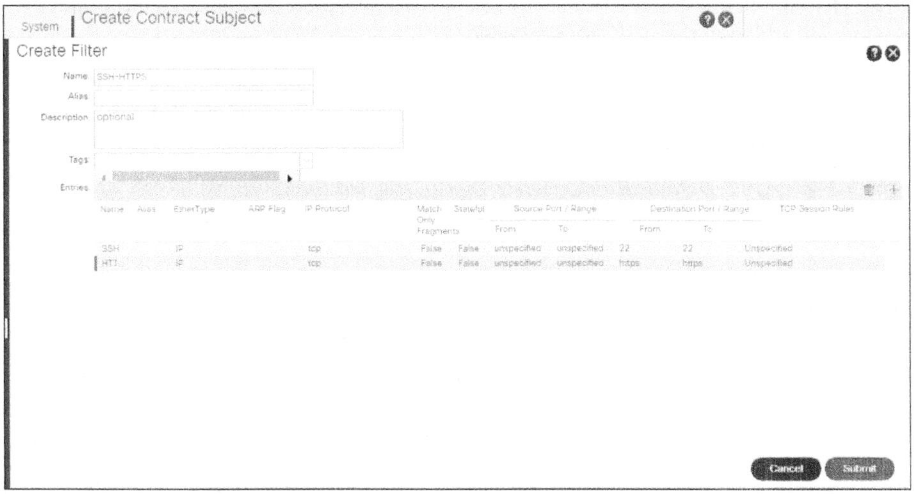

Figure 13-20 *Sample Filter That Classifies SSH and HTTPS Traffic*

Finally, the configuration cannot be considered complete until the contract has been allocated to the in-band EPG. Notice that Figure 13-21 adds the contract to the in-band EPG in the provided direction. This is because management hosts typically initiate SSH or HTTPS connections.

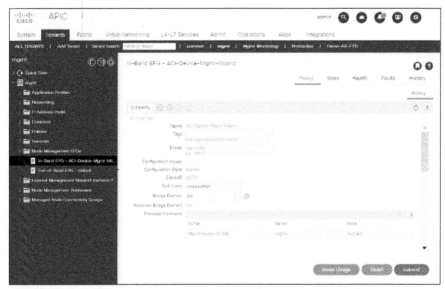

Figure 13-21   *Assigning Contracts to In-Band Management EPGs*

Evaluating APIC Connectivity Preferences

Remember that APICs are essentially servers and not routers. Servers do not segment routing tables via VRF instances. Therefore, a solution is needed to tweak outbound default routing metrics. Under System > System Settings > APIC Connectivity Preferences, you can do just that, ensuring that a specific management connection is preferred unless a more specific route has been added to the APIC routing table.

In Example 13-2, the default route out of the APIC interface called oobmgmt has the lower and more preferred metric, whereas the in-band management connection over bond0.266 has a higher metric. This is because the APIC Connectivity Preferences parameter is set to ooband.

Example 13-2   *APIC Default Route Metric Lower Toward the OOB Network*

```
APIC1# bash
admin@APIC1:~> route -n
Kernel IP routing table
Destination     Gateway         Genmask         Flags   Metric Ref    Use    Iface
0.0.0.0         10.234.10.1     0.0.0.0         UG      16     0      0      oobmgmt
0.0.0.0         10.233.65.81    0.0.0.0         UG      32     0      0      bond0.266
10.233.60.0     10.233.60.30    255.255.252.0   UG      0      0      0      bond0.260
10.233.60.30    0.0.0.0         255.255.255.255 UH      0      0      0      bond0.260
10.233.65.80    0.0.0.0         255.255.255.240 U       0      0      0      bond0.266
10.233.65.81    0.0.0.0         255.255.255.255 UH      0      0      0      bond0.266
10.234.10.0     0.0.0.0         255.255.254.0   U       0      0      0      oobmgmt
169.254.1.0     0.0.0.0         255.255.255.0   U       0      0      0      teplo-1
169.254.254.0   0.0.0.0         255.255.255.0   U       0      0      0      1xcbr0
172.17.0.0      0.0.0.0         255.255.0.0     U       0      0      0      docker0
```

After the APIC Connectivity Preferences parameter is set to inband, the APIC updates its routing table to prefer the in-band connection unless a more specific route is available in the routing table (see Example 13-3).

Example 13-3 *APIC Default Route Metric Lower in the In-Band Network*

```
admin@APIC1:~> route -n
Kernel IP routing table
Destination     Gateway        Genmask          Flags   Metric Ref   Use   Iface
0.0.0.0         10.233.65.81   0.0.0.0          UG      8      0     0     bond0.266
0.0.0.0         10.234.10.1    0.0.0.0          UG      16     0     0     oobmgmt
10.233.60.0     10.233.60.30   255.255.252.0    UG      0      0     0     bond0.260
10.233.60.30    0.0.0.0        255.255.255.255  UH      0      0     0     bond0.260
10.233.65.80    0.0.0.0        255.255.255.240  U       0      0     0     bond0.266
10.233.65.81    0.0.0.0        255.255.255.255  UH      0      0     0     bond0.266
10.234.10.0     0.0.0.0        255.255.254.0    U       0      0     0     oobmgmt
169.254.1.0     0.0.0.0        255.255.255.0    U       0      0     0     teplo-1
169.254.254.0   0.0.0.0        255.255.255.0    U       0      0     0     1xcbr0
172.17.0.0      0.0.0.0        255.255.0.0      U       0      0     0     docker0
```

NOTE In quite a few ACI configurations that reference management and monitoring stations such as SNMP, syslog, and AAA servers, you are asked to enter a management EPG. This is like configuring source interfaces for such services on NX-OS switches. If the APIC Connectivity Preferences parameter has been toggled to inband and an out-of-band management EPG is selected for outbound communications with management and monitoring systems, the selection of the management EPG can be invalidated. On the flipside, if the APIC Connectivity Preferences parameter has been toggled to ooband, an in-band management EPG can be selected in ACI configurations for connectivity toward such servers, as long as the APIC routing tables have routes pointing to the subnets in which these servers reside.

Out-of-Band Management Contracts in Review

Recall from Chapter 3 that contracts for out-of-band management are defined under a different folder than are in-band contracts. Figure 13-22 shows that OOB contracts are configured under the Out-of-Band Contracts folder. These contracts are not interchangeable with standard contracts used for in-band management.

Figure 13-22 *Configuration of an Out-of-Band Contract*

Just as in the case of in-band connectivity, contracts need to be applied to the relevant management EPG. Figure 13-23 shows a minor difference in the application of contracts to out-of-band EPGs compared to in-band EPGs. Contracts can only be applied to OOB EPGs in the provided direction. Another difference that is not shown, however, is that OOB contracts do not support logging of traffic matching a particular filter chain.

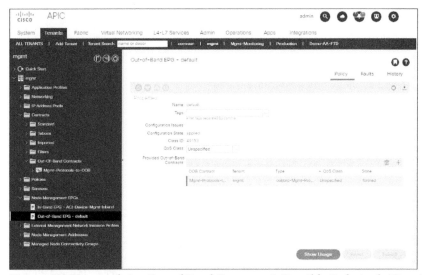

Figure 13-23   *Applying Out-of-Band Contracts Is Possible Only in the Provided Direction*

Finally, another difference is that restricting management access to a subset of subnets over OOB interfaces is configured at the external management network interface profile level. This is the same object to which OOB contracts need to be applied in the consumed direction (see Figure 13-24). The concept of an external management network interface profile does not exist for in-band connectivity.

Figure 13-24   *Object Representing Management Hosts Connecting to OOB Interfaces*

Chapter 14, "Monitoring ACI Using Syslog and SNMP," includes further examples of contracts for the out-of-band network.

Exam Preparation Tasks

As mentioned in the section "How to Use This Book" in the Introduction, you have a couple of choices for exam preparation: Chapter 17, "Final Preparation," and the exam simulation questions on the companion website.

Review All Key Topics

Review the most important topics in this chapter, noted with the Key Topic icon in the outer margin of the page. Table 13-2 lists these key topics and the page number on which each is found.

Table 13-2   Key Topics for Chapter 13

Key Topic Element	Description	Page Number
Paragraph	Describes the fundamental benefit of out-of-band management in ACI	464
Paragraph	Summarizes the key use cases for OOB management in ACI	465
Paragraph	Describes the fundamental benefit of in-band management in ACI	465
Paragraph	Outlines the primary drawback of in-band management in ACI	467
Paragraph	Describes the Cisco recommendation for IP addressing when implementing in-band and OOB management side by side	467
List	Lists the steps necessary to effectively deploy in-band management in ACI	467
Figure 13-4	Illustrates the AAEP configurations required for switch-facing APIC LOM ports in in-band management deployments	468
Figure 13-5	Illustrates the interface policy group configurations needed for switch-facing APIC LOM ports in in-band management deployments	469
Figure 13-8	Demonstrates the configuration of static IP addressing for in-band management	470
Figure 13-12	Shows a configuration example for the default node management policy	472
Figure 13-13	Demonstrates how to configure a node management connectivity group	473
Figure 13-14	Shows how to configure a dynamic IP address pool	473
Paragraph	Describes the significance of the APIC Connectivity Preferences setting	478

Memory Tables

There are no memory tables or lists in this chapter.

Define Key Terms

There are no key terms for this chapter.

Monitoring ACI Using Syslog and SNMP

This chapter covers the following topics:

Understanding System Messages: This section explains what system messages are and how ACI structures them.

Forwarding System Messages to Syslog Servers: This section walks through the process of configuring ACI for system message forwarding to syslog servers.

Using SNMP in ACI: This section provides a basic understanding of SNMP as well as SNMP capabilities supported in ACI.

Configuring ACI for SNMP: This section explores the process of configuring ACI to respond to SNMP read queries and forward system messages as traps.

This chapter covers the following exam topic:

■ 5.2 Utilize syslog and snmp services

Chapter 4, "Exploring ACI," touches on how ACI provides feedback to users through faults, event logs, health scores, and audit logs. This chapter details how ACI structures faults, events, and other log records into system messages for forwarding to syslog servers and SNMP managing systems.

This chapter also covers the ACI configurations necessary to allow remote devices to poll ACI switches and APICs via SNMP read queries.

This chapter revisits the MIM and reinforces your understanding of the ACI object model, enabling you to develop highly customized monitoring policies.

"Do I Know This Already?" Quiz

The "Do I Know This Already?" quiz allows you to assess whether you should read this entire chapter thoroughly or jump to the "Exam Preparation Tasks" section. If you are in doubt about your answers to these questions or your own assessment of your knowledge of the topics, read the entire chapter. Table 14-1 lists the major headings in this chapter and their corresponding "Do I Know This Already?" quiz questions. You can find the answers in Appendix A, "Answers to the 'Do I Know This Already?' Questions."

Table 14-1 "Do I Know This Already?" Section-to-Question Mapping

Foundation Topics Section	Questions
Understanding System Messages	1, 2
Forwarding System Messages to Syslog Servers	3–6
Using SNMP in ACI	7, 8
Configuring ACI for SNMP	9, 10

1. True or false: ACI can only generate system messages for faults.
    a. True
    b. False
2. Which system message format provides the most granularity?
    a. Syslog
    b. NX-OS
    c. ACI
    b. Fault
3. Which set of monitoring policies needs to be modified to enable syslog forwarding for server port failures, assuming that no custom monitoring policies will be enforced?
    a. Fabric > Fabric Policies > Policies > Monitoring > Common Policies
    b. Fabric > Fabric Policies > Policies > Monitoring > default
    c. Fabric > Access Policies > Policies > Monitoring > default
    d. Tenant > common > Policies > Monitoring > default
4. An ACI administrator has been tasked with troubleshooting why a syslog server is not receiving syslog messages from ACI. Which of the following could be possible causes for syslog traffic not arriving on the syslog server? (Choose all that apply.)
    a. The syslog server's IP address has not been included as an external syslog data collector.
    b. ACI supports only syslog Version 9.
    c. A contract permitting all traffic into and out of the management EPG has been assigned, but an explicit contract for syslog has not been created.
    d. No syslog sources have been defined.
5. An administrator has configured a new syslog destination monitoring group and wants to ensure that system messages for a specific tenant are redirected to the new syslog destination group. After configuring a new set of syslog monitoring policies and a syslog source within the monitoring policies, no log forwarding seems to be taking place for problems that occur within the tenant. What went wrong? (Choose the best answer.)
    a. Custom monitoring policies cannot be configured in ACI.
    b. The monitoring policies need to be assigned to the tenant in the Policy tab.
    c. A firewall in the path toward the syslog server is blocking port 161.
    d. A load balancer has been defined as an L4-L7 device within the tenant.

6. Which APIC CLI command signals an APIC or ACI switch to generate a system message for transmission toward a syslog server?

    a. moquery

    b. grep

    c. logit

    d. syslog

7. An ACI administrator has configured ACI for SNMP and is trying to use MIBs to execute a configuration change in the fabric but is unable to do so. What is the most likely reason for this?

    a. ACI has been configured for SNMPv3, but an SNMPv3 user has not been configured.

    b. ACI contract issues need to be resolved.

    c. A firewall is blocking communication between the SNMP manager and ACI.

    d. SNMP write commands are not supported in ACI.

8. What are feasible reasons an ACI configuration to a specific SNMP manager may be failing or suboptimal? (Choose all that apply.)

    a. Contracts have been defined on the management EPG, but they are not specific enough.

    b. The out-of-band EPG is used, but static node management addresses have not been configured.

    c. The administrator has configured 12 trap destinations.

    d. Client entries in the SNMP policy include the IP address of the SNMP manager but not the subnet default gateway.

9. An ACI administrator is testing an SNMP configuration that has just been deployed. SNMP read queries related to fabric policies and access policies tend to work fine. However, the administrator is unable to perform read queries related to EIGRP for a specific tenant. What is a possible problem?

    a. The SNMP pod policy has not been configured correctly.

    b. The SNMP contracts associated to the management EPG should be deleted.

    c. SNMP contexts need to be associated with VRF instances in the tenant.

    d. SNMP read queries are not supported on ACI leaf switches, and EIGRP runs on switches.

10. With default SNMP manager settings, which IP protocols and ports should be configured in a contract to allow full SNMP read queries and traps?

    a. UDP 161 and TCP 162

    b. UDP 161 and UDP 514

    c. UDP 161 and UDP 162

    d. TCP 161 and UDP 514

Foundation Topics

Understanding System Messages

A *system message* is a specially formatted message that typically contains a subset of information about a fault, an event, or another log record in the fabric. When certain faults and events occur, ACI can forward system messages to the console, external syslog servers, external SNMP servers, call home servers, or, alternatively, log the system message locally on the devices that generate the message.

Both APICs and ACI switches can generate system messages. ACI can structure system messages in a format similar to NX-OS switches, or it can structure system messages in a new ACI-oriented format. The default preferred system message format is the ACI structure because it includes more data.

System messages following the NX-OS format use the following syntax:

```
timestamp Nexus: FACILITY-SEVERITY-MNEMONIC: Message-text
```

This syntax includes the following variables and fixed strings:

- **timestamp:** The year, month, date, and time of day of system message generation
- **Nexus:** A fixed string
- **FACILITY:** Two or more uppercase letters that indicate the affected hardware device, protocol, or module of the system software
- **SEVERITY:** A single-digit code from 0 to 7 that reflects the severity of the condition, as outlined in Table 14-2
- **MNEMONIC:** A code that uniquely identifies the error message
- **Message-text:** A description of the problem encountered or the event that occurred

Table 14-2 NX-OS System Message Severity Levels

Level	Severity Level (NX-OS)	ITU Level (ACI)	Description
0	Emergency	—	System unusable
1	Alert	Critical	Immediate action required
2	Critical	Major	Critical condition
3	Error	Minor	Error condition
4	Warning	Warning	Warning condition
5	Notification	Cleared	Normal but significant condition
6	Informational	—	Informational message only
7	Debugging	—	Messages that appear during debugging only

Generally, system messages reflecting a lower severity level tend to point to conditions or events that have a higher potential for impacting an ACI fabric or endpoints within the fabric.

Example 14-1 shows a system message generated by an ACI switch. The syslog severity 5 has been logged.

Example 14-1   *Sample System Message for a Fault in NX-OS Format*

```
2014 Jan 25 21:42:07 Nexus: ETHPORT-5-IF_DOWN_ADMIN_DOWN:
Interface Ethernet3/1 is down (Administratively down))
```

System messages following the ACI format use the following syntax:

```
timestamp host %LOG_LOCALn-severity-SYSTEM_MSG [code][lifecycle
state][rule][severity text][DN of affected MO]
```

```
Message-text
```

This syntax includes the following variables and fixed strings:

- **timestamp:** The year, month, date, and time of day of system message generation

- **host:** The IP address or hostname of the device that generated the system message

- **%LOG_LOCALn:** A single-digit code from 0 to 7 that reflects the local facility of the message and is sometimes used to sort received messages

- **severity:** A single-digit code from 1 to 5 following the ITU perceived severity values described in RFC 5674 reflecting the severity of the condition

- **SYSTEM_MSG:** A fixed string

- **code:** The unique fault or event code associated with the message

- **lifecycle state:** The current state in the fault lifecycle; output is omitted when a message is being generated for an event

- **rule:** The action or condition that caused the event, such as a component failure or a threshold crossing

- **severity text:** The text translation of the numeric severity values (for example, major), as indicated in Table 14-3

- **DN of affected MO:** The distinguished name (DN) of the managed object (MO) affected by the fault condition or event

- **Message-text:** A description of the problem encountered or the event that occurred

Table 14-3   ACI System Message Severity Levels

Level	ITU Level (ACI)	Description
0	—	System is unusable
1	Critical	Immediate action required
2	Major	Critical condition
3	Minor	Error condition
4	Warning	Warning condition
5	Cleared	Normal but significant condition
6	Informational	Informational message only
7	—	Messages that appear during debugging only

Example 14-2 shows a sample system message generated in ACI format for a fault on a switch with node ID 102, indicating that the APIC named apic1 has lost connectivity to the switch.

Example 14-2   *Sample ACI-Structured System Message for a Fault*

```
July 22 22:45:28 apic1 %LOG_LOCAL0-2-SYSTEM_MSG [F0110] [soaking] [node-failed]
[critical] [topology/pod-1/node-102/fault-F0110]
Node 102 not reachable. unknown
```

Example 14-3 presents a sample system message generated in ACI format for an event logging the transition of a fabric port on node 101 to an optimal status from the view of apic1.

Example 14-3   *Sample ACI-Structured System Message for an Event*

```
July 22 22:45:27 apic1 %LOG_LOCAL0-6-SYSTEM_MSG [E4208219] [link-state-change] [info]
[subj-[topology/pod-1/lnkcnt-1/lnk-101-1-1-to-1-1-3]/rec-4294968577]
Link State of Fabric Link is set to ok
```

Forwarding System Messages to Syslog Servers

Administrators can configure ACI to forward system messages to external syslog servers using the following simple process:

Step 1.   Apply necessary contracts to allow syslog forwarding.

Step 2.   Configure syslog monitoring destination groups.

Step 3.   Configure syslog sources for desired monitoring policies.

Step 4.   Verify syslog forwarding to desired syslog servers.

These steps do not need to be completed in the order presented. However, it does make sense to create syslog monitoring destination groups first because syslog sources need to reference the syslog monitoring destination groups. Furthermore, there is little reason to verify until the configuration has been completed.

Although the process seems very straightforward, it tends to challenge engineers on their understanding of monitoring policies and the ACI object hierarchy because syslog sources for all desired monitoring policies need to be configured for proper syslog forwarding to take place. Therefore, the following sections provide some details to make these steps clearer.

Apply Necessary Contracts to Allow Syslog Forwarding

Chapter 13, "Implementing Management," outlines the procedure for applying contracts to the out-of-band ACI subnet by limiting the sources for communication to all private IP addresses.

This chapter outlines the process for enabling a contract that allows communication with syslog servers. However, unlike the procedure described in Chapter 13, this procedure attempts to further lock down access to UDP port 514 by specifying the syslog server IP addresses in a dedicated external management instance profile.

NOTE   Some earlier ACI code revisions did not require syslog ports to be opened via contracts for out-of-band communication. However, the application of an out-of-band contract to limit communication has always been considered a Cisco best practice. Where in-band management is used to forward traffic to syslog servers, explicit contract enforcement *is* required.

The first step in creating out-of-band contracts for syslog is to create a filter to classify syslog traffic. Figure 14-1 shows how users can launch the filter creation wizard by navigating to the mgmt tenant, opening the Contracts folder, right-clicking on Filters, and selecting Create Filter.

Figure 14-1 *Launching the Create Filter Wizard from the mgmt Tenant*

In the Create Filter window, enter a filter name, create a filter entry, and click Submit. Figure 14-2 shows two filters, named syslog-dest and syslog-src, that classify all port 514 traffic in both the source and destination port directions. By default, syslog servers listen on port 514, but they can also communicate outbound via port 514, even though they do not send acknowledgments for client messages.

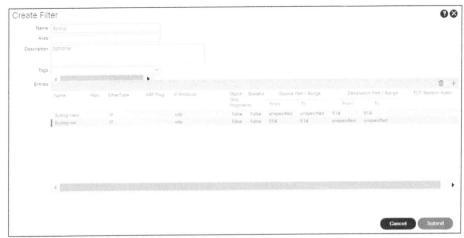

Figure 14-2 *Creating a Filter for Syslog Traffic*

Next, create an out-of-band contract by navigating to Contracts, right-clicking Out-of-Band Contracts, and selecting Create Out-of-Band Contracts. Select a name for the new contract and click on the + sign to create a subject for syslog traffic (see Figure 14-3).

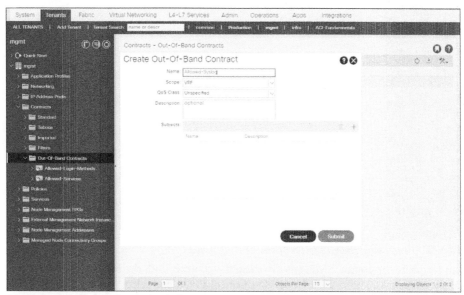

Figure 14-3 *Launching the Subject Creation Page from the Create Out-of-Band Contract Window*

Name the new subject, click the + sign next to Filters, associate the syslog filter with the subject, and then click Update and OK (see Figure 14-4).

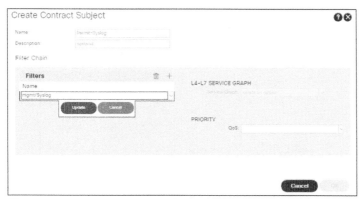

Figure 14-4 *Associating a Filter with a New Subject*

Once the subject has been created, it appears on the Create Out-of-Band Contract page. Click Submit to finalize creation of the new contract (see Figure 14-5).

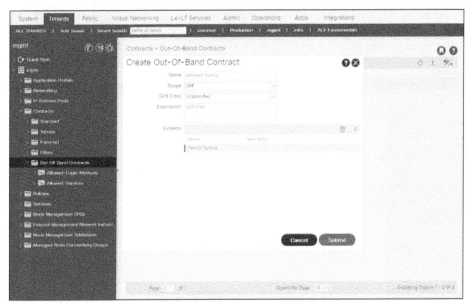

Figure 14-5 *Finalizing the Creation of the Out-of-Band Contract*

After you create the contract, you can associate the contract with the out-of-band EPG. To do so, navigate to mgmt, click Node Management EPGs, and select Out-of-Band EPG - default. Then select the newly created contract in the Provided Out-of-Band Contracts view and click Update (see Figure 14-6). Finally, click Submit to update the OOB EPG.

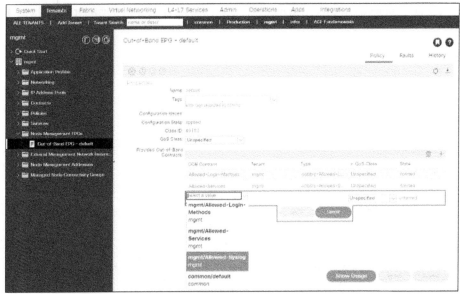

Figure 14-6 *Associating a Contract with an Out-of-Band EPG*

Next, a new external EPG needs to be created to represent the syslog servers. Remember that creating a specific external EPG for syslog servers is not a requirement, but this section demonstrates how it can be done. In this example, the syslog contract will be consumed by the new external EPG.

To create an external EPG, which is called an external management network instance profile within the management tenant, navigate to mgmt, right-click External Management Network Instance Profiles, and select Create External Management Network Instance Profiles. Enter the external EPG name, the new contract, and host routes for the syslog server, as shown in Figure 14-7, and click Submit to complete the contract creation process.

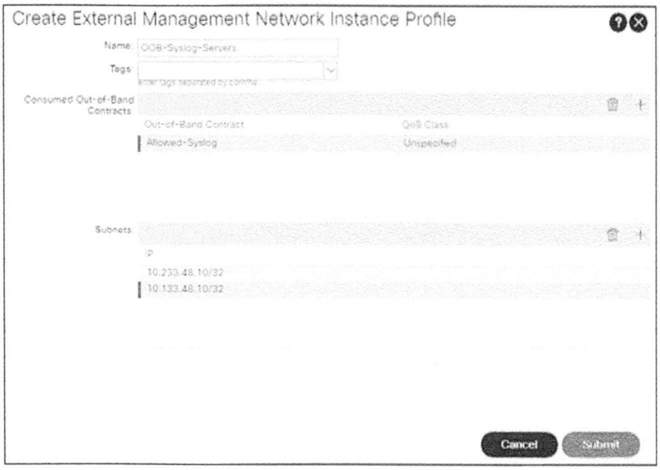

Figure 14-7   *Creating a New External Management Network Instance Profile*

NOTE   It is not necessary to create a separate external management network instance profile for each traffic type. A single external EPG can classify all traffic arriving on OOB interfaces. However, if you need different management or monitoring endpoints to have different levels of access to the fabric, this is most feasibly done through specificity and by defining separate EPGs that each classify different sets of external endpoints.

NOTE   So how would contract enforcement be different if in-band management were used? The contract itself would be the same, but it would need to be configured under **mgmt > Contracts > Standard** instead. Because in-band management allows contract allocation in both the provider and consumer directions, the contract direction becomes more important. With the contract filters shown in Figure 14-2, the contract would need to be applied on an external EPG associated with an L3Out in the provider direction and on the in-band management EPG in the consumer direction.

Configuring Syslog Monitoring Destination Groups

Syslog *monitoring destination groups* are used to define and group syslog servers together. The reason for grouping syslog servers together is that a company may want one set of servers to be used for monitoring system messages involving fabric and access policies. A specific department within the company or perhaps a customer or partner may request that system messages related to a specific tenant they manage be forwarded to a dedicated set of servers they also manage.

To configure a syslog monitoring destination group, navigate to the Admin menu, select External Data Collectors, and under Monitoring Destinations, right-click on the Syslog folder and select Create Syslog Monitoring Destination Group, as shown in Figure 14-8.

Figure 14-8 *Navigating to the Syslog Monitoring Destination Group Wizard*

Enter a name for the syslog monitoring destination group, select the desired system message format, determine the granularity of timestamps and whether they should be precise to the millisecond, and toggle Admin State to enabled. If system messages should also be logged on the device console and within the local file systems, set Admin State for these parameters to enabled and determine the desired message logging severity (see Figure 14-9). Note that setting console logging severity to a value that generates an exorbitant number of messages is discouraged due to the potential for impact on device CPU utilization.

Figure 14-9 *Configuring a Syslog Monitoring Destination Group, Step 1*

Next, create an entry for each syslog server in the destination group, as demonstrated in Figure 14-10. Note that a different system message severity level, destination port, forwarding facility, and source interface can be selected for each syslog server, if desired.

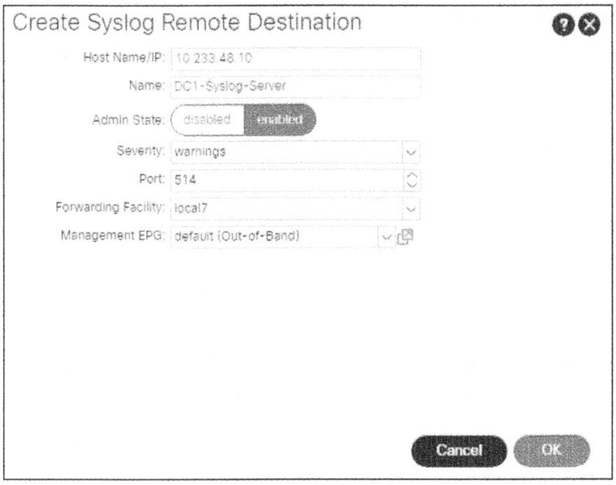

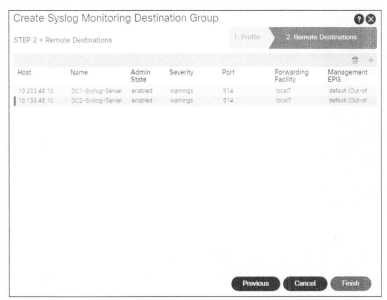

Figure 14-10 *Creating a Syslog Remote Destination, Step 2*

When all syslog servers that are members of the destination group have been defined, as shown in Figure 14-11, click Finish to move on to configuring syslog sources.

Figure 14-11 *Verifying the Syslog Remote Destinations Configured in a Syslog Monitoring Destination Group*

Configuring Syslog Sources for Desired Monitoring Policies

After any planned syslog monitoring destination groups have been configured, monitoring sources need to be configured to point to the destination groups.

As a review, there are four default monitoring groups in ACI. Each addresses a different set of faults, events, and logs. The default monitoring groups can be found in the following locations as of ACI Release 4.2(1):

- Fabric > Fabric Policies > Policies > Monitoring > Common Policies

- Fabric > Fabric Policies > Policies > Monitoring > default

- Fabric > Access Policies > Policies > Monitoring > default

- Tenant > common > Policies > Monitoring > default

By right-clicking on a desired monitoring policy and selecting Create Syslog Source, as shown in Figure 14-12, you can trigger the launch of the Create Syslog Source wizard.

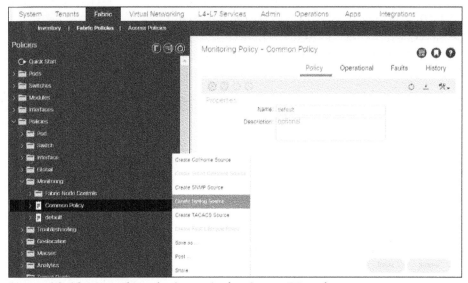

Figure 14-12 *Launching the Create Syslog Source Wizard*

In the Create Syslog Source screen, enter a name for the syslog source object. Then select the types of events, faults, and log records to convert to system messages by selecting the appropriate Include checkboxes. Determine the minimum message severity level for which ACI should forward messages and then select a syslog monitoring destination group from the Dest Group pull-down. Finally, click Submit. Figure 14-13 shows the creation of a syslog source for the monCommonPol class.

Figure 14-13 *Creating a Syslog Source*

Remember that even though this book demonstrates steps for the creation of a single syslog source, it is important to create syslog sources for each class of active monitoring policies within the fabric if the intent is to forward syslog messages pertinent to all aspects of the fabric.

Note that when configuring syslog sources in some of the monitoring policies, you may not be able to create the syslog source object by right-clicking the top-level menu. In such cases, you need to navigate to the CallHome/Smart CallHome/SNMP/Syslog/TACACS submenu for the monitoring policy, select Syslog, and then create syslog sources by clicking the + sign on the right side of the screen, as shown in Figure 14-14.

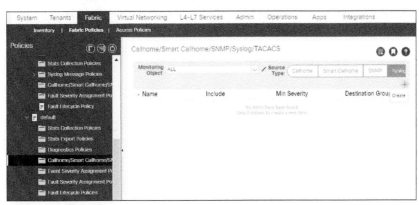

Figure 14-14 *Alternative Method for Creating Syslog Sources*

Note that the use of the four default monitoring policies in these configuration examples assumes that ACI administrators are not customizing monitoring policies. However, in multitenant environments, monitoring policy customization is very common. This section goes over some common examples of monitoring policy customization—namely, interface-level and tenant-level syslog customizations.

Say that an administrator of a tenant named DCACI wants all system messages relevant to the tenant he or she manages to be forwarded to a dedicated group of syslog servers. A fabric administrator has already created a syslog monitoring destination group named DCACI-syslog that enables syslog forwarding and references the syslog servers managed by the tenant administration team. The next step would be for the tenant administrator to create custom monitoring policies. Figure 14-15 shows the creation of a new monitoring policy called DCACI-monitoring and the association of a child monitoring source named DCACI-syslog-source with the new syslog monitoring destination group.

Figure 14-15 *Associating Syslog Sources with Custom Monitoring Policies*

At this point, you might think that the configuration is complete. Just because a new set of monitoring policies has been created within a tenant, however, does not mean the tenant or objects within the tenant are associated with it. Figure 14-16 shows how you can verify which monitoring policies are associated with an object. In this figure, the distinguished name of the monitoring policy object associated with the DCACI tenant is still uni/tn-common/monepg-default, which is the set of default monitoring policies of class monEPGPol from the common tenant.

Figure 14-16 *Checking the Monitoring Policies Associated with an Object*

NOTE Figure 14-16 provides an important example of why administrators should familiarize themselves with the ACI object model. Verification of traditional network configurations is possible using simple CLI commands. In ACI, on the other hand, it can sometimes be difficult to understand where a configuration went wrong without knowledge of the object model.

To modify the active set of monitoring policies for a tenant, you must navigate to the tenant in question, open the Policy tab, select the new policy from the Monitoring Policy dropdown, and then click Submit (see Figure 14-17).

Figure 14-17 *Assigning Custom Monitoring Policies to a Tenant*

As a result of making this change, the tenant as well as any child objects, such as bridge domains and EPGs, begin to reference the custom monitoring policies through inheritance, as indicated by the updated distinguished name in Figure 14-18.

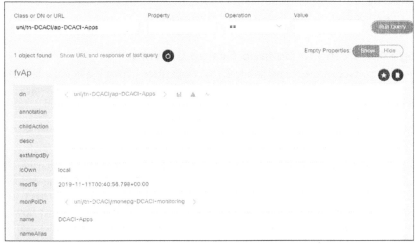

Figure 14-18 *Verifying Assignment of Custom Monitoring Policies*

> **NOTE**   Certain attributes flow downward in the hierarchical object structure according to the location of objects within the tree.

So how are custom monitoring policies assigned to objects in the fabric policies and access policies view? There is always a possibility that a customer or department might own a physical server or even several ACI switches within a fabric and might therefore expect to be able to receive syslog data pertinent to incidents involving hardware, such as ports bouncing or a switch port failure. In such cases, custom fabric and access monitoring policies need to be defined and associated with the highest-level object in the hierarchy below which the customer needs to monitor. Through inheritance, the monPolDn attribute of child objects then reflects the custom monitoring policies. Figure 14-19 shows how a custom set of access monitoring policies can be applied to an interface policy group. Note that monitoring policies for switches and modules can also be modified via switch and module policy groups.

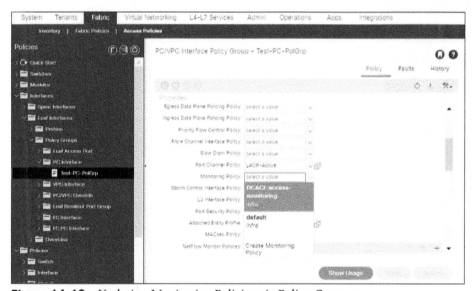

Figure 14-19   *Updating Monitoring Policies via Policy Groups*

Verify Syslog Forwarding to Desired Syslog Servers

Configuration of syslog forwarding is often a task that takes place during the initial buildout of an ACI fabric. It is important for administrators not to assume that all desired messages will be forwarded correctly; it is also important that this theory be properly validated.

The first thing to verify is IP connectivity between the ACI out-of-band or in-band management interfaces and the syslog servers.

After verifying IP connectivity, it is a good idea to test whether the syslog service on each node in the fabric can forward traffic properly to each syslog server configured in the syslog monitoring destination groups by using the APIC CLI command **logit severity** {*severity*} **dest-grp** {*destGroup*} **server** {*remoteDest*}{*message*} (**node** {*id*}). Example 14-4 shows how a user can prompt the APIC to signal nodes 101 and 102 to generate a test system message using severity level 1 and forward it to each of the configured syslog servers in the Syslog-Servers destination group configured earlier.

Example 14-4   *Using* logit *to Test System Message Submission*

```
apic1# logit severity 1 dest-grp Syslog-Servers server 10.233.48.10 "This is a test"
  node 101
apic1# logit severity 1 dest-grp Syslog-Servers server 10.233.48.10 "This is a test"
  node 102
apic1# logit severity 1 dest-grp Syslog-Servers server 10.133.48.10 "This is a test"
  node 101
apic1# logit severity 1 dest-grp Syslog-Servers server 10.133.48.10 "This is a test"
  node 102
```

If syslog messages are indeed received by the syslog server, the communication path, the syslog service, and the health of the syslog server have been sufficiently validated.

After verifying the syslog monitoring destination groups, you can verify the syslog source configuration to ensure that all necessary configurations are in place to forward desired system messages to syslog servers. The most reliable way to verify that syslog sources are in place is to trigger various types of failures within the system and ensure that system messages arrive on syslog servers. Just remember that triggers need to be identified for each monitoring class for which syslog sources have been configured.

One way to verify syslog configurations on all nodes in a fabric is to use the MOQuery tool. To query for all syslog sources (class syslogSrc) configured in a fabric, use the command **moquery -c syslogSrc**. To also verify whether the syslog sources have been assigned to the desired destination groups, you can add the **-x** option with the argument **'rsp-subtree=children'**. This ensures that child objects are also included in the query. Example 14-5 shows how this is possible. In this example, the output has been piped via **grep** to exclude certain output for brevity. This output shows that four syslog sources have been configured: common-syslog, fabric-syslog, access-syslog, and tenant-syslog. These sources correlate to the four out-of-the-box monitoring groups in ACI and are all the syslog sources configured in this specific fabric.

Example 14-5   *Using MOQuery to Validate Syslog Source Configurations*

```
apic1# moquery -c syslogSrc -x 'rsp-subtree=children' | grep -E "name
  |dn|incl|monPolDn|tDn|^$"

name         : common-syslog
dn           : uni/fabric/moncommon/slsrc-common-syslog
incl         : all,audit,events,faults,session
monPolDn     : uni/fabric/moncommon

  dn          : uni/fabric/moncommon/slsrc-common-syslog/rsdestGroup
  monPolDn    : uni/fabric/moncommon
  tDn         : uni/fabric/slgroup-Syslog-Servers

name         : fabric-syslog
dn           : uni/fabric/monfab-default/slsrc-fabric-syslog
```

```
incl            : all,audit,events,faults,session
monPolDn        : uni/fabric/monfab-default

  dn                : uni/fabric/monfab-default/slsrc-fabric-syslog/rsdestGroup
  monPolDn          : uni/fabric/monfab-default
  tDn               : uni/fabric/slgroup-Syslog-Servers

name            : access-syslog
dn              : uni/infra/moninfra-default/slsrc-access-syslog
incl            : all,audit,events,faults,session
monPolDn        : uni/infra/moninfra-default

  dn                : uni/infra/moninfra-default/slsrc-access-syslog/rsdestGroup
  monPolDn          : uni/infra/moninfra-default
  tDn               : uni/fabric/slgroup-Syslog-Servers

name            : tenant-syslog
dn              : uni/tn-common/monepg-default/slsrc-tenant-syslog
incl            : all,audit,events,faults,session
monPolDn        : uni/tn-common/monepg-default

  dn                : uni/tn-common/monepg-default/slsrc-tenant-syslog/rsdestGroup
  monPolDn          : uni/tn-common/monepg-default
  tDn               : uni/fabric/slgroup-Syslog-Servers
```

The MOQuery tool can also display the syslog server destinations that have been configured. The **syslogRemoteDest** class pertains to syslog servers configured in the fabric, as shown in Example 14-6.

Example 14-6   *Using MOQuery to Validate Syslog Destination Groups*

```
apic1# moquery -c syslogRemoteDest | grep -E '#|host|adminState|epgDn|severity'
# syslog.RemoteDest
host            : 10.133.48.10
adminState      : enabled
epgDn           : uni/tn-mgmt/mgmtp-default/oob-default
severity        : warnings
# syslog.RemoteDest
host            : 10.233.48.10
adminState      : enabled
epgDn           : uni/tn-mgmt/mgmtp-default/oob-default
severity        : warnings
```

Using SNMP in ACI

Simple Network Management Protocol (SNMP) allows third-party applications to monitor network devices. The application that performs the monitoring is called an *SNMP manager*; the system being managed is referred to as an *SNMP agent*.

SNMP managers initiate SNMP read queries for SNMP agents to send certain information. If supported, SNMP managers can also send configuration changes to SNMP agents through SNMP write commands.

Whether an SNMP agent supports read queries, write commands, or both, the information that a remote system can request from the agents is defined in an object called a *Management Information Base (MIB)*.

When important system events occur on an SNMP-enabled device, the SNMP agent can send *SNMP notifications* in the form of traps and informs to the SNMP manager. An *SNMP trap* is an unreliable message that does not require an acknowledgment from the SNMP manager. An *inform* is a message that is sent reliably, as it is stored in memory until the SNMP manager issues a response.

Events of interest for SNMP notifications may include a module crashing or an interface going down.

There are three major versions of SNMP. SNMPv1 and SNMPv2c use community strings. SNMPv3 adds encryption and authentication capabilities and is considered the most secure but also generally consumes more CPU and memory resources. SNMPv3 uses a concept called security levels to define the level of security to be enforced. SNMPv3 security level definitions along with keywords used for each security level in ACI are as follows:

- **auth:** Authenticates users but does not encrypt traffic

- **noauth:** Does not authenticate or encrypt traffic and uses a username match

- **priv:** Both authenticates SNMPv3 users and encrypts traffic

The default ports involved in SNMP communication are UDP ports 161 and 162. SNMP agents listen for SNMP manager read queries on port 161. SNMP managers listen for traps on port 162.

ACI Support for SNMP

ACI switches and APICs run SNMP agents and support SNMPv1, v2, and v3, including both MIBs and notifications (traps). However, ACI does *not* support SNMP write commands.

SNMP support in ACI can be summarized as follows:

- SNMP read queries (Get, Next, Bulk, Walk) are supported by leaf and spine switches and by APICs. Only MIBs specific to ACI are supported.

- SNMP write commands (Set) are not supported in ACI.

- SNMP traps (v1, v2c, and v3) are supported by leaf and spine switches and by APICs. When system messages are sent to an SNMP manager, these messages are in the form of SNMP traps, and so the configuration of SNMP trap forwarding is very similar to the process for forwarding syslog messages.

- ACI supports a maximum of 10 trap receivers. If more than 10 trap receivers are configured, some of them do not receive notifications.

- ACI supports both IPv4 and IPv6 SNMP trap destinations.

> **NOTE** Cisco has specially developed a plethora of MIBs for ACI to enable very granular monitoring. To obtain the list of MIBs supported in ACI, visit the ACI MIB Support List at https://www.cisco.com/c/dam/en/us/td/docs/Website/datacenter/aci/mib/mib-support.html.

ACI SNMP Configuration Caveats

Administrators need to authorize SNMP managers that should be allowed to query ACI via SNMP. To do so, SNMP manager IP addresses need to be configured in a field called Client Entries in an SNMP client group profile. Adding SNMP manager IP addresses to the Client Entries list is like permitting endpoints via an access list. Although a subnet can be used to define the SNMP managers, a broad subnet such as 0.0.0.0/0 should not be used in the Client Entries field.

The SNMP client group profile configuration needs to be applied at the pod level through an SNMP policy. Any SNMP community strings or SNMPv3 user credentials that the SNMP manager will be using to execute read queries against ACI also need to be configured in this same SNMP policy.

An important thing to note about ACI MIBs is that they are divided into two categories:

- **Global scope:** A *global scope MIB* is an MIB whose scope is not limited to a specific VRF instance and that touches on broader aspects of the fabric. Examples of MIBs of a global scope are those that request data related to the status of switch power supplies, interface or port channel statuses, CPU utilization, and memory utilization.

- **VRF specific:** A *VRF-specific MIB* is an MIB whose scope is limited to a VRF. Examples of VRF-specific MIBs are those involving IP addresses or endpoints residing in a VRF or route peerings out of a specific VRF.

When using VRF-specific MIBs, an extra configuration step is necessary. A VRF-specific SNMP context needs to be created, and one or more SNMP community profiles need to be associated with the SNMP context. The SNMP community then becomes bound to the SNMP context and can only be used for SNMP read queries involving the specific VRF, regardless of whether the SNMP community was previously associated with a global scope at the SNMP pod policy level.

A prerequisite for proper SNMP implementation for APICs is for nodes to have static management IP addresses assigned. The process for configuring static out-of-band addresses is covered in Chapter 3.

Configuring ACI for SNMP

The following steps are required to configure ACI to respond to SNMP read queries and forward traps:

Step 1. Apply necessary contracts for SNMP.

Step 2. Associate SNMP policy with pod policy.

Step 3. (Optional) Associate SNMP contexts with desired VRF instances.

Step 4.   Configure SNMP monitoring destination groups.

Step 5.   Configure SNMP sources for all desired monitoring policies.

Step 6.   Verify SNMP forwarding to desired SNMP servers.

Although these steps generally do not need to be done in order, configuration of monitoring destination groups should take place before SNMP sources are configured. This is because each SNMP source configuration needs to reference an SNMP monitoring destination group. Furthermore, there is little point in verifying SNMP configuration before full implementation. Also, note that these steps assume that either out-of-band or in-band management has been fully set up with static node management addresses. The following sections provide some details to make these steps clearer.

Apply Necessary Contracts for SNMP

As noted earlier in this chapter, contracts should allow UDP ports 161 and 162 to enable SNMP communication. Figure 14-20 shows filter entries that satisfy requirements for SNMP. These filters need to be associated with a subject that permits traffic forwarding and has the Reverse Filter Ports option enabled. For in-band management, you need to also enable the Apply Both Directions option.

Figure 14-20   *Filters Needed for SNMP Reads and Traps*

NOTE   Under certain conditions, either these filters or contract directionality may need to be tweaked. For example, if in-band management is used and L3Out external EPGs are explicit in the IP addresses allowed to communicate via SNMP, a contract with this same filter can be both consumed and provided by both the external EPG and the in-band EPG to ensure full SNMP communication.

Associate an SNMP Policy with a Pod Policy

To enable remote SNMP managers to query the fabric, a pod SNMP policy needs to be configured. Navigate to Fabric, click Fabric Policies, double-click Policies, open Pod, double-click SNMP, and edit the desired SNMP policy. Figure 14-21 shows the default SNMP policy that is already applied to all pods within the fabric being modified.

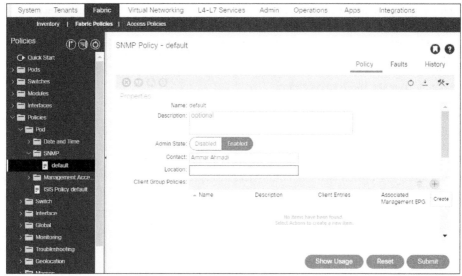

Figure 14-21 *Filters Needed for SNMP Reads and Traps*

Enable SNMP by toggling the Admin State parameter. Then enter the desired contact details and click the + sign in the Client Group Policies portion of the window to create a client SNMP group profile, as shown in Figure 14-22. Associate a management EPG to the client SNMP group profile and enter addresses for the SNMP managers. Finally, click Submit.

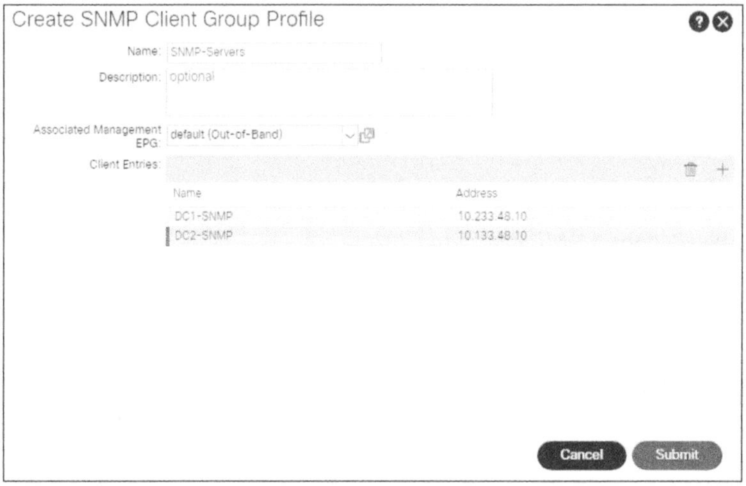

Figure 14-22 *Creating an SNMP Client Group Profile*

After defining the client SNMP group profile, scroll down in the SNMP policy and configure either SNMPv3 users or SNMP community strings to allow read queries. Figure 14-23 shows that two SNMP community strings have been defined. One of these community policies will be allocated to an SNMP context that will be bound to a VRF instance called DCACI. Once this binding takes place, the VRF-specific SNMP string cannot be used for queries involving MIBs that are of a global scope.

Figure 14-23 *Creating SNMP Community Policies and/or SNMPv3 Users*

Scroll down further within the SNMP policy to define servers that will receive SNMP traps and the port on which these servers listen for traps. Figure 14-24 shows that an SNMP server at 10.233.48.10 has been defined as a trap receiver that listens on port 162. Click Submit to apply the changes to the SNMP policy.

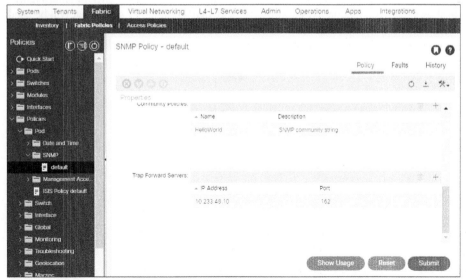

Figure 14-24 *Defining Servers That Will Receive SNMP Traps*

Remember that for the SNMP policy to take effect, it has to be assigned to an active pod policy group. Click Show Usage to ensure that the SNMP policy is active. If it is not, navigate to the pod policy group of interest and update the SNMP policy the pod policy group references.

Associate SNMP Contexts with Desired VRF Instances

To create an SNMP context to enable VRF-specific MIB queries from a remote SNMP manager, navigate to the tenant of interest, right-click the desired VRF instance, and select Create SNMP Context (see Figure 14-25).

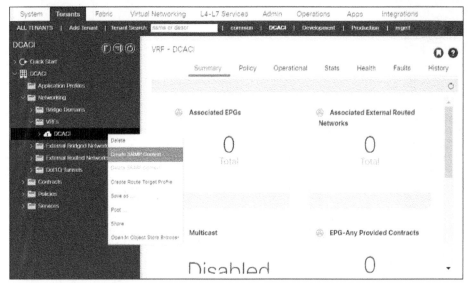

Figure 14-25 *Creating an SNMP Context*

In the Create SNMP Context window, enter a context name, define the community string that will be used to query ACI for information specific to the VRF, and click Submit. Figure 14-26 shows that DCACI-context-password is the SNMP community string that will be used for this SNMP context. This string can no longer be used for queries of MIBs of a global scope, even though this string was also defined under the pod SNMP policy.

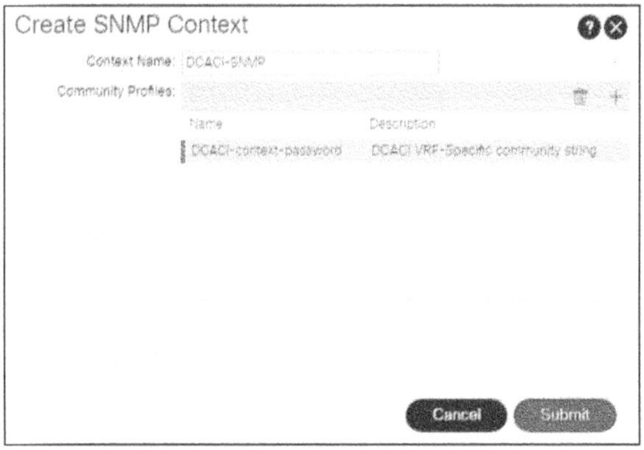

Figure 14-26 *Dedicating a Community String to an SNMP Context*

Configure SNMP Monitoring Destination Groups

Just as with syslog configuration, SNMP trap forwarding requires the definition of SNMP monitoring destination groups. You also need to define the SNMP protocol version used for trap forwarding on a per-server basis. Navigate to Admin, select External Data Collectors, open Monitoring Destinations, right-click SNMP, and select Create SNMP Monitoring Destination Group. Figure 14-27 shows the first page of the wizard, where you select a name for the object and click Next.

Figure 14-27 *Launching the Create SNMP Monitoring Destination Group Wizard*

Create entries for each SNMP manager that should receive traps. The information required includes destination addresses, ports, SNMP version, and community strings to use for trap forwarding. Figure 14-28 shows that an administrator has configured two servers for trap forwarding. Click Finish to complete the configuration.

Create SNMP Monitoring Destination Group

STEP 2 > Trap Destinations

Host Name/IP	Port	Version	Security Name	v3 Security level	Management EPG
10.233.48.10	162	v2c	HelloWorld	noauth	default (Out-of-Ba...
10.133.48.10	162	v2c	HelloWorld	noauth	default (Out-of-Ba...

Previous   Cancel   Finish

Figure 14-28 *Adding Servers to SNMP Monitoring Destination Group for Trap Forwarding*

Note that DNS names can be used in SNMP monitoring destination groups. If SNMPv3 is used, an SNMPv3 security level needs to also be selected. Instead of a community string, SNMPv3 trap forwarding requires that the SNMPv3 username be entered as the community. The GUI sometimes refers to the SNMPv3 username as a security name.

Configure SNMP Sources for All Desired Monitoring Policies

Much as with syslog, SNMP system message forwarding in the form of traps necessitates that SNMP sources be configured for four default monitoring groups in ACI. Each group addresses a different set of faults, events, and logs. The default monitoring groups can be found in the following locations:

- Fabric > Fabric Policies > Policies > Monitoring > Common Policy

- Fabric > Fabric Policies > Policies > Monitoring > default

- Fabric > Access Policies > Policies > Monitoring > default

- Tenant > common > Policies > Monitoring > default

Figure 14-29 shows the SNMP source creation wizard being launched for the common policy.

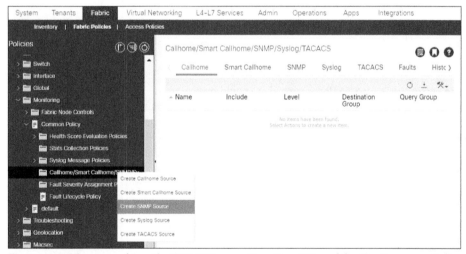

Figure 14-29 *Launching the SNMP Source Creation Wizard for the Common Policy*

In the wizard, name the SNMP source, map the previously created SNMP monitoring destination group to the SNMP source, and click Submit. Figure 14-30 shows the creation of an SNMP source named common-snmp.

Create SNMP sources for each of the desired monitoring policy classes. Custom SNMP sources can also be used to achieve additional granularity.

Figure 14-30   *Creating an SNMP Source*

14

Verify SNMP Forwarding to Desired SNMP Servers

The best way to verify SNMP read queries is to actually execute read queries using the SNMP manager. Command-line tools available on most SNMP managers (for example, snmp-get and snmpwalk) can execute queries against an SNMP agent. Trap receipt is also best validated on the SNMP manager itself.

Example 14-7 shows how the basic SNMP policy applied at the pod level can be verified using the **show snmp** APIC CLI command.

Example 14-7   *Verifying Operational Status of SNMP Pod Policy Settings*

```
apic1# show snmp
(...output truncated for brevity...)
Input Statistics:
    34 SNMP packets input
    0 Trap PDUs received
    48 Get-next PDUs
    0 General Errors
    0 Set-request PDUs
    44 Number of requested variables
Output Statistics:
    0 Get-request PDUs generated
    58 Get-responses PDUs generated
    0 Set-requests PDUs generated
    34 SNMP packets output
Other Statistics:
    0 Silent Drops
    0 Proxy Drops
    Disabled Authentication Traps Status
Name               Admin State  Location          Contact             Description
------------------ ----------   ---------------   -----------------   -------------
default            enabled                        Ammar Ahmadi
```

Other commands that can be used to verify SNMP configurations using the APIC CLI include **show snmp clientgroups, show snmp community, show snmp hosts,** and **show snmp users.** The command **show snmp summary** is also very helpful (see Example 14-8).

Example 14-8 *Verifying SNMP Configuration Settings*

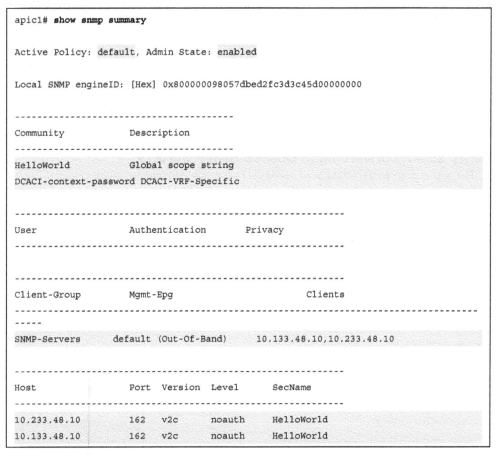

Finally, the MOQuery tool can be used to validate SNMP source configurations. You can query the ACI object hierarchy for SNMP source configurations by using the class snmpSrc. Example 14-9 shows that only a single set of monitoring policies has been configured for the fabric in this case.

Example 14-9 *Verifying SNMP Source Configurations*

```
apic1# moquery -c snmpSrc -x 'rsp-subtree=children'
Total Objects shown: 1
(...output truncated for brevity...)
# snmp.Src
name         : common-snmp
dn           : uni/fabric/moncommon/snmpsrc-common-snmp
incl         : events,faults
```

```
monPolDn     : uni/fabric/moncommon
rn           : snmpsrc-common-snmp

# snmp.RsDestGroup
  dn           : uni/fabric/moncommon/snmpsrc-common-snmp/rsdestGroup
  monPolDn     : uni/fabric/moncommon
  tDn          : uni/fabric/snmpgroup-SNMP-Monitoring-Servers
```

Exam Preparation Tasks

As mentioned in the section "How to Use This Book" in the Introduction, you have a couple of choices for exam preparation: Chapter 17, "Final Preparation," and the exam simulation questions in the Pearson Test Prep Software Online.

Review All Key Topics

Review the most important topics in this chapter, noted with the Key Topic icon in the outer margin of the page. Table 14-4 lists these key topics and the page number on which each is found.

Table 14-4 Key Topics for Chapter 14

Key Topic Element	Description	Page Number
Paragraph	Describes system messages	485
Table 14-2	Lists NX-OS system message severity levels	485
Table 14-3	Lists ACI system message severity levels	486
List	Outlines steps for configuring ACI for syslog forwarding	487
Paragraph	Describes syslog monitoring destination groups	492
Paragraph	Revisits the default monitoring policies and where each of them can be found in the GUI	494
Paragraph	Describes the significance of configuring syslog sources for all active monitoring policies	495
List	Outlines the level of support within ACI for SNMP	501
List	Describes types of ACI MIBs from a scope perspective and defines each of them	502
Paragraph	Lists requirement for static node management addresses for SNMP	502
List	Outlines the steps necessary for proper SNMP configuration	502
List	Lists the classes of monitoring policies available for SNMP source configuration	508

Complete Tables and Lists from Memory

There are no memory tables or lists for this chapter.

Define Key Terms

Define the following key terms from this chapter and check your answers in the glossary:

system message, monitoring destination group, monitoring source, Management Information Base (MIB), SNMP notification, SNMP trap, global scope MIB, VRF-specific MIB

CHAPTER 15

Implementing AAA and RBAC

This chapter covers the following topics:

> **Implementing Role-Based Access Control (RBAC):** This section addresses the technical tools ACI offers for RBAC enablement.

> **Integrating with External AAA Servers:** This section details how ACI integrates with TACACS+, RADIUS, and LDAP servers.

This chapter covers the following exam topic:

- 5.4 Implement AAA and RBAC

This book has placed a lot of emphasis on multitenancy as a key feature of ACI. Multitenancy is used to lock down and separate data plane traffic, and it also enables a level of fault isolation from a configuration standpoint.

In the world of multitenancy, management plane lockdown is critical. Where IT is expected to *not* function as a cost center but an enabler and seller of new services to the business, everyone becomes a customer. Tenants then become a powerful tool in the IT arsenal for isolating or restricting customer traffic. At times, the service offered may be to allow business units to independently deploy new services in the tenants they are assigned. This may require central IT organizations to provide customers a good deal of management access to ACI fabrics, but central IT still needs to be able to restrict access to functions that may enable customers to break ACI fabrics. To sum up, the demands placed on the new world of networking necessitate very granular role-based access control (RBAC). ACI meets such demands head on through its robust RBAC and AAA capabilities.

"Do I Know This Already?" Quiz

The "Do I Know This Already?" quiz allows you to assess whether you should read this entire chapter thoroughly or jump to the "Exam Preparation Tasks" section. If you are in doubt about your answers to these questions or your own assessment of your knowledge of the topics, read the entire chapter. Table 15-1 lists the major headings in this chapter and their corresponding "Do I Know This Already?" quiz questions. You can find the answers in Appendix A, "Answers to the 'Do I Know This Already?' Questions."

Table 15-1 "Do I Know This Already?" Section-to-Question Mapping

Foundation Topics Section	Questions
Implementing Role-Based Access Control (RBAC)	1–7
Integrating with External AAA Servers	8–10

1. A user has been assigned to a security domain called Production and a domain called Production. The security domain has been mapped to two tenants, named Prod1 and Prod2. In the security domain assignment for the user, the tenant-admin role was selected, and it has access privilege type Write. Which the following items may the user still be unable to do?

   a. Create bridge domains, application profiles, and EPGs in the Prod1 tenant

   b. View basic objects within the common tenant

   c. Map an EPG in the Prod2 tenant to a port on a leaf

   d. Create service graphs in the Prod2 tenant

2. Which of the following roles may be most suitable for a user who needs basic visibility into ACI for the purpose of monitoring and troubleshooting?

   a. ops

   b. fabric-admin

   c. nw-svc-admin

   d. tenant-admin

3. A user needs full read-only visibility into an ACI fabric. Which predefined security domain can be used to enable such visibility?

   a. common

   b. all

   c. infra

   d. fabric

4. True or false: RBAC rules can be used to explicitly deny an offending user access to a portion of the ACI object hierarchy.

   a. True

   b. False

5. True or false: A privilege enables access to a particular function within a system. A role is simply a collection of privileges.

   a. True

   b. False

6. When creating an RBAC rule, which three parameters must be entered?

   a. Object name, domain, and associated user

   b. DN, domain, and whether the rule grants write access

   c. Object name, domain, and security domain

   d. DN, security domain, and whether the rule grants write access

7. Which role is best suited for a user who needs to manage access policies available under the Fabric menu?

   a. tenant-admin

   b. read-only

   c. access-admin

   d. fabric-admin

8. How can users who are successfully authenticated against LDAP be authorized for ACI access? (Choose all that apply.)

   a. The LDAP server can be configured to assign users specially formatted Cisco AV pairs and return them in the queries ACI runs against the schema.

   b. ACI cannot use LDAP data for authorization purposes.

   c. ACI provides users a basic level of read-only access to the common tenant if Remote User Login Policy has been set to Assign Default Role and authorization data is missing.

   d. ACI can be configured to map user group membership to the desired user access levels.

9. What Cisco AV pair authorizes a user to create an EPG in a tenant named Prod?

   a. shell:domains = all//admin

   b. shell:domains = all/aaa/tenant-admin

   c. shell:domains = all/admin/

   d. domains:shell = admin//all/

10. True or false: When Default Authentication Realm has been set to an external AAA service, and all AAA providers are unavailable to service requests or respond to ICMP traffic, users need to re-initialize the fabric to regain management access.

   a. True

   b. False

Foundation Topics

Implementing Role-Based Access Control (RBAC)

RBAC is a method of restricting and authorizing access to a system based on the roles of individuals within a company. For ACI to grant a user management access to fabric resources, that user must be assigned the following parameters:

■ **One or more security domains:** A security domain identifies the portions of the hierarchical object tree the user can access.

- **One or more roles:** A role is a collection of privileges and determines the set of actions the user can take within the scope of the security domains.

- **An access level for each role:** The access level or access privilege type indicates whether the user has read-only or read/write access to carry out the functions associated with the role within the specified subtrees of the ACI object hierarchy.

In addition to local user authentication, ACI supports external user authentication via LDAP, TACACS+, RADIUS, SAML, and RSA.

The majority of configurations related to RBAC can be performed via the GUI in subtabs or submenus of the AAA page by navigating to **Admin > AAA**.

Understanding Security Domains

ACI objects are designed to enable the templatization of configurations, where possible, to encourage future policy reuse. A security domain is a form of template that enables administrators to identify desired subtrees of the ACI object hierarchy to which one or multiple users should be granted access.

In more technical terms, a *security domain* is a tag that references one or more subtrees in the ACI object hierarchy. An ACI administrator who creates a security domain can then assign it to tenants and domains. For more granular references, an administrator can map an object subtree using the parent distinguished name (DN) to a security domain. A user who is subsequently mapped to the security domain gains a level of access to the referenced subtrees of the object hierarchy.

Remember that the level of access to the security domain subtrees that is afforded to a user is determined by the roles and access privilege types for the roles assigned to each individual user. Therefore, it is important to understand that security domain assignment by itself does not enable access rights.

By default, an ACI fabric includes several special predefined security domains that can be used for access assignment to users:

- **all:** Allows access to the entire ACI object hierarchy

- **common:** Allows access to the common tenant

- **mgmt:** Allows access to the management tenant

Figure 15-1 shows the creation of a new security domain called Production via the Create Security Domain window, which you can access by navigating to **Admin > AAA > Security > Security Domains** and selecting Create Security Domain from the pull-down menu.

After creating a security domain tag, you need to assign the desired tenants, domains, and any other taggable objects to the security domain. Figure 15-2 shows how you can navigate to the Policy subtab of a tenant to add one or more security domains to the tenant. To add a security domain called Production, you enter the name and click Update to accept the change. In this way, you effectively assign the object tree for the tenant named Production to the security domain called Production.

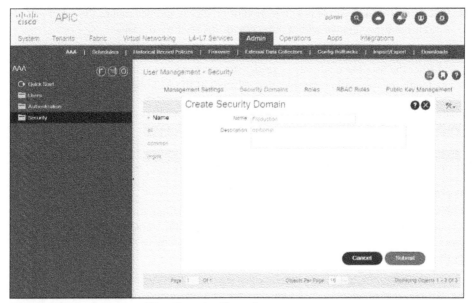

Figure 15-1   *Creating a New Security Domain*

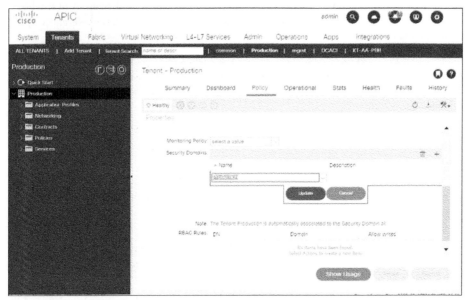

Figure 15-2   *Assigning a Tenant to a Security Domain*

For a user to gain access to the tenant named Production, the user needs to be assigned to the Production security domain using a role and access level that provides the ability to carry out the desired tenant functions.

Understanding Privileges and Roles

A *privilege* enables access to a particular function within a system. An ACI fabric enforces access privileges at the managed object (MO) level.

A *role* is a collection of privileges. ACI has a set of predefined roles. An ACI administrator can modify the predefined roles or expand on default ACI roles by creating custom roles.

You can explore the set of privileges assigned to each role by navigating to **Admin > AAA > Security > Roles**. Figure 15-3 shows that the fabric-admin role is a collection of 12 privileges.

Figure 15-3 *Exploring the Privileges Assigned to Each Role*

The fabric-equipment privilege, for example, is one of the privileges ACI assigns to the fabric-admin role; it is used for atomic counter, diagnostic, and image management policies on leaf and spine switches within ACI.

Another common privilege is tenant-security, which enables users who are assigned the tenant-admin role to create contracts within tenants.

> **NOTE** As of the time of writing, a total of 62 privileges can be found in ACI. It is unlikely that DCACI candidates will be expected to know the function of each and every privilege; however, privilege names are somewhat descriptive of the functions that they enable. DCACI candidates *are* encouraged to create various users with different privileges to better understand the privileges available in ACI.

Table 15-2 describes the predefined ACI roles that can be assigned to users.

Table 15-2 Predefined Roles in ACI

Role Name	Description
aaa	Aids in configuring authentication, authorization, accounting, and import/export policies
access-admin	Enables administration and configuration of access policies
admin	Provides full access to an ACI fabric
fabric-admin	Enables administration and configuration of fabricwide settings and also firmware management
nw-svc-admin	Allows users to configure L4–L7 network service insertion and orchestration
nw-svc-params	Grants access to the parameters governing the configuration of external L4–L7 devices
ops	Provides network operator privileges to an ACI fabric to allow for monitoring and troubleshooting functionality in ACI
read-all	Provides read-only visibility into an ACI fabric
tenant-admin	When assigned to a limited security domain, allows configuration of most attributes inside a tenant but does not allow changes to fabricwide settings that can potentially impact other tenants
tenant-ext-admin	Allows the configuration of external connectivity, such as L3Outs, for ACI tenants; a subset of the tenant-admin role
vmm-admin	Grants access to ACI integrations with virtualization environments such as Microsoft Hyper-V, OpenStack, and VMware vSphere

While you cannot create custom privileges, you can define custom roles if the out-of-the-box roles outlined in Table 15-2 do not fit your requirements. Figure 15-4 shows how you can navigate to the Create Role page by going to **Admin > AAA > Security > Roles** and clicking on the Create Role option from the pull-down menu.

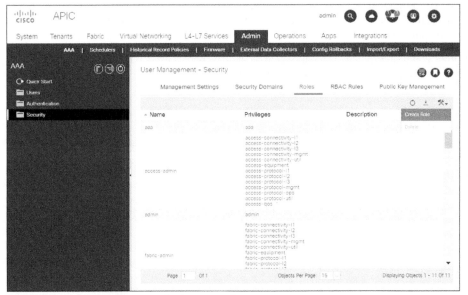

Figure 15-4 *Navigating to the Create Role Page*

Figure 15-5 show how a new role called EPG-Admin can be created from the Create Role page through assignment of the tenant-EPG privilege. In a role with this privilege, a user can create EPGs, delete them, and bind them to domains from within the tenant view, map them to encapsulations, and assign them to ports (to which the user has visibility).

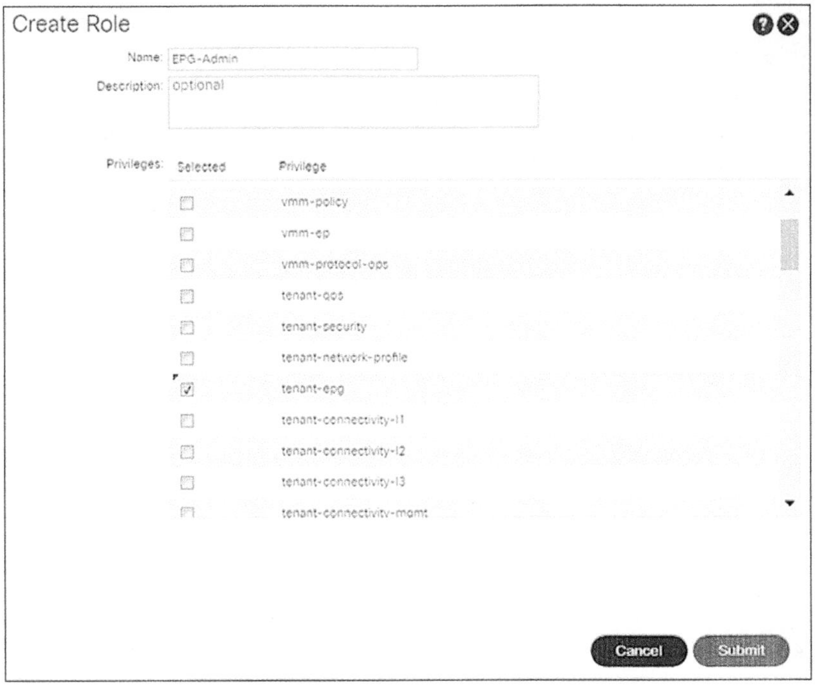

Figure 15-5   *Creating a Custom Role*

Creating Local Users and Assigning Access

Let's say that an IT department has just hired a new engineer named Bob. The IT department has decided that Bob should be allowed access to create and delete EPGs within the tenant named Production but should not be allowed access to modify any other objects within the tenant. After careful consideration, IT has decided that Bob can also be provided complete read-only access to the Production tenant and full access to modify any object within another tenant called Development. Note that these requirements are very basic and do not necessitate the creation of custom RBAC roles. These requirements can be enforced using the read-all and tenant-admin roles, respectively.

A security domain that grants access to the tenant called Production has already been created (refer to Figure 15-2), and a custom RBAC role called EPG-Admin has also been created (refer to Figure 15-5), but a new security domain and a reference to the security domain by the Development tenant is also needed. Once this new security domain is created, the AAA administrator can create a user for Bob and begin to allocate the required access. Figure 15-6 shows how you navigate to **Admin > AAA > Security > Users** and select Create Local User from the pull-down menu to create a user for Bob.

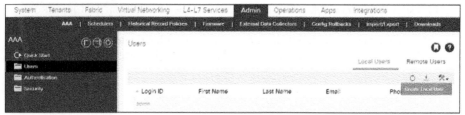

Figure 15-6 *Opening the Create Local User Wizard*

In the Create Local User window, you select a user ID and password for Bob. Figure 15-7 shows the first page of the Create Local User wizard, where you enter user identity data.

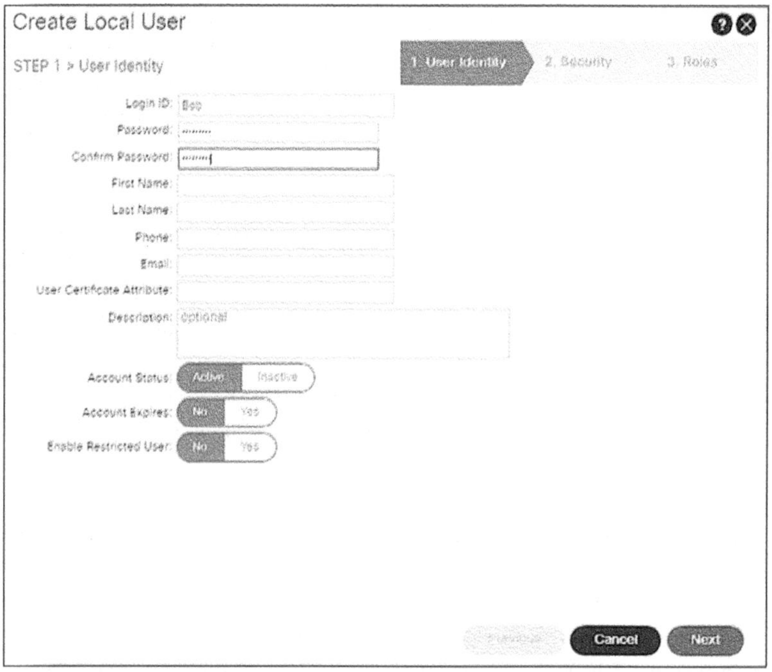

Figure 15-7 *Entering User Identity Information in the Create Local User Page*

Most of the fields in the User Identity page are self-explanatory. However, the following points are worthy of note:

- **Login ID requirements:** Login IDs can be up to 32 characters long. Letters, numbers, underscores, dashes, and dots are acceptable characters for login IDs.

- **Default ACI password requirements:** By default, the ACI password strength check necessitates that passwords be at least eight characters in length and have fewer than three consecutive repeated characters. Passwords can contain lowercase or uppercase letters, digits, and symbols. Passwords cannot be those that can be easily predicted using a dictionary attack, cannot be permutations of words like cisco, and cannot be the reverse of the username. You can disable password strength check for non-production use cases by using the **no password pwd-strength-check** APIC CLI command, or you can modify the strength check to reflect corporate password strength policies. To create a custom policy, navigate to **Admin > AAA > Security > Management Settings** and select Create Password Strength Policy from the pull-down menu. If password strength check has been disabled via the APIC CLI, the implementation of a modified password strength policy requires that the password strength check be reenabled first.

- **User Certificate Attribute setting:** This is the client certificate user identity used to enable certificate-based authentication.

- **Account Status setting:** This parameter determines whether the user is active and able to log in to the fabric or is temporarily disabled. The account status field can be toggled whenever there is a need to manually disable or enable an account.

- **Account Expires setting:** By setting the Account Expires option to Yes, you can define an expiration date and time for the user object. ACI does not delete the user account when the expiration date is hit, but it does disable logins into the fabric from the expired user account.

As shown in Figure 15-8, the second page in the Create Local User wizard is where you assign security domains to a user. Because the requirements for the user Bob involved both the Development tenant and the Production tenant, both security domains should be added here.

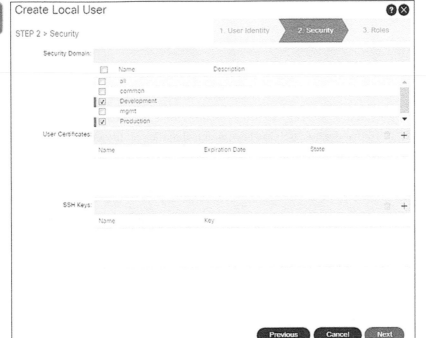

Figure 15-8 *Assigning a User to Security Domains*

After mapping the user Bob to the two security domains, you need to fulfill the access requirements by assigning Bob the custom EPG-Admin role for the Production security domain using the access privilege type Write. Bob also needs read-only access to the entire tenant named Production. This can be accomplished by mapping the Production security domain to the role named read-all with access privilege type Read. Bob also needs full access to the Development tenant, which can be accomplished by mapping Bob to the role tenant-admin and the Write access privilege type. These three changes are reflected in Figure 15-9. Click Finish to execute the user creation.

Figure 15-9 *Mapping Access Levels to Security Domains for a Local User*

Notice in Figure 15-10 that the user Bob has been assigned to the security domains, roles, and access privilege types specified. However, he has also been assigned read-only access to the common tenant.

Figure 15-10 *ACI Grants Local Users Read-Only Access to the Common Tenant*

ACI automatically grants locally created tenant-focused ACI users read-only access to the common tenant because objects within the common tenant can be consumed by all other tenants.

When the user Bob logs in to ACI, he realizes that he does not have visibility into all the menus within the fabric. Figure 15-11 illustrates that Bob does not have access to the Fabric menu, for example. Figure 15-11 also shows that the user Bob can create EPGs within the Production tenant, as indicated by the fact that the Create Application EPG menu option is not grayed out.

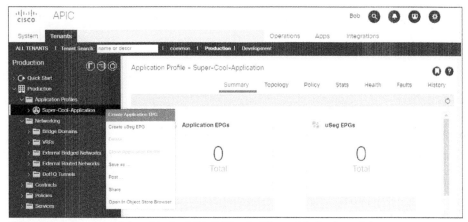

Figure 15-11 *Verifying Limited Visibility in Line with Assigned Access*

Tweaking Roles and User Access

Bob currently has the access he needs. If the organization someday decides, however, that users like Bob need expanded access to the Production tenant, the custom EPG-Admin role can be modified to include a broader number of privileges. This can pose some new problems if not all the users that have already been assigned to the EPG-Admin role are expected to have such elevated privileges. If this is the case and the EPG-Admin role cannot be modified, a new role should be created with elevated privileges, and it should be mapped to Bob and any other relevant users.

Figure 15-12 shows how the IT department could elevate users like Bob to a whitelisting and security administrator role by expanding the privileges associated with the custom EPG-Admin role to also include the tenant-security and tenant-network-profile privileges. After this change, users like Bob are able to not only create new application profiles but also create filters, filter entries, subjects, and contracts. They are also able to assign the security constructs they create to EPGs within the tenants to which they have been assigned write access via the EPG-Admin role.

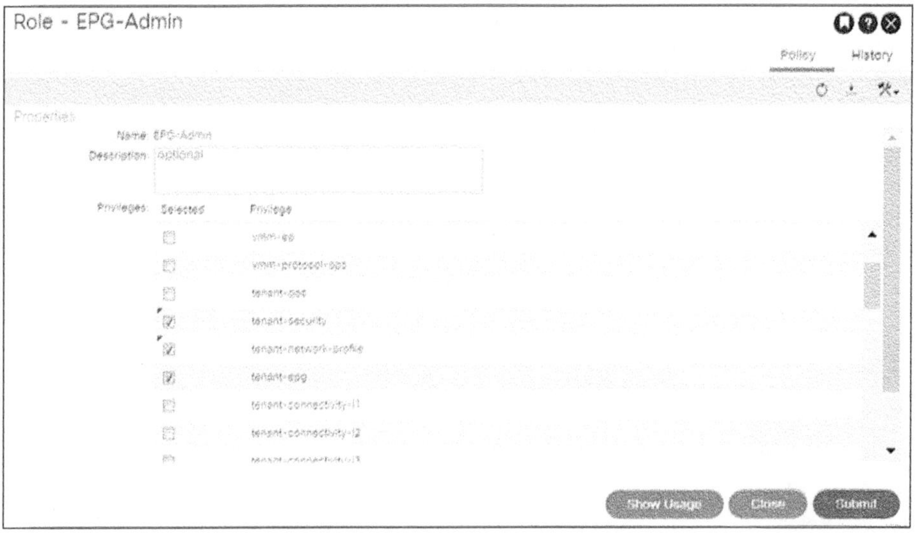

Role - EPG-Admin

Properties

Name: EPG-Admin
Description: optional

Privileges:

Selected	Privilege
☐	vmm-ep
☐	vmm-protocol-ops
☐	tenant-qos
☑	tenant-security
☑	tenant-network-profile
☑	tenant-epg
☐	tenant-connectivity-l1
☐	tenant-connectivity-l2
☐	tenant-connectivity-l3

Figure 15-12 *Expanding Privileges Associated with a Role*

Let's say that tenant-focused users like Bob are also expected to be able to map EPGs to physical ports and encapsulations in the ACI fabric. There are two obstacles to achieving this level of access. First, Bob and like users have not yet been mapped to a security domain that grants them visibility into the relevant domain subtrees of the ACI hierarchical object tree. Second, even if they did have visibility to a domain, they would also need to have visibility to the port configurations to be able to select the port to which the EPG should be assigned.

The problem of lack of access to a domain can be easily resolved. In Figure 15-13, the fabric admin user navigates to the domain named Production-Domain and adds a reference to the security domain named Production, to which Bob has already been assigned.

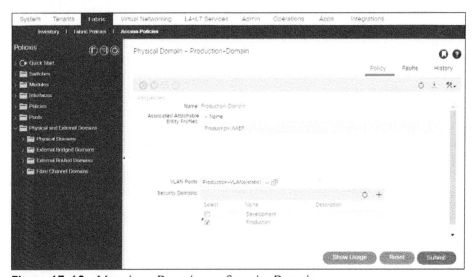

Figure 15-13 *Mapping a Domain to a Security Domain*

Once the domain named Production-Domain is mapped to the Production security domain, Bob is able to bind EPGs within the tenant named Production to the domain called Production-Domain. To bind an EPG to a domain, Bob navigates to **Tenants > Production > Application Profiles** and then drills down to the relevant application profile, drills down into the relevant EPG, opens up the Domains folder, and selects Add Physical Domain Association from the pull-down menu (see Figure 15-14).

Figure 15-14   *Binding an EPG to a Domain in the Tenant View*

The reason Bob selects Add Physical Domain Association and not the other pull-down menu options is that Bob intends to map the EPG to encapsulations for bare-metal servers. The process of enabling Bob to add VMM domain associations to EPGs is similar to the process shown previously. Figure 15-15 shows that Bob now has visibility to the domain called Production-Domain, which he adds and clicks Submit.

Figure 15-15   *Binding a Domain to an EPG*

While the first obstacle to allowing Bob to assign EPGs to ports has been resolved, and EPGs like the one called Web-Tier can now be bound to a domain, Bob is still unable to assign the EPGs in the Production tenant to ports. This, you will find, is due to lack of access privileges to the underlying infrastructure. Figure 15-16 demonstrates this challenge and how Bob is unable to select ports to make EPG assignments even though he may be able to select a VLAN encapsulation now that a domain-to-security domain mapping is in place.

Figure 15-16 *Challenges with Lack of Visibility to Underlying Ports*

One potential solution to this challenge could be to provide Bob read-only access to the pre-defined domain called all; however, this may not be an acceptable solution for service providers or in IT environments in which tenant access is granted to partners. Another possible solution is for ACI administrators to create a custom RBAC rule that enables more granular access to the specific portion of the ACI object hierarchy without exposing details of the fabric view to users like Bob.

Custom RBAC Rules

If your organization needs more granular RBAC over resources than is possible via privileges, roles, and security domains, you can create custom RBAC rules.

RBAC rules allow granular control on top of the existing RBAC framework and conform to the following principles:

- RBAC rules are additive and associative.

- RBAC rules cannot be used to deny access to portions of the ACI object hierarchy.

- Effective use of RBAC rules requires that you gain knowledge of the ACI object hierarchy and learn how to find DNs for any given object.

- When creating an RBAC rule, ACI only validates for DN format and not for the existence of the specified DN. This makes the pre-staging of RBAC prior to full policy deployment a possibility.

- During creation of an RBAC rule, you need to select whether users assigned to relevant security domains will have read-only access or full control of the object subtree.

For Bob and other tenant security administrators to be able to map EPGs to physical ports, an RBAC rule can be created to grant the security domain named Production read-only access to a portion of the ACI object hierarchy called topology. Figure 15-17 shows how you navigate to **Admin > AAA > Security > RBAC Rules > Explicit Rules** and select Create RBAC Rule to open the Create RBAC Rule wizard.

Figure 15-17   *Navigating to the Create RBAC Rule Wizard*

Figure 15-18 shows how you expose the topology subtree to all users who have access to the Production security domain without allowing such users to make any changes to the topology subtree.

Figure 15-18   *Creating a Custom RBAC Rule*

The user Bob needs to log out and log back in for access changes to take effect.

With the custom RBAC rule in place, Bob and other users assigned to the Production security domain should have access to map EPGs within the Production tenant to any physical server or appliance whose port configuration references the AAEP called Production-AAEP, using any encapsulation in the VLAN ID range defined by the VLAN pool called Production-VLANs.

Figure 15-19 shows Bob trunking the EPG called Web-Tier to port 1/20 on a leaf switch identified as Leaf 301, using an encapsulation of VLAN ID 505.

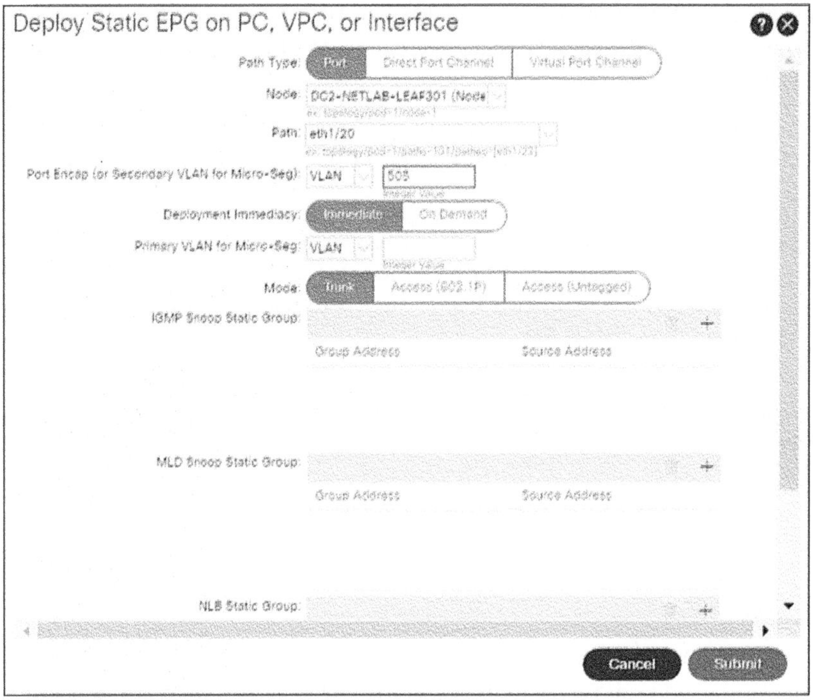

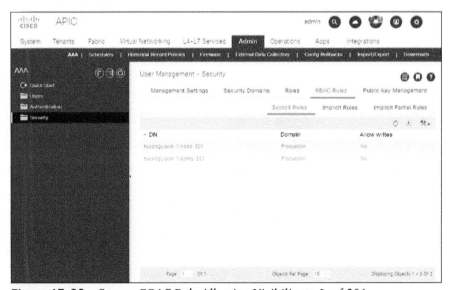

Figure 15-19   *Successfully Mapping an Encapsulation to a Port*

If you do not want to grant read-only access to the entire topology hierarchy, you can assign access to a specific subset of fabric nodes. Figure 15-20 demonstrates how alternative custom RBAC rules could be created to assign access to Node 301 and its paths (ports), thereby restricting the access of users like Bob to ports on Leaf 301.

Figure 15-20   *Custom RBAC Rule Allowing Visibility to Leaf 301*

As a result of this change, Bob sees only Leaf 301 as an option for mapping encapsulations to underlying switch ports. Other leaf switches, such as Leaf 302, are unavailable to Bob (see Figure 15-21).

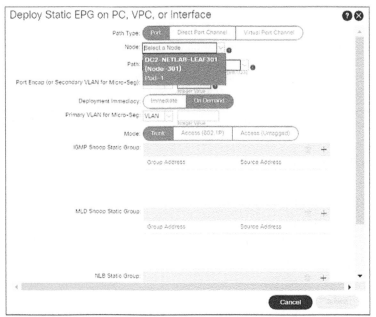

Figure 15-21   *User Visibility Restricted to Leaf 301 and Its Ports*

A Common RBAC Pitfall

Where security policies dictate that users be allocated the minimum level of access necessary to perform their job duties, it is especially important to define RBAC to fulfill the expected granularity requirements.

It is possible to use the predefined roles with security domains to enforce a good level of control, but it is just as important for administrators to fully understand the privileges that are being granted as a result of role assignments and to design RBAC accordingly.

For example, if a AAA administrator decides to allocate a user access to the tenant-admin role using the predefined security domain all, it may be assumed that the user would only have access to tenant-specific functions due to the name of the role assigned. This assumption would be far from the truth. In reality, the tenant-admin role grants the majority of privileges available in an ACI fabric to the new user. When this is combined with the security domain all, the user has capabilities that come very close to the predefined admin user capabilities in an ACI fabric.

The safest approach to RBAC in environments that demand clear delineation between roles is to start with a restrictive approach and gradually add privileges and visibility to additional subtrees of the ACI object hierarchy when additional requirements are identified.

Integrating with External AAA Servers

This chapter has so far touched on RBAC deployment using local users. This section addresses how ACI can integrate with external AAA servers via the TACACS+, RADIUS, and LDAP protocols.

> **NOTE** The scope of the Implementing Cisco Application Centric Infrastructure DCACI 300-620 exam is limited to ACI-side configurations only. Knowledge of products such as Cisco Identity Service Engine (ISE) is not tested on the exam. Therefore, this book does not cover the low-level details of ISE configuration for ACI device administration but instead provides a high-level explanation of the ISE configuration process in an effort to avoid confusion around the authentication and authorization process.

Configuring ACI for TACACS+

ACI configuration for TACACS+ involves three basic steps:

Step 1. Create the desired TACACS+ providers.

Step 2. If using ACI versions prior to Release 4 or configuring ACI via the APIC CLI, create a TACACS+ provider group.

Step 3. Create a TACACS+ login domain.

A TACACS+ provider is a reference to an individual TACACS+ server that details how ACI nodes communicate with the specified server. Table 15-3 describes the configuration options available in a TACACS+ provider definition.

Table 15-3 Configuration Parameters for TACACS+ Providers

Configuration Parameter	Description
Host Name or IP Address	ACI allows you to reference a TACACS+ server using either its IP address or DNS address.
Port	This is the TCP port number ACI needs to use to connect to the TACACS+ daemon. The range is from 1 to 65535. The default is 49.
Authorization Protocol	TACACS+ authorization protocols include PAP, MS-CHAP, and CHAP. The default TACACS+ authorization protocol is PAP.
Key	This is the shared secret key that ACI nodes and the TACACS+ server use for encrypting and decrypting traffic between one another.
Timeout	This is the number of seconds the ACI node waits for a response from the TACACS+ provider before timing out. The acceptable range is from 5 to 60 seconds. The default is 5 seconds.
Retries	This is the number of times ACI automatically retries login attempts for a single authentication submission. The acceptable range is from 1 to 5 retries. The default is 1.

Configuration Parameter	Description
Management EPG	This is the management EPG (in-band or out-of-band) from which ACI should source requests to the TACACS+ server.
Server Monitoring	This parameter can be set to either Enabled or Disabled. When it is enabled for a TACACS+ provider, the APICs periodically attempt to execute login attempts against the TACACS+ provider to verify that the TACACS+ service is alive on the server. When enabled, ACI asks administrators to additionally enter a username and password. By default, Server Monitoring is set to Disabled. Server monitoring checks are exclusive to APICs. To enable monitoring checks that leafs and spines are also able to perform, use of the Ping Check option under the AAA Policy view is more common.

To navigate to the TACACS+ provider creation page, click the Admin menu, select AAA, and then select Authentication followed by TACACS. Finally, right-click the Tools menu and select Create TACACS+ Provider, as shown in Figure 15-22.

Figure 15-22 *Navigating to the Create TACACS+ Provider Page*

Figure 15-23 shows the creation of a TACACS+ provider that references a server at 10.233.48.60, using mostly default settings.

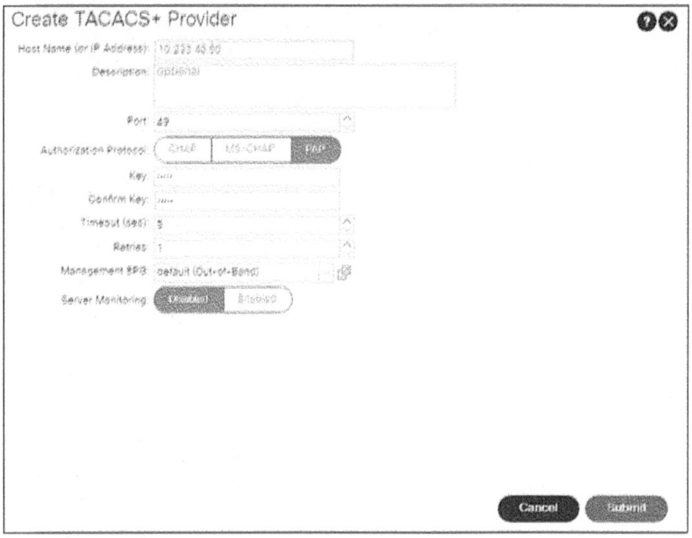

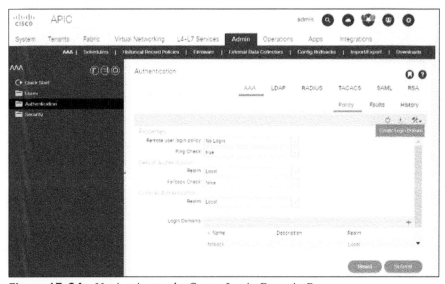

Figure 15-23   *Configuring a TACACS+ Provider*

In this deployment, the ACI software version does not require creation of a TACACS+ provider group. Therefore, you can move on to step 3 of the process and create a login domain referencing any desired TACACS+ providers. It is only after a TACACS+ login domain is created that users are able to authenticate and authorize against TACACS+ servers.

To create a login domain, navigate to Admin, click AAA, select Authentication, choose the AAA submenu, select Policy, select the Tools menu, and click Create Login Domain, as shown in Figure 15-24.

Figure 15-24   *Navigating to the Create Login Domain Page*

On the Create Login Domain page, enter the name that is expected to appear in the login drop-down box, select the desired realm (the AAA method), and select the providers associated with the login domain. You can prioritize the use of a specific provider by using the Priority field. If ACI deems all listed providers as healthy via the Ping Check or Server Monitoring features, ACI attempts to authenticate against the AAA providers in the ranked priority configured. Figure 15-25 shows a login domain configuration that prioritizes the TACACS+ server at 10.233.48.60.

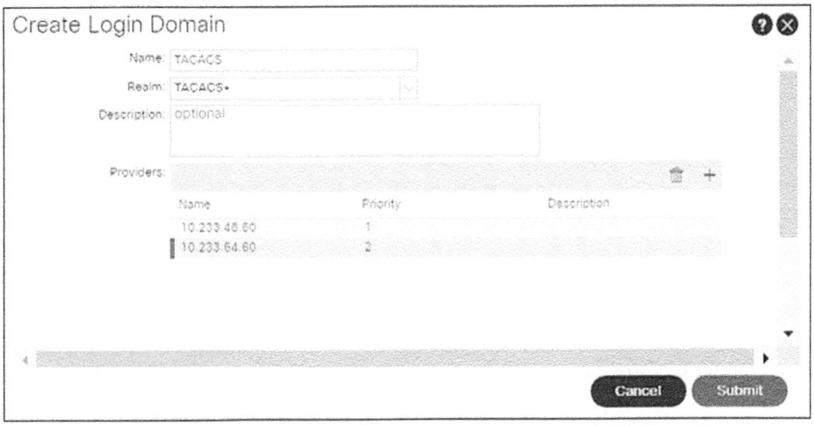

Figure 15-25   *Configuring a TACACS+ Login Domain*

Once the TACACS+ login domain is created, users can select it from the Domain drop-down box to authenticate against the configured providers. Figure 15-26 shows the user Bob trying to authenticate against the TACACS+ login domain.

Figure 15-26   *Selecting a Custom Domain During GUI Login*

The GUI-based configurations presented in Figure 15-22 through Figure 15-25 can also be done using the APIC CLI. Example 15-1 presents the commands needed.

Example 15-1 *Configuring ACI for TACACS+ via the APIC CLI*

```
APIC1(config)# show run
(...output truncated for brevity...)
  tacacs-server host "10.233.48.60"
    exit
  tacacs-server host "10.233.64.60"
    exit
  aaa group server tacacsplus TACACS
    server 10.233.48.60 priority 1
    server 10.233.64.60 priority 2
    exit
  aaa authentication login domain TACACS
    realm tacacs
    group TACACS
    exit
```

Note in this example that new ACI software still groups TACACS servers together behind the scenes, but the GUI abstracts this step from users. Also, notice that the key values involving passwords do not appear in **show** command output.

Configuring ISE to Authenticate and Authorize Users for ACI

The high-level process for configuring ISE to allow authentication and authorization of ACI users is as follows:

NOTE In these steps, references to menu items are valid for ISE Release 2.7. Other releases of ISE may require slightly different steps.

Step 1. **Enable Device Admin Service:** For ISE to perform TACACS+ operations, ensure that the Enable Device Admin Service checkbox is enabled under **Administration > System > Deployment**.

Step 2. **Configure AAA clients:** Navigate to **Administration > Network Resources > Network Devices** and create entries for ACI nodes. It is recommended that a specific device type be defined for ACI nodes under **Administration > Network Resources > Network Device Groups** beforehand. Configuring a specific network device group for ACI nodes enables ISE administrators to group ACI authentication and authorization rules based on a device type condition.

Step 3. **Configure user identity groups:** Think of user identity groups in the context of ACI authorization as a grouping of users with the same expected level of access. The user Bob, for instance, is a junior administrator who is expected to have different levels of access for several different security domains. For example, he might be categorized into a junior-admin user identity group. To fulfill the needs of a hypothetical deployment that requires a group of ACI administrators, a group of ACI network operators, and a group of junior engineers, three user identity groups can be used.

Step 4.   **Configure users and associate each of them with a user identity group:** Users can be created locally on ISE servers, or ISE can integrate with external user databases. Each user needs to be assigned to a user identity group so that ISE can map the user to an authorization rule.

Step 5.   **Create a TACACS profile for each user identity group:** A TACACS profile includes a custom attribute that specifies the security domains, roles, and privilege types associated with each user identity group. TACACS profiles are sometimes also referred to as shell profiles. A TACACS profile does not directly point to a user identity group. user identity group-to-TACACS profile mappings result from authorization rules.

Step 6.   **Create a device admin policy set for ACI:** An ACI-specific device admin policy set enables ISE administrators to group authentication and authorization rules for ACI nodes. The authentication condition for the policy set may be the device type. Each authorization rule may be simply map a TACACS profile (shell profile) to a specific user identity group.

Figure 15-27 shows a TACACS profile for ACI that includes the string *shell:domains* followed by a set of three comma-separated security domain assignments. The information entered here has been specially formatted for ACI.

Figure 15-27   *Authorization Data Configuration Through a TACACS Profile*

To map the TACACS profiles with users, you can use authorization rules like the ones in Figure 15-28.

Figure 15-28   *Mapping TACACS Profiles to Users Based on Group Membership*

As a result of the ACI and ISE configurations, the user Bob should be able to log in to the fabric by using the TACACS login domain and be assigned the correct Cisco attribute/value (AV) pair. Figure 15-29 verifies that ISE has passed the parameters configured in the desired shell profile to ACI, providing Bob with the access he requires. You can navigate to **Admin > AAA > Users > Remote Users** and double-click the desired user to verify that the proper Cisco AV pair has been allocated to a user.

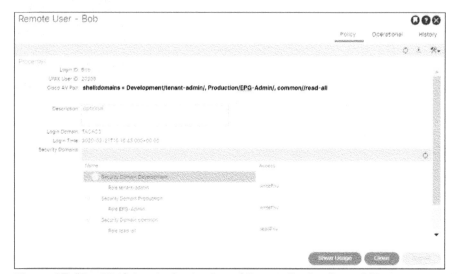

Figure 15-29   *Verifying Authorization of Externally Configured Users*

Expected Cisco AV Pair Formatting for ACI

For ACI to assign users the correct level of access, the Cisco AV pair returned by the external servers needs to be specially formatted. The following two formats are valid for ACI:

NOTE   The Cisco AV pair string is case-sensitive.

Format 1:

```
shell:domains = domainA/writeRole1|writeRole2|writeRole3/
readRole1|readRole2,
```

```
domainB/writeRole1|writeRole2|writeRole3/readRole1|readRole2
```

Format 2:

```
shell:domains = domainA/writeRole1|writeRole2|writeRole3/
readRole1|readRole2,
```

```
domainB/writeRole1|writeRole2|writeRole3/
readRole1|readRole2(userId)
```

Note here that the / character is a separator between write roles and read roles for each login domain and is required even if only one type of role needs to be assigned.

The only difference between the two formats is that the second one also specifies a trailing UNIX user ID. Cisco recommends assigning a unique user ID in the range 16000 to 23999. This is especially important for users who need to log in to switches or APICs via the CLI to create files or run scripts against the system. It ensures that key users have separate home directories and that any files or processes a user creates get associated with the user's unique user ID.

The Cisco AV pair formatting required by ACI can be best understood through examples, such as those presented in Table 15-4.

Table 15-4   Examples of *shell:domains* Value Assignments

Value Assigned to *shell:domains*	User Access
all//read_all	The user gains access to the all security domain via the read_all role, using the privilege type Read. Notice that the privilege type is interpreted to be Read if there are two instances of the / character between the security domain and role.
all/admin/(16005)	The user gains access to the all security domain via the admin role, using privilege type Write. Notice that the privilege type is interpreted to be Write if there is only one instance of the / character between the security domain and role. ACI assigns UNIX user ID 16005 to the user(s).
all//admin	The user gains access to the all security domain via the admin role, using the privilege type Read. Assignment of this value is beneficial when a network operator needs read-only access to the entire fabric but also needs to log in to switches. Logging in to ACI switches via the command line requires the admin role.
all/aaa/read-all	The user gains access to the all security domain via the aaa role, using the privilege type Write. In addition, the user gains access to the all security domain via the read-all role, using the privilege type Read.

15

Value Assigned to *shell:domains*	User Access
all/fabric-adminlaccess-admin/	The user gains access to the all security domain via both the fabric-admin and access-admin roles, using the privilege type Write.
Development/tenant-admin/, Production/EPG-Admin/, common//read-all	The user gains access to the Development security domain via the tenant-admin role, using the privilege type Write. The user also gains access to the Production security domain via the custom-defined EPG-Admin role, using the privilege type Write. The user also gains access to the common security domain via the read-all role, using the privilege type Read.

The Cisco AV pair formatting expected for authorization is the same regardless of whether TACACS+, RADIUS, or LDAP is used.

Configuring ACI for RADIUS

ACI configuration for RADIUS is very similar to ACI configuration for TACACS+ and involves the following three basic steps:

Step 1. Create the desired RADIUS providers.

Step 2. If using ACI versions prior to Release 4 or configuring via the APIC CLI, create a RADIUS provider group.

Step 3. Create a RADIUS login domain.

Table 15-5 describes the configuration options available in a RADIUS provider definition.

Table 15-5 Configuration Parameters for RADIUS Providers

Configuration Parameter	Description
Host Name or IP Address	ACI allows administrators to reference a RADIUS server by using either its IP address or DNS address.
Authorization Port	This is the service port number for the RADIUS service. The range is from 1 to 65535. The default is 1812.
Authorization Protocol	RADIUS authorization protocols include PAP, MS-CHAP, and CHAP. The default RADIUS authorization protocol is PAP.
Key	This is the shared secret key that ACI nodes and the RADIUS server use for encrypting and decrypting passwords between one another. In contrast with TACACS+, which encrypts the entire payload, RADIUS encrypts passwords only.
Timeout	This is the number of seconds the ACI node waits for a response from the RADIUS provider before timing out. The acceptable range is from 5 to 60 seconds. The default is 5 seconds.
Retries	This is the number of times ACI automatically retries login attempts for a single authentication submission. The acceptable range is from 1 to 5 retries. The default is 1.

Configuration Parameter	Description
Management EPG	This is the management EPG (in-band or out-of-band) from which ACI should source requests to the RADIUS server.
Server Monitoring	This parameter can be set to either Enabled or Disabled. When it is enabled for a RADIUS provider, the APICs periodically attempt to execute login attempts against the RADIUS provider to verify that the RADIUS service is alive on the server. When enabled, ACI asks administrators to additionally enter a username and password. By default, Server Monitoring is set to Disabled. Server monitoring checks are exclusive to APICs. To enable monitoring checks that leafs and spines are also able to perform, use of the Ping Check option under the AAA Policy view is more common.

Example 15-2 presents the commands needed for configuring RADIUS via the APIC CLI.

Example 15-2 *Configuring ACI for RADIUS via the APIC CLI*

```
APIC1(config)# show run
(...output truncated for brevity...)
  radius-server host "10.233.48.67"
    exit
  aaa group server radius RADIUS
    server 10.233.48.67 priority 1
    exit
  aaa authentication login domain RADIUS
    realm radius
    group RADIUS
    exit
```

Note in this example that new ACI software also groups RADIUS servers together behind the scenes even though the GUI abstracts this step from users. Again, key values do not appear in **show** command output.

Configuring ACI for LDAP

ACI configuration for LDAP integration involves the following basic steps:

Step 1. Configure the desired LDAP providers.

Step 2. Configure LDAP group map rules unless the LDAP providers have been configured to return Cisco AV pairs.

Step 3. Configure an LDAP group map.

Step 4. Create an LDAP login domain.

Table 15-6 describes the configuration options available in an LDAP provider definition.

Table 15-6 Configuration Parameters for LDAP Providers

Configuration Parameter	Description
HostName or IP Address	ACI allows administrators to reference an LDAP server by using either its IP address or DNS address.
Port	This is the service port number for the LDAP service. The range is from 1 to 65535. The default is 389.
Bind DN	This is a string referencing an account on an LDAP server that is able to query at least a portion of the LDAP directory hierarchy. This account should ideally be a system account with a non-expiring password. In non-production environments leveraging LDAP servers with anonymous bind capabilities, this field can be left empty. LDAP server administrators need to provide ACI administrators the exact Bind DN string.
Base DN	This is a string referencing the container and subtree under which ACI is able to execute queries for matching users using the bind account. LDAP server administrators need to provide ACI administrators the exact Base DN string.
Password	This is the password of the LDAP account specified in the Bind DN field.
Timeout	This is the number of seconds ACI nodes wait for a response from the LDAP provider server. The acceptable range is from 5 to 60 seconds. The default is 30 seconds.
Retries	This is the number of times ACI automatically retries login attempts for a single authentication submission. The acceptable range is from 1 to 5 retries. The default is 1.
Enable SSL	This checkbox allows administrators to enforce SSL-based connections with the LDAP provider.
SSL Certificate Validation Level	Acceptable values for this option are Permissive and Strict. Permissive certificate checking relaxes requirements around certificate validation, making it an ideal option in deployments that use self-signed certificates. Strict certificate validation is ideal in production environments.
Attribute	ACI determines the level of user authorization from the Attribute field. The two most common values for this field are memberOf and CiscoAVPair. When using the memberOf option, configuration of LDAP group map rules is mandatory.
Filter Type	Filters define how ACI queries an LDAP schema and interprets the existence of a user. The LDAP provider configuration page provides three options for the Filter Type parameter: Default, Microsoft AD, and Custom.
Custom Filter	This is a custom filter value.
Management EPG	This is the management EPG (in-band or out-of-band) from which ACI should source requests to the LDAP server.
Server Monitoring	This parameter can be set to either Enabled or Disabled. When it is enabled for an LDAP provider, the APICs periodically attempt to execute login attempts against the LDAP provider to verify that the LDAP service is alive on the server. When enabled, ACI asks administrators to additionally enter a username and password. By default, Server Monitoring is set to Disabled. Server monitoring checks are exclusive to APICs. To enable monitoring checks that leafs and spines are also able to perform, use of the Ping Check option under the AAA Policy view is more common.

The Filter Type option requires further explanation. If you select the Default filter type in a GUI-based LDAP provider configuration, ACI does not ask users to enter a custom filter. Instead, it uses the string cn=$userid as the filter. This is suitable for most LDAP implementations that define users as common name (cn) objects. In Microsoft Active Directory implementations, selection of the Microsoft AD filter type prompts ACI to configure sAMAccountName=$userid as the filter. For any LDAP schema that requires use of a different filter, select the Custom filter type to expose the Custom Filter field and enter a filter that is more suitable to the LDAP implementation.

Figure 15-30 shows how to open the LDAP provider creation wizard by navigating to **Admin > AAA >Authentication > LDAP > Providers**, clicking the Tools menu, and selecting Create LDAP Provider.

Figure 15-30 *Navigating to the Create LDAP Provider Page*

Notice in Figure 15-31 that the memberOf attribute is used in the LDAP configuration. This tells ACI that it should expect the LDAP server to return the LDAP-based group membership of the users instead of a Cisco AV pair. In addition, Filter Type is set to Custom, and the Custom Filter field is set to cn=$userid in. However, you could instead set Filter Type to Default.

In addition to having LDAP providers defined, ACI needs to know how to map LDAP group memberships with ACI RBAC constructs to determine the level of authorization. To define such mappings, you open the Create LDAP Group Map Rules wizard, as shown in Figure 15-32.

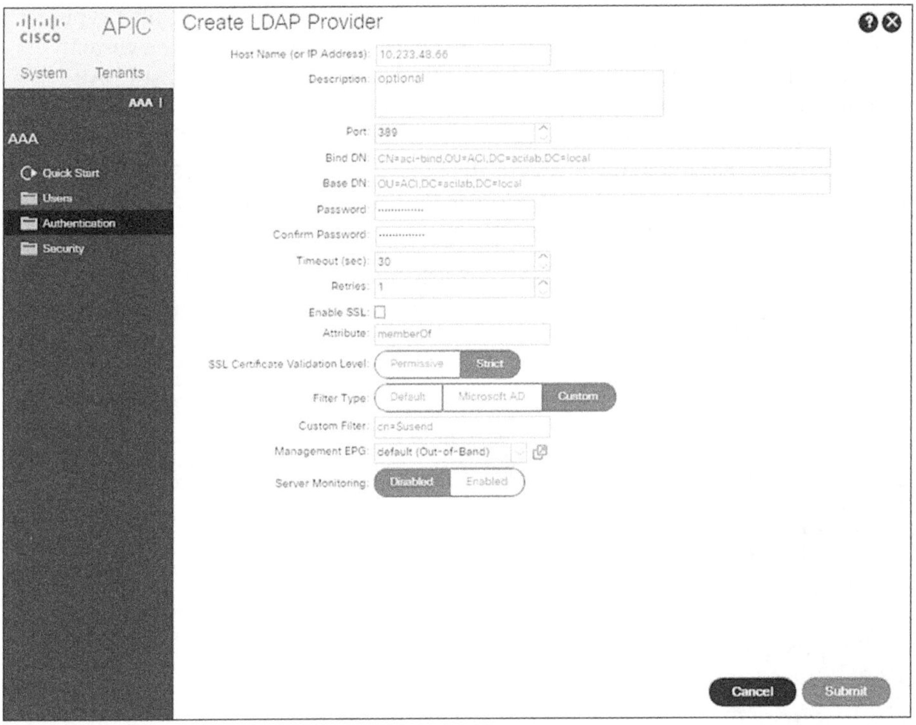

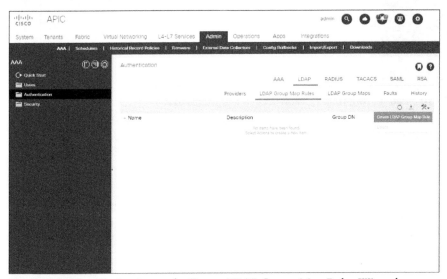

Figure 15-31 *Defining an LDAP Provider*

Figure 15-32 *Navigating to the Create LDAP Group Map Rules Wizard*

The first page in the Create LDAP Group Map Rules wizard asks for the group DN the LDAP servers will return for a given group defined on the LDAP servers. ACI also needs to know what security domains users with the specified group membership should be able to access. Figure 15-33 shows the LDAP Group DN setting and the security domains ACI should correlate with the specified LDAP group.

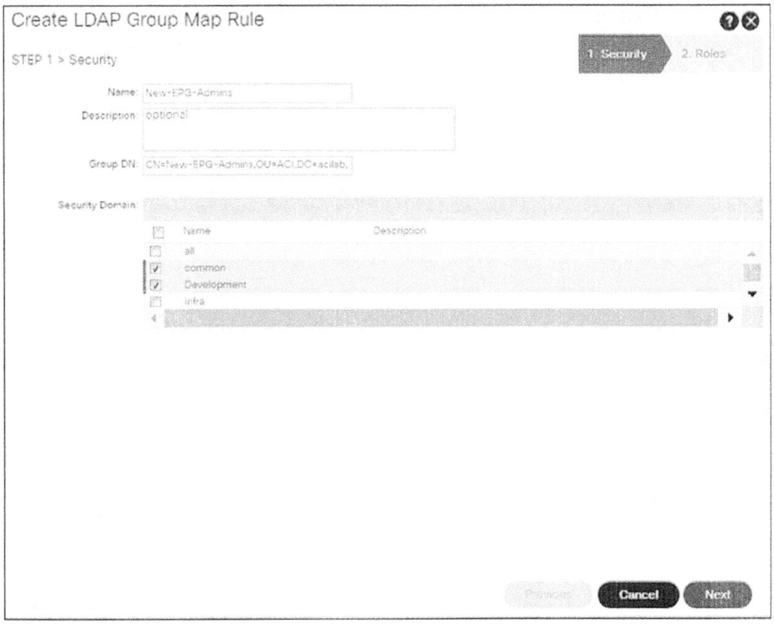

Figure 15-33   *The Create LDAP Group Map Rules Wizard, Page 1*

Figure 15-34 shows how to associate roles and privileges with each security domain specified.

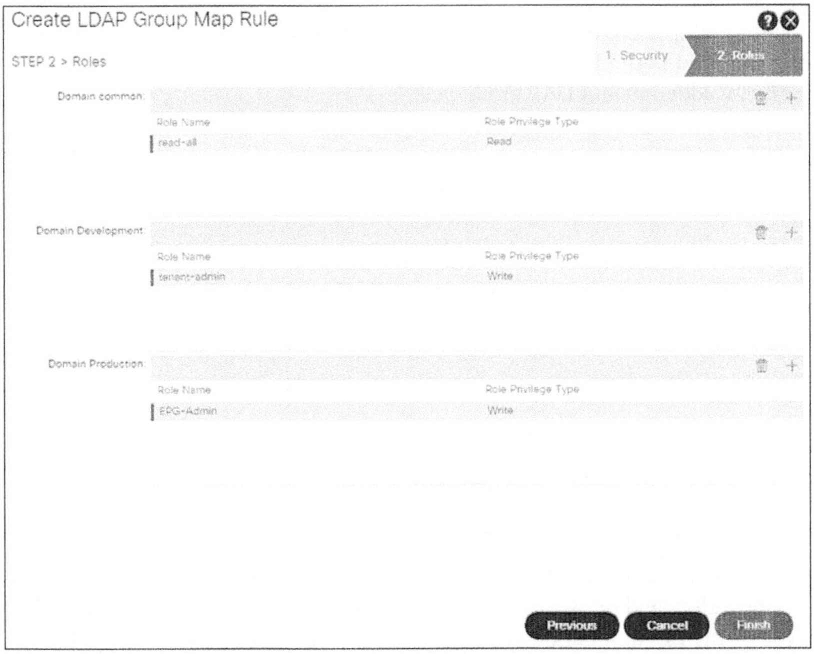

Figure 15-34   *The Create LDAP Group Map Rules Wizard, Page 2*

By the end of the process, LDAP group-to-ACI access level mappings should have been configured for each family of ACI users that will be authenticated and authorized via LDAP. Figure 15-35 shows a deployment with three sets of mapping rules.

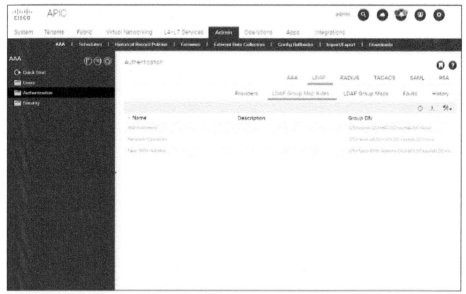

Figure 15-35   *LDAP Group Map Rules*

The LDAP mapping rules can then be grouped together into an LDAP group map. When a deployment requires multiple LDAP login domains, administrators can associate a different LDAP group map to each LDAP login domain. Figure 15-36 shows the three LDAP group map rule entries being added to an LDAP group map.

Figure 15-36   *Configuring an LDAP Group Map*

Finally, you need to configure an LDAP login domain by selecting the authorization method, the desired LDAP providers, and the associated LDAP group map for user login. Figure 15-37 shows an example of the LDAP login domain configuration. This example uses LDAP group mappings for user authorization. In cases where LDAP can associate Cisco AV pairs with users, the LDAP login domain and provider can leverage CiscoAVPair for authorization, which does not require the configuration of LDAP group map rules.

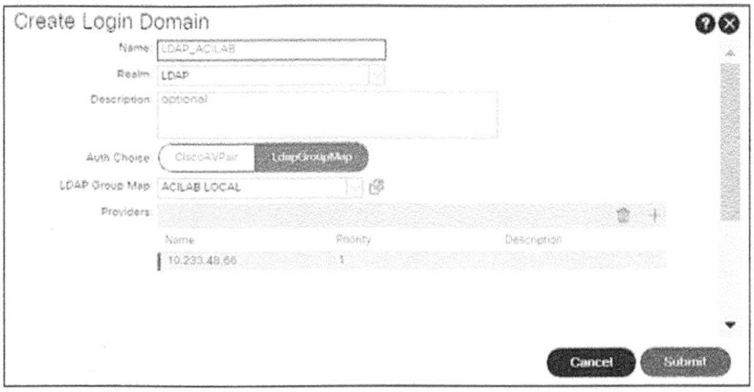

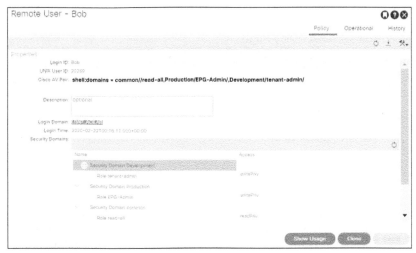

Figure 15-37   *Configuring an LDAP Login Domain*

When a user logs in to the fabric using an LDAP login domain, the level of access granted to the user can be validated in the Remote User screen. Regardless of the configured authorization method, the Remote User screen shows the associated Cisco AV pair, as shown in Figure 15-38.

Figure 15-38   *Verifying the Level of Access for LDAP-Authenticated Users*

AAA Authentication Policy Settings

There are several global AAA configuration settings that users can tweak at **Admin > AAA > Authentication > AAA > Policy**. Figure 15-39 shows these settings.

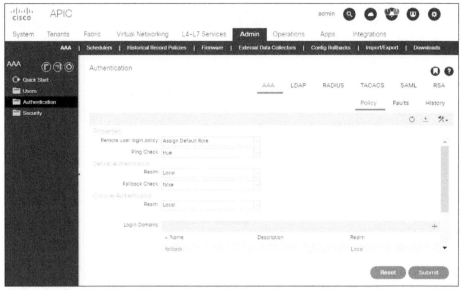

Figure 15-39 *Configuration Options on the AAA Policy Page*

Table 15-7 describes these settings and the drop-down list values users can choose for each setting.

Table 15-7   Settings on the AAA Policy Page

Setting	Description
Remote User Login Policy	There are two acceptable values for this setting. Assign Default Role ensures that any remotely authenticated user with a bad or missing Cisco AV pair gets assigned to the common security domain using the read-all role and the privilege type Read. No Login, on the other hand, ensures that such users cannot log in to the fabric. The default value for this setting is No Login.
Ping Check	ACI performs ICMP health checks against AAA providers. The Ping Check setting can be set to either True or False. ACI continues to run ICMP health checks against all AAA providers, regardless of the value chosen. If Ping Check is set to True, ACI removes inaccessible providers from the authentication process and authenticates against operational providers instead. If ICMP traffic cannot reach AAA servers due to firewall rules, the Ping Check setting should be set to False to ensure that ACI continues to authenticate against all servers, regardless of the result of ICMP health checks.
Default Authentication Realm	This setting governs the login domain ACI uses when a user does not select a domain when logging in to the fabric. It also determines the login domain used when a user attempts to log in to the fabric by using the DefaultAuth domain. You can select Local, LDAP, RADIUS, TACACS+, RSA, or SAML for Default Authentication Realm. Local is selected by default. When you select a setting other than Local, an additional Login Domain field appears, allowing selection of the intended domain.

Setting	Description
Fallback Check	ACI comes with a preconfigured login domain called fallback that is set to local authentication by default. The Fallback Check setting, which can be set to True or False, enables or disables reliance on the AAA provider ICMP health check for activation of the fallback domain. If fallback check is set to True and the configured AAA providers respond to ICMP traffic but are unable to authenticate users, the fallback login domain will be unavailable, and users may remain locked out of the fabric. For this reason, Fallback Check is often kept at its default value of False.
Console Authentication Realm	This parameter allows users to specify the authentication method for console logins to ACI nodes. By default, it is set to Local. Other valid options are LDAP, RADIUS, TACACS+, and RSA. When you select a setting besides Local, ACI exposes an additional field for you to specify the login domain.

Figure 15-40 shows Default Authentication Realm set to TACACS+ and a login domain called TACACS. Fallback Check has been kept at its default value of False. The figure also shows all the available login domains in a particular fabric.

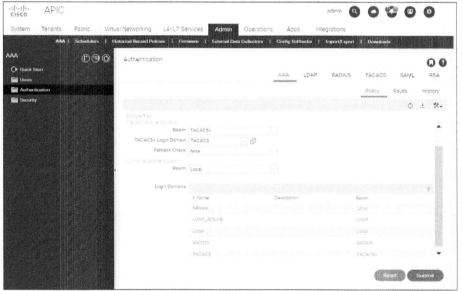

Figure 15-40 *Login Domains and Global AAA Settings Configured in a Fabric*

As a result of these settings, the login domain DefaultAuth, as shown in Figure 15-41, references the login domain called TACACS. Remember from Figure 15-40 that there is no explicit domain called DefaultAuth, as this refers to any domain set for Default Authentication Realm.

Figure 15-41 *DefaultAuth Domain Shown in ACI Login Page*

Before changing the value of the Default Authentication Realm parameter, ensure that the AAA providers associated with the preferred login domain are available and that those providers authorize users as expected.

Regaining Access to the Fabric via Fallback Domain

To use the fallback domain to regain access to a fabric due to AAA connectivity or configuration issues, use the syntax *apic:fallback\\username* in the GUI User ID field. Use the syntax *apic#fallback\\username* when logging in via the CLI.

Exam Preparation Tasks

As mentioned in the section "How to Use This Book" in the Introduction, you have a couple of choices for exam preparation: Chapter 17, "Final Preparation," and the exam simulation questions on the companion website.

Review All Key Topics

Review the most important topics in this chapter, noted with the Key Topic icon in the outer margin of the page. Table 15-8 lists these key topics and the page number on which each is found.

Table 15-8 Key Topics for Chapter 15

Key Topic Element	Description	Page Number
List	Lists the elements associated with users that collectively determine the level of management access a user has to an ACI fabric	516
Paragraph	Defines security domains	517
List	Lists the predefined out-of-the-box security domains	517
Paragraph	Defines privileges in ACI	519
Paragraph	Defines roles in ACI	519
Table 15-2	Lists and describes predefined roles in ACI	520
Figure 15-8	Demonstrates how to assign a local user to security domains	523
Figure 15-9	Demonstrates how to map roles and role privilege types to a local user	524

Key Topic Element	Description	Page Number
Paragraph	Explains that all users created in ACI gain read-only access to the common tenant	525
Paragraph/List	Defines RBAC rules and describes their characteristics	528
Figure 15-18	Shows how an RBAC rule can be created	529
List	Explains the high-level steps involved in configuring ACI for integration with TACACS+	532
Table 15-3	Describes the settings available for TACACS+ provider configurations	532
Paragraph	Documents the two Cisco AV pair formats ACI accepts from external AAA servers	539
List	Explains the high-level steps involved in configuring ACI for integration with RADIUS	540
Table 15-5	Describes the settings available for RADIUS provider configurations	540
List	Explains the high-level steps involved in configuring ACI for integration with LDAP	541
Table 15-6	Describes the settings available for LDAP provider configurations	542
Table 15-7	Describes the global AAA settings that administrators can tweak	548

15

Complete Tables and Lists from Memory

Print a copy of Appendix C, "Memory Tables" (found on the companion website), or at least the section for this chapter, and complete the tables and lists from memory. Appendix D, "Memory Tables Answer Key" (also on the companion website), includes completed tables and lists you can use to check your work.

Define Key Terms

Define the following key terms from this chapter and check your answers in the glossary:

security domain, privilege, role, RBAC rule

CHAPTER 16

ACI Anywhere

This chapter covers the following topics:

ACI Multi-Site Fundamentals: This section reviews ACI Multi-Site terminology and describes, at a high level, how ACI Multi-Site works.

Building Primary and Disaster Recovery Data Centers with ACI: This section explains why ACI Multi-Site shines in primary and DR data center designs.

Building Active/Active Data Centers with ACI: This section contrasts the use of ACI Multi-Pod and the use of ACI Multi-Site when designing active/active data centers.

Extending ACI to Remote Locations and Public Clouds: This section describes some additional use cases for ACI Multi-Pod and Multi-Site.

This chapter covers the following exam topics:

- 6.1 Describe multipod
- 6.2 Describe multisite

This book has looked closely at many of the details of ACI constructs and single-pod fabric deployments. Modern data centers, however, often need to extend beyond the confines of single-pod fabrics and into other environments. The network and whitelisting policies that have been defined for applications also need to extend into other environments. Enter ACI Anywhere.

ACI Anywhere is a marketing term that highlights not just the evolution of ACI but also all the places Cisco has been taking ACI. This term encompasses a host of solutions, including ACI Multi-Pod, ACI Multi-Site, ACI Multicloud, Remote Leaf, vPod, and other solutions yet to come. The common theme that underpins all these solutions is that together they extend the ACI operational framework across data centers, across remote locations, across bare-metal clouds, and even into public cloud environments. Together, ACI Anywhere solutions transform ACI into a true hybrid cloud solution.

Although those interested in implementation guidance need to search outside this book, this chapter shines light on some of the key use cases for ACI Multi-Pod and ACI Multi-Site. Which one best fits into your data center strategy? As you will see in this chapter, sometimes the answer can be both.

"Do I Know This Already?" Quiz

The "Do I Know This Already?" quiz allows you to assess whether you should read this entire chapter thoroughly or jump to the "Exam Preparation Tasks" section. If you are in doubt about your answers to these questions or your own assessment of your knowledge of the topics, read the entire chapter. Table 16-1 lists the major headings in this chapter and their corresponding "Do I Know This Already?" quiz questions. You can find the answers in Appendix A, "Answers to the 'Do I Know This Already?' Questions."

Table 16-1 "Do I Know This Already?" Section-to-Question Mapping

Foundation Topics Section	Questions
ACI Multi-Site Fundamentals	1–5
Building Primary and Disaster Recovery Data Centers with ACI	6, 7
Building Active/Active Data Centers with ACI	8, 9
Extending ACI to Remote Locations and Public Clouds	10

CAUTION The goal of self-assessment is to gauge your mastery of the topics in this chapter. If you do not know the answer to a question or are only partially sure of the answer, you should mark that question as wrong for purposes of the self-assessment. Giving yourself credit for an answer you correctly guess skews your self-assessment results and might provide you with a false sense of security.

1. Which protocol does ACI Multi-Site use to advertise information about an endpoint in a stretched subnet to an adjacent fabric?

   a. COOP

   b. OSPF

   c. MP-BGP EVPN

   d. EIGRP

2. Which protocol establishes the underlay for ISN connectivity in an ACI Multi-Site deployment?

   a. COOP

   b. OSPF

   c. MP-BGP EVPN

   d. EIGRP

3. True or false: Administrators should refrain from configuring access policies locally within a fabric after integrating the fabric into ACI Multi-Site.

   a. True

   b. False

4. True or false: A schema defines a unit of change within ACI Multi-Site.

   a. True

   b. False

5. How do you make application traffic flow over the ISN between two ACI fabrics that have been integrated into ACI Multi-Site?

    a. Put in place contracts between the desired EPGs and ensure that the route is known in both the source and destination VRF instances.

    b. Navigate to Configure Infra in ACI Multi-Site and ensure that all configuration parameters are correct.

    c. ACI Multi-Pod needs to also be deployed for application communication to function.

    d. ACI Multi-Site is only used for stretching EPGs, not for allowing communication.

6. What feature can ACI Multi-Pod and ACI Multi-Site use to optimize ingress routing for stretched subnets into data centers over the WAN?

    a. Contracts

    b. Access policies

    c. COOP

    d. Host-based routing

7. True or false: ACI Multi-Site can enable IP mobility across data centers without the need to flood broadcast, unknown unicast, and multicast traffic.

    a. True

    b. False

8. A company needs to perform VMM integration, conduct cross-data center vMotion, and leverage vSphere DRS in a multi-data center design. Which solution best fits these requirements?

    a. ACI Multi-Pod

    b. ACI Multi-Site

    c. Remote leaf

    d. ACI Multi-Tier

9. A company wants to deploy active/active firewall clustering across two data centers. Which solution supports this requirement?

    a. ACI Multi-Pod

    b. ACI Multi-Site

    c. Remote leaf

    d. ACI Multi-Tier

10. A company wants to integrate its on-premises ACI fabrics with public cloud environments. Which of the following ACI solutions can support such an integration? What solution, if any, needs to be deployed in the cloud to make this integration work?

    a. ACI Multi-Pod and Cisco ASR 1000

    b. ACI Multi-Site and Cisco Cloud APIC

    c. ACI Multi-Pod and Cisco Cloud APIC

    d. ACI Multi-Site and Cisco ASR 1000

Foundation Topics

ACI Multi-Site Fundamentals

ACI Anywhere extends the confines of the data center network to anywhere an organization owns data. ACI Multi-Site is often the glue that enables such extension. Therefore, we address ACI Multi-Site first.

Chapter 2, "Understanding ACI Hardware and Topologies," covers what a valid ACI Multi-Site topology looks like as well as the reasons second-generation spines are required for deploying ACI Multi-Site. But beyond hardware and topologies, there are other questions about these two solutions that beg answers. For example, what protocols do ACI Multi-Site fabrics use to interconnect? What new terminology does ACI Multi-Site introduce? What new constructs are required to integrate multiple ACI fabrics? Finally, how do you choose between ACI Multi-Pod and ACI Multi-Site for a given use case? To develop the context needed to answer these questions, a basic understanding of ACI Multi-Site fundamentals is required.

Interconnecting ACI Fabrics with ACI Multi-Site

As mentioned earlier in this book, ACI Multi-Site requires the deployment of an intersite network (ISN) between sites that supports OSPF on the last-hop routers facing the spines in each site. OSPF establishes the underlay for cross-site communication.

To configure ACI to form OSPF adjacencies with the ISN, you need to configure access policies on spines locally within each fabric for ports that connect to the ISN. In addition, you need to define APIC addresses for each fabric as sites within the Multi-Site Orchestrator (MSO) cluster. Then you can use the MSO cluster to deploy a special L3Out in the infra tenant. This L3Out is very similar to L3Outs that enable IPN functionality in ACI Multi-Pod deployments, but you should refrain from manually modifying ACI Multi-Site L3Outs.

Table 16-2 describes some of the cross-site connectivity concepts related to ACI Multi-Site.

Table 16-2   ACI Multi-Site Cross-Site Connectivity Configuration Concepts

Term	Definition
Site	Each independent ACI fabric. To be able to add a site and deploy policy to it, MSO needs to know the name to allocate to the specified fabric, the URLs of APICs within the fabric, and the site ID.
Site ID	A unique numeric identifier for each fabric. Once selected, the site ID cannot be changed. Note that this setting has no relationship to the fabric ID value that administrators need to enter during fabric initialization.
Overlay multicast TEP	A single anycast tunnel endpoint configured within each fabric (site) for ingress replication of cross-site data plane BUM traffic.
BGP autonomous system number (ASN)	The BGP ASN configured within the fabric or site for route reflection. MSO pulls the BGP ASN configured in each site when users define sites in MSO.
Overlay unicast TEP	A single anycast TEP address assigned to each pod within each fabric for forwarding of cross-site unicast traffic.

Term	Definition
BGP EVPN router ID	An ID for each spine that has been enabled for ACI Multi-Site forwarding that enables route peering across sites.
CloudSec encryption	Encryption used when traffic is egressing a fabric through Multi-Site spines and is destined for spines in another fabric and needs to be encrypted. Note that not all spines and not all spine ports support CloudSec. This is a VTEP-to-VTEP encryption feature.

Figure 16-1 shows the Fabric Connectivity Infra page, which can be accessed in current MSO versions at Sites > Configure Infra. This screenshot depicts an ACI Multi-Site deployment with two sites defined: DC1 and DC2. In this figure, you can see the connectivity details at the site (fabric) level for the DC1 fabric. Recall from Table 16-2 that some configuration parameters, such as overlay multicast TEP, are configured at the fabric level. Users can further drill down to pod-specific configurations within each site or to spine-specific configurations.

Figure 16-1 *Configuring ACI Multi-Site for Connectivity to the ISN*

With the proper ACI Multi-Site L3Outs in place, spines within each fabric that have been enabled for Multi-Site functionality can establish MP-BGP EVPN adjacencies with one another. ACI fabrics can then advertise endpoint and other routing information to each other. ACI uses Type 2 EVPN updates to communicate endpoint information to other fabrics. The COOP database on spines in each site can easily differentiate between remote fabric endpoints and endpoints within the local fabric by referencing the overlay unicast TEP of the target site for all remote fabric endpoint entries. A fabric never needs to update remote fabrics of endpoint moves that stay local to the fabric. If an endpoint moves between fabrics, EVPN Type 2 update messages are used to synchronize endpoint data within all relevant fabrics.

The establishment of Layer 3 connectivity between fabrics does not by itself mean that user traffic will start to flow over the ISN. ACI Multi-Site constructs need to be used to explicitly enable cross-site communication through contracts or preferred group settings. For this to happen, administrators configure intersite policies using schemas, templates, and other ACI Multi-Site constructs.

New ACI Multi-Site Constructs and Configuration Concepts

Table 16-3 lists a number of new terms that need to be understood to effectively make use of ACI Multi-Site.

Table 16-3 New ACI Multi-Site Constructs and Concepts

Term	Description
Schema	A collection of configuration templates and the assignment of each template to sites that have been defined in the Multi-Site deployment. A schema can cover policies defined for a single tenant or policies for multiple tenants.
Template	A child of a schema that contains configuration objects that are either shared between sites or site specific. Each template gets associated with a single tenant.
Stretched	Objects, such as tenants, VRF instances, EPGs, bridge domains, subnets, or contracts, that are deployed to multiple sites.
Template conformity	A feature of ACI Multi-Site that runs checks to validate that configurations under a template pushed to multiple sites by the MSO have not been altered within a given fabric by administrators. When templates are stretched across sites, their configuration details are shared and standardized across sites.
Intersite L3Out	In current MSO releases, a feature that enables endpoints located in one site to use a remote L3Out to connect to entities in an external network. Early versions of ACI Multi-Site required locally configured L3Outs in each ACI fabric to route traffic out of the fabric.
Import	A process through which the majority of tenant objects within a production ACI fabric are brought into ACI Multi-Site.

Locally Governed Versus MSO-Governed Configurations

Some configurations are governed by MSO, and others continue to be governed by local fabrics.

ACI Multi-Site does *not* make any changes to access policies or fabric policies. ACI Multi-Site is strictly concerned with objects under the Tenants menu. Furthermore, even under this menu, ACI Multi-Site does not currently deal with the creation of certain objects, such as local L3Outs and L4–L7 device configurations. In addition, there is no requirement to import all tenants into ACI Multi-Site. It is okay to have a mixed deployment in which some tenants remain site local and others are imported into ACI Multi-Site.

Schemas and Templates in Practice

It may not be vital for DCACI candidates to fully understand all the concepts in this chapter, but understanding schemas and templates can definitely help Implementing Cisco

Application Centric Infrastructure DCACI 300-620 exam candidates get an idea of the power and flexibility of ACI Multi-Site. Figure 16-2 shows a schema called Production, under which three templates have been created. In this case, all three of these templates have been associated with a stretched tenant called BusinessApps. The template names are locally significant to the MSO. One of the templates, BApps-Stretched, houses all stretched objects, including a VRF, and can be seen to have been associated with both DC1 and DC2 fabrics. The template named BApps-DC1 contains objects for the tenant that are local to DC1, and BApps-DC2 manages objects specific to DC2.

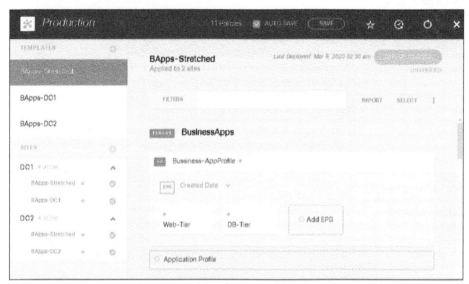

Figure 16-2 *A View of a Schema, Templates, and Sites in ACI Multi-Site*

The schema could combine templates from multiple tenants. A schema is not much more than a container for grouping templates and related policies together. Templates, on the other hand, are very significant. A template defines the unit or scope of a configuration change. When you navigate to the BApps-Stretched template view and select Deploy to Sites, any changes in the template from the last configuration push are simultaneously submitted to all sites associated with the template. If you make changes locally within the sites to any objects pertinent to the template, those configuration changes are modified to reflect the current configuration state of the MSO template.

Building Primary and Disaster Recovery Data Centers with ACI

Business requirements such as business continuity and disaster recovery sometimes necessitate the deployment of separate data center fabrics. These fabrics still need to be interconnected. But which ACI solution is ideal for disaster recovery data centers?

While ACI Multi-Pod can be used for primary and disaster recovery data center deployments, the assumption in disaster recovery sometimes is that infrastructure within each data center needs to be completely separate, and the data centers need to have zero dependencies on one another. Because each ACI Multi-Pod deployment uses a single APIC cluster and some configuration changes can potentially impact all pods within a deployment, ACI Multi-Pod can sometimes be ruled out as a potential option.

In general, ACI Multi-Site has some strengths in this area that make it a more valid solution for enabling disaster recovery.

Centralized Orchestration and Management of Multiple Fabrics

One important benefit of ACI Multi-Site is that MSO is yet another management tool in a network engineer's toolbelt. MSO can help validate the operational state of multiple fabrics. It allows you to audit whether there is significant configuration drift between sites and whether changes have been made that may have broken configuration conformity. Figure 16-3, for example, shows the status of sites integrated into ACI Multi-Site, faults that administrators should evaluate, and the results of schema and template verifications performed by MSO.

> **NOTE**   Although MSO is a management tool, it is only used in ACI Multi-Site deployments. It is not meant to be used for general management of single-fabric or single-pod ACI deployments.

Figure 16-3   *Fault Management Across Multiple Data Centers with ACI Multi-Site*

These centralized orchestration and management capabilities are important for managing primary and disaster recovery data centers because they ensure that policy is in sync and that the disaster recovery data center is always ready or can be made ready quickly if disaster strikes.

Tweaking Broadcast and Stretch Settings on a Per-BD Basis

Traditional cross-site VLAN stretching solutions do not offer a lot of granularity in terms of how traffic is stretched across sites. Solutions such as Cisco Overlay Transport Virtualization (OTV) block a few select protocols, but data center solutions today generally lack the configuration knobs needed to have different policies at an individual subnet level. With ACI, however, stretch settings can be tweaked for any given requirement. Figure 16-4 illustrates how a bridge domain named BD-BApps can be configured as a stretched subnet without the need for intersite broadcast, unknown unicast, and multicast (BUM) forwarding to take place. Settings such as Intersite BUM Traffic Allow ensure that subnets can be stretched without flooding remote data centers with packets that can adversely impact performance and reliability. This is a critical requirement for a lot of disaster recovery data centers today.

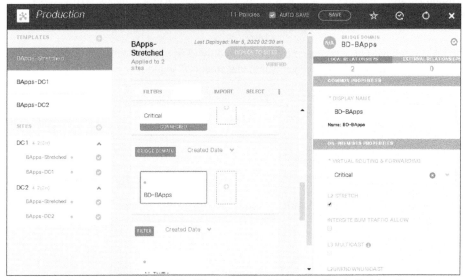

Figure 16-4 *Preventing BUM Traffic Across an ISN for a Single Bridge Domain*

Important per-bridge domain tweaks to consider when designing primary and disaster recovery data centers include the following:

- **Layer 3 only across sites:** For this type of scenario, the L2 Stretch checkbox is disabled. If the bridge domain is placed in a stretched template, different Layer 3 subnets can be assigned to the bridge domain in each site. This conforms closely with a lot of primary/disaster recovery data center designs.

- **IP mobility without BUM flooding:** This involves the ability to perform vMotion across sites without cross-site flooding by enabling the L2 Stretch setting and disabling the Intersite BUM Traffic Allow setting.

- **Layer 2 flooding across sites:** Where flooding across sites may be a requirement for a subnet (for example, some type of cross-site clustered service), the L2 Stretch and Intersite BUM Traffic Allow settings can both be selected.

Cross-Data Center Ingress Routing Optimizations

To direct traffic to the right data center over the WAN, ACI enables the advertisement of host routes out L3Outs. This is also supported with ACI Multi-Site. Figure 16-5 shows how the Host Route feature is configured at the individual site level. This enables some interesting designs. For example, an administrator can enable host-based routing out only the disaster recovery data center, while the subnet itself is only advertised out the primary data center. A route map can then be used to prevent advertisement of the subnet itself from the disaster recovery data center. If, at any point, endpoints within the subnet need to be migrated to the disaster recovery data center, routing tables converge to prefer the more specific host routes for endpoints that have been moved to the disaster recovery fabric. This provides an easy way to ensure that traffic is sent to the right data center while keeping enterprise routing tables manageable.

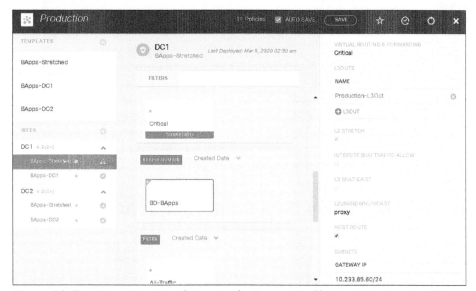

Figure 16-5 *Using Host-Based Routing for Ingress Traffic Optimization in ACI Multi-Site*

Simultaneous or Independent Policy Deployment to Sites

One top-of-mind issue for a lot of engineers who design and support primary and disaster recovery data centers is to guarantee that configuration changes can be made independently to data centers, so that if a change goes bad, both data centers are not affected.

While templates and tenants do allow for some control over the scope of changes, verifications within MSO also confirm which objects will be created, deleted, or modified as a result of a change. Figure 16-6 shows a relatively safe change in which the only object being modified is a bridge domain named BD-BApps. MSO also confirms that the changes will only be applied to DC1.

Figure 16-6 *Confirming Configuration Changes Prior to Deployment to Sites*

Note that ACI Multi-Site stretched templates currently make configuration changes simultaneously across multiple sites. However, new features are being introduced to enable configurations impacting multiple data centers to be pushed to one fabric at a time. This feature will make ACI Multi-Site a powerful orchestration tool for primary and disaster recovery data centers.

Building Active/Active Data Centers with ACI

Whereas primary and disaster recovery environments are typically loosely coupled data centers with limited stretched subnets, active/active designs involve tightly coupled data centers and sometimes involve stretching all subnets between data centers. Active/active data centers are usually deployed short distances from one another to accommodate the hitless migration of workloads from one data center to another. The focus with active/active data centers is disaster avoidance and prevention.

There are multiple definitions for active/active data centers today. Some engineers identify deployment of active/active firewall clustering or breaking up active/standby firewall pairs across the data centers as a requirement for acknowledging a design as being active/active. The thought process is that minimal or no loss of firewall state information should occur in such data centers upon the loss of one of the data centers. Other engineers believe data centers that rely on global server load balancing and placement of active workloads in each data center are active/active designs. With this definition, loosely coupled primary and disaster recovery data centers that have no stretched subnets or any ability to proactively migrate workloads could also be called active/active data centers.

This book defines active/active a bit in between these two definitions. For a network design to be considered active/active, all or the majority of subnets should exist in both data centers, and the network should be able to direct traffic to the intended firewalls and other stateful services appliances at all times—even if an entire data center is lost. This definition does not necessarily require that active/active clustering be used or that TCP transaction state never be lost. However, workloads should be able to easily migrate from one data center to another with ease for disaster avoidance and prevention. Using this definition, ACI Multi-Pod often wins against ACI Multi-Site as the ideal solution for active/active design requirements. (This is not meant to imply that ACI Multi-Site cannot be used for active/active data center design.)

VMM Integrations Applicable to Multiple Data Centers

One of the reasons ACI Multi-Pod is ideal in active/active designs is that ACI Multi-Pod has a single APIC cluster spread across sites and can therefore have a single VMM integration for each vCenter data center object, even if the ESXi hosts within the data center object reside in both data centers. With ACI Multi-Site, however, separate APIC clusters in each data center also mean that each data center has to perform VMM integration separately with each vCenter instance.

Using ACI Multi-Site to implement separate integrations in each data center does not rule out cross-vCenter vMotion capabilities; however, it does make some features, such as cross-site vSphere high availability, fault tolerance, and distributed resource scheduling, impossible when VMM integration is performed. This is because separate DVS instances are deployed to each data center.

In many active/active designs deployed across short distances, such as in stretched metro cluster designs, the idea is to use advanced features such as vSphere high availability, fault tolerance, and distributed resource scheduling to avoid disasters in the first place. And, in these designs, ACI Multi-Pod often becomes the solution of choice.

Stateful Services Integration in ACI Multi-Pod and Multi-Site

There are three primary stateful services integration models that can be used to attach devices directly to ACI Multi-Pod or Multi-Site fabrics:

- **Each active/standby appliance pair deployed across data centers:** In this connectivity model, each pair of active/standby appliances is broken up and attached to the fabric in separate data centers. This is a common design in data centers where there is no sensitivity to asymmetric traffic flows because one appliance will always be actively forwarding traffic while the other will be in a ready state, waiting to take over in the case of an outage. ACI Multi-Pod fully supports this attachment model, but ACI Multi-Site supports this model only when the firewalls are running in L3 or L2 mode and function as the default gateway for endpoints.

- **Active/active stateful services clustering across data centers:** In this model, stateful services appliances are deployed in an active/active cluster across sites. This attachment model requires that ACI be able to learn the same endpoint data (MAC address and IP information) in both sites at the same time. While this connectivity model is fully supported with ACI Multi-Pod today, ACI Multi-Site does not support active/active clustering as of the time of this writing.

- **Independent active/standby appliances in each data center:** When there is no requirement for proactive migration of endpoints between data centers, engineers can deploy separate firewall pairs in each data center and use either PBR or host-based routing to direct traffic to the right firewall pair. Both ACI Multi-Pod and ACI Multi-Site support use of independent active/standby stateful services appliances in each

16

data center. However, use of independent firewall pairs in each data center is often seen more as a use case for ACI Multi-Site deployments due to the loss of firewall state information during failures or during cross-site workload migrations.

Of these three attachment models, the first two are more in line with the objectives of active/active data centers because they are able to ensure preservation of firewall state information during failures. This is why ACI Multi-Pod is often the platform of choice for active/active data center designs. This should not be understood as a rule but as general guidance. This also does not mean that ACI Multi-Site will never be needed as a tool to enable disaster recovery capabilities for the active/active pods. Furthermore, there is also the issue of product development. As ACI Multi-Site continues to mature, it may one day support a broader number of stateful services connectivity models.

Extending ACI to Remote Locations and Public Clouds

The increasing popularity of public cloud offerings and the desire to place workloads closer to users mean that engineers need to be more flexible about the changing boundaries of data centers. ACI Anywhere has options to extend data center boundaries to meet these types of new requirements without the need to sacrifice security, stability, or agility.

Extending ACI into Public Clouds with ACI Multi-Site

Companies that embrace ACI within the data center can integrate public cloud environments such as AWS and Azure into ACI Multi-Site and manage these environments as additional sites within the overall deployment. This integration requires use of an additional product called the Cisco Cloud APIC, which translates ACI Multi-Site constructs into the relevant public cloud constructs and deploys policy into the public cloud by using cloud-native APIs.

The benefits of this approach include consistent network policies and security posture across clouds and on-premises data centers; secure automated connectivity and network stitching, centralized orchestration, visibility, and monitoring; and seamless workload migration across environments.

This solution requires the use of the Cisco Cloud Service Router (CSR) 1000V.

Extending ACI into Bare-Metal Clouds with vPod

In addition to extension into popular public clouds, ACI can extend into bare-metal clouds by using the vPod solution. At the time of this writing, vPod cannot be configured as an independent site in ACI Multi-Site and needs to be configured as a pod within a larger ACI Multi-Pod deployment.

The vPod solution consists of virtual leaf (vLeaf), virtual spine (vSpine), and ACI Virtual Edge (AVE). The vPod solution can also be deployed in data centers that are too small to justify the cost of an ACI fabric deployment.

Integrating Remote Sites into ACI Using Remote Leaf Switches

Remote leaf switches significantly ease application migrations for the purpose of data center exits. They are also great for permanent use at locations where small numbers of servers need to be housed. They are also very easy to deploy.

One aspect of remote leafs, however, is failover. Engineers deploying remote leaf switches associate remote leafs with a pod. If remote leafs are deployed in ACI Multi-Pod environments that span multiple data centers, they can potentially fail over to another data center if there is an outage within the original data center or pod to which the leafs were associated.

ACI remote leaf does not support failover across sites within Multi-Site deployments as of the time of writing. Cross-data center failover is currently a remote leaf use case for ACI Multi-Pod only.

Exam Preparation Tasks

As mentioned in the section "How to Use This Book" in the Introduction, you have a couple of choices for exam preparation: Chapter 17, "Final Preparation," and the exam simulation questions on the companion website.

Review All Key Topics

Review the most important topics in this chapter, noted with the Key Topic icon in the outer margin of the page. Table 16-4 lists these key topics and the page number on which each is found.

Table 16-4 Key Topics for Chapter 16

Key Topic Element	Description	Page Number
Table 16-2	Defines some key ACI Multi-Site cross-site configuration parameters	555
Table 16-3	Defines a number of new constructs and concepts that are unique to ACI Multi-Site	557
List	Lists some key tweaks that can be made at the bridge domain level using the MSO to make ACI Multi-Site ideal for primary/DR data centers	560
List	Describes the supported stateful services attachment models for ACI Multi-Pod and ACI Multi-Site	563

Memory Tables

There are no memory tables or lists in this chapter.

Define Key Terms

Define the following key terms from this chapter and check your answers in the glossary:

site, site ID, overlay multicast TEP, overlay unicast TEP, BGP EVPN router ID, CloudSec encryption, schema, template, stretched, template conformity, intersite L3Out

CHAPTER 17

Final Preparation

The first 16 chapters of this book cover the technologies, protocols, design concepts, and considerations required to be prepared to pass the Implementing Cisco Application Centric Infrastructure DCACI 300-620 exam. While these chapters supply the detailed information, most people need more preparation than simply reading the first 16 chapters of this book. This chapter details a set of tools and a study plan to help you complete your preparation for the exam.

This short chapter has several main sections. The first section helps you get ready to take the exam, and the second section lists exam preparation tools that can be useful at this point in the study process. The final section provides a suggested study plan you can use now that you have completed all the earlier chapters in this book.

Getting Ready

Here are some important tips to keep in mind to ensure that you are ready for this rewarding exam:

- **Build and use a study tracker:** Consider using the exam objectives shown in this chapter to build a study tracker for yourself. Such a tracker can help ensure that you have not missed anything and that you are confident for your exam. As a matter of fact, this book offers a sample study planner as Appendix E on the companion website.

- **Think about your time budget for questions on the exam:** When you do the math, you will see that, on average, you have one minute per question. While this does not sound like a lot of time, keep in mind that many of the questions will be very straightforward, and you will take 15 to 30 seconds on those. This leaves you extra time for other questions on the exam.

- **Watch the clock:** Check in on the time remaining periodically as you are taking the exam. You might even find that you can slow down pretty dramatically if you have built up a nice block of extra time.

- **Get some earplugs:** The testing center might provide earplugs but get some just in case and bring them along. There might be other test takers in the center with you, and you do not want to be distracted by their screams. I personally have no issue blocking out the sounds around me, so I never worry about this, but I know it is an issue for some.

- **Plan your travel time:** Give yourself extra time to find the center and get checked in. Be sure to arrive early. As you test more at a particular center, you can certainly start cutting it closer time-wise.

- **Get rest:** Most students report that getting plenty of rest the night before the exam boosts their success. All-night cram sessions are not typically successful.

- **Bring in valuables but get ready to lock them up:** The testing center will take your phone, your smartwatch, your wallet, and other such items and will provide a secure place for them.

- **Take notes:** You will be given note-taking implements and should not be afraid to use them. I always jot down any questions I struggle with on the exam. I then memorize them at the end of the test by reading my notes over and over again. I always make sure I have a pen and paper in the car, and I write down the issues in my car just after the exam. When I get home—with a pass or fail—I research those items!

Tools for Final Preparation

This section lists some information about the available tools and how to access the tools.

Pearson Cert Practice Test Engine and Questions on the Website

Register this book to get access to the Pearson IT Certification test engine (software that displays and grades a set of exam-realistic multiple-choice questions). Using the Pearson Cert Practice Test Engine, you can either study by going through the questions in Study mode or take a simulated (timed) exam.

The Pearson Test Prep practice test software comes with two full practice exams. These practice tests are available to you either online or as an offline Windows application. To access the practice exams that were developed with this book, please see the instructions in the card inserted in the sleeve in the back of the book. This card includes a unique access code that enables you to activate your exams in the Pearson Test Prep software.

Accessing the Pearson Test Prep Software Online

The online version of this software can be used on any device with a browser and connectivity to the Internet including desktop machines, tablets, and smartphones. To start using your practice exams online, simply follow these steps:

Step 1. Go to http://www.PearsonTestPrep.com.

Step 2. Select **Pearson IT Certification** as your product group.

Step 3. Enter your email and password for your account. If you don't have an account on PearsonITCertification.com or CiscoPress.com, you need to establish one by going to PearsonITCertification.com/join.

Step 4. In the My Products tab, click the **Activate New Product** button.

Step 5. Enter the access code printed on the insert card in the back of your book to activate your product. The product is then listed in your My Products page.

Step 6. Click the **Exams** button to launch the exam settings screen and start the exam.

Accessing the Pearson Test Prep Software Offline

If you wish to study offline, you can download and install the Windows version of the Pearson Test Prep software. You can find a download link for this software on the book's companion website, or you can just enter this link in your browser:

http://www.pearsonitcertification.com/content/downloads/pcpt/engine.zip

To access the book's companion website and the software, simply follow these steps:

Step 1. Register your book by going to PearsonITCertification.com/register and entering the ISBN: **9780136602668**.

Step 2. Respond to the challenge questions.

Step 3. Go to your account page and select the **Registered Products** tab.

Step 4. Click on the **Access Bonus Content** link under the product listing.

Step 5. Click the **Install Pearson Test Prep Desktop Version** link in the Practice Exams section of the page to download the software.

Step 6. When the software finishes downloading, unzip all the files onto your computer.

Step 7. Double-click the application file to start the installation and follow the onscreen instructions to complete the registration.

Step 8. When the installation is complete, launch the application and click the **Activate Exam** button on the My Products tab.

Step 9. Click the **Activate a Product** button in the Activate Product Wizard.

Step 10. Enter the unique access code from the card in the sleeve in the back of your book and click the **Activate** button.

Step 11. Click **Next** and then click the **Finish** button to download the exam data to your application.

Step 12. You can now start using the practice exams by selecting the product and clicking the **Open Exam** button to open the exam settings screen.

Note that the offline and online versions sync together, so saved exams and grade results recorded on one version will be available to you in the other version as well.

Customizing Your Exams

When you are in the exam settings screen, you can choose to take exams in one of three modes:

- Study mode
- Practice Exam mode
- Flash Card mode

Study mode allows you to fully customize an exam and review answers as you are taking the exam. This is typically the mode you use first to assess your knowledge and identify information gaps. Practice Exam mode locks certain customization options in order to present a realistic exam experience. Use this mode when you are preparing to test your exam readiness. Flash Card mode strips out the answers and presents you with only the question stem. This mode is great for late-stage preparation, when you really want to challenge yourself to provide answers without the benefit of seeing multiple-choice options. This mode does not provide the detailed score reports that the other two modes provide, so it is not the best mode for helping you identify knowledge gaps.

In addition to these three modes, you will be able to select the source of your questions. You can choose to take exams that cover all of the chapters, or you can narrow your selection to just a single chapter or the chapters that make up specific parts in the book. All chapters are selected by default. If you want to narrow your focus to individual chapters, simply deselect all the chapters and then select only those on which you wish to focus in the Objectives area.

You can also select the exam banks on which to focus. Each exam bank comes complete with full exams of questions that cover topics in every chapter. You can have the test engine serve up exams from all four banks or just from one individual bank by selecting the desired banks in the exam bank area.

There are several other customizations you can make to your exam from the exam settings screen, such as the time allowed for taking the exam, the number of questions served up, whether to randomize questions and answers, whether to show the number of correct answers for multiple-answer questions, and whether to serve up only specific types of questions. You can also create custom test banks by selecting only questions that you have marked or questions on which you have added notes.

Updating Your Exams

If you are using the online version of the Pearson Test Prep software, you should always have access to the latest version of the software as well as the exam data. If you are using the Windows desktop version, every time you launch the software, it will check to see if there are any updates to your exam data and automatically download any changes that have been made since the last time you used the software. This requires that you be connected to the Internet at the time you launch the software.

Sometimes, due to a number of factors, the exam data might not fully download when you activate your exam. If you find that figures or exhibits are missing, you might need to manually update your exams.

To update a particular exam you have already activated and downloaded, simply select the Tools tab and click the Update Products button. Again, this is only an issue with the desktop Windows application.

If you wish to check for updates to the Windows desktop version of the Pearson Test Prep exam engine software, simply select the Tools tab and click the Update Application button. Doing so allows you to ensure that you are running the latest version of the software engine.

Premium Edition

In addition to the free practice exam provided on the website, you can purchase additional exams with expanded functionality directly from Pearson IT Certification. The Premium Edition of this title contains an additional two full practice exams and an eBook (in both PDF and ePub format). In addition, the Premium Edition title also has remediation for each question to the specific part of the eBook that relates to that question.

Because you have purchased the print version of this title, you can purchase the Premium Edition at a deep discount. There is a coupon code in the book sleeve that contains a one-time-use code and instructions for where you can purchase the Premium Edition.

To view the premium edition product page, go to www.informit.com/title/9780136602668.

Suggested Plan for Final Review/Study

This section lists a suggested study plan from the point at which you finish reading through Chapter 16 until you take the DCACI 300-620 exam. You can ignore this plan, use it as is, or take suggestions from it.

The plan involves four steps:

Step 1. **Review Key Topics and "Do I Know This Already?" (DIKTA) Questions:** You can use the table that lists the key topics in each chapter or just flip the pages looking for key topics. Also, reviewing the DIKTA? questions from the beginning of the chapter can be helpful for review.

Step 2. **Complete Memory Tables:** Open Appendix C, "Memory Tables" (found on the companion website), and print the entire appendix or print the tables by major part. Then complete the tables.

Step 3. **Gain hands-on experience:** Nothing can replace real experience with an ACI fabric. The best way to gain hands-on experience is to administer an ACI fabric or use a lab environment.

Step 4. **Use the Pearson Test Prep Practice Test engine to practice:** The Pearson Test Prep practice test engine enables you to study using a bank of unique exam-realistic questions available only with this book.

Summary

The tools and suggestions listed in this chapter have been designed with one goal in mind: to help you develop the skills required to pass the DCACI 300-620 exam. This book has been developed from the beginning to not just tell you the facts but to also help you learn how to apply the facts. No matter what your experience level leading up to when you take the exam, it is our hope that the broad range of preparation tools, and even the structure of the book, will help you pass the exam with ease. We hope you do well on the exam.

Answers to the "Do I Know This Already?" Questions

Chapter 1

1. A, C, D. Level of expertise, number of managed endpoints, and difficulty of information correlation across devices all contribute to management complexity. However, open standards *do not* contribute to management complexity, even though different vendor interpretations of open standards do contribute to network management complexity.

2. A. 12 header bits are used in the definition of VLAN IDs. Out of the resulting 4096 VLAN IDs, 2 are reserved and cannot be used for data traffic, resulting in 4094 usable VLAN IDs.

3. B. Firewalls in traditional networks are primarily used for securing north–south traffic flows.

4. B. Internally, ACI uses VXLAN. VLANs are primarily used to classify inbound traffic into EPGs and also to enable trunking to servers.

5. D. Multi-Site Orchestrator (MSO) is used to orchestrate configurations across multiple ACI fabrics.

6. A. Stateless networking involves using node IDs as the identities of switches and APICs and allows a device to be decommissioned and another device commissioned with minimal changes to the network.

7. A. Blacklisting is the practice of allowing all traffic except that which is denied through security mechanisms like access lists. Blacklisting is a feature of traditional switching and routing solutions.

8. B. ACI has been built around policy reuse, which enables companies that do not have a strong desire for automation to still achieve better agility.

9. C. In ACI multipod, each pod forms its own control plane. While each site in an ACI multisite deployment also forms separate control planes, each site is also considered a distinct fabric.

10. D. Microsegmentation can be accomplished within a single tenant and is not by itself a technical driver for deploying multiple tenants.

Chapter 2

1. B. If new spines cannot be deployed at the remote site, then ACI Multi-Pod and Multi-Site are not valid options. Furthermore, ACI Multi-Tier generally assumes that cables will be run directly between spines and leaf switches or, alternatively, between

Tier 1 and Tier 2 leaf switches without the use of an ISN or IPN. ACI Remote Leaf, on the other hand, can be deployed at remote locations through an IPN and therefore does not require dedicated cross-site circuits or fiber.

2. D. The requirement for Multicast PIM-Bidir is unique to ACI Multi-Pod. ACI Multi-Site, on the other hand, uses the ingress replication function of the spine nodes in the source site to replicate BUM traffic to all remote sites to which a given cross-site BUM-enabled bridge domain has been stretched.

3. D. APIC-to-leaf connectivity as well as leaf-to-spine connectivity have been valid connectivity options since the first shipments of ACI hardware. With ACI Multi-Tier leaf-to-leaf cabling is acceptable as long as the cabling connects a Tier 1 leaf to a Tier 2 leaf. As of the time of this writing, there are no use cases for spine-to-spine connectivity. ACI disables spine-to-spine connections when it detects them.

4. A, C. Ingress replication of BUM traffic and namespace normalization are both functionalities that are enabled by second-generation spine hardware. IP fragmentation is not supported in ACI. Multicast forwarding via PIM-Bidir applies to ACI Multi-Pod and not ACI Multi-Site.

5. A. Border leaf switches provide Layer 2 and Layer 3 connectivity to outside networks, meaning connectivity to non-ACI switches and routers.

6. B. At the time of this book's publication, a cluster of at least four L3 APICs is necessary to scale to 200 leaf switches. Sharding is a result of the evolution of what is called horizontal partitioning of databases. In an ACI deployment that has three or more APICs, there will always be three shards for each attribute in the APIC database. Standby APICs do not actively synchronize data with active APICs. They are passive players in an ACI fabric that need to be manually activated to replace a failed APIC and restore the APIC quorum.

7. B, C. Nexus 93180YC-EX is a cloud-scale leaf switch. Nexus 9364C is a second-generation spine and supports ACI Multi-Site. Nexus 9736C-FX is a line card that can be populated into a Nexus 9500 Series spine and supports ACI Multi-Site. The Nexus 9396PX is a first-generation leaf switch.

8. A, C. The Nexus 9336PQ is a first-generation spine. It does not support the namespace normalization required for ACI Multi-Site support. It does, however, support 40 Gbps connectivity. Therefore, an upgrade from Nexus 9336PQ would not help increase bandwidth unless 100 Gbps leaf-to-spine connectivity is the desired target. This upgrade would allow enablement of CloudSec. ACI Multi-Pod is supported in first-generation hardware.

9. A. All interfaces with speeds of 10 Gbps or higher on leaf switches whose model numbers end with FX support MACsec.

10. D. The Nexus 9348GC-FXP is well positioned for low-bandwidth 100 Mbps and 1 Gigabit Ethernet use cases that rely on RJ-45 transceiverless connectivity.

Chapter 3

1. D. The first three options listed are spine switches and therefore do not allow APIC connectivity. The Nexus 93180YC-FX, on the other hand, is a leaf, and in-band APIC ports can therefore be connected to it to allow fabric discovery.

2. A, C. If the infrastructure VLAN ID or fabric ID needs to change, a fabric rebuild is required. However, APIC OOB IP addresses can be changed after initialization. The active or standby status of a controller may necessitate that an individual APIC be re-initialized with a standby APIC node ID, but it does not necessitate the re-initialization of an entire fabric.

3. B. Following the establishment of encrypted IFM communication channels, APICs are able to push configuration changes to ACI switches. It is at this point that a switch is considered to have become activated and fully operational.

4. B, C. A seed leaf needs to be activated first before a spine can be activated. In-band APIC interfaces function in an active/standby mode. If the APIC interface that is active is not connected to an ACI leaf switch, the discovery will fail. For an APIC to add a switch to the Fabric Membership tab to allow administers to authorize the switch to join the fabric, the APIC needs to see LLDP packets from the seed leaf and must also be able to process DHCP Discover packets from it. APICs cannot possibly form a cluster until at least a seed leaf has been discovered.

5. B. All options listed except B have minimal impact on the fabric discovery process. However, the network mode should remain set to Dedicated. Otherwise, unexpected connectivity problems can occur.

6. D. Out of the options listed, Proxy-TEP is the only option that exclusively references spine switches.

7. C. Atomic Replace allows the replacement of all current settings with configurations from a file. Atomic Merge and Best Effort Merge both enable merging configurations with currently configured settings. There is no such thing as a Best Effort Replace.

8. B, C, D. ACI supports forwarding of backups and restoration of backups via FTP, SFTP, and SCP.

9. D. Using four upgrade groups—two for spines and two for leafs with node ID-based separation into groups based on odd and even node IDs—tends to enable the most resilient setup. Option A results in fabricwide outages. Option B can result in zero downtime, but a number of spines and leafs are under upgrade simultaneously. Option C with random node assignment can easily lead to downtime.

10. A. By tying the export operation to a scheduler, an administrator can have ACI perform automated scheduled backups.

Chapter 4

1. C. Logging in to the CLI via a non-default login domain requires the special login syntax of apic#*domain**username*.

2. B. The APICs are the brains of an ACI network. For the most part, the switch CLI only allows use of **show** and **debug** commands that enable verification that desired configurations have been pushed to a device and also verification of device function.

3. B. An administrator can enable or disable supported management protocols or change the ports associated with the enabled management access methods by editing the management access policy associated with active pod policy groups.

4. C. Access policies primarily govern the configuration and operation of non-fabric (access) ports, including parameters such as link speed and other port-level configurations, including LLDP and LACP.

5. C. Fabric policies govern configurations that apply more holistically at the switch or pod level.

6. A, D. MOQuery is a CLI-based tool used for querying the ACI object hierarchy, and Visore is the GUI-based equivalent.

7. B. The Raised state almost always suggests the existence of an active problem in the network. Faults in the Raised state remain in this state until the underlying condition is resolved.

8. A, D. Answer A is correct because acknowledgment of a fault whose underlying condition has been resolved leads to the deletion of the fault. Answer D is also correct. The default amount of time faults are retained after their underlying conditions are resolved is 3600 seconds, and this interval is called the retention interval. Note that while events are immutable and serve as the permanent record of occurrences in the system, faults follow a lifecycle.

9. D. The Common policy has a global fabricwide scope and deals with monitoring of objects such as the APIC controllers and fabric nodes. The policies configured in this class are also used when there is no corresponding policy under the more specific infra or tenant scopes.

10. B. Health scores are meant to provide a means for periodic reporting of the health and operational status of ACI objects, tenants, pods, or entire fabrics.

Chapter 5

1. C. Fabric APICs push policy to leaf switches via in-band connections into the infra tenant. The infra tenant forms both the underlay and overlay for intra-fabric communication. The infra tenant does not get exposed to the user space (tenants), and it has its own private network space and bridge domains.

2. C. The common tenant is a special tenant whose purpose is to provide common services to other tenants in an ACI fabric. The common tenant enables the creation of shared L3Outs, shared bridge domains, and shared VRF instances.

3. D. An endpoint group is a grouping of physical or virtual network endpoints that reside within a single bridge domain and have similar policy requirements. ACI can classify both IP-based and non-IP-based endpoints into EPGs. An EPG does not necessarily define a broadcast domain, and it is bridge domains that best correlate to broadcast domains.

4. B. An application profile is a container that allows EPGs to be grouped according to their relationship with one another to enable easier configuration and auditing of relevant policies or to make policy reuse possible.

5. D: The command **show ip route** needs to be followed up with the name of the intended tenant and the VRF. Hence, the command **show ip route CCNP:DCACI** displays the routes in a VRF named DCACI, which resides in a tenant named CCNP.

6. C. A filter matches interesting traffic and consists of a series of filter entries. A subject determines the action to be taken on traffic that is matched, and a contract is directionally applied to EPGs to determine the traffic flows to which the contract applies.

7. B. The setting Intra EPG Isolation allows an administrator to enforce traffic isolation between endpoints that reside in an EPG. This feature is configured at the EPG level.

8. D. Where a client is requesting a service from another system, the client is a consumer of the server-side service, and the server is the provider of the service.

9. A. An external EPG is a special type of EPG that represents endpoints outside an ACI fabric, such as user laptops, campus IoT devices, or Internet users. External EPGs are applied at the VRF instance level on an object called an L3Out.

10. A. There is an *n*:1 relationship between filters and tenants, meaning that large numbers of filters can be created in each tenant.

Chapter 6

1. D. A physical domain governs the attachment of bare-metal servers and appliances that need static VLAN allocations.

2. B. Even if an administrator assigns a VLAN pool to an AAEP and assigns the AAEP to ports, the VLANs in the pool do *not* get activated on the switch ports. The VLAN pool, in itself, just defines the potential list of VLAN IDs that a tenant administrator can use to map EPGs to switch ports. For traffic to flow over VLANs, one or more EPGs still need to be mapped to ports either by a tenant administrator or via direct mappings on the AAEP, which is called an AAEP EPG.

3. A. VMM domains allow both static and dynamic mapping of EPGs to VLANs for virtualized environments. The use of dynamic mapping of EPGs is recommended.

4. D. A tenant administrator who wants to map an EPG to ports and encapsulations should first bind the EPG to a domain. The domain association by the tenant administrator acts as authorization that the endpoints within the specified EPG are indeed meant to connect to the fabric via the method specified by the domain. The domains that are bound to the EPG also indicate which VLAN IDs are acceptable encapsulations for the EPG.

5. B. An EPG can be bound to multiple domains, but the domains should ideally not reference overlapping VLAN pools. This is especially important if there are leaf switches that have the EPG mapped to an encapsulation using more than one of the domains. EPGs can be bound statically to physical ports for bare-metal connectivity. EPGs are not directly associated with VRF instances. The construct that does get mapped directly to a VRF is called a bridge domain.

6. C. ACI uses MisCabling Protocol (MCP) for loop prevention.

7. B. When port channel interface policy groups are reused on a switch, ACI interprets the reuse as an intention to add the new ports to the previous port channel bundle. Interface policy groups involving aggregations should generally not be reused.

8. A. Interface policy groups pertaining to non-aggregated ports can be reused—without caveats.

9. A. A switch can be assigned more than one interface profile.

10. C. A switch profile is a logical object that represents one or more physical switches from a configuration standpoint and directly points to node IDs. The use of switch profiles provides part of the basis for stateless networking in ACI.

Chapter 7

1. C. The out-of-service status appears when access policies have been successfully deployed for a port but there are no EPG mappings to the port, and therefore the port is not actively forwarding traffic.

2. A. vPC domains or vPC explicit protection groups are configured at Fabric > Access Policies > Policies > Switch > Virtual Port Channel default. Another confusing location, Fabric > Access Policies > Policies > Switch > VPC Domain, is where vPC peer dead intervals are configured.

3. B. Leaf access port policy groups can only be used for individual (non-aggregated) ports. To configure a port channel, configure a port channel interface policy group instead and associate it with leaf switch ports.

4. B. Switches encapsulate traffic destined to an endpoint behind a vPC and send it to the destination loopback 1 IP address, which is common across both vPC peers.

5. B. Interface policies can typically enable CDP without the need for overrides.

6. A. This is an accurate statement.

7. A. This is an accurate statement.

8. B, C, D. MCP needs to be enabled globally and at the interface level. When MCP PDUs need to also be sent out on a tagged VLAN, Enable MCP PDU per VLAN options needs to be checked.

9. B. This is true only if some sub-ports are left unused.

10. B. By default, ACI attempts only to preserve DSCP settings.

Chapter 8

1. C. When an endpoint attaches to a leaf, the endpoint is considered local to the leaf. A leaf that learns an endpoint through local attachment is the most significant source of truth for the endpoint information in ACI, and therefore the leaf learns both the MAC address and any associated IP addresses for the endpoint.

2. B. When a bridge domain does not have unicast routing enabled and a default gateway to leaf switches and BD L2 unknown unicast has been set to hardware proxy, ARP gleaning cannot take place, and traffic destined toward the silent host is

dropped at the spine. Consequently, BD L2 unknown unicast should always be set to flood when an L2 BD houses a silent host.

3. B. An endpoint in ACI is defined as a single MAC address and all IP addresses associated with it. If an IP address is flapping between MAC addresses, ACI detects a MAC duplication. This can impact endpoint learning and consequently lead to disruption of traffic toward and from the endpoint. If the issue is transient, it could indicate that an appliance failover has taken place and likely does not indicate an issue. If, on the other hand, the problem is non-transient, it should be investigated. Note that answers A and C are incorrect because a MAC address can have multiple IP address associations.

4. A. The leaf to which an endpoint attaches propagates the endpoint information to the spines and thus is the holder of the single source of truth in the fabric.

5. A. This is a large part of the definition of hardware proxy forwarding.

6. B. With hardware proxy, ACI still needs ARP, but it is able to unicast ARP traffic from endpoints unless ARP flooding has been turned on.

7. B. In ACI, traffic is flooded based on an FTag tree to ensure a loop-free topology. Each ACI fabric contains multiple FTag trees.

8. D. The Deployment Immediacy parameter setting On Demand delays enforcement of policy in hardware until ACI receives its first packet on the associated port. This can cause a minor delay in forwarding.

9. C. Apply Both Directions and Reverse Filter Ports are both needed. Apply Both Directions signals to ACI that it needs to create a reverse rule. Reverse Filter Ports tells ACI to swap the source and destination ports when creating the reverse rule.

10. B. Log is a directive.

Chapter 9

1. A. When connecting ACI to a router (as opposed to a Layer 3 switch), there is very little to no benefit gained when using SVIs. There is also no use case for floating SVIs in this situation because there is minimal potential for workload movement when connecting to physical routers. Use of routed interfaces rules out deployment of further L3Outs from other VRFs on the same interface(s). Routed subinterfaces, on the other hand, enable reuse of physical interfaces for Layer 3 extension of regular user VRFs. Each encapsulation can be tied to a different L3Out.

2. D. A route profile for interleak does not create Deny prefix-list entries and therefore does not prevent entry of routes that have already been learned on an L3Out and added to a leaf RIB from being distributed into BGP. Therefore, A is not an acceptable answer. Answers B and C would prevent the border leaf switches from learning the 10.0.0.0/8 subnet in the first place and are therefore incorrect. Answer D is correct because BGP route reflection is the basis for external route distribution in ACI fabrics.

3. C. In this case, a vPC can be configured for connectivity to the firewall, and an L3Out can be deployed using SVIs to enable peering with the firewall. Floating SVIs is not the best choice because the question specifies that the firewall is a physical

appliance, and therefore there is no expectation for firewall connections to move between switches.

4. C. The only parameters administrators need to enter for BGP route reflection in ACI are the BGP ASN the fabric should use and the spines in each pod that should function as route reflectors. All other configuration occurs in the background, without user input.

5. B, D. In this case, the administrator is experiencing a common problem. If the requirement is to implement multiple L3Outs in a single VRF, the administrator is advised to either use BGP to benefit from a separate route map per L3Out or to implement the EIGRP and OSPF L3Outs on different switches. This problem may at some point be resolved through an enhancement.

6. A. To use an ASN other than the route reflector ASN, an administrator needs to use a *local-as* configuration in the BGP peer connectivity profile to make its BGP AS look like something else to the peer.

7. A, D. EIGRP cannot be used on BGP L3Outs. For BGP loopback reachability, use OSPF or static routes on BGP L3Outs. B is incorrect because the BGP dynamic neighbor feature in ACI does not attempt to start a BGP session but waits for the other side to try to initiate a session. Without explicit configuration on the other side, a session will never be established. Therefore, C is incorrect. A and D are the correct answers.

8. B, C. Administrative distances for SPF are configured via an OSPF timer policy and are applied at the VRF level for all address families or at the VRF level for an individual address family. Therefore, A is incorrect. ACI does support OSPF authentication, which needs to be configured under an OSPF interface profile, so B is correct. Any border leaf L3Out leverages VRF-lite to extend routing to the outside world. Answer C is correct. ACI does support OSPFv3, but the system makes it mostly transparent from the user perspective. Just assign an IPv6 address to an L3Out, and the routing process reflects OSPFv3. For this reason, D is incorrect.

9. A, D. BFD is not supported on BGP prefix peers and loopback addresses as of the time of writing. It is supported on non-loopback interfaces and all configurable routing protocols in ACI.

10. A. The route profile type Match Routing Policy Only has more similarities with the **route-map** command in other solutions, but the default route profile type Match Prefix and Routing Policy does merge implicit and explicit route maps together.

Chapter 10

1. B. In endpoint migration scenarios, it is best to set L2 Unknown Unicast setting to Flood to ensure similar forwarding behavior across ACI and the traditional network.

2. D. Because an any-to-any contract typically creates a full mesh of relationships, this can impact the policy CAM.

3. C. vzAny allows a one-to-many contract relationship within the scope of a VRF instance.

4. A. Multi Destination Flooding is primarily concerned with forwarding of broadcast, L2 multicast, and link-local traffic.

5. B. When implementing a bridge domain extension, only a single external Layer 2 EPG is allowed per bridge domain.

6. A, C, D. There is no such thing as AAEP extension. AAEP EPG is a variant of EPG extension. The other three answers are all correct.

7. B, C, D. Once the default gateway moves into ACI, the Layer 2 connection is irrelevant. Therefore, A is incorrect. However, if the L3Out has not been associated with the BD (or EPG) or the subnet Scope parameter has not been set to Advertised Externally, the subnet is not advertised out of ACI. For this reason, B and C are correct. Another possible reason for the communication outage may be contracts. With EPG extension, it is not ACI but the traditional network switches that initially control access to the subnet. But when the default gateway moves into ACI, contracts govern communication with the EPGs. For this reason, D is also a correct answer.

8. A. Port Local Scope can be used to enable multiple EPGs to use the same encapsulation across different ports on a given leaf switch.

9. D. All endpoints in a common flooding domain simultaneously experiencing performance degradation could signal the possibility of a Layer 2 loop. Answer A is incorrect because if MCP had taken action, any offending ports would have been disabled. Answers B and C are incorrect because no administrative action is required to enable ACI to flood Rapid PVST+ BPDUs out all ports associated with the same EPG and encapsulation. Answer D is correct because the point-to-point Spanning Tree Protocol link type can lead to faster Spanning Tree Protocol convergence than what may be safe given the hub-like nature of ACI from a Spanning Tree Protocol perspective.

10. A. ACI does need special configuration to ensure that MST BPDUs arriving in the native VLAN on interswitch links are not dropped, so answer A is correct. Answers B and C are incorrect because ACI does not run Spanning Tree Protocol, participate in the Spanning Tree Protocol topology, or even halt the flooding of BPDUs due to bridge domain setting modification. Answer D is a recipe for utter disaster. BPDU filtering, when used to prevent BPDU entry into ACI from outside switches, should only be implemented on external switches on interfaces that face ACI. This is because BPDU filtering prevents outbound advertisement of BPDUs. It should be used only when there will never be a second entry point for a VLAN into an ACI fabric.

Chapter 11

1. D. Creating a port group for vCenter and its dependencies using the port binding setting Ephemeral allows the administrator to reassign the vCenter VM to the specified port group in the event that certain failure scenarios occur.

2. B. The vSphere distributed switch is more advanced than the vSphere standard switch. Nexus 1000v and the AVS are not owned and managed by VMware.

3. A. VMkernel adapters are logical interfaces that enable transmission, receipt, or processing of hypervisor system traffic. Examples of ESXi system traffic include management, vMotion, IP storage, fault tolerance, and vSAN.

4. A, D. The only correct answers are A and D.

5. C. The answer is data center.

6. B. The VMM domain profile can be understood to be analogous with the VDS. A VDS needs to be generated before it can be consumed by ESXi hosts.

7. A, B, D. The only incorrect answer is C because ACI does not push bridge domains into a VDS; it pushes EPGs into a VDS.

8. C. The resolution immediacy setting Pre-Provision ensures that the policy is downloaded to the leaf switches with operational access policies involving the AAEP associated with the VMM domain, regardless of the status of hypervisors or LLDP and CDP neighbor relationships. The deployment immediacy setting Immediate would be needed to complement this.

9. A. VDS names need to be unique across each vCenter instance.

10. A. By creating an enhanced LAG policy and updating EPG VMM domain associations, an ACI administrator can create uplink port channels on an ACI-generated VDS and control the path that traffic takes.

Chapter 12

1. D. Device packages designed for service policy mode typically enable a wide range of changes, sometimes to the extent that the entire appliance may be configured by ACI.

2. B. Device packages are the foundation of both service policy mode and service manager mode.

3. B. This statement accurately describes service graphs with PBR. Non-PBR service graphs, on the other hand, expect that users insert the services device into the topology using VLAN or VRF stitching.

4. A. This process of operationalizing an instance of a service graph is called rendering.

5. C. Go-through mode relates to deployment of transparent mode firewalls. Bridging between a single subnet with this deployment mode requires at least two bridge domains.

6. D. A device selection policy determines which L4–L7 services device can be used for a given contract and service graph template.

7. D. Setting the Locked attribute to True for a given parameter prevents users who need to consume a function profile from modifying the parameter via ACI.

8. B. A service graph template is meant to be generic and does not specify EPGs. Instead, the instantiations of service graphs and the L4–L7 service graph to contract subject assignments determine the exact EPGs to which a function or service chain applies.

9. A. When you select Virtual, ACI exposes a drop-down that necessitates selection of a VMM domain.

10. D. Cluster interfaces, also called logical interfaces, are user-friendly mappings to a set of concrete interfaces. The use of cluster interfaces allows other ACI configurations to reference something that is more memorable to users. It reduces the possibility of configuration mistakes because it limits the need to reference concrete interfaces after initially mapping them to cluster interfaces. Note that provider and consumer connectors themselves map back to cluster interfaces.

Chapter 13

1. A. Out-of-band interfaces have been designed to be very difficult to impact through everyday configuration changes.

2. B. In-band configurations are reliant on access policies. Hence, they are a lot more closely tied to configurations in the access policies view. Something like removing the in-band management encapsulation from the pertinent VLAN pool can theoretically trigger an outage within the in-band network.

3. B. ACI does not allow leaking of data plane traffic into the oob VRF instance. However, it does allow leaking of traffic to and from the inb VRF.

4. A. Cisco recommends that dynamic and static IP addressing not be combined when OOB and in-band management are deployed together.

5. B. OOB management is designed to be simple. In-band management, on the other hand, allows more advanced constructs and features such as the deployment of L3Outs.

6. C. NTP is not a prerequisite for in-band management.

7. A. Managed node connectivity groups are constructs that map IP address pools to management EPGs. Therefore, the configuration of at least one managed node connectivity group is mandatory when using dynamic IP addressing.

8. B. APICs function much like any other servers. They are not VRF aware and use route metrics to prefer one route over another.

9. B. In-band contracts are standard contracts and are very much like contracts applied elsewhere within user VRFs. Out-of-band contracts offer less functionality. For example, they do not support the Log directive. They can also only be applied to OOB EPGs in the provided direction. Therefore, they do have minor differences.

10. A. The APIC Connectivity Preferences setting changes the preferred management interface for outbound connections by manipulating route metrics.

Chapter 14

1. B. System messages can also be generated for events and logs—specifically audit logs and session logs.

2. C. System message formats include ACI and NX-OS. Of the two, the ACI system message structure is the more granular.

3. C. Monitoring policies under the Access Policies view (the monInfraPol class) govern issues related to downlink (non-fabric) port failures. Access Policies also governs VMM management.

4. A, D. For syslog communication to be possible, the syslog server needs to be configured as an external syslog collector or in a syslog monitoring destination group. Furthermore, syslog source groups that reference the monitoring destination group need to be configured. Syslog is documented in RFC standards and is not associated with versions. Contracts for syslog are not always needed, especially when out-of-band is used as the management EPG. Regardless, answer C is incorrect because a permit-all contract would still enable syslog communication.

5. B. Custom monitoring policies do not take effect until they are manually allocated to a parent object. Through inheritance, all child objects that themselves do not have custom monitoring policy allocations then get assigned to the new custom monitoring policies.

6. C. **logit** is used to test syslog configurations within a fabric through submission of a test system message.

7. D. Regardless of the configuration status or whether there is full communication between ACI and the SNMP manager, ACI does not support SNMP write commands. Therefore, an SNMP manager would never be able to use SNMP to make configuration changes to ACI.

8. B, C. Answer A is not a possible reason for communication to fail. Contracts just need to be broad enough to allow the desired communication. Answer B is a reason for SNMP communication failing. ACI supports a maximum of 10 trap receivers. If more are configured, two of the receivers will not function. The SNMP policy enforces ACL-like security, and the *only* client entries that must be populated in the Client Entries field are the IP addresses of the SNMP managers.

9. C. Certain MIBs that touch on VRF-specific parameters require that the VRF instance be associated with an SNMP context for SNMP read queries to function.

10. C. By default, SNMP get or read queries take place over UDP port 161, and SNMP traps flow over UDP port 162.

Chapter 15

1. C. The tenant-admin role maps to a wide range of privileges, which means it is a very powerful default role within ACI. With this role and the access privilege type set to Write, there is very little a user cannot do within the specified tenants. For example, the user can create L4–L7 devices within the Prod1 and Prod2 tenants as long as the user has also been associated with relevant domains, and the user can apply service graphs. The user can also create basic objects within these tenants. However, the user cannot map encapsulations to switch ports unless he has also been granted access to the underlying hardware. Note that all tenant users gain read-only access to the common tenant by default.

2. A. The ops role provides network operator privileges to an ACI fabric, enabling basic monitoring and troubleshooting functionalities.

3. B. Several security domains are predefined: all, mgmt, and common. The predefined security domain all provides access to the entire ACI object hierarchy.

4. B. RBAC rules cannot be used to deny users access. If a user has too much access, the roles, privileges, security domains, and privilege types allocated to the user should be revisited.

5. A. A privilege enables access to a particular function within the system. An ACI fabric enforces access privileges at the managed object (MO) level. A role is simply a collection of privileges.

6. D. Just as with almost everything else in ACI, the goal with RBAC rules is to templatize configurations. ACI therefore attempts to enable users to expand security domain access to users associated with the security domain by allowing access to additional DNs. Therefore, parameters required for creating an RBAC rule consist of the DN of the additional object, the security domain to be expanded, and whether to grant users write or simply read-only access to the new portion of the object hierarchy.

7. C. The access-admin role enables administration and configuration of access policies.

8. A, C, D. The answers are self-explanatory.

9. C. The first option provides the user administrative access to the entire ACI object hierarchy but with read-only privileges, which is mostly useful for network operator CLI access. The second option provides the user the aaa role with write privileges and the tenant-admin role fabricwide but with read-only privileges. The third option provides full administrative access to the fabric. The fourth option is incorrectly formatted.

10. B. Users can still leverage the fallback login domain. If the fallback login domain has not been modified from its default setting, users can authenticate against the local database within ACI by using a special login syntax.

Chapter 16

1. C. MP-BGP EVPN handles cross-site endpoint information advertisements.

2. B. ACI Multi-Site uses OSPF to build the underlay.

3. B. ACI Multi-Site only governs tenants. Access policies continue to be configured locally within APICs. Not all tenant objects can currently be deployed from MSO, but when a tenant has been imported into MSO, administrators should refrain from making changes to objects within the MSO-managed tenant.

4. B. ACI Multi-Site defines a unit and scope of a change using templates.

5. A. If the fabrics have already been integrated into ACI Multi-Site, the only thing you need to do is to create a schema with templates underneath it and then add the necessary contracts to the EPGs to enable communication. Proper routing within VRF instances should also be set up.

6. D. Host-based routing can allow for optimization of ingress traffic, ensuring that traffic ingresses the data center where the endpoint resides.

7. A. ACI Multi-Site enables IP mobility across sites without the need to carry over performance-limiting and dangerous forwarding methods such as flooding.

Appendix A: Answers to the "Do I Know This Already?" Questions   585

A

8.   A. ACI Multi-Pod is a good fit for a lot of active/active use cases such as DRS. These requirements are not supported with ACI Multi-Site.

9.   A. ACI Multi-Pod is a good fit for a lot of active/active use cases such as active/active firewall clustering. This requirement is not currently supported with ACI Multi-Site.

10.   B. ACI Multi-Site integrates with the Cisco Cloud APIC and manages the public cloud deployment as yet another site under its management.

CCNP Data Center Application Centric Infrastructure DCACI 300-620 Exam Updates

Over time, reader feedback allows Pearson to gauge which topics give our readers the most problems when taking the exams. To assist readers with those topics, the authors create new materials clarifying and expanding on those troublesome exam topics. As mentioned in the Introduction, the additional content about the exam is contained in a PDF on this book's companion website, at http://www.ciscopress.com/title/9780136602668.

This appendix is intended to provide you with updated information if Cisco makes minor modifications to the exam upon which this book is based. When Cisco releases an entirely new exam, the changes are usually too extensive to provide in a simple update appendix. In those cases, you might need to consult the new edition of the book for the updated content. This appendix attempts to fill the void that occurs with any print book. In particular, this appendix does the following:

- Mentions technical items that might not have been mentioned elsewhere in the book

- Covers new topics if Cisco adds new content to the exam over time

- Provides a way to get up-to-the-minute current information about content for the exam

Always Get the Latest at the Book's Product Page

You are reading the version of this appendix that was available when your book was printed. However, given that the main purpose of this appendix is to be a living, changing document, it is important that you look for the latest version online at the book's companion website. To do so, follow these steps:

Step 1. Browse to www.ciscopress.com/title/9780136602668.

Step 2. Click the **Updates** tab.

Step 3. If there is a new Appendix B document on the page, download the latest Appendix B document.

NOTE The downloaded document has a version number. Comparing the version of the print Appendix B (Version 1.0) with the latest online version of this appendix, you should do the following:

- **Same version:** Ignore the PDF that you downloaded from the companion website.

- **Website has a later version:** Ignore this Appendix B in your book and read only the latest version that you downloaded from the companion website.

Technical Content

The current Version 1.0 of this appendix does not contain additional technical coverage.

GLOSSARY

A

access policy   A policy that primarily governs the configuration and operation of non-fabric (access) ports. Configuration of parameters such as link speed, CDP, LLDP, and LACP for connectivity to downstream servers, appliances, or non-ACI switches, as well as routers all fall into the realm of access policies. Access policies also include mechanisms to allow or block the flow of tenant traffic on access ports.

ACI Multi-Pod   The natural evolution of the ACI stretched fabric design in which spine and leaf switches are divided into pods, and different instances of IS-IS, COOP, and MP-BGP protocols run inside each pod to enable a level of control plane fault isolation.

ACI Multi-Site   A solution that interconnects multiple ACI fabrics for the purpose of homogenous policy deployment across ACI fabrics, homogenous security policy deployment across on-premises ACI fabrics and public clouds, and cross-site stretched subnet capabilities, among others.

Any EPG (vzAny)   A one-to-all EPG relationship that provides a convenient way of associating all endpoint groups (EPGs) in a VRF instance with one or more contracts.

APIC Cisco IMC   A controller that allows lights-out management of the physical server, firmware upgrades, and monitoring of server hardware health.

APIC cluster   A set of three or more servers that connects to leaf switches within an ACI fabric and functions as the central management point for the entire fabric.

APIC in-band port   APIC VIC adapters that need to be directly cabled to ACI leaf switches to allow fabric initialization and switch discovery. The VIC adapters used for in-band communication operate at 10 or 25 Gigabit Ethernet speeds.

APIC OOB port   An embedded LAN on motherboard (LOM) port for out-of-band management of an APIC. In third-generation APICs, these dual LAN ports support both 1 and 10 Gigabit Ethernet. The OOB ports are the default avenue for management access to an ACI fabric.

application profile   A container that allows EPGs to be grouped according to their relationship with one another to simplify configuration and auditing of relevant policies and to enable a level of policy reuse.

ARP gleaning   A process in which ACI attempts to "tickle" potential silent hosts by sending ARP traffic toward them, enabling ACI to then learn of such hosts in the data plane. Also known as silent host detection.

attachable access entity profile (AAEP)   A construct that fabric administrators use to authorize the placement of endpoint traffic on external entities, such as bare-metal servers, virtual machine hypervisors, switches, and routers. ACI can connect to external entities using individual ports, port channels, or vPCs.

audit log   A record of user actions in ACI, such as logins, logouts, object creations, object deletions, and any other configuration changes (object attribute changes).

B

BGP EVPN router ID   An ID for each spine that has been enabled for ACI Multi-Site forwarding that enables route peering across sites.

blacklisting   The practice of forwarding all traffic except traffic that is blocked using tools like access lists. The default behavior of traditional switches and routers is to blacklist traffic.

border leaf   A leaf switch that provides Layer 2 and Layer 3 connectivity to outside networks. Border leaf switches are often the point of policy enforcement between internal and external endpoints.

bridge domain (BD)   A Layer 2 forwarding construct that is somewhat analogous to a VLAN and has to be associated with a VRF instance.

C

class   One or more objects in the MIM that are of a similar type.

CloudSec encryption   Encryption used when traffic is egressing a fabric through multisite spines and is destined for spines in another fabric and needs to be encrypted. This is a VTEP-to-VTEP encryption feature.

compute leaf   An ACI leaf switch that connects to a server. Compute leaf switches are the point of policy enforcement when traffic is being sent between local endpoints.

concrete device   An L4–L7 services appliance that is used in a service graph.

consumer   In a client/server communication, the device initiating a communication request.

contract   A mechanism that references one or more subjects and is associated directionally with EPGs to determine which traffic flows are bound by the contract. Contracts are scope limited and can also be configured to modify traffic QoS markings.

contract scope   A condition that determines whether a contract can be enforced between EPGs. Contract scope options include application profile, VRF, tenant, and global.

D

deployment immediacy   When policies, such as VLANs, VXLAN bindings, contracts, and filters, have been downloaded to a leaf switch, factors that specify when a policy is actually pushed into the hardware policy content-addressable memory (CAM).

device manager   A configuration that tells ACI how to access an L4–L7 services device management solution for services appliance configuration in service manager mode. A device manager configuration includes the IP address, communication protocol, and credentials for the L4–L7 management solution.

device selection policy   A policy that associates or ties one or more L4–L7 devices to a graph template and contract. Also known as a logical device context.

distinguished name (DN)   A unique name that describes an ACI-managed object and locates its place in the ACI object hierarchy.

domain   The central link between the access policies hierarchy and the tenant hierarchy. A domain is the glue that binds tenant EPGs to access and virtual networking policies. With the help of pools, domains determine whether a tenant administrator is allowed to map an EPG to a certain encapsulation and underlying infrastructure. Each domain points to and consumes a single VLAN pool.

dynamic breakout port   A high-bandwidth port on certain hardware platforms that is split into multiple lower-speed connections, allowing customers to use a greater amount of the forwarding capacity of a high-bandwidth port even when there is a need to attach lower-bandwidth endpoints.

dynamic tunnel endpoint (DTEP)   Dynamically learned TEP addresses that include PTEPs and spine proxy addresses.

dynamic VLAN allocation   ACI's automatic choice of a VLAN ID out of a range of VLANs associated with a VLAN pool mapped to an EPG.

E

endpoint   Especially in the context of local endpoint learning, one MAC address and zero or more IP addresses associated with the MAC address. In remote endpoint learning, a cached IP address or MAC address of a device.

endpoint group (EPG)   A group of physical or virtual network endpoints that reside within a single bridge domain and have similar policy requirements. Endpoints within an EPG may be directly or indirectly attached to ACI leaf switches but communicate in some fashion over an ACI fabric.

event record   An object that is created by a system to log the occurrence of a specific condition that might be of interest to ACI administrators.

external bridge domain   A type of domain used in attachments to switches outside ACI for Layer 2 connectivity.

external bridged network   A bridge domain extension out an ACI fabric. Also referred to as an L2Out.

external EPG   A special type of EPG that represents endpoints outside an ACI fabric, such as user laptops, campus IoT devices, or Internet users. External EPGs allow the application of different security policies to different sets of outside users. External EPGs classify outside traffic using subnets, but the subnets can be as granular and numerous as needed.

external routed domain   A type of domain used in attachments to switches and routers outside ACI for Layer 2 connectivity.

F

fabric policy   A policy that governs configurations that apply more holistically at the switch or pod level. Fabric policies also include the operation and configuration of switch fabric ports.

fabric port   An interface that is used to interconnect spine and leaf switches within a fabric. By default, all spine switch interfaces besides the mgmt0 port and a number of leaf uplink ports are configured as fabric ports.

fabric tunnel endpoint (FTEP)   A single fabricwide pervasive IP address. ACI creates loopback 1023 interfaces on all leaf switches for assignment of FTEP addresses. The FTEP address represents the entire fabric and is used to encapsulate traffic in VXLAN to and from AVS and AVE virtual switches, if present.

fault   A potential problem in a fabric or the lack of required connectivity outside the fabric. Each fault has a weight and a severity and is registered into the ACI object hierarchy as a child object to the MO primarily associated with the fault.

fault lifecycle policy   A policy that specifies the timer intervals that govern fault transitions between states in the lifecycle. Fault lifecycle policies can be specified in the Common policy, in default policies, or in a custom monitoring policy.

filter   A mechanism that matches interesting traffic flows. The EtherType, Layer 3 protocol type, and Layer 4 ports involved in communication flows can all be used to match interesting traffic using filter entries.

floating SVI   A feature that enables users to configure an L3Out without locking the L3Out down to specific physical interfaces. This feature enables ACI to establish routing adjacencies with virtual machines without having to build multiple L3Outs to accommodate potential VM movements.

forwarding tag (FTag) tree   A predefined topology based on which ACI is able to forward multi-destination traffic. Each FTag tree does not necessarily use all fabric uplinks. That is why ACI creates multiple FTag trees and load balances multi-destination traffic across them.

function profile   The main mechanism by which L4–L7 services device administrators define configuration parameters in ACI to feed back to services devices.

G

global scope MIB   An MIB whose scope is not limited to a specific VRF instance and that touches on broader aspects of the fabric. Examples of MIBs of a global scope are those that request data related to the status of switch power supplies, interface or port channel statuses, CPU utilization, and memory utilization.

H

health scores   Scores that enable an organization to evaluate and report on the health and operation of managed objects, switches, tenants, pods, or the entire ACI fabric. By associating a weight with each fault, ACI provides a means for allocating health scores to objects. An object whose children and associated objects are not impacted by faults has a health score of 100. As faults occur, the health score of the object diminishes until it trends toward 0. With the resolution of all related faults, the health score returns to 100.

I–J–K

infrastructure VLAN   A VLAN that is used for control communication between ACI fabric nodes (leaf switches, spine switches, and APICs). This VLAN is also used for extending an ACI fabric to AVS or AVE virtual switches. The infra VLAN should be unique and should not be used elsewhere in the environment. Acceptable infra VLAN IDs are 2 through 4094.

interface policy   In ACI, configuration parameters that dictate interface behavior. Examples of interface policies include port speeds, enabled or disabled protocols or port-level features, and monitoring settings.

interface policy group   A port configuration template that aligns with link types. Each individual physical interface or link aggregation within ACI derives two critical configuration components from an interface policy group: a collection of interface policies and an AAEP. Some types of interface policy groups are fully reusable, and others are semi-reusable.

interface profile   A collection of interface mappings that gets bound to switch IDs through its association with one or more switch profiles.

interface selector   A child object of an interface profile that ties an interface policy group to one or more port IDs. Since switch associations are determined by switch profiles and not interface profiles, interface selectors only determine port ID associations and not the list of switches to which the interface policy groups should be assigned.

interleak   Redistribution of all L3Out-learned routes within user VRF instances into BGP for advertisement across the fabric. If an L3Out is using BGP, no redistribution (interleak) is required.

intersite L3Out   In current MSO releases, a feature that enables endpoints located in one site to use a remote L3Out to connect to entities in an external network.

intra-fabric messaging (IFM)   An encrypted in-band communication channel between APICs and switches over the infrastructure VLAN. When APICs push policy to switches, all relevant communication rides the IFM channel.

IP storage leaf   An ACI leaf switch that connects to an IP storage system. IP storage leaf switches can be a point of policy enforcement for traffic to and from local endpoints.

L

L2 Unknown Unicast   A setting for unicast traffic destined to an endpoint whose MAC address cannot be found in the ACI endpoint table.

L3Out   An object that defines a routed connection or a series of routed connections outside an ACI fabric to allow route propagation between a VRF instance within ACI and the outside world. BGP, OSPF, and EIGRP are all supported protocols for use on L3Outs. Static routes pointing outside ACI can also be configured on L3Outs.

L3Out bridge domain (BD)   A domain that ACI creates internally for an SVI to provide a Layer 2 flooding domain. This BD is called an L3Out BD or external BD and is not visible to ACI administrators.

leaf   A type of switch that is used as an attachment point for a server. APICs also connect to leaf switches.

leaf interface override   A policy that allows interfaces that already have interface policy group assignments to apply an alternate interface policy group.

Link Debounce Interval   A link-level policy setting that delays reporting of a link-down event to a switch supervisor.

local endpoint   An endpoint that an ACI leaf learns from an access (non-fabric) port, even if the endpoint is not directly attached to the leaf.

logical device   Physical devices clustered together. Also known as a clustered device.

logical interface profile   A profile that consists of one or more logical interface profiles defining L3Out interfaces, interface IP addresses, MTU values for routing protocol peering, and any other interface-specific configuration parameters.

logical node profile   An object that specifies which switches will establish routed connectivity to external devices for a given L3Out.

M

managed object (MO)   An object or group of objects within a hierarchical tree. MOs are abstractions of fabric resources. An MO can represent a physical object, such as a switch, an interface, or a logical object, such as an application profile, an endpoint group, or a fault.

Management Information Base (MIB)   An object that defines the information that a remote SNMP manger can request from an SNMP agent.

Management Information Model (MIM)   An object hierarchy that is managed by and stored on the APICs that represents both physical and logical components of the ACI fabric.

MisCabling Protocol (MCP)   An ACI protocol that detects loops caused by devices attached to an ACI fabric and that can be applied on both physical Ethernet interfaces and port channel interfaces.

monitoring destination group   A syslog group that is used to define and group together syslog servers or SNMP servers.

monitoring source   A definition added to a monitoring policy that points to the monitoring destination groups, thereby defining which server and server settings should be used for each set of monitoring policies.

monPolDn   An object attribute that references a monitoring policy object.

MOQuery   The CLI-based equivalent of Visore, which can be used to gain an understanding of the object hierarchy in ACI.

Multi Destination Flooding   A setting that primarily addresses forwarding of broadcast, L2 multicast, and link-local traffic. The three configuration options for the Multi Destination Flooding parameter are Flood in BD, Drop, and Flood in Encapsulation.

multitenancy   The ability to logically separate management as well as data plane forwarding of different logical environments that reside on top of common physical infrastructure.

N

network policy mode   A service graph management model which requires that ACI configure network connectivity to an L4–L7 services device but not the L4–L7 device itself.

node ID   A logical representation of an ACI switch or APIC that can be associated with or disassociated from physical hardware.

O

overlay multicast TEP   A single anycast tunnel endpoint within each fabric (site) for ingress replication of cross-site data plane BUM traffic.

overlay unicast TEP   A single anycast TEP address assigned to each pod within each fabric for forwarding of cross-site unicast traffic.

P–Q

pervasive gateway   An anycast default gateway that ACI leaf switches install to allow local endpoints to communicate beyond their local subnets.

pervasive route   A route to a BD subnet that points to the spine proxy TEP as its next-hop IP address. The function of a pervasive route is to ensure that a leaf switch knows that a particular destination is expected to be inside the fabric.

physical domain   A domain that governs the attachment of bare-metal servers and appliances that need static VLAN allocations.

physical tunnel endpoint (PTEP)   A type of IP address that ACI assigns to the loopback 0 interface of a given switch. Tunnels established between leaf switches for the purpose of data plane traffic forwarding are sourced from and destined to PTEP addresses.

platform-independent VLAN (PI VLAN)   A VLAN ID that is locally significant to each leaf switch and represents a bridge domain or EPG for internal operations. PI VLANs are not used for traffic forwarding.

pod policy group   A group of individual protocol settings that is collectively applied to a pod.

pod profile   A construct that specifies date and time, podwide SNMP, Council of Oracle Protocol (COOP) settings, and IS-IS and Border Gateway Protocol (BGP) route reflector policies for one or more pods. Pod profiles map pod policy groups to pods by using pod selectors.

pod selector   An object that references the pod IDs to which pod policies apply. Pod policy groups get bound to a pod through a pod selector.

Policy Universe   The top level of the MIM hierarchical object tree. It is not the true root of the tree but is a key branch of the overall hierarchy representing the bulk of user-configurable policies.

port binding   A setting that determines when virtual machines in a port group get allocated to a virtual port on a VDS.

port channel member override   A policy used when an override needs to be applied to one or more links that are part of a port channel or vPC but not necessarily the entire port channel or vPC. Examples of port channel member overrides are implementation of LACP fast timers and modification of LACP port priorities.

port encapsulation VLAN   A VLAN ID an administrator uses when mapping an EPG to a switch port. Both static path mapping and AAEP EPGs leverage this VLAN type. The term *port encapsulation* implies that the VLAN encapsulation used appears on the wire. Also known as an access encapsulation VLAN.

port group   A group of ports with similar policy requirements.

preferred group member   A feature that allows a set of EPGs within a VRF instance to have open communication with one another without the need for contracts while continuing to enforce contract requirements on all other EPGs within the VRF instance.

privilege   An authorization that enables access to a particular function within a system. An ACI fabric enforces access privileges at the managed object (MO) level.

provider   In a client/server communication, the device responding to a client communication request.

R

RBAC rule   A rule that allows granular control on top of the existing RBAC framework within ACI. An RBAC rule allows the addition of desired subtrees of the ACI object hierarchy to a security domain to enable broader visibility to users who may be granted access to a given security domain.

remote endpoint   An endpoint that a leaf learns by checking the source MAC and/or source IP header of a packet that arrives on a fabric port (over tunnel interfaces).

resolution immediacy   Factors in ACI that define when policies such as VLANs, VXLAN bindings, contracts, and filters are downloaded to leaf switches.

role   A collection of privileges in ACI. ACI has a set of predefined roles, but you can modify the predefined roles or expand on default ACI roles by creating custom roles.

route profile   A profile that enables users to add user-defined match rules or set rules for route filtering or route manipulation. They are sometimes referred to as route control profiles or route maps.

route reflector   A BGP speaker that is allowed to advertise iBGP-learned routes to certain iBGP peers. Route reflection bends the rules of BGP split horizon just a little, introducing a new set of BGP attributes for route loop prevention. In ACI, spines can be configured as route reflectors.

S

scheduler   Software that allows administrators to specify a window of time for ACI to execute certain operations such as switch upgrades and configuration backups. Schedulers can be triggered on a one-time-only basis or can recur on a regular basis.

schema   A collection of configuration templates and the assignment of each template to sites defined in the Multi-Site deployment.

secondary IP address   An IP address that is used when an external device behind an L3Out needs to point a static route to a common IP address that a pair of border leaf switches respond to.

security domain   A tag that references one or more subtrees in the ACI object hierarchy. After you create a security domain, you can assign it to tenants and domains. For more granular references, you can map a distinguished name (DN) in the ACI object hierarchy to a security domain. A user who is subsequently mapped to the security domain gains a level of access to the referenced subtrees of the object hierarchy.

service chain   A succession of functions enforced through contracts.

service graph   A graph of communication flows that are enforced via contracts to mandate the flow of traffic between a given pair of EPGs through a series of services functions.

service graph template   A template that defines the desired functions through which certain traffic should flow without actually specifying the traffic (EPGs) to which it applies.

service leaf   A leaf switch that connects to Layer 4–7 services appliances, such as firewalls and load balancers.

service manager mode   A service graph management model that enables services administrators to make services configuration changes in the L4–L7 management tool provided by a device vendor. ACI automates configuration to the services device but only minimally configures the L4–L7 services device itself.

service policy mode   A service graph management model that requires ACI to configure both network connectivity to an L4–L7 services device and also the L4–L7 device itself.

shadow EPG   Any form of EPG that is automatically generated by ACI, typically for the purpose of automating enforcement of contracts between two components.

sharding   Horizontal partitioning of databases that involves distributing a database across multiple instances of the schema. Sharding increases both redundancy and performance because a large partitioned table can be split across multiple database servers. It also enables a scale-out model involving adding to the number of servers as opposed to having to constantly scale up servers through hardware upgrades.

site   An independent ACI fabric.

site ID   A unique numeric identifier for each fabric. Once selected, the site ID cannot be changed.

SNMP notification   A notification that an SNMP agent sends to configured SNMP managers when an important system event occurs on an SNMP-enabled device.

SNMP trap   An unreliable message that does not require an acknowledgment from the SNMP manager.

spine   A type of switch that serves to interconnect leaf switches at high speeds and also handle certain control plane functions within a fabric.

squelching   The process of suppressing faults or events of a specific fault code or event type, which helps reduce the noise from a monitoring perspective and allows a company to focus on the faults that really matter.

static VLAN allocation   An administrator's static mapping of a specific EPG to a VLAN ID on a port, a port channel, a virtual port channel, or all ports on a switch.

stretched   Objects, such as tenants, VRF instances, EPGs, bridge domains, subnets, or contracts, that are deployed to multiple sites.

stretched ACI fabric   A partially meshed design that connects ACI leaf and spine switches distributed in multiple locations. The stretched ACI fabric design helps lower deployment costs when full-mesh cable runs between all leaf and spine switches in a fabric tend to be cost-prohibitive.

subject   A mechanism that determines the actions taken on interesting traffic or defines whether corresponding ports for return traffic should be opened.

system message   A specially formatted message that typically contains a subset of information about a fault, an event, or another log record in the fabric.

switch profile   A collection of switch policy group-to-node ID mappings that binds policy to switch IDs using switch selectors. Switch profiles reference interface profiles and deploy the port configurations defined in the interface profiles to switches to which the switch profile is bound. There are two types of switch profiles: leaf profiles and spine profiles.

switch selector   A child object of a switch profile that associates a switch policy group to one or more node IDs.

T

template   A child of a schema that contains configuration objects that are either shared between sites or are site specific. Each template gets associated with a single tenant. A template defines the unit or scope of a configuration change.

template conformity   A feature of ACI Multi-Site that runs checks to validate that configurations under a template pushed to multiple sites by the MSO have not been altered within a given fabric by administrators.

tenant   In ACI, a secure and exclusive virtual computing environment that forms a unit of isolation from a policy perspective but does not represent a private network.

TEP pool   A subnet used for internal fabric communication. This subnet can potentially be advertised outside ACI over an IPN or ISN or when a fabric is extended to virtual environments using the AVS or AVE. TEP pool subnets should ideally be unique across an enterprise environment. Cisco recommends that TEP pool subnet sizes be between /16 and /21. TEP pool sizes impact pod scalability. Each pod should be assigned a separate TEP pool.

transit leaf   A leaf switch that provides connectivity between two sites in a stretched fabric design. Transit leaf switches connect to spine switches in both sites. No special configuration is required for transit leaf switches. At least one transit leaf switch must be provisioned in each site for redundancy reasons.

U–V–W

user tenant   A tenant that does not come out of the box with ACI and is created by a user.

Virtual Machine Manager (VMM) domain   A type of domain that enables the deployment of EPGs and corresponding encapsulations into virtualized environments.

virtual routing and forwarding (VRF) instance   A mechanism used to partition a routing table into multiple routing tables for the purpose of enabling Layer 3 segmentation over common hardware. In ACI, each tenant can contain multiple VRF instances.

Visore   A GUI-based tool that can be used to gain an understanding of the object hierarchy in ACI.

VLAN pool   The range of VLAN IDs that are acceptable for application to ACI access (non-fabric) ports for a particular function or use.

VM vNIC   Virtual network adapters configured within VMs and associated with port groups.

VMkernel adapter   A logical interface that enables transmission, receipt, or processing of hypervisor system traffic. Examples of ESXi system traffic include management, vMotion, IP storage, fault tolerance, and vSAN. Like virtual machines, VMkernel adapters need to be associated with port groups.

vmnic   A physical network interface card that connects an ESXi server to a physical switch. You can think of a vmnic as a string used in the naming of virtual switch uplinks within ESXi hypervisors.

vPC peer dead interval   The amount of time a leaf switch waits following a vPC peer switch failure before it assumes the role of vPC master. The default peer dead interval in ACI is 200 seconds. This value can be tuned to between 5 and 600 seconds through configuration of a vPC domain policy.

VRF-specific MIB　An MIB whose scope is limited to a VRF instance. Examples of VRF-specific MIBs are those involving IP addresses or endpoints residing in a VRF or route peerings out of a specific VRF.

vSphere distributed switch (VDS)　A virtual switch that is created and centrally managed by vCenter, with the switch data plane residing within the ESXi hypervisors.

vSphere load balancing　Load balancing in vSphere that enables administrators to choose how uplink ports on a virtual switch are used to distribute network traffic originating from virtual machines and VMkernel interfaces.

vSphere standard switch (vSwitch)　A basic Layer 2 virtual switch instantiated by and limited in scope to a single hypervisor. It can be used to enable ESXi host IP connectivity with other hosts or endpoints. It can also enable basic connectivity for virtual machines.

whitelisting　The practice of dropping all traffic unless it is explicitly allowed via contracts. The default behavior of ACI and firewalls is to support whitelisting.

X–Z

zero trust security　An approach to network security in which communication is allowed only if there is a justification for the traffic flows. ACI supports a zero-trust architecture through whitelisting and the ability to selectively punt traffic to firewalls for identity verifications, where necessary.

Index

D

F

J-K

L

P

Q-R

S

T

W

X-Y-Z

CISCO

Connect, Engage, Collaborate

The Award Winning
Cisco Support Community

Attend and Participate in Events

Ask the Experts
Live Webcasts

Knowledge Sharing

Documents
Blogs
Videos

Top Contributor Programs

Cisco Designated VIP
Hall of Fame
Spotlight Awards

Multi-Language Support

https://supportforums.cisco.com

Pearson

Where are the companion content files?

Thank you for purchasing this
Premium Edition version of
CCNP Data Center Application Centric
Infrastructure DCACI 300-620 Official Cert Guide

This product comes with companion content. You have access to these files by following the steps below:

1. Go to **ciscopress.com/account** and log in.

2. Click on the "Access Bonus Content" link in the Registered Products section of your account page for this product, to be taken to the page where your downloadable content is available.

Please note that many of our companion content files can be very large, especially image and video files.

If you are unable to locate the files for this title by following the steps at left, please visit **ciscopress.com/support** and select the chat, phone, or web ticket options to get help from a tech support representative.

The Professional and Personal Technology Brands of Pearson

Addison Wesley   **Cisco Press**   **informIT**   PEARSON IT Certification   **que**   **sAms**